Management

Skills and Application

Thirteenth Edition

Leslie W. Rue

Professor Emeritus of Management
Robinson College of Business
Georgia State University

Lloyd L. Byars

Professor Emeritus of Management
College of Management
Georgia Institute of Technology

Boston Burr Ridge, IL Dubuque, IA New York San Francisco St. Louis
Bangkok Bogotá Caracas Kuala Lumpur Lisbon London Madrid Mexico City
Milan Montreal New Delhi Santiago Seoul Singapore Sydney Taipei Toronto

The McGraw·Hill Companies

MANAGEMENT: SKILLS AND APPLICATION

Published by McGraw-Hill/Irwin, a business unit of The McGraw-Hill Companies, Inc., 1221 Avenue of the Americas, New York, NY, 10020.

This book is printed on acid-free paper.

1 2 3 4 5 6 7 8 9 0 WCK/WCK 0 9 8

ISBN 978-0-07-338150-3
MHID 0-07-338150-0

Vice president and editor-in-chief: *Brent Gordon*
Publisher: *Paul Ducham*
Managing developmental editor: *Laura Hurst Spell*
Editorial assistant: *Jane Beck*
Executive marketing manager: *Rhonda Seelinger*
Project manager: *Kathryn D. Mikulic*
Senior production supervisor: *Debra R. Sylvester*
Design coordinator: *Joanne Mennemeier*
Senior photo research coordinator: *Jeremy Cheshareck*
Photo researcher: *Gary Overstreet*
Media project manager: *Suresh Babu, Hurix Systems Pvt. Ltd.*
Cover design: *Brittany Skwierczynski*
Typeface: *10/12 Times New Roman*
Compositor: *ICC Macmillan Inc.*
Printer: *Quebecor World Versailles Inc.*

Library of Congress Cataloging-in-Publication Data

Rue, Leslie W.
Management : skills and application / Leslie W. Rue, Lloyd L. Byars.—13th ed.
p. cm.
Includes index.
ISBN-13: 978-0-07-338150-3 (alk. paper)
ISBN-10: 0-07-338150-0 (alk. paper)
1. Management. I. Byars, Lloyd L. II. Title.
HD31.R797 2009
658--dc22

2008041188

www.mhhe.com

To Penny and Linda, our wonderful wives of 41 and 39 years, respectively.

Preface

We are extremely pleased that this book has gone into thirteen editions. We believe the book's endurance is due largely to the feedback and assistance we have received from instructors and students who have used the book. Relying on the suggestions of these groups as well as our own thoughts, we have attempted to improve the book with each new edition.

NEW TO THIS EDITION

In addition to the normal updates of statistics, referenced research studies, and general concepts, the following changes were emphasized in this edition:

- Global chapter organization has been changed to improve the flow of material. Operations Control and Planning are now consolidated with Operations Management.
- New Skill-Building Exercises and experiential cases have been added throughout the book. Many of the new activities emphasize the development of writing skills.
- Approximately two-thirds of the Management Illustrations used throughout the text have been revised, making them very up-to-date.
- Most of the Chapter Previews are either new or significantly updated in this edition.
- Key subject areas have been expanded and revised, including Setting Objectives, Delegation, and Outsourcing.
- Links have been added to show the contribution of major theorists to various models and methods.

STRUCTURE OF THE CHAPTERS

Most of the text's pedagogy has been retained from the last edition. Look for these features in each chapter:

- Learning Objectives—chapter-opening guidelines for students to use as they read. This list of key objectives provides the reader a roadmap for venturing into the text.
- Chapter Previews—real-life, up-to-date vignettes that illustrate one or more of the major points covered in the respective chapters. Preview analysis questions are presented at the end of each vignette to help the student relate the chapter material to the preview.
- Management Illustrations—brief, chapter-related actual corporate examples found in boxes throughout the chapters. These illustrations present more than 60 examples of concepts contained in the text, and most contain urls of the companies detailed in them.
- Corporate/Organization References—more than 200 references to actual corporations and organizations. We are extremely proud of these references that will best serve to bridge the gap between theory and practice. Look for them in the text itself, chapter previews, and management illustrations.
- Margin Glossary—key terms defined where mentioned in the text. This feature is especially helpful to students reviewing chapter material for study and/or testing.
- Review Questions—these questions, at the end of each chapter, tie directly back to the learning objectives. By tying the chapter concepts together from beginning to end, students can evaluate their understanding of key constructs and ideas.
- Skill-Building Questions—end-of-chapter questions designed to promote critical thinking. These questions ask students to get to a deeper level of understanding by applying, comparing, contrasting, evaluating, and illustrating ideas presented in the chapter.

- Skill-Building Exercises—end-of-chapter tools for students and instructors. These exercises can be assigned on the spot in class or as homework.
- Case Incidents—end-of-chapter short cases for students. These incidents present life-like situations requiring management decisions related to the material covered in the respective chapters. As with the skill-building exercises, these can be assigned in class or as homework.

THE TEACHING PACKAGE

A variety of support materials help the instructor in teaching this dynamic field of management. These key items are available for the thirteenth edition from the Online Learning Center at www.mhhe.com/rue13e:

- Lecture Resource Manual and Test Bank

  The Lecture Resource Manual and Test Bank is the instructor's tool box for enhancing student learning. The instructor's manual contains brief chapter overviews; lecture outlines that include topical headings; definitional highlights; coordination points for key terms, review questions, and learning objectives; suggested answers to in-text questions; and transparency masters. The popular "Barriers to Student Understanding" feature addresses areas that are most often stumbling blocks for students. In this section, a series of suggestions guide the instructor in preparing for difficulties, covering easily misunderstood concepts, and aiding the student learning experience through directed discussion. The Test Bank section, completely revised and updated, includes true-false, multiple-choice, and essay questions tied to the chapter learning objectives and classified according to their level of difficulty, and with page references.
- PowerPoint presentations contain key points, tables, and graphs from the text as well as extra material.
- **Principles of Management Video DVD Vol. 1** (ISBN 0073364142) & NEW! Vol. 2 (ISBN 0073364231) Now offering more than 70 video clips from sources such as BusinessWeek TV, PBS, NBC, BBC, CBS, and McGraw-Hill are provided on two DVD sets. These company videos are organized by the four functions of management: planning, leading, organizing, and controlling, and they feature companies such as Playstation, Panera Bread, Patagonia, Mini Cooper, and the Greater Chicago Food Depository in 2½- to 15-minute clips.
- **EXPANDED! Manager's Hot Seat Online!** Now instructors can put students in the hot seat with access to an interactive program, including six brand new segments. Students are given an introduction to a situation, view a dossier of related management materials, and then watch 21 real managers apply their years of experience when confronting unscripted issues. As the scenario unfolds, questions about how the manager is handling the situation pop up, forcing the student to make decisions along with the manager. At the end of the scenario, students watch a post-interview with the manager, view how their responses matched up to the manager's decisions, and then submit a report critiquing the manager's choices while defending their own. Access to this online program is provided as part of the Premium Online Learning Access of this text. Access can also be purchased as a stand-alone program.
- ***Management in the Movies* DVD** (ISBN 0073317713) This faculty DVD makes it easy to bring that captivating power of big screen movies to your classroom! Each video clip illustrates a specific management topic in less than 2½ minutes via a scene from major movies or a TV show. For example, Groups—*13 Going On 30,* Ethics—*John Q,* Global

Management—*Gung Ho*. The *Management in the Movies* DVD is available exclusively for current users of McGraw-Hill *Principles of Management,* OB and HRM texts and is supported by an instructor's manual with suggestions for usage of the clip, video summaries, and discussion questions for each segment!

- **Group and Video Resource Manual: An Instructor's Guide to an Active Classroom** (ISBN 0073044342) Authored by Amanda Johnson and Angelo Kinicki of Arizona State University, the Group & Video Resource Manual was created to help instructors create a livelier and stimulating classroom environment. The manual contains interactive in-class group and individual exercises to accompany Build Your Management Skills assessments on the OLC, additional group exercises for each chapter and comprehensive notes and discussion questions to accompany the Manager's Hot Seat. This valuable guide includes information and material to help instructors successfully execute additional group exercises and the Manager's Hot Seat into their classrooms. For each exercise, the manual includes learning objectives, unique PowerPoint slides to accompany the exercises, and comprehensive discussion questions to facilitate enhanced learning. The manual also includes lecturettes to supplement and expand material presented for each exercise.

FOR STUDENTS

- **Online Learning Center, www.mhhe.com/rue13e**—Students can freely access self-grading quizzes and chapter review materials in the student resource center of the Online Learning Center. Premium online content includes access to self-assessment and Manager's Hot Seat exercises (Premium Content Code Card—ISBN 0077300386).

Acknowledgments

We think the McGraw-Hill/Irwin sales staff is the best in the industry, and we thank them for their continued efforts on our behalf. Our thanks, also, to the members of the McGraw-Hill/Irwin in-house staff who have provided their support throughout this revision.

We have relied on the assistance of so many people throughout this book's history. As we come now to the thirteenth edition, we wish to thank all of those who have been involved with this project and to make special mention of those involved in the most recent reviewing and marketing research processes:

Dennis Brode
Sinclair Community College

Nancy Higgins
Montgomery College

Robert Osborne
Park University

Frank Tomassi
Johnson & Wales University

Patty Worsham
Riverside Community College

We are indebted to our families, friends, colleagues, and students for the numerous comments, ideas, and support that they have provided. A special thanks goes to our assistant, Charmelle Todd, for her work on this revision.

In our continuing efforts to improve this text, we earnestly solicit your feedback. You are the reason for this book's endurance!

Leslie W. Rue

Lloyd L. Byars

About the Authors

LESLIE W. RUE

is professor emeritus of management and former holder of the Carl R. Zwerner chair of Family Owned Enterprises in the Robinson College of Business at Georgia State University. He received his Bachelor of Industrial Engineering (with honor) and his Master of Industrial Engineering from Georgia Institute of Technology. He received his Ph.D. in Management from Georgia State University.

Prior to joining Georgia State University, Dr. Rue was on the faculty of the School of Business, Indiana University at Bloomington, Indiana. He has worked as a data processing project officer for the U.S. Army Management Systems Support Agency, in the Pentagon, and as an industrial engineer for Delta Airlines. In addition, Dr. Rue has worked as a consultant and trainer to numerous private and public organizations in the areas of planning, organizing, and strategy.

Dr. Rue is the author of over 50 published articles, cases, and papers that have appeared in academic and practitioner journals. In addition to this book, he has coauthored numerous other textbooks in the field of management. Several of these books have gone into multiple editions.

Dr. Rue will soon celebrate his 41st wedding anniversary. He has two daughters, a son, and seven grandchildren. His hobbies include the restoration of antique furniture and antique wooden speedboats.

LLOYD L. BYARS

received his Ph.D. from Georgia State University. He also received a Bachelor of Electrical Engineering and a Master of Science in Industrial Management from the Georgia Institute of Technology. He has taught at Georgia State University, Clark Atlanta University, and is currently professor of management, College of Management at the Georgia Institute of Technology.

Dr. Byars has published articles in leading professional journals and is also the author of four textbooks that are used in colleges and universities. He has served on the editorial review board of the *Journal of Systems Management* and the *Journal of Management Case Studies.*

Dr. Byars has worked as a trainer and consultant to many organizations, including Duke Power Company, Georgia Kraft Company, Kraft, Inc., South Carolina Electric and Gas Company, the University of Florida–Medical School, the Department of the Army, and the U.S. Social Security Administration. Dr. Byars also serves as a labor arbitrator, certified by both the Federal Mediation and Conciliation Service and the American Arbitration Association. He has arbitrated cases in the United States, Europe, Central America, and the Caribbean.

Dr. Byars has been married to Linda S. Byars for 39 years. They have two daughters, a son, one grandson, and one granddaughter.

Brief Outline of Contents

Contents

Foundations

1. Management in a Diverse Workplace
2. The Management Movement
3. Developing Communication Skills
4. Decision-Making Skills

Chapter **One**

Management in a Diverse Workplace

Learning Objectives

After studying this chapter, you will be able to:

1. Define management.
2. Describe the levels of management.
3. Discuss the functions of management.
4. Explain the roles of a manager.
5. Describe the skills required to perform the work of management.
6. Explain how principles of management are developed.
7. Define the glass ceiling.
8. Explain diversity.
9. Define entrepreneur.
10. Define small business.
11. Outline three requirements for encouraging entrepreneurship in medium-sized and large organizations.

Chapter Preview

Warren Buffett is often referred to as the world's second-richest man with a fortune of $44 billion dollars. He knows how to grow a business. He turned a failing textile company into an investment powerhouse. He still lives in the same house in Omaha, Nebraska, which he bought in 1958 for $31,500. Mr. Buffett is known for "value investing," picking undervalued stocks that may suffer short-term losses, but due to their intrinsic worth will usually grow over the long term. His philosophy about business is summarized in the following quote: "In business you look for the easy things to do."

In 2006 Warren Buffett stunned the world when he announced that much of his $44 billion fortune will go to improve world health and education.

Source: Adapted from "The Monitor's View," *The Christian Science Monitor*, June 29, 2006, p. 8.

Analyzing Management Skills

Go to the Internet and find articles relating to the management style of Warren Buffett. What is the style of management used by Buffett?

Applying Management Skills

In the jobs you have held either prior to entering college or during your college career, what skills did effective managers have?

Organizations today operate in a world of constant change. Technology and society are changing more rapidly than ever before. Concern for the environment has forced companies to think about how their actions affect the quality of the air, land, and water. Competition is fiercer than ever, because organizations from all over the world now try to sell their products and services to the same customers. Workplaces have become increasingly diverse, as minorities, women, and new immigrants participate in growing numbers. All these changes have created new challenges for managers.

WHAT IS MANAGEMENT?

management
A form of work that involves deciding the best way to use an organization's resources to produce goods or provide services.

Management is a form of work that involves deciding the best way to use an organization's resources to produce goods or provide services. An organization's resources include its employees, equipment, and money. In performing this work managers engage in some basic activities which include planning, organizing, staffing, leading, and controlling. These activities are discussed in more detail throughout this textbook.

Although the definition is simple, the job of management is quite complex. Management must make good decisions, communicate well with people, make work assignments, delegate, plan, train people, motivate people, and appraise employees' job performances. The varied work of management is extremely difficult to master. Yet mastery of management is vital to organizational success.

LEVELS OF MANAGEMENT

top or senior management
Establishes the objectives of the organization, formulates the actions necessary to achieve them, and allocates the resources of the organization to achieve the objectives.

middle management
Responsible for implementing and achieving organizational objectives; also responsible for developing departmental objectives and actions.

All organizations, from one-person businesses to giant corporations, need managers. Small businesses may be managed by one or just a few managers. Large and medium-sized companies may have many levels of management.

Senior Management

The highest level is known as **top or senior management.** Senior management has several important functions. First, it establishes the goals, or objectives, of the organization.[1] Second, it decides what actions are necessary to meet those goals. Finally, it decides how to use the organization's resources. This level of management usually includes the chairperson of the company's board of directors, the chief executive officer (CEO), the chief operating officer (COO), and the company's senior vice presidents. Senior managers are not involved in the company's day-to-day problems. Instead, they concentrate on setting the direction the company will follow. Management Illustration 1.1 describes decisions that are made by senior management.

Middle Management

Middle management is responsible for meeting the goals that senior management sets. This level of management sets goals for specific areas of the organization and decides what

Management Illustration 1.1

STARBUCKS

Starbucks ousted CEO Jim Donald on January 7, 2008. Howard Schultz, the chairman of the board of directors, has taken on the additional role of CEO. Mr. Schultz, 54 years old, came to the Seattle, Washington, coffee company in 1982 when it had four locations. Serving as CEO from 1987 to 2000, he presided over the company as it grew to more than 15,000 locations around the globe. Starbucks now has products on supermarket shelves and even has its own record label.

Mr. Schultz plans to slow down the pace of new store openings in the United States and to close struggling locations. The company had planned to open 1,600 stores in the United States during 2008. He also plans to improve the customer experience at U.S. stores, streamline management, and accelerate expansion overseas. In a letter to employees, Mr. Schultz said the company must shift its focus away from bureaucracy and back to customers. The question is whether his solutions will be drastic enough to improve the company's results. Furthermore, some of the objectives stated in the letter, such as "reigniting the emotional attachment with customers," are so difficult to measure that it may be hard for investors to know whether they are being met.

Ms. Sharon Zackfia, an analyst at William Blair & Co, says as follows, "If anyone's going to figure out how to make this train get back on the rails, even in these tough economic times, it's going to be Howard."

Source: Adopted from Janet Adamy, "Schultz Takes Over to Try to Perk Up Starbucks," *The Wall Street Journal* (Eastern edition), January 8, 2008, p. B1.

the employees in each area must do to meet those goals. For example, senior management might set a goal of increasing company sales by 15 percent in the next year. To meet that objective, middle management might develop a new advertising campaign for one of the organization's products/services.

Supervisory Management

supervisory management
Manages operative employees; generally considered the first level of management.

The lowest level of management is **supervisory management.** Supervisory managers make sure that the day-to-day operations of the organization run smoothly. They are in charge of the people who physically produce the organization's goods/services. Forepersons and crew leaders are examples of supervisory managers.

Large companies usually have all three kinds of managers. Supervisors are responsible for making sure that the daily operations of the company run well. Middle managers are responsible for making sure that all supervisors under their authority are performing well. Middle managers also may suggest ideas for increasing sales, improving service, or reducing costs. Senior managers include the company's CEO and senior vice presidents. These managers make decisions about the company's policies, products, and organizational strategy. A decision to increase salaries throughout the company would be made by senior management, for example.

The three levels of management form a *hierarchy.* As can be seen in Figure 1.1, the management hierarchy is shaped like a pyramid, with very few senior managers at the top and many supervisory managers at the bottom. Figure 1.2 further describes the different levels of management.

THE MANAGEMENT PROCESS

role
Set of behaviors associated with a particular job.

There are several ways to examine how management works. One way is to divide the tasks managers perform into categories. A second way is to look at the roles different types of managers play in a company. A **role** is a set of behaviors associated with a particular job. A third way is to look at the skills managers need to do their jobs. Each of these ways of thinking about management will help you better understand the management process.

FIGURE 1.1
The Management Pyramid

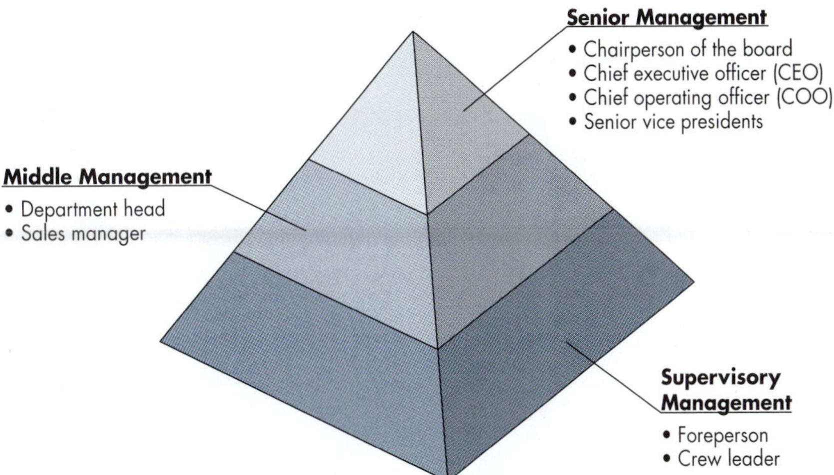

planning
Deciding what objectives to pursue during a future period and what to do to achieve those objectives.

organizing
Grouping activities, assigning activities, and providing the authority necessary to carry out the activities.

staffing
Determining human resource needs and recruiting, selecting, training, and developing human resources.

leading
Directing and channeling human behavior toward the accomplishment of objectives.

Management Tasks

Managers in all organizations—from small businesses to large companies—engage in some basic activities. These activities can be divided into five categories:

1. **Planning.** A manager decides on goals and the actions the organization must take to meet them. A CEO who sets a goal of increasing sales by 10 percent in the next year by developing a new software program is engaged in planning.
2. **Organizing.** A manager groups related activities together and assigns employees to perform them. A manager who sets up a team of employees to restock an aisle in a supermarket is organizing.
3. **Staffing.** A manager decides how many and what kind of people an organization needs to meet its goals and then recruits, selects, and trains the right people. A restaurant manager's staffing duties include interviewing and training waiters.
4. **Leading.** A manager provides the guidance employees need to perform their tasks. This helps ensure that organizational goals are met. A manager leads by keeping the lines of communication open. Holding regular staff meetings where employees can ask questions about their projects and responsibilities is a good example of leading.
5. **Controlling.** A manager measures how the organization performs to ensure that financial goals are being met. Controlling requires a manager to analyze accounting records and to make changes if financial standards are not being met.

FIGURE 1.2
Levels of Management
Large organizations usually have at least three levels of management. Each level is responsible for a different set of functions.

1. **Senior Management**

   Senior management is responsible for setting objectives for the organization, deciding what actions are necessary to meet them, and determining how best to use resources. This level of management usually includes the chairperson of the board of directors, the CEO, the COO, and the organization's senior vice presidents.

2. **Middle Management**

   Middle management is responsible for achieving the goals set by senior management.

3. **Supervisory Management**

   Supervisory management is responsible for the people who physically produce the organization's products or provide its services. Crew leaders and forepersons are examples of supervisors.

FIGURE 1.3
Relative Emphasis Placed on Function of Management at Each Level of Management

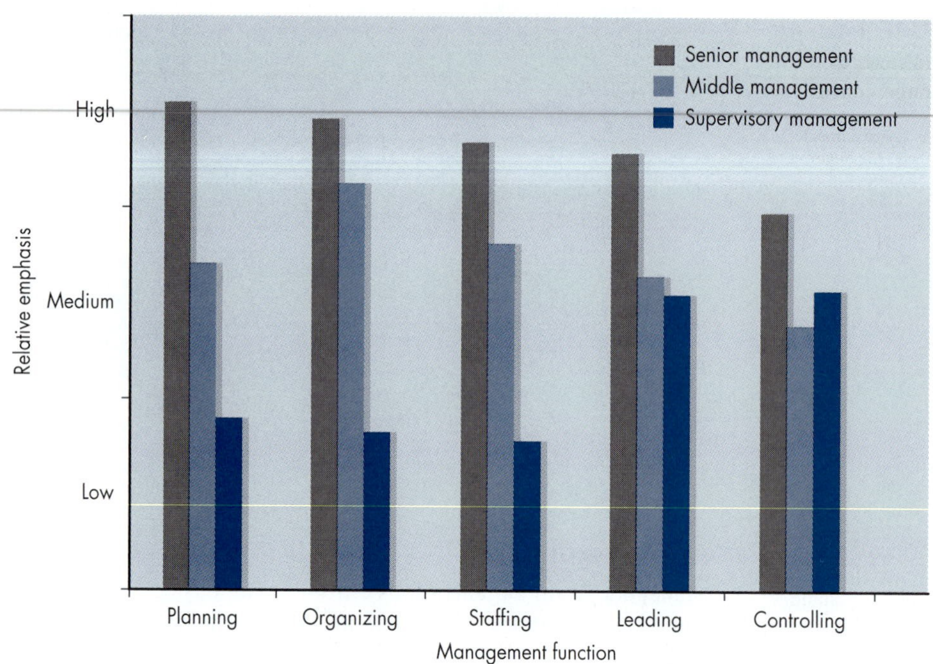

controlling
Measuring performance against objectives, determining the causes of deviations, and taking corrective action where necessary.

Many management activities overlap. Organizing, for example, is difficult without a plan. Keeping good employees on the job is difficult if a workplace is poorly organized and lacks leadership.

Figure 1.3 shows how different levels of management focus on different activities. Senior managers divide their time about equally among the five activities. Middle managers spend most of their time leading and controlling. Supervisory managers spend little time planning and a lot of time controlling.

Management Roles

Managers have authority, or power, within organizations and use it in many ways. To best use their authority, managers take on different roles. Most management roles fall into one of three categories: interpersonal roles, information-related roles, and decision-making roles.[2]

Interpersonal roles include a manager's relationships with people. A manager plays an interpersonal role by providing leadership within the organization or interacting with others outside the organization.

Information-related roles require a manager to provide knowledge, news, or advice to employees. A manager fills this role by holding meetings or finding other ways of letting employees know about important business activities. *Decision-making roles* are those a manager plays when making changes in policies, resolving conflicts, or deciding how best to use resources. Figure 1.4 gives examples and definitions of the three types of roles.

conceptual skills
Involve understanding the relationship of the parts of a business to one another and to the business as a whole. Decision making, planning, and organizing are specific managerial activities that require conceptual skills.

Management Skills

A third way of looking at the management process is by examining the kinds of skills required to perform a particular job.[3] Three types of skills have been identified.

1. **Conceptual skills** are those that help managers understand how different parts of an organization relate to one another and to the organization as a whole. Decision making, planning, and organizing are managerial activities that require conceptual skills.

FIGURE 1.4
Definitions of Management Roles

Source: Adapted from Henry Mintzberg, *The Nature of Managerial Work* (New York: Harper & Row, 1972), pp. 54–99.

Interpersonal Roles	Information-Related Roles	Decision-Making Roles
Figurehead: Manager serves as official representative of the organization. *Relationship builder:* Manager interacts with peers and with people outside the organization to gain information. *Leader:* Manager guides and motivates staff and acts as a positive influence in the workplace.	*Monitor:* Manager receives and collects information. *Communicator:* Manager distributes information within the organization. *Spokesperson:* Manager distributes information outside the organization.	*Entrepreneur:* Manager initiates change. *Disturbance handler:* Manager decides how conflicts between subordinates should be resolved and steps in when a subordinate suddenly leaves or an important customer is lost. *Resource director:* Manager decides how the organization will use its resources. *Negotiator:* Manager decides to negotiate major contracts with other organizations or individuals.

human relations skills
Involve understanding people and being able to work well with them.

technical skills
Involve being able to perform the mechanics of a particular job.

2. **Human relations skills** are those that managers need to understand and work well with people. Interviewing job applicants, forming partnerships with other organizations, and resolving conflicts all require good human relations skills.
3. **Technical skills** are the specific abilities that people use to perform their jobs. Operating a word processing program, designing a brochure, and training people to use a new budgeting system are all technical skills.

Not all management skills are easy to place in a single category. Most fall into more than one. In order to develop a company advertisement, for example, a manager must have conceptual, human relations, and technical skills. Managers would need conceptual skills to develop the advertisement's message. They would need human relations skills to assemble and motivate the team of people who create the advertisement. Training the team by teaching them a computer graphics program would require technical skills.

All levels of management require some combination of these skills. Different skills are more important at different levels of management, as Figure 1.5 shows. Conceptual skills are most important at the senior management level. Technical skills are most important at lower levels of management, particularly at the supervisory level. Human relations skills are important at all levels of management.

PRINCIPLES OF MANAGEMENT

principle
A basic truth or law.

A **principle** is a basic truth or law. The principle, or law, of gravity explains why objects fall to the ground when they are dropped. The principle of inertia explains why objects at rest remain at rest. Scientists prove that principles are true by performing controlled experiments. These experiments test a *hypothesis,* or an idea about the way something works. Once the experiment has been repeated many times with the same results, the hypothesis is accepted as a law, or principle.

Developing principles of management is more complicated than developing scientific principles. Carrying out a controlled experiment in the business world is difficult to do, because researchers cannot control all of the factors the way they can in a laboratory. To test the effect of a particular business practice, researchers would need to study companies that were exactly alike in every way except the business practice being studied. In the real world, however, companies differ in many ways. It is unlikely that researchers would find identical companies to study.

FIGURE 1.5
Mix of Skills Used at Different Levels of Management

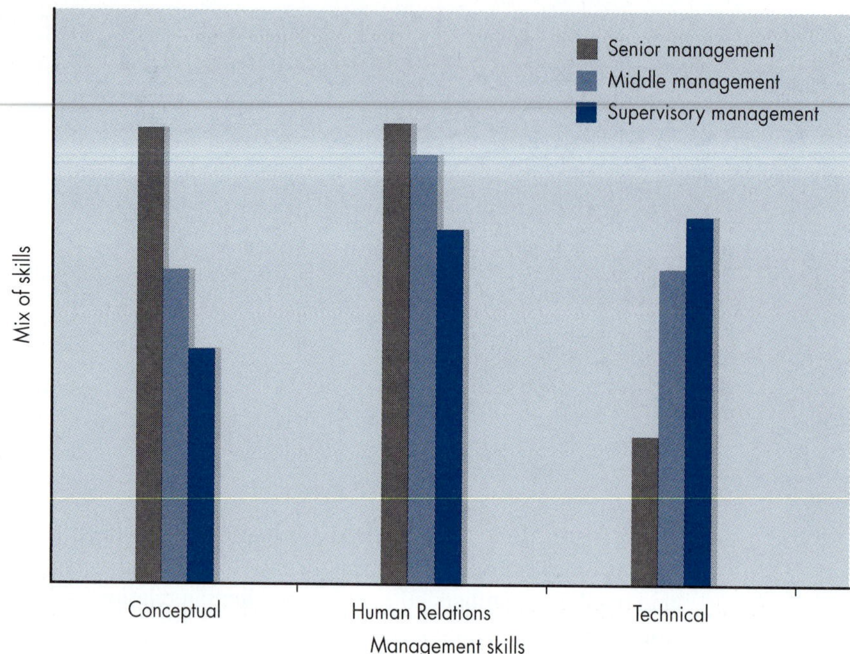

Because controlled management experiments are so difficult to carry out, most management principles are developed through observation and deduction. *Deduction* is the process of drawing a general conclusion from specific examples. For instance, a researcher may observe that employees in 15 companies work more efficiently when their supervisors treat them well. In this case, the researcher may deduce that a pleasant work environment contributes to productivity. This conclusion might then become a management principle.

Management principles are more likely to change than physical principles. They also are likely to be interpreted differently by different people. For this reason management principles are best viewed as guides to action rather than rigid laws. A manager follows management principles most of the time. If, however, a principle clearly does not apply to a specific situation, an experienced manager will not use it. An important part of being a manager is recognizing when a principle should be followed and when it should not. Being able to change and adapt, particularly during times of uncertainty, is an important management skill.

Until recently, many managers followed the management principle that all employees need to arrive at work at the same time. They also believed that people who worked in offices needed to dress a certain way. In the past several years, managers at many companies adopted a new way of thinking about work schedules. Many companies now allow their employees to work flexible schedules, or flextime. Some even allow their employees to work at home. Attitudes about dress codes also have changed, with many businesses allowing their employees to dress casually.

THE CHANGING NATURE OF THE MANAGER'S ENVIRONMENT

Anyone who reads a newspaper recognizes that rapid changes are occurring in lifestyles, resources, information availability, and the work environment, including diversity in the workplace. This section reviews some of these changes and examines their impact on management.

Video conferencing is one of the many ways new data and information are being provided at accelerating rates.

Changes in Information Availability

Because of the increasing sophistication of communication systems and the rapid increase in the use of computers, new data and information are being provided at an accelerating rate. For example:

- Access to the Internet provides a wide array of information that previously was unavailable and/or difficult to obtain.
- Cell phones, e-mail, and teleconferencing enhance the opportunities for improved communications within businesses.

The rapid increase in information availability increases technological change. Increases in information availability and technological change require managers to have increased technical skills. Furthermore, these changes require more skilled and trained employees. This then increases the importance of the manager's role in training. Higher levels of skill and training require new approaches to motivation and leadership. Thus, the manager needs more skill in the human relations area.

Changes in Outlook toward the Work Environment

Some forecasters predict that there will be more emphasis on the quality of work life in the future. The factors that can improve the quality of work life include:

1. Safe and healthy working conditions.
2. Opportunity to use and develop individual capabilities.
3. Opportunity for personal and professional growth.
4. Work schedules, career demands, and travel requirements that do not regularly take up family and leisure time.
5. The right to personal privacy, free speech, equitable treatment, and due process.

Because some of these factors fall within the scope of management, changes affecting them will have a direct impact on the manager's job.

Changes in Demographics

One of the more significant changes in today's environment is the increasing diversity of the American population. The latest demographic data show that the United States is becoming more diverse. Figure 1.6 shows the projected population of the United States by race to the year 2050. It is interesting to note that as of today Hispanics have grown to be the largest ethnic group.

Diversity and Management

For many years, the managers of most large and medium-sized U.S. organizations were almost exclusively white males. As recently as the 1960s and 1970s, women in the workforce filled primarily service and support roles, acting as secretaries, teachers, salesclerks, and waitresses, for instance. Many minority workers were confined to menial jobs such as custodial work and manual labor. In the last two decades of the twentieth century, however, more and more women and minorities have joined the workforce. They also have attained positions as high-level managers in organizations of all sizes. Furthermore, they presently serve in senior-level management jobs in the federal, state, and local governments.

FIGURE 1.6
Projected Population of the United States, by Demographic Group: 2010 to 2050

Source: U.S. Census Bureau, 2004, "U.S. Interim Projections by Age, Sex, Race, and Hispanic Origin," <http://www.census.gov/ipc/www.usinterimproj/>, Internet Release Date: March 18, 2004.

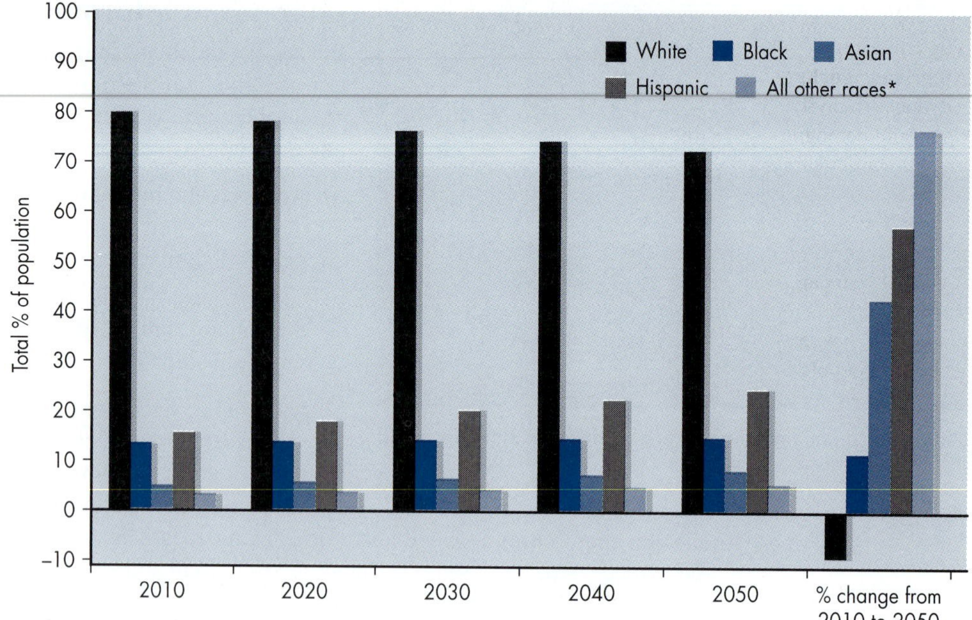

*Includes Native American and Alaska Native, Native Hawaiian and Other Pacific Islander, and two or more races.

glass ceiling
Refers to a level within the managerial hierarchy beyond which very few women and minorities advance.

Despite these changes, most senior managers in the country are still white men. The problems women and minorities have had winning promotions to senior management positions gave rise to the term **glass ceiling.** This is the invisible barrier that prevents women and minorities from moving up in the organizational hierarchy.

As in many other fields, such as sports and space exploration, the glass ceiling is steadily becoming a window of opportunity. Top managers, especially CEOs, are highly visible and often inseparable from their companies. It also can be the spark that is needed to trigger more promotions of women to senior managerial positions. As businesses and government agencies downsize, or lay off workers to cut costs, many of those opting for attractive retirement benefits are senior white males. Their departure opens the door for women and minorities eager to move into the highest ranks of management.

What Is Diversity?

diversity
Including people of different genders, races, religions, nationalities, ethnic groups, age groups, and physical abilities.

Diversity in the workforce means including people of different genders, races, religions, nationalities, ethnic groups, age groups, and physical abilities. The increasing diversity of the workplace represents a major social change in the United States.

The trend toward greater diversity is expected to continue over the next 50 years, as the proportion of nonwhites and immigrants in the U.S. population grows. By creating a culture that is open to different behavioral styles and that incorporates a wide range of views, diversity can improve decision making. Greater diversity allows an organization to respond not only to diverse groups of employees but also to diverse groups of customers.

Another dimension of diversity is related to the increasing globalization of many companies. As companies become more global, diversity must be defined in global and not just Western terms. Defining diversity in global terms means looking at all people and everything that makes them different from one another, as well as the things that make them similar. Differentiating factors often go beyond race and language and may include such things as values and customs. The changing American workplace is described in Figure 1.7.

FIGURE 1.7
The Changing American Workplace
Advances in civil rights and demographic changes in the United States have made the workplace much more diverse than it was 30 years ago. Today, managers must understand how to work with people from diverse backgrounds.

1. **The Workplace in the 1960s**

   Until the 1970s, white males dominated most businesses in the United States. For the most part, managers managed people who came from backgrounds that were similar to their own.

2. **The Workplace in the Year 2008**

   By the year 2008, most workplaces included women and minorities. Increasing diversity has helped companies understand the needs of their increasingly diverse customer bases.

3. **The Workplace in the Mid-Twenty-First Century**

   By the middle of the twenty-first century, minorities will make up almost half of the population. In response to these changes, the workplace is expected to become even more diverse than it is today.

A multicultural workplace presents challenges for both employees and supervisors. For example, religious holidays, which are celebrated at different times throughout the year by Muslims, Christians, Jews, and other religious groups, have the potential to be a source of conflict among employees. Managers need to be sensitive to the needs of their employees when it comes to these holidays. On the other hand, employees should be responsible about arranging to take these days off.

What challenges and contributions does the increasingly diverse workforce present? From an overall viewpoint, organizations must get away from the tradition of fitting employees into a single corporate mold. Everyone will not look and act the same. Organizations must create new human resource policies to explicitly recognize and respond to the unique needs of individual employees.

Greater diversity will create certain specific challenges but also make some important contributions. Communication problems are certain to occur, including misunderstandings among employees and managers as well as the need to translate verbal and written materials into several languages. An increase in organizational factionalism will require that increasing amounts of time be dedicated to dealing with special-interest and advocacy groups.

In addition to creating the above challenges, greater diversity presents new opportunities. Diversity contributes to creating an organization culture that is more tolerant of different behavioral styles and wider views. This often leads to better business decisions. Management Illustration 1.2 shows the value of having a diverse group of suppliers.

ENTREPRENEURSHIP AND MANAGEMENT

professional manager
An individual who performs the basic management functions for the ongoing organization.

Senior, middle, and supervisory managers are all **professional managers.** Professional managers are paid to perform management functions within a company. Like other employees, they receive salaries for the work they do. Professional managers work for businesses, but they do not own them.

Entrepreneurs are people who launch and run their own businesses. When they start out, they must perform many of the basic management functions that professional managers perform. As their companies grow, they sometimes hire professional managers.

Many large companies, including Estée Lauder, Kellogg, and General Electric, were started by entrepreneurs. Gary Comer, for example, started a small mail-order company in 1963. Today his company, Lands' End, is a multimillion dollar company whose clothing is

Management Illustration 1.2

SUPPLIER DIVERSITY IN AT&T

Anyone wondering about the business case for supplier diversity programs should talk to Joan Kerr. The executive director of supplier diversity at AT&T says that in 2006 the company documented that supplier diversity was a factor in generating $11 billion in revenue. Beyond generating revenue, Kerr adds that diverse suppliers can act as powerful advocates for the company sourcing from them, especially since some diverse suppliers are politically active in their communities.

A recent study by the Women's Business Enterprise National Council and management consulting firms SB Services reveals that 80 percent of female consumers polled who were between the ages of 35 and 55 would be compelled to try a company's product or service if the parent company sourced from a women-owned business. The same percentage said sourcing from women-owned business would increase their brand loyalty.

For years, many top-tier companies have rolled out their supplier diversity programs at every stage of their buying process and have been quietly reaping the financial benefits. Many companies point to globalization as a strong reason to get more diverse suppliers on board.

Source: Adapted from Maria Varmazis, "Supplier Diversity Yields Growth," *Purchasing*, August 16, 2007, p. 57.

entrepreneur
An individual who conceives the idea of what product or service to produce, starts the organization, and builds it to the point where additional people are needed.

sold all over the world. The company has thousands of employees and many professional managers.

Being an entrepreneur is much more risky than being a professional manager. Without the right skills and a lot of hard work, entrepreneurs can go out of business and lose all the money invested in their company. Starting and owning a company can be more rewarding than working for a company, however. Successful entrepreneurs can create prosperous businesses that provide large incomes and a feeling of personal accomplishment.

Entrepreneurs and professional managers often have different personal characteristics. Entrepreneurs tend to be more independent than managers, and they may have less formal education. Some entrepreneurs jump from job to job before starting their own businesses.

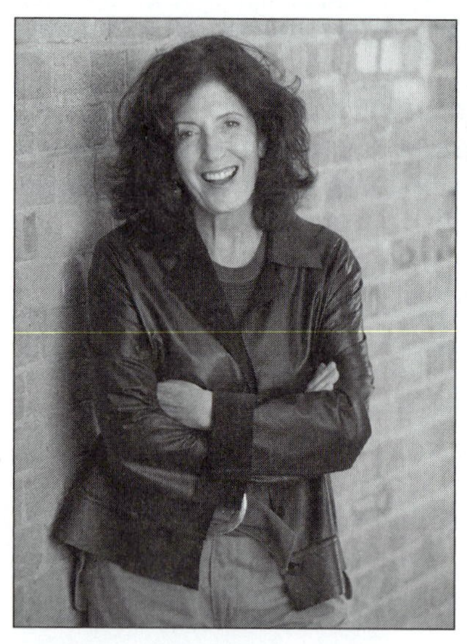

The late Anita Roddick was the founder of the Body Shop, one of the world's most successful retailers of cosmetics and other body products. The Body Shop has had a reputation for supporting social and environmental causes due to Roddick's belief in social responsibility.

Entrepreneurs start with an idea for creating or modifying a product or service that they believe in. Entrepreneurs like the idea of making decisions and being their own bosses. They often find tremendous satisfaction in their work, and their financial rewards can be great. Being an entrepreneur means working long hours and making decisions about every aspect of a business. It also means taking risks. Unlike professional managers, entrepreneurs invest money in their businesses and risk losing all of it if their business does not succeed. Without entrepreneurs, there would be no new businesses and fewer exciting developments, or innovations, in business and industry. Management Illustration 1.3 describes what one company does to encourage entrepreneurship.

Entrepreneurs own their businesses, but they can choose among several different types of ownership. Some entrepreneurs are *sole proprietors,* or people who run their businesses single-handedly. Certain types of work are particularly well suited to this form of ownership—medicine, dentistry, and accounting, for example. Many store owners are also sole proprietors. Other entrepreneurs may form partnerships, especially when a large sum of money is involved. One or more partners may supply the money while another runs the business. Two or more people may also run a business together. Still other small businesses may choose to *incorporate,* or become a corporation, to avoid being held personally liable for financial losses. Some entrepreneurs choose to own franchises.

Management Illustration 1.3

IDEABLOB UNIVERSITY

Ideablob University (www.ideablob.com/university), is an extension of ideablob.com and a first-of-its-kind tool that empowers professors and students to create, share, and evolve business ideas online.

Ideablob is an active online community where small business owners and entrepreneurs share business ideas in exchange for feedback, advice, and votes from the community. Advanta, one of the nation's largest credit card issuers (through Advanta Bank Corp.) in the small business market owns Ideablob and awards a $10,000 monthly prize to the best idea, as determined by the voting. To date, Advanta has paid out prize money to a Chicago-based software developer and a Philadelphia-based non-profit company founder.

A 2006 study by the Johnson Center for Entrepreneurship and Innovation at Indiana University found a 533 percent growth in the number of schools offering courses and programs in entrepreneurship since the 1980s. During the early 1980s, more than 300 universities reported courses in small business and entrepreneurship. Today, entrepreneurial education includes more than 2,200 courses at more than 1,600 schools, 277 endowed faculty positions, 44 academic journals, and nearly 150 research centers.

Source: Adapted from *Business Wire*, New York, January 11, 2008.

IMPORTANCE OF SMALL BUSINESSES

small business
A company that is independently owned and operated and is not dominant in its field; generally has fewer than 100 employees.

A **small business** is a company that is independently owned and operated. Some small businesses, such as neighborhood flower shops, restaurants, or dry-cleaning stores, serve local areas. Other small businesses, such as mail-order and Internet companies, serve customers all over the world. Owners of small businesses often perform all management tasks.

The Small Business Administration (SBA), the government agency that lends money to small businesses, considers a business small if it has fewer than 100 employees. According to this definition, more than 98 percent of the businesses in the United States are small businesses. These small businesses play an important role in the U.S. economy. They employ millions of American workers and sell billions of dollars of products and services.

Small businesses tend to produce more innovations than larger businesses. Many of the most important high-technology companies in the country, including Intel, Apple, and Microsoft, began as small businesses. Microsoft is one of the largest companies in the world, and its founder, Bill Gates, is one of the world's richest people. Some of today's small companies may eventually become corporate giants. Management Illustration 1.4 describes a unique small business.

Entrepreneurship in Large and Medium-Sized Businesses

Many large and medium-sized organizations have begun to encourage their managers to become more innovative and to take more risks. At Dell Computer, for example, CEO and founder Michael Dell encourages his employees to take risks by allowing them to work independently, make mistakes, and learn from the process. He sets hard-to-meet targets and encourages his employees to stretch themselves to meet them. His approach has helped Dell become one of the most successful companies in the country.

intrapreneurship
Entrepreneurship within a large or medium-sized company.

Businesses that want to encourage managers to think more like entrepreneurs must find ways to support and encourage people who develop new products and services. Like Michael Dell, they must be willing to accept failure and to encourage people even after a new idea fails. Entrepreneurship within a large or medium-sized company is sometimes called **intrapreneurship.** Intrapreneurs take risks, but not with their own investments.

Management Illustration 1.4

CATHY RICHMAN—A WOMEN IN BUSINESS

Cathy Richman, founder, chief executive officer, director, and chairwoman of Angels Foster Family Network, embraces the spirit of love, grace, and giving of the heart just for the sake of giving. Richman has donated her time as CEO and chairwoman since she founded Angels in 1998. Richman is involved in every element of Angels, from fundraising and administration, to training and child placement.

A mother of three and former foster parent, Richman spent five years as a volunteer court-appointed special advocate in San Diego County Juvenile courts. During that time she witnessed firsthand the problems and failures of county-run foster care.

Drawing on her experiences as a child advocate and her research in child development, Richman developed her own vision for foster care. She envisioned a select corps of foster parents whose motives for fostering arose out of love for children and who would commit to nurturing foster babies for long periods of time. She dreamed of a day when all foster babies would be properly nurtured and given all the necessary tools to grow up to be healthy, productive members of society.

The Angels Foster Family Network is a nonprofit, licensed foster family agency that specializes in placing infants and toddlers with exceptional, loving, and committed families in San Diego and Riverside Counties. The Angels Mission is to rescue abused, abandoned, and neglected young children, match them up with a select group of screened foster parents, and ensure the maximum emotional, social, and intellectual development of each child.

Angels Foster Family Network has placed more than 205 babies and toddlers in loving foster care families. 65 percent of the children less than three years old in the Angels program are adopted. Only 11 percent of the children in traditional foster care are adopted.

Source: Adapted from Anonymous, "Women Who Mean Business: Cathy Richman, Angels Foster Family Network," *San Diego Business Journal*, November 5, 2007, p. A8.

THE CHALLENGE OF THE NEW INFORMATION AGE

Successful implementation of the basic planning, organizing, and controlling functions of management requires that managers have adequate information. This means managers must first identify and then acquire the necessary information. Identifying and acquiring adequate information historically have been two of the biggest challenges of managers. The advent of the computer age has greatly altered not only the availability of information but also the manner in which it is identified and acquired.

The phenomenal improvements in computer hardware have been accompanied by improvements in software and user compatibility. Modern computers are much more user friendly than those of the past. Managers today do not need to know sophisticated programming languages and computer jargon to use computers. The use of computers in the management process is discussed throughout this book.

ORGANIZATION OF THIS BOOK

This book is divided into seven sections:

- Part I: Foundations
- Part II: Contemporary Issues
- Part III: Planning and Organizing Skills
- Part IV: Staffing Skills
- Part V: Directing Skills
- Part VI: Controlling Skills
- Part VII: Operations Management Skills

Part I provides an overview of the management process. Chapter 1 defines management and describes the functions and skills of management. Chapter 2 presents a historical view of management. Chapter 3 describes the importance of communication skills in management. Chapter 4 focuses on the decision-making skills required in management.

Part II analyzes contemporary issues in management. Chapter 5 focuses on ethics and social responsibility. Chapter 6 describes the internationalization of business.

Part III focuses on planning and organizing skills. Chapter 7 discusses the basics of planning and strategic management. Chapter 8 describes the organizing skills of management. Chapter 9 explains the development of organizational structures. Chapter 10 discusses the role of formal and informal work groups in organizations.

Part IV focuses on the staffing skills of management. Chapter 11 describes the staffing process. Chapter 12 analyzes the process of training and developing employees and managers.

Part V analyzes the directing skills of management. Chapters 13 and 14 examine motivation and the importance of leadership in improving organizational performance. Chapter 15 describes approaches to managing conflict and stress. Chapter 16 focuses on managing change and culture.

Part VI explores the controlling skills of management. Chapter 17 describes the controlling function of management. Chapter 18 discusses appraising and rewarding performance.

Part VII analyzes operations management skills. Chapter 19 discusses operations management and planning. Chapter 20 explores operations control.

Summary

1. *Define management.* Management is a form of work that involves coordinating an organization's resources—land, labor, and capital—to accomplish organizational objectives.
2. *Describe the levels of management.* Three levels of management exist. Top management establishes the goals of the organization and the actions necessary to achieve them. Middle management develops departmental goals and actions necessary to achieve organizational objectives. Supervisors manage operative employees.
3. *Discuss the functions of management.* The functions of management are
   - Planning: deciding what objectives to pursue during a future period and what to do to achieve those objectives.
   - Organizing: grouping activities, assigning activities, and providing the authority necessary to carry out the activities.
   - Staffing: determining human resource needs and recruiting, selecting, training, and developing human resources.
   - Leading: directing and channeling human behavior toward the accomplishment of objectives.
   - Controlling: measuring performance against objectives, determining causes of deviations, and taking corrective action where necessary.
4. *Explain the roles of a manager.* The roles of a manager fall into three major categories: interpersonal, informational, and decisional. Formal authority and status together generate certain interpersonal roles. The interpersonal roles, in turn, determine the informational roles of the manager. Finally, access to information, authority, and status place the manager at a central point in the organizational decision-making process.

5. *Describe the skills required to perform the work of management.* The three skills required in management are
   - Conceptual skills: involve understanding the relationship of the parts of a business to one another and to the business as a whole. Decision making, planning, and organizing are separate managerial activities that require conceptual skills.
   - Human relations skills: involve understanding people and being able to work well with them.
   - Technical skills: involve being able to perform the mechanics of a particular job.
6. *Explain how principles of management are developed.* Typically, principles are developed through a controlled experiment process. However, management principles are developed through observation and deduction.
7. *Define the glass ceiling.* The glass ceiling refers to a level within the managerial hierarchy beyond which very few women and minorities advance.
8. *Explain diversity.* Diversity means including people of different genders, races, religions, nationalities, ethnic groups, age groups, and physical abilities.
9. *Define entrepreneur.* An entrepreneur conceives the idea of what product or service to produce, starts the organization, and builds it to the point where additional people are needed.
10. *Define small business.* A small business is a company that is independently owned and operated and is not dominant in its field. As a rule, small businesses have fewer than 100 employees.
11. *Outline three requirements for encouraging entrepreneurship in medium-sized and large businesses.* Organizations must develop a system that supports and encourages people to champion their new ideas or products; they must tolerate failures; and they must have effective communication systems.

Review Questions

1. What is management?
2. Describe the levels of management.
3. Name and describe the basic management functions.
4. Define the basic skills required in management.
5. How are principles of management developed?
6. Explain how the composition of the workforce is changing.
7. Define glass ceiling and give examples of how it affects women and minorities.
8. Define diversity.
9. Define entreneurship.
10. Distinguish between a professional manager and an entrepreneur.
11. What is a small business?
12. What are three essential characteristics for developing an entrepreneurial spirit in larger corporations?

Skill-Building Questions

1. Management has often been described as a universal process, meaning the basics of management are transferable and applicable in almost any environment. Do you believe a good manager in a bank could be equally effective in a college or university? Explain your reasoning.

2. How does one decide who is and who is not a manager in a given organization? For example, is the operator of a one-person business, such as a corner grocery store, a manager? Explain.
3. Do you think management can be learned through books and study or only through experience?
4. Discuss the following statement: All entrepreneurs are managers, but not all managers are entrepreneurs.
5. Explain how you would deal with the difficulties and challenges of the glass ceiling.

SKILL-BUILDING EXERCISE 1.1
Managerial Characteristics

Take a few minutes to recall the best manager for whom or with whom you ever worked. Identify a specific individual (as opposed to a general type of person). You could have worked with or for this person several years ago or very recently. It could have been on a full- or part-time job. Once you have identified your manager by name, make a list of about six characteristics that you think made this person an outstanding manager.

Take a few minutes to recall the worst manager for whom or with whom you ever worked. Identify a specific individual (as opposed to a general type of person). You could have worked with or for this person several years ago or very recently. It could have been on a full- or part-time job. Once you have identified your manager by name, make a list of about six characteristics that you think made this person a bad manager.

Questions

1. Did you have difficulty identifying both a good and a poor manager?
2. Were the characteristics of the managers you selected similar to those of others described in the class?
3. Do you believe that successful managers have many common characteristics?

SKILL-BUILDING EXERCISE 1.2
Success of a Business

Have each student locate the Web site of any entrepreneurial and/or small business. Each student should be prepared to comment on what can be learned from the organization's Web site. Possible sources of information include *Venture, Inc., BusinessWeek,* or *The Wall Street Journal.*

SKILL-BUILDING EXERCISE 1.3
Online Research

In this chapter, you have learned about the field of management. For more information, go to *BusinessWeek* online at www.businessweek.com. Locate an article on a business that interests you. Write a summary of the article and present your findings to the class.

SKILL-BUILDING EXERCISE 1.4
Are You an Entrepreneur?

In recent years, entrepreneurs, or folks who do things their own way, have become a highly analyzed species, but often the data uncovered have been so voluminous as to confuse rather than clarify.

Among the most confused, perhaps, are thousands of would-be entrepreneurs whose friends tell them they aren't equipped with the qualities for success.

Recognizing this, Northwestern Mutual Life Insurance Co., which considers its own agents to be entrepreneurial, wondered what it is that makes a good entrepreneur. And so it commissioned a test.

Professor John Braun, a psychologist at the University of Bridgeport, is the author of this somewhat revealing—if not entirely scientific—quiz that aims to clarify your understanding.

- Significantly high numbers of entrepreneurs are children of first-generation Americans. If your parents were immigrants, add one to your score. If not, subtract one.
- As a rule, successful entrepreneurs weren't top achievers in school. If you were a top student, deduct four. If not, add four points.
- Entrepreneurs weren't especially enthusiastic about group activities in school. If you enjoyed such activities, subtract one. If not, add it.

- As youngsters, entrepreneurs often preferred to be alone. Did you prefer aloneness? If so, add one. Otherwise, subtract it.
- Those who started childhood enterprises, such as lemonade stands, or who ran for elected office at school can add two because enterprise is easily traced to an early age. Those who weren't enterprising must subtract two.
- Stubbornness as a child seems to translate into determination to do things one's own way. If you were stubborn enough to learn the hard way, add one. Otherwise, subtract it.
- Caution may involve unwillingness to take risks. Were you a cautious child? If so, drop four points. Otherwise, add them.
- If you were more daring than your playmates, add four.
- If the opinions of others matter a lot to you, subtract one. Add one otherwise.
- Weariness with daily routine is sometimes a motivating factor in starting a business. If this would be a factor in your desire to go out on your own, add two points. Otherwise, deduct them.
- If you enjoy work, are you willing to work overnight? Yes, add two. No, deduct six.
- Add four more if you would be willing to work as long as it takes with little or no sleep to finish a job. No deductions if you wouldn't.
- Entrepreneurs generally enjoy their activity so much they move from one project to another without stopping. When you complete a project successfully, do you immediately begin another? Yes, plus two. No, minus two.
- Would you be willing to spend your savings to start a business? If so, add two, and deduct that many if you aren't.
- Add two more if you'd be willing to borrow from others to supplement your own funds. If not, you lose two points.
- If you failed, would you immediately work to start again? Yes gives you four, no takes that many away.
- Subtract another point if failure would make you look for a good-paying job.
- Do you believe entrepreneurs are risky? Yes, minus two. No, plus two.
- Add a point if you write out long-term and short-term goals. Otherwise, subtract one.
- You win two points if you think you have more knowledge and experience with cash flow than most people. You lose them if you don't.
- If you're easily bored, add two. Deduct two points if you aren't.
- If you're an optimist, add two. If you're a pessimist, erase two.

Scoring

If you score 35 or more, you have everything going for you. Between 15 and 35 suggests you have background, skills, and talent to succeed. Zero to 15 indicates you ought to be successful with application and skill development.

Zero to minus 15 doesn't rule you out, but it indicates you would have to work extra hard to overcome a lack of built-in advantages and skills. And if you score worse than minus 15, your talents probably lie elsewhere.

Source: Northwest Mutual Life Insurance Company. Used with permission.

Case Incident 1.1

The Expansion of Blue Streak

Arthur Benton started the Blue Streak Delivery Company five years ago. Blue Streak initially provided commercial delivery services for all packages within the city of Unionville (population 1 million).

Art started with himself, one clerk, and one driver. Within three years, Blue Streak had grown to the point of requiring 4 clerks and 16 drivers. It was then that Art decided to expand and provide statewide service. He figured this would initially require the addition of two new offices, one located at Logantown (population 500,000) in the southern part of the state and one at Thomas City (population 250,000) in the northern part of the state. Each office was staffed with a manager, two clerks, and four drivers. Because both Logantown and Thomas City were within 150 miles of Unionville, Art was able to visit each office at least once a week and personally coordinate the operations in addition to providing general management assistance. The statewide delivery system met with immediate success and reported a healthy profit for the first year.

The next year, Art decided to expand and include two neighboring states. Art set up two offices in each of the two neighboring states. However, operations never seemed to go smoothly in the neighboring states. Schedules were constantly being fouled up, deliveries were lost, and customer complaints multiplied. After nine months, Art changed office managers in all four out-of-state offices. Things still did not improve. Convinced that he was the only one capable of straightening out the out-of-state offices, Art began visiting them once every two weeks. This schedule required Art to spend at least half of his time on the road traveling between offices.

After four months of this activity, Art began to be tired of the constant travel; operations in the two neighboring states still had not improved. In fact, on each trip Art found himself spending all his time putting out fires that should have been handled by the office managers.

Art decided to have a one-day meeting that all of his office managers would attend to discuss problems and come up with some answers. At the meeting, several issues were raised. First, all of the managers thought Art's visits were too frequent. Second, most of the managers did not seem to know exactly what Art expected them to do. Finally, each of the managers believed they should have the authority to make changes in their office procedures without checking with Art before making the change.

Questions

1. What suggestions would you offer to Art to improve his operation?
2. What management skills must Art master if he is to resolve his problems and continue to grow?

Case Incident 1.2

Wadsworth Company

Last year, Donna Carroll was appointed supervisor of the small parts subassembly department of Wadsworth Company. The department employed 28 people. Donna had wanted the promotion and thought her 15 years of experience in various jobs at the company qualified her for the job.

Donna decided to have two group leaders report to her. She appointed Evelyn Castalos and Bill Degger to these new positions. She made it clear, however, that they retained their present operative jobs and were expected to contribute to the direct productive efforts. Evelyn is ambitious and a highly productive employee. Bill is a steady, reliable employee.

Work assignment decisions were to be made by Evelyn. She took on this responsibility with great enthusiasm and drew up work-scheduling plans covering a period of one month. She believed productivity could be increased by 8 percent due primarily to work assignment improvements. She went regularly from workplace to workplace, checking the finished volume of work at each station. Bill assumed, at the suggestion and support of Donna, the task of training new employees or retraining present employees on new work coming into the department.

Donna spent most of her time preparing and reading reports. She made certain to be friendly with most of the other supervisors. She talked with them frequently and helped them fill out forms and reports required by their jobs. She also frequently circulated among the employees of her department, exchanging friendly remarks. However, when an employee asked a question concerning work, Donna referred the person to either Evelyn or Bill.

Some of the employees complained among themselves that the work assignments were unfair. They contended that favorites of Evelyn got all the easy jobs and, although the present volume of work had increased, no extra help was being hired. Several times the employees talked with Donna about this, but Donna referred them to Evelyn each time. Likewise, many of the employees complained about Bill's performance. They based their opinions on the apparent lack of knowledge and skill the new employees had after receiving training from Bill.

Questions

1. Do you think the duties Evelyn and Bill are handling should have been delegated by Donna?
2. What difficulties do you see for Evelyn and Bill in being both group leaders and operative employees?
3. Do you consider Evelyn and Bill to be managers? Why or why not?

References and Additional Readings

1. Throughout this book, the terms *objectives* and *goals* will be used interchangeably.
2. Henry Mintzberg, "The Manager's Job: Folklore and Fact," *Harvard Business Review,* March–April 1990, pp. 163–76.
3. See Robert L. Katz, "The Skills of an Effective Administrator," *Harvard Business Review,* March/April 1986, p. 178.

Chapter Two

The Management Movement

Learning Objectives

After studying this chapter, you will able to:

1. Explain why management did not emerge as a recognized discipline until the twentieth century.
2. Describe the three facets of the U.S. Industrial Revolution.
3. Discuss the role the captains of industry played in the development of modern organizations.
4. Define scientific management, and outline the role Frederick W. Taylor and his contemporaries played in its development.
5. Summarize Henri Fayol's contributions to modern management.
6. Discuss the human relations thrust in management, with emphasis on the role of the Hawthorne experiments.
7. Define the management process period, the management theory jungle, the systems approach, and the contingency approach.
8. Compare the major differences in the American, Japanese, and Theory Z organizations.
9. Summarize the eight characteristics of excellent companies identified by Peters and Waterman.
10. Explain why the international aspects of management are currently being emphasized.
11. Discuss some predictions as to how managers might manage in the twenty-first century.

Chapter Preview

Throughout history, successful leaders have been those that practiced sound management principles. As early as the sixth century B.C., Chinese general Sun Tzu wrote about marshaling his army into subdivisions, of gradations of rank among officers, and of using gongs, flags, and signal fires for communication. Sun Tzu also advocated lengthy deliberations and in-depth plans before going into battle: "Thus do many calculations (plans) lead to victory, and few calculations to defeat."

The great contributors to management thought described in this chapter all had unique ideas, often went against the established thoughts of their day, learned from their peers, were never willing to accept defeat, and persevered when criticized. Their gift to contemporary business managers is the set of tools with which to mold and create the ideas and success of the future. Our responsibility is to use the tools wisely.

Sources: Daniel Wren, *The Evolution of Management Thought,* 2nd edition (New York: John Wiley & Sons, 1979), p. 17; and Lionel Giles (ed. and trans.), *Sun Tzu on the Art of War,* (London: Luzac and Co., 1910) p. 5.

Analyzing Management Skills

What are the benefits of understanding how management theory and practice have changed over the past 100 years? How might you use this information as a manager?

Applying Management Skills

Recall or imagine a workplace task that you found inefficient or tedious. Imagine that your manager asks you for suggestions to improve the procedure for completing the task. What would be your general approach for improving the procedure?

A knowledge of the history of any discipline is necessary for understanding where the discipline is and where it is going. Management is no exception. For example, how often have you read a news story covering a particular incident and formed an opinion only to change it when you understood the events leading up to the incident? Many of today's managerial problems began during the early management movement. Understanding the historical evolution of these problems helps the modern manager cope with them. It also helps today's managers develop a feel for why the managerial approaches that worked in earlier times do not necessarily work today. The challenge to present and future managers is not to memorize historical names and dates; it is to develop a feel for why and how things happened and to apply this knowledge to the practice of management.

Some forms of management have existed since the beginning of time. Ever since one human tried to direct another, management thought has been developing. While there are numerous isolated examples of very early management practices and theories (see Figure 2.1

FIGURE 2.1
Very Early References to Management

Source: Daniel Wren, *The Evolution of Management Thought,* 3rd ed. (New York: John Wiley & Sons, 1987), pp. 13–18.

1792–1750 B.C.	King Hammurabi of Babylon issued a unique code of 282 laws that governed business dealings and a host of other societal matters.	551–479 B.C.	Confucius of China advocated that governmental offices should go to men based on merit and proven ability.
1750 B.C.	Viziers were created in Egypt. Viziers acted as a type of professional manager for the king.	469–399 B.C.	Socrates of Greece observed that managerial skills were transferable.
1300 B.C.	Moses of the Bible was counseled by Jethro, his father-in-law, as to how to organize his people.	384–322 B.C.	Aristotle of Greece exhibited numerous insights into management, touching on the topics of specialization, departmentalization, centralization, and leadership.

Management Illustration 2.1

A VERY EARLY MANAGEMENT THEORIST

www.philosophypages.com/ph/macv.htm

Niccolo Machiavelli (1469–1527) was born in Florence, Italy, into an old Tuscan family. In his late twenties, Machiavelli became a leading figure in the Republic of Florence where he served as first secretary of the council of the republic for 14 years. Following a shift in power in the republic, Machiavelli was dismissed from his office, arrested, tortured, and imprisoned. Orders from Pope Leo X resulted in Machiavelli finally being released from prison. Machiavelli spent the last 14 years of his life in retirement in Florence. During these retirement years, Machiavelli wrote several books on history and politics. He is best known for his book *The Prince,* written in 1513 (but not published until 1532).

Machiavelli's basic assumption was that all people are bad and ever ready to display a vicious nature, whenever they may find an opportunity to do so. Therefore, Machiavelli reasoned that rulers and leaders were justified in using any management style that suited their purpose. In other words, he believed that the ends always justified the means. He believed that rulers should not be concerned with being virtuous but rather should use whatever means, no matter how wicked, to achieve the desired results of making people obey. It is in this light that *Machiavellian* has come to mean an unscrupulous, crafty, and cunning management style.

Sources: Daniel A. Wren, *The Evolution of Management Thought,* 2nd ed. (New York: John Wiley & Sons, 1979), p. 35; and *The World Book Encyclopedia* (Chicago: World Book—Childcraft International Inc., 1979), p. 10.

and Management Illustration 2.1), the development of management thought as we know it is a relatively modern concept. The age of industrialization in the nineteenth century and the subsequent emergence of large organizations called for new approaches to management. The environment that led up to and surrounded the emergence of management thought is the subject of this chapter.

U.S. INDUSTRIAL REVOLUTION

As the name suggests, the U.S. Industrial Revolution encompassed the period when the United States began to shift from an almost totally agrarian society to an industrialized society. The year 1860 is generally thought of as the start of the Industrial Revolution in this country.

Daniel Wren has described the Industrial Revolution in America as having three facets: power, transportation, and communication.[1] Many new inventions, such as the steam engine, allowed industries to expand and locate in areas that at one time were devoid of factories and other signs of progress. Industry was no longer dependent on water and horses for its power.

Transportation moved through periods of industrial and commercial traffic on canals, railroads, and eventually efficient road systems. However, progress always brings its own set of unique problems. Communication lines were extended, decisions had to be made within a rapidly changing framework, scheduling difficulties arose, and new markets developed. All of these changes required new management skills.

Communication by way of the telegraph, telephone, and radio changed the way U.S. organizations functioned. Speed and efficiency dramatically increased. The trend away from an agrarian society forced many behavioral changes on the workers of the land. Schedules, work tasks, workloads, compensation, and safety were hotly debated issues well into the twentieth century.

CAPTAINS OF INDUSTRY

Once industrialization began, it continued at a rapid pace. By the end of the nineteenth century, the economy had shifted from a mainly agrarian one to an economy heavily involved with manufactured goods and industrial markets.[2]

During the last quarter of the nineteenth century, American business was dominated and shaped by captains of industry. These captains of industry included John D. Rockefeller (oil), James B. Duke (tobacco), Andrew Carnegie (steel), and Cornelius Vanderbilt (steamships and railroads). In contrast to the laissez-faire attitudes of previous generations, these individuals often pursued profit and self-interest above all else. Although their methods have been questioned, they did obtain results. Under these individuals, giant companies were formed through mergers in both the consumer and producer goods industries. They created new forms of organizations and introduced new methods of marketing. For the first time, nationwide distributing and marketing organizations were formed. The birth of the corporate giant also altered the business decision-making environment.

For the empire building and methods of the captains of industry, previous management approaches no longer applied. Government began to regulate business. In 1890, the Sherman Antitrust Act, which sought to check corporate practices "in restraint of trade," was passed.

By 1890, previous management methods were no longer applicable to U.S. industry. No longer could managers make on-the-spot decisions and maintain records in their heads. Corporations had become large scale, with national markets. Communication and transportation had expanded and spurred great industrial growth. Technological innovations contributed to industrial growth: The invention of the internal combustion engine and the use of electricity as a power source greatly speeded industrial development at the close of the nineteenth century.

However, despite what seemed to be an ideal climate for prosperity and productivity, wages were low.[3] Production methods were crude, and worker training was almost nonexistent. There were no methods or standards for measuring work. Work had not been studied to determine the most desirable way to complete a task. The psychological and physical aspects of a job such as boredom, monotony, and fatigue were not studied or even considered in the design of most jobs.

At this point in the development of management, the engineering profession made significant contributions. Engineers designed, built, installed, and made operative the production systems. It was only natural, then, for them to study the methods used in operating these systems.

SCIENTIFIC MANAGEMENT AND FREDERICK W. TAYLOR

The development of specialized tasks and of departments within organizations had come with the rapid industrial growth and the creation of big business. One person no longer performed every task but specialized in performing only a few tasks. This created a need to coordinate, integrate, and systematize the work flow. The time spent on each item could be significant if a company was producing several thousand items. Increased production plus the new need for integrating and systematizing the work flow led engineers to begin studying work flows and job content.

The spark generally credited with igniting the interest of engineers in general business problems was a paper presented in 1886 by Henry Towne, president of the Yale and Towne Manufacturing Company, to the American Society of Mechanical Engineers. Towne

Management Illustration 2.2

THE MAN WHO CHANGED WORK FOREVER

www.eldritchpress.org/fwt/taylor.html

Frederick Winslow Taylor was born in Germantown, Pennsylvania, in 1856 of Quaker-Puritan stock. From his boyhood, Taylor had sought to improve everything he saw. Other kids viewed him as weird, since he seemed more interested in laying out the ball field correctly than in playing the game.

His parents wanted him to be a lawyer like his father and hence enrolled him at Phillips Exeter Academy to prepare for Harvard. Though Taylor passed the Harvard exams with honors, his poor health and eyesight forced him to take up an apprenticeship as a pattern maker and machinist with the Enterprise Hydraulic works at Philadelphia in 1874. At the end of his apprenticeship period, Taylor joined Midvale Steel as a common laborer and rose to machinist, to gang boss of the machinists, to foreman of the shop, to master mechanic in charge of repairs and maintenance throughout the plant, and to chief engineer in the short span of six years.

After a three-year stint as general manager at Manufacturing Investment Company, Taylor set up practice as a consulting engineer for management. It was as a consultant to Bethlehem Steel Company that Taylor made his greatest contribution to management with his time and motion studies. Employees willing to follow Taylor's "one best way" of doing a job found that their productivity soared and that they could double or even triple their old pay. As the pace of work accelerated, some employees rebelled, and complaints against Taylor by organized labor even landed him in front of a Senate investigatory panel in 1912.

Recently, some scholars have challenged the methodology and accuracy of Taylor's studies. The assertion is that Taylor drew erroneous conclusions by simplifying his experiments and data collection. Even if these recent accusations are true, Taylor's imprint on management cannot be denied. As stated by populist critic Jeremy Rifkin, "His work principles have been transported to every sector of the globe and have been responsible for converting much of the world's population to the modern time frame."

The world of management was indeed poorer when Taylor died of pneumonia a day after his fifty-ninth birthday. The epitaph on his grave in Philadelphia reads "Frederick W. Taylor, Father of Scientific Management" and rightly so.

Sources: Daniel A. Wren, *The Evolution of Management Thought* (New York: Ronald Press, 1972); Alan Farnham, "The Man Who Changed Work Forever," *Fortune,* July 21, 1997, p. 114; John Greco, "Frederick Winslow Taylor (1856–1915): The Science of Business," *Journal of Business Strategy,* September–October 1999, p. 28; and Charles D. Wrege and Richard M. Hodgetts, "Frederick W. Taylor's 1899 Pig Iron Observations: Examining Fact, Fiction and Lessons for the New Millennium," *Academy of Management Journal,* December 2000, pp. 1283–91. For more information about Bethlehem Steel Company, please visit its Web site at www.bethsteel.com. You can read more about Frederick Winslow Taylor by visiting the Taylor Archive Web site at www.lib.stevens-tech.edu.

stressed that engineers should be concerned with the financial and profit orientations of the business as well as their traditional technical responsibilities.[4] A young mechanical engineer named Frederick Winslow Taylor was seated in the audience. Towne's talk sparked an idea in Taylor's mind for studying problems at Midvale Steel Company. During his years at Midvale Steel Company, Taylor worked with and observed production workers at all levels. It did not take him long to figure out that many workers put forth less than 100 percent effort. Taylor referred to this tendency to restrict output as **soldiering.** Because soldiering conflicted with Taylor's Quaker-Puritan background (Management Illustration 2.2 discusses Taylor's background), it was hard for him to understand and accept. He decided to find out why workers soldiered.

soldiering
Describes the actions of employees who intentionally restrict output.

Taylor quickly saw that workers had little or no reason to produce more; most wage systems of that time were based on attendance and position. Piece-rate systems had been tried before but generally failed because of poor use and weak standards. Taylor believed a piece-rate system would work if the workers believed the standard had been fairly set and management would stick to that standard. Taylor wanted to use scientific and empirical methods rather than tradition and custom for setting work standards. Taylor's efforts became the true beginning of scientific management.

scientific management Philosophy of Frederick W. Taylor that sought to increase productivity and make the work easier by scientifically studying work methods and establishing standards.

Taylor first formally presented his views to the Society of Mechanical Engineers in 1895.[5] His views were expanded in book form in 1903 and again in 1911.[6] **Scientific management,** as developed by Taylor, was based on four main principles:

1. The development of a scientific method of designing jobs to replace the old rule-of-thumb methods. This involved gathering, classifying, and tabulating data to arrive at the "one best way" to perform a task or a series of tasks.
2. The scientific selection and progressive teaching and development of employees. Taylor saw the value of matching the job to the worker. He also emphasized the need to study worker strengths and weaknesses and to provide training to improve employee performance.
3. The bringing together of scientifically selected employees and scientifically developed methods for designing jobs. Taylor believed that new and scientific methods of job design should not merely be put before an employee; they should also be fully explained by management. He believed employees would show little resistance to changes in methods if they understood the reasons for the changes and saw a chance for greater earnings for themselves.
4. A division of work resulting in an interdependence between management and workers. Taylor believed if they were truly dependent on each other, cooperation would naturally follow.[7]

For both management and employees, scientific management brought a new attitude toward their respective duties and toward each other.[8] It was a new philosophy about the use of human effort. It emphasized maximum output with minimum effort through the elimination of waste and inefficiency at the operative level of the organization.[9] A methodological approach was used to study job tasks. This approach included research and experimentation methods (scientific methods). Standards were set in the areas of personnel, working conditions, equipment, output, and procedures. The managers planned the work; the employees performed it. The result was closer cooperation between managers and employees.

The scientific study of work also emphasized specialization and division of labor. Thus, the need for an organizational framework became more and more apparent. The concepts of line and staff emerged. In an effort to motivate employees, wage incentives were developed in most scientific management programs. Once standards were set, managers began to monitor actual performance and compare it with the standards. Thus began the managerial function of control.

Scientific management is a philosophy about the relationship between people and work, not a technique or an efficiency device. Taylor's ideas and scientific management were based on a concern not only for the proper design of the job but also for the worker. This aspect has often been misunderstood. Taylor and scientific management were (and still are) attacked as being inhumane and aimed only at increasing output. In this regard, scientific management and Taylor were the targets of a congressional investigation in 1912.[10] The key to Taylor's thinking was that he saw scientific management as benefiting management and employees equally: Management could achieve more work in a given amount of time; the employee could produce more—and hence earn more—with little or no additional effort. In summary, Taylor and other scientific management pioneers believed employees could be motivated by economic rewards, provided those rewards were related to individual performance. Management Illustration 2.3 provides an interesting story related to Frederick Taylor.

Other Scientific Management Pioneers

Several disciples and colleagues of Taylor helped to promote scientific management. Carl Barth was often called the most orthodox of Taylor's followers. He worked with Taylor at

Management Illustration 2.3

A STEELWORKER MADE MANAGEMENT HISTORY

In 1899, a man named Henry Noll loaded 48 tons of pig iron in one day as part of a scientific management experiment conducted by Frederick W. Taylor for Bethlehem Steel. From that experiment, Taylor developed a high-incentive work program with a set sequence of work and rest motions. The program—described in Taylor's *Principles of Scientific Management*—was designed to more than triple the amount a worker could load in a day. The Taylor method was adopted by companies all over the country.

When the results of the experiment were published, Henry Noll—under the pseudonym "Schmidt"—was described only as an ambitious and healthy 27-year-old man. In a social commentary published 12 years later, Upton Sinclair described Taylor's method as inhumane and accused him of unfairly inducing "Schmidt" to perform 362 percent more work for 61 percent more pay.

In response to the criticism, Taylor and others made several unsuccessful attempts to find Henry Noll, and rumors began to surface that he had died of overexertion. In 1914, he was finally found and pronounced healthy by a physician. Henry Noll—"Schmidt"—died of a natural death in 1925.

Source: Ann Kovalenko, *The Sunday Call-Chronicle,* Allentown, PA, December 6, 1964.

Bethlehem Steel and followed him as a consultant when Taylor left Bethlehem. Barth did not alter or add to scientific management to any significant degree; rather, he worked to popularize Taylor's ideas.

Morris Cooke worked directly with Taylor on several occasions. Cooke's major contribution was the application of scientific management to educational and municipal organizations. Cooke worked hard to bring management and labor together through scientific management. His thesis was that labor was as responsible for production as management was. Cooke believed increased production would improve the position of both.[11] Thus, Cooke broadened the scope of scientific management and helped gain the support of organized labor.

Lillian Gilbreth, the First Lady of Management, spent over 50 years of her life emphasizing concern for employees and showed how scientific management should foster rather than stifle employees.

Henry Lawrence Gantt worked with Taylor at both Midvale Steel and Bethlehem Steel. Gantt is best known for his work in production control and his invention of the Gantt chart, which is still in use today. The Gantt chart graphically depicts both expected and completed production. (Gantt charts are discussed in Chapter 8.) Gantt was also one of the first management pioneers to state publicly the social responsibility of management and business. He believed the community would attempt to take over business if the business system neglected its social responsibilities.[12]

Frank and Lillian Gilbreth were important to the early management movement both as a husband-and-wife team and as individuals. The Gilbreths, inspired by Taylor and scientific research, were among the first to use motion picture films to study hand and body movements to eliminate wasted motion. Frank Gilbreth's major area of interest was the study of motions and work methods. Lillian Gilbreth's primary field was psychology. Following Frank's untimely death in 1924 (he was in his mid-50s), Lillian continued their work for almost 50 years until her death in 1972. During this time, Lillian's work emphasized concern for the worker, and she showed how scientific management should foster rather than stifle employees. Because of her many achievements (see Figure 2.2), Lillian Gilbreth became known as the First Lady of Management. By combining motion study and psychology, the Gilbreths contributed greatly to research in the areas of fatigue, monotony, micromotion study, and morale.

FIGURE 2.2
Lillian M. Gilbreth: First Lady of Management

Source: From Daniel A. Wren, *Evolution of Management Thought*, 4/e, 1994, p. 143. Reprinted with permission of John Wiley & Sons, Inc.

- First female member of the Society of Industrial Engineers (1921).
- First female member of the American Society of Mechanical Engineers.
- First female selected to attend the National Academy of Engineering.
- First woman to receive the degree of Honorary Master of Engineering (University of Michigan).
- First female professor of management at an engineering school (Purdue University, 1935).
- First female professor of management at Newark College of Engineering.
- First and only female recipient of the Gilbreth Medal (1931).
- First female awarded the Gantt Gold Medal.
- First and only recipient of the CIOS Gold Medal.
- Received over 20 honorary degrees and served five U.S. presidents as an adviser.

FAYOL'S THEORY OF MANAGEMENT

Henri Fayol, a Frenchman, was the first to issue a complete statement on a theory of general management. Though popular in Europe in the early 1900s, the theory did not really gain acceptance in America until the late 1940s. Today, Fayol's greatest contribution is considered to be his theory of management principles and elements. Fayol identified the following 14 principles of management:

1. *Division of work:* concept of specialization of work.
2. *Authority:* formal (positional) authority versus personal authority.
3. *Discipline:* based on obedience and respect.
4. *Unity of command:* each employee should receive orders from only one superior.
5. *Unity of direction:* one boss and one plan for a group of activities having the same objective.
6. *Subordination of individual interests to the general interest:* a plea to abolish the tendency to place individual interest ahead of the group interest.
7. *Remuneration:* the mode of payment of wages was dependent on many factors.
8. *Centralization:* the degree of centralization desired depended on the situation and the formal communication channels.
9. *Scalar chain* (line of authority): shows the routing of the line of authority and formal communication channels.
10. *Order:* ensured a place for everything.
11. *Equity:* resulted from kindness and justice.
12. *Stability of tenured personnel:* called for orderly personnel planning.
13. *Initiative:* called for individual zeal and energy in all efforts.
14. *Esprit de corps:* stressed the building of harmony and unity within the organization.

Fayol developed his list of principles from the practices he had used most often in his own work. He used them as general guidelines for effective management but stressed flexibility in their application to allow for different and changing circumstances.

Fayol's real contribution, however, was not the 14 principles themselves (many of which were the products of the early factory system) but his formal recognition and synthesis of these principles. In presenting his principles of management, Fayol was probably the first to outline what today are called the *functions of management*. In essence, he identified planning, organizing, commanding, coordinating, and controlling as elements of management. He most heavily emphasized planning and organizing because he viewed these elements as essential

FIGURE 2.3
Significant Events Contributing to the Solidification of Management

- First conference on Scientific Management, October 1911.
- First doctoral dissertation on subject of scientific management by H. R. Drury at Columbia University, 1915.
- Founding of professional management societies: Society to Promote the Science of Management, 1912; Society of Industrial Engineers, 1917; American Management Association, 1923; Society for Advancement of Management, 1936.
- First meeting of management teachers, December 1924.

to the other functions. Recent translations and interpretations of some of Fayol's very early papers have further reinforced the fact that Fayol was ahead of his time in recognizing the role of administration (management) in determining the success of an organization.[13]

The works of Taylor and Fayol are essentially complementary. Both believed proper management of personnel and other resources is the key to organizational success. Both used a scientific approach to management. The major difference is in their orientation. Taylor stressed the management of operative work, whereas Fayol emphasized the management of organization.

PERIOD OF SOLIDIFICATION

period of solidification
A period in the 1920s and 1930s in which management became recognized as a discipline.

The 1920s and most of the 1930s were a **period of solidification** and popularization of management as a discipline. The acceptance of management as a respectable discipline was gained through several avenues. Universities and colleges began to teach management; by 1925, most schools of engineering were offering classes in management.[14] Professional societies began to take an interest in management. Much of the management pioneers' work was presented through the American Society of Mechanical Engineers. After the turn of the century, many other professional societies began to promote management. By the mid-1930s, management was truly a recognized discipline. Figure 2.3 summarizes the major events leading to this recognition.

THE HUMAN RELATIONS THRUST

The Great Depression of 1929–32 saw unemployment in excess of 25 percent. Afterward, unions sought and gained major advantages for the working class. In this period, known as the Golden Age of Unionism, legislatures and courts actively supported organized labor and the worker. The general climate tended to emphasize understanding employees and their needs (as opposed to focusing on the methods used to conduct work). Figure 2.4 summarizes several of the most important pro-union laws passed during the 1920s and 1930s. A major research project, known as the Hawthorne studies, is generally recognized as igniting the interest of business in the human element of the workplace.[15]

FIGURE 2.4
Significant Pro-Union Legislation during the 1920s and 1930s

Railway Labor Act of 1926	Gave railway workers the right to form unions and engage in collective bargaining; established a corresponding obligation for employers to recognize and collectively bargain with unions.
Norris–La Guardia Act of 1932	Severely restricted the use of injunctions to limit union activity.
National Labor Relations Act of 1935 (Wagner Act)	Resulted in full, enforceable rights of employees to join unions and to engage in collective bargaining with their employer, who was legally obligated to do so.
Fair Labor Standards Act of 1938	Established minimum wages and required that time-and-a-half be paid for hours worked over 40 in one week.

Management Illustration 2.4

THE HAWTHORNE STUDIES

The Hawthorne studies were comprised of four major categories of experiments. The illumination experiments took place before the Harvard researchers were involved. In these experiments, the level of illumination was altered in one test group, and the resulting outputs were then compared to the outputs of another group not subjected to changes in illumination. Only when the intensity of illumination was reduced to moonlight level was there any appreciable decline in productivity. The relay assembly test room experiments were concerned with evaluating the effects of improved material conditions, methods of work, relief from fatigue, reduced monotony, and wage incentives on group output. All of these factors were found to have little effect on output. The interview program involved interviewing over 20,000 workers to gain information about their attitudes and sentiments. Out of these interviews came the first insights as to the influence of the work group on the outputs of the group's individual members. The bank wiring observation room experiments were designed to further investigate the influence of the group on individual group members. This experiment tested the effect of a group piecework incentive pay plan on the output of the work group in a bank wiring room. The researchers concluded from this experiment that output is actually a form of social behavior, and that, if a worker is to be accepted, he or she must act in accordance with the standards of the group.

Source: Alan C. Filley and Robert J. House, *Managerial Process and Organizational Behavior* (Glenview, IL: Scott, Foresman and Co., 1969), pp. 19–21. For more information on studies conducted by the National Academy of Sciences, go to its Web site at www.nas.edu.

Hawthorne studies
Series of experiments conducted in 1924 at the Hawthorne plant of Western Electric in Cicero, Illinois; production increased in relationship to psychological and social conditions rather than to the environment.

The Hawthorne Studies

The **Hawthorne studies** began in 1924 when the National Research Council of the National Academy of Sciences began a project to define the relationship between physical working conditions and worker productivity. The Hawthorne plant of Western Electric in Cicero, Illinois, was the study site. First, the researchers lowered the level of lighting, expecting productivity to decrease. To their astonishment, productivity increased. Over the next several months, the researchers repeated the experiment by testing many different levels of lighting and other variables. Regardless of the level of light, output was found to increase.

Baffled by the results, in early 1927 the researchers called in a team of psychologists from Harvard University led by Elton Mayo. Over the next five years, hundreds of experiments were run involving thousands of employees. In these experiments, the researchers altered such variables as wage payments, rest periods, and length of workday. The results were similar to those obtained in the illumination experiments: Production increased, but with no obvious relationship to the environment. After much analysis, the researchers concluded that other factors besides the physical environment affected worker productivity. They found that employees reacted to the psychological and social conditions at work, such as informal group pressures, individual recognition, and participation in decision making.

The researchers also discovered that the attention shown to the employees by the experimenters positively biased their productivity. This phenomenon has since become known as the *Hawthorne effect*. Yet another finding was the significance of effective supervision to both productivity and employee morale. While the methods used and the conclusions reached by the Hawthorne researchers have been questioned, they did generate great interest in the human problems in the workplace and focused attention on the human factor.[16] Management Illustration 2.4 describes the specific phases of the Hawthorne studies.

EARLY CHAMPIONS OF HUMAN RELATIONS

Mary Parker Follett was not a businesswoman in the sense that she managed her own business. However, through her writings and lectures, she had a great impact on many business and government leaders. While concerned with many aspects of the management process, her basic theory was that the fundamental problem of any organization is to build and maintain dynamic yet harmonious human relations within the organization.[17]

In 1938, Chester Barnard, president of New Jersey Bell Telephone for many years, published a book that combined a thorough knowledge of organizational theory and sociology.[18] Barnard viewed the organization as a social structure and stressed the psychosocial aspects of organizations. Effectively integrating traditional management and the behavioral sciences, Barnard's work had a great impact on managers and teachers of management.

THE PROFESSIONAL MANAGER

The career manager, or professional manager, did not exist until the 1930s. Until this time, managers were placed into one of three categories: owner-managers, captains of industry, or financial managers. The owner-managers dominated until after the Civil War. The captains of industry controlled organizations from the 1880s through the turn of the century. The financial managers operated in much the same ways the captains of industry did, except that they often did not own the enterprises they controlled and operated. The financial managers dominated from around 1905 until the early 1930s, when the Great Depression severely weakened public confidence in business organizations.

In the late 1930s, the professional manager emerged. The *professional manager* is a career person who does not necessarily have a controlling interest in the enterprise for which he or she works. Professional managers realize their responsibility to three groups: employees, stockholders, and the public. With expanded technology and more complex organizations, the professional manager became more and more prevalent.

CHANGING STYLES OF MANAGEMENT

As organizations grew in size and complexity, managers began stressing the importance of employees and their needs. As managers studied the employees and developed theories about employees' behavior, new styles and methods of managing emerged.

One innovative style of managing was developed by James F. Lincoln of Lincoln Electric Company in 1913. Lincoln realized that effective cooperation requires rewards. Thus, he designed a plan that coupled an incentive system with a request for cooperation. Lincoln emphasized the basic need of all individuals to express themselves. Specifically, the plan contained the following components:

1. An advisory board of employees.
2. A piece-rate method of compensation wherever possible.
3. A suggestion system.
4. Employee ownership of stock.
5. Year-end bonuses.
6. Life insurance for all employees.
7. Two weeks of paid vacation.
8. An annuity pension plan.
9. A promotion policy.

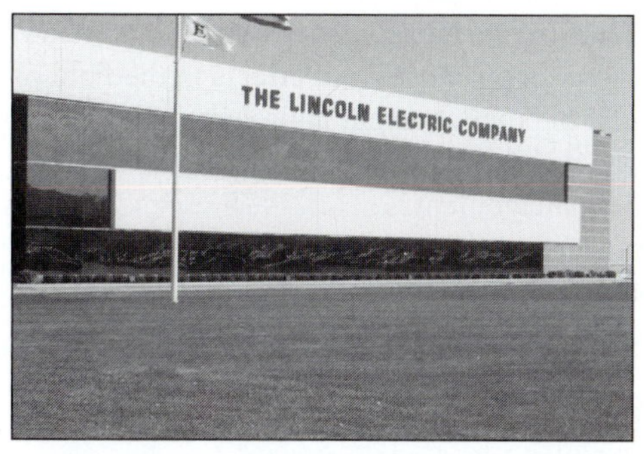

James F. Lincoln of Lincoln Electric Company was one of the first to realize that if incentives were given to employees for a job well done, those employees will continue to work hard. Ninety-five years later, Lincoln Electric employees are still among the highest paid in their industry, www.lincolnelectric.com.

Management Illustration 2.5

115 YEARS OF EXCELLENCE AT LINCOLN

The Lincoln Electric Company began in 1893 as a manufacturer of electric motors. The company made its first welding set in 1909, and by 1922, welding products surpassed electric motors as the company's primary business.

Lincoln Electric employs an "incentive management" system. Many of Lincoln's production workers are paid by piecework. Bonuses are given for reliability and suggestions and have averaged 100 percent of base pay in many years. The company also practices a policy of continuous employment–guaranteed lifetime employment for all full-time employees who have been there at least three years.

Why haven't guaranteed work and high wages put Lincoln in a poor competitive position in its industry? The primary reason is high productivity. According to Lincoln, output per employee has always been 100 percent to 150 percent above that of most other companies.

Lincoln's financial performance has reflected its success with the sales exceeding $1 billion for the first time in 1995. Over the past 15 years, Lincoln has transformed itself from the leading U.S. manufacturer of welding products to the leading global manufacturer in the industry. Today, Lincoln has 35 manufacturing locations, including operations, manufacturing alliances, and joint ventures in 19 countries and a worldwide network of distributors and sales offices covering more than 160 countries.

Sources: William Baldwin, "This is the Answer," *Forbes,* July 5, 1982, pp. 50–52; Maryann Mrowca, "Ohio Firm Relies on Incentive Pay System to Motivate Workers and Maintain Profits," *The Wall Street Journal,* August 12, 1983, p. 50; Daniel Eisenberg, "Where People Are Never Let Go," *Time,* June 18, 2001, p. 40; and "Lincoln Electric Declares 25 Cent Dividend," *Financial Wire,* November 29, 2007, p. 1.

The development of Lincoln Electric Company can be attributed to its innovative management. It certainly has been successful. For several decades, Lincoln workers have consistently been among the highest paid in their industry in the world, averaging almost double the total pay of employees in competing companies. Lincoln's selling price has consistently been lower than that of any comparable product, and the company has consistently paid a dividend since 1918. Management Illustration 2.5 provides some additional information about Lincoln Electric.

Another innovative manager, Henry Dennison (1877–1952), believed the strengths of an organization come from its members and the sources of power are the incentives, habits, and traditions that influence people in an organization.[19] Dennison believed an organization has the greatest strength if all of its members are strongly motivated; their actions do not lose effectiveness through friction, conflicts, or imbalance; and their actions move in a single direction, reinforcing one another. He believed management's primary purpose is to provide conditions under which employees work most readily and effectively. Instead of designing an organizational structure first, Dennison advocated finding "like-minded" people, grouping them, and then developing the total organizational structure. In summary, Dennison believed management's attention must focus on causes and effects in the field of human behavior. Dennison successfully practiced his management approach in the 1920s and 1930s at Dennison Manufacturing Company, which was also one of the early companies to implement the Taylor system of scientific management.

McCormick multiple-management plan
Developed by Charles McCormick, a plan that uses participation as a training and motivational tool by selecting promising young employees from various company departments to form a junior board of directors.

Charles McCormick and William Given, Jr., were top managers who worked independently and who both applied a human relations philosophy to their organizations. Both McCormick's and Given's styles of management were based on employee involvement in the decision-making process.

McCormick, a manufacturer of spices and extracts, developed and made famous the **McCormick multiple-management plan.**[20] This plan used participation as a training and motivating tool by selecting 17 promising young people from various departments within the company to form a junior board of directors. The junior board met with the senior board once a month and submitted its suggestions. Besides the immediate benefit of providing suggestions, the junior board provided early identification of management talent, opened communication lines, and relieved senior board members of much of the detailed

bottom-up management
Philosophy popularized by William B. Given that encouraged widespread delegation of authority to solicit the participation of all employees from the bottom to the top of the organization.

Scanlon plan
Incentive plan developed in 1938 by Joseph Scanlon to give workers a bonus for tangible savings in labor costs.

planning and research. The huge success of the junior board led to the creation of sales and factory boards that operated in much the same way. McCormick's model of developing junior executive boards was used in numerous companies by 1938 and in nearly 400 companies by the late 1940s.[21]

Shoe and Foundry Company encouraged widespread delegation of authority to gain the involvement of "all those down from the **bottom up.**"[22] Given's approach promoted considerable managerial freedom in decision making, the free interchange of ideas, and the recognition that managerial growth involves some failure. Given believed the judgment, initiative, and creativeness of all employees in an organization provide a better end result than the autocratic administration of any single individual.

In 1938, Joseph Scanlon developed a productivity plan that gave employees a bonus for tangible savings in labor costs. The **Scanlon plan** was unique in at least three respects. First, joint management and union committees were formed to discuss and propose labor-saving techniques. Second, group rewards, rather than individual rewards, were made for suggestions. Third, employees shared in reduced costs rather than increased profits.[23] Scanlon believed participation was desirable not only to create a feeling of belonging but also to show clearly the role of employees and unions in suggesting improvements.

MANAGEMENT PROCESS PERIOD

process approach to management
Focuses on the management functions of planning, controlling, organizing, staffing, and leading.

The participative forms of management developed in the 1930s gave rise to the **process approach to management** in the late 1940s.[24] This approach attempted to identify and define a process for attaining desired objectives. The process approach led management to become concerned primarily with identifying and refining the functions or components of the management process. For this reason, the process approach is sometimes referred to as the *functional approach*.

As we have said, Henri Fayol was the first management scholar to present explicitly a functional analysis of the management process. Fayol identified planning, organizing, commanding, coordination, and control as functions of management. However, Fayol's work was not readily available in English until 1949, so his ideas were virtually unknown in this country until then.

Oliver Sheldon, an Englishman, also gave an early breakdown of the management process.[25] In 1923, Sheldon defined management as the determination of business policy, the coordination of the execution of policy, the organization of the business, and the control of the executive.

In 1935, Ralph C. Davis was the first American to publish a functional breakdown of the management process.[26] He subdivided it into three functions: planning, organizing, and controlling.

All of these management scholars made early reference to a functional approach to management. But the concept was not widely accepted until an English translation made Fayol's work widely available in 1949. Thus, Fayol was truly responsible for founding the process approach to management.

OTHER APPROACHES

The late 1950s saw a new era in the study of management. Uneasy with the process approach to management, production managers and industrial engineering scholars began testing mathematical and modeling approaches to quantify management. As a result, mathematical and decision theory schools of thought developed for the study of management. The decision theory school was based largely on economic theory and the theory of consumer choice. The mathematical school viewed management as a system of mathematical relationships.

At about the same time that these quantitative approaches were flourishing, behavioral scientists were studying management in terms of small-group relations; they depended heavily on psychology and social psychology. Drawing on the work of Chester Barnard and sociological theory, another school saw management as a system of cultural interrelationships. An empirical school of thought was developed by those scholars using the case approach. Their basic premise was that effective management can be learned by studying the successes and failures of other managers.

management theory jungle
Term developed by Harold Koontz referring to the division of thought that resulted from the multiple approaches to studying the management process.

Harold Koontz was the first management scholar to discuss this fragmentation movement in detail.[27] Koontz accurately referred to this division of thought as the **management theory jungle.** Many conferences and discussions followed Koontz's analysis in an attempt to untangle the theory jungle and unite the various schools of thought. While some progress was made, a unified theory of management has yet to be realized.

THE SYSTEMS APPROACH

The fragmentation period of the late 1950s and early 1960s was followed by an era of attempted integration. Many management theorists sought to use a systems approach to integrate the various management schools. A system is "an assemblage or combination of things or parts forming a complex or unitary whole."[28]

systems approach to management
A way of thinking about the job of managing that provides a framework for visualizing internal and external environmental factors as an integrated whole.

The **systems approach to management** was viewed as "a way of thinking about the job of managing … [which] provides a framework for visualizing internal and external environmental factors as an integrated whole."[29] Under this approach, the organization is seen as an open system that is influenced by its internal and external environmental factors. The organization then, in turn, influences these same internal and external environmental factors; hence, a dynamic interplay is created. In essence, the manager is asked to view the human, physical, and informational facets of the manager's job as linked in an integrated whole.

One popular thrust was to use a systems approach to integrate the other schools of management into the traditional functional approach. The idea was to integrate the human relations and mathematical approaches into the appropriate functional areas. Thus, while studying planning, a systems approach might include mathematical forecasting techniques.

THE CONTINGENCY APPROACH

contingency approach to management
Theorizes that different situations and conditions require different management approaches.

The 1970s were characterized by the so-called contingency approach. In the **contingency approach to management,** different situations and conditions require different management approaches. Proponents believe there is no one best way to manage; the best way depends on the specific circumstances. Recognizing the rarity of a manager who thinks one way to manage works best in all situations, one might ask, "What is new about this approach?" What is new is that contingency theorists have often gone much further than simply saying, "It all depends." Many contingency theories outline in detail the style or approach that works best under certain circumstances. Contingency theories, many of which are discussed in this book, have been developed in areas such as decision making, organizational design, leadership, planning, and group behavior.

FIGURE 2.5
Comparison of Japanese, American, and Theory Z Organizations

Source: Adapted from William Ouchi, *Theory Z* (Reading, MA: Addison-Wesley Publishing, Inc., 1984), pp. 58, 71–88.

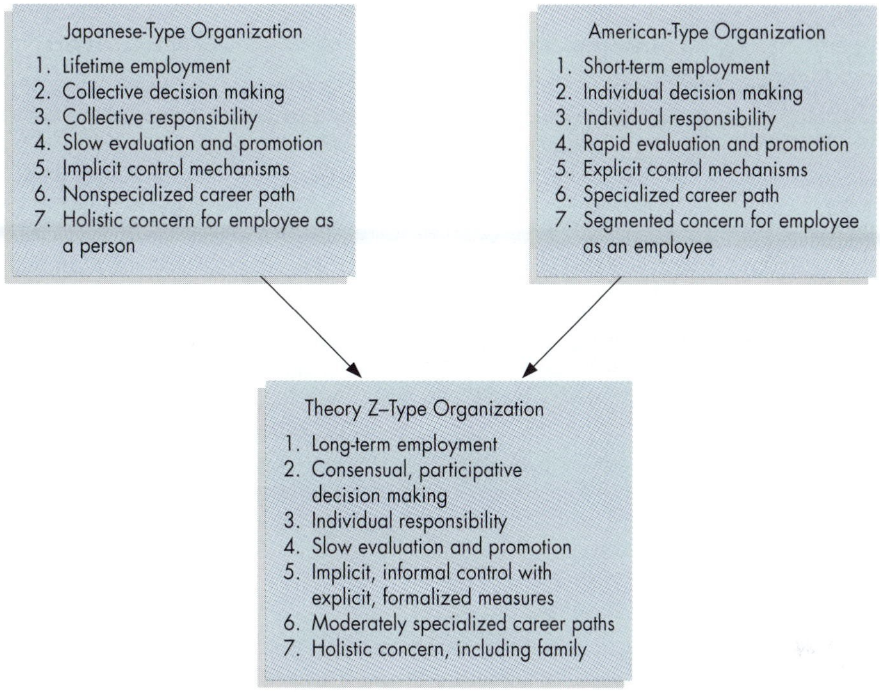

Japanese-Type Organization
1. Lifetime employment
2. Collective decision making
3. Collective responsibility
4. Slow evaluation and promotion
5. Implicit control mechanisms
6. Nonspecialized career path
7. Holistic concern for employee as a person
American-Type Organization
1. Short-term employment
2. Individual decision making
3. Individual responsibility
4. Rapid evaluation and promotion
5. Explicit control mechanisms
6. Specialized career path
7. Segmented concern for employee as an employee
Theory Z–Type Organization
1. Long-term employment
2. Consensual, participative decision making
3. Individual responsibility
4. Slow evaluation and promotion
5. Implicit, informal control with explicit, formalized measures
6. Moderately specialized career paths
7. Holistic concern, including family

THE JAPANESE MANAGEMENT MOVEMENT AND THEORY Z

Theory Z
A theory developed by William Ouchi that attempts to integrate American and Japanese management practices by combining the American emphasis on individual responsibility with the Japanese emphasis on collective decision making, slow evaluation and promotion, and holistic concern for employees.

The tremendous economic success many Japanese companies enjoyed following World War II drew worldwide attention to their management practices. As management scholars studied Japanese management, they identified certain characteristics that differed somewhat from traditional American approaches. In general terms, Japanese managers encouraged more employee participation in decision making, they showed a deeper concern for the personal well-being of employees, and they placed great emphasis on the quality of their products and services. Top management acted more as a facilitator of decision making than as an issuer of edicts. The flow of information and initiatives from the bottom to the top of the organization was emphasized. Japanese organizations also tended to be characterized by lifetime employment and nonspecialized career paths for employees.

Realizing there are many valuable lessons to be learned from the Japanese, William Ouchi developed a theory, called **Theory Z,** that attempts to integrate American and Japanese management practices.[30] Theory Z combines the American emphasis on individual responsibility with the Japanese emphasis on collective decision making, slow evaluation and promotion, and holistic concern for employees. Other factors recommended by Ouchi, such as length of employment and career path characteristics, represent compromises between traditional American and Japanese practices. Figure 2.5 summarizes the profile of traditional American and Japanese organizations as well as Ouchi's Theory Z organization.

SEARCH FOR EXCELLENCE

In 1982, Thomas J. Peters and Robert H. Waterman, Jr., released a book, ***In Search of Excellence,*** that soon became the best-selling management-related book ever published.[31] Working as management consultants at a time when Japanese management

FIGURE 2.6
Peters and Waterman's Eight Characteristics of Excellent Companies

Source: Thomas J. Peters and Robert H. Waterman, Jr., *In Search of Excellence* (New York: Harper & Row, 1982), pp. 13–16.

Characteristics of Excellence	Description of Characteristics
1. A bias for action	A tendency to get on with things; a willingness to experiment.
2. Close to the customer	The provision of unparalleled quality/service; a willingness to listen to the customer.
3. Autonomy and entrepreneurship	Encouragement of practical risk taking and innovation; tolerance of a reasonable number of mistakes as a part of the innovative process.
4. Productivity through people	Rank-and-file employees are viewed as the root source of quality and productivity gains; employees are treated with respect and dignity; enthusiasm and trust are encouraged.
5. Hands on; value driven	The company philosophy and values are clearly communicated; managers take a hands-on approach.
6. Stick to the knitting	Companies diversify only into businesses that are closely related; emphasis is on internal growth as opposed to mergers.
7. Simple form; lean staff	Companies have simple structure with clear lines of authority; headquarters staff is kept small.
8. Simultaneous loose-tight properties	Autonomy is pushed down to the lowest levels, but at the same time certain core values are not negotiable.

In Search of Excellence
Book by Thomas J. Peters and Robert H. Waterman, Jr., that identifies 36 companies with an excellent 20-year performance record. The authors identified eight characteristics of excellence after interviewing managers in each company.

styles were receiving worldwide attention (in the late 1970s), Peters and Waterman asked, "Can't we learn something from America's most successful companies?" Using a combination of subjective criteria and six measures of financial success covering a 20-year period (1961 through 1980), the authors identified a final subsample of 36 American companies. According to the authors' criteria, these companies had demonstrated excellent performance over the 20-year time frame studied. Most of the 36 companies in the final subsample were well-known companies such as IBM, McDonald's, Delta Air Lines, and Eastman Kodak. After interviewing each company in the subsample and analyzing their findings, Peters and Waterman identified eight "attributes of excellence," summarized in Figure 2.6.

While Peters and Waterman's work has been criticized as being overly subjective and not based on sound research methods, it has caused many managers to rethink their ways of doing things.[32] Specifically, Peters and Waterman reemphasized the value of on-the-job experimentation and creative thinking, the need to place the customer first, and the need to treat employees as human beings.

THE EMPHASIS ON QUALITY

Beginning in the late 1970s, gathering steam throughout the 1980s, and reaching its height in the early 1990s was an emphasis on overall quality of the product or service. The quality of American products and services had reached a low by the early 1970s. This phenomenon, coupled with the quality successes of the Japanese, forced managers to look to the quality issue as one way of improving the position of American products and services.

The major change that resulted from this increased attention to quality was a shift from finding and correcting mistakes or rejects to *preventing* them. This led to the development of total quality management (TQM), which is a management philosophy that emphasizes "managing the entire organization so that it excels in all dimensions of products and services that are important to the customer."[33] TQM is discussed at length in Chapter 20.

THE INTERNATIONAL AND GLOBAL MOVEMENT

In the past few decades, many U.S. companies have turned to the international arena for new markets and opportunities. Well-known U.S. companies such as Wal-Mart, McDonald's, and Disney have expanded into international markets. It is a fact that a significant number of the largest U.S. multinationals realize more than 50 percent of their revenues from international markets.

Even companies that do not trade directly in the international and global markets are often greatly affected by foreign competition, alliances, and investment. As a result, U.S. managers are being forced to think in terms of international and global rather than local or national markets. Business emphasis will likely continue to shift to the international scene throughout the intermediate future. International management is discussed in greater detail in Chapter 6.

MANAGEMENT IN THE TWENTY-FIRST CENTURY

As summarized in this chapter, there is little doubt that significant changes occurred in the twentieth century in all facets of American organizations and the manner in which they are managed. From a management perspective, what changes are likely to occur as we move into the twenty-first century?

The authors of the book *Beyond Workplace 2000* have made some interesting projections as to what organizations and management might look like in the twenty-first century.

- Most American companies will find that they no longer can gain a competitive advantage from further improvements in quality, service, cost, or speed, since the gap between rivals on these traditional measures of performance will all but close.
- Every American business and every employee who works for an American business will be forced to become agile, flexible, and highly adaptive, since the product or service they provide and the business processes they employ will be in a constant state of change.
- Every American company will be forced to develop a much better understanding of what it does truly well and will invest its limited resources in developing and sustaining superiority in that unique knowledge, skill, or capability.
- Organizational structures will become extremely fluid. No longer will there be departments, units, divisions, or functional groups in most American businesses. There will only be multidisciplinary and multiskilled teams, and every team will be temporary.
- There will be a meltdown of the barriers between leader and follower, manager and worker. Bosses, in the traditional sense, will all but disappear. While there will be a few permanent leaders external to work and project teams, these people will act more as coordinators of team activities than as traditional leaders.[34]

Other, more recent, projections about organizations and management in the future reinforce the central theme that future organizations will be more fluid and less rigid than in the past.[35] These projections proclaim that organizations of the future will have to adapt to their employees, not the other way around.[36]

Time will tell if these predictions do, in fact, come true. One thing for certain is that the rate of change will continue to accelerate, and both organizations and managers will be required to adapt to these changes.

CONCLUSION

This chapter has summarized the major events that affected management discipline from the nineteenth century to the present. But the discipline did not develop and mature at the same rate in all parts of the country. Similarly, it did not develop from a series of discrete happenings; rather, it grew from a series of major and minor events. Figure 2.7 presents a chronological summary of the major and related events in the management movement.

FIGURE 2.7
Major Components and Related Events of the Management Movement

Major Management Movements	Related Events
U.S. Industrial Revolution (before 1875)	Steam power (1790–1810) Railroad boom (1830–1850) Telegraph (1844)
Captains of industry (1875–1900)	Formation of corporate giants: John D. Rockefeller (oil) James B. Duke (tobacco) Andrew Carnegie (steel) Cornelius Vanderbilt (shipping and railroads)
Scientific management era (1895–1920)	Henry Towne, "The Engineer as Economist," 1886 Frederick W. Taylor's work (1895–1915): Carl Barth Morris Cooke Henry Lawrence Gantt Frank and Lillian Gilbreth Henry Fayol, *Administration Industrielle et Generale,* 1916
Period of solidification (1920 to early 1930s)	Founding of professional management societies (1920s)
Human relations movement (1931 to late 1940s)	Hawthorne studies, led by Elton Mayo (1924–1932) Mary Parker Follett (1920–1933) Chester Barnard, *Functions of the Executive,* 1938
Management process period (early 1950s to early 1960s)	Widely circulated English translation of Fayol's work (1949) Ralph Davis, *Top Management Planning,* 1951 Early principles of management texts
Management theory jungle (early to late 1960s)	Process approach Quantitative approaches Behavioral approaches
Systems approach (late 1960s to early 1970s)	Integrates the various approaches to the study of management
Contingency approach (1970s)	Theorizes that different situations and conditions require different management approaches
Theory Z (1980s)	Combines certain characteristics of traditional Japanese and American management styles
Search for excellence (1980s)	Attempt to learn management lessons from a group of U.S. companies that experienced certain success over the 1961–1980 time span
Emphasis on quality, TQM (1980s–1990s)	Emphasis on overall quality of the product or service
International movement (1990s–present)	Increased awareness of international and global markets and managerial approaches
Management into twenty-first century	Extremely fluid organizations; multidisciplinary and multiskilled teams

Summary

1. *Explain why management did not emerge as a recognized discipline until the twentieth century*. Just as traffic lights were not needed before cars, management, as it now exists, was not needed before organizations became complex. Before the late nineteenth and twentieth centuries, most organizations were relatively simple. Industrialization and mass production brought large and complex organizations.
2. *Describe the three facets of the U.S. Industrial Revolution*. The three major facets of the U.S. Industrial Revolution are (1) power, (2) transportation, and (3) communication.
3. *Discuss the role the captains of industry played in the development of modern organizations*. The captains of industry, who included John D. Rockefeller, James B. Duke, Andrew Carnegie, and Cornelius Vanderbilt, built great companies. They introduced nationwide distribution and marketing methods. Because of the size and dominance of these companies, the relationship between business and government changed forever. Government passed legislation to check corporate practices in restraint of trade.
4. *Define scientific management, and outline the role Frederick W. Taylor and his contemporaries played in its development*. Scientific management is a philosophy about the use of human effort. It seeks to maximize output with minimum effort through the elimination of waste and inefficiency at the operative level. Frederick W. Taylor was the major figure responsible for popularizing scientific management through his writings and consulting. Several contemporaries of Taylor helped spread Taylor's philosophy through their own efforts. The most prominent included Carl Barth, Morris Cooke, Henry Gantt, and Frank and Lillian Gilbreth.
5. *Summarize Henri Fayol's contributions to modern management*. Henri Fayol made many contributions, but the most significant was his development of management principles and elements. The 14 principles Fayol developed are still applicable today, and his five management elements are very similar to today's functions of management.
6. *Discuss the human relations thrust in management, with emphasis on the role of the Hawthorne experiments*. Following the Great Depression, more emphasis began to be placed on understanding workers and their needs. The Hawthorne studies, which began in 1924 and lasted until 1932, focused attention on human relations and specifically on the psychological and sociological aspects of work. Mary Parker Follett also helped to popularize the human relations movement.
7. *Define the management process period, the management theory jungle, the systems approach, and the contingency approach*. The management process period took place between the late 1940s and the late 1950s. During this period, management thought focused primarily on identifying and refining the functions or components of the management process. The management theory jungle, first clearly identified by Harold Koontz, referred to the many different approaches being taken to the study of management in the late 1950s and early 1960s. The systems approach attempted to integrate the various approaches to management. The systems approach is a way of thinking about the job of managing that provides a framework for visualizing internal and external environmental factors as an integrated whole. The contingency approach to management theorizes that different situations and conditions require different management approaches and that no one approach works best in all situations.
8. *Compare the major differences in the American, Japanese, and Theory Z organizations*. In general terms, American organizations place emphasis on individual responsibility, whereas Japanese organizations place more emphasis on collective decision making, slow evaluation and promotion, and holistic concern for employees. Theory Z

attempts to combine the American emphasis on individual responsibility with the Japanese emphasis on collective decision making and responsibility. Figure 2.5 summarizes the major points of each type of organization.

9. *Summarize the eight characteristics of excellent companies identified by Peters and Waterman.* In their book *In Search of Excellence,* Peters and Waterman identified eight characteristics of excellent companies (see Figure 2.6). In general, these eight characteristics emphasize the value of on-the-job experimentation and creative thinking, the need to place the customer first, and the need to treat employees as human beings.
10. *Explain why the international aspects of management are currently being emphasized.* Many of today's U.S. companies have turned to the international arena for new markets and profits. Even those companies that do not trade internationally are often greatly affected by imports or exports from other countries. Thus, almost all companies today are affected to some degree by the international aspects of management.
11. *Discuss some predictions as to how managers might manage in the twenty-first century.* Organization structures may become extremely fluid with no structured departments, units, divisions, or functional groups. The barriers between leader and follower, manager and worker will disappear. Managers will act as coordinators of team activities. Organizations will be more fluid and less rigid and will have to adapt to their employees.

Review Questions

1. What were the three facets of the Industrial Revolution in America? Discuss the impact of each of these facets on the development of today's industry.
2. What effect did the captains of industry have on the relationships between government and industry?
3. What is scientific management? Discuss the four main principles of scientific management.
4. Discuss the major contribution to scientific management of Morris Cooke, Henry Lawrence Gantt, and Frank and Lillian Gilbreth.
5. What was Henri Fayol's major contribution to the management movement?
6. Discuss the impact of the Hawthorne studies on management thought.
7. Describe in detail the following approaches to the management process: Lincoln Electric Company, the McCormick multiple-management plan, bottom-up management, and the Scanlon plan.
8. What is the process approach to management? Discuss some of the major contributors to this approach.
9. Discuss the factors that led to the management theory jungle.
10. What is the systems approach to the management process?
11. Describe the period beginning in the late 1970s where significant emphasis was placed on the quality of products and services.
12. Describe the contingency approach to management.
13. What is Theory Z?
14. Identify the eight characteristics of successful companies reported by the authors of *In Search of Excellence.*
15. How are companies that do not trade internationally affected by international markets?
16. Discuss several predictions concerning how organizations might be structured and managed in the twenty-first century.

Skill-Building Questions

1. From the viewpoint of a practicing manager, what do you see as the major lessons to be learned from the evolution of management thought?
2. Why do you think many people have misinterpreted Frederick W. Taylor's scientific management principles as being inhumane?
3. Offer some general guidelines for applying scientific management principles in a manner that would be positively received by employees.
4. What challenges do you think will be presented by the continued internationalization of companies?

SKILL-BUILDING EXERCISE 2.1
What Have We Learned*

Following are excerpts from a speech made by Frederick W. Taylor in 1911:

> If any of you will get close to the average workman in this country—close enough to him so that he will talk to you as an intimate friend—he will tell you that in his particular trade if, we will say, each man were to turn out twice as much work as he is now doing, there could be but one result to follow: Namely, that one-half the men in his trade would be thrown out of work.
>
> This doctrine is preached by almost every labor leader in the country and is taught by every workman to his children as they are growing up; and I repeat, as I said in the beginning, that it is our fault more than theirs that this fallacy prevails.
>
> While the labor leaders and the workmen themselves in season and out of season are pointing out the necessity of restriction of output, not one step are we taking to counteract that fallacy; therefore, I say, the fault is ours and not theirs.

1. Do you think Taylor's position is equally applicable today? Be prepared to justify your answer.

The founder and chairman of APQC (formerly known as the American Productivity and Quality Center) in Houston, C. Jackson Grayson, warned several years ago that if management and labor cannot make their relationship less adversarial, "then we won't get the full, long-term kick in productivity that we desperately need."†

2. Looking at Taylor's and Grayson's remarks, which were made approximately 73 years apart, one has to wonder what we have learned. Many similar comparisons could be made. Why do you think managers don't seem to learn as much as they could from the past?

SKILL-BUILDING EXERCISE 2.2
Finding the One Best Way

Suppose you have been assigned the simple task of stuffing 1,000 two-page flyers (8½" × 11") into a normal size envelope (4" × 9½"). The envelopes come in boxes of 250, and the flyer pages are in stacks of 1,000 each. The flyers must first be stapled together, folded, and then placed into the envelopes.

a. Get a stapler, a few envelopes, and several 8½ × 11" sheets of paper, and determine how you might accomplish this task. Identify where each component will be positioned and exactly how you will perform the task.

b. After you have tried your first method, see if you can determine any ways in which it might be improved.

c. Compare your method with those of others in your class.

Questions

1. Were you able to improve your first method in step *b*?
2. Did you pick up further improvements from others in your class (step *c*)?

**Scientific Management: Address and Discussions at the Conference on Scientific Management at the Amos Tuck School of Administration and Finance* (Norwood, MA: Plimpton Press, 1912), pp. 23–24.

†"The Revival of Productivity," *BusinessWeek,* February 13, 1984, p. 100.

Case Incident 2.1

Granddad's Company

J.R.V. Company, which manufactures industrial tools, was founded in 1945 by James R. Vail, Sr. Currently, James R. Vail, Jr., is the president of the company; his son Richard is executive vice president. James Jr. has run the company for the past 30 years in a fashion very similar to that of his father.

When the company was founded, James Sr. had been a big supporter of scientific management. He had organized the work very scientifically with the use of time and motion studies to determine the most efficient method of performing each job. As a result, most jobs at J.R.V. were highly specialized and utilized a high degree of division of labor. In addition, there was always a heavy emphasis on putting people in jobs that were best suited for them and then providing adequate training. Most employees are paid on a piece-rate incentive system, with the standards set by time and motion studies. James Jr. has largely continued to emphasize scientific management since he took over. All employees now receive two weeks' paid vacation and company health insurance. Also, employees are generally paid an average wage for their industry. The present J.R.V. building was constructed in 1970, but it has had several minor improvements, such as the addition of improved lighting and an employees' lunchroom.

James Jr. is planning to retire in a few years. Recently, he and Richard, his planned successor, have disagreed over the management of the company. Richard's main argument is that times have changed and time and motion studies, specialization, high division of labor, and other company practices are obsolete. James Jr. counters that J.R.V. has been successful under its present management philosophy for many years, and change would be "foolish."

Questions

1. Do you agree with Richard? Why or why not?
2. Are the principles of scientific management applicable in today's organization? Explain your answer.

Case Incident 2.2

Return to Scientific Management

Recently, a professor at State University was lecturing in a management development seminar on the topic of motivation. Each of the participants candidly discussed problems that existed in their respective organizations. Problem areas mentioned included absenteeism, turnover, and poor workmanship. The participants managed a variety of employees such as automobile assembly workers, clerical workers, computer operators, sanitation workers, and even some middle-level managers.

During the discussion, one of the participants made the following statement: "What we need to stop all of these problems is a little scientific management."

Questions

1. What do you think the person means?
2. Do you agree? Discuss.
3. Take one of the jobs in the above case and show how you could apply scientific management.

References and Additional Readings

1. Daniel Wren, *The Evolution of Management Thought,* 2nd ed. (New York: John Wiley & Sons, 1979), p. 90.
2. Alfred D. Chandler, Jr., "The Beginnings of 'Big Business' in American Industry," *Business History Review,* Spring 1959, p. 3.
3. Harry Kelsey and David Wilderson, "The Evolution of Management Thought" (unpublished paper, Indiana University, Bloomington, IN, 1974), p. 7.
4. Henry R. Towne, "The Engineer as Economist," *Transactions, ASME* 7 (1886), pp. 428–32.
5. Frederick W. Taylor, "A Piece-Rate System," *Transactions, ASME* 16 (1895), pp. 856–83.
6. Frederick W. Taylor, *Shop Management* (New York: Harper & Row, 1903); and Frederick W. Taylor, *The Principles of Scientific Management* (New York: Harper & Row, 1911).
7. *Scientific Management: Address and Discussions at the Conference on Scientific Management at the Amos Tuck School of Administration and Finance* (Norwood, MA: Plimpton Press, 1912), pp. 32–35.
8. John F. Mee, *Management Thought in a Dynamic Economy* (New York: New York University Press, 1963), p. 411.
9. John F. Mee, "Seminar in Business Organization and Operation" (unpublished paper, Indiana University, Bloomington, IN), p. 5.
10. Wren, *The Evolution of Management Thought*, pp. 136–40.
11. Ibid., p. 188.
12. Henry L. Gantt, *Organizing for Work* (New York: Harcourt Brace Jovanovich, 1919), p. 15.
13. Daniel A. Wren, "Henri Fayol As Strategist: A Nineteenth Century Corporate Turnaround," *Management Decision,* vol. 39, issue 5–6, 2001, pp. 475–87; and Daniel A. Wren, Arthur G. Bedeian, and John D. Breeze, "The Foundations of Henri Fayol's Administrative Theory," *Management Decision,* vol. 40, issue 9, 2002, pp. 906–18.
14. John F. Mee, "Management Teaching in Historical Perspective," *Southern Journal of Business,* May 1972, p. 21.
15. For a detailed description of the Hawthorne studies, see Fritz G. Roethlisberger and William J. Dickson, *Management and the Worker* (Cambridge, MA: Harvard University Press, 1939).
16. For example, see Alex Carey, "The Hawthorne Studies: A Radical Criticism," *American Sociological Review,* June 1967, pp. 403–16.
17. Henry C. Metcalf and L. Urwick, eds., *Dynamic Administration: The Collected Papers of Mary Parker Follett* (New York: Harper & Row, 1940), p. 21.
18. Chester I. Barnard, *The Functions of the Executive* (Cambridge, MA: Harvard University Press, 1938).
19. Henry S. Dennison, *Organization Engineering* (New York: McGraw-Hill, 1931).
20. Charles P. McCormick, *Multiple Management* (New York: Harper & Row, 1949).
21. Ibid., p. viii; and Charles P. McCormick, *The Power of People* (New York: Harper & Row, 1949).
22. William B. Given, Jr., *Bottom-Up Management* (New York: Harper & Row, 1949).
23. Joseph Scanlon, "Enterprise for Everyone," *Fortune*, January 1950, pp. 41, 55–59; and Wren, *The Evolution of Management Thought*, p. 330.
24. Mee, *Management Thought,* p. 53.
25. Oliver Sheldon, *The Philosophy of Management* (London: Sir Isaac Pitman & Sons, 1923).
26. Ralph C. Davis, *The Principles of Business Organizations and Operations* (Columbus, OH: H. L. Hedrick, 1935), pp. 12–13.
27. Harold Koontz, "The Management of Theory Jungle," *Academy of Management Journal,* December 1961, pp. 174–88.
28. *Webster's Collegiate Dictionary* (New York: Random House, 1991), p. 1356.

29. Richard A. Johnson, Fremont E. Kast, and James E. Rosenzweig, *The Theory of Management Systems* (New York: McGraw-Hill, 1963), p. 3.
30. William C. Ouchi, *Theory Z* (Reading, MA: Addison-Wesley, 1981).
31. Thomas J. Peters and Robert H. Waterman, Jr., *In Search of Excellence* (New York: Harper & Row, 1982).
32. For a criticism of *In Search of Excellence*, see Daniel T. Carroll, "A Disappointing Search for Excellence," *Harvard Business Review,* November–December 1983, pp. 78–88.
33. Richard B. Chase and Nicholas J. Aquilano, *Production and Operations Management: A Life Cycle Approach,* 6th ed. (Homewood, IL: Richard D. Irwin, 1992), pp. 186–87.
34. Joseph H. Boyett and Jimmie T. Boyett, *Beyond Workplace 2000* (New York: Penguin Books, 1995), pp. xiii–xiv.
35. Peter Senior, "Where Organization and Management May Be Headed," *Consulting to Management,* June 2004, pp. 50–56.
36. Peter Coy, "COG or Co-Worker? The Organization Man Isn't Extinct or Even Endangered—But the Role Has Been Refined over the Past 100 Years," *BusinessWeek,* August 20, 2007, p. 58.

Chapter Three

Developing Communication Skills

Learning Objectives

After studying this chapter, you will able to:

1. Define communication.
2. Describe the interpersonal communication process.
3. Describe problems that could arise from conflicting or inappropriate assumptions made in interpersonal communication.
4. Define semantics, and explain its role in interpersonal communication.
5. Define perception.
6. Explain how emotions may affect communication.
7. Explain the concept of feedback in communication.
8. Explain active listening.
9. Describe the grapevine.
10. Define and briefly discuss the e-mail process.
11. Define the Internet and intranets.
12. Discuss two factors that complicate communications in international business activities.

Chapter Preview

Eraser Man seemed like a harmless gimmick to promote lean manufacturing throughout the global operations of Columbia, Maryland-based W. R. Grace & Co. The pink eraser mascot was supposed to convey a simple message: Eradicate or "erase" waste. But when the $2.8 billion specialty chemicals manufacturer introduced Eraser Man during a focus-group session in China, the company's Asian staff was perplexed and perhaps a little miffed. That's because in China, erase actually means invisible.

"They said, 'do you really want this program to be invisible?'" recalls Michael Piergrossi, W. R. Grace's vice president of human resources. "Of course, the answer is no."

Also at issue was the color pink. "Pink is just not an acceptable color in China; it's feminine. No self-respecting man would want to be associated with a program that's marked by the color pink," Piergrossi explained.

Grace's cultural gaffe wasn't unique. In fact, it's becoming all too common for manufacturers as they go global. Fortunately for Grace, the mistake was easily corrected. (Eraser Man is now tan instead of pink and employees in China are asked to "simplify" or "reduce" rather than erase). But other manufacturers worldwide can face much more serious consequences when they don't prepare for the varying customs and workplace practices of their foreign operations. The potential fallout includes trust issues between employees at home and abroad, along with safety and quality standards that don't quite match up with those within domestic operations.

Source: Adapted from Jonathan Katz, "Worlds of Difference," *Industry Week,* December 2007, p. 39.

Analyzing Management Skills

Most people have heard the statement: Actions speak louder than words. What does this statement mean? Do you agree or disagree with the statement?

Applying Management Skills

Go on the Internet and find an example of communications within an organization. Be prepared to describe what you find.

communication
The act of exchanging information.

Communication is the act of exchanging information. It can be used to inform, command, instruct, assess, influence, and persuade other people. Communication skills are important in all aspects of life, including business.

Managers use communication every day. In fact, they spend as much as three-quarters of their time communicating (see Figure 3.1). Good managers develop effective communication skills. They use these skills to absorb information, motivate employees, and deal effectively with customers and co-workers. Good communication can significantly affect a manager's success.

COMMUNICATION AS A MANAGEMENT SKILL

Communicating effectively is an important management skill for several reasons:

- *Managers must give direction to the people who work for them.* Managers who fail to give clear guidance often find that employees perform their jobs poorly because they do not understand what is expected of them.
- *Managers must be able to motivate people.* Good managers use their ability to communicate to get other people excited about their jobs.

FIGURE 3.1
Communicating in the Business World

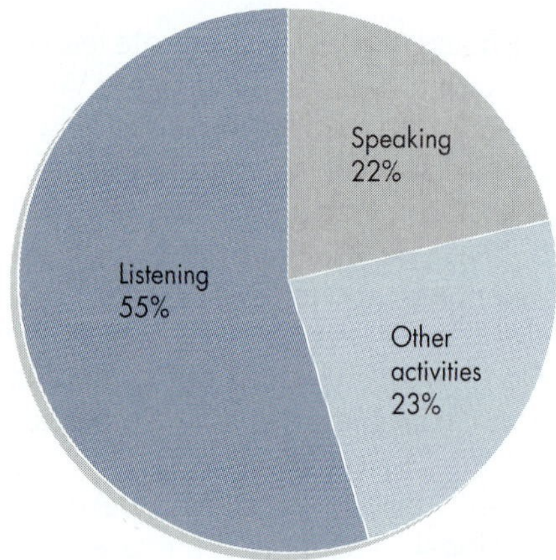

- *Managers must be able to convince customers that they should do business with them.* Effective communication is the key to convincing a customer to purchase a product or service. Without good communication skills, managers will find it difficult to attract customers, even if their companies' products or services meet the customer's needs.
- *Managers must be able to absorb the ideas of others.* Business managers interact with many people, including co-workers, customers, and suppliers. To be effective, they must be able to understand and accept other people's viewpoints.
- *Managers must be able to persuade other people.* Managers often have ideas that others oppose. To persuade other people to accept their ideas, managers must be able to communicate effectively.

INTERPERSONAL COMMUNICATION

Effective communication between individuals, especially between a manager and subordinates, is critical to achieving organizational objectives and, as a result, to managing people effectively. Estimates vary, but it is generally agreed that since managers spend much of their time with their subordinates, effective communication is critical to the wise and effective use of their time.

interpersonal communication
An interactive process between individuals that involves sending and receiving verbal and nonverbal messages.

Interpersonal communication is an interactive process between individuals that involves sending and receiving verbal and nonverbal messages. The basic purpose of interpersonal communication is to transmit information so that the sender of the message is understood and understands the receiver. Figure 3.2 diagrams this dynamic and interactive process. An event or a condition generates information. The desire to share the information, or inform another person about it, creates the need to communicate. The sender then creates a message and communicates it both verbally and nonverbally. The receiver, in turn, perceives and interprets the message and (hopefully) creates a reply message as a response to it. This reply message may generate a response by the sender of the initial message, and the process continues in this fashion.

Often, however, many factors interfere and cause this process to fail. Some causes of interpersonal communication failure are conflicting or inappropriate assumptions, different interpretations of the meanings of words (semantics), differences in perception, emotions either preceding or during communication, poor listening habits, inadequate communication skills, insufficient feedback, and differences in the interpretations of nonverbal communications. Management Illustration 3.1 shows the consequences of communication breakdown.

FIGURE 3.2
Interpersonal Communication Process

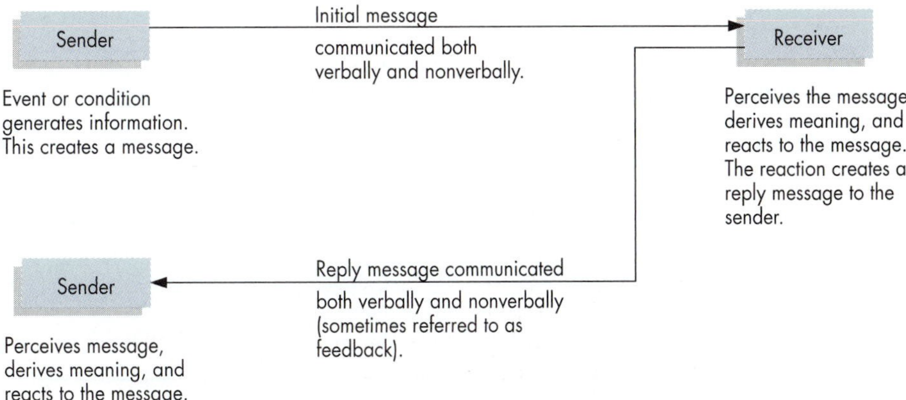

Management Illustration 3.1

COMMUNICATION BREAKDOWN

A communication error was blamed for a near collision at Los Angeles International Airport. The incident occurred when two airliners came within 8,000 feet of each other on a Los Angeles International Airport runway after an air traffic controller miscommunicated with the pilots, the FAA said.

The runway incursion on December 26 involved an American Airlines plane arriving from Mexico and a Mexicana Airlines plane preparing for takeoff. The arriving plane had just landed on the outer runway and was about to cross the inner runway where an Airbus A319 was about to take off for Morelia, Mexico.

The traffic controller told the American Airlines pilot to stop before crossing the inner runway. The pilot apparently misheard the direction and read back that he would go ahead and cross the runway. The controller did not catch the pilot's statement and cleared the Mexicana flight for takeoff before realizing that the American Airlines jetliner was about to roll onto the runway.

Source: Adapted from Jack Gillum, "TIA Tower-Plane Problems Cited," *Tribune Business News,* January 1, 2008, Wire Feed.

Conflicting or Inappropriate Assumptions

Have you ever thought you were being understood when you were really not? This is a common mistake made by couples, teachers, superiors, and parents. If one assumes that communication is flowing as intended, one tends to move on with the dialogue without allowing feedback to indicate whether clarity of expression and communication has been achieved. Good managers always seek verbal or nonverbal feedback, before continuing the communication process. Remember that interpretation of meaning can always be a problem when assumptions are involved. Messages such as "Stop," "Do this right now," and "Please don't" never seem to have the same meanings to children that the adult sender intended. Sound communication usually flows from ensuring that the sender and the receiver see and understand assumptions in the same way.

Semantics

semantics
The science or study of the meanings of words and symbols.

Semantics is the science or study of the meanings of words and symbols. Words themselves have no real meaning. They have meaning only in terms of people's reactions to them. A word may mean very different things to different people, depending on how it is used. In addition, a word may be interpreted differently based on the facial expressions, hand gestures, and voice inflections used.

The problems involved in semantics are of two general types. Some words and phrases invite multiple interpretations. For example, Figure 3.3 shows different interpretations of the word *fix*. Another problem is that groups of people in specific situations often develop their own technical language, which outsiders may or may not understand. For example,

FIGURE 3.3
Interpretations of the Word *Fix*

An Englishman visits America and is completely awed by the many ways we use the word *fix*. For example,

1. His host asks him how he'd like his drink fixed. He meant *mixed.*
2. As he prepares to leave, he discovers he has a flat tire and calls a repairperson, who says he'll fix it immediately. He means *repair*.
3. On the way home, he is given a ticket for speeding. He calls his host, who says, "Don't worry, I'll fix it." He means *nullify*.
4. At the office the next day, he comments on the cost of living in America, and one of his colleagues says, "It's hard to make ends meet on a fixed income." She means *steady* or *unchanging*.
5. He has an argument with a co-worker. The latter says, "I'll fix you." He means *seek revenge*.
6. A cohort remarks that she is in a fix. She means *condition* or *situation*.

Management Illustration 3.2

CROSS-BORDER TRUCKING

It all comes down to the word "establish." In the latest battle over cross-border trucking, the U.S. Department of Transportation, the Teamsters Union, and Congress are at loggerheads over whether to allow trucks from Mexico to cross freely into the United States.

The transportation department has decided to continue its pilot program despite a law against it that Congress passed in December. DOT's argument is that the law prohibits the government from spending any money to "establish" the program—but it began the program in September and simply is continuing it.

The law says: "None of the funds made available under this act may be used to establish a cross-border motor carrier demonstration program to allow Mexico-domiciled motor carriers to operate beyond the commercial zones along the international border between the United States and Mexico."

Semantics aside, the fact that Mexican trucks still are rolling into the United States has rankled the Teamsters Union, which filed a letter in the 9th Circuit Court of Appeals in San Francisco claiming: "The Bush administration broke yet another law in continuing to allow long-haul trucks from Mexico to use U.S. highways." "The lawlessness, recklessness, and sheer arrogance of the Bush administration just blows my mind," Teamsters General President Jim Hoffa said in a statement.

Source: Adapted from Meena Thiruvengadam, *McClatchy-Tribune Business News,* January 10, 2008, Wire Feed.

physicians, government workers, and military employees are often guilty of using acronyms and abbreviations that only they understand.

Words are the most common form of interpersonal communication. Because of the real possibility of misinterpretation, words must be carefully chosen and clearly defined for effective communication. Management Illustration 3.2 illustrates a problem in semantics.

Perception

perception
The mental and sensory processes an individual uses in interpreting information received.

Perception deals with the mental and sensory processes an individual uses in interpreting information she or he receives. Since each individual's perception is unique, people often perceive the same situation in different ways.

Perception begins when the sense organs receive a stimulus. The stimulus is the information received, whether it is conveyed in writing, verbally, nonverbally, or in another way. The sense organs respond to, shape, and organize the information received. When this information reaches the brain, it is further organized and interpreted, resulting in perception. Different people perceive the same information differently because no two people have the same personal experiences, memories, likes, and dislikes. In addition, the phenomenon of selective perception often distorts the intended message: People tend to listen to only part of the message, blocking out the rest for any number of reasons.

Examine Figure 3.4 on page 50 and answer the following questions:

1. In Figure 3.4(a), describe in writing the physical characteristics and age of the woman you see. After writing the physical characteristics and age, turn to page 59 and see how accurate you are.
2. In Figure 3.4(b), which shape is larger?
3. In Figure 3.4(c), which line—AX, CX, CB, or XD—is the longest?

Obviously, if differences exist in how physical objects are perceived, the potential for differences in perception in interpersonal communication is even greater. Differences in perception can occur between younger and older employees, college graduates and noncollege graduates, and supervisors and subordinates. A manager should never assume that his or her actions and words will be perceived exactly as they were intended. In fact, it is probably safer to assume that they will *not* be perceived as they were intended. Feedback is the most effective method for reducing differences in perception.

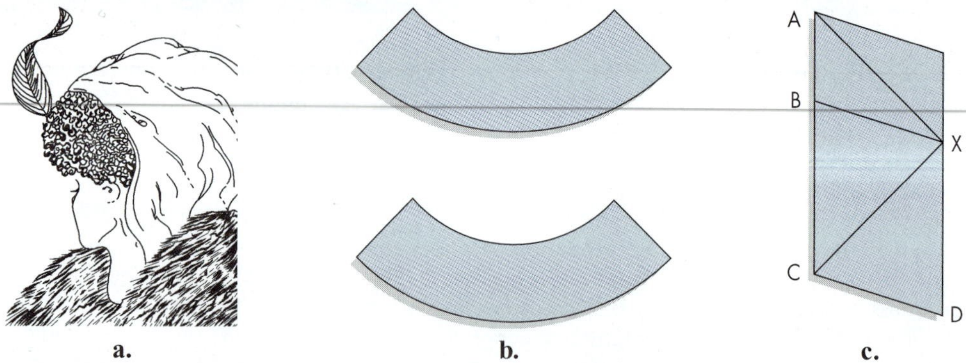

FIGURE 3.4
Illustrations of Perceptual Distortions

Sources: (a) Edwin G. Boring, "New Ambiguous Figure." *American Journal of Psychology*, July 1930, p. 444. Also see Robert Leeper, "A Study of a Neglected Portion of the Field of Learning—the Development of Sensory Organization," *Journal of Genetic Psychology*, March 1935, p. 62. Originally drawn by cartoonist W. E. Hill and published in *Puck*, November 8, 1915. (b) and (c) Gregory A. Kimble and Normal Gamezy, *General Psychology* (New York: Ronald Press, 1963), pp. 324–25.

Emotions Either Preceding or During Communication

Just as perception affects our cognitive processes during communication, emotions affect our disposition to send and receive the communication. Anger, joy, fear, sorrow, disgust, or panic (to mention only a few emotions) can all affect the way we send or receive messages. Emotional disposition is like the stage on which the communication piece plays its part: The stage can be perfectly prepared or in total disarray. The setting for the communication piece is obviously important. Communications during periods of high emotion usually have difficulty succeeding. Therefore, managers with good communication skills strive to manage the emotional as well as the physical communication environment.

LEARNING TO COMMUNICATE

Managers communicate in writing and verbally. Before they can master either form of communication, they must be able to identify the audience, develop good listening skills, and understand the importance of feedback and nonverbal communication.

Understanding the Audience

Managers communicate with many different kinds of people. Hotel managers, for example, communicate with hotel guests, food and beverage employees, housekeepers, maintenance people, architects, travel agents, and many other types of people. They also may deal with senior management from the hotel's corporate office. Each of these groups of people represents a different audience.

To communicate effectively, managers need to determine their audience. Specifically, they need to be able to answer the following questions:

1. What does the audience already know?
2. What does it want to know?
3. What is its capacity for absorbing information?
4. What does it hope to gain by listening? Is it hoping to be motivated? Informed? Convinced?
5. Is the audience friendly or hostile?

Hotel managers communicate with the hotel's housekeeping staff about complaints by guests. In doing so, they must inform the staff of the problem and motivate them to work harder to prevent complaints in the future. They would not need to provide background material on the nature of the housekeeper's role. The audience already understands what that role includes.

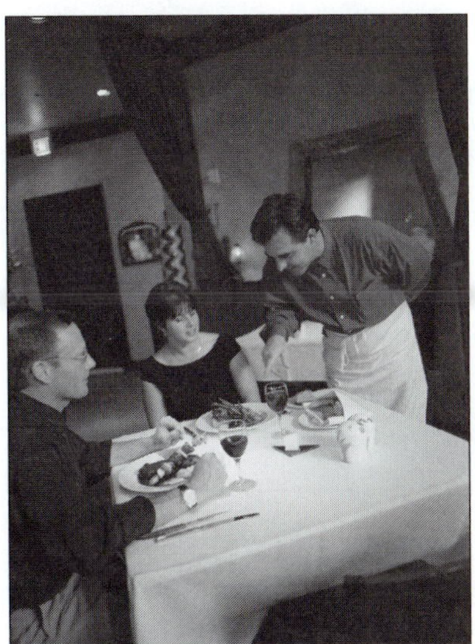

In the restaurant industry, managers need to be able to communicate with many different audiences: from the customer to the hostess, from the bartender to the server, from the chef to the food company and on down the line. Managers need to identify their audience in order to communicate with them effectively.

If a lawsuit is filed against a hotel, managers of the hotel must inform senior management about the situation. In communicating with the hotel's senior management, they would describe what was being done to deal with the situation. They would also provide detailed background information that would allow the corporate officers to fully understand the situation.

Developing Good Listening Skills

One of the most important skills a manager can develop is the ability to listen (see Figure 3.5). Good listening skills enable managers to absorb the information they need, recognize problems, and understand other people's viewpoints.

Managers need to learn to listen actively. **Active listening** involves absorbing what another person is saying and responding to the person's concerns (see Figure 3.6). Learning to listen actively is the key to becoming a good communicator.

Most people do not listen actively. Tests indicate that immediately after listening to a 10-minute oral presentation, the average listener has heard, comprehended, accurately evaluated, and retained about half of what was said. Within 48 hours, the effectiveness level drops to just 25 percent. By the end of a week, listeners recall only about 10 percent or less of what they heard.

Managers need to work at being active listeners. Many people daydream or think about an unrelated topic when someone else is talking. Some people become angry by a speaker's remarks and fail to fully absorb what the person is saying. Others become impatient and interrupt, preferring to talk rather than listen.

Learning to listen actively involves the following steps:

active listening
Absorbing what another person is saying and responding to the person's concerns.

1. *Identify the speaker's purpose.* What is the speaker trying to achieve? Why is the speaker speaking?
2. *Identify the speaker's main ideas.* Which of the points are the key points? Which points need to be addressed by the listener?
3. *Note the speaker's tone as well as his or her body language.* Is the speaker angry? Nervous? Confident?
4. *Respond to the speaker with appropriate comments, questions, and body language.* Use facial expressions and body language to express the emotions you want to express. Establish eye contact, sit up straight, and lean toward the speaker to show interest. Ask a question or make a comment from time to time to show that you are listening attentively.

Feedback

feedback
The flow of information from the receiver to the sender.

Effective communication is a two-way process. Information must flow back and forth between sender and receiver. The flow from the receiver to the sender is called **feedback.** It informs the sender whether the receiver has received the correct message; it also lets the

FIGURE 3.5
Are You a Good Listener?

- Are you open to what other people say to you, or do you make up your mind about things before you hear other people's views?
- Do you become bored when other people speak?
- Do you interrupt people when they are speaking?
- Do you daydream at meetings?
- Are you hesitant to ask clarifying questions?

FIGURE 3.6
Using Active Listening

1. **Listening**

   Knowing how to listen is an important part of dealing with customers. Using active listening skills helps managers understand why customers are dissatisfied.

2. **Responding**

   The way managers respond to complaints can be just as important as the way they solve the customer's problem. Businesspeople should always be courteous and friendly when dealing with customers. They should demonstrate interest in determining what went wrong and figuring out what they can do to solve the problem.

3. **Making Sure the Customers Are Satisfied**

   Managers need to determine whether they have satisfied the customers' needs. To do so, they must interpret the feedback they receive from the customers.

receiver know if he or she has received the correct message. For example, asking a person if she or he understands a message often puts the person on the defensive and can result in limited feedback. Instead of asking if a person understands a message, it is much better to request that the receiver explain what he or she has heard.

In an experiment designed to show the importance of feedback in the communication process, one person was asked to verbally describe to a group of people the layout of the rectangles shown in Figure 3.7. The group members were required to draw the layout based on the verbal description. The experiment was conducted in two ways. First, the group was not allowed to ask questions while the layout was being described, and the person describing the layout was hidden from view so the group could not see the person's facial expressions or other nonverbal communications. Thus, no feedback was present. In the second trial, the group was allowed to ask questions as the layout was being described, and the speaker was openly facing the group. Thus, feedback was present. The results showed the layout was described more quickly to the group when no feedback was allowed. However, feedback greatly improved the accuracy and the group's degree of confidence in the accuracy of their drawings.

Understanding the Importance of Nonverbal Communication

paralanguage
A form of nonverbal communication that includes the pitch, tempo, loudness, and hesitations in the verbal communication.

People have a great capacity to convey meaning through nonverbal means of expression. One form of nonverbal communication, called **paralanguage,** includes the pitch, tempo, loudness, and hesitations in the verbal communication. People also use a variety of gestures in nonverbal communication. In America, for example, one can raise an eyebrow to indicate disapproval, interest, concern, or attention. In Japan, however, that raised eyebrow would be considered an obscene gesture.

FIGURE 3.7
Rectangles in Communication Experiment

Source: From Harold J. Leavitt, *Managerial Psychology,* 1972. Reprinted with permission of The University of Chicago Press.

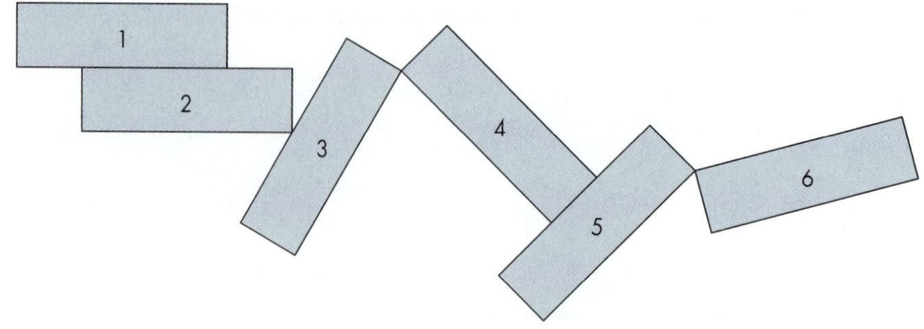

Management Illustration 3.3

WHAT'S THAT ABOUT COMMUNICATIONS?

The newly hired traveling salesman wrote his first sales report to the home office. It stunned the brass in the sales department. Obviously, the new "hope" was a blithering illiterate, for here's what he had written:

> I have seen this outfit which they ain't never bought a dimes worth of nothing from us, and I sole them a couple hundred thousand dollars of guds. I am now going to Chicawgo.

But before the illiterate itinerant could be given the heave-ho by the sales manager, along came another letter.

> I cum hear and sole them haff a millyon.

Fearful if he did, and fearful if he didn't fire the illiterate peddler, the sales manager decided to dump the problem in the lap of the president.

The following morning, the members of the ivory tower were flabbergasted to see the two letters posted on the bulletin board and this letter from the president tacked above:

> We've been spending two much time trying two spel instead of trying to sel. Lets wach those sails. I want ever boddy should read these letters from Gooch who is on the rode doing a grate job for us, and you should go out and do like he done.

Source: unknown.

People also communicate nonverbally by how close they stand to each other. Body posture and eye contact also communicate messages. For example, lack of eye contact can communicate indifference or shyness.

In summary, nonverbal communication is an important supplement to verbal communication and sometimes can even change the meaning of verbal communication. Nonverbal communication is an effective way to communicate emotions. When combined with verbal communication, it gives managers powerful tools for transmitting information to employees.

WRITTEN COMMUNICATION

Managers communicate in writing every day. They send e-mails, write letters, and draft reports. To communicate effectively, managers must be able to write clearly, concisely, and persuasively. Management Illustration 3.3 gives a humorous example of a person who communicated effectively, but whose writing skills were lacking.

Before actually writing a business document, managers need to think about what they want to achieve. They must identify the purpose of the document, the audience, and the main point they want to convey. Using a form like that shown in Figure 3.8 can help them work through this stage of the writing process.

FIGURE 3.8
Identifying the Purpose, Audience, and Main Point of a Document

Purpose

- Why am I writing this document?
- What action do I want the reader to take after reading it?

Audience

- Who will read this document?
- How much does the reader already know about the topic?
- How will the reader use the document?
- Are there any special sensitivities of which I should be aware?

Main Message

- What is the main message I want to convey in this document?
- How will I support that message?

FIGURE 3.9 **Suggestions for Improving Written Communication Skills**

	Examples	
Tips	**Weak Writing**	**Strong Writing**
Use language that is easy to understand. Avoid using jargon or bureaucratic language.	Interfacing with foreign counterparts is likely to continue in the future at an accelerated pace.	We plan to work closely with foreign partners.
Use short, simple sentences.	After three years of declining sales, corporate management decided to adopt a quality-improvement program, which was instituted in all production units last month, with plans for expansion throughout the company by early April.	Sales fell for three consecutive years. In response, corporate management put a quality-improvement program in place in all production units. By April, it hopes to expand the program throughout the company.
Use restrained, moderate language that is not overly emotional.	Sales were terrible this year!	Sales were weaker than management had expected.
Avoid the passive voice in favor of the active voice.	The decision was made to create two new brochures.	The marketing department decided to create two new brochures.
Use gender-neutral language. Avoid sexist language.	Every man in this company does his best to increase company profits.	Everyone in our company does his or her best to increase company profits.

Principles of Good Writing

Many business managers have difficulty writing well. To improve their writing, managers can apply several basic principles:

1. *Write as simply and clearly as possible.* Avoid writing in a way that is difficult to understand.
2. *Be sure that the content and tone of the document are appropriate for the audience.* Do not waste readers' time communicating information they already know. However, do not assume they are as familiar with the topic as you are. Always use a polite tone, especially when writing to customers.
3. *Proofread the document.* If you are using a computer, use the spell-check function. If you are not using a computer, use a dictionary to check the spelling of words you do not know. Always read the document for incorrect grammar or usage.

Figure 3.9 offers suggestions for improving written communication skills.

ORAL COMMUNICATION

Not all business communication is done in writing. In fact, most business communication is done orally.

Some oral communication is formal and takes place at meetings or interviews. Most oral communication is informal. It takes place in offices and hallways, next to the water fountain, in the cafeteria, and over the telephone.

The Importance of Oral Communication

Communicating well verbally is important for managers. Successful managers use their oral communication skills to give clear instructions, motivate their staffs, and persuade other people.

FIGURE 3.10 Techniques for Speaking Effectively

Technique	Example
Enumeration (listing key points)	Our department is looking for people with excellent technical ability, outstanding communication skills, and the desire to contribute to a team.
Generalization followed by examples	We continue to demonstrate our commitment to staff education. Last year we sent almost half of our employees to seminars and training sessions. This year, we expect to include up to 75 percent of all employees in staff education.
Cause and effect	We increased our sales force by 25 percent in the Northeast region in 2001. As a result, sales rose by more than $2 million.
Comparison and contrast	Our newest portable computer is as light as our competitors' and has as much computing power. However, it is $400 less expensive than our competitors' products.

Being able to communicate effectively also is important because it can set the tone within a department or company. In some departments, managers say "good morning" to as many co-workers as they can. They invite their employees to discuss problems with them. In other departments, managers isolate themselves from lower-level employees and make no effort to communicate. These small differences can have a big effect on employee morale.

Developing Oral Communication Skills

All businesspeople need to be able to speak effectively (see Figure 3.10). Whether they are talking to a colleague or presenting a keynote address before thousands of people, they need to follow the same rules of thumb:

1. *Make emotional contact with listeners by addressing them by name where possible.* When talking face-to-face, establish eye contact.
2. *Avoid speaking in a monotone.* Use your voice to emphasize important words within a sentence.
3. *Be enthusiastic and project a positive outlook.* Focus on what is going right, rather than what is going wrong.
4. *Avoid interrupting others.* Even if you know what the other person is going to say, avoid cutting other people off or finishing their sentences for them.
5. *Always be courteous.* Avoid getting angry when other people are talking, even if you disagree with what they are saying.
6. *Avoid empty sounds or words, such as "uh," "um," "like," and "you know."* Sprinkling your speech with empty fillers will make you sound unprofessional.

CHOOSING THE BEST METHOD OF COMMUNICATION

Managers need to master both written and verbal communication skills. They also need to understand when to use each kind of skill. In general, verbal communication is most appropriate for sensitive communications. Written communication is most appropriate for communicating routine information, such as changes in company policies or staff. Choosing the best method of communication will help you relay information in an appropriate and professional manner. Figure 3.11 summarizes the most appropriate method of communication for specific situations.

FIGURE 3.11
Choosing the Best Method of Communication

Method of Communication	Most Appropriate Method of Communication
Oral Communication Alone	• Reprimanding employees • Resolving disputes within the company
Written Communication Alone	• Communicating information requiring future action • Communicating information of a general nature
Oral Communication Followed by Written Communication	• Communicating information requiring immediate action • Communicating directives or orders • Communicating information about an important policy change • Communicating with one's immediate superior about a work-related problem • Praising an employee for outstanding performance

COMMUNICATING WITHIN THE ORGANIZATION

In order to be an effective manager, the importance of the grapevine and e-mail must be understood.

The Grapevine

grapevine
Informal channels of communication within an organization

Many informal paths of communication also exist in organizations. These informal channels are generally referred to as the **grapevine.** During the Civil War, intelligence telegraph lines hung loosely from tree to tree and looked like grapevines. Messages sent over these lines were often garbled; thus, any rumor was said to be from the grapevine. Grapevines develop within organizations when employees share common hobbies, home towns, lunch breaks, family ties, and social relationships. The grapevine always exists within the formal organizational structure. However, it does not follow the organizational hierarchy; it may go from secretary to vice president or from engineer to clerk. The grapevine is not limited to nonmanagement personnel; it also operates among managers and professional personnel.

One of the problems with communicating by "the grapevine" is that information tends to get distorted as it travels to each person and can lead to gossip and rumors.

The grapevine generally has a poor reputation because it is regarded as the primary source of distorted messages and rumors. However, management must recognize that the grapevine is often accurate. Management must also recognize that information in the grapevine travels more rapidly than information in the formal channels of communication. Finally, management must recognize the resilience of the grapevine. No matter how much effort is spent improving the formal channels of communication, grapevines will always exist.

Because the grapevine is inevitable, management should use it to complement formal channels of communication. In utilizing the grapevine, honesty is always the best policy. Rumors and distorted messages will persist, but honest disclaimers by management will stop the spread of inaccurate information.[1]

E-mail

Especially valuable to communication in today's organizations is the use of electronic mail systems, or e-mail, provided by networked and online systems. The e-mail system provides for high-speed exchange of written messages through the use of computerized text processing and computer-oriented communication networks. The primary advantages of this system are that it saves time, eliminates wasted effort (such as unanswered or repeat phone calls), provides written records (if necessary) of communications without the formality of memos, and enables communication among individuals who might not communicate otherwise.

The Internet

Internet
A global collection of independently operating, but interconnected, computers.

The **Internet** is a global collection of independently operating, but interconnected, computers.[2] Frequently referred to as the *information superhighway,* the Internet is actually a network of computer networks. Think of the Internet as analogous to the interstate highway system; just as the interstate system connects to different cities via many different routes, the Internet connects computers around the world via a number of different electronic pathways.

The real value of the Internet to managers is the information that it makes available. Through the Internet, managers can access massive amounts of information by accessing computers around the world that are linked together through the Internet. E-mail uses the Internet.

Intranets

intranet
A private, corporate, computer network that uses Internet products and technologies to provide multimedia applications within organizations.

An **intranet** is a private, corporate, computer network that uses Internet products and technologies to provide multimedia applications within organizations. An intranet connects people to people and people to information and knowledge within the organization; it serves as an "information hub" for the entire organization. Most organizations set up intranets primarily for employees, but they can extend to business partners and even customers with appropriate security clearance. Research has found that the biggest applications for intranets today are internal communications, followed by knowledge sharing and management information systems.[3]

COMMUNICATION IN INTERNATIONAL BUSINESS ACTIVITIES

Communication in international business activities becomes more complicated in both the verbal and nonverbal communication processes. In verbal communication, the obvious problem of dealing with different languages exists. More than 3,000 languages are spoken, and about 100 of these are official languages of nations. English is the leading international language, and its leadership continues to grow. However, as anyone who has studied a modern language knows, verbally communicating with a person in another language complicates the communication process.

The nonverbal communication process is even more complicated. Cultural differences play a significant role in nonverbal communication. For example, in the United States, people tend to place themselves about three feet apart when standing and talking. However, in the Middle East, individuals are likely to stand only a foot or so apart while conversing. This closeness obviously could intimidate an American manager.

There are no simple answers to the problems in communicating in international business activities. However, there are two things the manager should do: (1) learn the culture of the people with whom he or she communicates and (2) write and speak clearly and simply. Most people will have learned English in school and will not understand jargon or slang. As expansion into international business continues, these simple rules will become

Management Illustration 3.4

CULTURAL DIFFERENCES

For North Americans, body language in India can be challenging to understand. Indians say yes and shake their head from side to side, which Westerners misinterpret as no. For no, Indians toss their heads back, similar to the American gesture for yes.

The handshake is used to communicate in many cultures. However, hand contact between men and women is unacceptable in the Islamic world. While carrying on a conversation in Italy, a flailing of the hands and arms would probably go unnoticed. In Japan, however, it may be considered threatening. Furthermore, in the Middle East eating food with the left hand is considered to be unclean.

Source: Various sources.

increasingly important. Management Illustration 3.4 describes several methods of communicating in the international setting.

Summary

1. *Define communication.* Communication is the act of transmitting information.
2. *Describe the interpersonal communication process.* Interpersonal communication occurs between individuals. It is an interactive process that involves a person's effort to attain meaning and respond to it. It involves sending and receiving verbal and nonverbal messages.
3. *Describe problems that could arise from conflicting or inappropriate assumptions made in interpersonal communication.* Misunderstandings can occur when a speaker thinks he or she was being clear or was understood. Questions that go unanswered, points that are misunderstood, and meanings that are misinterpreted are examples of potential problems.
4. *Define semantics, and explain its role in interpersonal communication.* Semantics is the science or study of the meanings of words and symbols. Because of the possibility of misinterpretation, words must be carefully chosen and clearly defined to enable effective communication.
5. *Define perception.* Perception deals with the mental and sensory processes an individual uses in interpreting information received.
6. *Explain how emotions may affect communication.* Emotions affect one's disposition to send and receive communication. Anger, joy, fear, sorrow, disgust, or panic can all affect the way one sends and receives messages. Communications during periods of high emotion are often subject to distortion.
7. *Explain the concept of feedback in communication.* Feedback is the flow of information from the receiver to the sender. For communication to be effective, information must flow back and forth between sender and receiver.
8. *Explain active listening.* Active listening involves absorbing what another person is saying and responding to the person's concerns.
9. *Describe the grapevine.* The grapevine consists of the informal channels of communication that develop within the organization as a result of common hobbies, home towns, lunch breaks, family ties, and social relationships among employees.
10. *Define and briefly discuss the e-mail process.* The electronic mail, or e-mail, system provides for high-speed exchange of written messages through the use of computerized text processing and computer-oriented communication networks.
11. *Define the Internet and intranets.* The Internet is a global collection of independently operating, but interconnected, computers. An intranet is a private, corporate, computer network that uses Internet products and technologies to provide multimedia applications within organizations.

12. *Discuss two factors that complicate communications in international business activities.* Communicating in a foreign language complicates the communication process. Cultural differences exhibited through nonverbal communications are also complicating factors.

Solutions to Perception Questions for Figure 3.4

1. About 60 percent of the people viewing the picture in Figure 3.4(a) for the first time see a young, attractive, and apparently wealthy woman. About 40 percent see an old, ugly, and apparently poor woman. The figure below clarifies the profiles of the two women.

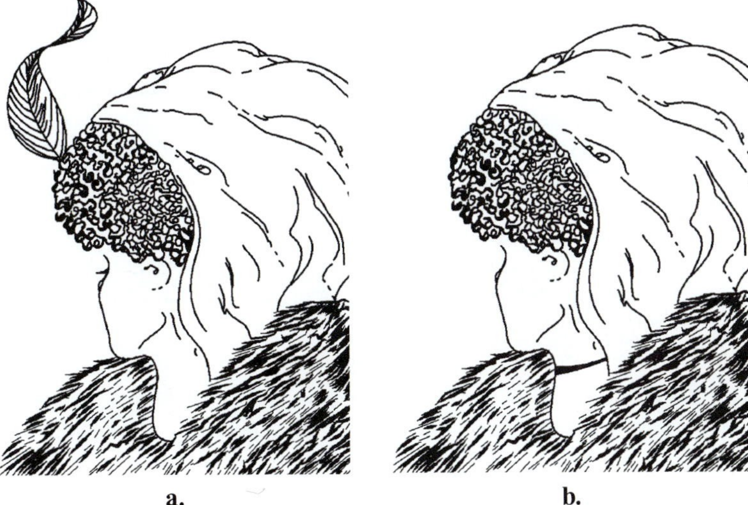

a. Profile of Young Woman
b. Profile of Old Woman

Source: Robert Leeper, "A Study of a Neglected Portion of the Field of Learning—the Development of Sensory Organization," *Journal of Genetic Psychology,* March 1935, p. 62.

2. Shapes are same size.
3. AK, CK, CB, and XD are same length.

Review Questions

1. What is communication?
2. Define interpersonal communication.
3. Give an illustration of a conflicting assumption.
4. What is semantics?
5. What is perception, and what role does it play in communication?
6. How should one deal with emotions in communication?
7. What is feedback, and how does it affect the communication process?
8. What is active listening?
9. Explain the importance of nonverbal communication in interpersonal communication.
10. Describe the following organizational communication systems:
    a. E-mail communication system
    b. Grapevine
11. Define the Internet and intranets.
12. Describe two factors that complicate communications in international business.

Skill-Building Questions

1. Describe some ways the grapevine can be used effectively in organizations.
2. Explain why many managers frequently raise the following question: "Why didn't you do what I told you to do?"
3. Discuss the following statement: Meanings are in people, not words.
4. "Watch what we do, not what we say." Is this a good practice in organizations? Explain.
5. Poor communication of the organization's objectives is often given as the reason for low organizational performance. Do you think this is usually a valid explanation? Why or why not?

SKILL-BUILDING EXERCISE 3.1
Writing Skills

You have been asked by GP&R to write a report describing your company's operations. Here are some facts: There are five project managers, 10 engineers, 14 surveyors, 20 supervisors, 150 heavy equipment operators, 55 laborers, and 33 traffic directors. Equipment includes 24 dump trucks, 25 steam rollers, 38 front-end loaders, 47 backhoes, 39 graders, 35 bulldozers, 27 steam shovels, and six asphalt layers.

You are currently under contract to widen two state highways from two to four lanes; one is 22 miles and the other is 39 miles. You just bid on a job to resurface 113 miles of two-lane state routes. Eighty-eight percent of the equipment is operable at any given time, and your equipment is valued at around $34 million. Payroll is about $300,000 per week. Depending on the size of the job, there are 1–2 project managers, 2–3 engineers, and 4–7 supervisors at the job site.

Write a report explaining your operations to GP&R using the facts given. Feel free to embellish in necessary.

SKILL-BUILDING EXERCISE 3.2
What's Your Communication Style?

Carefully read each statement and its four endings. Grade these by assigning a 4 to the ending that most describes you, a 3 to the next ending most like you, a 2 to the next ending most like you, and a 1 to the ending least like you. Once you have assigned a number, you may not use that number again in the set of four endings. For example, you may not assign a grade of 4 to both 1*a* and 1*b*.

1. I am most likely to impress my co-workers as
   - *a*. Down to earth, practical, and to the point. *a* ____
   - *b*. Emotional, sensitive to my own and others' feelings. *b* ____
   - *c*. Cool, logical, patient. *c* ____
   - *d*. Intellectual and somewhat aloof. *d* ____
2. When I am assigned a project, I am most concerned that the project will be
   - *a*. Practical, with definite results that will justify my time and energy on it. *a* ____
   - *b*. Stimulating, involving lively interaction with others. *b* ____
   - *c*. Systematically or logically developed. *c* ____
   - *d*. Breaking ground and advancing knowledge. *d* ____
3. In reacting to individuals whom I meet socially, I am likely to consider whether
   - *a*. They are assertive and decisive. *a* ____
   - b. They are caring. *b* ____
   - *c*. They seem thorough and exact. *c* ____
   - *d*. They seem highly intelligent. *d* ____
4. When confronted by others with a different opinion, I find it most useful to
   - *a*. Pinpoint the key differences, and develop compromises so that speedy decisions can be made. *a* ____
   - *b*. Put myself in the others' shoes, and try to understand their point of view. *b* ____
   - *c*. Keep calm and present my material clearly, simply, and logically. *c* ____
   - *d*. Create new proposals. *d* ____

5. Under pressure, I suspect I may come through to others as being
   a. Too concerned with wanting immediate action, and pushing for immediate decisions. *a* ____
   b. Too emotional and occasionally carried away by my feelings. *b* ____
   c. Highly unemotional, impersonal, too analytical and critical. *c* ____
   d. Snobbish, condescending, intellectually superior. *d* ____
6. When lecturing to a group, I would like to leave the impression of being
   a. A practical and resourceful person who can show the audience how to, for example, streamline a procedure. *a* ____
   b. A lively and persuasive individual who is in touch with the audience's emotions and moods. *b* ____
   c. A systematic thinker who can analyze the group's problems. *c* ____
   d. A highly innovative individual. *d* ____

Now transcribe the numbers that you wrote beside each ending to the appropriate spaces below. Total the columns for questions 1–3 and for questions 4–6. The initials at the bottom of the columns—S, F, T, and I—stand for the different communication styles: senser, feeler, thinker, and intuitor. The column with the highest total for questions 1–3 is your communication style under relaxed conditions, and the column with the highest total for questions 4–6 is your style under stress conditions. Once you have defined your particular style, check the table at the end of the exercise for the positive and negative traits associated with it. Note that you may have the positive traits without the negative ones or vice versa.

	a	*b*	*c*	*d*
1.	____	____	____	____
2.	____	____	____	____
3.	____	____	____	____
Total	**S**	**F**	**T**	**I**

	a	*b*	*c*	*d*
4.	____	____	____	____
5.	____	____	____	____
6.	____	____	____	____
Total	**S**	**F**	**T**	**I**

Source: Phyllis Kuhn, "Sharpening Your Communication Skills," *Medical Laboratory Observer,* March 1987. Used with permission from Medical Laboratory Observer. Copyright © 1987 by Nelson Publishing, Inc., www.mlo-online.com.

Some Traits Linked to Each Communication Style

Positive	**Negative**
Intuitor	
Creative	Fantasy-bound
Idealistic	Impractical
Intellectual	Too theoretical
Feeler	
Caring	Wishy-washy
Conscientious	Guilt-ridden
Persuasive	Manipulative
Thinker	
Exact, precise	Nitpicker
Deliberate	Rigid
Weighs all alternatives	Indecisive
Senser	
Decisive	Impulsive
Assertive	Aggressive
Enjoys producing quick results	Lacks trust in others' ability
Technically skillful	Self-involved, status seeking

SKILL-BUILDING EXERCISE 3.3 Effective Listening

Are you an effective listener? Ask a peer that you communicate with regularly and who you know will answer honestly to respond yes or no to these 10 questions. Do not answer the questions yourself. We often view ourselves as great listeners when, in fact, others know that we are not.

1. During the past two weeks, can you recall an incident where you thought I was not listening to you?
2. When you are talking to me, do you feel relaxed at least 90 percent of the time?
3. When you are talking to me, do I maintain eye contact with you most of the time?
4. Do I get defensive when you tell me things with which I disagree?
5. When talking to me, do I often ask questions to clarify what you are saying?
6. In a conversation, do I sometimes overreact to information?
7. Do I ever jump in and finish what you are saying?
8. Do I often change my opinion after talking something over with you?
9. When you are trying to communicate something to me, do I often do too much of the talking?
10. When you are talking to me, do I often play with a pen, pencil, my keys, or something else on my desk?

Use your peer's answers to grade your listening skills. If you received 9 or 10 correct answers, you are an excellent listener; seven or eight correct answers indicates a good listener; five or six correct answers means you possess average listening skills; and less than five correct answers is reflective of a poor listener. The answers most often given for effective listeners are (1) no, (2) yes, (3) yes, (4) no, (5) yes, (6) no, (7) no, (8) yes, (9) no, (10) no.

Source: From Tom D. Lewis and Gerald Graham, "7 Tips for Effective Listening." This excerpt was reprinted with permission from the August 2003 issue of *Internal Auditor,* published by The Institute of Internal Auditors, Inc., www.theiia.org.

SKILL-BUILDING EXERCISE 3.4

We Americans supposedly speak the English language. However, anyone who has ever visited England knows that the English often use different words and phrases than we do. Can you identify what the English words or phrases in Part A below would be if spoken by an American?

A. English phrases

_____ chemist	_____ half five	_____ porter
_____ phone engaged	_____ mind your step	_____ tin
_____ ring-up	_____ a bit dear	_____ lift
_____ round up	_____ way out	_____ queue
_____ wines and spirits	_____ bonnet	_____ lorry
_____ chipped potatoes	_____ stall	_____ rates
_____ give way	_____ flat	_____ braces
_____ to let	_____ kiosk	_____ gangway
_____ ta!	_____ ironmonger	_____ underground
_____ it's mommy's go	_____ pillar box	

B. American equivalents

a. elevator	*e.* can	*i.* taxes
b. mailbox	*f.* subway	*j.* suspenders
c. orchestra seat	*g.* hood	*k.* aisle
d. line	*h.* newsstand	*l.* apartment

m. janitor	*s.* too expensive	*x.* french fries
n. hardware dealer	*t.* watch your step	*y.* yield
o. truck	*u.* call	*z.* for rent
p. exit	*v.* go halfway around circle and straight up	*aa.* bid adieu
q. drugstore		*bb.* it's mommy's turn
r. busy	*w.* liquor store	*cc.* five-thirty

SKILL-BUILDING EXERCISE 3.5
Perception Test

Take a maximum of 10 minutes to complete the following test.

1. In 1963, if you went to bed at 8 o'clock PM and set the alarm to get up at 9 o'clock the next morning, how many hours of sleep would you get?
2. If you have only one match and enter a room in which there is a kerosene lamp, an oil stove, and a wood-burning stove, which would you light first?
3. Some months have 30 days; some have 31. How many have 28 days?
4. If a doctor gave you three pills and told you to take one every half-hour, how long would they last?
5. A man builds a house with four sides, and it is rectangular in shape. Each side has a southern exposure. A big bear comes wandering by. What color is the bear?
6. I have in my hand two U.S. coins that total 55 cents in value. One is not a nickel. Please bear that in mind. What are the two coins?
7. Divide 30 by ½ and add 10. What is the answer?
8. Take two apples from three apples, and what do you have?
9. An archaeologist found some gold coins dated 34 B.C. How old are they?
10. How many animals of each species did Moses take aboard the ark with him?

SKILL-BUILDING EXERCISE 3.6
Sexist/Nonsexist Language

As part of communicating that an organization is truly committed to supporting a highly qualified and diverse workforce, managers should take every opportunity to demonstrate the use of nonsexist language.

1. Try to identify a nonsexist word to use in place of each of the following words that may carry a sexist connotation:

Man-hours	Layout man	Foreman
Watchman	Man-made	Draftsman
Girl Friday	Salesman	Policeman
Repairman	Spokesman	Freshman

2. List additional words or terms that you think might carry a sexist connotation.

Case Incident 3.1
Can You Manage This?

Bill Sterling had been reviewing the financial reports for the last quarter. Bill was president of the Advantage Company, makers of high-quality sports apparel. He was unhappy with the cost of materials for a popular line of shorts, shirts, and pants, and thought the company was paying too much for the cotton-knit fabric. He then called Debby Wood, vice president of manufacturing, and told her to cut fabric costs. She in turn called Eddie Perez, the purchasing supervisor, and said, "Mr. Sterling is upset about the cost of the cotton knit you're using and wants it brought down! Do what you need to do. You've let this get out of hand."

Eddie was a bit perplexed. Didn't they know the cost of cotton knit had risen from $1.77 to $2.20 per yard? But he had been instructed to cut costs, so he found a supplier who could sell the fabric for $1.85 per yard and ordered 120 yards, about enough for two weeks of sewing. When the cotton knit arrived, Eddie could tell that the fabric was a lower quality than they had been using, but it could be used.

The next month Heather Schotsky, the assembly supervisor, asked Eddie about the cotton knit they were using. It stretched out during the sewing process, making the garments look baggy. Eddie explained that Mr. Sterling had sent word to cut the fabric cost. "This was the best cotton knit I could find at the lower cost," said Eddie.

When Bill Sterling reviewed the next quarter's financial reports, he found that sales had dropped for their popular Gear Down line of shirts, shorts, and pants. To find out why, he called Keesha Freeman, the marketing director.

"Sears, the Sports Authority, and Belk have all cut back on orders, Bill," Keesha said. "They're saying the garments they've received lately just aren't selling. Customers complain they look baggy, and the fabric feels thinner than before. I talked to Debby, and she said you told her to cut fabric costs. So she told Eddie to do so."

Bill immediately called Debby and reversed his decision to cut fabric costs. He said, "Tell Eddie to start purchasing the better quality fabric." When Debby finally talked to Eddie, he asked her what to do with the lower grade fabric.

"That's your problem, Eddie. You shouldn't have ordered so much," Debby replied. Bill Sterling had really scolded her, and she was still angry about it.

Fortunately, Eddie found another company willing to buy the fabric for $1.45 per yard. He sold it to make room for the new shipment of cotton knit he just ordered.

Three days later Debby called Eddie into her office to find out why he sold the lower grade fabric. "Who told you it was OK to sell that fabric?"

"No one. I thought you said it was my decision. I needed to make room for the new fabric and this was the best price I could get," Eddie answered.

"With decisions like that, this company could end up in the tank. Maybe we could've used that fabric for another line," said Debbie. "Don't let this happen again."

Questions

1. Explain the communications problem?
2. Was the problem handled well?

Case Incident 3.2

Tardy Tom

On September 30, 2007, a large national automobile-leasing firm in Columbus, Ohio, hired Tom Holland as a mechanic. Tom, the only mechanic employed by the firm in Columbus, was to do routine preventive maintenance on the cars. When he first began his job, he was scheduled to punch in on the time clock at 7 AM On October 30, 2007, Tom's supervisor, Russ Brown called him to his office and said, "Tom I've noticed during October that you've been late for work seven times. What can I do to help you get here on time?"

Tom replied, "It would be awfully nice if I could start work at 8 AM instead of 7 AM."

Russ then stated, "Tom I'm very pleased with your overall work performance, so it's OK with me if your workday begins at 8 AM."

During the month of November 2007, Tom was late eight times. Another conversation occurred similar to the one at the end of October. As a result of it, Tom's starting time was changed to 9 AM.

On January 11, 2008, Russ Brown posted the following notice on the bulletin board:

Any employee late for work more than two times in any one particular pay period is subject to termination.

On January 20, 2008, Russ called Tom into his office and gave him a letter that read, "During this pay period, you have been late for work more than two times. If this behavior continues, you are subject to termination." Tom signed the letter to acknowledge that he had received it.

During February 2008, Tom was late eight times and between March 1 and March 11, five times. On March 11, 2008, Russ notified Tom that he had been fired for his tardiness.

On March 12, 2008, Tom came in with his union representative and demanded that he get his job back. Tom alleged that there was another employee in the company who had been late as many times as he had, or more. Tom further charged that Russ was punching the time clock for this employee because Russ was having an affair with her. The union representative stated that three other people in the company had agreed to testify, under oath, to these facts. The union representative then said, "Russ, rules are for everyone. You can't let one person break a rule and penalize someone else for breaking the same rule. Therefore, Tom should have his job back."

Questions

1. Was the manager communicating a message to Tom?
2. Should Tom get his job back?
3. What would you do if you were an arbitrator in this dispute?

References and Additional Readings

1. For additional information, see Mandy Thatcher, "The Grapevine: Communication Tool or Thorn in Your Side?" *Strategic Communication Management,* August 2003, pp. 30–34.
2. For more information on the Internet, see *"The Oxford Dictionary of the Internet"* by Rachel Singer Gordon, *Library Journal,* December 2001, p. 12.
3. For more information see Darlene Fichter, "Making Your Intranet Live Up to Its Potential," *Online,* January/February 2006, pp. 51–53.

Chapter Four

Decision-Making Skills

Learning Objectives

After studying this chapter, you will be able to:

1. Explain the difference between decision making and problem solving.
2. Distinguish between programmed and nonprogrammed decisions.
3. Explain the intuitive approach to decision making.
4. Discuss two rational approaches to decision making.
5. List the different conditions under which managers make decisions.
6. Explain the role values play in making decisions.
7. Summarize the positive and negative aspects of group decision making.
8. Define creativity and innovation, and outline the basic stages in the creative process.
9. Identify several specific tools and techniques that can be used to foster creative decisions.
10. List the six stages in creative decision making.
11. Explain the role of a management information system (MIS).

Chapter Preview

Phil Knight, a former collegiate runner, began selling Japanese-manufactured running shoes shortly after graduating from college in the early 1960s. When, in 1971, his Japanese supplier tried to take over his business, Knight broke away and began manufacturing his own shoes, called Nike, designed by his former college running coach.

After much success over the next twelve years, Knight handed off the role of president to a longtime employee and took off for an extended trip through China in the spring of 1983. The company almost immediately began to sputter and Knight returned as president in the fall of 1984. By mid-1997, Nike had become a giant, controlling over 40 percent of the U.S. footwear market. Once again, Knight checked out, spending less and less time at Nike. In a very short time Nike's sales stagnated. By 1999 Knight was back and once again revived the company. In early 2005, Knight named Bill Perez, who formerly headed the privately held household products company, S. C. Johnson & Son Inc., as his replacement and the new CEO of Nike. Perez lasted a mere 13 months until he was pressured to leave by Knight. Knight immediately appointed a company insider and longtime lieutenant, Mark Parker, as president and chief executive officer.

Sources: Daniel Roth, "Can Nike Still Do It Without Phil Knight?" *Fortune*, April 4, 2005, pp. 58–66; and Helen Jung, "Nike Tries to Find the Right Fit," *Knight Ridder Business Tribune*, January 24, 2006, p. 1.

Analyzing Management Skills

What are some of the decision-making skills that are necessary for a manager like Phil Knight to be successful?

Applying Management Skills

Suppose you are a CEO and were in charge of naming your replacement. What type of information would you need and what factors would you consider before making your decision?

Some authors use the term *decision maker* to mean *manager*. However, although managers are decision makers, not all decision makers are managers. For example, a person who sorts fruit or vegetables is required to make decisions, but not as a manager. However, all managers, regardless of their positions in the organization, must make decisions in the pursuit of organizational goals. In fact, decision making pervades all of the basic management functions: planning, organizing, staffing, leading, and controlling. Although each of these functions requires different types of decisions, all of them require decisions. Thus, to be a good planner, organizer, staffer, leader, and controller, a manager must first be a good decision maker. The approach of this chapter is to first present some theoretical approaches and foundations for making decisions, to discuss many of the major factors that might impact decision makers, and finally to introduce several tools that can be used to help managers make decisions.

decision process
Process that involves three stages: intelligence, design, and choice. Intelligence is searching the environment for conditions requiring a decision. Design is inventing, developing, and analyzing possible courses of action. Choice is the actual selection of a course of action.

Herbert Simon, a Nobel prize winner, has described the manager's **decision process** in three stages: (1) intelligence, (2) design, and (3) choice.[1] The intelligence stage involves searching the environment for conditions requiring a decision. The design stage entails inventing, developing, and analyzing possible courses of action. Choice, the final stage, refers to the actual selection of a course of action.

The decision process stages show the difference between management and nonmanagement decisions. Nonmanagement decisions are concentrated in the last (choice) stage. The fruit/vegetable sorter has to make a choice regarding only the size or quality of the goods. Management decisions place greater emphasis on the intelligence and design stages. If the decision-making process is viewed as only the choice stage, managers spend very little time making decisions. If, however, the decision-making process is viewed as not only the actual choice but also the intelligence and design work needed to make the choice, managers spend most of their time making decisions.

DECISION MAKING VERSUS PROBLEM SOLVING

decision making
In its narrowest sense, the process of choosing from among various alternatives.

problem solving
Process of determining the appropriate responses or actions necessary to alleviate a problem.

The terms *decision making* and *problem solving* are often confused and therefore need to be clarified. As indicated earlier, **decision making,** in its narrowest sense, is the process of choosing from among various alternatives. A *problem* is any deviation from some standard or desired level of performance. **Problem solving,** then, is the process of determining the appropriate responses or actions necessary to alleviate a problem. Problem solving necessarily involves decision making, since all problems can be attacked in numerous ways and the problem solver must decide which way is best. On the other hand, not all decisions involve problems (such as the person sorting fruit and vegetables). However, from a practical perspective, almost all managerial decisions do involve solving or at least avoiding problems.

PROGRAMMED VERSUS NONPROGRAMMED DECISIONS

programmed decisions
Decisions that are reached by following an established or systematic procedure.

nonprogrammed decisions
Decisions that have little or no precedent; they are relatively unstructured and generally require a creative approach by the decision maker.

Decisions are often classified as programmed or nonprogrammed. **Programmed decisions** are reached by an established or systematic procedure. Normally, the decision maker knows the situation in a programmable decision. Routine, repetitive decisions usually fall into this category. Managerial decisions covered by organizational policies, procedures, and rules are programmed in that established guidelines must be followed in arriving at the decision.

Nonprogrammed decisions have little or no precedent. They are relatively unstructured and generally require a more creative approach by the decision maker; the decision maker must develop the procedure to be used. Generally, nonprogrammed decisions are more difficult to make than programmed decisions. Deciding on a new product, a new piece of equipment, and next year's goals are all nonprogrammed decisions.

THE INTUITIVE APPROACH TO DECISION MAKING

intuitive approach
Approach used when managers make decisions based largely on hunches and intuition.

When managers make decisions solely on hunches and intuition (the **intuitive approach**), they are practicing management as though it were wholly an art based only on feelings. While intuition and other forms of judgment do play a role in many decision situations, problems can occur when managers ignore available facts and rely only on feelings. When this happens, managers sometimes become so emotionally attached to certain positions that almost nothing will change their minds. They develop the "don't bother me with the facts—my mind is made up" attitude. George Odiorne isolated the following emotional attachments that can hurt decision makers:

1. Fastening on unsubstantiated facts and sticking with them.
2. Being attracted to scandalous issues and heightening their significance.
3. Pressing every fact into a moral pattern.
4. Overlooking everything except what is immediately useful.
5. Having an affinity for romantic stories and finding such information more significant than any other kind, including hard evidence.[2]

Such emotional attachments can be very real and can lead to poor decisions. They most often affect managers or decision makers who are "living in the past" and either will not or cannot modernize their thinking. An example is the manager who insists on making decisions just as the founder of the company did 40 years ago.

Odiorne offers two suggestions for managers and decision makers engulfed by emotional attachments.[3] First, become aware of biases and allow for them. Undiscovered biases do the most damage. Second, seek independent opinions. It is always advisable to ask the opinion of some person who has no vested interest in the decision. Intuition does play a role in decision making. The key is to not ignore facts when they are available. "Good companies not only can learn. They've also learned to forget," says Professor C. K. Prahalad of the University of Michigan in his coauthored book *Competing for the Future*.[4]

RATIONAL APPROACHES TO DECISION MAKING

Approaches to decision making that attempt to evaluate factual information through the use of some type of deductive reasoning are referred to as *rational approaches*. The following sections discuss two types of rational approaches.

The Optimizing Approach

optimizing approach
Includes the following steps: recognize the need for a decision; establish, rank, and weigh criteria; gather available information and data; identify possible alternatives; evaluate each alternative with respect to all criteria; and select the best alternative.

The physical sciences have provided a theoretical approach to decision making that can be adapted to management problems. The **optimizing approach** (sometimes called the *rational* or *scientific approach*) to decision making includes the following steps:

1. Recognize the need for a decision.
2. Establish, rank, and weigh the decision criteria.
3. Gather available information and data.
4. Identify possible alternatives.
5. Evaluate each alternative with respect to all criteria.
6. Select the best alternative.

Once the need to make the decision is known, criteria must be set for expected results of the decision. These criteria should then be ranked and weighed according to their relative importance.

Next, factual data relating to the decision should be collected. After that, all alternatives that meet the criteria are identified. Each is then evaluated with respect to all criteria. The final decision is based on the alternative that best meets the criteria.

Limitations of the Optimizing Approach

The optimizing approach to decision making is an improvement over the intuitive approach, but it is not without its problems and limitations. The optimizing approach is based on the concept of "economic man." This concept postulates that people behave rationally and their behavior is based on the following assumptions:

1. People have clearly defined criteria, and the relative weights they assign to these criteria are stable.
2. People have knowledge of all relevant alternatives.
3. People have the ability to evaluate each alternative with respect to all the criteria and arrive at an overall rating for each alternative.
4. People have the self-discipline to choose the alternative that rates the highest (they will not manipulate the system).

Consider the following difficulties with the above approach. First, these assumptions are often unrealistic; decision makers do not always have clearly defined criteria for making decisions. Second, many decisions are based on limited knowledge of the possible alternatives; even when information is available, it is usually less than perfect. Third, there is always a temptation to manipulate or ignore the gathered information and choose a favored (but not necessarily the best) alternative.

Due to the limitations of the optimizing approach, most decisions still involve some judgment. Thus, in making decisions, the manager generally uses a combination of intuitive and rational approaches.

The Satisficing Approach

Believing the assumptions of the optimizing approach to be generally unrealistic, Herbert Simon, in attempting to understand how managerial decisions are actually made, formulated his **principle of bounded rationality.** This principle states, "The capacity of the human mind for formulating and solving complex problems is very small compared with the size of the problems whose solution *is* required for objectively rational behavior—or even for a reasonable approximation to such objective rationality."[5] Basically, the principle of bounded rationality states that human rationality has definite limits. Based on this principle, Simon proposed a decision model of the "administrative man," which makes the following assumptions:

principle of bounded rationality
Assumes people have the time and cognitive ability to process only a limited amount of information on which to base decisions.

1. A person's knowledge of alternatives and criteria is limited.
2. People act on the basis of a simplified, ill-structured, mental abstraction of the real world; this abstraction is influenced by personal perceptions, biases, and so forth.
3. People do not attempt to optimize but will take the first alternative that satisfies their current level of aspiration. This is called *satisficing*.
4. An individual's level of aspiration concerning a decision fluctuates upward and downward, depending on the values of the most recently identified alternatives.

optimizing
Selecting the best possible alternative.

satisficing
Selecting the first alternative that meets the decision maker's minimum standard of satisfaction.

level of aspiration
Level of performance that a person expects to attain; determined by the person's prior successes and failures.

The first assumption is a synopsis of the principle of bounded rationality. The second assumption follows naturally from the first. If limits to human rationality do exist, an individual must make decisions based on limited and incomplete knowledge. The third assumption also naturally follows from the first assumption: If the decision maker's knowledge of alternatives is incomplete, the individual cannot optimize but can only satisfice. **Optimizing** means selecting the best possible alternative; **satisficing** means selecting the first alternative that meets the decision maker's minimum standard of satisfaction. Assumption four is based on the belief that the criteria for a satisfactory alternative are determined by the person's current level of aspiration. **Level of aspiration** refers to the level of performance a person expects to attain, and it is impacted by the person's prior successes and failures.

Figure 4.1 represents the satisficing approach to decision making. If the decision maker is satisfied that an acceptable alternative has been found, she or he selects that alternative. Otherwise the decision maker searches for an additional alternative. In Figure 4.1, the

FIGURE 4.1
Model of the Satisficing Approach

Source: Adapted from James G. March and Herbert A. Simon, *Organizations*, 1958, John Wiley & Sons.

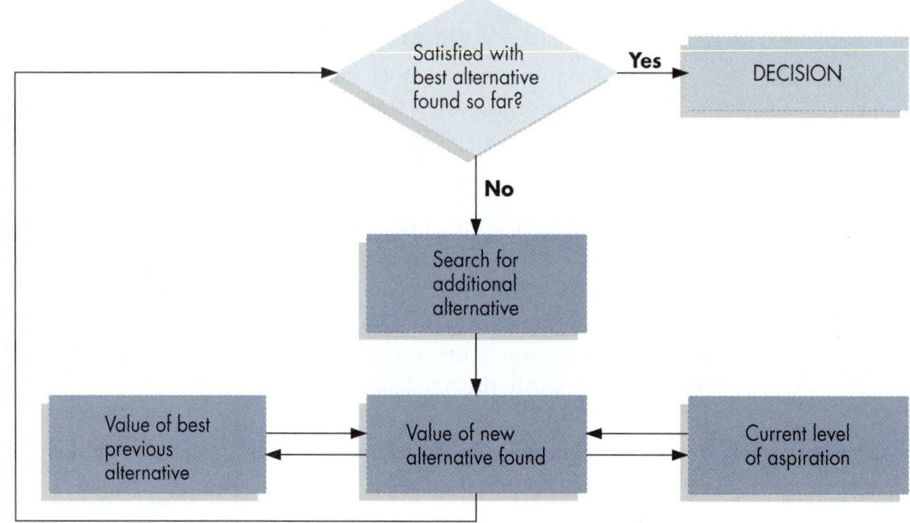

double arrows indicate a two-way relationship: The value of the new alternative is influenced by the value of the best previous alternative; the value of the best previous alternative is in turn influenced by the value of the new alternative. As the arrows indicate, a similar two-way relationship exists between the value of the new alternative and the current level of aspiration. The net result of this evaluation determines whether or not the decision maker is satisfied with the alternative. Thus, the "administrative man" selects the first alternative that meets the minimum satisfaction criteria and makes no real attempt to optimize.

THE DECISION MAKER'S ENVIRONMENT

A manager's freedom to make decisions depends largely on the manager's position within the organization and on its structure. In general, higher-level managers have more flexibility and discretion. The patterns of authority outlined by the formal organization structure also influence the flexibility of the decision maker.

Another important factor in decision-making style is the purpose and tradition of the organization. For example, a military organization requires a different style of decision making than a volunteer organization does.

The organization's formal and informal group structures also affect decision-making styles. These groups may range from labor unions to advisory councils.

The final subset of the environment includes all of the decision maker's superiors and subordinates. The personalities, backgrounds, and expectations of these people influence the decision maker.

Figure 4.2 shows the major environmental factors within an organization that affect decision makers in an organization. In addition to these major organizational factors, there are always other factors in the general environment that can impact a decision maker. Some of these factors might include industry norms, the labor market, the political climate, and competition. Successful managers must develop an appreciation for the different environmental forces that both influence them and are influenced by their decisions.

FIGURE 4.2
Environmental Factors Influencing Decision Making in an Organization

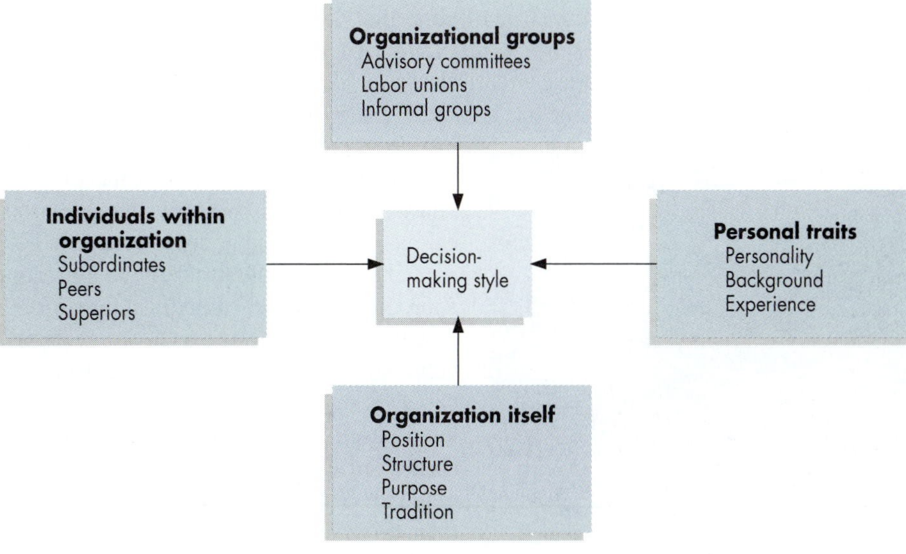

FIGURE 4.3
Umbrella Decision Alternatives and Outcomes

Alternative	State of Nature: No Rain	State of Nature: Rain
Take umbrella	Dry, but inconvenient	Dry
Do not take umbrella	Dry, happy	Wet

CONDITIONS FOR MAKING DECISIONS

Decisions are not always made with the same amount of available information. The best decision often depends on what happens later. Consider the simple decision of whether to take an umbrella when going outside. The more desirable alternative is determined by whether or not it rains, but this is not under the control of the decision maker. Figure 4.3 gives combinations of alternatives and states of nature and their respective outcomes for the individual trying to decide whether or not to take an umbrella when going outside.

Certainty

situation of certainty
Situation that occurs when a decision maker knows exactly what will happen and can often calculate the precise outcome for each alternative.

Knowing exactly what will happen places the decision maker in a **situation of certainty.** In such a situation, the decision maker can calculate the precise outcome for each alternative. If it is raining, the person knows the outcome of each alternative and therefore can choose the best alternative (take an umbrella). Rarely, however, are decisions made in today's organizations under a condition of certainty. A manager deciding between a delivery by air (taking a set time to arrive at a set cost) or one by truck (also taking a set time to arrive at a set cost) would be an example of a decision made under a condition of certainty.

Risk

situation of risk
Situation that occurs when a decision maker is aware of the relative probabilities of occurrence associated with each alternative.

Unfortunately, the outcome associated with each alternative is not always known in advance. The decision maker can often obtain—at some cost—information regarding the different possible outcomes. The desirability of getting the information is figured by weighing the costs of obtaining the information against the information's value. A decision maker is in a **situation of risk** if certain reliable but incomplete information is available. In a situation of risk, some ideas of the relative probabilities associated with each outcome are known. If the weather forecaster has said there is a 40 percent chance of rain, the decision maker is operating in a situation of risk.

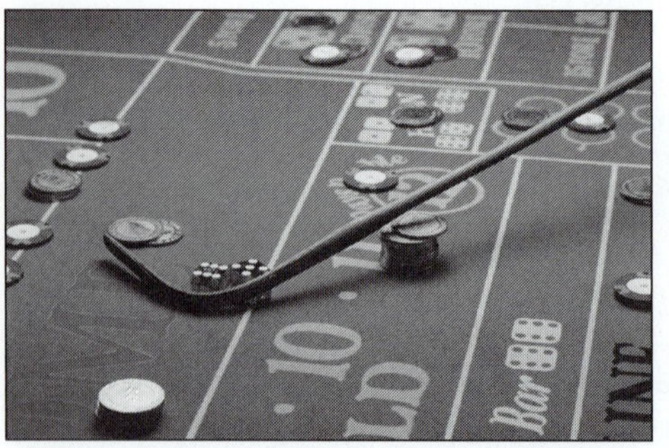

A decision maker in a company, as with a gambler, is at a situation of risk if certain reliable but incomplete information is available.

The precise probabilities of the various outcomes usually are not known. However, reasonably accurate probabilities based on historical data and past experiences often can be calculated. When no such data exist, it is difficult to estimate probabilities. In such cases, one approach is to survey individual opinions.

Under conditions of risk, the decision maker can use expected value analysis to help arrive at a decision. With this technique, the expected payoff of each known alternative is mathematically calculated based on its probability of occurrence. One potential shortcoming of expected value analysis is that it represents the average outcome if the event is repeated many times. That is of little help if the act occurs only once. For example, airplane passengers are not

FIGURE 4.4
Possible Approaches to Making Decisions under Uncertainty

Approach	How It Works	Related to the Umbrella Example
Optimistic or gambling approach (maximax)	Choose the alternative whose best possible outcome is the best of all possible outcomes for all alternatives.	Do not take umbrella.
Pessimistic approach (maximin)	Compare the worst possible outcomes of each of the alternatives, and select the alternative whose worst possible outcome is least undesirable.	Take umbrella.
Risk-averting approach	Choose the alternative that has the least variation among its possible alternatives.	Take umbrella.

interested in average fatality rates; rather, they are interested in what happens on their particular flight.

situation of uncertainty
Situation that occurs when a decision maker has very little or no reliable information on which to evaluate the different possible outcomes.

maximax approach
Selecting the alternative whose best possible outcome is the best of all possible outcomes for all alternatives; sometimes called the *optimistic* or *gambling approach* to decision making.

maximin approach
Comparing the worst possible outcomes for each alternative and selecting the one that is least undesirable; sometimes called the *pessimistic approach* to decision making.

risk-averting approach
Choosing the alternative with the least variation among its possible outcomes.

Uncertainty

When the decision maker has very little or no reliable information on which to evaluate the different possible outcomes, he or she is operating in a situation of uncertainty. Under a **situation of uncertainty,** the decision maker has no knowledge concerning the probabilities associated with different possible outcomes. For example, a person who is going to New York and has not heard a weather forecast for New York will have no knowledge of the likelihood of rain and hence will not know whether or not to carry an umbrella.

If the decision maker has little or no knowledge about which state of nature will occur, one of several basic approaches may be taken. The first is to choose the alternative whose best possible outcome is the best of all possible outcomes for all alternatives. This is an optimistic, or gambling, approach and is sometimes called the **maximax approach.** A decision maker using this approach would not take the umbrella because the best possible outcome (being dry without being inconvenienced) could be achieved only with this alternative.

A second approach for dealing with uncertainty is to compare the worst possible outcomes for each alternative and select the one that is least bad. This is a pessimistic approach and is sometimes called the **maximin approach.** In the umbrella example, the decision maker would compare the worst possible outcome of taking an umbrella to that of not taking an umbrella. The decision maker would then decide to take an umbrella because it is better to be dry than wet.

A third approach is to choose the alternative with the least variation among its possible outcomes. This is a **risk-averting approach** and results in more effective planning. If the decision maker chooses not to take an umbrella, the outcomes can vary from being dry to being wet. Thus, the risk-averting decision maker would take an umbrella to ensure staying dry.

Figure 4.4 summarizes the different approaches to making a decision under conditions of uncertainty. Management Illustration 4.1 discusses the major risks faced by large U.S. Companies according to a recent study.

TIMING THE DECISION

To properly time a decision, the need for a decision must be recognized. That is not always easy. The manager may simply not be aware of what is going on, or the problem requiring a decision may be camouflaged. Some managers always seem to make decisions on the

Management Illustration 4.1

MAJOR RISKS FACED BY LARGE U.S. COMPANIES

The 2007 U.S. Risk Barometer study surveyed 150 senior-level executives divided equally between Fortune 1000 and Fortune 2000 companies. The study was released by Protiviti Inc., a subsidiary of Robert Half International, Inc., and a leading provider of independent risk consulting and internal audit services. While the top risk varied by industry groupings, competitor risk ranked the highest overall. Customer satisfaction, the regulatory environment, information systems and IT security, and changing markets made up the other top risks as identified by the study.

The good news is that 53 percent of the companies surveyed perceived themselves to be "very effective" at managing risk. This was a 15 percent increase in the percentage of companies managing risk very effectively since the 2006 survey. The survey also found that "quicker identification of risk" was the most often cited benefit of better risk management, followed closely by "better risk information and measures" and "improvements in process performance." Of those companies that rated themselves as "not very effective" at managing risk, 77 percent plan on at least some changes to their risk management capabilities over the next two years.

Source: "Large U.S. Companies Getting Better at Managing Risks According to New Protiviti U.S. Risk Barometer, Nearly Half of Companies Rate Themselves 'Not Very Effective' at Using Risk Management Best Practices," *P.R. Newswire*, August 7, 2007.

spot; others tend to take forever to decide even a simple matter. The manager who makes quick decisions runs the risk of making bad decisions. Failure to gather and evaluate available data, consider people's feelings, and anticipate the impact of the decision can result in a quick but poor decision. Just as risky is the other extreme: the manager who listens to problems, promises to act, but never does. Nearly as bad is the manager who responds only after an inordinate delay. Other familiar types are the manager who never seems to have enough information to make a decision, the manager who frets and worries over even the simplest decisions, and the manager who refers everything to superiors.

Knowing when to make a decision is complicated because different decisions have different time frames. For instance, a manager generally has more time to decide committee appointments than he or she has to decide what to do when three employees call in sick. No magic formula exists to tell managers when a decision should be made or how long it should take to make it. The important thing is to see the importance of properly timing decisions. Management Illustration 4.2 discusses how video games can be used to train managers to make timely decisions.

THE ROLE OF VALUES/ETHICS IN DECISION MAKING

value
A conception, explicit or implicit, that defines what an individual or a group regards as desirable. People are not born with values; rather, they acquire and develop them early in life.

ethics
A set of moral principles or values that govern behavior.

A **value** is a conception, explicit or implicit, defining what an individual or a group regards as desirable.[6] A value may also be defined as a moral principle. **Ethics** are a set of moral principles or values that govern behavior. Values and ethics play an important role in the decision-making process. People are not born with values, but rather they acquire and develop them early in life. Parents, teachers, relatives, and other influence an individual's values and ethics. As result, every manager and every employee brings a certain set of values and ethics to the workplace.

A person's values have an impact on the selection of performance measures, alternatives, and choice criteria in the decision process. Differences in values often account for the use of different performance measures. For example, a manager concerned primarily with economic values would probably measure performance differently than a manager concerned mainly with social values. The former might look only at profit; the latter might think only of customer complaints.

Management Illustration 4.2

USING VIDEO GAMES TO IMPROVE DECISION MAKING

Jim Gee, a professor of education, and Kurt Squire, an assistant professor of education, of the University of Wisconsin, believe that video games are a good way to teach players an array of important skills such as making quick and timely decisions. Gee and Squire believe that the 30-and-under generation who were raised on video games and are now entering the workforce often prefer that learning be interactive and absorbing. The professors are quick to point out that the U.S. Army has invested heavily in video game training and that the games provide real training benefits.

The professors refute the often-held belief that only reclusive kids who lack social skills and real-world maturity play video games. Gee and Squire point out that most of the newer video games are meant to be played with others and that most kids who now play video games play them with others.

Source: Dinesh Ramde, "Professors Laud Potential of Video Games as Training Tools," *Knight Ridder Tribune Business News,* April 27, 2005, p. 1.

Differences in values may also generate different alternatives. A viable alternative to one person may be unacceptable to another because of differences in values. Because the final choice criteria depend on the performance measures used, they are also affected by values. For example, consider the question of laying off employees. Managers with dominant economic values would probably lay them off sooner than would managers with high social values.

Twenty-five years ago, George England, who conducted very extensive research on the role of values in the decision-making process, identified three major categories of values:

Pragmatic mode	Suggests that an individual has an evaluative framework that is guided primarily by success–failure considerations.
Ethical/moral mode	Implies an evaluative framework consisting of ethical considerations influencing behavior toward actions and decisions that are judged to be right and away from those judged to be wrong.
Affect, or feeling, mode	Suggests an evaluative framework that is guided by hedonism: One behaves in ways that increase pleasure and decrease pain.[7]

The work of England and others clearly establishes the important role values and ethics play in managers' decision-making processes. England's and other, more recent studies show that values and ethics may differ from culture to culture and that these differences may have a profound effect on resulting decisions.[8] To make sound decisions, today's managers must not only be aware of their own values and ethics but also know those of others inside and outside the organization.

PARTICIPATION IN DECISION MAKING

Most managers have opportunities to involve their subordinates and others in the decision-making process. One pertinent question is: Do groups make better decisions than individuals? Another is: When should subordinates be involved in making managerial decisions?

Group or Team Decision Making

Everyone knows the old axiom that two heads are better than one. Empirical evidence generally supports this view, with a few minor qualifications. Group performance is

Team decision making can often be successfully used to develop innovative and creative solutions to problems. What are some other positive aspects to team decision making? What are some negative aspects?

frequently better than that of the average group member.[9] Similarly, groups can often be successfully used to develop innovative and creative solutions to problems. Groups also often take longer to solve problems than does the average person.[10] Thus, group decisions are generally better when avoiding mistakes is more important than speed.

Group performance is generally superior to that of the average group member for two reasons. First, the sum total of the group's knowledge is greater. Second, the group has a much wider range of alternatives in the decision process.

One facet of group or team decision making compares the risk people will take alone with the risk they will take in a group. Laboratory experiments have shown that unanimous group decisions are consistently riskier than the average of the individual decisions.[11] This is somewhat surprising, since group pressures often inhibit the members. Possibly people feel less responsible for the outcome of a group decision than when they act alone. Additional research has found that groups make decisions best described as more polar than do individuals acting alone.[12] "More polar" means that groups tend to make decisions that are more extreme than those they would make as individuals. Figure 4.5 summarizes the positive and negative aspects of group decision making. Figure 4.6 lists some basic guidelines that managers can use to encourage employee participation in the decision-making process.

FIGURE 4.5
Positive and Negative Aspects of Group (Team) Decision Making

Positive Aspects	Negative Aspects
1. The sum total of the group's knowledge is greater.	1. One individual may dominate or control the group.
2. The group possesses a much wider range of alternatives in the decision process.	2. Social pressures to conform can inhibit group members.
3. Participation in the decision-making process increases the acceptance of the decision by group members.	3. Competition can develop to such an extent that winning becomes more important than the issue itself.
4. Group members better understand the decision and the alternatives considered.	4. Groups have a tendency to accept the first potentially positive solution while giving little attention to other possible solutions.

FIGURE 4.6
Basic Guidelines for Encouraging Employee Participation in Making Decisions

1. Don't criticize ideas.
2. Implement good employee ideas.
3. Give employees credit for ideas.
4. Never make employees feel stupid.

BARRIERS TO EFFECTIVE DECISION MAKING

Although it is desirable to study how to make decisions, managers must also work to remove barriers that limit the effectiveness of those decisions. Daniel Wheeler and Irving Janis identified four basic barriers to effective decision making. Barrier one is *complacency:* The decision maker either does not see danger signs or opportunity or ignores data from the environment that would affect decision making. Barrier two is called *defensive avoidance:* The decision maker denies the importance of danger, the opportunity, or the responsibility for taking action. *Panic* is the third barrier: Frantic attempts to solve a problem rarely produce the best results. The final barrier is *deciding to decide:* Accepting the responsibility and challenge of decision making is critical to overall effectiveness.[13] All of these barriers must be dealt with to create an environment that stimulates effective and creative decision making.

MAKING CREATIVE DECISIONS

If the optimizing approach to decision making is based on unrealistic assumptions and the intuitive and satisfying approaches often result in less than optimal decisions, what can managers do to improve their decision-making processes? One option that has produced positive results in numerous organizations is to encourage creative decisions and innovation at all levels within the organization. A recent study by PricewaterhouseCoopers found that almost half (45 percent) of lucrative ideas—whether breakthrough products or services, new uses for old ones, or ways to cut costs—come from employees.[14] The other half come from customers, suppliers, and competitors. This section discusses several techniques that can be used to foster creative decision-making within an organization.

The Creative Process

creativity
Coming up with an idea that is new, original, useful, or satisfying to its creator or to someone else.

innovation
Process of applying a new and creative idea to a product, service, or method of operation.

Creativity and innovation may seem similar but are actually quite different processes. **Creativity** is the thinking process involved in producing an idea or a concept that is new, original, useful, or satisfying to its creator or to someone else. **Innovation** refers to doing new things. Creativity involves coming up with a new idea, whereas innovation involves implementing the new idea. The challenge for today's managers is to establish an environment that encourages both creativity and innovation. The most successful managers are not necessarily those that are personally very creative but those that establish environments that encourage creativity among the employees. The following five-step process is generally thought to help establish an environment for creative decision making:

1. *Preparation*. The manager investigates thoroughly to make sure that all parts of the problem are fully understood and that all facts and ideas relevant to the problem have been identified.
2. *Concentration*. The manager commits to solving the problem in a timely manner.
3. *Incubation of ideas and information*. The manager recognizes that the accepted way of solving a problem is not always the best way. (Allow the creative spark to catch fire.)
4. *Illumination*. The manager connects a problem with an acceptable solution. (This step is often called the *Eureka connection*.)
5. *Verification*. The manager tests the solution and accepts the result.[15]

Although these steps often overlap, they provide a sound beginning point for the development of creative solutions that are critical to the success of the modern organization.

Establishing a Creative Environment

Probably the single most important factor that influences creativity and innovation by organizational members is the climate, or environment, in which they work. Certainly a manager's boss can have an impact on the type of climate established, but ultimately it is the individual manager who sets the tone for his or her area of responsibility. If a manager is genuinely interested in creative ideas, most employees are aware of it. The opposite is also true: Most employees realize when a manager is not interested in creativity.

People-based management skills and positive leadership can encourage a climate of creativity. To avoid hampering creativity, the manager must:

- Instill trust—eliminate the fear of failure of an idea.
- Develop effective internal and external communication. Upward and lateral communication encourage innovation.
- Seek a mix of talent within the organization. A blend of different personality types and interactions encourages creative problem solving.
- Reward useful ideas and solutions.
- Allow for some flexibility in the existing organizational structure so that new ideas and creative solutions will not be eliminated by tradition.

Tools to Foster Creativity

In addition to establishing the proper environment, managers can use several techniques to encourage creativity. The following sections describe some of these techniques.

Brainstorming

brainstorming
Presenting a problem to a group and allowing group members to produce a large quantity of ideas for its solution; no criticisms are allowed initially.

Alex F. Osborn developed brainstorming as an aid to producing creative ideas for an advertising agency. Basically, **brainstorming** involves presenting a problem to a group of people and allowing them to present ideas for a solution to the problem. Brainstorming is intended to produce a large quantity of ideas or alternatives and generally follows a definite procedure.

In the first phase, members of the group are asked to present ideas off the tops of their heads. Group members are told that quantity rather than quality of ideas is the goal. Questions submitted by the group leader usually include, How can we use this differently? How can we change? How can we substitute this? or How can we combine this? Four basic rules for the first phase are as follows:

1. No criticism of ideas is allowed.
2. No praise of ideas is allowed.
3. No questions or discussion of ideas is allowed.
4. Combinations of and improvements on ideas that have been previously presented are encouraged.

During the second phase, the merits of each idea are reviewed. This review often leads to additional alternatives. Furthermore, alternatives with little merit are eliminated in this phase. In the third phase, one of the alternatives is selected, frequently through group consensus. Management Illustration 4.3 describes how online brainstorming is currently being used by IBM.

Gordon Technique

William J. J. Gordon developed a technique for the consulting firm of Arthur D. Little, Inc., to spur creative problem solving. The technique was initially devised to get

Management Illustration 4.3

ONLINE BRAINSTORMING AT BIG BLUE

The use of online brainstorming is not new at IBM. The company used online brainstorming sessions to identify new business opportunities in 2001, to exchange ideas about good management in 2002, and to discuss IBM values in 2003. However, the current brainstorming event, led by CEO Samuel J. Palmisano, is by far the most ambitious to date.

Palmisano hopes to solicit the inputs of 100,000 minds in an open-source format. IBM is inviting clients, consultants, and employees' family members to tinker with its technologies in pursuit of new ideas. Palmisano says the company will put up to $100 million behind the strongest ideas generated. According to Palmisano it is the first time "a technology company takes its most valued secrets, opens them up to the world and says, OK, world, you tell us what to do with them."

There is danger in IBM's open-source approach to this brainstorming jam. Competitors could lurk in virtual chat rooms and listen in on new ideas. Responding to these fears, Ed Bevin, vice president of communications for IBM research and one of the jam's chief architects, said: "Without risk, there is no innovation." The event could produce payoffs beyond new ideas by building IBM's image as a forward-thinking global competitor.

Source: Jessi Hempel, "Big Blue Brainstorm," *BusinessWeek*, August 7, 2006, p. 70.

Gordon technique Differs from brainstorming in that no one but the group leader knows the exact nature of the real problem under consideration. A key word is used to describe a problem area.

creative ideas on technical problems. The **Gordon technique** differs from brainstorming in that no one but the group leader knows the exact nature of the real problem under consideration. A key word is used to describe a problem area; the group then explores that area, using the key word as a starting point. For instance, the word *conservation* may be used to start a discussion on energy conservation. The key word would direct discussion and suggestions on conservation to other areas in addition to the one under question. Proponents of the Gordon technique argue that it generates better-quality ideas because the discussion is not limited to one particular area as is the case with brainstorming.

Nominal Group Technique

nominal group technique (NGT) Highly structured technique for solving group tasks; minimizes personal interactions to encourage activity and reduce pressures toward conformity.

The **nominal group technique (NGT)** is a highly structured technique designed to keep personal interactions at a minimum. It involves the following steps:

1. *Listing.* Each group member, working alone, develops a list of probable solutions to a group task.
2. *Recording.* Each member offers an item from his or her listing in a round-robin manner to the group leader, who records the ideas on a master list in full view of the group. Some organizations today even have specially designed rooms with computers that project responses onto a large screen for all participants to see. The round-robin process continues until the leader has recorded all items on each person's list.
3. *Voting.* Each member records on an individual ballot his or her preference with respect to the priority or importance of the items appearing on the master list.

No verbal interaction is allowed during the first three steps. The results of the voting are tabulated, and scores are posted on the master list. Then the process continues as follows:

4. *Discussion.* Each item is discussed for clarification and valuation.
5. *Final voting.* Each member votes a second time with respect to the priority of the ideas generated.[16]

The NGT has been found to generate more unique ideas than brainstorming. However, both the NGT and brainstorming suffer from the problem occurring when the participants are so close to the problem under study that they are blind to what appear to be obvious solutions. As with brainstorming, NGT is now being used successfully online.[17]

Brainwriting

brainwriting
Technique in which a group is presented with a problem situation and members anonymously write down ideas, then exchange papers with others, who build on the ideas and pass them on until all members have participated.

In the **brainwriting** approach, group members are presented with a problem situation and then asked to jot their ideas on paper without any discussion. The papers are not signed. The papers are then exchanged with others, who build on the ideas and pass the papers on again until all members have had an opportunity to participate. Brainwriting can be a useful complement to brainstorming because it can eliminate some of the social forces that can inhibit idea generation, and it requires less facilitator expertise.[18]

Synectics

synectics
Creative problem-solving technique that uses metaphorical thinking to "make the familiar strange and the strange familiar."

Synectics is a relatively new technique used in creative problem solving. Synectics uses metaphorical thinking to "make the familiar strange and the strange familiar." Analogies are the best method for doing this. There appear to be several basic forms from which to springboard ideas:

- *Personal analogies*. Place yourself in the role of the object.
- *Direct analogies*. Make direct comparisons.
- *Symbolic analogies*. Look at the problem in terms of symbols.
- *Fantasy analogies*. Imagine the most perfect solution.

As an illustration of the fantasy analogy method, or "goal wishing," the participants fantasize about how a particular problem could be solved if there were no physical constraints. After developing a list of wishful solutions, the participants are encouraged to come up with the most absurd solutions they can imagine. Often at least one or two of these solutions can be refined into practical solutions.

A word of caution is in order regarding all of these techniques. Much controversy exists regarding their effectiveness as aids to creativity. Two researchers addressed this issue: "The evidence on balance does not seem encouraging enough to propose that managers who are seeking an extremely creative idea to help them on a problem situation should resort to a brainstorming session."[19] On the other hand, these same researchers concluded that brainstorming may generate a wider variety of solutions to a problem.

In conclusion, none of the previously described techniques is a complete answer for improving creativity within organizations. Each should be viewed as a tool that can help in some situations when the proper environment has been established. Management Illustration 4.4 describes one program used by Fallon Worldwide to encourage creativity among its employees.

A Model for Creative Decision Making

This section presents a practical model that can lead to better and more creative decisions.[20] While this model incorporates parts of the rational approach, its emphasis is on encouraging the generation of new ideas. Figure 4.7 outlines the stages of this model.

Stage 1: Recognition

When a problem or a decision situation exists, it is useful to first describe the circumstances in writing. An effective approach is to simply write out the facts in narrative form. This stage should include a description of the present situation, as well as when and where pertinent events occurred or will occur.

Management Illustration 4.4

ENCOURAGING EMPLOYEE CREATIVITY

For over 26 years Fallon Worldwide has been a very successful advertising agency with its U.S. base in Minneapolis. While much has been written and said about Fallon and its culture of encouraging creativity, not a lot has been said about its "dreamcatching" employee program. Kathy Spraitz, who spent 12 years at Fallon in different roles, says that employees are not only enabled, but encouraged by the company to take a leave of absence to pursue other non-advertising-related interests. "People would walk out for weeks to learn Flamenco dancing or write a novel or go run with the bulls. You could do anything."

The only requirement for participating in the program is that once employees return to work, they must share their experience, stories, and insights the hiatus generated. "It has nothing to do with ads and everything to with taking care of people," says Spraitz. Fallon management obviously believes that their "dreamcatching" program helps encourage creativity throughout the company.

Source: Jonathan Link, "Creativity Without Borders," *Boards*, February 2007, p. 40.

FIGURE 4.7
Model for Creative Decision Making

Source: Bruce Meyers, unpublished paper, Western Illinois University, 1987.

Stage		Activity
1	Recognition	To investigate and eventually define a problem or decision situation.
2	Fact finding	
3	Problem finding	
4	Idea finding	To generate possible alternatives or solutions (ideas).
5	Solution finding	To identify criteria and evaluate ideas generated in stage 4.
6	Acceptance finding	To work out a plan for implementing a chosen idea.

Stage 2: Fact Finding

After the decision situation has been described in written form, the next step is to systematically gather additional information concerning the current state of affairs. Questions asked in this stage usually begin with *who, what, where, when, how many, how much,* or similar words. The intent of the fact-finding stage is to organize available information about the decision situation.

Stage 3: Problem Finding

The fact-finding stage is concerned primarily with the present and the past; the problem-finding stage is oriented toward the future. In a sense, this stage might be viewed as problem redefining or problem analysis. The overriding purpose of this stage is to rewrite or restate the problem in a manner that will encourage more creative solutions. In light of stages 1 and 2, the decision maker should attempt to restate the problem in several different ways, with the ultimate goal of encouraging a broader range of solutions. For example, the decision situation "Shall I use my savings to start a new business?" could be restated, "In what ways might I finance my new business?" The first statement elicits a much narrower range of possible solutions than does the second. Similarly, "Shall I fire this employee?" could be restated, "Should I transfer, punish, retrain, or fire this employee, or should I give him/her another chance?"

After listing several restatements of the problem, the decision maker should select the one that most closely represents the real problem and has the greatest number of potential solutions. At this point, the decision situation should be defined in a manner that suggests multiple solutions.

Stage 4: Idea Finding

This stage aims to generate a number of different alternatives for the decision situation. In this stage, a form of brainstorming is used, following two simple rules: (1) no judgment or evaluation is allowed and (2) all ideas presented must be considered. The purpose of these rules is to encourage the generation of alternatives, regardless of how impractical they seem at first. A good approach is for the decision maker to list as many ideas as possible that relate to the problem. The decision maker should then go back and consider what might be substituted, combined, adopted, modified, eliminated, or rearranged to transform any of the previously generated ideas into additional ideas.

Stage 5: Solution Finding

The purpose of this stage is to identify the decision criteria and evaluate the potential ideas generated in stage 4. The first step for the decision maker is to develop a list of potential decision criteria by listing all possibilities. Once a list of potential criteria has been developed, the decision maker should pare down the list by selecting the most appropriate criteria. Naturally, the decision maker should aim for a manageable number of criteria (normally fewer than seven). The next step is to evaluate each idea generated in stage 4 against the selected criteria. Usually many ideas from stage 4 can be eliminated by simple inspection. The remaining ideas should then be evaluated against each criterion using some type of rating scale. After each idea has been evaluated against all criteria, the best solution usually becomes obvious.

Stage 6: Acceptance Finding

This final stage attempts to identify what needs to be done to successfully implement the chosen idea or solution. This stage not only addresses the *who, when, where,* and *how* questions but should also attempt to anticipate potential objections to the decision.

While the above model is certainly not perfect, it does encourage managers to go beyond bounded rationality and to make better decisions than they would by following the satisficing approach.

DECISION MAKING WITH COMPUTERS/MANAGEMENT INFORMATION SYSTEMS

With the continuing increase in technology, computers are being used more and more to help managers make decisions. E-mail, the Internet, and the intranet, which were discussed in Chapter 3, all provide information used by managers to help make decisions. As information system is a system for acquiring, organizing, storing, manipulating, and transmitting information.[21] A **management information system (MIS)** is an information system used by managers to support the day-to-day operational and tactical decision-making needs of managers. A MIS is designed to produce information needed for the successful management of a process, department, or business. A MIS provides information that managers have specified in advance as adequately meeting their information needs. Usually the information made available by a MIS is in the form of periodic reports, special reports, and outputs of mathematical simulations.

management information system (MIS)
An information system used by managers to support the day-to-day operational and tactical decision making needs of managers.

In the broader sense, management information systems have existed for many years, even before computers. However, in most people's minds the term *MIS* implies the use of computers to process data that managers will use to make operational decisions. The information an MIS provides describes the organization or one of its major parts in terms of what has happened in the past, what is happening now, and what is likely to happen in the future.

FIGURE 4.8
Characteristics of an MIS

Source: From *Information Technology in Business*, 2nd edition, by J. A. Senn. Copyright © 1998 by Pearson Education, Inc. Reprinted by permission of Pearson Education, Inc., Upper Saddle River, NJ.

- Uses data captured and stored as a result of transaction processing.
- Reports data and information rather than details of transaction processing.
- Assists managers in monitoring situations, evaluating conditions, and determining what actions need to be taken.
- Supports recurring decisions.
- Provides information in prespecified report formats, either in print or on-screen.

data processing
Capture, processing, and storage of data.

transaction-processing system
Substituting computer processing for manual recordkeeping procedures.

It is important to note that a MIS is not the same as data processing. **Data processing** is the capture, processing, and storage of data, whereas a MIS uses those data to produce information for management in making decisions to solve problems. In other words, data processing provides the database of the MIS.

Transaction-processing systems substitute computer processing for manual record-keeping procedures. Examples include payroll, billing, and inventory record systems. By definition, transaction processing requires routine and highly structured decisions. It is actually a subset of data processing. Therefore, an organization can have a very effective transaction-processing system and not have a MIS. Figure 4.8 summarizes the characteristics of management information systems.

Many MISs have been developed for use by specific organizational subunits. Examples of MISs intended to support managers in particular functional areas include operational information systems, marketing information systems, financial information systems, and human resource information systems. Several specific MISs used by organizational subunits are discussed in later chapters.

Summary

1. *Explain the difference between decision making and problem solving.* In its narrowest sense, decision making is the process of choosing from among various alternatives. Problem solving is the process of determining the appropriate responses or actions necessary to alleviate a deviation from some standard or desired level of performance. From a practical perspective, almost all managerial decisions involve solving or avoiding problems, and therefore, it is not necessary to distinguish between managerial decision making and managerial problem solving.
2. *Distinguish between programmed and nonprogrammed decisions.* Programmed decisions are reached by following an established or systematic procedure. Nonprogrammed decisions have little or no precedent and generally require a more creative approach by the decision maker.
3. *Explain the intuitive approach to decision making.* In the intuitive approach, managers make decisions based on hunches and intuition. Emotions and feelings play a major role in this approach.
4. *Discuss two rational approaches to decision making.* One rational approach, optimizing, involves the following six steps: (1) Recognize the need for a decision; (2) Establish, rank, and weigh the criteria; (3) Gather available information and data; (4) Identify possible alternatives; (5) Evaluate each alternative with respect to all criteria; and (6) Select the best alternative. A second rational approach, satisficing, is based on the principle of bounded rationality. In the satisficing approach, the decision maker selects the first alternative that meets his or her minimum standard of satisfaction.
5. *List the different conditions under which managers make decisions.* Managers normally make decisions under the conditions of certainty, risk, or uncertainty.

6. *Explain the role that values and ethics play in making decisions.* A manager's values define his or her ethics and affect the selection of performance measures, alternatives, and choice criteria in the decision process.
7. *Summarize the positive and negative aspects of group decision making.* Positive aspects include the following: (1) The sum total of the group's knowledge is greater; (2) the group possesses a much wider range of alternatives in the decision process; (3) participation in the decision-making process increases the acceptance of the decision by group members; and (4) group members better understand the decision and the alternatives considered. Negative aspects include the following: (1) One individual may dominate or control the group; (2) Social pressures to conform can inhibit group members; (3) Competition can develop to such an extent that winning becomes more important than the issue itself; and (4) Groups have a tendency to accept the first potentially positive solution while giving little attention to other possible solutions.
8. *Define creativity and innovation, and outline the basic stages in the creative process.* Creativity is the thinking process involved in producing an idea or a concept that is new, original, useful, or satisfying to its creator or to someone else. Innovation is doing new things. The creative process generally has five stages: (1) preparation, (2) concentration, (3) incubation, (4) illumination, and (5) verification.
9. *Identify several specific tools and techniques that can be used to foster creative decisions.* Tools to foster creative decisions include brainstorming, the Gordon technique, the nominal group technique, brainwriting, and synectics.
10. *List the six stages in creative decision making.* The model for creative decision making encompasses the following six steps: (1) recognition, (2) fact finding, (3) problem finding, (4) idea finding, (5) solution finding, and (6) acceptance finding.
11. *Explain the role of a management information system (MIS).* A MIS is an information system used by managers to support their day-to-day operational and tactical decision-making needs. A MIS provides information that managers have specified in advance as adequately meeting their information needs. Usually the information made available by a MIS is in the form of periodic reports, special reports, and outputs of mathematical simulations.

Review Questions

1. What are the three stages in the decision-making process?
2. What is the difference between decision making and problem solving?
3. Discuss the intuitive approach to decision making.
4. Discuss the optimizing approach to decision making.
5. What criticisms can be made concerning the optimizing approach to decision making?
6. Discuss the satisficing approach to decision making, and explain the difference between satisficing and optimizing.
7. Distinguish among the decision situations of certainty, risk, and uncertainty.
8. What are values? What relationship exists between values and ethics?
9. Outline some positive and negative aspects of group decision making.
10. List several guidelines for encouraging employee participation in making decisions.
11. What are the four barriers to effective decision making?

12. Describe the five-step process for creating an environment that fosters creative decision making.
13. Describe the following aids to creativity:
    a. Brainstorming
    b. Gordon technique
    c. Nominal group technique
    d. Brainwriting
    e. Synectics
14. Describe the six-stage model of creative decision making.
15. How does a transaction-processing system differ from an MIS?

Skill-Building Questions

1. Identify a significant decision recently made by management of a major company (you might look in *BusinessWeek* or *The Wall Street Journal*). In the decision you identify, did the manager or managers satisfice or optimize?
2. What factors do you think affect the amount of risk a manager is willing to take when making a decision?
3. Comment on the following statement: "Groups always make better decisions than individuals acting alone."
4. How many creative uses can you think of for a brick? Now ask a five- to seven-year-old child the same question. How do you account for the differences? Why do you think children might be more creative than adults?
5. Think of a new form of a product or service to solve something that bugs you, for example, trash can lids that won't stay shut. (Many primary-grade creativity classes do this as a learning exercise in creativity.)
6. When you go into a fast-food store and the salesperson keys your order into the cash register, how might this information be used as part of a MIS?

SKILL-BUILDING EXERCISE 4.1

Lost at Sea

You are adrift on a private yacht in the South Pacific. Due to a fire of unknown origin, much of the yacht and its contents have been destroyed. The yacht is now slowly sinking. Your location is unclear because critical navigational equipment was destroyed and you and the crew were distracted in trying to bring the fire under control. Your best estimate is that you are approximately 1,000 miles south-southwest of the nearest land.

Following is a list of 15 items that are intact and undamaged after the fire. In addition to these articles, you have a serviceable rubber life raft with oars large enough to carry yourself, the crew, and all the items listed. The total contents of all survivors' pockets are a package of cigarettes, several books of matches, and five one-dollar bills.

Your task is to rank the following 15 items in terms of their importance to your survival. Place the number 1 by the most important item, the number 2 by the second most important, and so on through number 15, the least important.

______ Sextant
______ Shaving mirror
______ Five-gallon can of water
______ Mosquito netting
______ One case of U.S. Army C rations
______ Maps of the Pacific Ocean
______ Seat cushion (flotation device approved by the Coast Guard)
______ Two-gallon can of oil-gas mixture

_______ Small transistor radio
_______ Shark repellent
_______ 20 square feet of opaque plastic
_______ One quart of 160-proof Puerto Rican rum
_______ 15 feet of nylon rope
_______ Two boxes of chocolate bars
_______ Fishing kit

After everyone has completed the above rankings, your instructor will divide the class into teams or groups. Your group is to then rank the same items, using a group consensus method. This means the ranking for each of the 15 survival items must be agreed on by each group member before it becomes part of the group decision. Consensus is difficult to reach. Therefore, not every ranking will meet with everyone's complete approval. As a group, try to make each ranking one with which all group members can at least partly agree. Here are some guides to use in reaching consensus:

1. Avoid arguing for your own individual judgments. Approach the task on the basis of logic.
2. Avoid changing your mind for the sole purpose of reaching agreement and avoiding conflict. Support only solutions with which you agree at least somewhat.
3. Avoid conflict-reducing techniques such as majority vote, averaging, or trading.
4. View differences of opinion as a help rather than a hindrance in decision making.

Source: Adapted from John E. Jones and J. William Pfeiffer, eds., *The 1975 Annual Handbook for Group Facilitators* (La Jolla, CA: University Associates, Inc., 1975).

SKILL-BUILDING EXERCISE 4.2
Creativity Exercise

Most of us believe we are more creative than we really are. Take a maximum of four minutes each on solving the following three problems.

a. Draw four straight lines connecting the dots in the following diagram without lifting your pencil (or pen) off the paper. You are permitted to cross a line, but you cannot retrace any part of a line.

• • •

• • •

• • •

b. What do the following words have in common (other than they are all in the English language)?

CALMNESS	FIRST
CANOPY	SIGHING
DEFT	STUN

c. Place 10 circles of the same size in five rows with four circles in each row.

After you have attempted each of the above problems, be prepared to discuss the following questions:

1. Why do you think these "simple" problems were difficult for you?
2. Do you think grade school children tend to do better or worse than adults on problems such as these? Why?

SKILL-BUILDING EXERCISE 4.3

Risk Aversion

This exercise illustrates how different decision makers react differently to similar risks. Draw the following set of axes on a piece of paper:

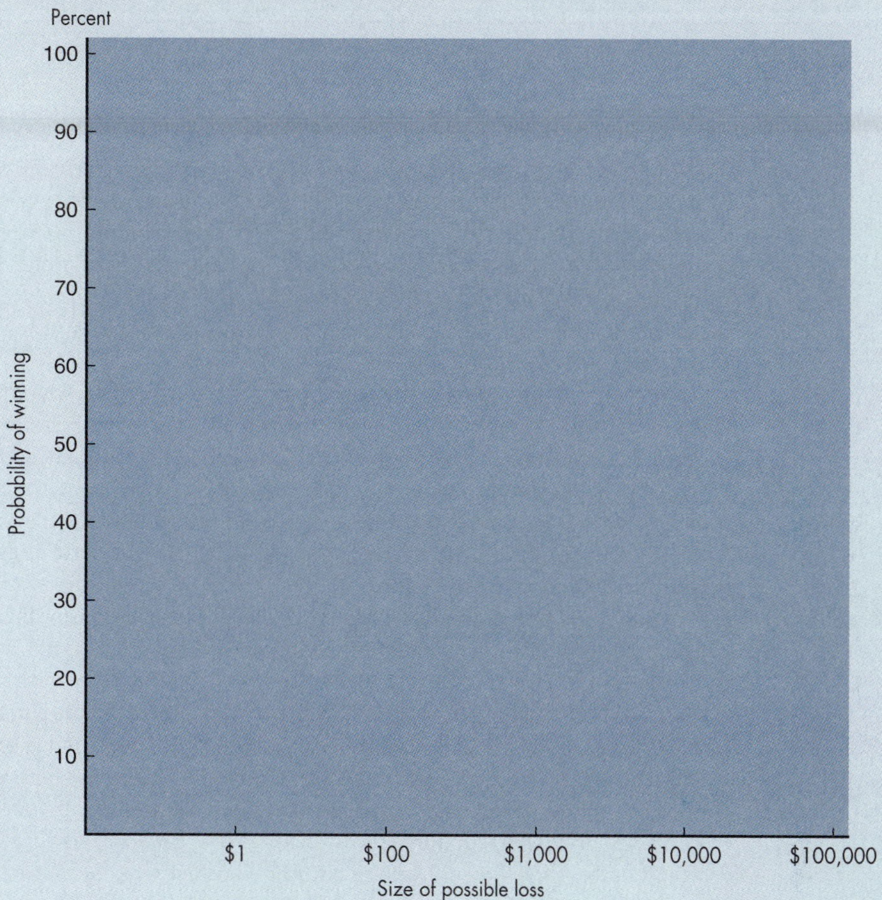

Assume you are faced with a decision on whether to play or not to play a game of chance. You will play the game once and only once. If you win, you will get $2. If you lose, you will have to pay $1. Would you be willing to play if the probability of winning the game is 80 percent? How about 50 percent? 40 percent? 30 percent? Find the lowest probability of winning for which you would be willing to play the game for one time only. Put a dot above the $1 on the graph at the probability that you select. Repeat the process for each of the following games:

Reward for Winning	Penalty for Losing
$ 20	$ 10
200	100
2,000	1,000
20,000	10,000
200,000	100,000

Note: Players cannot declare bankruptcy if they lose. They must give up one third of their earnings until the debt is fully paid.

1. Connect the dots on your graph and compare the curves drawn by various individuals in the class.

2. Do you consider yourself to be a risk taker or a risk averter?
3. How do you think that your affinity for risk might affect your ability to be a good manager?

Case Incident 4.1

Getting Out of the Army

Jay Abbott is confident that his future will be secure and financially rewarding if he decides to remain in the Army. He entered more than 10 years ago as a commissioned officer after completing his college education on an ROTC scholarship. At age 32, Jay has progressed to the rank of captain and is currently being considered for promotion to major. He has no reason to believe he will not be promoted. He has been successful in all of his appointments, is well liked by everyone—his peers, superiors, and subordinates—and has an unblemished record.

However, at the 10-year mark, Jay had second thoughts about staying in the Army and has been thinking about leaving ever since. He has felt more and more resentful that the Army has affected a large part of his personal life. Although he had always preferred to wear his hair shorter than most young men do, he resented the fact that even if he wanted to let it grow out or grow sideburns, he couldn't do it. It was the principle of the whole idea: the intrusion of the Army into his personal life. That this intrusion extended to his wife and children bothered him even more.

Jay's wife, Ellen, was finishing her master's thesis. This took up a large portion of her free time; yet her lack of involvement in the officers' clubs was frowned on. There was just no such thing as a private family life in Jay's position. He didn't even have much time to spend with the family. His job required long hours of work, including weekend duty, which left little time for his wife and two daughters, ages seven and nine. Another problem was that Ellen, who held a degree in design engineering, was unable to pursue any kind of real career, something that was important to both of them.

These thoughts raced through Jay's mind over and over again as he tried to decide what would be best for himself and his family. The Army had a lot of positive aspects, he kept reminding himself: He was already earning $49,000 a year, and with his nearly certain promotion, this would rise to $55,000. Also, he was being recommended for the Army's command and general staff college. There was little chance he would not be approved; completing the program would make his future even brighter. If he stayed, he would be able to retire in just 10 more years (at age 42) with a permanent retirement income of half his final salary plus free medical and dental coverage. By then, he figured, he would probably be a lieutenant colonel with a base pay of about $65,000; at worst, he would retire a major. At 42, he would have plenty of time to devote to a second career if he so desired.

On the other hand, regardless of how attractive the benefits seemed, salaries in the armed services had not kept pace with the rising rate of inflation: Congress had held the lid on raises at less than 3 percent, and no changes in this position were evident for the next few years. In fact, Jay had read several newspaper articles indicating that Congress was considering reducing benefits for the armed services, the 20-year retirement income specifically.

After doing some checking, Jay learned that the training and experience received in the Army were valuable to civilian employers. Commissioned in the signal corps, he had vast experience in the area of telecommunications. He had recently completed a tour as an instructor in a service school. He had also been in many positions of leadership during his term in the Army. At 32, he probably had more firsthand managerial experience than most civilian managers. He knew that large organizations were currently hiring young ex-military officers at salaries $10,000 to $15,000 higher than those of recent college graduates.

Questions

1. What should Jay do?
2. What factors should Jay consider in his decision?
3. What role would values play in Jay's decision?

Case Incident 4.2

Going Abroad

You supervise 12 engineers. Their formal training and work experience are very similar, so you can use them interchangeably on projects. Yesterday, your manager informed you that an overseas affiliate has requested four engineers to go abroad on extended loan for six to eight months. For a number of reasons, he argued and you agreed, this request should be met from your group.

All your engineers are capable of handling this assignment; from the standpoint of present and future projects, there is no special reason any one engineer should be retained over any other. Somewhat complicating the situation is the fact that the overseas assignment is in a generally undesirable location.

Questions

1. How would you select who should go abroad on extended loan?
2. What are some major factors that would influence your decision process?

Source: Victor H. Vroom, "A New Look at Managerial Decision Making," *Organizational Dynamics,* Spring 1973.

References and Additional Readings

1. Herbert A. Simon, *The New Science of Management Decision* (New York: Harper & Row, 1960), p. 2.
2. George S. Odiorne, *Management and the Activity Trap* (New York: Harper & Row, 1974), pp. 128–29; and George S. Odiorne, *The Change Resisters* (Englewood Cliffs, NJ: Prentice Hall, 1981), pp. 15–25.
3. Odiorne, *Management and the Activity Trap*, pp. 142–44.
4. "Go-Go Goliaths," *BusinessWeek*, February 13, 1995, p. 66.
5. Herbert A. Simon, *Model of Man* (New York: John Wiley & Sons, 1957), p. 198.
6. William D. Guth and Renato Tagiuri, "Personal Values and Corporate Strategy," *Harvard Business Review*, September–October 1965, pp. 124–25.
7. George England, "Personal Value Systems of Managers and Administrators," *Academy of Management Proceedings*, August 1973, pp. 81–94.
8. For example, see H. S. Badr, E. R. Gray, and B. L. Kedia, "Personal Values and Managerial Decision Making: Evidence from Two Cultures," *Management International Review*, Fall 1982, pp. 65–73; and H. J. Davis and S. A. Rasool, "Values Research and Managerial Behavior: Implications for Devising Culturally Consistent Managerial Styles," *Management International Review*, July 1988, pp. 11–19.
9. Irving Lorge, David Fox, Joel Davitz, and Martin Brenner, "A Survey of Studies Contrasting the Quality of Group Performance and Individual Performance, 1930–1957," *Psychological*

Bulletin, November 1958, pp. 337–72; Frederick C. Miner, Jr., "Group versus Individual Decision Making: An Investigation of Performance Measures, Decision Strategies, and Process Losses/Gains," *Organizational Behavior and Human Performance,* February 1984, pp. 112–24; and Alan S. Blinder and John Morgan, "Are Two Heads Better Than One? Monetary Policy by Committee," *Journal of Money, Credit, and Banking*, October 2005, p. 789.

10. M. E. Shaw, "A Comparison of Individuals and Small Groups in the National Solution of Complex Problems," *American Journal of Psychology*, July 1932, pp. 491–504; Lorge et al., "A Survey of Studies"; and W. E. Watson, K. Kumar, and L. K. Michaelson, "Cultural Diversity's Impact on Interaction Process and Performance: Comparing Homogeneous and Diverse Task Groups," *Academy of Management Journal*, June 1993, pp. 590–602.
11. M. Wallach, N. Kogan, and D. J. Bem, "Group Influence on Individual Risk Taking," *Journal of Abnormal and Social Psychology*, August 1962, pp. 75–86; and N. Kogan and M. Wallach, "Risk Taking as a Function of the Situation, the Person, and the Group," in *New Directions of Psychology*, Vol. 3, ed. G. Mardler (New York: Holt, Rinehart & Winston, 1967).
12. D. G. Meyers, "Polarizing Effects of Social Interaction", in *Group Decision Making*, ed. H. BranStatter, J. Davis, and G. Stock-Kreichgauer (New York: Academic Press, 1982).
13. Daniel D. Wheeler and Irving L. Janis, *A Practical Guide for Making Decisions* (New York: Macmillan, 1980), pp. 17–36.
14. Anne Fisher, "Get Employees to Brainstorm Online," *Fortune*, November 29, 2004, p. 72.
15. Graham Walles, *The Art of Thought* (New York: Harcourt Brace Jovanovich, 1976), p. 80.
16. Gene E. Burton, Dev S. Pathok, and David R. Burton, "The Gordon Effect in Nominal Grouping," *University of Michigan Business Review*, July 1978, p. 8; and Nells Zuech, "Identifying and Ranking Opportunities for Machine Vision in a Facility," *Industrial Engineering*, October 1992, pp. 42–44.
17. Pitar Pazos Lago, Mario G. Beruvides, Jiun-Yin Jian, Ana Maria Canto, et al., "Structuring Group Decision Making in a Web-Based Environment by Using the Nominal Group Technique," *Computers & Industrial Engineering*, March 2007, p. 277.
18. Chauncey E. Wilson, "Brainstorming Pitfalls and Best Practices," *Interactions*, September/October 2006, p. 50.
19. T. Richards and B. L. Freedom, "Procedures for Managers in Idea-Deficient Situations: An Examination of Brainstorming Approaches," *Journal of Management Studies*, February 1978, pp. 43–55.
20. The basis for this model and much of this discussion were contributed by Bruce Meyers, associate professor of management at Western Illinois University.
21. E. Turban, *Decision Support and Expert Systems* (New York: Macmillan, 1988).

Contemporary Issues

Chapter Five

Ethical, Social, and Legal Responsibilities of Management

Learning Objectives

After studying this chapter, you will be able to:

1. Define ethics.
2. Explain a code of ethics.
3. Identify four categories of laws relating to ethics in business.
4. Explain social responsibility.
5. Identify the six areas of law that affect business organizations.
6. Identify the types of taxes that affect business profits.
7. Explain the differences between copyrights, patents, and trademarks.
8. Define intellectual property.

Chapter Preview

One of the most interesting issues in the field of business ethics is whistle-blowing. In 1986 Congress passed amendments to the False Claims Act of 1863 which offer whistle-blowers financial rewards for disclosing fraud committed against the federal government. The Sarbanes-Oxley Act passed in 2002 provides new protections for whistle-blowers in business. The Securities and Exchange Commission has proposed regulations that would in certain cases require lawyers to blow the whistle on corporations they serve that engage in securities fraud. Employees who can prove that they have been terminated or otherwise penalized for whistle-blowing are entitled to reinstatement and up to two times the amount of back pay, plus interest.

Some whistle-blowers under the False Claims Act have reaped very large rewards. Chester Walsh, who blew the whistle against General Electric for defense contractor fraud, received a payout in excess of $13 million. Gwendolyn Cavanaugh and Virginia Lanford split $8.2 million as a reward for reporting Medicare fraud by their employer, Vencor, a health care company. For the period of 1997 to 2001, it is estimated that whistle-blowers received $680 million for their share of recoveries.

Source: Adapted from Thomas L. Carson, Mary Ellen Verdu, and Richard E. Wokutch, "Whistle-Blowing for Profit: An Ethical Analysis of the Federal False Claims Act," *Journal of Business Ethics,* pp. 362–376.

Analyzing Management Skills

Do you feel that whistle-blowers should be financially rewarded?

Applying Management Skills

What actions could your school or workplace take to make it more socially responsible?

ethics
A system of right and wrong.

Ethics can be defined as a system of right and wrong. Ethics assist individuals in deciding when an act is moral or immoral, socially desirable or not. There are many sources of ethics. These include: religious beliefs, national and ethnic beliefs, community standards, family practices, educational experiences, and friends. Business ethics is the application of ethical standards to commercial enterprise.

The role of ethics in management decisions is difficult. Management issues often are emotionally charged, and many types of ethical problems may arise in business situations. What should managers do if they are aware of unethical practices in their businesses? Should they blow the whistle and risk their jobs? Should they quit and allow unethical practices to continue? Should they ignore the practices? These are only a few of the difficult ethical decisions managers face.[1]

CODES OF ETHICS

code of ethics
A document that outlines the principles of conduct to be used in making decisions within an organization.

To help managers know how to respond ethically to different business situations, many companies have developed codes of ethics. A **code of ethics** is a document that outlines the principles of conduct to be used in making decisions within an organization. Most corporations in the United States have codes of ethics.

Content of Ethical Codes

Codes of ethics are formal documents that are shared with all employees. Some of the areas they cover include the following:

- Honesty.
- Adherence to the law.
- Product safety and quality.
- Health and safety in the workplace.
- Conflicts of interest.
- Employment practices.
- Selling and marketing practices.
- Financial reporting.
- Pricing, billing, and contracting.
- Trading in securities/using confidential information.
- Acquiring and using information about competitors.
- Security.
- Payments to obtain business.
- Political activities.
- Protection of the environment.

Management Illustration 5.1

DESTRUCTION OF STATE E-MAILS

A new lawsuit claims that two of the top aides of Matt Blunt, governor of Missouri, ordered all departments in the administration to regularly delete e-mails so potentially damaging messages wouldn't be available to the public.

The suit was filed by former Blunt lawyer Scott Eckersley. It says the governor's chief counsel at the time, Henry Herschel, called a meeting of staff attorneys and instructed them that "all e-mail should be deleted"—ignoring protests from some in the room that e-mails are public records. The suit also claims that the governor's chief of staff, Ed Martin, told staff members "to make sure they deleted their e-mails in both the inbox and trash files to ensure they did not have to be turned over to the press or public."

Eckersley, who was deputy counsel when he was fired, has claimed he was ousted after run-ins with Herschel, Martin, and other Blunt aides about the handling of e-mails. He also has accused them of leading a smear campaign against him. His lawsuit says he peppered the aides with warnings that their orders violated state laws on how records should be retained and made available to the public. In an electronic age, e-mails sent on government computers or accounts are considered vital records.

The suit, filed in Jackson County Circuit Court, accuses the governor's office of defaming Eckersley and claims his firing violated state law protecting whistle-blowers. It asks for unspecified monetary damages.

Source: Adapted from Jo Mannies, "Suit Alleges Illegal Destruction of State E-mails," *McClatchy—Tribune Business News,* January 10, 2008, Wire Feed.

Merely establishing a code of ethics does not prevent unethical behavior. To be effective, codes of ethics must be enforced. In fact, ethical codes that are not enforced probably do more harm than good. For this reason, it is important that companies discipline employees who violate their codes of ethics.

BEHAVING ETHICALLY

Businesspeople regularly make ethical decisions. These decisions have important consequences for both individuals and their companies. Behaving unethically can hurt, or even end, a businessperson's career. It can cause a company to lose millions of dollars or even go out of business altogether. Behaving ethically helps employees gain the trust of the people with whom they work. It can also help businesses gain the trust of customers, suppliers, and others.

Behaving Honestly

In many situations, the ethical course of action is clear-cut. Ethical employees never steal from their employers. They never lie about the hours they work. They never falsify documents. Management Illustration 5.1 describes an ethical issue involving e-mail.

Employee Theft

Employers trust their employees not to steal from them. Employees who behave ethically do not violate that trust.

Dishonest employees steal from their employers in a variety of ways. Some embezzle money or steal supplies or inventory from their employers. Some accept bribes from people who want to do business with their company. Others submit false expense accounts.

Lying about Hours Worked

Employees who behave ethically are honest about the hours they work. Employees who work at home, for example, accurately report how long they work. They do not take advantage of the fact that their managers cannot check to see if they are actually at their desks.

Ethical employees also show up at work unless they are ill or need to be away from their jobs for a legitimate reason. They do not pretend to be sick in order to stay home when they should be at work.

FIGURE 5.1
Solving Ethical Dilemmas

Source: L. Nash, "Ethics without the Sermon," *Harvard Business Review* 59 (1981), p. 78.

1. Have you defined the problem accurately?
2. How would you define the problem if you stood on the other side of the fence?
3. Whom could your decision or action injure? Can you discuss the problem with the affected parties before you make your decision?
4. Are you confident that your position will be as valid over a long period of time as it seems now?
5. Could you disclose without qualm your decision or action to your boss, your CEO, the board of directors, your family, and society as a whole?

Falsifying Records

One of the worst ethical lapses an employee can commit is falsifying records. This can cause very grave damage to a company's reputation. It can even cause people to become ill or die. A manager at a pharmaceutical company, for example, who falsifies records documenting the side effects of the drugs the company produces can cause people who take the drug to die. A production supervisor who falsifies documents to indicate that computer parts were checked can cause his company to sell defective products. Years of excellent corporate performance can be wiped out by these kinds of unethical actions.

Dealing with Ethical Dilemmas

Ethical dilemmas are situations in which the ethical course of action is not clear. Such situations arise regularly in the business world. Consider the following examples:

1. Your boss informs you confidentially that one of your friends is going to be fired. Your friend is about to buy a house. Should you warn your friend that he is about to be fired even though you promised your boss that you would not?
2. Your colleague has been violating your company's code of ethics by accepting expensive gifts from a salesperson who does business with your company. Should you notify your supervisor?
3. One of your employees has not been performing her job properly. You know that she has been having serious personal problems, and you have tried to be understanding. However, your entire staff is suffering because of poor performance by this key team member. What should you do?

One way of approaching ethical dilemmas like these is to answer the series of questions shown in Figure 5.1. Talking to people you trust can also help you develop solutions to ethical problems. Figure 5.2 explains some of the ethical problems in business.

FIGURE 5.2
Ethical Problems in the Business World
Having a code of ethics and a personal sense of what is right and wrong can help business managers choose the right course of action.

1. **Normal Interactions between Business Acquaintances**

   Many interactions between people doing business together are considered a normal part of doing business. Managers often take clients out to lunch or invite them to play golf, for example. These kinds of interactions help businesspeople get to know each other.

2. **Questionable Interactions between Business Acquaintances**

   Some interactions between business acquaintances are questionable. A manager who sends a client an expensive gift, for example, could be seen as trying to bribe the client into doing business with his or her company. Businesses often provide their employees with guidelines on the types of gifts they consider acceptable.

3. **Illegal Interactions between Business Acquaintances**

   Paying bribes to attract business is unethical and illegal. Managers who engage in this kind of activity could face legal action and go to jail.

LAWS RELATING TO ETHICS IN BUSINESS

Over the years, various laws have been enacted that directly relate to the issue of ethics in business. These laws apply to competitive behavior, corporate governance, consumer protection, and environmental protection.

Competitive Behavior

Since the late nineteenth century the federal government has regulated companies to make sure that they do not engage in anticompetitive behavior. All companies operating in the United States must abide by these laws. Enforcement of these laws is handled by the Antitrust Division of the Justice Department and by the Federal Trade Commission.

The Sherman Act

As you learned in Chapter 2, the Sherman Antitrust Act of 1890 makes it illegal for companies to monopolize trade. Under the law, mergers can be prohibited if the new company that results from the merger will control too large a share of the market. The purpose of the law is to ensure that companies remain able to compete fairly.

The Clayton Act

The Clayton Act of 1914 makes it illegal to charge different prices to different wholesale customers. This means that a manufacturer of steel, for example, cannot charge one price to General Motors and another price to Chrysler.

The Clayton Act also bans the practice of requiring a customer to purchase a second good. Manufacturers of computer hardware, for example, cannot require customers to purchase software as well.

The Wheeler-Lea Act

The Wheeler-Lea Act of 1938 bans unfair or deceptive acts or practices, including false advertising. Under the act, businesses must inform consumers of possible negative consequences of using their products. Labeling of cigarette packages is an example of the kind of disclosure required by the Wheeler-Lea Act.

Sarbanes-Oxley Act

The Public Company Accounting Reform and Investor Protection Act (Sarbanes-Oxley Act) was passed in 2002. The act is also called SOX. SOX includes requirements for auditor independence, restriction on firms engaging accounting firms for both auditing and consulting services, independence of firms' board committees, management's assessment of internal controls, and personal certification of financial reports by firms' CEOs and CFOs. Retaliation for whistle-blowing and altering or destroying documents to impede a federal investigation is generally illegal. Under SOX, employees can file complaints with the Occupational Safety and Health Administration (OSHA) if they have been retaliated against by their employer for reporting suspected corporate fraud or other activities related to fraud against shareholders. Management Illustration 5.2 describes a financial settlement under the Sarbanes-Oxley Act. Figure 5.3 summarizes the major points of the Sarbanes-Oxley Act.

Consumer Protection

Several laws protect consumers in the United States against unethical and unsafe business practices. These laws cover food and drugs, other manufactured products, and loans.

Management Illustration 5.2

BACKDATING OF STOCK OPTIONS

William McGuire ascended to the helm of what was then a regional health care company in 1989. Through a series of acquisitions, he turned UnitedHealth Group into a managed-care leader. Today the company serves more than 71 million people nationwide through traditional health plans, as well as Medicare and Medicaid programs, and health-related financial products.

In December 2006, McGuire left, along with two other UnitedHealth executives after an investigation commissioned by the company's board concluded that he had received stock option grants that were "likely backdated" to allow insiders to maximize financial gains.

The controversy was touched off by a *Wall Street Journal* report last year that questioned whether UnitedHealth and other companies had dated executives' options—after they were granted—to when the prices of the shares dipped particularly low in order to maximize the recipients' gains. The newspaper reported that McGuire received options on the days UnitedHealth's share price hit annual lows in 1997, 1999, and 2000—timing that was all but impossible by chance.

During McGuire's 17-year tenure, UnitedHealth's share price increased fiftyfold. At the same time, he amassed a potential fortune in unexercised stock options that became the focus of probes by U.S. and state regulators. His shares were valued at one point at $1.6 billion.

In the settlement, McGuire agreed to return over $320 million in options. He also is forgoing the full value of his fully vested Supplemental Executive Retirement Plan (SERP), which is worth nearly $92 million, and about $8.1 million of incentive compensation benefits in a deferred compensation plan, said his lawyer, David M. Brodsky. McGuire already has repaid $198 million by repricing options, bringing his total giveback to more than $600 million. McGuire's settlement is the first under the Sarbanes-Oxley Act.

Source: Adapted from *Lisa Girion,* "Compensation; Ex-CEO to Make Huge Repayment; UnitedHealth Group's McGuire Agrees to Give Back $468 Million in Backdating Settlement," *Los Angeles Times,* Los Angeles, California: December 7, 2007. p. C1.

FIGURE 5.3
Major Points of the Sarbanes-Oxley Act of 2002

Source: Reprinted by permission of CPE, Inc., 3700 Reed Road, Suite 227, Broomall, PA 19008, 800-514-1114, www.cpeonline.com.

The SEC will direct the NYSE and NASDAQ to prohibit listing any public company whose audit committee does not comply with a new list of requirements affecting auditor appointment, compensation, and oversight. The audit committee must consist solely of independent directors.

CEOs and CFOs must certify in each periodic report containing financial statements that the report fully complies with Sections 13(a) and 15(d) of the Securities Exchange Act of 1934 and that the information fairly presents the company's financial condition and results of operations.

Certifying officers will face penalties for false certification of $1,000,000 and/or up to 10 years' imprisonment for "knowing" violation and $5,000,000 and/or up to 20 years' imprisonment for "willing" violation.

No public company may make, extend, modify, or renew any personal loan to its executive officers or directors, with limited exceptions.

The act sets a deadline for insiders to report any trading in their companies' securities to within two business days after the execution date of the transaction.

Each company must disclose "on a rapid and current basis" additional information about the company's financial condition or operations as the SEC determines is necessary or useful to investors or in the public interest.

All annual reports filed with the SEC containing financial statements must include all material corrections identified by a public accounting firm.

The act creates several new crimes for securities violations, including

- Destroying, altering, or falsifying records with the intent to impede or influence any federal investigation or bankruptcy proceeding.
- Knowing and willful failure by an accountant to maintain all audit or workpapers for five years.
- Knowingly executing a scheme to defraud investors in connection with any security.

Food and Drugs

The Federal Food, Drug, and Cosmetic Act of 1938 bans the sale of impure, improperly labeled, falsely guaranteed, and unhealthful foods, drugs, and cosmetics. The law is enforced by the Food and Drug Administration (FDA), which has the power to force manufacturers to stop selling products it considers unsafe.

Consumer Products

The Consumer Product Safety Commission (CPSC) was established in 1972. It establishes minimum product safety standards on consumer products. If a product is found to be defective, the Consumer Product Safety Commission has the authority to force the manufacturer to recall the product. For example, in 1999 the CPSC recalled a quarter of a million Nike water bottles. The bottles were recalled because the cap was not attached properly, possibly causing users to choke.

Loans

A series of laws protects U.S. consumers against unfair lending practices. Under the Truth in Lending Act of 1968, creditors are required to let consumers know how much they are paying in finance charges and interest. The Equal Credit Opportunity Act of 1975 prohibits creditors from making credit decisions on the basis of discriminatory practices.

Environmental Protection

Since the late 1960s, environmental protection has been an important social and economic issue in the United States. This concern has been reflected in the many laws designed to protect the environment.

The National Environmental Policy Act of 1969

The key piece of legislation in environmental protection is the National Environmental Policy Act of 1969. This law created the Environmental Protection Agency (EPA), whose mission is to protect human health and safeguard the air, water, and land.

Since 1969, many environmental laws affecting businesses have been passed. These laws include the Clean Air Act, the Toxic Substances Control Act, and the Clean Water Act. All of these laws are enforced by the EPA.

The Clean Air Act of 1970

The Clean Air Act of 1970 is the comprehensive federal law that regulates air emissions. The original act set maximum air pollution standards for each of the 50 states. In 1990, the act was amended to deal with problems of acid rain, ground-level ozone, stratospheric ozone depletion, and toxic substances in the air.

The Toxic Substances Control Act of 1976

The Toxic Substances Control Act of 1976 was enacted to give the EPA the ability to track the 75,000 industrial chemicals currently produced in or imported into the United States. The EPA screens these chemicals and can require reporting or testing of those that may pose an environmental or human health hazard.

The Clean Water Act of 1977

The Clean Water Act of 1977 gives the EPA the authority to set standards on the type and quantity of pollutants that industries can put into bodies of water. The law makes it illegal to discharge any pollutant into navigable waters unless a permit is obtained.

ETHICAL STANDARDS AND CULTURE

Standards of business ethics differ around the world. This means that business practices that are acceptable in one country may be considered unethical in others.

Business managers working in foreign countries must be aware of these different ethical standards. They must set guidelines for their companies on how to operate both within their own culture and in other cultures.

Corporate Gift Giving

Gift-giving customs differ around the world. In some cultures, gifts are expected; failure to present them is considered an insult. In Japan, for example, lavish gift giving is an important part of doing business. Gifts are usually exchanged at the first meeting.

In the United States, government officials are not allowed to accept expensive gifts from businesses. Regardless of local practices, American managers operating abroad must abide by the standards set in the United States.

Intellectual Property

intellectual property
Ownership of ideas; gives creators of the intellectual property the exclusive right to market and sell their work.

Intellectual property refers to ownership of ideas, such as inventions, books, movies, and computer programs. In many countries, including the United States, creators of intellectual property have the exclusive right to market and sell their work. These rights are guaranteed through patent, trademark, and copyright laws. These types of protection ensure that only the creators of intellectual property profit from their work.

Intellectual property protection is very important to business. Without such laws, a computer company could market a best-selling game created by another computer company. A pharmaceutical company could manufacture and sell drugs developed by another drug company.

Although the United States has tough laws governing intellectual property, enforcing those laws is a problem, particularly in the software industry. In 1999, the Justice Department, the FBI, and the Customs Service began cracking down on piracy and counterfeiting of computer software and other products in the United States.

Rules concerning intellectual property rights differ in some countries. In China and India, for example, the government does not enforce such rights. As a result, some Chinese companies copy and sell foreign computer programs. Some publishers in India reprint foreign textbooks, selling them as if they had published them themselves. In the United States, someone who engages in this practice is guilty of plagiarism and can be sued in a court of law. Intellectual property must be respected in the American workplace.

SOCIAL RESPONSIBILITY

social responsibility
The obligation that individuals or businesses have to help solve social problems.

Social responsibility refers to the obligation that individuals or businesses have to help solve social problems. Most companies in the United States feel some sense of social responsibility.[2]

Businesses' concepts of their role in society have changed dramatically over the past century. Views toward social responsibility evolved through three distinct schools of thought: profit maximization, trusteeship management, and social involvement.

Profit Maximization

In the nineteenth and early twentieth centuries, business owners in the United States believed that their role was simply to maximize the profits their companies earned. Dealing with social problems was not considered a legitimate business activity.

Trusteeship Management

Thinking about the role of business changed in the 1920s and 1930s, when a philosophy known as *trusteeship management* became popular. This philosophy recognized that owners of businesses had obligations to do more than just earn profits. They also had obligations to their employees, their customers, and their creditors. Most businesses continued to hold this view until the 1960s.

Social Involvement

During the 1960s, many people began to believe that corporations should use their influence and financial resources to address social problems. They believed corporations should help solve problems such as poverty, crime, environmental destruction, and illiteracy.

According to this view, businesses should be responsible corporate citizens, not just maximizers of profit. Businesses have obligations to all of the people affected by their actions, known as stakeholders. **Stakeholders** include a company's employees, customers, suppliers, and the community.

stakeholders
The people—employees, customers, suppliers, and the community—who are affected by the actions of a business.

Corporations have increasingly demonstrated their commitment to social change. One example of this commitment is the increased diversity in the workplace. Most corporations have made efforts to diversify their workforces by hiring and promoting more women and minorities. Many businesses also have established workshops to help their employees understand people from different backgrounds.

MEASURING SOCIAL RESPONSIBILITY

Corporations demonstrate their sense of social responsibility in various ways. Performance in each of these areas is measured as part of a social audit.

Philanthropy and Volunteerism

One way a company demonstrates its sense of social responsibility is by contributing time and money to charitable, cultural, and civic organizations. Corporate philanthropy, or efforts to improve human welfare, can take many forms. Computer giant Compaq (now merged with Hewlett-Packard), for example, provides technology, product, and cash contributions to organizations throughout the United States. It also has planted seedlings in Australia, supported an institute for people with disabilities in India, and refurbished a school in Brazil. All of these activities reflect the company's sense of social responsibility.

Some companies grant employees paid time off to participate in charitable activities. Many high-tech companies, for example, allow their employees to volunteer for the U.S. Tech Corps, which sends employees from technology companies to work in public schools. Other corporations allow employees time off to donate blood, participate in food and clothing drives, or raise money for such causes as the United Way.

Many corporations also donate money by matching charitable donations made by their employees. In this way companies both encourage employee giving and make their own contributions to philanthropic causes. Management Illustration 5.3 describes the relationship between Warren Buffett and Bill Gates on contributions to charity.

Environmental Awareness

Another way companies demonstrate their sense of social responsibility is by limiting the damage their operations cause to the environment. They do so by creating production processes that are as environmentally friendly as possible.

Management Illustration 5.3

THE $44 BILLION DOLLAR GIFT

In the Chapter 1 preview Warren Buffett announced a $44 billion gift to charity. It is interesting to see that he chose the Bill & Melinda Gates Foundation as the main recipient of the gift. Bill Gates is the founder of Microsoft Corporations.

The Gates Foundation began in 1994 with a corporate eye on the bottom line, maintaining lean staffing and renting a nondescript building in Seattle. Its work is focused, concentrating on disease prevention in poor countries and improving education—especially by promoting small classroom sizes in the United States. It seeks to leverage its dollars by working in partnership with other charities and governments, and applies a system of standards to evaluate the success of projects.

A good philanthropy takes the more entrepreneurial, long view, and embraces risk in pursuit of projects of general benefit to mankind, or of help to those underserved by society, business, or government. Indeed, the Gates Foundation has made mistakes—it has a mixed record in education, for instance—but Buffett likes that. "In business," he said, "you look for the easy things to do. In philanthropy, you take on important problems and it is a tougher game."

The Buffett–Gates arrangement also presents a challenge. To the Gates Foundation, it's a challenge to stay efficient despite doubling its size. To other wealthy individuals, it's an invitation to give more. And to everyone else, it's a call to catch the spirit of Buffett's selfless generosity (he didn't start a charity in his name). In the end, it truly is a billion-dollar heart, not wallet, that makes a difference.

Source: Adapted from "The Monitor's View," *The Christian Science Monitor,* Boston, MA, June 29, 2006, p. 8.

Businesses also can affect the environment by establishing policies that reduce pollution. Encouraging employees to carpool, for example, reduces toxic emissions and conserves gasoline. Using biodegradable products also helps protect the environment.

Sensitivity to Diversity and Quality of Work Life

One of the most important ways a company can demonstrate its sense of social responsibility is through its workforce. Socially responsible businesses maintain ethnically diverse workforces that reflect the societies in which they operate. McDonald's, for example, has created a diverse work environment. At least 70 percent of McDonald's restaurant management and 25 percent of the company executives are minorities and women.

Companies also can demonstrate their social responsibility by adopting policies that contribute to the quality of life of their employees. Flexible work hours, for example, allow workers to better meet their families' needs. On-site day care centers make life easier for employees with young children.

Actions Necessary to Implement Social Responsibility

The biggest obstacle to organizations assuming more social responsibility is pressure by financial analysts and stockholders who push for steady increases in earnings per share on a quarterly basis. Concern about immediate profits makes it difficult to invest in areas that cannot be accurately measured and still have returns that are long run in nature. Furthermore, pressure for short-term earnings affects corporate social behavior; most companies are geared toward short-term profit goals. Budgets, objectives, and performance evaluations are often based on short-run considerations. Management may state a willingness to lose some short-term profit to achieve social objectives. However, managers who sacrifice profit and seek to justify these actions on the basis of corporate social goals may find stockholders unsympathetic.

Organizations should also carefully examine their cherished values, short-run profits, and others, to ensure that these concepts are in tune with the values held by society. This should be a constant process, because the values society holds are ever-changing.

Management Illustration 5.4

FRONTIER AIRLINES AND SOCIAL RESPONSIBILITY

Currently in its 14th year of operations, Frontier Airlines is the second-largest jet service carrier at Denver International Airport, employing approximately 6,000 aviation professionals. Frontier has 60 aircraft and one of the youngest Airbus fleets in North America.

On January 18, 2008, Frontier Airlines received the Martin Luther King, Jr. Business Social Responsibility Award: a high honor bestowed upon individual business people, corporations, and nonprofit organizations who have contributed to the Denver community.

Each year, the award committee rewards the nominees who best represent the spirit of the life of Dr. Martin Luther King, Jr., embracing concepts of equal opportunity for all, promotion of good will toward people and encouragement of programs which make the world a better place.

"Frontier believes strongly in the concept of corporate responsibility and we strive to instill that value in everything we do," said Frontier manager of community relations, Jennifer Gunn. "While we are extremely honored to receive this award and to be mentioned in the same sentence as a great man like Martin Luther King, Jr., we are also grateful to have the opportunity to give back to the Denver community for all the support it has shown Frontier. Thank you to all the Frontier employees who helped us earn this prestigious award, and we look forward to many more years of giving back to our hometown of Denver."

The award ceremony took place in Denver at the 23rd annual Martin Luther King, Jr. Business Social Responsibility Award Luncheon, hosted by the Marriott City Center Hotel. Proceeds from this event will be donated to the Colorado Scholarship Coalition, who will select and award Martin Luther King, Jr. Scholarships.

Source: Adapted from *Anonymous,* "Frontier Airlines Wins Business Social Responsibility Award," *PR Newswire,* New York: Jan 18, 2008.

Organizations should reevaluate their long-range planning and decision-making processes to ensure that they fully understand the potential social consequences. Plant location decisions are no longer merely economic matters. Environmental impact and job opportunities for disadvantaged groups are examples of other factors to consider.

Organizations should seek to aid both governmental agencies and voluntary agencies in their social efforts. This should include technical and managerial help as well as monetary support. Technological knowledge, organizational skills, and managerial competence can all be applied to solving social problems.

Organizations should look at ways to help solve social problems through their own businesses. Many social problems stem from the economic deprivation of a fairly large segment of our society. Attacking this problem could be the greatest social effort of organizations.

Another major area in which businesses are active is corporate philanthropy. Corporate philanthropy involves donations of money, property, or work by organizations to socially useful purposes. Many companies have directed their philanthropic efforts toward education, the arts, and the United Way. Contributions can be made directly by the company, or a company foundation can be created to handle the philanthropic program. Management Illustration 5.4 describes the approach of Frontier Airlines to social responsibility.

Conducting a Social Audit

social audit
A method used by management to evaluate the success or lack of success of programs designed to improve the social performance of the organization.

One method of measuring the success of a firm is to conduct a social audit. A **social audit** allows management to evaluate the success or lack of success of programs designed to improve the social performance of the organization. Rather than looking exclusively at economic and financial measures, the social audit can be a beginning point for encouraging environmental and social strategies that really work.

One suggested method for accomplishing the social audit and reacting to the information includes the following steps:

1. Examine social expectations, sensitivity, and past responses.
2. Examine and then set social objectives and meaningful priorities.

3. Plan and implement strategies and objectives in each program area.
4. Set budgets for resources necessary for social action and make a commitment to acquire them.
5. Monitor accomplishments or progress in each program area.

To ensure that stockholders, stakeholders, and the general public know about the commitment and accomplishments of social programs, most large corporations publish their successes in their annual reports. These firms make social responsibility an integral part of their mission statements. True commitment goes beyond the self-serving and selective nature of public relations. Most experts agree that socially responsible firms will eventually be rewarded by their markets and stakeholders.

LEGAL RESPONSIBILITY

Congress and state and local legislatures pass many laws that regulate businesses. The federal, state, and local governments enforce these laws. If businesses do not comply with these laws, they may be subject to legal sanctions, such as fines, penalties, loss of license, or even jail. Many companies hire a government affairs manager, who makes sure that the company knows the laws that regulate its activities. The government affairs manager also makes sure that the company keeps up with new laws and does not become liable for their actions.

regulations
Rules that government agencies issue to implement laws.

Regulations are rules that government agencies issue to implement laws. Businesses spend a lot of time and money making sure they comply with laws and regulations and do not face unwanted liability.

There are six important areas of law that affect business operations:

1. *Corporate law.* Corporate law regulates how businesses can set themselves up to operate as companies.
2. *Tax law.* Tax law regulates how much money businesses must pay the government to help provide services for the public.
3. *Intellectual property law.* Intellectual property law regulates how businesses can protect inventions and new products.
4. *Consumer law.* Consumer law protects individuals against business activities that might be harmful to them.
5. *Commercial law.* Commercial law regulates how businesses enter into contracts with other businesses and with consumers.
6. *Licensing and zoning law.* Licensing laws regulate who can go into certain businesses. Zoning laws regulate where they can establish operations.

CORPORATE LAW

Not all businesses are alike. Some companies are enormous, with more than 100,000 employees and offices in many states and even in other countries. Some are small, with only a couple of partners working together in a single office. Still others are run by just one person. There are laws regulating four kinds of business entities or ownership: sole proprietorships, partnerships, corporations, and limited liability company (LLC).

sole proprietorship
A business owned by a single individual, or proprietor.

Sole Proprietorships

The simplest kind of business is a **sole proprietorship.** A sole proprietorship is a business owned by a single individual, or proprietor. Small businesses often are sole proprietorships, and entrepreneurs often are sole proprietors. Sole proprietors set up businesses after checking with state and local officials about licenses, zoning regulations, and other requirements. Sole proprietors have many advantages. First, they control the entire business and keep all the profits. Second, sole proprietors can make decisions quickly. Additionally, sole proprietors usually pay fewer taxes than other kinds of businesses.

There are several disadvantages of sole proprietorship, however. Sole proprietors have full responsibility for the business. If the business runs into financial trouble, for instance, the owner has full liability for all debts. A sole proprietor may have to use personal savings or even sell a house or car to pay debts from a business. In addition, sole proprietorships can fail entirely if, for example, the owner becomes ill or disabled. Despite these disadvantages, sole proprietorships are popular in the United States.

Partnerships

partnership
An association of two or more persons who jointly own a for-profit business.

A **partnership** is an association of two or more persons who jointly own a for-profit business. The Uniform Partnership Act, which governs general partnerships, requires them to meet two requirements. First, a partnership must be owned by two or more persons. Under the law, a "person" can be a corporation or another organization as well as an individual. Second, partners must share the profits from their business.

A partnership allows partners to combine their talents and their financial resources. Partners share responsibility for making decisions, and a partnership pays less in taxes than a corporation. With two people rather than one, a partnership may have an easier time getting a loan than a sole proprietorship.

The biggest disadvantage of a partnership is that the partners, like sole proprietors, have unlimited liability for business debts. Even if only one partner is responsible for a business's debts, all the partners are responsible for paying them. A second disadvantage is that partners may disagree on how the business should be run or how profits should be shared. Such disagreements can hurt the business.

limited liability partnership (LLP)
a partnership where liability is limited to the amount of money invested in the business or any guarantees given.

Another form of partnership is referred to as **limited liability partnership (LLP).** With an LLP, liability is limited to the amount of money invested in the business and any personal guarantees it may give.

Corporations

corporation
A business formed under state or federal statutes that is authorized to act as a legal person.

A **corporation** is a business formed under state or federal statutes that is authorized to act as a legal person. A corporation exists apart from its owners and can be taxed and sued like an individual. Corporate owners have limited liability. This means they cannot lose their personal resources if the corporation fails. Only the corporation loses.

Corporations have many advantages. Like partnerships, they offer stockholders limited liability and a share of the profits. Stockholders have no management responsibilities. Corporations can raise money by selling stock. They generally have an easier time getting credit than any other type of business.

Corporations have two major disadvantages, however. First, they must comply with many more federal and state laws than either sole proprietorships or partnerships. Corporations must register with a state government agency to begin a business, while a sole proprietor can begin a business at any time. Second, corporations pay more taxes than any other type of business. They pay special taxes to the state and federal governments as well as a tax on profits.

limited liability company (LLC)
Similar to a corporation, owners have limited personal liability for the debts and actions of the LLC.

Limited Liability Company (LLC)

A **Limited Liability Company (LLC)** is a relatively new business structure. LLCs are popular because, similar to a corporation, owners have limited personal liability for the debts and actions of the LLC. Other features of LLCs are more like those of a partnership, providing management flexibility and the benefit of pass-through taxation.

Owners of an LLC are called members. Since most states do not restrict ownership, members may include individuals, corporations, other LLCs, and foreign entities. There is no maximum number of members. Most states also permit "single member" LLCs, those having only one owner. A few types of businesses generally cannot be LLCs, such as banks and insurance companies.

TAX LAW

The type of ownership managers choose for their businesses often depends on the types of taxes involved. Taxes are monies paid by corporations and individuals and are used to fund government programs and services, such as highways and schools.

Income Tax

income tax
A tax levied against a business's profits.

Businesses pay several different types of taxes, but the most important tax is called an income tax. An **income tax** is a tax levied against a business's profits. For example, if a business earns $100,000 in profits this year, and the income tax rate is 30 percent, the business will pay the government $30,000 in taxes.

Property Tax

property tax
Tax levied against the property, buildings, and land owned by a business.

Businesses also must pay property taxes. **Property taxes** are taxes levied against the property, buildings, and land owned by a business. Property taxes are based on an assessed valuation of the building or land. An *assessed valuation* is the amount that a piece of property is worth, according to a tax assessor. For example, the assessed valuation of land and buildings in the heart of Manhattan in New York City is extremely high because there is very little space to construct new buildings. The business owners of property and land in New York City would pay more in taxes than business owners in many other parts of the country.

Taxes may hurt businesses by taking away part of their profits. To make up for these losses, businesses often pass on costs by charging consumers more money for products.

Withholding Federal Taxes

Businesses also collect taxes from employees. The government requires businesses to withhold income taxes from employees' earnings and send them to the federal government. Without the help of business, it would be very difficult for the federal government to collect taxes from working people.

Managers make important decisions because of taxes. For example, a manager may decide to relocate the business's operations because of more favorable taxes in another state. In the late 1990s, for example, the Caterpillar Corporation, a major equipment manufacturer, moved its operations from Illinois to Texas because the taxes were more favorable in the state of Texas. When managers develop strategic plans for making profits, they always need to take the effect of taxes into account.

INTELLECTUAL PROPERTY LAWS

Taxes can cut into a company's profits, but there are also laws that protect business profit. For example, businesses are protected by intellectual property laws. Intellectual property laws protect the inventions and new ideas of businesses.

Our society could not survive without new inventions. Inventions lead to advances in fields such as medicine that improve our quality of life. In the business world, inventions lead to new products. The three kinds of intellectual property protections are patents, trademarks, and copyrights.

Patents

Inventors and companies come up with thousands of inventions every year. Just think about it—television, CDs, cellular phones, bar codes at grocery stores—our world is full of new technological devices made possible by creative inventors.

patent
The document the federal government issues to inventors and companies that gives them the exclusive right to their inventions for 17 years.

Some inventors work on their own, while others work for companies. A company can protect its inventions by applying for a patent. A **patent** is the document the federal government issues to inventors and companies that gives them the exclusive right to make, use, and sell their inventions for 17 years. When the 17 years are up, other companies can begin selling that invention. The inventor of each type of new product must apply for another patent.

Trademarks

trademark
A word, name, symbol, or slogan a business uses to identify its own goods.

A **trademark** is a word, name, symbol, or slogan a business uses to identify its own goods and set them apart from others. Companies apply to the federal government's patents and trademark office when they want to establish a new trademark. Once a company owns its trademark, no other company can use it. Registered trademarks are good for 10 years, and companies can renew them every additional 10 years.

Trademarks are powerful selling tools. Nike puts its trademark on every item of athletic wear it makes, from shoes to underwear. In many countries of the world, wearing Nike goods is a status symbol.

Copyrights

copyright
The protection provided to a creative work.

John Grisham's novels are widely read in the United States and abroad. When Grisham writes a novel, he copyrights the manuscript so that no one else can publish his work without his permission. A **copyright** is the protection provided to a creative work. It can be used to protect literary works, musical compositions, plays, dances, paintings, movies, maps, and computer programs. The owner of the copyright, usually the person who creates the work, is the only one with the legal right to reproduce the work, sell it, or allow others to use it. Under copyright law, photocopying pages of a book can be illegal without the author's or publisher's permission.

CONSUMER LAW

Some laws, such as intellectual property laws, protect businesses. Other laws are designed to protect consumers. *Consumers* are individuals who buy goods and services for their own use. You and the members of your family are consumers every time you buy food, clothing, drugs, or any other item from a business. To protect consumers from unfair business practices, the federal and state governments have established consumer protection laws.

Consumers should understand consumer laws so they know their rights when dealing with businesses. For example, many consumers who buy used cars from dealerships may not know that the law requires dealers to tell buyers certain things about that car, including how many miles it has been driven. Knowing what a car dealer must tell you about buying a car protects both you and the dealer.

The Federal Trade Commission

If you think that someone in business has treated you unfairly, you can write a letter of complaint to the Federal Trade Commission (FTC).

The FTC, an agency of the federal government, will take action against a company if it receives enough consumer complaints to establish a "pattern of wrongdoing." For example, if a large number of people complain that a catalog company is making false promises about its merchandise, the FTC will investigate the complaint.

The FTC has many rules governing all kinds of sales. For instance, the Used Car Rule requires dealers to tell customers important information about a used car. The Telemarketing Sales Rule helps protect consumers from being bombarded with unwanted telemarketing calls by placing limitations on companies that sell or promote by telephone. Some of the FTC rules have been very successful. For example, many consumers would be surprised to find an article of clothing without a care label that tells you how to wash and dry the clothing.

Other Rules That Protect Consumers

There are other laws and agencies that protect consumers as well. For example, the Food and Drug Administration (FDA) protects consumers against problems with mislabeled and impure foods, drugs, cosmetics, and medical devices. The FDA approves all new drugs before they are sold. The Fair Packaging and Labeling Act requires manufacturers of foods, drugs, cosmetics, and medical devices to clearly label products with the name of the manufacturer, the contents, and the amount the package contains. Labels on packaged foods must provide complete nutritional information as well.

COMMERCIAL LAW

In addition to complying with laws regulating their dealings with consumers, businesses must comply with commercial laws that regulate their contracts and dealings with other businesses. The basic commercial law document is called the Uniform Commercial Code.

Contracts

contract
An agreement between two parties to carry out a transaction.

Businesses must follow laws governing how they can enter into contracts. A **contract** is an agreement between two parties to carry out a transaction, such as the sale of goods from a seller to buyer. Contracts create an obligation between the parties, or those agreeing to the contract, that can be enforced in a court of law. For example, when McDonald's agrees to purchase orange juice from Minute Maid to sell in its restaurants, the two companies enter into a contract that is legally enforceable.

Most people enter into different kinds of contracts during their lives. When they buy cars, expensive pieces of furniture, computers, and houses, they generally sign a contract. The contract describes the item being sold, sets out the terms of payment, and states whether the item can be returned.

Businesses enter into contracts daily. Like individuals, they buy things, such as office supplies and computer equipment. They also may lease items, such as furniture or even temporary employees. In each instance, they become a party to a contract.

Contracts must follow very specific rules if they are to stand up in a court of law. Anyone signing a contract—an individual, a representative of a group, the manager of a company—must know exactly what is in the contract and make sure the contract is properly prepared.

Contracts are often difficult to break. If you sign a contract and do not live up to your end of the bargain, the other party can take you to court. You have the same option if the other party does not complete the contract. It's always best to review contracts carefully beforehand. Knowing what you are signing is the best way to avoid problems with a contract later on.

Because most businesses deal in amounts of goods worth more than $500, most business sales contracts are written contracts. To satisfy the Uniform Commercial Code, written contracts must contain certain information. They must state that the parties involved have agreed to the sale and must give the quantity of the goods involved. The exact quantity is important because courts will enforce a contract only for the amount of the goods listed in the contract.

Business Sales Contracts

Business sales contracts are often short, simple documents that meet the requirements of the Uniform Commercial Code. When businesses write a contract for a very large quantity of goods, however, the contract often is many pages long. Suppose the National Aeronautic and Space Administration (NASA), a branch of the federal government, orders parts to build a new shuttle from Boeing Corporation. A space shuttle is a complicated machine that must be extremely safe. The contract must describe the parts using exact measurements that may be tiny fractions of an inch. It must list everything used to make the parts. Because the parts may have more than one component, the contract must provide details for each component. It must break down the costs so that NASA can see what it is paying for each item, no matter how small.

LICENSING AND ZONING LAW

Government passes rules on commercial law to make sure that businesses follow rigid standards when they make deals with other businesses. In addition, state and local governments pass licensing and zoning laws that regulate who can operate a business and where owners can set up shop.

State and local governments use licensing as a way to limit and control people who plan to enter certain types of businesses. For example, if you wanted to start a restaurant, you would need to apply for a license from the local department of food and beverage control. The government may deny your application if it thinks there already are more than enough restaurants in the area.

Government officials can take away a license from a business that is not complying with laws and regulations. For example, the department of sanitation inspects local restaurants to make sure that they are complying with health codes, such as storing foods properly and keeping bathrooms sanitary. If the restaurant is not complying with the rules, the department of sanitation will issue a warning or possibly suspend the restaurant's license to operate. A government agency also has the power to completely revoke a restaurant's license, which means that the restaurant would have to close and go out of business altogether.

Local governments also may regulate businesses through building codes, which regulate physical features or structures of buildings. Building codes may regulate the maximum height, minimum square feet of space, and the types of materials that can be used in constructing an office. Finally, local governments regulate where a building can be built through zoning ordinances and regulations. For example, businesses can operate in commercially zoned areas but not residential areas. Finally, it is important to note that other legislation that affects businesses and management is discussed throughout this book.

Summary

1. *Define ethics.* Ethics are a set of moral principles or values that govern behavior.
2. *Explain a code of ethics.* A code of ethics is a written document that outlines the principles of conduct to be used in making decisions within an organization.
3. *Identify four categories of laws relating to ethics in business.* These laws apply to competitive behavior, corporate governance, consumer protection, and environmental protection.
4. *Explain social responsibility.* Social responsibility refers to the role of business in solving current social issues over and above legal requirements.
5. *Identify the six areas of law that affect business organizations.* The six areas of law that affect business organizations are corporate law, tax law, intellectual property law, consumer law, commercial law, and licensing and zoning law.
6. *Identify the types of taxes that affect business profits.* These are income taxes, property taxes, and withholding federal taxes.
7. *Explain the differences between copyrights, patents, and trademarks.* A patent is the document the federal government issues to inventors and companies that gives them the exclusive right to make, use, and sell their inventions for 17 years. A trademark is a word, name, symbol, or slogan a business uses to identify its own goods and set them apart from others. Companies apply to the federal government's patents and trademark office when they want to establish a new trademark. Once a company owns its trademark, no other company can use it. Registered trademarks are good for 10 years, and companies can renew them every additional 10 years. A copyright is the protection provided to a creative work.
8. *Define intellectual property.* Intellectual property laws protect the inventions and new ideas of businesses. The three kinds of intellectual property protections are patents, trademarks, and copyrights.

Review Questions

1. Define ethics.
2. What is a code of ethics?
3. What is intellectual property?
4. Identify the laws that deal with ethical issues in business.
5. Explain social responsibility.
6. What are the six areas of law that affect business organizations?
7. Explain the laws regulating the three kinds of business entities or ownership.
8. Describe the three kinds of intellectual property protections.
9. What is the Uniform Commercial Code?

Skill-Building Questions

1. Why does the government regulate businesses?
2. What are three ways in which corporations can demonstrate a sense of social responsibility?
3. Why are ethical codes more common today than they were 50 years ago?
4. James F. Lincoln stated: "'Do unto others as you would have them do unto you' is a proper labor–management policy." Do you agree or disagree? Why?

SKILL-BUILDING EXERCISE 5.1
Where Do You Stand?

Read each of the following situations and decide how you would respond. Be prepared to justify your position in a class discussion.

Situation 1: Family versus Ethics
Jim, a 56-year-old middle manager with children in college, discovers that the owners of his company are cheating the government out of several thousand dollars a year in taxes. Jim is the only employee in a position to know this. Should Jim report the owners to the Internal Revenue Service at the risk of endangering his own livelihood, or should he disregard the discovery to protect his family's livelihood?

Situation 2: The Roundabout Raise
When Joe asks for a raise, his boss praises his work but says the company's rigid budget won't allow any further merit raises for the time being. Instead, the boss suggests the company "won't look too closely at your expense accounts for a while." Should Joe take this as authorization to pad his expense account because he is simply getting the money he deserves through a different route, or should he not take this roundabout "raise"?

Situation 3: The Faked Degree
Bill has done a sound job for over a year; he got the job by claiming to have a college degree. Bill's boss learns Bill actually never graduated. Should his boss dismiss him for a false résumé? Should he overlook the false claim, since Bill is otherwise conscientious and honorable and dismissal might ruin Bill's career?

Situation 4: Sneaking Phone Calls
Helen discovers that a co-worker makes about $100 a month in personal long-distance telephone calls from an office telephone. Should Helen report the employee or disregard the calls, since many people make personal calls at the office?

Situation 5: Cover-Up Temptation
José discovers that the chemical plant he manages is creating slightly more water pollution in a nearby lake than is legally permitted. Revealing the problem will bring negative publicity to the plant, hurt the lakeside town's resort business, and scare the community. Solving the problem will cost the company well over $100,000. It is unlikely that outsiders will discover the problem. The violation poses no danger whatever to people; at most, it will endanger a small number of fish. Should José reveal the problem despite the cost to his company, or should he consider the problem as a mere technicality and disregard it?

Situation 6: Actual Salary
Dorothy finds out that the best-qualified candidate for a job really earned only $18,000 a year in his last job, not the $28,000 he claimed. Should Dorothy hire the candidate anyway, or should she choose someone considerably less qualified?

Source: *The Wall Street Journal* by Roger Rickles. Copyright (©) 1983 by Dow Jones & Co., Inc. via Copyright Clearance Center.

SKILL-BUILDING EXERCISE 5.2
Truthfulness in Advertising

Advertising claims may be totally inaccurate ("sticker price is a low $11,998" may omit all transportation costs, state taxes, dealer charges, and factory options, which together add 25 percent to 30 percent to the price of a car). Other claims are greatly exaggerated ("12-hour relief from sore throat pain"), verbally misleading ("you'll have to eat 12 bowls of Shredded Wheat to get the vitamins and nutrition in 1 bowl of Total"), or visually misleading (healthy, active people shown in pleasant social situations to advertise liquor, beer, or cigarettes).

Questions
From magazines, newspapers, or television, select an advertisement you believe to be untruthful.

1. Why do you think the claims are untruthful?
2. Into what group (inaccurate, exaggerated, or misleading) do you think they fall?

Source: La Rue Tone Hosmer, *The Ethics of Management* (Homewood, IL: Richard D. Irwin, 1987), p. 86.

SKILL-BUILDING EXERCISE 5.3
Code of Ethics

Most companies develop a code of ethics to help managers respond to different business situations. A code of ethics is a written document that outlines the principles of conduct to be used in making decisions within an organization. Managers should be aware, however, that merely establishing a code of ethics does not prevent unethical behavior. To be effective, ethical codes must be enforced.

You are president of Acme Corporation, which produces and markets copy equipment. You are planning to develop a code of ethics for your president of company. Prepare an outline of topics that you want to include in the code of ethics.

Questions

1. How difficult was it to develop a code of ethics?
2. Do you feel that a code of ethics can be used by a company or is it just something nobody pays any attention to?

SKILL-BUILDING EXERCISE 5.4
Debating the Sarbanes-Oxley Act

The major points of the Sarbanes-Oxley Act of 2002 are summarized in Figure 5.3. Carefully study Figure 5.3 and develop an argument either supporting the rise and necessity of the act or in opposition to the act. Your instructor may allow you to gather additional information through library or Internet research. Summarize your argument points in outline form, and be prepared to debate classmates who take the other side of the argument.

Case Incident 5.1
Lightbulb Sellers

You receive the following telephone call: "Hello, Mr. Smith. This is Sam. I am a handicapped person." Sam wants to sell you a high-priced lightbulb, guaranteed to last up to five years. He may also want to sell you vitamins and household cleaning solutions. The lightbulbs sold in this manner cost about twice as much as they do at a local hardware store.

However, few of the lightbulb sales organizations are charities. They are for-profit companies whose business is selling lightbulbs by phone. United Handicapped Workers, Lifeline Industries Inc., Handicapped Workers of America, United Handicapped Workers of Charlotte (North Carolina), and American Handicapped Workers are among the larger for-profit companies selling lightbulbs by phone.

The people who make the phone calls are normally paid an hourly wage, a commission, or some combination of the two. The fact that you are dealing with a for-profit business is not always clear, even though the caller may say, "We're not asking for charity or a handout."

Questions

1. Do you believe the practices of these organizations are ethical? Explain.
2. What are the pros and cons of these practices?

Source: "Lightbulb Sellers' Employers Often Not Charity," *Atlanta Journal and Constitution,* May 28, 1990, p. B3.

Case Incident 5.2

Padding the Expense Account?

Principals:

Rick Bell—residence accounts manager in Midland for United Electric Company. Rick is 25 years old, is considered to have good potential as a manager, and was promoted to his present job one month ago.

Stan Holloway—district manager for United Electric in Midland. He is 33 years old and has been in his present job 2½ years. His district, Midland, has strong political influence in the company, as the current president of United Electric was raised in Midland.

Stan is Rick's boss.

Chester "Chet" House—division manager for United. He is 61 years old and is located at company headquarters about 30 miles from Midland. He is Stan's boss and is also a close personal friend of the president of United.

At 7:45 AM on the 28th of March, Rick Bell was preparing to leave Stan Holloway's office after chatting with him for a few minutes about the week's activities.

Rick: Oh, I almost forgot. As soon as I have my monthly expense voucher typed, I'll send it to you for signature so it can be forwarded to disbursing.

Stan: I'm glad you mentioned that. I had meant to talk to you about your voucher this month. I have about $100 worth of items I want you to include on your voucher. This month my voucher is really loaded, and I hate to submit an extremely high amount in light of the emphasis being placed on personal expense control. Since I have signature authority on your voucher, nobody will look at it, and when you get your check back you can give me the extra amount to cover my additional expenses. Here is an itemized list of expenses and dates incurred for inclusion.

Also, don't forget that Chet House is coming by today, and we are to go to lunch with him.

Rick Bell leaves Stan's office with the itemized list in his hand. During the morning, Rick gives much thought to Stan's request. At about 10 AM, Stan calls Rick on the intercom and informs him that he (Stan) won't be able to go to lunch with them (Rick and Chet) that day because the local congressman is making an unscheduled stop in Midland to confer with some selected business leaders on some local issues that will be dominant in the upcoming fall election. He asks Rick to take Chet out to lunch and give him his regrets and to tell Chet that he (Stan) will see them after lunch around 2 PM When Chet arrives, he and Rick leave for lunch and during the meal, the following conversation ensues:

Rick: Mr. House, What would you do if you were ever approached to include expenses on your expense voucher that were not yours?

Chet: Well son, that's a hard thing to theorize on. I guess the best approach would be to look at the consequences for different courses of action. If you did it and got caught in the yearly audit (a slim but possible chance), you could be reprimanded or even fired if the violation were flagrant enough. Of course, if you didn't get caught, you would be home free unless you were repeatedly asked to do it. And if you refuse to do it and the person asking you happens to be your boss, funny things sometimes begin to happen. People get labeled as being uncooperative and nobody wants to be thought of as being uncooperative.

> So I guess that every man at some time has to make a decision that determines his survival among the fittest. This situation could be one of them.

Rick and Chet finished their meal in relative silence and went back to the office where they met Stan for their conference. After the conference, Rick went back to his office and gave some thought to the events of the day. That evening after work Rick went back to Stan's office with the results of his decision.

Questions

1. What would you have done if you were Rick?
2. Do you agree with Mr. House's response to Rick?

References and Additional Readings

1. See Dennis W. Organ, "Business Ethics 101?" *Business Horizons,* January–February 2003, pp. 1–2.
2. For additional information, see Ronald Paul Hill, Debra Stephens, and Iain Smith, "Corporate Social Responsibility: An Examination of Individual Firm Behavior," *Business and Society Review,* September 2003, pp. 339–64.

Chapter Six

International Business

Learning Objectives

After studying this chapter, you will be able to:

1. Explain why countries trade with each other.
2. Explain why companies export and import.
3. Explain how and why countries restrict international trade.
4. Describe a global economy.
5. Explain e-commerce.
6. Describe a free trade area.
7. Describe the strategies organizations use to compete in the global economy.
8. Describe various ways used by companies to sell their products or services in the international market.

Chapter Preview

Examples of Foreign Business Practices

Country	Business Practice
China	Food is extremely important. All business transactions require at least one and usually two evening banquets. The first banquet is given by the host, the second by the guest.
Indonesia	Even foreigners are expected to arrive late to social occasions. It is generally appropriate to arrive about 30 minutes after the scheduled time.
Singapore	Businesspeople exchange business cards in a formal manner, receiving the card with both hands and studying it for a few moments before putting it away.
Saudi Arabia	Businesspeople greet foreigners by clasping their hand, but they do not shake hands.
Switzerland	Business is conducted very formally. Humor and informality are inappropriate.

Analyzing Management Skills

How has the Internet made it easier to market products to foreign customers?

Applying Management Skills

As a manager for an American e-commerce company, what effects might increased Internet access in China have on your business?

international trade
The exchange of goods and services by different countries.

Today, instead of being separated by distance, time, transportation, and communications barriers, nations have become increasingly interdependent. **International trade** consists of the exchange of goods and services by different countries. It includes the purchase of American blue jeans in China and the purchase of Belgian chocolate in the United States. The growth of international trade over the past several decades has been both a primary cause and effect of globalization. The volume of internatinoal trade has increased at a steady pace. This increase in the trade of manufactured goods often exceeds the increase in the rate of the production of these goods. As a result, consumers around the world now enjoy a broader selection of products than ever before. A whole host of U.S. and foreign government agencies and international institutions have been established to help manage with ever-growing flow of trade.

Although increased international trade has spurred tremendous economic growth across the globe, by raising incomes, creating jobs, reducing prices, and increasing workers' earning power, international trade can also bring economic, political, and social disruptions. Developments in transportation and communication have revolutionized economic exchange, not only increasing its volume but also widening its geographical scope. As trade expanded in geographic scope, diversity, and quantity, the channels of trade also became more complex. Improvement in communications such as the Internet have expanded international trade making sellers and buyers more interconnected.

Most of the world today depends on international trade to maintain its standard of living. American manufacturers sell automobiles, heavy machinery, clothing, and electronic goods abroad. Argentine cattle ranchers ship beef to consumers in dozens of foreign countries. Saudi Arabian oil producers supply much of the world with oil. In return, they purchase food, cars, and electronic goods from other countries.

Countries trade for several different reasons. One country may not be able to produce a good it wants. France, for example, cannot produce oil because it has no oil fields. If it wants to consume oil, it must trade with oil-producing countries. Countries also may trade because they have an advantage over other countries in producing particular goods or services.

ABSOLUTE ADVANTAGE

absolute advantage
The ability to produce more of a good than another producer.

Different countries are endowed with different resources. Honduras, for example, has fertile land, a warm and sunny climate, and inexpensive labor. Compared with Honduras, Great Britain has less fertile soil, a colder and rainier climate, and more expensive labor. Given the same combination of inputs (land, labor, and capital), Honduras would produce much more coffee than Great Britain. It has an absolute advantage in the production of coffee. An **absolute advantage** is the ability to produce more of a good than another producer with the same quantity of inputs.

COMPARATIVE ADVANTAGE

law of comparative advantage
Producers should produce the goods they are most efficient at producing and purchase from others the goods they are less efficient at producing.

Countries need not have an absolute advantage in the production of a good to trade. Some countries may be less efficient at producing *all* goods than other countries. Even countries that are not very efficient producers are more efficient at producing some goods than others, however. The **law of comparative advantage** states that producers should produce the goods they are most efficient at producing and purchase from others the goods they are less efficient at producing. According to the law of comparative advantage, individuals, companies, and countries should specialize in what they do best.

EXPORTING AND IMPORTING

exports
Goods and services that are sold abroad.

imports
Goods and services purchased abroad.

International trade takes place when companies sell the goods they produce in a foreign country or purchase goods produced abroad. Goods and services that are sold abroad are called **exports.** Goods and services that are purchased abroad are called **imports.**

The United States is the largest exporter in the world, exporting about $700 billion worth of goods and services a year. It also is the world's largest importer, purchasing about $900 billion worth of foreign goods and services annually.

Exports

Exports represent an important source of revenue for many companies. IBM earns almost 40 percent of its revenues abroad.

Why Do Companies Export?

About 95 percent of the world's consumers live outside the United States. Companies that sell their products exclusively within the United States miss out on the opportunity to reach most of the world's consumers. To increase their sales, companies like Procter & Gamble spend millions of dollars trying to identify what customers in foreign countries want.

Companies also seek out export markets in order to diversify their sources of revenue. *Diversification* is engaging in a variety of operations. Businesses like to diversify their sales so that sluggish sales in one market can be offset by stronger sales elsewhere.

How Do Companies Identify Export Markets?

To determine if there is sufficient demand for their products or services overseas, companies analyze demographic figures, economic data, country reports, consumer tastes, and competition in the markets they are considering. Business managers contact the International Trade Administration of the U.S. Department of Commerce, foreign consulates and embassies, and foreign and international trade organizations. They also visit the countries they are considering and conduct surveys in order to assess consumer demand.

Businesses also need to find out what restrictions they may face as exporters. All countries require exporters to complete certain kinds of documents. Some countries also insist that foreign companies meet specific requirements on packaging, labeling, and product safety. Some also limit the ability of exporters to take money they earn from their exports out of the country.

Imports

American companies import billions of dollars worth of goods and services every year. They import consumer goods, such as television sets and automobiles, and industrial goods, such as machines and parts. They import raw materials, such as petroleum, and

Companies import products they can resell in their own companies. Wholesalers and retailers will, for example, import cheeses from France because customers want to purchase them.

food products, such as fruits and vegetables. They import these goods in order to use them to produce other goods or to sell them to customers.

Imports of Materials

Many companies import some or all of the materials they use in order to reduce their production costs. Manufacturers of appliances, for example, import steel from Japan because it is less expensive than steel manufactured in the United States.

Some companies use imported inputs because domestically made inputs are not available or their quality is not as good as that of imported goods. Jewelry designers import diamonds and emeralds, which are not produced in the United States. Fashion designers use imported cashmere wool, which is softer than domestic wool.

Imports of Consumer Goods

Companies also import products that they can resell in their own countries. Automobile dealers import cars and trucks from Europe and Asia. Wholesalers and retailers import clothing from Thailand, electronic goods from Japan, and cheese from France.

Companies import these goods because consumers want to purchase them. Some of these goods, such as garments from Asia, are less expensive than domestically manufactured products. Others, such as Saabs and Volvos, are popular despite costing more than domestically produced goods.

Balance of Trade

balance of trade
Difference between the value of the goods a country exports and the value of the goods it imports.

The **balance of trade** is the difference between the value of the goods a country exports and the value of the goods it imports. A country that exports more than it imports runs a *trade surplus.* A country that imports more than it exports runs a *trade deficit.*

For many years the United States has run a trade deficit. This means that the value of the goods and services it buys from other countries exceeds the value of the goods and services it sells to other countries. Other countries, such as China, have run huge trade surpluses. In these countries, the value of exports exceeds the value of imports. Management Illustration 6.1 describes China's balance of trade.

Foreign Exchange

Companies that purchase goods or services from foreign countries must pay for them with foreign currency. If a U.S. company purchases goods from Japan, for example, it must pay for them in yen. If it purchases goods from Switzerland, it must pay for them in Swiss francs.

Companies purchase foreign currency from banks, which convert each currency into dollars. The value of one currency in terms of another is the foreign exchange rate.

Exchange rates can be quoted in dollars per unit of foreign currency or units of foreign currency per dollar. The exchange rate for the Swiss franc, for example, might be 1.5 to the dollar. This means that one dollar is worth 1.5 Swiss francs and one Swiss franc is worth 1/1.5 dollar, or $0.67.

Most exchange rates fluctuate from day to day. Managers involved in international trade must follow these fluctuations closely, because they can have a dramatic effect on profits. Consider, for example, an American electronics store that wants to purchase 10 million yen worth of Japanese stereos, camcorders, and cameras. If the exchange rate of the yen is 115 to the dollar, the U.S. company must pay $86,956 to purchase 10 million yen worth of Japanese equipment (10 million yen/115 yen per dollar). If the value of the yen rises so that a dollar is worth only 100 yen, the company would have to spend $100,000 to purchase the same value of Japanese goods (10 million yen/100 yen per dollar).

Management Illustration 6.1

EXPORTS AND IMPORTS IN CHINA

In 2007, China's biggest trade gap was again with the United States. By China's count, that surplus amounted to $163 billion, up 13 percent from 2006. That was a slower growth rate than in recent years, as China's imports from the United States last year grew faster than its exports to America.

It was the reverse for the European Union. China's trade surplus with the EU widened 46 percent in 2007 to $134 billion. That has prompted stronger calls from EU leaders for Beijing to let the value of China's currency rise significantly, which would tend to make Chinese goods more expensive in overseas markets.

By product category, China's exports in 2007 were led by shipments of computers and other data-processing equipment and parts, which totaled $123 billion, an increase of 33 percent from 2006. Many of these goods, as well as other products with imported components, are assembled in China. China's exports of apparel continued to show sharp increases, climbing 21 percent last year to $115 billion. Chinese steel shipments totaled $44 billion, up a whopping 68 percent from 2006.

For all of last year, Chinese exports of toys showed few ill effects from the problems over lead-tainted products. Last year, China shipped toys valued at $8.5 billion, up 20 percent from 2006. Full-year figures for food exports weren't available, but statistics through November show that Chinese farm products and food exports increased 17 percent to $32.5 billion.

As in past years, China's leading imports continued to be commodities and resources to support the nation's furious building of infrastructure, factories, and other development. Imports of iron ore jumped 62 percent to $33.8 billion, and copper imports rose 58.5 percent to $19.7 billion.

Source: Adapted from Don Lee, "China's Global Trade Surplus Up 47%," *Los Angeles Times,* January 12, 2008, p. C3.

PROTECTIONISM

International trade can benefit all trading partners. It also may hurt some domestic producers, however. A U.S. manufacturer of watches may find it difficult to compete with a Taiwanese producer, who pays his workers a fraction of what workers in the United States earn. Competition from the Taiwanese producer may force the U.S. company out of business.

To help domestic manufacturers compete against foreign companies, governments sometimes impose protectionist measures, such as tariffs, quotas, and other types of restrictions. All of these measures reduce the volume of international trade. Management Illustration 6.2 describes the World Trade Organization (WTO) and its efforts to eliminate barriers to international trade.

Tariffs

tariffs
Government-imposed taxes charged on goods imported into a country.

A **tariff** is a tax on imports. The purpose of a tariff is to raise the price of foreign goods in order to allow domestic manufacturers to compete. The United States imposes tariffs on many goods. This means that a Korean company that sells men's shirts in the United States must pay an import tax on every one of its shirts that enters the country. The purpose of this tax is to make it more difficult for foreign manufacturers to compete with American companies in the United States.

Quotas

quota
Establishes the maximum quantity of a product that can be imported or exported during a given period.

Quotas are restrictions on the quantity of a good that can enter a country. The United States imposes quotas on many kinds of goods. For example, it allows just 1.6 million tons of raw sugar to enter the country from abroad. This quota has raised the price of raw sugar, making goods that use sugar, such as candy and cold cereal, more expensive. It has hurt American companies and individuals that consume sugar, but helped American companies and individuals that produce sugar.

Management Illustration 6.2

WORLD TRADE ORGANIZATION (WTO)

FUNCTIONS

The WTO's overriding objective, is to help trade flow smoothly, freely, fairly, and predictably. It does this by:

- Administering trade agreements.
- Acting as a forum for trade negotiations.
- Settling trade disputes.
- Reviewing national trade policies.
- Assisting developing countries in trade policy issues, through technical assistance and training programmes.
- Cooperating with other international organizations.

STRUCTURE

The WTO has 150 members, accounting for over 97 percent of world trade. Around 30 others are negotiating membership. Decisions are made by the entire membership. This is typically by consensus. A majority vote is also possible but it has never been used in the WTO, and was extremely rare under the WTO's predecessor, GATT. The WTO's agreements have been ratified in all members' parliaments.

The WTO's top level decision-making body is the Ministerial Conference which meets at least once every two years. Below this is the General Council (normally ambassadors and heads of delegation in Geneva, but sometimes officials sent from members' capitals) which meets several times a year in the Geneva headquarters. The General Council also meets as the Trade Policy Review Body and the Dispute Settlement Body. At the next level, the Goods Council, Services Council, and Intellectual Property (TRIPS) Council report to the General Council.

Numerous specialized committees, working groups and working parties deal with the individual agreements and other areas such as the environment, development, membership applications and regional trade agreements.

SECRETARIAT

The WTO Secretariat, based in Geneva, has around 637 staff members and is headed by a director-general. It does not have branch offices outside Geneva. Since decisions are taken by the members themselves, the Secretariat does not have the decision-making role that other international bureaucracies are given.

The Secretariat's main duties are to supply technical support for the various councils and committees and the ministerial conferences, to provide technical assistance for developing countries, to analyze world trade, and to explain WTO affairs to the public and media. The Secretariat also provides some forms of legal assistance in the dispute settlement process and advises governments wishing to become members of the WTO. The annual budget is roughly 182 million Swiss francs.

Source: Adapted from information on the Internet.

Embargoes

embargo
Involves stopping the flow of exports to or imports from a foreign country.

An **embargo** is a total ban on the import of a good from a particular country. Embargoes usually are imposed for political rather than economic reasons. Since 1961, for example, the United States has imposed an embargo on Cuba, whose regime it opposes. This embargo bans the importation of goods from Cuba and the export of U.S. goods to Cuba.

THE RISE OF THE GLOBAL ECONOMY

global economy
Economy in which companies compete actively with businesses from around the world.

Many factors have led to the rise of the **global economy,** an economy in which companies compete actively with businesses from all over the world. These factors include improvements in communications technology, the rise in democracy in the world, and the elimination of trade restrictions.[1]

Improvements in Telecommunications Technology

Improvements in telecommunications technology have had an enormous impact on international trade. Exchanges of information that once took weeks now take seconds, as a result of the development of fax machines and e-mail.

Development of the Internet also has led to *e-commerce,* or sales made over the World Wide Web. E-commerce has enabled even small companies to reach consumers in foreign countries by marketing their products on Web sites.

Management Illustration 6.3

STALLING MEXICAN TRUCKS

Congress voted to halt funding for a pilot program that allows selected Mexican 18-wheelers to begin traveling freely into the United States as part of the 1994 North American Free Trade Agreement. The Department of Transportation contends that the congressional action permits the current program to continue while banning any new program. The Federal Motor Carrier Safety Administration, the DOT agency that regulates the program, quietly acknowledged last week that the program is still underway, adding that it has issued permits to 11 Mexican companies with a total of 56 trucks. Most Mexican trucks were previously confined to a 25-mile border zone.

The 1.4 million-member International Brotherhood of Teamsters, which represents U.S. long-haul truckers, expressed outrage and vowed to press ahead with a lawsuit against the program, which is pending in a federal appeals court in San Francisco. "We're not happy," Teamsters spokeswoman Leslie Miller said. "We believe they are breaking the law."

Under the program, launched in the fall, up to 500 trucks from 100 Mexican companies could travel into the interior of the United States over the next year. The agreement also allows 100 U.S. companies to send their trucks beyond a restrictive border zone in Mexico. Four U.S. companies with a total of 41 trucks have been cleared to travel into the Mexican interior.

Source: Adapted from Dave Montgomery, "Vote Doesn't Stall Mexican Trucks," *McClatchy-Tribune Business News,* January 4, 2008, Wire Feed.

Since the end of the cold war, American brands have earned billions of dollars selling products and services in markets where they were once excluded. Holiday Inn, for example, now runs a hotel in Warsaw.

Political Changes

The political changes that have taken place have dramatically increased opportunities for businesses. As a result of the end of the cold war with Russia and the thawing of relations with China, American companies have earned billions of dollars selling products and services in markets from which they were once excluded. Holiday Inn, for example, now runs a hotel in Warsaw. Colgate-Palmolive has a facility in Huangpu, China. Both of these companies, and thousands of others, have benefited from the spread of capitalism.

Free Trade Areas

To promote international trade and limit protectionism, countries create free trade areas. A **free trade area** is a region within which trade restrictions are reduced or eliminated.

free trade area
A region within which trade restrictions are reduced or eliminated.

North American Free Trade Agreement (NAFTA)
NAFTA allows businesses in the United States, Mexico, and Canada to sell their products anywhere in North America without facing major trade restrictions.

The largest free trade area in the world is in North America. Under the terms of the **North American Free Trade Agreement (NAFTA)** of 1994, businesses in the United States, Mexico, and Canada can sell their products anywhere in North America without facing major trade restrictions. Management Illustration 6.3 describes one disagreement concerning NAFTA.

Consumers in all three countries have benefited from lower prices on North American imports. The price of a blouse imported from Canada or a pair of shoes imported from Mexico, for example, is lower than it used to be, because the price no longer includes a tariff.

Many producers have also benefited from NAFTA by increasing their exports within North America. American grain farmers, for example, have increased their sales to Mexico as a result of NAFTA. U.S. automobile sales to Mexico also have risen.

NAFTA has forced some American workers to lose their jobs. Companies have reduced their workforces in this country to take advantage of lower labor costs in Mexico.

FIGURE 6.1 European Countries and Applicants

The *European Union* (*EU*) is a union of 27 European countries, known as member states. Figure 6.1 provides a map of the member states. A key activity of the EU is the establishment of a common single market within the member states.

DOING BUSINESS GLOBALLY

Thousands of U.S. businesses, large and small, participate in the global marketplace. Some companies, such as Benetton, build factories in foreign countries or set up retail outlets overseas. Others, such as Harley-Davidson, export their products throughout the world and import materials from other countries.

Forms of International Operations

Companies can sell their products or services in foreign countries in various ways. Small companies often work through local companies, which are familiar with local markets. Large companies often establish sales, manufacturing, and distribution facilities in foreign countries.

Working through a Foreign Intermediary

Companies that are not willing or able to invest millions of dollars in operations abroad often export their products through foreign intermediaries. A *foreign intermediary* is a wholesaler or agent who markets products for companies that want to do business abroad. In return for a commission, the agent markets the foreign company's product.

Working through a foreign intermediary saves a company the expense of setting up facilities in a foreign country. It also ensures that the company is represented by someone familiar with local conditions. Foreign intermediaries usually work for many foreign companies at a time, however. Thus, they are not likely to devote as much time to a single company's products as the company's own sales force would.

Signing a Licensing Agreement with a Foreign Company

Another way companies can reach foreign consumers is by licensing a foreign company to sell their products or services abroad. A *licensing agreement* is an agreement that permits one company to sell another company's products abroad in return for a percentage of the company's revenues.

TGI Friday's, a Dallas-based restaurant company, has used licensing agreements to expand its operations overseas. Signing such agreements enabled it to open branches in Singapore, Indonesia, Malaysia, Thailand, Australia, and New Zealand. Without such agreements, it might not have been able to penetrate those markets.

Forming a Strategic Alliance

Some companies can expand into foreign markets by forming *strategic alliances* with foreign companies. A strategic alliance involves pooling resources and skills in order to achieve common goals. Companies usually form strategic alliances to gain access to new markets, share research, broaden their product lines, learn new skills, and expand cross-cultural knowledge of management groups.

Becoming a Multinational Corporation

Companies willing to make a significant financial commitment often establish manufacturing and distribution facilities in foreign countries. A business with such facilities is known as a **multinational corporation (MNC)** (see Figure 6.2).

multinational corporation (MNC)
Business that maintains a presence in two or more countries, has a considerable portion of its assets invested in and derives a substantial portion of its sales and profits from international activities, considers opportunities throughout the world, and has a worldwide perspective and orientation.

Businesses become multinational corporations for several reasons. Some do so in order to sell their products or services in other countries. McDonald's, for example, maintains restaurants in 116 foreign countries. Sales to customers in these countries represent half of the company's total revenue.

Companies also expand abroad in order to take advantage of inexpensive labor costs. For example, Tarrant Apparel, a U.S. manufacturer of blue jeans, weaves most of its fabric in Mexico. It also has most of its jeans sewn in Mexico, where labor is cheaper than in the United States.[2]

Challenges of Working in an International Environment

Working for a multinational corporation presents many challenges. Managers must learn to deal with customers, producers, suppliers, and employees from different countries. They

FIGURE 6.2
Multinational Corporations
There are many ways for companies to do business globally. Multinational corporations often purchase their materials abroad or manufacture or assemble their products abroad. They also sell their products in foreign countries.

1. **Imported Materials**

   Multinational corporations may import materials used to manufacture their products. General Motors (GM), the largest automobile producer in the United States, works with more than 30,000 suppliers worldwide. Many of these suppliers are overseas.

2. **International Production**

   Multinational companies may produce their products in other countries. GM has manufacturing, assembly, or component operations in 50 countries. It operates abroad in order to improve service or reduce costs.

3. **International Sales**

   Multinational companies sell their products in other countries. GM cars and trucks are sold in Africa, Asia and the Pacific, Europe, the Middle East, and North America. Foreign sales represent a significant share of the company's total sales.

must become familiar with local laws and learn to respect local customs. They must try to understand what customers and employees want in countries that may be very different from the United States.

Understanding Foreign Cultures

Business managers from different countries see the world differently. Japanese managers, for example, tend to be more sensitive to job layoffs than American managers. Asian and African managers often have different views about the role of women in the workplace than American managers do.

Managers who work in foreign countries need to be aware of different cultural attitudes. They also need to understand business customs in different countries. Not knowing how to act in a foreign country can cause managers embarrassment, and it can cause them to miss out on business opportunities. Showing up for a business meeting without a tie might be acceptable in Israel, for example, but it would be completely out of place in Switzerland. Demonstrating great respect to a superior would be appreciated in Indonesia, but it would send the wrong signal in the Netherlands, where equality among individuals is valued.

Coalitions of Cooperating Countries and Trading Blocs

International businesses must also deal with coalitions of cooperating countries that are established to improve the economic conditions of the member countries. One coalition is the European Union, which was briefly discussed earlier in this chapter. Its purpose is to reduce tariffs on goods sold among member countries. Also, it is an attempt to eliminate the fiscal, technical, and border barriers between member countries that over several decades have increased the costs of goods and services in Europe and reduced the international competitiveness of European companies. Europe was to be a single market with exciting potential for multinational corporations. Many problems still exist in implementing the changes necessary for Europe to become one market. The democratic movement in Eastern Europe, the reunification of Germany, and the breakup of the Soviet Union have resulted in some of those countries and republics joining the European Union.

Another coalition is the Organization of Petroleum Exporting Countries (OPEC), which includes many of the oil-producing countries of the world. Its purpose is to control oil prices and production levels among member countries. Today, OPEC's effectiveness is limited because several member countries sell and produce at levels considerably different from official OPEC standards.

Management Illustration 6.4

HUMAN RIGHTS

With nine divisions that do everything from firearms training to protecting U.S. politicians who visit Iraq—Blackwater, is virtually a private army. The company employs around 2,000 security contractors and employs about 600 people at its headquarters. Among Blackwater's affiliates and business units, Blackwater Security Consulting protects military and civilian personnel, convoys, and assets.

An estimated 35,000 private security contractors work in Iraq for 181 companies, providing security for military bases, private businesses, foreign dignitaries, and the U.S. State Department. They're part of a larger force of some 180,000 private contractors, more people than the American military has in the country.

There have been several allegations of human rights abuses, the most recent by a group of Blackwater U.S. guards escorting a convoy through Baghdad. Iraqi officials say the guards killed 17 civilians and wounded 24 without provocation in Nisoor Square.

Justice Department investigators warned congressional staff in a private meeting that they might have little legal justification for prosecuting the case. At that meeting officials said it would be difficult, though not impossible, to hold the guards accountable for the deaths under current law.

An international human-rights organization, Human Rights First, said that a lack of political will—not a fuzzy legal framework—was primarily to blame for the dearth of prosecutions of private security contractors accused of abuses in Iraq. Human Rights First made several recommendations. They include asking the Justice Department to take the lead in prosecuting abuses in federal courts, coordinating investigations with the Defense Department, and holding companies accountable through their written federal contracts.

Source: Adapted from Barbara Barrett, "Rights Group Slams U.S. over Private Security Contractors in Iraq," *McClatchy-Tribune Business News,* January 17, 2008, Wire Feed.

Today, three large trading blocks exist: European Union; the North American Alliance of the United States, Canada, and Mexico (NAFTA); and Pacific Asia (Pacific Rim countries), with Japan being the dominant country in that region. Other members of the Pacific Rim trading bloc are China, Korea, Taiwan, Indonesia, Malaysia, the Philippines, Thailand, Hong Kong, and Singapore. These three large trading blocs will provide many opportunities and pose many threats for multinational organizations.

Political Changes

One of the most dramatic illustrations of how political changes influence the international business environment was the breakup of the Soviet Union and the fall of communist governments in Eastern Europe in the early 1990s. In addition, the political and economic upheavals in Bulgaria, Hungary, Poland, Romania, and the countries formerly known as Czechoslovakia and Yugoslavia have caused significant changes in how these countries conduct their own international business activities and how they relate to businesses from foreign countries.

Human Rights and Ethics

Should multinational firms close their plants in countries where human rights abuses are common and accepted ethical boundaries are violated? This is a valid issue, but U.S. managers must remember that business ethics have not yet been globalized; the norms of ethical behavior continue to vary widely even in Western capitalist countries. Thus, questions such as, Should Coca-Cola establish minimum labor standards for all of its bottlers around the world to prevent abuses of workers in certain countries? seem highly appropriate in the United States. However, such questions present dilemmas for multinational firms that are accompanied by ethical predicaments and hard choices. In each situation, the multinational firm must strike a balance among the values and ideals of all of its various publics. No clear and easy choices exist. Management Illustration 6.4 summarizes possible human rights violations by employees of an American firm.

Summary

1. *Explain why countries trade with each other.* Countries trade for several different reasons. One country may not be able to produce a good it wants. Another reason is that one of the countries may have an absolute advantage over another country. Another reason is that countries produce according to the law of comparative advantage.
2. *Explain why companies export and import.* One reason for exporting is to increase sales. Companies also export to diversify their sources of revenue. Companies import goods in order to use them to produce other goods or to sell them to customers. Companies also import products that they can resell in their own countries.
3. *Explain how and why countries restrict international trade.* To help domestic manufacturers compete against foreign companies, governments sometimes impose protectionist measures, such as tariffs, quotas, and other types of restrictions.
4. *Describe a global economy.* A global economy is one in which companies compete actively with businesses from all over the world.
5. *Explain e-commerce.* E-commerce refers to sales made over the World Wide Web.
6. *Describe a free trade area.* A free trade area is a region within which trade restrictions are reduced or eliminated.
7. *Describe the strategies organizations use to compete in the global economy.* Companies can sell their products or services in foreign countries in various ways. Small companies often work through local companies, which are familiar with local markets. Large companies often establish sales, manufacturing, and distribution facilities in foreign countries.
8. *Describe various ways used by companies to sell their products or services in the international market.* Companies sell their products by working through a foreign intermediary, signing a licensing agreement with a foreign company, forming a strategic alliance, or becoming a multinational corporation.

Review Questions

1. Define international trade.
2. What is absolute advantage? Law of comparative advantage?
3. Define export. Import.
4. What is the balance of trade?
5. What does foreign exchange mean?
6. What is a tariff? A quota? An embargo?
7. What is a global economy?
8. Describe a free trade area.
9. What ways can companies use to sell their products or services in foreign countries?

Skill-Building Questions

1. Do you think the old saying "When in Rome, do as the Romans do" applies to international business activities? Explain your answer.
2. What problems might you face if you were asked to serve as a manager in a foreign country?
3. What are some typical U.S. management practices that would be difficult to apply in foreign countries?
4. The fastest-growing market for U.S. cigarette manufacturers is in international markets. What ethical problems do you see in exporting cigarettes to foreign markets?

5. What do you think could be some potential pitfalls of entering into a strategic alliance?
6. Do you think NAFTA is a good idea? Develop five pro arguments and five con arguments for the establishment of NAFTA. What do you think will be the next country to join the NAFTA agreement? Justify your answer.

SKILL-BUILDING EXERCISE 6.1
Exchange Rates

Your company imports 3 million pounds of chocolate from Switzerland a year at a cost of 3 Swiss francs a pound. Last year the value of the Swiss franc was 1.5 francs per dollar. How much did your imports cost in dollars? If the value of the Swiss franc goes to 1.2 francs per dollar this year, how much will your imports cost?

SKILL-BUILDING EXERCISE 6.2
Free Trade

Free trade agreements, such as NAFTA (the North American Free Trade Agreement) and GATT (the General Agreement on Tariffs and Trade), may reduce trade restrictions within a designated region, as well as allow for increased sales and lower-priced goods. However, much criticism has also been voiced by consumer, labor, health, and environmental groups, such as the Alliance for Democracy, Public Citizen in Washington, D.C., and the Fair Trade Network. They believe that unrestricted, "corporate-managed" trade will do more harm than good. Do research on the Internet to answer the following questions:

1. Be prepared to discuss positives and negatives of NAFTA and GATT.
2. Be prepared to describe the purpose of:
   a. Alliance for Democracy.
   b. Public Citizen in Washington, D. C.
   c. Fair Trade Network.

SKILL-BUILDING EXERCISE 6.3
Geography of International Trade

Organize the class into teams of three students per team. Have each team either create or obtain a map of the world. Identify and highlight on the map the five countries that are the leading importers of U.S. goods and the five countries that are the leading exporters of goods to the United States. Each team should then explain why they feel that the top importer and top exporter is in that position.

SKILL-BUILDING EXERCISE 6.4
Blockbuster Video

Blockbuster Video is considering expanding into 10 new countries. The company's chief executive officer has asked you to analyze which countries might represent good choices. First, you should find out where Blockbuster has already expanded internationally. Then you should prepare a one-page report in which you identify all of the issues you think the company should consider. Be sure to discuss the importance of international trade agreements, economic and competitive issues, and cultural and political issues.

Case Incident 6.1

International Trade Decision

The Castle Company is a small yet fairly profitable American company that raises animals for their wool—merino wool sheep for merino wool, angora goats for cashmere, and alpacas for alpaca wool. The company also cleans, dyes, and spins the wool. Because of the high quality of the wool fibers, the Castle Company can command top dollar for the product. The retail prices per pound for dyed and natural yarns are: merino wool—$25; alpaca wool—$35; merino wool and alpaca blend—$40; and cashmere and merino wool blend—$50.

Jack Castle, the Castle Company president, believes their product line would sell well in Canada. Currently the exchange rate for the Canadian dollar is 0.9354 to one U.S. dollar. He has been considering two options.

The first option is to sell his yarns through a wholesaler in Montreal. Rather than receiving a commission, the wholesaler wants to pay the Castle Company a wholesale price in U.S. dollars that is 75 percent of the U.S. retail price. Presently the Castle Company receives a wholesale price of 80 percent of the retail price from its distributors in the United States. The Montreal wholesaler is also willing to pay for the yarns up front, that is, before it sells them.

The second option is for Jack to sign a licensing agreement with a chain of stores that specializes in craft products, like yarn and knitting needles. The chain's headquarters is in Toronto. The licensing agreement states that it would market and sell the Castle Company yarns for 5 percent of the Canadian retail price.

Other differences between the Montreal wholesaler and the chain craft store from Toronto involve their markets and the breadth of their distribution. The Toronto craft store is part of a 25-store chain throughout Canada, and it sells supplies for all kinds of crafts—from painting to jewelry making to sewing to needlepoint. The Montreal wholesaler sells only to yarn sellers and some specialty craft stores in Quebec.

After reviewing both offers, Jack chooses the wholesaler in Montreal. He believes the wholesaler would sell his yarns to the most appropriate market—specialty weavers and knitters.

Questions

1. Do you agree with Jack Castle's decision?
2. Are their any other options Jack should consider?

Case Incident 6.2

Imposed Quotas

A labor union official was alleged to have made the following statement:

> Foreign imports of textiles have cost American jobs and tax revenues. In order to slow down the disruptive impacts on American society, quotas should be placed on imports into the United States for those goods and products that are displacing significant percentages of U.S. production and employment.

Questions

1. Do you agree with the union official? Explain.
2. Do you believe import quotas should be established for certain industries? Which ones?
3. Does the United States benefit or lose from international trade?

References and Additional Readings

1. See, for example, V. Kumar and Anish Nagpal, "Segmenting Global Markets: Look before You Leap," *Marketing Research* 13, no. 1 (2001), pp. 8–19.
2. For more information on multinational companies, see Foley J. Bernard, "Multinationals and Global-Capitalism: From the Nineteenth to the Twenty-First Century," *The Economic History Review,* November 2005, p. 874.

Part **Three**

Planning and Organizing Skills

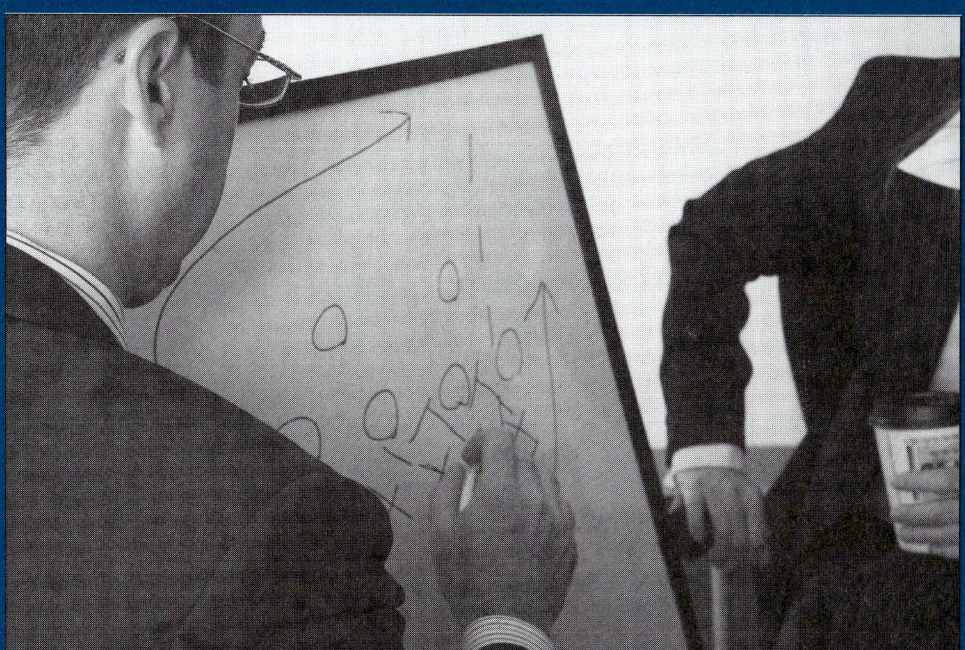

Chapter **Seven**

The Basics of Planning and Strategic Management

Learning Objectives

After studying this chapter, you will be able to:

1. Define planning and distinguish between formal and functional plans.
2. Contrast strategic planning with operational planning.
3. Explain the differences between objectives, policies, procedures, and rules.
4. Define the management by objectives (MBO) process.
5. Define strategy and explain the various levels of strategies.
6. Define strategic management and explain the strategic management process.
7. Define organizational mission and explain how mission relates to long- and short-range objectives.
8. Discuss the components of a SWOT analysis.
9. Define a strategic business unit (SBU).
10. Discuss what organizational factors need to be evaluated in implementing a strategic plan.

Chapter Preview

In the early 1980s, Howard Schultz predicted that consumers would support a new type of "coffee bar," serving specialty coffee and espresso products. Under his leadership, Starbucks grew from a homey little coffee shop in Seattle into a multimillion dollar corporation. In its early years, the company focused on domestic growth, infrastructure, and product development. In 1992, the company first went public, raising $29 million for expansion. A secondary offering in late 1994 netted around $180 million. Since going public, Starbucks has raised almost $500 million.

Speaking in 2000, Schultz said, "Five years ago our strategic intent was to build the leading brand of specialty coffee in North America. Five years later we have fulfilled that promise. And our strategic objectives now are much different, and that is to maintain our leadership position in North America and to build an enduring global brand around the world."

In September 2005, the company opened its 10,000th store, with plans to eventually have 30,000 stores worldwide (15,000 in the United States and 15,000 internationally). As of February 2005, Starbucks was in 35 countries. By October 2006, Starbucks had revised its estimate to 20,000 stores internationally with about half of them in Asia. At this same time, Starbucks was planning to open at least 100 stores per year in China which Starbucks believes will eventually become its second largest market in the world, second only to North America. As of January 2008, Starbucks had a significant and growing presence in 43 countries.

Sources: Karyn Stauss, "Howard Schultz: Starbucks' CEO Serves a Blend of Community, Employee Commitment," *Nation's Restaurant News,* January 2000, pp. 162–63; Gretchen Weber, "Preserving the Counter Culture," *Workforce Management,* February 2005, pp. 28–33; "Richard McGregor, "Starbucks Brews Up China Expansion," *Financial Times,* October 25, 2006; and "Starbucks Announces Strategic Initiatives to Increase Shareholder Value; Chairman Howard Schultz Returns as CEO," *Business Wire,* January 7, 2008.

Analyzing Management Skills

Why do you think it is important for a company like Starbucks to regularly refine and update its strategic objectives? What other functions might annual strategic planning sessions serve?

Applying Management Skills

What trends do you think will influence businesses in the next 10 years? If you opened a business today, what things would you do to plan for its future success?

THE PLANNING PROCESS

planning
Process of deciding what objectives to pursue during a future time period and what to do to achieve those objectives.

Planning is the process of deciding what objectives to pursue during a future time period and what to do to achieve those objectives. It is the primary management function and is inherent in everything a manager does. This chapter discusses the basics of the planning function and how this function relates to strategic management.

Why Plan?

It is futile for a manager to attempt to perform the other management functions without having a plan. Managers who attempt to organize without a plan find themselves reorganizing on a regular basis. The manager who attempts to staff without a plan will be constantly hiring and firing employees. Motivation is almost impossible in an organization undergoing continuous reorganization and high employee turnover.

Planning enables a manager or an organization to actively affect rather than passively accept the future. By setting objectives and charting a course of action, the organization commits itself to "making it happen." This allows the organization to affect the future. Without a planned course of action, the organization is much more likely to sit back, let things happen, and then react to those happenings in a crisis mode.

Planning provides a means for actively involving personnel from all areas of the organization in the management of the organization. Involvement produces a multitude of benefits. First, input from throughout the organization improves the quality of the plans; good suggestions can come from any level in the organization. Involvement in the planning process also enhances the overall understanding of the organization's direction. Knowing the big picture can minimize friction among departments, sections, and individuals. For example, through planning, the sales department can understand and appreciate the objectives of the production department and their relationship to organizational objectives. Involvement in the planning process fosters a greater personal commitment to the plan; the plan becomes "our" plan rather than "their" plan. Positive attitudes created by involvement also improve overall organizational morale and loyalty.

Planning can also have positive effects on managerial performance. Studies have demonstrated that employees who stress planning earn high performance ratings from supervisors.[1] They have also shown that planning has a positive impact on the quality of work produced.[2] While some have proven inconclusive, several studies have reported a positive relationship between planning and certain measures of organizational success, such as profits and goals.[3] One explanation that would fit all the findings to date is that good planning, as opposed to the mere presence or absence of a plan, is related to organizational success.

A final reason for planning is the mental exercise required to develop a plan. Many people believe the experience and knowledge gained throughout the development of a plan force managers to think in a future- and contingency-oriented manner; this can result in great advantages over managers who are static in their thinking. The age-old saying "If you don't know where you are going, any road will get you there," sums it up.

Formal Planning

formal plan
Written, documented plan developed through an identifiable process.

All managers plan. The difference lies in the methods they employ and the extent to which they plan. Most planning is carried out on an informal or casual basis. This occurs when planners do not record their thoughts but carry them around in their heads. A **formal plan** is a written, documented plan developed through an identifiable process. The appropriate degree of sophistication depends on the needs of the individual managers and the organization itself. The environment, size, and type of business are factors that typically affect the planning needs of an organization.

Functional Plans

functional plans
Originate from the functional areas of an organization such as production, marketing, finance, and personnel.

Plans are often classified by function or use. The most frequently encountered types of **functional plans** are sales and marketing plans, production plans, financial plans, and personnel plans. Sales and marketing plans are for developing new products or services and selling both present and future products or services. Production plans deal with producing the desired products or services on a timely schedule. Financial plans deal primarily with meeting the financial commitments and capital expenditures of the organization. Personnel plans relate to the human resource needs of the organization. Many functional plans are interrelated and interdependent. For example, a financial plan would obviously be dependent on production, sales, and personnel plans.

The Planning Horizon: Short Range, Intermediate, and Long Range

short-range plans
Generally cover up to one year.

long-range plans
Typically span at least three to five years; some extend as far as 20 years into the future.

The length of the planning horizon is relative and varies somewhat from industry to industry, depending on the specific environment and activity. What may be long range when operating in a rapidly changing environment, such as the electronics industry, may be short range when operating in a relatively static environment, such as the brick manufacturing industry. In practice, however, **short-range plans** generally cover up to one year, whereas **long-range plans** span at least three to five years, with some extending as far as 20 years into the future. While long-range planning is possible at any level in the organization, it is carried out primarily at the top levels.

Intermediate plans cover the time span between short-range and long-range plans. From a pragmatic standpoint, intermediate plans generally cover from one to three or one to five years, depending on the horizon covered by the long-range plan. Usually intermediate plans are derived from long-range plans and short-range plans are derived from intermediate plans. For example, if the long-range plan calls for a 40 percent growth in sales by the end of five years, the intermediate plan should outline the necessary steps to be taken over the time span covering one to five years. Short-range plans would outline what actions are necessary within the next year.

strategic planning
Analogous to top-level long-range planning; covers a relatively long period; affects many parts of the organization.

operations or tactical planning
Short-range planning; done primarily by middle- to lower-level managers, it concentrates on the formulation of functional plans.

contingency plans
Address the what-ifs of the manager's job; gets the manager in the habit of being prepared and knowing what to do if something does go wrong.

objectives
Statements outlining what the organization is trying to achieve; give an organization and its members direction.

Operational versus Strategic Plans

Strategic planning is analogous to top-level, long-range planning. It is the planning process applied at the highest levels of the organization, covering a relatively long period and affecting many parts of the organization. **Operations** or **tactical planning** is short-range planning and concentrates on the formulation of functional plans. Production schedules and day-to-day plans are examples of operational plans.

However, the distinctions between strategic and operations planning are relative, not absolute. The major difference is the level at which the planning is done. Strategic planning is done primarily by top-level managers; operational planning is done by managers at all levels in the organization and especially by middle- and lower-level managers.

Contingency Plans

Regardless of how thorough plans are, there will always be things that go wrong. What goes wrong is often beyond the control of the manager. For example, the economy takes an unexpected dip, a machine breaks down, or the arrival of a new piece of equipment is delayed. When such things happen, managers must be prepared with a backup, a contingency, plan. **Contingency plans** address the what-ifs of the manager's job. Contingency planning gets the manager in the habit of being prepared and knowing what to do if something does go wrong. Naturally, contingency plans cannot be prepared for all possibilities. What managers should do is identify the most critical assumptions of the current plan and then develop contingencies for problems that have a reasonable chance of occurring. A good approach is to examine the current plan from the point of view of what could go wrong. Contingency planning is most needed in rapidly changing environments. Management Illustration 7.1 describes some of the contingency plans developed and used by FedEx.

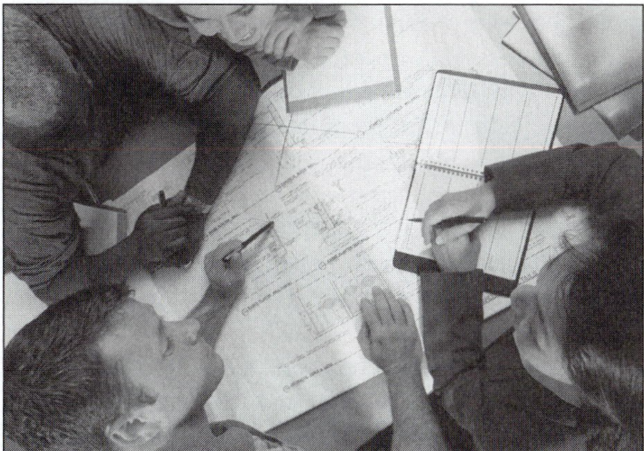

Strategic planning is done primarily by top-level managers, while operational planning is done by managers at all levels of the organization.

Objectives

If you don't know where you're going, how will you know when you get there? **Objectives** are statements outlining what you are trying to achieve; they give an organization and its members direction and purpose. Few managers question the importance of objectives, only what the objectives should be. Management cannot be properly practiced without pursuing specific objectives. Managers today and in the future must concentrate on where they and their organizations are headed.

It is also important to realize that managers and employees at all levels in an organization should have objectives; everyone should know what he or she is trying to achieve. One key for organizational success is for the objectives at all different levels to mesh together.

Management Illustration 7.1

CONTINGENCY PLANNING AT FEDEX

Every day of the year FedEx is faced with some type of disruption to its operations. In 2005 the company had to activate contingency plans for 30 tropical storms. In addition, FedEx had to deal with an air-traffic controller strike in France in March and a power blackout in Los Angeles in September. FedEx conducts disaster drills several times a year—for all types of events from big earthquakes to bioterrorism to a monster typhoon hitting the company's hub in the Philippines. Eight disaster kits, each containing two tons of supplies such as fuel and communications gear, stand ready in Memphis in the event that a facility is in need of repair. Every night, five empty FedEx planes roam the skies standing by to replace a broken-down plane or assist with an unexpected surge in volume.

Before hurricane Katrina hit, FedEx positioned 30,000 bags of ice, 30,000 gallons of water, and 85 home generators outside Baton Rouge and Tallahassee so that it could move quickly after the storm to relieve employees. Even though FedEx was ready for Katrina's high winds, the subsequent flooding and chaos presented some unexpected problems. FedEx learned from those problems and will be even more prepared next time. FedEx has recently teamed up with the American Red Cross to leverage its planning expertise to benefit small businesses in their disaster preparedness efforts.

Sources: Ellen Florian Kratz, "For FedEx, It Was Time to Deliver," *Fortune*, October 3, 2005, pp. 83–84; and "American Red Cross and FedEx Announce Collaboration to Help Small Businesses Get Prepared for Disaster; National Survey Reveals Majority of Small Businesses Are Unprepared," *PR Newswire*, September 13, 2007.

Long-Range Objectives

long-range objectives
Go beyond the current fiscal year; must support and not conflict with the organizational mission.

Long-range objectives generally go beyond the organization's current fiscal year. Long-range objectives must support and not conflict with the organizational mission. However, they may be quite different from the organizational mission, yet still support it. For instance, the organizational mission of a fast-food restaurant might be to provide rapid, hot-food service to a certain area of the city. One long-range objective might be to increase sales to a specific level within the next four years. Obviously, this objective is quite different from the organizational mission, but it still supports the mission.

Short-Range Objectives

short-range objectives
Generally tied to a specific time period of a year or less and are derived from an in-depth evaluation of long-range objectives.

Short-range objectives are generally tied to a specific time period of a year or less and should be derived from an in-depth evaluation of long-range objectives. Such an evaluation should result in a listing of priorities of the long-range objectives. Then short-range objectives can be set to help achieve the long-range objectives.

Normally, multiple objectives should be used to reflect the desired performance of a given organizational unit or person. From a top-level perspective, objectives should span all major areas of the organization. A problem with one overriding objective is that it is often achieved at the expense of other desirable objectives. For example, if production is the only objective, quality may suffer in attempts to realize maximum production. While objectives in different areas may serve as checks on one another, they should be reasonably consistent among themselves.

Objectives for organizations usually fall into one of four general categories: (1) profit oriented, (2) service to customers, (3) employee needs and well-being, and (4) social responsibility. Even nonprofit organizations must be concerned with profit in the sense that they generally must operate within a budget. Another scheme for classifying organizational objectives is (1) primary, (2) secondary, (3) individual, and (4) societal. Primary objectives relate directly to profit. Secondary objectives apply to specific units of the organization (e.g., departmental objectives). Individual objectives directly concern the organization's employees. Finally, societal objectives relate to the local, national, and global communities. The following section outlines areas for establishing objectives in most organizations:[4]

1. *Profitability*. Measures the degree to which the firm is attaining an acceptable level of profits; usually expressed in terms of profits before or after taxes, return on investment, earnings per share, or profit-to-sales ratios.
2. *Markets*. Reflects the firm's position in its marketplace, expressed in terms of share of the market, dollar or unit volume in sales, or niche in the industry.
3. *Productivity*. Measures the efficiency of internal operations expressed as a ratio of inputs to outputs, such as number of items or services produced per unit of time.
4. *Product*. Describes the introduction or elimination of products or services; expressed in terms of when a product or service will be introduced or dropped.
5. *Financial resources*. Reflects goals relating to the funding needs of the firm; expressed in terms of capital structure, new issues of common stock, cash flow, working capital, dividend payments, and collection periods.
6. *Physical facilities*. Describes the physical facilities of the firm; expressed in terms of square feet of office or plant space, fixed costs, units of production, or similar measurements.
7. *Research and innovation*. Reflects the research, development, or innovation aspirations of the firm; usually expressed in terms of dollars to be expended.
8. *Organization structure*. Describes objectives relating to changes in the organizational structure and related activities; expressed in terms of a desired future structure or network of relationships.
9. *Human resources*. Describes the human resource assets of the organization; expressed in terms of absenteeism, tardiness, number of grievances, and training.
10. *Social responsibility*. Refers to the commitments of the firm regarding society and the environment; expressed in terms of types of activities, number of days of service, or financial contributions.

How to State/Write Objectives

The SMART criteria offer helpful guidelines for stating and writing objectives.[5] SMART stands for *specific, measurable, achievable, relevant,* and *time-based*. Each of these criterion is discussed below.

Specific. Specific in this context means that an observable action, behavior, or achievement is described *and* linked to a rate, number, percentage, or frequency. "Answer all written customer complaints quickly" is a precise description of behavior, but it is not linked to a rate, number, or percentage of frequency. "Answer all written customer complaints within 48 hours" is specific and linked to a rate.

Measurable. A system, method, or procedure must exist that allows the tracking and recording of the specific action, behavior, or achievement upon which the objective is focused. Using the previous example, a system must exist for measuring just how long it is taking to answer written customer complaints.

Achievable. Objectives should be set so that people are capable of achieving them. Some think that objectives should be set just slightly higher than can be attained. The thought here is to keep the employee stretching and to avoid the letdown that might occur once the objective has been reached. One problem with this approach is that it takes only a short time for employees to figure out that the objective is unattainable. This can quickly demotivate employees. On the other hand, most people are turned on, not off, when they reach a challenging goal. The key is for the objective to be challenging and realistic. Employees should be required to stretch, but the objective should be within their capabilities.

Relevant. Relevant in this context means the objective is viewed by affected employees as being important to the organization and as something that they can impact or change. If employees perceive an objective as unimportant or as something they can't impact or change, they are going to psychologically dismiss the objective.

Time-based. Somewhere in the stated objective there should be a specific date (day/month/year) or time frame for reaching or "achieving the objective.

In addition to the above SMART characteristics, objectives should be regularly updated and assigned priorities. All too often, objectives are not regularly reviewed and updated. Pursuing outdated objectives wastes resources. Objectives should be reviewed periodically. Those that are no longer of value should be discarded. Others will need revising in light of recent changes. Because objectives are of differing importance, both the manager and employees should know an objective's relative importance. Everyone should know which objectives are most important and which are least important. Then, if problems occur, everyone will be able to budget time accordingly.

management by objectives (MBO)
Management by objectives is a philosophy based on converting organizational objectives into personal objectives. MBO works best when the objectives of each organizational unit are derived from the objectives of the next higher unit in the organization.

policies
Broad, general guides to action that constrain or direct the attainment of objectives.

Management by Objectives (MBO)

One approach to setting objectives that has enjoyed considerable popularity is the concept of **management by objectives (MBO).** MBO originated from the writings of Peter Drucker in the 1950s. MBO is a philosophy based on converting organizational objectives into personal objectives. It assumes that establishing personal objectives elicits employee commitment, which leads to improved performance. MBO has also been called management by results, goals and control, work planning and review, and goals management. All of these programs are similar and follow the same basic process.

MBO works best when the objectives of each organizational unit are derived from the objectives of the next higher unit in the organization. Thus, the objective-setting process requires involvement and collaboration among the various levels of the organization; this joint effort has beneficial results. First, people at each level become more aware of organizational objectives. The better they understand the organization's objectives, the better they see their roles in the total organization. Second, the objectives for an individual are jointly set by the person and the superior; there are give-and-take negotiating sessions between them. Achieving self-formulated objectives can improve motivation and, thus, job performance. MBO is discussed in further depth in Chapter 18.

The primary purpose of a rule such as "No smoking in the building" is to provide guidance. What is the difference then between a rule and a procedure?

Policies

To help in the objective-setting process, the manager can rely to some extent on policies and procedures developed by the organization. **Policies** are broad, general guides to action that constrain or direct objective attainment. Policies do not tell organizational members exactly what to do, but they do establish the boundaries within which they must operate. For example, a policy of "answering all written customer complaints in writing within 10 days" does not tell a manager exactly how to respond, but it does say it must be done in writing within 10 days. Policies create an understanding among members of a group that makes the actions of each member more predictable to other members.

procedure
Series of related steps or tasks expressed in chronological order for a specific purpose.

rules
Require specific and definite actions to be taken or not to be taken in a given situation.

Procedures and rules differ from policies only in degree. In fact, they may be thought of as low-level policies. A **procedure** is a series of related steps or tasks expressed in chronological order for a specific purpose. Procedures define in step-by-step fashion the methods through which policies are achieved. Procedures emphasize details. **Rules** require specific and definite actions to be taken or not to be taken in a given situation. Rules leave little doubt about what is to be done. They permit no flexibility or deviation. Unlike procedures, rules do not have to specify sequence. For example, "No smoking in the building" is a rule. In reality, procedures and rules are subsets of policies. The primary purpose is guidance. The differences lie in the range of applicability and the degree of flexibility. A no-smoking rule is much less flexible than a procedure for handling customer complaints. However, a rule can have a clear relationship to an objective. For example, a no-smoking rule may help the organization reach a stated objective of "a cleaner and safer corporate environment."

STRATEGY

strategy
Outlines the basic steps management plans to take to reach an objective or a set of objectives; outlines how management intends to achieve its objectives.

The word *strategy* originated with the Greeks about 400 B.C.; it pertained to the art and science of directing military forces.[6] A **strategy** outlines the basic steps that management plans to take to reach an objective or a set of objectives. In other words, a strategy outlines how management intends to achieve its objectives.

Levels of Strategy

Strategies exist at three primary levels in an organization and are classified according to the scope of what they are intended to accomplish. The three levels are corporate, business, and functional strategies.

Corporate Strategies

corporate (grand) strategies
Address which businesses an organization will be in and how resources will be allocated among those businesses.

growth strategy
Used when the organization tries to expand, as measured by sales, product line, number of employees, or similar measures.

Strategies that address which businesses the organization will be in and how resources will be allocated among those businesses are referred to as **corporate strategies.** Corporate strategies are sometimes called **grand strategies.** They are established at the highest levels in the organization, and they involve a long-range time horizon. Corporate strategies are concerned with the overall direction of the organization, specifically tied to mission statements, and generally formulated by top corporate management. Four basic corporate strategy types are recognized: growth, stability, defensive, and combination.

Growth strategies are used when the organization tries to expand in terms of sales, product line, number of employees, or similar measures. Under this concept, an organization can grow through concentration of current businesses, vertical integration, and diversification. Kellogg and McDonald's use concentration strategies—focusing on extending the sales of their current products or services—very successfully. A. G. Bass (maker of the famous "preppie" shoe, Bass Weejuns) believes vertical integration, in which a company moves into areas it previously served either as a supplier to or as a customer for its current products or services, to be a superior growth strategy. The final growth strategy is exemplified by Coca-Cola's purchase of Minute Maid Orange Juice in the early 1980s and its later purchase of Dasani spring waters. Diversification can take several forms, but concentric (in related fields) is the most common.

stability strategy
Used when the organization is satisfied with its present course (status quo strategy).

Stability strategies are used when the organization is satisfied with its present course. Management will make efforts to eliminate minor weaknesses, but generally its actions will remain the status quo. Stability strategies are most likely to be successful in unchanging or very slowly changing environments. Growth is possible under a stability strategy, but it will be slow, methodical, and nonaggressive. Most organizations elect a stability strategy by default rather than by any conscious decision or plan.

Management Illustration 7.2

TURNAROUND STRATEGY AT HEWLETT-PACKARD

In the three years following Hewlett-Packard's (HP) acquisition of Compaq Computer, the price of the company's stock was a vast disappointment. In an effort to reverse HP's fortunes, Mark Hurd was hired from NCR to become the new CEO in the spring of 2005. Hurd had been with NCR for 25 years and had been CEO since 2003. When Hurd took over as CEO of NCR, the company's stock was trading at $10. After the implementation of an eight-quarter cost-cutting plan, NCR's stock had risen to $37 in early 2005.

Industry pros familiar with Hurd's style have outlined a three-step turnaround strategy that they believe will ultimately determine how successful Hurd is at HP. The three steps are as follows:

1. Cut until it hurts. This translates into a workforce reduction of 5 percent to 10 percent at an annual savings of 21 to 42 cents a share of stock.
2. Raise the bar. Hurd believes that HP is "off benchmark" in numerous areas and should not be satisfied to meet industry averages.
3. Keep his promises. Unlike its recent past, Hurd must meet his revenue and earnings projections to earn the confidence of the investment community.

In fiscal 2007, which ended October 31, HP's revenues topped $100 billion for the first time and the company surged past IBM as the world's largest technology company. By December 2007, HP's stock price had more than doubled since Hurd had taken over. The company expects revenues to reach $111.5 billion in fiscal 2008 and to range from $117.1 billion to $118.2 billion in fiscal 2009. In December 2007, Hurd, when referring to cost-cutting initiatives, said: "We have more to do."

Source: Excerpt from Adam Lashinsky, "Take a Look at HP," *Fortune*, June 13, 2005, pp. 117–19. Copyright © 2006 Time Inc., All rights reserved; and Steve Johnson, "Mark Hurd's HP Game Plan: CEO Delivers 'Prudent' Forecast for Developing Untapped Sectors," *McClatchy–Tribune Business News*, December 12, 2007.

defensive (retrenchment) strategy
Used when a company wants or needs to reduce its operations.

Defensive or **retrenchment strategies** are used when a company wants or needs to reduce its operations. Most often they are used to reverse a negative trend or to overcome a crisis or problem. The three most popular types are *turnaround* (designed to reverse a negative trend and get the organization back to profitability), *divestiture* (the company sells or divests itself of a business or part of a business), and *liquidation* (the entire company is sold or dissolved). Management Illustration 7.2 describes the turnaround strategy that Hewlett-Packard (HP) began to implement in 2005.

combination strategy
Used when an organization simultaneously employs different strategies for different parts of the company.

Combination strategies are used when an organization simultaneously employs different strategies for different parts of the company. Most multibusiness companies use some type of combination strategy, especially those serving several different markets. Coca-Cola, for example, pursued a combination strategy in 1989 when it divested its Columbia Pictures division while expanding its soft-drink and orange juice businesses.

Figure 7.1 summarizes the major types and subtypes of corporate strategies.

FIGURE 7.1
Major Types and Subtypes of Corporate Strategies

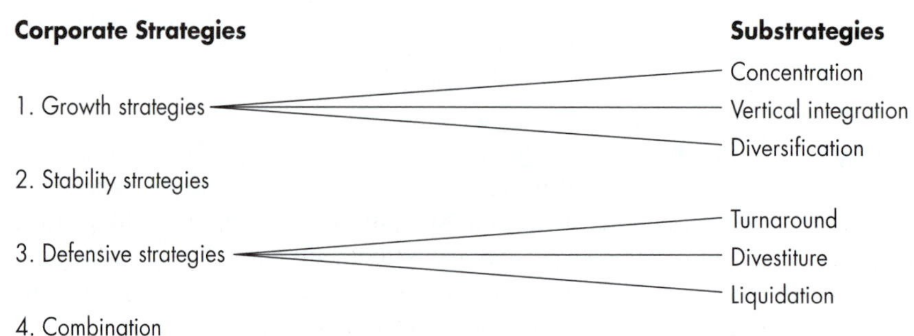

Business Strategies

business strategies
Focus on how to compete in a given business.

Business strategies, the second primary level of strategy formulation, are sometimes called competitive strategies. Business strategies focus on how to compete in a given business. Narrower in scope than a corporate strategy, a business strategy generally applies to a single business unit. Though usually situational in nature, most of these strategies can be classified as overall cost leadership, differentiation, or focus.[7]

Overall cost leadership is a strategy designed to produce and deliver the product or service for a lower cost than the competition. Cost leadership is usually attained through a combination of experience and efficiency. More specifically, cost leadership requires close attention to production methods, overhead, marginal customers, and overall cost minimization in such areas as sales and research and development (R&D). Achieving an overall low-cost position usually requires that the company develop some unique advantage or advantages over its competitors. Examples include a high market share, favorable access to raw materials, use of state-of-the-art equipment, or special design features that make the product easy to manufacture. Wal-Mart and Home Depot have adopted this strategy with great success.

Differentiation aims to make the product or service unique in its category, thus permitting the organization to charge higher-than-average prices. Differentiation can take many forms, such as design or brand image, quality, technology, customer service, or dealer network. The basic purpose of a differentiation strategy is to gain the brand loyalty of customers and a resulting lower sensitivity to price. Following a differentiation strategy does not imply that the business should have little concern for costs but, rather, that the major competitive advantage sought is through differentiation.

Depending on what is required to achieve differentiation, a company may or may not find it necessary to incur relatively high costs. For example, if high-quality materials or extensive research is necessary, the resulting product or service may be priced relatively high. When this is the case, the idea is that the uniqueness of the product or service will create a willingness on the part of the customers to pay the premium price. While such a strategy can be very profitable, it may or may not preclude gaining a high share of the market. For example, Rolex demands a very high price for its watches and makes a profit, but it has a very small market share.[8] Mercedes-Benz and Ralph Lauren Polo sportswear are other examples of products that used a differentiation strategy. Differentiation can be achieved through a superior product (Rolex), a quality image (Mercedes-Benz), or a brand image (Polo sportswear).

Focus is a third type of business strategy. Companies that use this method focus on, or direct their attention to, a narrow market segment. The segment may be a special buyer group, a geographical market, or one part of the product line. With a focus strategy, the firm serves a well-defined but narrow market better than competitors that serve a broader or less defined market. A "tall men's" clothing store is an example of a company following a focus strategy. Colgate-Palmolive, for example, has determined that to reach Hispanics successfully, it must capitalize on shared traits of this growing segment. Its 70 percent market share of toothpaste sold to Hispanics is largely attributed to understanding that three-quarters of Hispanics who watch TV or listen to radio do so with Spanish-language stations. Colgate-Palmolive has heavy sponsorship of favorite programs on these stations.[9]

Functional Strategies

functional strategies
Concerned with the activities of the different functional areas of the business.

The third primary level of strategy is functional strategies. **Functional strategies** are narrower in scope than business strategies and deal with the activities of the different functional areas of the business—production, finance, marketing, human resources, and the like. Functional strategies support the business strategies and are primarily concerned with

FIGURE 7.2
Levels of Strategies

Corporate Strategy

Addresses which businesses an organization will be in and how resources will be allocated among those businesses; describes the way the organization will pursue its objectives.

Business Strategy

Focuses on how to compete in a given business.

Functional Strategy

Concerned with the activities of the different functional areas of the organization, short-range step-by-step methods to be used (tactics).

how-to issues. Usually functional strategies are in effect for a relatively short period, often one year or less. Figure 7.2 summarizes the different levels of strategies.

THE STRATEGIC MANAGEMENT PROCESS

Strategic Management

strategic management Formulation, proper implementation, and continuous evaluation of strategic plans; determines the long-run directions and performance of an organization. The essence of strategic management is developing strategic plans and keeping them current.

The rapid rate of change in today's business world is making it increasingly necessary that managers keep their plans current. **Strategic management** is the application of the basic planning process at the highest levels of the organization. Through the strategic management process, top management determines the long-run direction and performance of the organization by ensuring careful formulation, proper implementation, and continuous evaluation of plans and strategies. The essence of strategic management is developing strategic plans and keeping them current as changes occur internally and in the environment. It is possible to prepare a formal plan with a well-defined strategy and not practice strategic management. In such a situation, the plan could become outmoded as changes occur in the environment. Practicing strategic management does not ensure that an organization will meet all change successfully, but it does increase the odds.

Although guided by top management, successful strategic management involves many different levels in the organization. For example, top management may ask middle- and lower-level managers for input when formulating top-level plans. Once top-level plans have been finalized, different organizational units may be asked to formulate plans for their respective areas. A proper strategic management process helps ensure that plans throughout the different levels of the organization are coordinated and mutually supportive.

Organizations that consciously engage in strategic management generally follow some type of formalized process for making decisions and taking actions that affect their future direction. In the absence of a formal process, strategic decisions are made in a piecemeal fashion. An informal approach to strategy, however, does not necessarily mean the organization doesn't know what it is doing. It simply means the organization does not engage in any type of formalized process for initiating and managing strategy.

The strategic management process includes setting the organization's mission; defining what business or businesses the organization will be in; setting objectives; developing, implementing, and evaluating strategies; and adjusting these components as necessary. While the basic process is similar in most organizations, differences exist in the formality of the process, levels of managerial involvement, and degree of institutionalization of the process.

Management Illustration 7.3

SUN TZU'S IDEAS ARE STILL BEING USED

The concept of using military strategy to improve business strategy formulation may be a relatively new idea in the western world, but it is certainly not new to our European and Asian trading partners. In fact, most American corporations' international competitors base their theory of business acumen on sound and proven military principles rather than on what we would call "business administration." According to Scott DeGarmo, senior editor of *Success* magazine, "While Westerners study the art of the spreadsheet to prepare for business careers, Asians study *The Art of War*."

Any enlightened strategist should undertake a reading of Sun Tzu's *The Art of War*. Many consider this 2,500-year-old work by a mysterious Chinese warrior-philosopher to be "the definitive work on strategy." The aim of Sun Tzu's philosophy is invincibility, victory without battle, and unassailable strength through the understanding of physics, politics, and the psychology of conflict.

Following are some of Sun Tzu's most valued ideas that can be incorporated into the formulation of modern corporate planning and strategy:

- All warfare is based on deception.
- Offer the enemy a bait to lure him; feign disorder and strike him.
- The enemy must not know where I intend to give battle. For if he does not know where I intend to give battle, he must prepare in a great many places.
- To win 100 victories in 100 battles is not the acme of skill. To subdue the enemy without fighting is the acme of skill.
- Attack an enemy's strategy, not his army.
- If you outnumber an opponent 10 to 1, surround them; if you outnumber them 5 to 1, attack them; and if you outnumber them 2 to 1, divide them.
- Knowing when to fight is the secret to winning.
- Surprise is a key element to victory.
- Be like a massive flood in a canyon. Direct your formation toward an objective with superior force.

Mercedes-Benz China has recently unleashed a new advertising campaign inspired by Sun Tzu's *Art of War*. The campaign is geared to the male consumers of Mercedes's M and GL class SUVs. The hope is to deepen the brands' connection with high-end customers and to differentiate the brands from those of its key competitors, BMW and Land Rover. The idea behind the campaign is to associate Sun Tzu's *Art of War* and the psychological satisfaction from owning a Mercedes SUV—making the owner feel like a strong and powerful man.

Sources: Joseph J. Romm, "The Gospel According to Sun Tzu," *Forbes*, December 9, 1991, pp. 154–156; and Benjamin Li, "Mercedes Draws on *Art of War*," *Media*, September 7, 2007, p. 8.

formulation phase
First phase in strategic management, in which the initial strategic plan is developed.

implementation phase
Second phase in strategic management, in which the strategic plan is put into effect.

evaluation phase
Third phase in strategic management, in which the implemented strategic plan is monitored, evaluated, and updated.

Although different organizations may use somewhat different approaches to the strategic management process, most successful approaches share several common components and a similar sequence. The strategic management process is composed of three major phases: (1) formulating the strategic plan, (2) implementing the strategic plan, and (3) evaluating the strategic plan. The **formulation phase** is concerned with developing the initial strategic plan. The **implementation phase** involves implementing the strategic plan that has been formulated. The **evaluation phase** stresses the importance of continuously evaluating and updating the strategic plan after it has been implemented. Each of these three phases is critical to the success of the strategic management process. A breakdown in any one area can easily cause the entire process to fail. Management Illustration 7.3 presents evidence that strategic management is not a new concept and in fact may have its roots in ancient China. This illustration also shows that these ancient strategies are still being used.

Formulating Strategy

The formulation stage of the strategic management process involves developing the corporate- and business-level strategies to be pursued. The strategies ultimately chosen are

FIGURE 7.3
Objectives of the Company Mission

Source: Adapted from William R. King and David I. Cleland, *Strategic Planning and Policy* (New York: Van Nostrand Reinhold, 1978), p. 124.

1. To ensure unanimity of purpose within the organization.
2. To provide a basis for motivating the use of the organization's resources.
3. To develop a basis, or standard, for allocating organizational resources.
4. To establish a general tone or organizational climate; for example, to suggest a businesslike operation.
5. To serve as a focal point for those who can identify with the organization's purpose and direction and to deter those who cannot do so from participating further in its activities.
6. To facilitate the translation of objectives and goals into a work structure involving the assignment of tasks to responsible elements within the organization.
7. To specify organizational purposes and the translation of these purposes into goals in such a way that cost, time, and performance parameters can be assessed and controlled.

shaped by the organization's internal strengths and weaknesses and the threats and opportunities the environment presents.

The first part of the formulation phase is to obtain a clear understanding of the current position and status of the organization. This includes identifying the mission, identifying the past and present strategies, diagnosing the organization's past and present performance, and setting objectives for the company's operation.

Identifying Mission

mission
Defines the basic purpose(s) of an organization: why the organization exists.

An organization's mission is actually the broadest and highest level of objectives. The **mission** defines the basic purpose or purposes of the organization (for this reason, the terms *mission* and *purpose* are often used interchangeably). Basically, an organization's mission outlines why the organization exists. A mission statement usually includes a description of the organization's basic products or services and a definition of its markets or sources of revenue. Figure 7.3 outlines the objectives of a typical mission statement. Figure 7.4 presents actual mission statements from three well-known companies.

Defining *mission* is crucial. It is also more difficult than one might imagine. Over 50 years ago, Peter Drucker emphasized that an organization's purpose should be examined and defined not only at its inception or during difficult times but also during successful periods.[10] If the railroad companies of the early 1900s or the wagon makers of the 1800s had made their organizational purpose to develop a firm position in the

FIGURE 7.4
Examples of Mission Statements

Company	Mission Statement
FedEx	FedEx Corporation will produce superior financial returns for its shareowners by providing high value-added logistics, transportation, and related information services through focused operating companies. Customer requirements will be met in the highest quality manner appropriate to each market segment served. FedEx Corporation will strive to develop mutually rewarding relationships with its employees, partners, and suppliers. Safety will be the first consideration in all operations. Corporate activities will be conducted to the highest ethical and professional standards.
Harley-Davidson	We fulfill dreams through the experience of motorcycling, by providing to motorcyclists and to the general public an expanding line of motorcycles and branded products and services in selected market segments.
Pfizer	We will become the world's most valued company to patients, customers, colleagues, investors, business partners, and the communities where we work and live.

transportation business, they might hold the same economic positions today that they enjoyed in earlier times.

Drucker argues that an organization's purpose is determined not by the organization itself but by its customers. Customer satisfaction with the organization's product or service defines the purpose more clearly than does the organization's name, statutes, or articles of incorporation. Drucker outlines three questions that need to be answered to define an organization's present business. First, management must identify the customers: where they are, how they buy, and how they can be reached. Second, management must know what the customer buys. For instance, does the Rolls-Royce owner buy transportation or prestige? Finally, what is the customer looking for in the product? For example, does the homeowner buy an appliance from Sears, Roebuck & Company because of price, quality, or service?

Management must also identify what the future business will be and what it should be. Drucker presents four areas to investigate. The first is market potential: What does the long-term trend look like? Second, what changes in market structure might occur due to economic developments, changes in styles or fashions, or competition? For example, how have oil prices affected the automobile market structure? Third, what possible changes will alter customers' buying habits? What new ideas or products might create new customer demand or change old demands? Consider the impact of the cell phone on the demand for pay telephones. Finally, what customer needs are not being adequately served by available products and services? The introduction of overnight package delivery by FedEx is a well-known example of identifying and filling a current customer need. Figure 7.5 presents several excerpts of actual mission statements as they relate to certain components.

FIGURE 7.5 Identifying Mission Statement Components: A Compilation of Excerpts from Actual Corporate Mission Statements

1. Customer-market	We believe our first responsibility is to the doctors, nurses, and patients, to mothers and all others who use our products and services. (Johnson & Johnson)
	To anticipate and meet market needs of farmers, ranchers, and rural communities within North America. (CENEX)
2. Product-service	AMAX's principal products are molybdenum, coal, iron ore, copper, lead, zinc, petroleum and natural gas, potash, phosphates, nickel, tungsten, silver, gold, and magnesium. (AMAX)
3. Geographic domain	We are dedicated to the total success of Corning Glass Works as a worldwide competitor. (Corning Glass)
4. Technology	Control Data is in the business of applying microelectronics and computer technology in two general areas: computer-related hardware and computing-enhancing services, which include computation, information, education, and finance. (Control Data)
	The common technology in these areas relates to discrete particle coatings. (NASHUA)
5. Concern for survival	In this respect, the company will conduct its operation prudently, and will provide the profits and growth which will assure Hoover's ultimate success. (Hoover Universal)
6. Philosophy	We are committed to improve health care throughout the world. (Baxter Healthcare)
	We believe human development to be the worthiest of the goals of civilization and independence to be the superior condition for nurturing growth in the capabilities of people. (Sun Company)
7. Self-concept	Hoover Universal is a diversified, multi-industry corporation with strong manufacturing capabilities, entrepreneurial policies, and individual business unit autonomy. (Hoover Universal)
8. Concern for public image	We are responsible to the communities in which we live and work and to the world community as well. (Johnson & Johnson)
	Also, we must be responsive to the broader concerns of the public, including especially the general desire for improvement in the quality of life, equal opportunity for all, and the constructive use of natural resources. (Sun Company)

Source: From John A. Pearce II and F. R. David, "Corporate Mission Statements: The Bottom Line," *Academy of Management Executive*, May 1987. Reprinted with permission.

Management Illustration 7.4

SAM'S RETURNS TO ORIGINAL STRATEGY

www.samsclub.com

The original business strategy of Sam's Club was to cater specifically to the needs of small business members as opposed to the needs of individual consumers. Over the years, Sam's drifted from its original strategy by eliminating core small business items from its product mix, increasing expenses by making the clubs more aesthetically pleasing, and focusing too much on individual members, known as Sam's Advantage Members.

Weak sales and profit performance by 2002 resulted in a management change. Kelvin Turner was made CEO and Doug McMillon was made executive vice president of merchandising and replenishment. This management team went back to putting emphasis on small business customers by making sure that its product mix included staple items frequently used by small businesses and restoring special business member hours. In fiscal 2005, Sam's reported that sales were up 17.1 percent since Kevin Turner took over. In August of 2005, Kevin Turner was made the Number Three executive at Microsoft and Doug McMillon was made CEO of Sam's.

By 2007, McMillon and Greg Spragg, who took McMillon's previous job, had decided that Sam's, while not leaving small business behind, needed a broader appeal to the individual consumer segment if the company were to continue the desired growth rate. Recently Sam's has attempted to blend business friendly features such as an enhanced click 'n pull department and a drive-through lane for merchandise pickups with female friendly changes to the tire department and prepared foods areas.

Sources: Mike Troy, "Sam's Rewrite Business Plan," *DSN Retailing Today*, June 9, 2003, p. 73; Robert A. Guth and Ann Zimmerman, "Microsoft Picks a Wal-Mart Vet to Be Its No. 3," *Wall Street Journal*, August 5, 2005, p. B1, and Mike Troy, "Sam's Softens Business Mantra in Favor of Reaching More Moms," *Retailing Today*, March 5, 2007, p. 42.

Identifying Past and Present Strategies

Before deciding if a strategic change is necessary or desirable, the past and present strategies used by the organization need to be clearly identified. General questions to be addressed include the following: Has past strategy been consciously developed? If not, can past history be analyzed to identify what implicit strategy has evolved? If so, has the strategy been recorded in written form? In either case, a strategy or a series of strategies, as reflected by the organization's past actions and intentions, can usually be identified.

Diagnosing Past and Present Performance

To evaluate how past strategies have worked and determine whether strategic changes are needed, the organization's performance record must be examined. How is the organization currently performing? How has the organization performed over the last several years? Is the performance trend moving up or down? Management must address all of these questions before attempting to formulate any type of future strategy. Evaluating an organization's performance usually involves some type of in-depth financial analysis and diagnosis. Management Illustration 7.4 describes how the business strategy of Sam's Club has changed over the last several years in response to its past performance.

Once management has an accurate picture of the current status of the organization, the next step in formulating strategy is to decide what the long-, intermediate-, and short-range objectives should be in light of the current mission. However, these objectives cannot be accurately established without examining the internal and external environments. Thus, establishing the long- and intermediate-range objectives and analyzing the internal and external environments are concurrent processes that influence each other.

Setting Objectives

Once the mission of the organization has been clearly established, the guidelines offered earlier in this chapter should be followed to determine the specific long- and short-range objectives of the different organizational units. In general, long-range organizational objectives should derive from the mission statement. These long-range organizational objectives should then lead to the establishment of short-range performance objectives for the organization. Derivative objectives are subsequently developed for each major division and department. This process continues down through the various subunits right down to the individual level.

SWOT Analysis

SWOT is an acronym for an organization's strengths, weaknesses, opportunities, and threats. A SWOT analysis is a technique for evaluating an organization's internal strengths and weaknesses and its external opportunities and threats. A major advantage of using a SWOT analysis is that it provides a general overview of whether the overall situation is healthy or unhealthy.[11] The underlying assumption of a SWOT analysis is that managers can better formulate a successful strategy after they have carefully reviewed the organization's strengths and weaknesses in light of the threats and opportunities the environment presents.

An organization's strengths and weaknesses are usually identified by conducting an internal analysis of the organization. The basic idea of conducting an internal analysis is to perform an objective assessment of the organization's current strengths and weaknesses. What things does the organization do well? What things does the organization do poorly? From a resource perspective, what are the organization's strengths and weaknesses?

external environment
Consists of everything outside the organization.

The threats and opportunities presented by the environment are usually identified by methodically assessing the organization's external environment. An organization's **external environment** consists of everything outside the organization, but the focus of this assessment is on the external factors that have an impact on its business. Such factors are classified by their proximity to the organization: They are either in its broad environment or in its competitive environment. Broad environmental factors are somewhat removed from the organization but can still influence it. General economic conditions and social, political, and technological trends represent major factors in the broad environment. Factors in the competitive environment are close to the organization and come in regular contact with it. Stockholders, suppliers, competitors, labor unions, customers, and potential new entrants represent members of the competitive environment.

Managers use many different qualitative and quantitative methods for forecasting broad environmental trends. Qualitative techniques are based primarily on opinions and judgments, whereas quantitative techniques are based primarily on the analysis of data and the use of statistical techniques. Both methods can be helpful depending on the circumstances and the information available.

The five forces model of competition is a tool developed by Michael Porter to help managers analyze their competitive environment. This model suggests that the competitive environment can be assessed by analyzing the impact of and interactions among five major forces in the competitive or industry environment: (1) suppliers, (2) buyers, (3) competitive rivalry among firms currently in the industry, (4) product or service substitutes, and (5) potential entrants into the industry.[12] By using this tool to access the competitive environment, managers can then better select the most appropriate business level strategy to pursue. Figure 7.6 summarizes the five forces model of competition.

An assessment of the external environment emphasizes the fact that organizations do not operate in a vacuum and are very much affected by their surroundings. Figure 7.7 lists several factors that managers should consider when assessing an organization's strengths and weaknesses and the threats and opportunities posed by the environment. The most important result of a SWOT analysis is the ability to draw conclusions about the attractiveness of the organization's situation and the need for strategic action.

FIGURE 7.6
Five Forces Model of Competition

Source: M. E. Porter, *Competitive Strategy* (New York: Free Press, 1980).

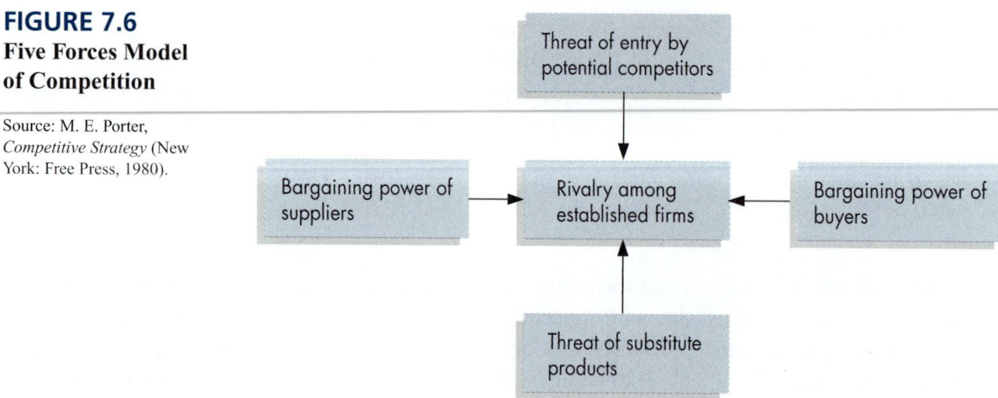

FIGURE 7.7 SWOT Analysis—What to Look For in Sizing Up a Company's Strengths, Weaknesses, Opportunities, and Threats

Potential Internal Strengths

- Core competencies in key areas
- Adequate financial resources
- Well-thought-of by buyers
- An acknowledged market leader
- Well-conceived functional area strategies
- Access to economies of scale
- Insulated (at least somewhat) from strong competitive pressures
- Proprietary technology
- Cost advantages
- Better advertising campaigns
- Product innovation skills
- Proven management
- Ahead on experience curve
- Better manufacturing capability
- Superior technological skills
- Other?

Potential External Opportunities

- Ability to serve additional customer groups or expand into new markets or segments
- Ways to expand product line to meet broader range of customer needs
- Ability to transfer skills or technological know-how to new products or businesses
- Integrating forward or backward
- Falling trade barriers in attractive foreign markets
- Complacency among rival firms
- Ability to grow rapidly because of strong increases in market demand
- Emerging new technologies

Potential Internal Weaknesses

- No clear strategic direction
- Obsolete facilities
- Subpar profitability because . . .
- Lack of managerial depth and talent
- Missing some key skills or competencies
- Poor track record in implementing strategy
- Plagued with internal operating problems
- Falling behind in R&D
- Too narrow a product line
- Weak market image
- Weak distribution network
- Below-average marketing skills
- Unable to finance needed changes in strategy
- Higher overall unit costs relative to key competitors
- Other?

Potential External Threats

- Entry of lower-cost foreign competitors
- Rising sales of substitute products
- Slower market growth
- Adverse shifts in foreign exchange rates and trade policies of foreign governments
- Costly regulatory requirements
- Vulnerability to recession and business cycle
- Growing bargaining power of customers or suppliers
- Changing buyer needs and tastes
- Adverse demographic changes
- Other?

Source: From Arthur A. Thompson, Jr., and A. J. Strickland III, *Strategic Management: Concepts and Cases,* 8th ed, 1995, p. 94. Reproduced with permission of The McGraw-Hill Companies.

FIGURE 7.8
SWOT Analysis Diagram

Source: John A. Pearce II and Richard B. Robinson, Jr., *Formulation, Implementation and Control of Competitive Strategy*, 10th edition (Burr Ridge, IL: McGraw-Hill/Irwin, 2007), p. 155.

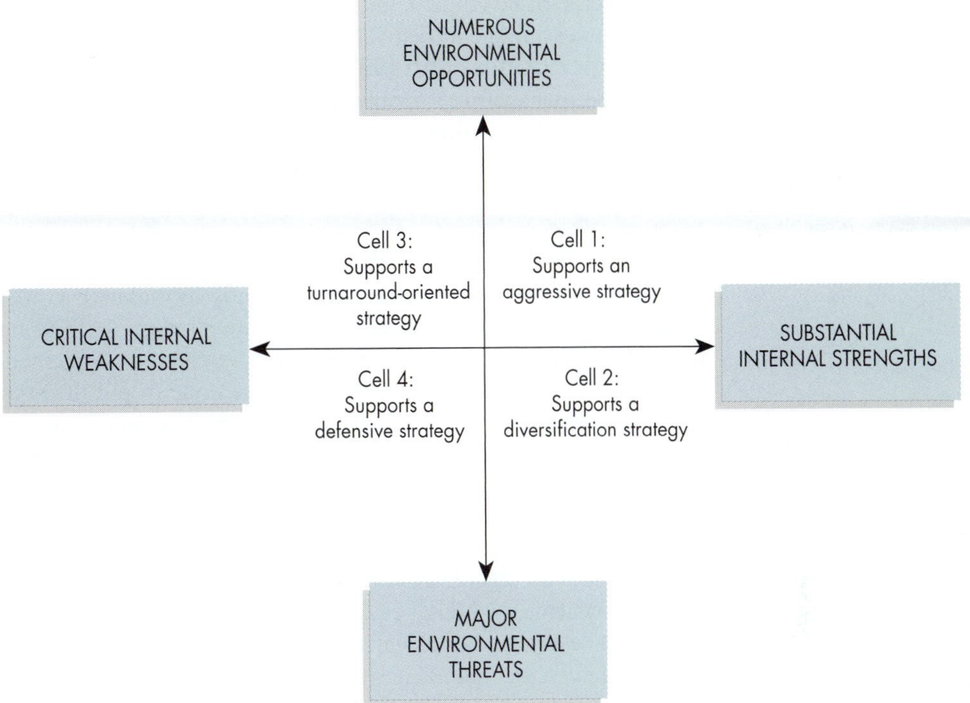

Comparing Strategic Alternatives

The goal in this stage of the formulation process is to identify the feasible strategic alternatives (in light of everything that has been done up to this point) and then select the best alternative. Given the mission and long-range objectives, what are the feasible strategic alternatives? The results of the SWOT analysis limit the feasible strategic alternatives. Figure 7.8 illustrates how the results of the SWOT analysis can be used to narrow down the feasible strategic alternatives.[13] Cell 1 is the most favorable situation with the organization facing several environmental opportunities with numerous internal strengths. This situation calls for aggressive and growth-oriented strategies to exploit the favorable match. In Cell 2, the organization has identified numerous internal strengths but, faces an unfavorable environment. This situation suggests diversification strategies to redeploy those resources and competencies in more opportunistic markets. An organization in Cell 3 faces very positive market opportunities but is constrained by relatively weak internal resources. Organizations in this situation should pursue some type of turnaround strategy so as to strengthen internal weaknesses and take advantage of the positive market opportunity. Cell 4 is the least favorable situation, with the organization facing major environmental threats with weak internal resources. This situation dictates some type of defensive strategy to reduce or redirect involvement in the current products or markets.

The evaluation and final choice of a specific strategic alternative involves the integration of the mission, objectives, and the SWOT analysis. In this phase, management attempts to select the corporate strategy that offers the organization its best chance to achieve its mission and objectives through actions that are compatible with its capacity for risk and its value structure. Once the corporate strategy has been identified, additional substrategies must be selected to support it.

In the case of diversified, multibusiness organizations, comparing strategic alternatives involves assessing the attractiveness of each business as well as the overall business mix. A **strategic business unit (SBU)** is a distinct business that has its own set of competitors and can be managed reasonably independently of other businesses within the organization.[14] The elements of an SBU vary from organization to organization but can be a division, a subsidiary, or a single product line. In a small organization, the entire company may be an SBU.

strategic business unit (SBU)
Distinct business that has its own set of competitors and can be managed reasonably independently of other businesses within the organization.

Implementing Strategy

After the corporate strategy has been carefully formulated, it must be translated into organizational actions. Given that the corporate strategy and business-level strategies have been clearly identified, what actions must be taken to implement them? Strategy implementation involves everything that must be done to put the strategy in motion successfully. Necessary actions include determining and implementing the most appropriate organizational structure, developing short-range objectives, and establishing functional strategies.

Organizational Factors

Not only does an organization have a strategic history; it also has existing structures, policies, and systems. Although each of these factors can change as a result of a new strategy, each must be assessed and dealt with as part of the implementation process.

Even though an organization's structure can always be altered, the associated costs may be high. For example, a reorganization may result in substantial hiring and training costs for newly structured jobs. Thus, from a practical standpoint, an organization's current structure places certain restrictions on strategy implementation.

The strategy must fit with current organizational policies, or the conflicting policies must be modified. Often past policies heavily influence the extent to which future policies can be altered. For example, A. T. Cross Company, manufacturer of world-renowned writing instruments, has a policy of unconditionally guaranteeing its products for life. Because customers have come to expect this policy, Cross would find it difficult to discontinue it.

Similarly, organizational systems that are currently in place can affect how the strategy might best be implemented. These systems can be either formal or informal. Examples include information systems, compensation systems, communication systems, and control systems.

Functional Strategies

As introduced earlier in this chapter, functional strategies are the means by which business strategies are operationalized. Functional strategies outline the specific short-range actions to be taken by the different functional units of the organization (production, marketing, finance, human resource, etc.) to implement the business strategies. The development of functional strategies generally requires the active participation of many levels of management. In fact, input by lower levels of management at the development stage is essential to the successful implementation of functional strategies.

Evaluating and Controlling the Strategic Plan

After the strategic plan has been put into motion, the next challenge is to monitor continuously the organization's progress toward its long-range objectives and mission. Is the corporate strategy working, or should revisions be made? Where are problems likely to occur? The emphasis is on making the organization's managers aware of the problems that are

FIGURE 7.9
The Strategic Management Process

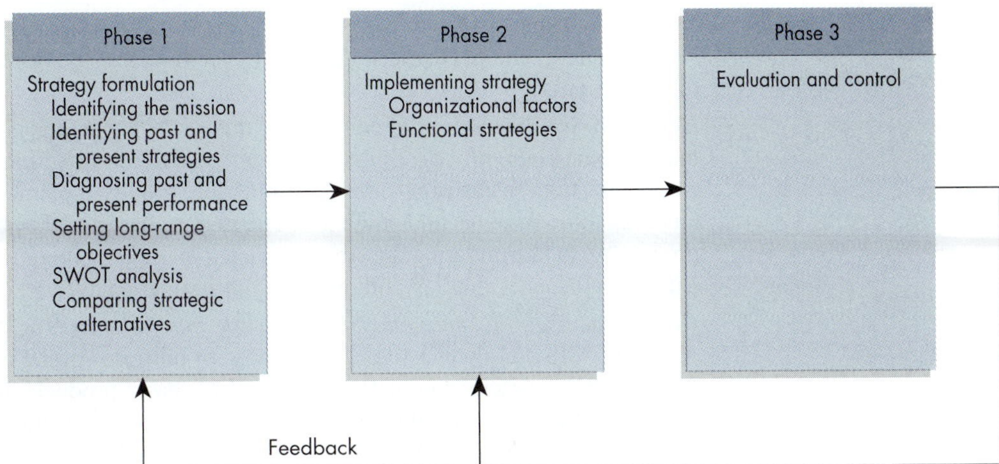

likely to occur and of the actions to be taken if they do arise. As discussed earlier in this chapter, continuously evaluating and responding to internal and environmental changes is what strategic management is all about.

Figure 7.9 summarizes the strategic management process and its major components.

Summary

1. *Define planning and distinguish between formal and functional plans.* Planning is the process of deciding which objectives to pursue during a future time period and what to do to achieve those objectives. Formal planning occurs when a written, documented plan is developed through an identifiable process. Functional plans originate from the functional areas of an organization, such as production, marketing, finance, and personnel.
2. *Contrast strategic planning with operational planning.* Strategic planning covers a relatively long period, affects many parts of the organization, and includes the formulation of objectives and the selection of the means for attaining those objectives. Operational or tactical planning is short range and concentrates on the formulation of functional strategies.
3. *Describe the differences between objectives, policies, procedures, and rules.* Objectives are statements outlining what the organization is trying to achieve; they give the organization and its members direction and purpose. Objectives can be long, intermediate, or short range in nature. Policies are broad, general guides to action that constrain or direct the attainment of objectives. Policies do not tell the organization what to do, but they do establish the boundaries within which it must operate. Procedures are a series of related steps or tasks expressed in chronological order for a specific purpose. Procedures emphasize details. Finally, rules require specific and definite actions to be taken or not to be taken in a given situation. Unlike procedures, rules do not have to specify sequence; they permit no flexibility or deviation.
4. *Define the management by objectives (MBO) process.* MBO is a philosophy based on converting organizational objectives into personal objectives. MBO is based on the belief that establishing personal objectives elicits employee commitment.
5. *Define strategy and explain the various levels of strategies.* A strategy outlines the basic steps management must take to reach an objective or a set of objectives. Corporate strategies (growth, stability, defensive, or combination) address what businesses an organization will be in and how resources will be allocated among those businesses. Business strategies (overall cost leadership, differentiation, and focus) concentrate on

how to compete in a given business or industry. Functional strategies (production, marketing, finance, and personnel) deal with the activities of the different functional areas of the business.

6. *Define strategic management and explain the strategic management process.* Strategic management is the process of determining the long-run direction and performance of an organization by ensuring careful formulation, proper implementation, and continuous evaluation of plans and strategies. The major phases of the strategic management process are (1) formulating the strategic plan, (2) implementing the strategic plan, and (3) continuously evaluating and updating the strategic plan.
7. *Define organizational mission and explain how mission relates to long- and short-range objectives.* Mission defines the basic purpose or purposes of the organization and usually includes a description of the organization's basic products and/or services and a definition of its markets and/or sources of revenue. An organization's mission is actually the broadest and highest level of objectives. It is from the mission that all long-range and short-range objectives are derived.
8. *Discuss the components of a SWOT analysis.* SWOT is an acronym for an organization's strengths, weaknesses, opportunities, and threats. A SWOT analysis is a technique for evaluating an organization's internal strengths and weaknesses and its external opportunities and threats. A major advantage of using a SWOT analysis is that it provides a general overview of the organization's strategic situation.
9. *Define a strategic business unit (SBU).* An SBU is a distinct business that has its own set of competitors and can be managed reasonably independently of other businesses within the organization.
10. *Discuss what organizational factors need to be evaluated in implementing a strategic plan.* Not only does an organization have a strategic history; it also has existing structures, policies, and systems. Although each of these factors can change as a result of a new strategy, each must be assessed and dealt with as part of the implementation process.

Review Questions

1. Define planning. What questions does planning answer?
2. Why is it necessary to plan? Distinguish between formal and functional planning. How is most planning conducted?
3. What is the difference between strategic planning and operational planning? Between long-range and short-range planning?
4. What is a contingency plan?
5. Define policy, procedure, and rule.
6. Define objectives and differentiate between long- and short-range objectives.
7. What are the SMART criteria for objectives?
8. What is management by objectives (MBO)?
9. Define strategy.
10. What are the major forms of strategy?
11. What are the four types of corporate strategy? What are the three forms of business strategy?
12. What are the steps in the strategic management process?
13. Define mission.

14. What does SWOT stand for?
15. Describe the four cells of the SWOT Analysis Diagram.
16. Define a strategic business unit (SBU).

Skill-Building Questions

1. Why should one plan? What are the benefits of planning?
2. If you were serving as a strategic management consultant, how might you respond to the following question: How can I plan for next year when I don't even know what I'm going to do tomorrow?
3. As discussed on page 140, strategic management is an activity that must emanate from top management. Given this, why should you, as a first-line or middle manager, be concerned with strategic management?
4. Comment on the following statement: Most organizations succeed or fail based on their ability to react to environmental changes.

SKILL-BUILDING EXERCISE 7.1
Setting SMART Objectives

Assess the objectives in Exhibit 1 (see page 152), then critique them. The purpose of the objective is described under the heading "Performance target." The person with whom the objective is being set is given in brackets. Review each of the objectives in Exhibit 1 against each of the SMART criteria, then make an entry in each box using the following key:

x = objective does not conform to this criteria
✓ = objective conforms to this criteria
? = difficult to tell if this conforms to this criteria.

SKILL-BUILDING EXERCISE 7.2
Developing a Personal Career Plan

One of the common threads many successful people share is that they developed a sense of direction relatively early in life. At the same time, it is common for people to enter and even graduate from college with little idea of what they want to do. Similarly, many people reach middle age only to ask, "How did I end up here?"

Questions

1. Apply the concepts discussed in this chapter and develop, in outline form, a 10-year plan for your own career.
2. Your outline need only be a few pages long. Begin with a statement of mission and work down through each step in the strategic management model. Be sure and include a SWOT analysis. Make your plan as realistic as possible.
3. Identify the major assumptions and environmental trends on which you based your plan.
4. What parts of your plan do you think will be the hardest to achieve?

The following article gives great guidance for developing your own career plan: Patricia Buhler, "Managing in the 90s," *Supervision*, May 1997, pp. 24–26.

SKILL-BUILDING EXERCISE 7.3
Most Admired Companies

Every year since 1983 *Fortune* magazine has published the results of a survey that attempts to identify the most admired among the largest companies in the United States. Recently the surveys have included approximately 600 companies. For the 2007 list, the companies identified as the 10 most admired (in descending order) were:

1. General Electric
2. Starbucks
3. Toyota Motor Corp.
4. Berkshire Hathaway
5. Southwest Airlines
6. FedEx
7. Apple
8. Google
9. Johnson & Johnson
10. Procter & Gamble

EXHIBIT 1
SMART Objectives

Source: Garry Platt, "SMART Objectives: What They Mean and How to Set Them." *Training Journal*, August 2002, p. 24.

	SPECIFIC	MEASURABLE	ACHIEVABLE	RELEVANT	TIME-BASED
Performance target: to improve profitability (department manager).					
1. Objective: to reduce overtime costs.					
Performance target: to improve customer care (receptionist).					
2. Objective: to ensure that 90 percent of items received (addressed to and for action by the receptionist) are replied to on day of receipt.					
Performance target: to improve leadership ability (team leader).					
3. Objective: to supervise the team better by 25 March 2009.					
4. Objective: to have agreed, set, and recorded three performance targets with each member of staff by the end of June 2009.					
Performance target: to reduce overall running costs (transport manager).					
5. Objective: to achieve a 500 percent reduction over previous year on transport costs (end of this week).					
6. Objective: to achieve a 5 percent reduction over previous year on transport costs.					
7. Objective: to achieve a 5 percent change over previous year on transport costs (by 2 March 2009).					
Performance target: to increase client base (marketing executive).					
8. Objective: to generate 15 new clients by 1 June 2009.					
9. Objective: to generate more clients.					
Performance target: to reduce waste and scrap output (production manager).					
10. Objective: by year-end (31 December 2009) to have reduced waste output by a reasonable amount.					
11. Objective: to adopt a just-in-time strategy for the stores.					

For the 2001 list, the companies identified as the 10 most admired (in descending order) were:

1. General Electric
2. Cisco System
3. Wal-Mart
4. Southwest Airlines
5. Microsoft
6. Home Depot
7. Berkshire Hathaway
8. Charles Schwab
9. Intel
10. Dell Computer

Over the six-year time span between the above lists, only three companies (General Electric, Berkshire Hathaway, and Southwest Airlines) were on both lists. Pick one of the companies that is on the 2001 list and not on the 2007 list and identify one or more trends or forces in the company's external or internal environment that might help explain why the company dropped off the list.

Sources: Ahmad Diba and Lisa Muñoz, "America's Most Admired Companies," *Fortune*, February 19, 2001, pp. 64–66; and Anne Fisher, "American's Most Admired Companies," *Fortune*, March 19, 2007, p. 88.

SKILL-BUILDING EXERCISE 7.4
Making Assumptions

Translate the demographic data below into a set of assumptions for (a) a small community hospital, (b) an urban school system, and (c) Ford Motor Company.

How does this demographic data rank in importance with other environmental trends that might affect each of these organizations?

Percentage Increase in Population by Age Groups, 1994–2009

Ages	1994–1999	1999–2004	2004–2009
Under 15	3.4	7.0	10.6
15–17	−11.6	−10.3	−20.1
18–24	−5.4	−9.7	−13.6
25–34	10.2	3.0	13.5
35–44	22.2	16.6	42.4
45–54	−0.9	12.4	11.5
55–65	2.4	−4.1	−1.9
Over 65	9.6	9.1	19.6

SKILL-BUILDING EXERCISE 7.5
Environmental Forces

Summarized below are the descriptions of two environmental forces that could have an influence on the automobile industry. Describe the potential threats and opportunities that might face General Motors as a result of these environmental forces.

Social

Studies of social and economic trends present the auto industry with an enormous population of buyers who are predisposed to purchase and will have the financial means to buy new cars on a regular basis. Three demographic groups that will be particularly significant to the industry are baby boomers, women, and the elderly.

Maturing baby boomers will have far more disposable income available for automobile purchases, and a sizable upscale segment will favor luxury cars and sport-utility vehicles. Baby boomers and the elderly also will increase demand for recreational vehicles (RVs) while reducing the need for station wagons and minivans as their families mature. A large and growing blue-collar segment of the boomers, however, favors pickup trucks and Japanese cars.

Women will increasingly become more involved in new-car purchases and are expected to exercise as much power in the automotive market as men. Automotive marketing successes of the future will be generated by advertising that prominently features women.

The final dominant group, which represents a "graying of America," is buyers 55 and older. They constitute 25 percent of new-car buyers, and this statistic will increase. Older buyers will look for features that make driving safer and easier, including electronic systems to warn drivers who are getting drowsy, nonglare instrument panels, and simplified electronic controls.

Technological

The rocketing price of gasoline has made efficiency a top priority with almost all buyers. The cars of tomorrow will be loaded with intelligent systems: smart computers that run the engine and transmission more efficiently, electronic suspension systems, radar obstacle detection to help drivers avoid accidents, and navigation systems that will help drivers avoid traffic jams while video screens indicate alternate routes. Self-tinting glass and infrared technology that enhances night vision also will be available. Antilock brakes, air bags, and traction control will become standard.

The use of space-age plastics will increase because they are lightweight, less expensive than steel, and noncorrosive. New techniques for making models and prototypes quickly and inexpensively using sophisticated computers are the wave of the future.

The extensive use of robotic technology in production will increase, and automobile manufacturers will develop cars for the future that will run on alternative fuels. The demand for electric and hybrid cars is expected to increase dramatically.

SKILL-BUILDING EXERCISE 7.6 Word Associations

This exercise is designed to demonstrate how the establishment of a realistic and specific goal can help you improve your performance. You will be given four words and your task is to identify a fifth word that has a common association with each of the four words in a given set. For example, what word has a common association with each of the following?

Sleeping contest spot shop

The answer is *beauty*.

Now that you understand the game, time yourself and see how many of the following sets you can do in *two* minutes.

1. cross	baby	blood	ribbon	________
2. touch	palate	soap	sell	________
3. tree	cup	cake	forbidden	________
4. dust	movie	gaze	sapphire	________
5. alley	date	snow	spot	________
6. rest	post	linen	fellow	________
7. opera	no	box	stone	________
8. storage	shoulder	comfort	cream	________
9. business	suit	wrench	shine	________
10. bug	rest	fellow	cover	________

Your instructor will give you the correct answers. Based on the number you got right, set the following goal for the next exercise:

If you got 1 or 2 correct, your new goal is 4.
If you got 3 or 4 correct, your new goal is 7.
If you got 5 or more correct, your new goal is 9.

Do you consider this new goal challenging? Impossible? Now, striving to make your new goal, see how many of the following sets you can do in *two* minutes.

1. days	biscuit	collar	ear	________
2. play	breast	pox	wire	________

3. guy	crack	up	man	__________
4. ball	trouser	fruit	house	__________
5. dress	good	star	prayer	__________
6. stone	jacket	fever	pages	__________
7. bathtub	wedding	telephone	key	__________
8. horse	brake	left	box	__________
9. right	pike	your	stile	__________
10. bulldog	cuff	toast	windows	__________

Your instructor will give you the correct answers. How did you do relative to your score on the first set? Do you think that having a specific goal affected your score on the second exercise?

Source: This exercise is adapted from Henry Tosi and Jerald W. Young, *Management Experiences and Demonstrations* (Homewood, IL: Richard D. Irwin, 1982), pp. 35–38, 166, 183.

Case Incident 7.1

First in the Market

Juan Peron is a process engineer employed by Vantage Engineering, Inc., and assigned to the research laboratory in the Advanced Products Division (APD). Vantage is a well-established manufacturer of military hardware. APD's general purpose is to conduct research to improve the company's military hardware products. However, the laboratory director was recently given permission to develop spin-off products for possible sale on the open market.

Juan spent his first year in APD assisting on various project assignments. At the end of that year, he was put in charge of a special project to research a chemically processed wood for specialty applications. During the initial stages of the project, Juan spent most of his time in the laboratory becoming familiar with the basic aspects of the treatment process. However, he soon tired of the long, tedious experimental work and became more and more eager to move quickly into the promotion and marketing of the product. This desire was soon realized. An article in a recent national trade publication had generated keen interest in a similar wood product, and as a result, Vantage immediately allocated several thousand dollars to the development and marketing of the chemically processed wood. Simultaneously, a minor reorganization occurred, placing Juan and his project under the direction of Greg Waites, a close friend of Juan's. Thus, Juan had an opportunity to get out of the lab and become more involved in the promotion and marketing aspects.

Juan and Greg soon began traveling nationally, discussing the new product with potential customers. Traveling enabled Juan to spend less and less time in the lab, and as a result many of the experiments required to determine the performance characteristics of the new product were left unfinished. As the number of companies demonstrating an interest in purchasing small quantities for trial applications grew, Juan suggested to Greg that a small pilot plant be constructed. In response to Greg's concerns regarding the performance characteristics of the wood, Juan assured him the preliminary tests indicated the wood could be successfully produced. Juan contended that Vantage had to get a head start on the newly created market before everyone else got into the game, that they should build the pilot plant immediately to fill the sudden influx of orders and then worry about completing the performance tests. Greg, seeing the advantages of getting into the market first, finally agreed, and construction of the pilot plant began shortly thereafter.

During construction, Juan and Greg continued traveling to promote the wood. When the pilot plant was near completion, Juan went to Vantage's human resource department and requested that three employees be hired to operate the plant. Juan intended to personally direct the technical operations and thus saw no need to establish elaborate job descriptions for the positions.

A week later, Juan had his three employees. Due to a workload reduction in the Electronics Division of Vantage, the employees filling these positions had taken these jobs to avoid being laid off. One had previously been a purchasing agent, and the others had been electronics technicians. At the beginning of the workday, Juan would drop by the plant and give directions to the crew for the entire day before departing to make sales calls. No formal leader had been appointed, and the three employees, knowing little about the chemical process involved, were instructed to "use common sense and ingenuity."

A month after the plant operations had gotten under way, a major producer of archery bows requested an order for 70,000 bow handles to be delivered in time to be sold for the upcoming hunting season. It was too good to be true! Juan knew that if they accepted the order, the first year of operations would be guaranteed to be in the black. On receiving the product specifications, Juan persuaded Greg to sign the contract, arguing that they would be throwing all their hard work down the drain if they didn't. Subsequently, a crash program was established at the plant to get the order out on time.

One month after the final shipment of handles had been made, Juan hired a junior engineer, Libby Adams, to conduct the performance experiments that had been disbanded while the plant was getting the rush order out. Libby examined some of the experimental handles and discovered hairline cracks at various stress points that had not appeared during the initial examination. She immediately went to Juan's office to inform him of the problem and found Juan and Greg sitting there with a telegram from the archery company. It stated that several retail merchants had returned bows with hairline cracks in the handles and that the archery company would seek a settlement for its entire investment in the handles.

Vantage paid the settlement and subsequently canceled the wood project.

Questions

1. What caused the wood project to fail?
2. Would a more effective strategy on the part of Juan and Greg have helped ensure the success of the project?
3. At what stage of the strategic management process did the breakdown occur?
4. What general observations can be made to prevent such a situation from occurring again?

Source: From Patricia Buhler, "Managing in the 90s," *Supervision*, May 1997. Reprinted by permission of © National Research Bureau, 320 Valley Street, Burlington, Iowa 52601.

Case Incident 7.2

Hudson Shoe Company

John Hudson, president of Hudson Shoe Company, and his wife spent the month of February on a long vacation in Santo Oro in Central America. After two weeks, Mr. Hudson became restless and started thinking about an idea he had considered for several years but had been too busy to pursue—entering the foreign market.

Mr. Hudson's company, located in a midwestern city, was started some 50 years earlier by his father, now deceased. It has remained a family enterprise, with his brother David in charge of production, his brother Sam the comptroller, and his brother-in-law Bill Owens taking care of product development. Bill and David share responsibility for quality control; Bill often works with Sam on administrative matters and advertising campaigns. Many competent subordinates are also employed. The company has one of the finest reputations in the shoe industry. The product integrity is to be envied and is a source of great pride to the company.

During John's stay in Santo Oro, he decided to visit some importers of shoes. He spoke to several and was most impressed with Señor Lopez of Bueno Compania. After checking Señor Lopez's bank and personal references, his impression was confirmed. Señor Lopez said he would place a small initial order if the samples proved satisfactory. John immediately phoned his office and requested the company rush samples of its best-sellers to Señor Lopez. These arrived a few days before John left for home. Shortly after arriving home, John was pleased to receive an order for 1,000 pairs of shoes from Señor Lopez.

John stayed in touch with Lopez by telephone; within two months after the initial order, Hudson Shoe received an order for 5,000 additional pairs of shoes per month. Business continued at this level for about two years until Señor Lopez visited the plant. He was impressed and increased his monthly order from 5,000 to 10,000 pairs of shoes.

This precipitated a crisis at Hudson Shoe Company, and the family held a meeting. They had to decide whether to increase their capacity with a sizable capital investment or drop some of their customers. They did not like the idea of eliminating loyal customers but did not want to make a major investment. David suggested they run a second shift, which solved the problem nicely.

A year later, Lopez again visited and left orders for 15,000 pairs per month. He also informed them that more effort and expense was now required on his part for a wide distribution of the shoes. In addition to his regular 5 percent commission, he asked John for an additional commission of $2 per pair of shoes. When John hesitated, Lopez assured him that Hudson could raise its selling price by $2 and nothing would be lost. John felt uneasy but went along because the business was easy, steady, and most profitable. A few of Hudson's smaller customers had to be dropped.

By the end of the next year, Lopez was placing orders for 20,000 pairs per month. He asked that Hudson bid on supplying boots for the entire police force of the capital city of Santo Oro. Hudson received the contract and within a year, was supplying the army and navy of Santo Oro and three other Central American countries with their needs.

Again, several old Hudson customers could not get their orders filled. Other Hudson customers were starting to complain of late deliveries. Also, Hudson seemed to be less willing to accept returns at the end of the season or to offer markdown allowances or advertising money. None of this was necessary with its export business. However, Hudson Shoe did decide to cling to its largest domestic customer—the largest mail-order chain in the United States.

In June of the following year, Lopez made a trip to Hudson Shoe. He informed John that in addition to his $2 per pair, it would be necessary to give the minister of revenue $2 per pair if he was to continue granting import licenses. Moreover, the defense ministers, who approved the army and navy orders in each country where they did business, also wanted $2 per pair. Again, selling prices could be increased accordingly. Lopez informed John that shoe manufacturers in the United States and two other countries were most eager to have this business at any terms. John asked for 10 days to discuss this with his partners. Lopez agreed and returned home to await their decision. The morning of the meeting of the board of directors of the Hudson Shoe Company, a wire was received from the domestic mail-order chain stating it would not be buying from Hudson next season. John Hudson called the meeting to order.

Questions

1. What were the objectives of Hudson Shoe Company?
2. What strategies do you think Hudson Shoe was following?
3. How would you evaluate John Hudson's plans?
4. What would you do if you were John Hudson?

References and Additional Readings

1. J. J. Hemphill, "Personal Variables and Administrative Styles," in *Behavioral Science and Educational Administration* (Chicago: National Society for the Study of Education, 1964), chap. 8.
2. A. L. Comrey, W. High, and R. C. Wilson, "Factors Influencing Organization Effectiveness: A Survey of Aircraft Workers," *Personnel Psychology* 8 (1955), pp. 79–99.
3. For a discussion of these studies, see John A. Pearce II, Elizabeth B. Freeman, and Richard D. Robinson, Jr., "The Tenuous Link between Formal Strategic Planning and Financial Performance," *Academy of Management Review*, October 1987, pp. 658–73; and Mike Schraeder, "A Simplified Approach to Strategic Planning," *Business Process Management Journal* 8, no. 1 (2002), pp. 11–21.
4. Anthony Raia, *Managing by Objectives* (Glenview, IL: Scott, Foresman, 1974), p. 38.
5. Much of this section is drawn from Garry Platt, "SMART Objectives: What They Mean and How to Set Them," *Training Journal*, August 2002, p. 23.
6. George A. Steiner, *Top Management Planning* (New York: Macmillan, 1969), p. 237.
7. Michael E. Porter, *Competitive Strategy: Techniques for Analyzing Industries and Competitors* (New York: Free Press, 1980).
8. Porter, *Competitive Strategy*, pp. 37–38.
9. Patricia Braus, "What Does 'Hispanic' Mean?" *American Demographics*, June 1993, pp. 46–49, 58.
10. Peter E. Drucker, *The Practice of Management* (New York: Harper & Row, 1954), p. 51.
11. Arthur A. Thompson, Jr., A. J. Strickland III, and John E. Gamble, *Crafting and Executing Strategy,* 15th edition (Burr Ridge, IL: McGraw-Hill/Irwin, 2007), p. 97.
12. Porter, *Competitive Strategy*.
13. Much of this section is drawn from John A. Pearce II and Richard B. Robinson, Jr., *Strategic Management,* 8th edition (New York: McGraw-Hill/Irwin, 2003), pp. 155–57.
14. George A. Steiner, John B. Miner, and Edmond R. Gray, *Management Policy and Strategy*, 2nd edition (New York: Macmillan, 1982), p. 189.

Chapter Eight

Organizing Work

Learning Objectives

After studying this chapter, you will be able to:

1. Define organization, and differentiate between a formal and an informal organization.
2. Explain the importance of the organizing function.
3. List the advantages and the major disadvantage of horizontal division of labor.
4. Distinguish between power, authority, and responsibility.
5. List four principles of organization that are related to authority.
6. Identify several reasons managers are reluctant to delegate.
7. Recount the major factors that affect a manager's span of management.
8. Explain the concept of centralization versus decentralization.
9. Define empowerment.
10. Name and define three workplace changes, in addition to decentralization and empowerment, that have affected the organizing function in today's organizations.

Chapter Preview

Home Depot began as a three-store start-up in 1979 and grew to a $45 billion chain by 2000, making it America's fastest growing retailer over that time period. In early 2000, Home Depot hired Bob Nardelli from GE as CEO following the retirement of cofounders Bernie Marcus and Arthur Blank. Mr. Nardelli was selected to bring GE-style discipline and focus to Home Depot's management team.

Over the next six years, Mr. Nardelli implemented centralization policies to make the company more efficient and hence to save money. These policies often limited employees' ability to make decisions. Home Depot also hired more and more part-timers. While Mr. Nardelli's centralization policies and part-time employees did save money, they also eroded the employees' entrepreneurial spirit and had a negative impact on customer service. Mr. Nardelli resigned amid pressure from stockholders in late 2006.

Sources: Andrew Ward, "Nardelli's Style Helps to Seal His Fate . . . How the Home Depot Chief's Approach Caused Tensions with Managers and Contributed to Investor Dissatisfaction," *Financial Times,* January 4, 2007, p. 22; and Gina Ruiz, "Home Depot's New HR Leader Faces Tall Order," *Workforce Management,* February 12, 2007, p. 4.

Analyzing Management Skills

How might taking away employees' authority for making decisions have a negative impact on the organization?

Applying Management Skills

Suppose you are in charge of building a homecoming display for your school with 10 volunteers. How would you organize them?

organization
Group of people working together in some concerted or coordinated effort to attain objectives.

organizing
Grouping of activities necessary to attain common objectives and the assignment of each grouping to a manager who has the authority necessary to supervise the people performing the activities.

informal organization
Aggregate of the personal contacts and interactions and the associated groupings of people working within the formal organization.

Most work today is accomplished through organizations. An **organization** is a group of people working together in some type of concerted or coordinated effort to attain objectives. As such, an organization provides a vehicle for implementing strategy and accomplishing objectives that could not be achieved by individuals working separately. The process of **organizing** is the grouping of activities necessary to attain common objectives and the assignment of each grouping to a manager who has the authority required to supervise the people performing the activities.[1] Thus, organizing is basically a process of division of labor accompanied by appropriate delegation of authority. Proper organizing results in more effective use of resources.

The framework that defines the boundaries of the formal organization and within which the organization operates is the organization structure. A second and equally important element of an organization is the informal organization. The **informal organization** refers to the aggregate of the personal contacts and interactions and the associated groupings of people working within the formal organization.[2] The informal organization has a structure, but it is not formally and consciously designed. Informal groups are discussed in-depth in Chapter 10.

REASONS FOR ORGANIZING

One of the primary reasons for organizing is to establish lines of authority. Clear lines of authority create order within a group. Absence of authority almost always leads to chaotic situations where everyone is telling everyone else what to do.

Second, organizing improves the efficiency and quality of work through synergism. *Synergism* occurs when individuals or groups work together to produce a whole greater than the sum of the parts. For example, synergism results when three people working together produce more than three people working separately. Synergism can result from division of labor or from increased coordination, both of which are products of good organization. Two organizations that appear to be very similar can experience very different levels of performance due to the synergy resulting from their organizational structures. Highly successful organizations generally achieve a high level of synergy as a result of the manner in which they are organized.

A final reason for organizing is to improve communication. A good organization structure clearly defines channels of communication among the members of the organization. Such a system also ensures more efficient communications.

Historically, the desire to organize led to the development of an organization. The use of an organization allows people to jointly (1) increase specialization and division of labor, (2) use large-scale technology, (3) manage the external environment, (4) economize on transaction costs, and (5) exert power and control.[3] When designed and coordinated effectively, these characteristics help the organization to serve its customers with a high degree of service and productivity.

Management Illustration 8.1

DIVISION OF LABOR

One man draws out the wire, another straightens it, and a third cuts it, a fourth points it, a fifth grinds it at the top for receiving the head; to make the head requires two or three distinct operations; to put it on is a peculiar business, to whiten the pins is another; it is even a trade by itself to put them into the paper, and the important business of making a pin is, in this manner, divided into 18 distinct operations, which, in some manufactories, are all performed by distinct hands; though in others the same man will sometimes perform two or three of them. I have seen a small manufactory of this kind where 10 men only were employed and where some of them consequently performed two or three distinct operations. But though they were very poor and therefore but indifferently accommodated with the necessary machinery, they could, when they exerted themselves, make among them about 12 pounds of pins a day.

Source: Adam Smith, *An Inquiry into the Nature and Causes of the Wealth of Nations,* vol. 1 (London: A. Strahan and T. Cadell, 1776), pp. 7–8.

DIVISION OF LABOR

Organizing is basically a process of division of labor. The merits of dividing labor have been known for centuries. Taking the simple task of manufacturing a pin, Adam Smith in 1776 demonstrated how much more efficiently the task could be performed through division of labor.[4] As explained in Management Illustration 8.1, Smith argued that it was more efficient to divide the different tasks or operations required to make an object than it was to have each employee make the entire object individually.

Labor can be divided either vertically or horizontally. Vertical division of labor is based on the establishment of lines of authority and defines the levels that make up the vertical organization structure. In addition to establishing authority, vertical division of labor facilitates the flow of communication within the organization. To illustrate how vertical division of labor can vary from company to company, consider the automobile industry in the early 1980s. At that time, Toyota had 5 levels between the chairperson and the first-line supervisor, whereas Ford had over 15.[5] For a more thorough description of the advantages of the "flat" organization, see Chapter 9.

Horizontal division of labor is based on specialization of work. The basic assumption underlying horizontal division of labor is that by making each worker's task specialized, more work can be produced with the same effort through increased efficiency and quality. Specifically, horizontal division of labor can result in the following advantages:

1. Fewer skills are required per person.
2. The skills required for selection or training purposes are easier to supply.
3. Practice in the same job develops proficiency.
4. Primarily utilizing each worker's best skills promotes efficient use of skills.
5. Concurrent operations are made possible.
6. More conformity in the final product results when each piece is always produced by the same person.

The major problem with horizontal division of labor is that it can result in job boredom and even degradation of the employee. An extreme example of horizontal division of labor is the automobile assembly line. Most people working on an automobile assembly line do a small number of very simple tasks over and over again. It usually doesn't take long for these employees to become bored. Once employees become bored, their productivity often declines, absenteeism and tardiness increase, and the quality of work goes down. Solutions to the problems created by horizontal division of labor include a reexamination of job scope, implementing job rotation, and balancing job simplification with job depth.

job scope
Refers to the number of different types of operations performed on the job.

Job scope refers to the number of different types of operations performed. In performing a job with narrow scope, the employee performs few operations and repeats the cycle frequently. The job of a toll booth operator on a major highway would be an example of a job with a narrow scope. The negative effects of jobs lacking in scope vary with the person performing the job, but they can include more errors and lower quality. Often job rotation, wherein workers shift in the planned sequence of activities, eliminates boredom and monotony and encourages multiple skills and cross training.

job depth
Refers to the freedom of employees to plan and organize their own work, work at their own pace, and move around and communicate as desired.

Job depth refers to the freedom of employees to plan and organize their own work, work at their own pace, and move around and communicate as desired. The job of a traveling salesperson would be an example of a job high in job depth. A lack of job depth can result in job dissatisfaction and work avoidance, which in turn can lead to absenteeism, tardiness, and even sabotage.

Division of labor is not more efficient or even desirable in all situations. At least two basic requirements must exist for the successful use of division of labor. The first requirement is a relatively large volume of work. Enough volume must be produced to allow for specialization and keep each employee busy. The second requirement is stability in the volume of work, employee attendance, quality of raw materials, product design, and production technology.

POWER, AUTHORITY, AND RESPONSIBILITY

power
Ability to influence, command, or apply force.

authority
Legitimate exercise of power; the right to issue directives and expend resources; related to power but narrower in scope.

responsibility
Accountability for the attainment of objectives, the use of resources, and the adherence to organizational policy.

Power is the ability to influence, command, or apply force. Power is usually derived from the control of resources. **Authority** is power derived from the rights that come with a position and represents the legitimate exercise of power. Thus, authority is one source of power for a manager. Lines of authority link the various organizational components. Unclear lines of authority can create major confusion and conflict within an organization.

Responsibility is accountability for the attainment of objectives, the use of resources, and the adherence to organizational policy. Once responsibility is accepted, performing assigned work becomes an obligation. The term *responsibility* as used here should not be confused with the term *responsibilities* as in the context of defining job duties.

Sources of Authority

As just mentioned, authority can be viewed as a function of position, flowing from top to bottom through the formal organization. According to this view, people hold authority because they occupy a certain position; once removed from the position, they lose their authority. Taking this theory one step further, one can say the American people, through the Constitution and laws, represent the ultimate source of authority in this country. The Constitution and laws guarantee the right of free enterprise. The owners of a free enterprise organization have the right to elect a board of directors and top management. Top management selects middle-level managers. This process continues down to the lowest person in the organization. This traditional view of authority is also called the *formal theory of authority.*

A second theory of authority was first outlined in 1926 by Mary Parker Follett and popularized in 1938 by Chester Barnard.[6] Called the *acceptance theory of authority,* this theory maintains that a manager's source of authority lies with his or her subordinates because they have the power to either accept or reject the manager's command. Presumably, if a subordinate does not view a manager's authority as legitimate, it does not exist.

Both Follett and Barnard viewed disobeying a communication from a manager as a denial of authority by the subordinate. In summary, the acceptance theory of authority recognizes that subordinates play an active role in determining lines of authority and are not merely passive recipients in the process. This idea is somewhat similar to the contention that without followers you can have no leaders. Both elements must be present and mutually recognized for true structure to exist. Companies with a high degree of employee involvement, responsibility, and accountability appear to recognize acceptance theory as being beneficial for mutual support and encouragement between labor and management.

PRINCIPLES BASED ON AUTHORITY

Because authority is a key element in managing organizations, several key concepts are relevant. Delegation, unity of command, the scalar principle, and the span of management historically have been the most important of these concepts.

Delegation: The Parity Principle

Delegation refers to the assigning of authority from one person to another. Delegation by a manager means that the manager grants or confers authority to one or more subordinates.

According to Herbert Engel, "As an abstract idea, delegation must be as old as the human race itself."[7] The apportioning of specific duties to members of a group by a leader seems almost as natural as it is necessary. Delegation normally occurs when one needs something done that one either cannot or chooses not to do oneself. The decision may be based on situations, skills, time, established order, or the expansion and growth of responsibilities as dictated by the group or the organization. Managers can delegate responsibility to subordinates in the sense of making subordinates responsible to them. However, this delegation to subordinates makes managers no less responsible to their superiors. Delegation of responsibility does not mean abdication of responsibility by the delegating manager. Responsibility is not like an object that can be passed from individual to individual.

parity principle
States that authority and responsibility must coincide.

The **parity principle** states that authority and responsibility must coincide. Management must delegate sufficient authority to enable subordinates to do their jobs. At the same time, subordinates can be expected to accept responsibility only for those areas within their authority.

Subordinates must accept both authority and responsibility before the delegation process has been completed. Management sometimes expects employees to seek and assume responsibility they have not been asked to assume and then bid for the necessary authority. Such a system leads to guessing games that do nothing but create frustration and waste energy.

A manager's resistance to delegating authority is natural. There are several reasons for this reluctance:

1. Fear that subordinates will fail in doing the task—"if you want it done right, do it yourself."
2. The belief that it is easier to do the task oneself rather than delegate it.
3. Fear that subordinates will look "too good."
4. Humans' attraction to power.
5. Comfort in doing the tasks of the previous job held.
6. Preconceived ideas about employees.
7. Desire to set the right example.

Despite all the reasons for not delegating, there are some very strong reasons for a manager to delegate. Several phenomena occur when a manager successfully delegates. First, the manager's time is freed to pursue other tasks, and the subordinates gain feelings of belonging and being needed. These feelings often lead to a genuine commitment on the part of the subordinates. Second, delegation is one of the best methods for developing subordinates and satisfying customers. Pushing authority down the organization also allows employees to deal more effectively with customers. For example, some department stores give their salespeople and authority to make exchanges and refunds right on the floor, while others require customers to go to the credit department. Most customers much prefer the first situation. Taco Bell went from a $500 million regional company in 1982 to a $3 billion national company in 10 years because it recognized that the way to ultimately reach and satisfy customers was to empower its lower-level employees to make changes in operational strategies and tactics.[8] Successful delegation involves delegating matters that stimulate subordinates.

How to Delegate

To successfully delegate, a manager must decide which tasks can be delegated. A good way for a manager to do this is to first analyze how he or she spends his or her time. This can usually be done by keeping a daily time log indicating how time is actually spent. By carefully studying a time log, a manager can often identify the functions and duties that can be delegated and those that cannot.

Once a manager has determined which tasks can be delegated, he or she should decide which subordinates can handle each task. In order to best assign tasks to subordinates, managers must be well-acquainted with the skills of their immediate subordinates. When a manager has decided what tasks can be delegated to whom, the next step is to grant authority to make commitments, use resources, and take the actions necessary to perform the tasks. This is often the most difficult step in the delegation process for all of the reasons mentioned in the previous section.

The final steps in the delegation process are to make the subordinates responsible and to control the delegation. Subordinates can be made responsible by clearly creating an obligation on their part. Controlling the delegation requires that the delegating manager periodically check to ensure that things are going as planned. The frequency of these checks should be cooperatively decided by the delegating manager and the affected employees. Checks should not be so frequent as to stifle the employees, but they should be frequent enough to provide necessary support and guidance. Figure 8.1 summarizes the steps in the delegation process. Clearly defining objectives and standards, involving subordinates in the delegation process, and initiating training that defines and encourages delegation tend to improve the overall delegation process.

Probably the most nebulous part of the delegation process centers around the question of how much authority to delegate. As mentioned previously, management must delegate sufficient authority to allow the subordinate to perform the job. Precisely what can and cannot be delegated depends on the commitments of the manager and the number and quality

FIGURE 8.1
Steps in the Delegation Process

1. Analyze how you spend your time.
2. Decide which tasks can be assigned.
3. Decide who can handle each task.
4. Delegate the authority.
5. Create an obligation (responsibility).
6. Control the delegation.

of subordinates. A rule of thumb is to delegate authority and responsibility to the lowest organization level that has the competence to accept them.

Failure to master delegation is probably the single most frequently encountered reasons managers fail. To be a good manager, a person must learn to delegate.

exception principle
States that managers should concentrate on matters that deviate significantly from normal and let subordinates handle routine matters; also called *management by exception.*

The **exception principle** (also known as *management by exception*) states that managers should concentrate their efforts on matters that deviate significantly from normal and let subordinates handle routine matters. The exception principle is closely related to the parity principle. The idea behind the exception principle is that managers should concentrate on those matters that require their abilities and not become bogged down with duties their subordinates should be doing. The exception principle can be hard to comply with when incompetent or insecure subordinates refer everything to their superiors because they are afraid to make a decision. On the other hand, superiors should refrain from making everyday decisions that they have delegated to subordinates. This problem is often referred to as *micromanaging*.

Unity of Command

unity of command principle
States that an employee should have one, and only one, immediate manager.

The **unity of command principle** states that an employee should have one, and only one, immediate manager. The difficulty of serving more than one superior has been recognized for thousands of years. Recall the biblical quote, "No man can serve two masters." In its simplest form, this problem arises when two managers tell the same employee to do different jobs at the same time. The employee is thus placed in a no-win situation. Regardless of which manager the employee obeys, the other will be dissatisfied. The key to avoiding problems with unity of command is to make sure employees clearly understand the lines of authority that directly affect them. Too often managers assume employees understand the lines of authority when in fact they do not. All employees should have a basic understanding of the organizational chart for their company and where they fit on it. An organizational chart frequently clarifies lines of authority and the chain of command.

More times than not, problems relating to the unity of command principle stem from the actions of managers rather than the actions of employees. This happens most often when managers make requests of employees who do not work directly for them.

Scalar Principle

scalar principle
States that authority in the organization flows through the chain of managers one link at a time, ranging from the highest to the lowest ranks; also called *chain of command.*

The **scalar principle** states that authority in the organization flows through the chain of managers one link at a time, ranging from the highest to the lowest ranks. Commonly referred to as the *chain of command,* the scalar principle is based on the need for communication and the principle of unity of command.

Problems arise when an employee has different managers pulling him or her in different directions, which is why the unity of command principle, having one manager to report to, is so effective.

The problem with circumventing the scalar principle is that the link bypassed in the process may have very pertinent information. For example, suppose Jerry goes directly above his immediate boss, Ellen, to Charlie for permission to take his lunch break 30 minutes earlier. Charlie, believing the request is reasonable, approves it, only to find out later that the other two people in Jerry's department had also rescheduled their lunch breaks. Thus, the department would be totally vacant from 12:30 to 1 o'clock. Ellen, the bypassed manager, would have known about the other rescheduled lunch breaks.

A common misconception is that every action must painstakingly progress through every link in the chain, whether its course is upward or downward. This point was refuted many years ago by Lyndall Urwick, an internationally known management consultant:

> Provided there is proper confidence and loyalty between superiors and subordinates, and both parties take the trouble to keep the other informed in matters in which they should have a concern, the "scalar process" does not imply that there should be no shortcuts. It is concerned with authority, and provided the authority is recognized and no attempt is made to evade or to supersede it, there is ample room for avoiding in matters of action the childish practices of going upstairs one step at a time or running up one ladder and down another when there is nothing to prevent a direct approach on level ground.[9]

As Henri Fayol stated years before Urwick, "It is an error to depart needlessly from authority, but it is an even greater one to keep to it when detriment to the business ensues."[10] Both Urwick and Fayol are simply saying that in certain instances, one can and should shortcut the scalar chain as long as one does not do so in a secretive or deceitful manner.

Span of Management

span of management
Number of subordinates a manager can effectively manage; also called *span of control.*

The **span of management** (also called the *span of control*) refers to the number of subordinates a manager can effectively manage. Although the British World War I general Sir Ian Hamilton is usually credited for developing the concept of a limited span of control, related examples abound throughout history. Hamilton argued that a narrow span of management (with no more than six subordinates reporting to a manager) would enable the manager to get the job accomplished in the course of a normal working day.[11]

In 1933, V. A. Graicunas published a classic paper that analyzed subordinate–superior relationships in terms of a mathematical formula.[12] This formula was based on the theory that the complexities of managing increase geometrically as the number of subordinates increases arithmetically.

Based on his personal experience and the works of Hamilton and Graicunas, Lyndall Urwick first stated the concept of span of management as a management principle in 1938: "No superior can supervise directly the work of more than five, or at the most, six subordinates whose work interlocks."[13]

Since the publication of Graicunas's and Urwick's works, the upper limit of five or six subordinates has been continuously criticized as being too restrictive. Many practitioners and scholars contend there are situations in which more than five or six subordinates can be effectively supervised. Their beliefs have been substantiated by considerable empirical evidence showing that the limit of five or six subordinates has been successfully exceeded in many situations.[14] Urwick has suggested these exceptions can be explained by the fact that senior workers often function as unofficial managers or leaders.[15]

In view of recent evidence, the span of management concept has been revised to state that the number of people who should report directly to any one person should be based on the complexity, variety, and proximity of the jobs, the quality of the people filling the jobs, and the ability of the manager.

While much effort is given to ensuring that a manager's span of management is not too great, the opposite situation is often overlooked. All too frequently in organizations, situations develop in which only one employee reports to a particular manager. While this situation might very well be justified under certain circumstances, it often results in an inefficient and top-heavy organization. The pros and cons of flat organizations (wide spans of management, few levels) versus tall organizations (narrow spans of management, many levels) are discussed at length in the next chapter. Figure 8.2 summarizes the factors affecting the manager's span of management.

FIGURE 8.2
Factors Affecting the Span of Management

Factor	Description	Relationship to Span of Control
Complexity	Job scope Job depth	Shortens span of control
Variety	Number of different types of jobs being managed	Shortens span of control
Proximity	Physical dispersion of jobs being managed	Lengthens span of control
Quality of subordinates	General quality of the employees being managed	Lengthens span of control
Quality of manager	Ability to perform managerial duties	Lengthens span of control

CENTRALIZATION VERSUS DECENTRALIZATION

There are limitations to the authority of any position. These limitations may be external, in the form of laws, politics, or social attitudes, or they may be internal, as delineated by the organization's objectives or by the job description. The tapered concept of authority states that the breadth and scope of authority become more limited as one descends the scalar chain (see Figure 8.3).

The top levels of management establish the shapes of the funnels in Figures 8.3 and 8.4. The more authority top management chooses to delegate, the less conical the funnel becomes. The less conical the funnel, the more decentralized the organization. **Centralization** and **decentralization** refer to the degree of authority delegated by upper management. This is usually reflected by the numbers and kinds of decisions made by the lower levels of management. As they increase, the degree of decentralization also increases. Thus, an organization is never totally centralized or totally decentralized; rather, it falls along a continuum ranging from highly centralized to highly decentralized. In Figure 8.4, the organization represented by the diagram on the left is much more centralized than that represented by the right-hand diagram.

centralization
Little authority is delegated to lower levels of management.

decentralization
A great deal of authority is delegated to lower levels of management.

The trend in today's organizations is toward more decentralization. Decentralization has the advantage of allowing for more flexibility and quicker action. It also relieves executives from time-consuming detail work. It often results in higher morale by allowing lower levels of management to be actively involved in the decision-making process. The major disadvantage of decentralization is the potential loss of control. Duplication of effort can also accompany decentralization. Management Illustration 8.2 describes how one company has realized outstanding results through decentralization.

FIGURE 8.3
Tapered Concept of Authority

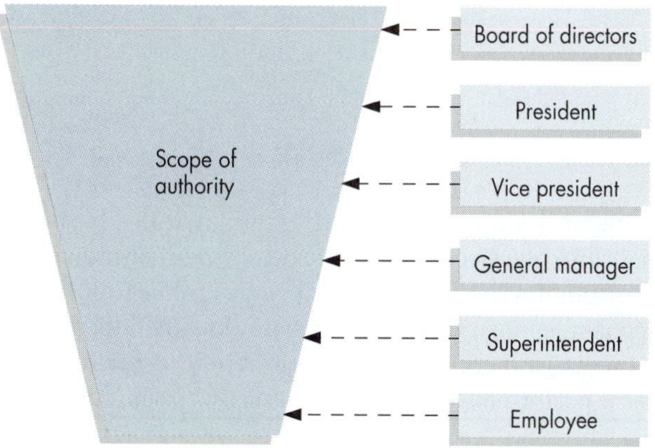

Management Illustration 8.2

DECENTRALIZATION AT STRYKER

www.strykercorp.com

John W. Brown became president and CEO of Stryker Corporation in 1977. Stryker is a $4.3 billion Kalamazoo, Michigan, global manufacturer of surgical devices, orthopedic implants, and hospital beds and stretchers. Stryker currently has 17 divisions and operates seven manufacturing plants in the continental United States, eight in Europe, and one each in Puerto Rico and Canada. When Brown became president and CEO, he set a staggering target of 20 percent annual growth in net earnings—a goal that was exceeded in 26 of the next 27 years.

One of Brown's keys to success was that he oversaw a decentralized organization with each of Stryker's 17 divisions focusing on a specific market. Brown left the day-to-day running of the business to his division heads, who operate the way they see fit. "It is tremendous autonomy, but responsibility with a capital R," says Brown. Decentralization works at Stryker because Brown made Stryker a very numbers-oriented company. The people who thrive at Stryker are those who are entrepreneurial but also willing to be measured and rewarded based on financial goals.

In January of 2005, Stephen R. MacMillan replaced Brown as president and CEO of Stryker. Brown remains on the board as the nonexecutive chairman. On June 12, 2007, Stryker was selected as one of twelve award-winning organizations at the Gallup Great Workplace Summit. The Gallup Great Workplace Awards recognize the best performing workforces in the world. Applicants' results are compared across a workplace research database comprised of millions of work teams in more than 100 countries.

Sources: Michael A. Verespej, "Recession? What Recession?" *Chief Executive,* June 2002, pp. 44–47; Kevin Lamiman, "Stryker Corporation," *Better Investing,* November 2005, pp. 44–46; and "Stryker Corporation Recipient of the Gallup Great Workplace Award 2007; Stryker Corporation Received Award as a Part of Gallup Great Workplace Summit," *PR Newswire,* June 22, 2007.

FIGURE 8.4
Centralized versus Decentralized Authority

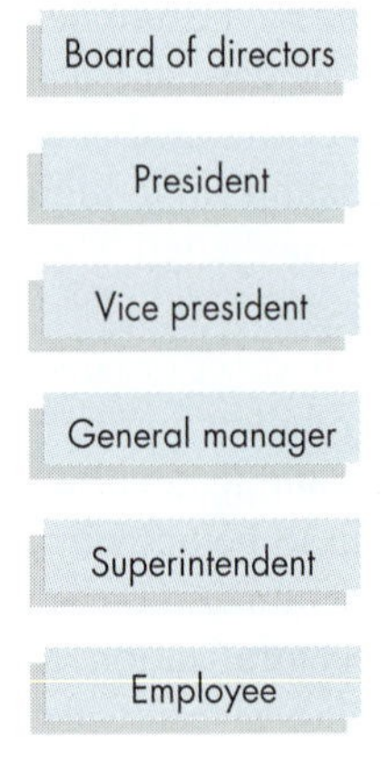

EMPOWERMENT

empowerment
Form of decentralization in which subordinates have authority to make decisions.

Empowerment is a form of decentralization that involves giving subordinates substantial authority to make decisions. Under empowerment, managers express confidence in the ability of employees to perform at high levels. Employees are also encouraged to accept personal responsibility for their work. In situations where true empowerment takes place, employees gain confidence in their ability to perform their jobs and influence the organization's performance. Under true empowerment, employees can bend the rules to

Management Illustration 8.3

EMPOWERING EMPLOYEES

Encouraging employees to "own" their work is paying off for the 125-year-old E. H. Wachs Company. Wachs began making steam boilers and piping in 1883, and has become a global supplier of on-site machining equipment for cutting pipe and tubing. "We try to empower our people," says Craig Lewandowski, vice president of manufacturing. "We encourage them to point out problems and suggest solutions. When they do, we respond quickly and positively. We're not interested in finding fault, we're interested in quickly spotting problems and then finding solutions. We have become very quick and dynamic in dealing with production problems."

At Wachs, if an operator incurs a problem while running a part, he or she can stop production and get the supervisor, manufacturing engineer, or even the design engineer involved in correcting the problem. "We have to get everyone involved in thinking about better ways to work," says Lewandowski, "because you never know where the next great idea is going to come from."

Source: Larry Haftl, "Empowering People: Key to Success," *American Machinist,* September 2006, p. 34.

do whatever they have to do to take care of the customer.[16] One result of empowerment is that employees demonstrate more initiative and perseverance in pursuing organizational goals. In order for empowerment to take root and thrive, the following four elements must be present:[17]

- *Participation.* Employees must be actively and willingly engaged in their respective jobs. They must want to improve their work processes and work relationship.
- *Innovation.* Employees must be given permission and encouragement to innovate and not do things the way they have always been done.
- *Access to information.* Employees at every level in the organization should make decisions about what kind of information they need to perform their job. This is different from traditional organizations where senior managers decide who gets what information.
- *Accountability.* Employees must be held accountable for their actions and the results achieved.

While the concept of empowerment looks relatively simple, it can be difficult to implement—especially in organizations where authority has traditionally flowed from top to bottom. Organizations can take several actions to help implement empowerment:[18]

- Whenever possible, restructure organizational units to be smaller, less complex, and less dependent on other units for decision making and action.
- Reduce to a minimum the number of hard rules for the organization.
- Emphasize a change throughout the organization that focuses on empowerment and personal accountability for delivering results.
- Provide the education and training necessary to enable people to respond to opportunities for improvement.

Accompanying the trend toward more decentralization in today's organizations is a trend toward increased empowerment of today's workforce. While some people believe that empowerment is praised loudly in public but seldom implemented, companies have experienced very positive results from having empowered their employees. Management Illustration 8.3 discusses how an 125-year-old company has empowered its production employees.

The basic idea of self-managed work teams is to motivate employees by having them participate in decisions that affect them and their work.

Self-Managed Work Teams

One method for empowering employees is through the use of *self-managed work teams.* Self-managed work teams (also called *self-directed* or *self-regulated work teams*) are work units without a frontline manager and empowered to control their own work.[19] The philosophy behind any type of work team is that teams can contribute to improved performance by identifying and solving work-related problems. The basic idea is to motivate employees by having them participate in decisions that affect them and their work. Self-managed work teams are teams of employees who accomplish tasks within their area of responsibility without direct supervision. Each team makes its own job assignments, plans its own work, performs equipment maintenance, keeps records, obtains supplies, and makes selection decisions of new members into the work unit.

There is no doubt that the use of self-managed work teams has grown dramatically over the last several years and will continue to grow in the future. Self-directed work teams are discussed further in Chapter 10, which is devoted to understanding all forms of work teams.

Workplace Changes in Organizations

Several changes are occurring in the workplace environment that can have an impact on how an entity might best be organized. Flextime, telecommuting, and job sharing are three such practices that are growing in popularity.

Flextime, or flexible working hours, allows employees to choose, within certain limits, when they start and end their workday. Usually the organization defines a core period (such as 10 AM to 3 PM) when all employees will be at work. It is then left to each employee to decide when to start and end the workday as long as the hours encompass the core period. Some flextime programs allow employees to vary the hours worked each day as long as they meet some specific total, which is usually 40 hours per week. The percentage of organizations offering flextime has increased dramatically over the last 15–20 years. A recent study by the Society for Human Resource Management found that 57 percent of employers offered some type of flextime in 2006.[20]

Flextime has the advantage of allowing employees to accommodate different lifestyles and schedules. Other potential advantages include avoiding rush hours and having less absenteeism and tardiness. From the employer's viewpoint, offering flextime can have the advantage of providing an edge in recruiting new employees and also retaining hard-to-find qualified employees. Also, organizations with flextime schedules have reported an average increase of 1 to 5 percent in productivity, as well as improved recruiting and retention.[21] On the downside, flextime can sometimes create communication and coordination problems for supervisors and managers.

Telecommuting is the practice of working at home, being able to interact with the office while traveling, or working at a satellite office. Today's information technology (PCs, the Internet, Blackberries, cellular phones, etc.) has made telecommuting a reality for many companies. According to the Telework Advisory Group for World at Work (formerly the International Telework Association and Council), approximately 45 million Americans worked from their home for some period during 2006, and approximately 12.4 million Americans worked from their home at least one day per month.[22]

Management Illustration 8.4

JOB SHARING FOR OVER 15 YEARS

Sharon Cercone and Linda Gladziszewski have shared a title and salary, a desk, a phone, and an e-mail account for the past 15 years. Over this time period, Sharon and Linda have shared seven human resources jobs at three different companies. Currently these women are compensation consultants at PNC Financial Services Group Inc. in Pittsburgh. Sharon works Mondays and Tuesdays. Linda works Thursdays and Fridays, and they alternate Wednesdays. They talk or exchange text messages several times a day and especially on Wednesdays. They also check with each other at night and keep project notes and a phone log. "We overcompensate so people understand that we don't let anything fall through the cracks," says Sharon. Both women receive the same recognition, and if one falters, both take the blame.

Source: Susan Berfield, "Two for the Cubicle," *BusinessWeek*, July 24, 2006, p. 88.

The earlier referenced 2006 survey by the Society for Human Resource Management found that 26 percent of its respondents offered some type of telecommuting.[23] Advantages of telecommuting include lower turnover, less travel time, avoiding rush hours, avoiding distractions at the office, being able to work flexible hours, and lower real estate costs for employers. Potential disadvantages of telecommuting are insurance concerns relating to the health and safety of employees working at home. Another drawback is that some state and local laws restrict what work can be done at home. The dramatic rise in the price of gasoline has made telecommuting even more attractive to millions of Americans.

Job sharing is a relatively new concept whereby two or more part-time employees perform a job that would normally be held by one full-time employee. Job sharing can be in the form of equally shared responsibilities, or split duties, or a combination of both. A 2005 survey by the Families and Work Institute found that 46 percent of organizations with 50 or more employees allowed some employees to job-share, while only 13 percent allowed all or most employees to do so.[24] A survey by Hewitt and Associates of 1,020 U.S. employers showed that slightly more than 25 percent offered job sharing.[25] Job sharing is especially attractive to people who want to work but not full-time. A critical factor relating to job sharing is how benefits are handled. Often benefits are prorated between the part-time employees. Some organizations allow job-sharing employees to purchase full health insurance by paying the difference between their prorated benefit and the premium for a full-time employee. Management Illustration 8.4 discusses an example of job sharing by two people who have shared seven different jobs in three different companies. Some well-known companies that utilize job sharing include Verizon Communications, Abbott Laboratories, IBM, and Xerox.

Summary

1. *Define organization, and differentiate between a formal and an informal organization.* An organization is a group of people working together in some type of concerted or coordinated effort to attain objectives. As such, an organization provides a vehicle for accomplishing objectives that could not be achieved by individuals working separately. The framework that defines the boundaries of the formal organization and within which the organization operates is the organization structure. The informal organization refers to the aggregate of the personal contacts and interactions and the associated groupings of people working within the formal organization. The informal organization has a structure, but it is not formally and consciously designed.

2. *Explain the importance of the organizing function.* The organizing function determines how organizational resources will be employed to achieve goals. It also establishes lines of authority, improves the efficiency and quality of work through synergism, and improves communication by defining channels of communication in the organization.
3. *List the advantages and the major disadvantage of horizontal division of labor.* Horizontal division of labor can result in the following advantages: (1) fewer skills are required per person; (2) it is easier to supply the skills required for selection or training purposes; (3) practice in the same job develops proficiency; (4) primarily utilizing each worker's best skills promotes efficient use of skills; (5) concurrent operations are made possible; and (6) there is more conformity in the final product if each piece is always produced by the same person. The major disadvantage of horizontal division of labor is that it can result in job boredom and even degradation of the worker.
4. *Distinguish between power, authority, and responsibility.* Power is the ability to influence, command, or apply force. Power is derived from the control of resources. Authority is power derived from the rights that come with a position; it is the legitimate exercise of power. Responsibility is accountability for the attainment of objectives, the use of resources, and the adherence to organizational policy. Once responsibility is accepted, performing assigned work becomes an obligation.
5. *List four principles of organization that are related to authority.* Four principles of organization related to authority are (1) the parity principle, (2) the unity of command principle, (3) the scalar principle, and (4) span of management.
6. *Identify several reasons managers are reluctant to delegate.* A manager's resistance to delegating authority is natural. Several reasons managers are reluctant to delegate include the following: (1) fear of subordinates failing; (2) it is easier for the manager to do the task than to teach a subordinate how to do it; (3) fear that subordinates will look "too good"; (4) humans' attraction to power; and (5) comfort in doing those tasks that should be delegated.
7. *Recount the major factors that affect a manager's span of management.* The major factors that affect a manager's span of management are (1) the complexity of the job being managed, (2) the variety among the jobs being managed, (3) the physical proximity of the jobs to one another, (4) the general quality of the subordinates being managed, and (5) the ability of the manager to perform the different managerial duties.
8. *Explain the concept of centralization versus decentralization.* Centralization and decentralization refer to the degree of authority delegated by upper management. This is usually reflected by the numbers and kinds of decisions made by the lower levels of management. As they increase, the degree of decentralization also increases. Thus, an organization is never totally centralized or totally decentralized: rather, it falls along a continuum ranging from highly centralized to highly decentralized.
9. *Define empowerment.* Empowerment is a form of decentralization that involves giving subordinates substantial authority to make decisions.
10. *Name and define three workplace changes, in addition to decentralization and empowerment, that have affected the organizing function in today's organizations.* The use of flextime, telecommuting, and job sharing has affected today's organizations. Flextime allows employees to choose, within certain limits, when they start and end their workdays. Telecommuting is the process of working away from a traditional office—usually at home. Job sharing is where two or more part-time employees perform a job that would normally be held by one full-time employee.

Review Questions

1. What is an organization? Define the management function of organizing. Define organization structure. What is an informal organization?
2. Discuss the reasons for organizing.
3. What is the difference between horizontal and vertical division of labor? What is the difference between job scope and job depth?
4. Define power, authority, and responsibility.
5. Discuss two approaches to viewing the sources of authority.
6. What is the parity principle? How does the parity principle relate to the exception principle?
7. Describe three components of the delegation process.
8. Why are many managers reluctant to delegate authority?
9. What is the unity of command principle?
10. What is the scalar principle?
11. What is the difference between a highly centralized and a highly decentralized organization?
12. Explain the concept of empowerment. What are self-managed work teams?
13. What is the span of management?
14. Define the following: flextime, telecommuting, and job sharing.

Skill-Building Questions

1. Do you think division of labor has been overemphasized in today's highly mechanized and efficient society?
2. Comment on the following statement, which is attributed to Robert Heinlein: "A human being should be able to change a diaper, plan an invasion, butcher a hog, conn a ship, design a building, write a sonnet, balance accounts, build a wall, set a bone, comfort the dying, take orders, give orders, cooperate, act alone, solve equations, analyze new problems, pitch manure, program a computer, cook a tasty meal, fight efficiently, and die gallantly. Specialization is for insects."
3. Identify and discuss a job that has a relatively wide job scope and narrow job depth. Identify a job that has a relatively narrow job scope and a wide job depth.
4. As a manager, would you prefer a relatively large (more than seven subordinates) or small (seven or fewer subordinates) span of management? Why? What are the implications of your choice?
5. Many people believe that the concept of empowerment receives a lot more talk than action. Why do you think this could be true?
6. Do you think you would like to telecommute? Why or why not?

SKILL-BUILDING EXERCISE 8.1

Promotion Possible: A Role Play

Your instructor will ask some class members to role play either the president or the current assistant sales manager in the following scenario.

The assistant sales manager of ABC Company has been in that job for six months. Due to poor sales over the past 18 months, the sales manager (his or her boss) has just been fired. The president of ABC then offers this job to the assistant sales manager subject to the following stipulations:

- You cannot increase the advertising budget.
- You must continue to let Metro-Media, Inc., handle the advertising.

- You cannot make any personnel changes.
- You will accept full responsibility for the sales for this fiscal year (which started two months ago).

The role play will simulate a meeting between the president and the assistant sales manager to discuss the offer. You can make any reasonable assumptions you think are necessary to play the role assigned to you.

SKILL-BUILDING EXERCISE 8.2
Minor Errors

Recently you have noticed that one of the staff members on the same level as your boss has been giving you a hard time concerning reports you submit to her. Having reviewed recent reports, you have discovered a few minor errors you should have caught; but in your opinion, they are not significant enough to warrant the kind of criticism you've been receiving. Your boss and this particular manager have a history of bad relations, which may be one reason for her attitude and actions.

As you think about how to best handle the situation, you consider these alternatives:

a. Talk to the manager in private and ask her why she is being so critical.

b. Do nothing. It is probably a temporary situation; to bring undue attention to it will only make matters worse.

c. Since your boss may get involved, discuss it with her and ask advice on what to do.

d. Work harder to upgrade the reports; make sure there will be nothing to criticize in the future.

e. Discuss it with your boss, but minimize or downplay the situation by letting her know that you believe constructive criticism of this type is usually healthy.

Other alternatives may be open to you, but assume these are the only ones you have considered.

1. *Without discussion* with anyone, decide which of these approaches you would take now. Be prepared to defend your choice.
2. What principle of organization most closely relates to this situation?
3. To what extent do you think this is an organizing problem as opposed to a personality problem?

Case Incident 8.1

A Good Manager?

Francis S. Russell is assistant general manager and sales manager for Webb Enterprises. At the moment, this self-styled perfectionist is sitting up in bed, checking his TTD sheet for tomorrow. The TTD (Things to Do) itemizes his daily activities, placing them on an exact time schedule. Never one to browbeat subordinates, Russell has his own special way of reminding people that time is money. Ever since the days when he was the best salesperson the company ever had, he had worked harder than the rest. It had paid off, too, because in only two years (when old Charlie retired), he was the heir apparent to the general managership. As this thought crossed Russell's mind, his immediate pride was replaced with a nagging problem. Where was he going to find the time to do all the things his position required? He certainly couldn't afford to just maintain the status quo. Then his mind forced him to plan tomorrow's activities and the problem was pushed into the background for future consideration.

(We see below a portion of Russell's well-planned day.)

TTD—October 16

7:15 Breakfast with Johnson (Purchasing). Get information on his cataloging system. Maybe combine with sales department and avoid duplication.

8:30 Meeting with Henry (assistant sales manager). Tell him exactly how the sales meeting for out-of-state representatives should be conducted. Caution—he's shaky on questions.

9:15 Discuss progress on new office procedures manual with Charlie (general manager). (He's irritated because I've dragged my heels on this. Let him know I've got Newman working on the problem.)

9:45 Assign Pat Newman the job of collecting data and sample copies regarding office manuals in other companies in our industry. Set up a system for him to use in analysis.

10:45 Call on Acliff Printing. A potentially big customer. (As Russell jotted down some information on this client, he reflected that it was a shame no one else on his staff could really handle the big ones the way he could. This thought was pleasing and bothersome at the same time.)

12:00 Lunch with J. Acliff (reservations at Black Angus).

3:00 Meet with Frank Lentz (advertising assistant) and check his progress on the new sales campaign. (Russell thought about Lentz's usual wild ideas and hoped that he had followed the general theme and rough sketches he had prepared.)

7:30 Chamber of Commerce meeting. (Look up Pierce Hansen—he may be able to help on the Acliff account.)

Questions

1. Do you think Francis is a highly motivated employee trying to do a good job? Explain your answer.
2. What problems do you see concerning Francis' effectiveness as a manager?
3. Assuming you were Charlie, the general manager, what solutions would you recommend?

Case Incident 8.2

The Vacation Request

Tom Blair has a week's vacation coming and really wants to take it the third week in May, which is the height of the bass fishing season. The only problem is that two of the other five members of his department have already requested and received approval from their boss, Luther Jones, to take off that same week. Afraid that Luther would not approve his request, Tom decided to forward his request directly to Harry Jensen, who is Luther's boss and who is rather friendly to Tom (Tom has taken Harry fishing on several occasions). Not realizing that Luther has not seen the request, Harry approves it. Several weeks pass before Luther finds out, by accident, that Tom has been approved to go on vacation the third week of May.

The thing that really bugs Luther is that this is only one of many instances in which his subordinates have gone directly to Harry and gotten permission to do something. Just last week, in fact, he overheard a conversation in the washroom to the effect that, "If you want anything approved, don't waste time with Luther, go directly to Harry."

Questions

1. What should Harry have done?
2. Who is at fault, Harry or Tom?
3. What if Luther confronts Harry with the problem and he simply brushes it off by saying he is really only helping?

References and Additional Readings

1. Harold Koontz and Cyril O'Donnell, *Management: A Systems and Contingency Analysis of Managerial Functions,* 6th ed. (New York: McGraw-Hill, 1976), p. 274.
2. Chester L. Barnard, *Functions of the Executive* (Cambridge, MA: Harvard University Press, 1938), pp. 114–15.
3. Gareth R. Jones, *Organizational Theory* (Reading, MA: Addison-Wesley, 1995), p. 9.
4. Adam Smith, *The Wealth of Nations* (New York: Modern Library, 1917); originally published in 1776.
5. Thomas J. Peters and Robert H. Waterman, Jr., *In Search of Excellence* (New York: Harper & Row, 1982), p. 313.
6. Mary Parker Follett, *Freedom and Co-Ordination* (London: Management Publication Trust, 1949), pp. 1–15 (the lecture reproduced in *Freedom and Co-Ordination* was first delivered in 1926); and Barnard, *Functions,* p. 163.
7. Herbert M. Engel, *How to Delegate* (Houston: Gulf, 1983), p. 6.
8. Michael Hammer and James Champy, *Reengineering the Corporation* (New York: Harper Business, 1993) pp. 180–81.
9. L. F. Urwick, *The Elements of Administration* (New York: Harper & Row, 1943), p. 46.
10. Henri Fayol, *General and Industrial Management* (London: Sir Isaac Pitman & Sons, 1949), p. 36; first published in 1916.
11. Sir Ian Hamilton, *The Soul and Body of an Army* (London: Edward Arnold, 1921), p. 229.
12. V. A. Graicunas, "Relationship in Organization," *Bulletin of the International Management Institute* (Geneva: International Labour Office, 1933); reprinted in *Papers on the Science of Administration,* ed. L. Gulick and L. F. Urwick (New York: Institute of Public Administration, 1937), pp. 181–87.
13. L. F. Urwick, "Scientific Principles and Organizations," *Institute of Management Series No. 19* (New York: American Management Association, 1938), p. 8.
14. For a brief discussion of such situations, see Leslie W. Rue, "Supervisory Control in Modern Management," *Atlanta Economic Review,* January–February 1975, pp. 43–44.
15. L. F. Urwick, "V. A. Graicunas and the Span of Control," *Academy of Management Journal,* June 1974, p. 352.
16. John Tschol, "Empowerment: The Key to Customer Service," *American Salesman,* November 1997, pp. 12–15.
17. John H. Dobbs, "The Empowerment Environment," *Training & Development,* February 1993, pp. 53–55.
18. Robert B. Shaw, "The Capacity to Act: Creating a Context for Empowerment," in *Organizational Architecture: Designs for Changing Organizations,* ed. David A. Nadler, Marc S. Gerstein, and Robert B. Shaw (San Francisco: Jossey-Bass, 1992), p. 169.

19. Renee Beckhams, "Self-Directed Work Teams: The Wave of the Future?" *Hospital Material Management Quarterly,* August 1998, pp. 48–60.

20. Stephanie Thompson, "Working Mothers Flex Their Scheduling Muscle," *Advertising Age,* November 6, 2006, p. 72.

21. Brian Gill, "Flextime Benefits Employees and Employers," *American Printer,* February 1998, p. 70; and Leah Carlson, "Firms Balance Workplace Flexibility and Business Demands," *Employee Benefit News,* April 1, 2005, p. 1.

22. http://www.workingfromanywhere.org/. Accessed on January 16, 2008.

23. Thompson, "Working Mothers Flex Their Scheduling Muscle."

24. "Have You Considered Job Sharing as a Retention Tool?" *HR Focus,* September 2006, pp. 10–11.

25. Pete Bach, "Job Sharing Can Make for Balanced Life," *Knight Ridder Tribune Business News,* January 31, 2006.

Chapter Nine

Organizational Structure

Learning Objectives

After studying this chapter, you will be able to:

1. Discuss the different stages an organization goes through as it grows and matures.
2. Explain what an organization chart is.
3. List several factors that can affect which structure is the most appropriate for a given organization.
4. Describe the general relationship between an organization's strategy and its structure.
5. Define outsourcing, and summarize its potential benefits as well as its potential drawbacks.
6. Describe a contingency approach to organizing.
7. Identify the different types of departmentalization.
8. Briefly describe each of the following types of organizational structure: line structure, line and staff structure, matrix structure, horizontal structure, and virtual organization.
9. Describe several trends that have taken place regarding the popularity of different types of organization structures.
10. Describe how committees can be made more effective.
11. Explain the difference between an inside and an outside board of directors.

Chapter Preview

PepsiCo recently announced a strategic realignment of its organizational structure. The two previous major operating units, PepsiCo North America and PepsiCo International are being transformed into three major operating units: PepsiCo America's Foods, PepsiCo America's Beverages, and PepsiCo International. "Given PepsiCo's robust growth in recent years, we are approaching a size which we can better manage as three units, instead of two," said Indra Nooyi, chairman and chief executive officer.

PepsiCo America's Foods includes Frito-Lay North America, Quaker, and all Latin American food and snack businesses. PepsiCo America's Beverages includes PepsiCola North America, Gatorade, Tropicana, and all Latin American beverage businesses. PepsiCo International includes all PepsiCo business in the United Kingdom, Europe, Asia, the Middle East and Africa. "Creating units that span North American and international markets, as well as developed and developing markets, allows us to better share best practices among our North American international businesses, while providing valuable development opportunities for our senior executives," stated Nooyi.

Source: "PepsiCo Reorganizes Structure, Creates Three Units," *Beverage Industry,* November 2007, p. 10.

Analyzing Management Skills

Do you think it is unusual for organizations to reorganize as they grow? What are some of the facotrs that might impact an organization's structure?

Applying Management Skills

Have you ever been in or observed a work situation where you felt customer service was being hindered by the organization's structure? What would you do differently if you could change the structure?

organization structure
Framework that defines the boundaries of the formal organization and within which the organization operates.

Organization structure is the framework that defines the boundaries of the formal organization and within which the organization operates. The structure of an organization reflects how groups compete for resources, where responsibilities for profits and other performance measures lie, how information is transmitted, and how decisions are made. Many people believe a good manager or a competent employee should be able to perform well regardless of the organization structure and environment. They believe that if managers or employees are good enough, they can overcome any obstacles the organization structure presents. Others believe that given the right organization structure, anyone should be able to perform in an acceptable fashion. The truth lies somewhere in between. An appropriate organization structure certainly helps foster good performance.

ORGANIZATION GROWTH STAGES

Figure 9.1 shows in general terms the stages an organization goes through as it grows and matures. The craft or family stage is characterized by the absence of formal policies, objectives, and structure. The operations of the organization at this stage generally center on one individual and one functional area. During the entrepreneurial stage, the organization grows first at an increasing and then a decreasing rate. An atmosphere of optimism pervades the entire organization as sales and profits rise rapidly. By the third stage of growth, the entrepreneur has been replaced by or evolved into a professional manager who performs the processes of planning, organizing, staffing, motivating, and controlling.[1] Profits are realized more from internal efficiency and less from external exploitation of the market. At this stage, the organization becomes characterized by written policies, procedures, and plans.

As the organization moves through the craft stage and into the entrepreneurial stage, an organization structure must be developed. This is a critical stage for the organization. If an

FIGURE 9.1
Organization Growth and Change

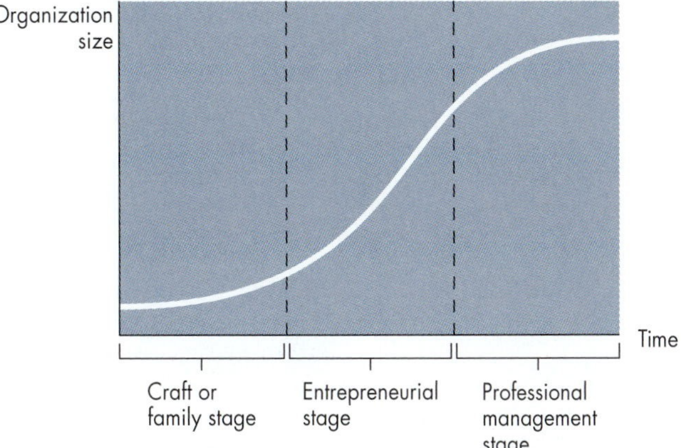

appropriate structure is not established and utilized, the entrepreneur may lose control and the entire organization may collapse. An organization structure must be developed that allows the organization to adapt to change in its environment.

ORGANIZATION CHARTS

An organization chart uses a series of boxes connected with one or more lines to graphically represent the organization's structure. Each box represents a position within the organization, and each line indicates the nature of the relationships among the different positions. Figure 9.2 presents an example of a basic organisation chart. As can seen in Figure 9.2, much information can be gleaned from an organization chart. Not only are specific relationships identified, but one can also get an overall sense of how the entire organization fits together. As organizations become larger and more complex, it becomes increasingly difficult to represent all of the relationships accurately.

FACTORS AFFECTING ORGANIZATION STRUCTURE

Several factors can affect which structure is the most appropriate for a given organization. A structure that is appropriate for a high-tech company that employs 50,000 people in eight countries will probably not be appropriate for a small retail business with just a dozen employees. Strategy, size, environment, and technology are some of the important factors found to be mostly closely related to organization structure.

Strategy

A major part of an organization's strategy for attaining its objectives deals with how the organization is structured. An appropriate structure will not guarantee success, but it will

FIGURE 9.2
Sample Organization Chart

Source: John A. Pearce II and Richard B. Robinson, Jr., *Strategic Management,* 8th ed. (Burr Ridge, IL: McGraw-Hill/Irwin, 2003), p. 314.

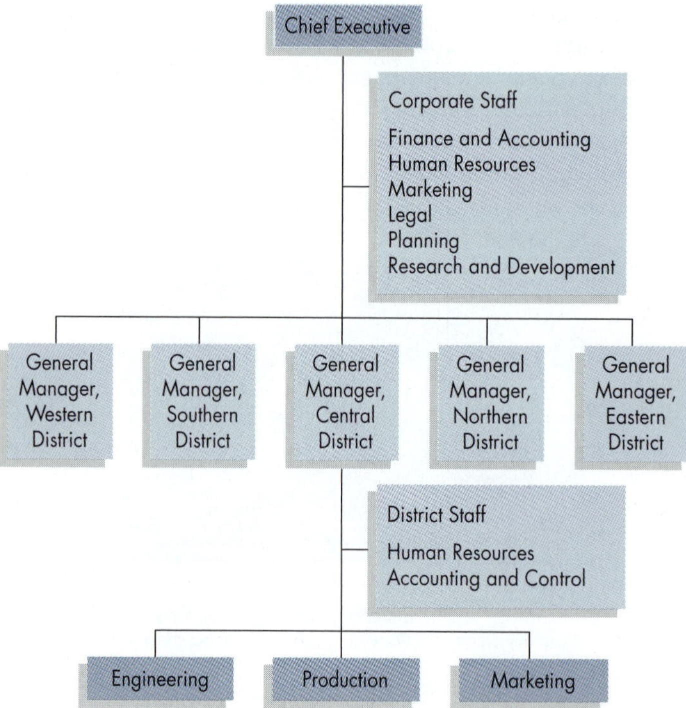

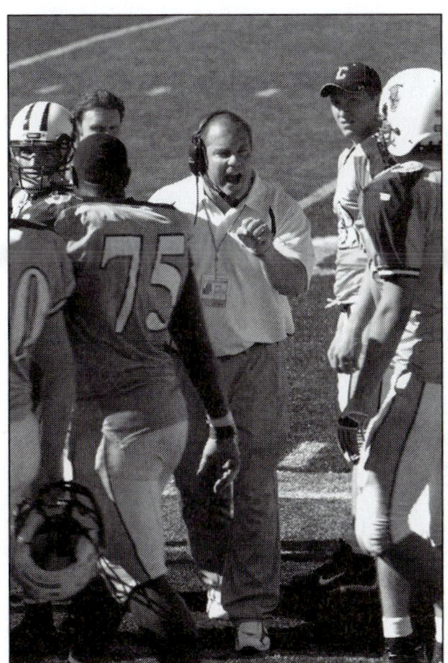

Managers, like coaches, need to realize that to succeed one must not only have a good strategy but also be prepared mentally and structurally.

enhance the organization's chances for success. Business leaders, athletic coaches, and military leaders all stress that to succeed one must not only have a good strategy but also be prepared to win (mentally and structurally). In addition to clarifying and defining strategy through the delegation of authority and responsibility, the organization structure can either facilitate or inhibit strategy implementation.

In a groundbreaking study of organizational strategy, Alfred D. Chandler described a pattern in the evolution of organizational structures.[2] The pattern was based on studies of Du Pont, General Motors, Sears, and Standard Oil Company, with corroborating evidence from many other firms. The pattern Chandler described was that of changing strategy, followed by administrative problems, leading to decline in performance, revised structure, and a subsequent return to economic health. In summary, Chandler concluded that structure follows strategy; in other words, changes in strategy ultimately led to changes in the organization's structure. Chandler's work related particularly to growth and to the structural adjustments made to maintain efficient performance during market expansion, product line diversification, and vertical integration.

Although subsequent research has supported the idea of a relationship between strategy and structure, it is clear that strategy is not the only variable that has a bearing on structure.[3] The process of matching structure to strategy is complex and should be undertaken with a thorough understanding of the historical development of the current structure and of other variables, including size, environment, and technology.

Size

There are many ways to measure the size of an organization, but sales volume and number of employees are the most frequently used factors. While no hard-and-fast rules exist, certain characteristics generally relate to an organization's size. Small organizations tend to be less specialized (horizontal division of labor), less standardized, and more centralized. Larger organizations tend to be more specialized, more standardized, and more decentralized. Thus, as an organization grows in size, certain structural changes naturally occur.

mechanistic systems
Organizational systems characterized by a rigid delineation of functional duties, precise job descriptions, fixed authority and responsibility, and a well-developed organizational hierarchy through which information filters up and instructions flow down.

organic systems
Organizational systems characterized by less formal job descriptions, greater emphasis on adaptability, more participation, and less fixed authority.

Environment

A landmark study relating organization to environment was conducted by Tom Burns and G. M. Stalker in the United Kingdom.[4] By examining some 20 industrial firms in both a changing industry and a more stable, established industry, Burns and Stalker focused on how a firm's pattern of organization was related to certain characteristics of the external environment. The researchers identified two distinct organizational systems. **Mechanistic systems** are characterized by a rigid delineation of functional duties, precise job descriptions, fixed authority and responsibility, and a well-developed organizational hierarchy through which information filters up and instructions flow down. **Organic systems** are characterized by less formal job descriptions, greater emphasis on adaptability, more participation, and less fixed authority. Burns and Stalker found that successful firms in stable and established industries tended to be mechanistic in structure, whereas successful firms in dynamic industries tended to be organic in structure. See Figure 9.3 for a more complete evaluation of the structural differences between mechanistic and organic systems.

Paul Lawrence and Jay Lorsch conducted a later study dealing with organization structure and its environment.[5] Their original study included 10 firms in three distinct industrial environments. Reaching conclusions similar to those of Burns and Stalker, Lawrence and

FIGURE 9.3
Structural Differences between Mechanistic and Organic Systems

Source: Adapted from Tom Burns and G. W. Stalker, *The Management of Innovation* (London: Tavistock, 1961), pp. 119–22.

Characteristics of Mechanistic and Organic Organizations

Mechanistic	Organic
Work is divided into narrow, specialized tasks.	Work is defined in terms of general tasks.
Tasks are performed as specified unless changed by managers in the hierarchy.	Tasks are continually adjusted as needed through interaction with others involved in the task.
Structure of control, authority, and communication is hierarchical.	Structure of control, authority, and communication is a network.
Decisions are made by the specified hierarchical level.	Decisions are made by individuals with relevant knowledge and technical expertise.
Communication is mainly vertical, between superior and subordinate.	Communication is vertical and horizontal, among superiors, subordinates, and peers.
Communication content is largely instructions and decisions issued by superiors.	Communication content is largely information and advice.
Emphasis is on loyalty to the organization and obedience to superiors.	Emphasis is on commitment to organizational goals and possession of needed expertise.

Lorsch found that to be successful, firms operating in a dynamic environment needed a relatively flexible structure, firms operating in a stable environment needed a more rigid structure, and firms operating in an intermediate environment needed a structure somewhere between the two extremes.

Numerous other studies have been conducted in the past several years investigating the relationship between organization structure and environment. In general, most have concluded that the best structure for a given organization is contingent on the organization's environment to some degree.[6] However, managerial style and corporate culture may also have an impact as interpretative agents of the environment. Microsoft's Bill Gates, Nike's Phil Knight, and Apple's Steve Jobs have all moved their companies in the direction of the organic model so they could swiftly move into new and as yet untapped markets and product lines.

Organization and Technology

Numerous studies have also been conducted investigating potential relationships between technology and organization structure. One of the most important of these studies was conducted by Joan Woodward in the late 1950s.[7] Her study was based on an analysis of 100 manufacturing firms in the southeast Essex area of England. Woodward's general approach was to classify firms along a scale of "technical complexity" with particular emphasis on three modes of production: (1) unit or small-batch production (e.g., custom-made machines), (2) large-batch or mass production (e.g., an automotive assembly plant), and (3) continuous flow or process production (e.g., a chemical plant). The unit or small-batch production mode represents the lower end of the technical complexity scale, while the continuous flow mode represents the upper end.

After classifying each firm into one of the preceding categories, Woodward investigated a number of organizational variables. Some of her findings follow:

1. The number of levels in an organization increased as technical complexity increased.
2. The ratio of managers and supervisors to total personnel increased as technical complexity increased.
3. Using Burns and Stalker's definition of organic and mechanistic systems, organic management systems tended to predominate in firms at both ends of the scale of technical complexity, while mechanistic systems predominated in firms falling in the middle ranges.
4. No significant relationship existed between technical complexity and organizational size.

A few years later, Edward Harvey undertook a similar study.[8] Rather than using Woodward's technical complexity scale, Harvey grouped firms along a continuum from technical diffuseness to technical specificity. Technically diffused firms have a wider range of products, produce products that vary from year to year, and produce more made-to-order products. Harvey's findings were similar to Woodward's in that he found significant relationships between technology and several organizational characteristics.

The general conclusion reached in the Woodward and Harvey studies was that a relationship clearly exists between organizational technology and a number of aspects of organization structure. Many additional studies have investigated the relationship between technology and structure. While some have reported conflicting results, most studies have found a relationship between technology and structure.

CHANGES AFFECTING ORGANIZATION STRUCTURE

outsourcing
Practice of subcontracting certain work functions to an independent outside source.

In recent years, dramatic improvements in communication technology have introduced new ways of conducting business. These new practices have affected the structure of many organizations. Outsourcing has resulted from improved communication technology and is having an effect on the structure of many organizations. **Outsourcing** is the practice of subcontracting certain work functions to an outside entity. Whether outsourcing is a response to downsizing, an attempt to cut costs, or an effort to increase service, it is a practice that is significantly affecting the workplace and organization charts. Work functions that are frequently being outsourced include accounting and finance functions, human resources, information technology, and even contract manufacturing. Outsourcing, which began in earnest less than 35 years ago, was estimated to be a $6 trillion a year business at the beginning of 2008.[9] Outsourcing in the United States was valued at approximately $45 billion in 2007 and estimated to grow to $130 billion by 2010.[10] It has been estimated that over 25 percent of the typical executive's budget goes to outsourcing supplies or services, and that is expected to grow considerably.[11] Outsourcing is a practice utilized by both large and small companies.

The International Association of Outsourcing Professionals estimates that almost 30 percent of all outsourcing in the United States is conducted by companies with less than $500 million in annual revenues.[12]

Outsourcing has numerous potential benefits, including the following:[13]

- Allowing the organization to emphasize its core competencies by not spending time on routine areas that can be outsourced.
- Reducing operating costs by utilizing others who can do the job more efficiently.
- Accessing top talent and state-of-the-art technology without having to own it.
- Fewer personnel headaches.
- Improving resource allocation by allowing growth to take place more quickly.

Of course, there are potential drawbacks to outsourcing.[14] One overriding concern is that a large number of jobs are being lost to other countries through outsourcing. For example, it has been estimated that more than 3 million jobs will leave the United States by 2015.[15] Other specific drawbacks include:

- Loss of control and being at the mercy of the vendor.
- Loss of in-house skills.
- Threat to the morale of the workforce if too many areas are dominated by outside vendors.
- No guarantee that it will save money or provide higher service standards.

Management Illustration 9.1

DIFFERENT REASONS FOR OUTSOURCING

When Delta Airlines outsourced its human resource functions to Affiliated Computers Services (ACS) in early 2005, it was strictly to save money. Delta, which filed for bankruptcy protection in September 2005, believed the deal could save it 25 percent over the seven years of the $120 million deal. The outsourcing also averted the need for Delta to spend $50 million on updating its human resources technology.

Not even two years into their seven-year outsourcing contract Delta and ACS changed the terms of their contract. According to a motion filed January 11, 2007, in U.S. Bankruptcy Court in New York, ACS agreed to make two cash payments of $6.6 million and $1.1 million to Delta "in settlement of certain disputes regarding Affiliated's performance of the services." The two companies also agreed to limit the scope of services that ACS will provide to Delta going forward. "Having a rift this early in a contract demonstrates how difficult the implementation stage can be for providers and buyers," says Jason Corsello, an analyst at Yankee Group.

Sources: Todd Henneman, "Measuring the True Benefit of Human Resources Outsourcing," *Workforce Management,* July 2005, pp. 76–77; and Jessica Marquez, "ACS Scales Back $120 Mil Delta HRO Agreement," *Workforce Management,* January 29, 2007, p. 7.

As with most management approaches, outsourcing is not a cure-all. Care must be taken that a long-term strategy evolves out of the use of outsourcing, not just a short-term fix to reduce costs. In the right situations, outsourcing can work well; but it almost always requires good management, good contracts, and realistic expectations. Management Illustration 9.1 discusses some of the difficulties that Delta Airlines experienced during the implementation phase of one outsourcing contract.

A CONTINGENCY APPROACH

contingency (situational) approach to organization structure
States that the most appropriate structure depends on the technology used, the rate of environmental change, and other dynamic forces.

The previous discussions emphasize the fact that several factors affect an organization's structure. The knowledge that there is no one best way to organize (i.e., the design is conditional) has led to a **contingency (situational) approach** to organizing. Figure 9.4 shows the previously discussed variables and others that can help determine the most appropriate organization structure. The contingency approach should be viewed as a process of assessing these relevant variables and then choosing the most appropriate structure for the situation. Because most of the relevant variables are dynamic, management should periodically analyze and appraise the organization's structure in light of any relevant changes.

FIGURE 9.4
Variables Affecting Appropriate Organization Structure

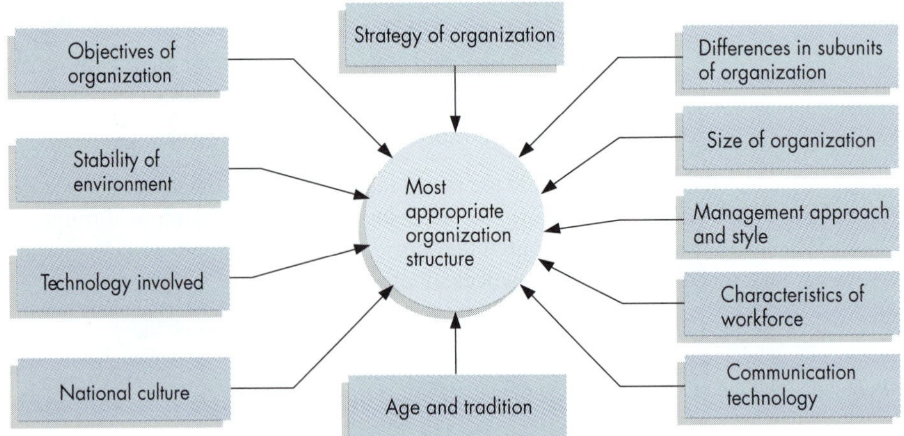

DEPARTMENTALIZATION

departmentalization
Grouping jobs into related work units.

While thousands of different organization structures exist, almost all are built on the concept of departmentalization. **Departmentalization** involves grouping jobs into related work units. The work units may be related on the basis of work functions, product, geography, customer, technique, or time.

Work Functions

functional departmentalization
Defining organizational units in terms of the nature of the work.

Functional departmentalization occurs when organization units are defined by the nature of the work. Although different terms may be used, most organizations have four basic functions: production, marketing, finance, and human resources. Production refers to the actual creation of something of value, either goods, services, or both. Marketing involves product or service planning, pricing the product or service with respect to demand, evaluating how to best distribute the good or service, and communicating information to the market through sales and advertising. Any organization, whether manufacturing or service, must provide the financial structure necessary for carrying out its activities. The human resources function is responsible for securing and developing the organization's people.

Each of these basic functions may be broken down as necessary. For instance, the production department may be split into maintenance, quality control, engineering, manufacturing, and so on. The marketing department may be grouped into advertising, sales, and market research. Figure 9.5 charts a typical functional departmentalization.

The primary advantage of functional departmentation is that it allows for specialization within functions. It also provides for efficient use of equipment and resources, potential economies of scale, and ease of coordination within the function itself. However, functional departmentalization can have some negative effects. For example, suboptimization of goals occurs when members of a functional group develop more loyalty to the functional group's goals than to the organization's goals. For example, the marketing department might be overzealous in selling products even when production cannot meet any additional demand. If the group's goals and the organization's goals are not mutually supportive, such activity can lead to problems. Conflict may also develop among different

FIGURE 9.5 **Functional Departmentalization**

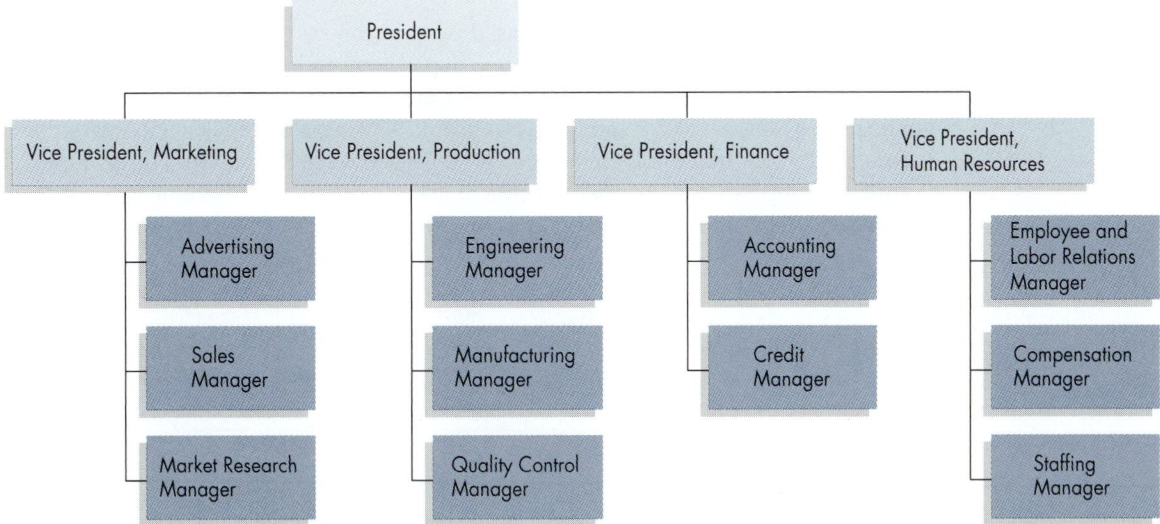

FIGURE 9.6
Product Departmentalization

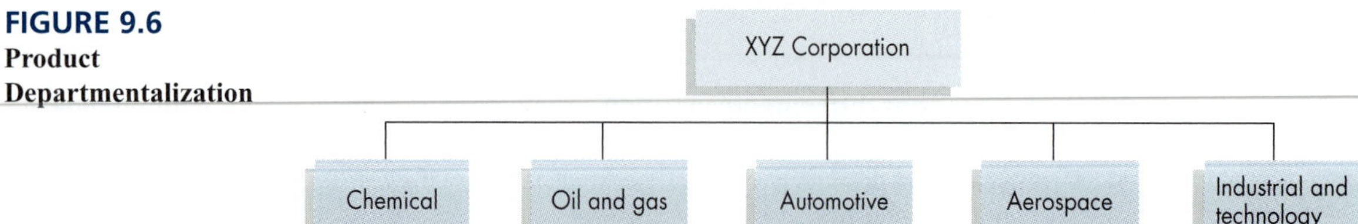

departments striving for different goals. In addition, employees who are locked into their functions have a restricted view of the organization. Finally, the rather narrow functional scope of managers may be a disadvantage when a multidisciplinary approach would be more advantageous.

Product

product departmentalization Grouping all activities necessary to produce and market a product or service under one manager.

Under **product departmentalization,** all the activities needed to produce and market a product or service are usually under a single manager. This system allows employees to identify with a particular product and thus develop esprit de corps. It also facilitates managing each product as a distinct profit center. Product departmentalization provides opportunities for training for executive personnel by letting them experience a broad range of functional activities. Problems can arise if departments become overly competitive to the detriment of the overall organization. A second potential problem is duplication of facilities and equipment. Product departmentalization adapts best to large, multiproduct organizations. Figure 9.6 illustrates how a company might be structured using product departmentalization.

Geographic

geographic departmentalization Defining organizational units by territories.

Geographic departmentalization is most likely to occur in organizations that maintain physically dispersed and autonomous operations or offices. Departmentalization by geography permits the use of local employees or salespeople. This can create customer goodwill and an awareness of local feelings and desires. It can also lead to a high level of service. Of course, having too many locations can be costly.

Customer

customer departmentalization Defining organizational units in terms of customers served.

Customer departmentalization is based on division by customers served. A common example is an organization that has one department to handle retail customers and one department to handle wholesale or industrial customers. Figure 9.7 shows departmentalization by customer for Johnson & Johnson. This type of departmentalization has the same advantages and disadvantages as product departmentalization. For example, if the professional group and the pharmaceutical group in Figure 9.7 became too competitive with each other for corporate resources, the organization's overall performance could suffer.

FIGURE 9.7
Customer Departmentalization

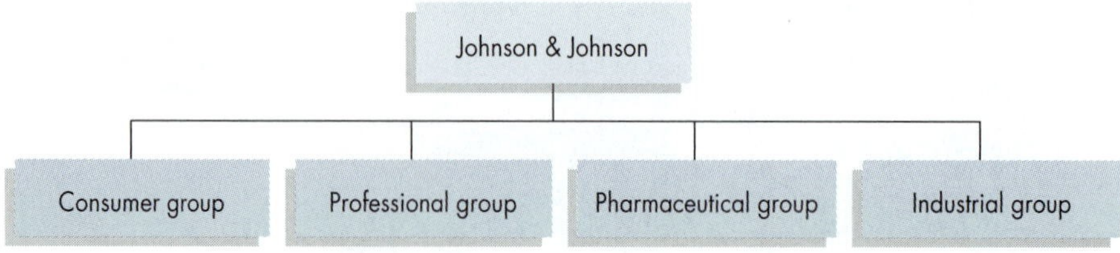

Other Types

Several other types of departmentalization are possible. Departmentalization by simple numbers is practiced when the most important ingredient for success is the number of employees. Organizing for a local United Way drive would be an example. Departmentalization by process or equipment is another possibility. A final type of departmentalization is by time or shift. Organizations that work around the clock may use this type of departmentalization.

Hybrid Departmentalization

hybrid departmentalization
Occurs when an organization simultaneously uses more than one type of departmentalization.

Typically, as an organization grows in size, it adds levels of departmentalization. A small organization may have no departmentalization at first. As it grows, it may departmentalize first on one basis, then another, and then another. For example, a large sales organization may use product departmentalization to create self-contained divisions; then each division might be further divided by geography and then by type of customer. **Hybrid departmentalization** occurs when an organization simultaneously uses more than one type of departmentalization. As Figure 9.8 illustrates, many different department

FIGURE 9.8 **Possible Departmentalization Mixes for a Sales Organization**

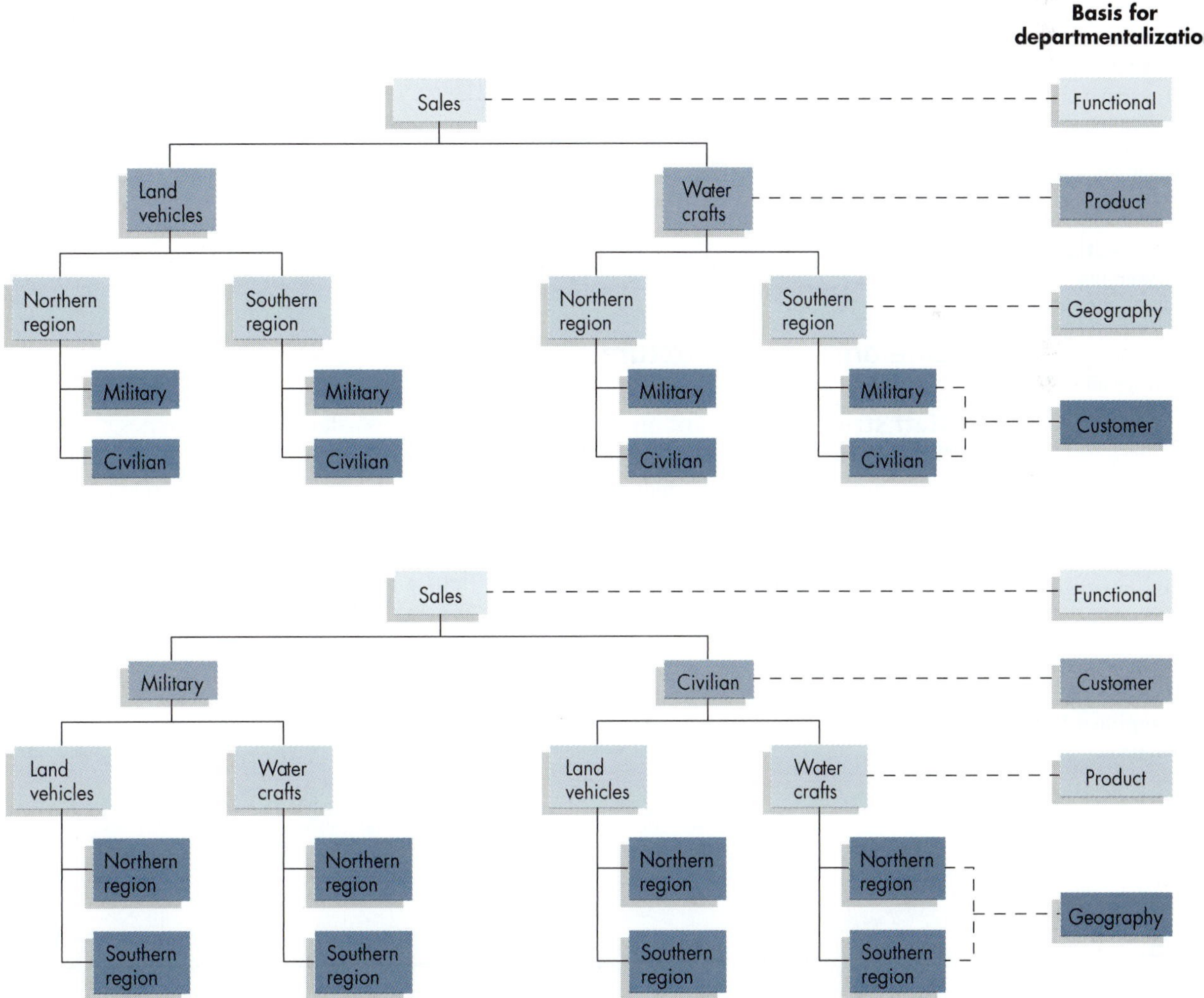

mixes are possible for a given organization. Which one is best depends on the specific situation.

TYPES OF ORGANIZATION STRUCTURES

There are several basic types of structures that organizations may use. Traditionally, these have been the line structure, the line and staff structure, or the matrix structure. Recently, new types of structures and organizations have evolved and are evolving to take advantage of the new communication and logistical technology available. These new structures include the horizontal structure and the virtual organization. Each of these types of structures is discussed in the following sections.

Line Structure

line structure
Organization structure with direct vertical lines between the different levels of the organization.

line and staff structure
Organization structure that results when staff specialists are added to a line organization.

staff functions
Functions that are advisory and supportive in nature; designed to contribute to the efficiency and maintenance of the organization.

line functions
Functions and activities directly involved in producing and marketing the organization's goods or services.

In a *line organization,* authority originates at the top and moves downward in a line. All managers perform *line functions,* or functions that contribute directly to company profits. Examples of line functions include production managers, sales representatives, and marketing managers.

The most important aspect of the **line structure** is that the work of all organizational units is directly involved in producing and marketing the organization's goods or services. This is the simplest organization structure and is characterized by vertical links between the different levels of the organization. All members of the organization receive instructions through the scalar chain. One advantage is a clear authority structure that promotes rapid decision making and prevents "passing the buck." A disadvantage is that it may force managers to perform too broad a range of duties. It may also cause the organization to become too dependent on one or two key employees who are capable of performing many duties. Because of its simplicity, line structure exists most frequently in small organizations. Figure 9.9 represents a simplified line structure.

Line and Staff Structure

The addition of staff specialists to a line-structured organization creates a **line and staff structure.** As a line organization grows, staff assistance often becomes necessary. **Staff functions** are advisory and supportive in nature; they contribute to the efficiency and maintenance of the organization. **Line functions** are directly involved in producing and marketing the organization's goods or services. They generally relate directly to the attainment of major organizational objectives, while staff functions contribute indirectly. Staff people are generally specialists in one field, and their authority is normally limited to making recommendations to line people. Typical staff functions include research and

FIGURE 9.9
A Simplified Line Structure

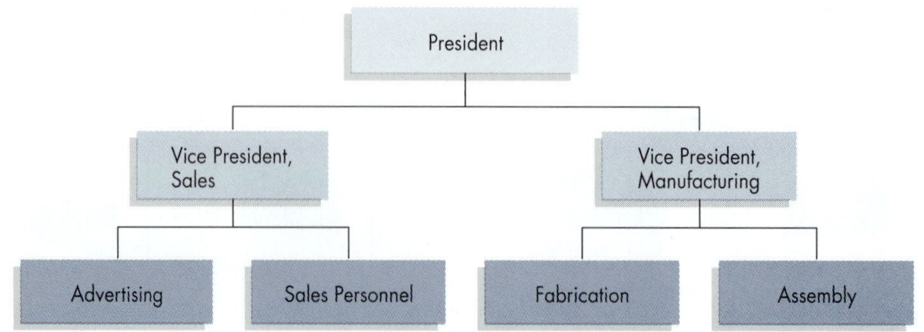

FIGURE 9.10
A Simplified Line and Staff Structure

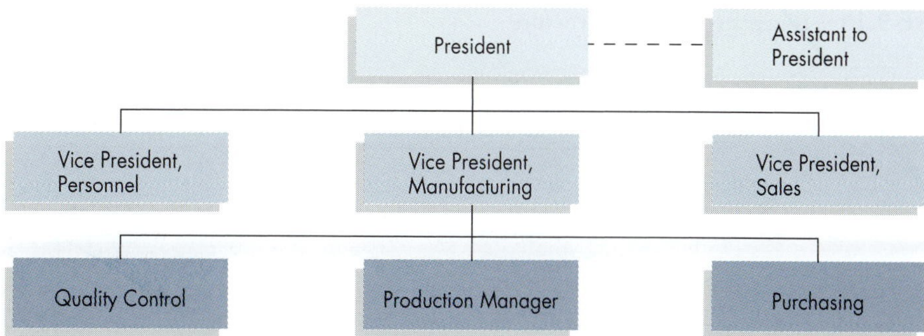

development, personnel management, employee training, and various "assistant to" positions. Figure 9.10 shows a simplified line and staff organization structure.

Line and Staff Conflict

The line and staff organization allows much more specialization and flexibility than does the simple line organization; however, it sometimes creates conflict. Some staff specialists resent the fact that they may be only advisers to line personnel and have no real authority over the line. At the same time, line managers, knowing they have final responsibility for the product, are often reluctant to listen to staff advice. Many staff specialists think they should not be in a position of having to sell their ideas to the line. They believe the line managers should openly listen to their ideas. If the staff specialist is persistent, the line manager often resents even more that the staff "always tries to interfere and run my department." The staff specialist who does not persist often becomes discouraged because "no one ever listens."

Matrix Structure

The matrix (sometimes called *project*) form of organization is a way of forming project teams within the traditional line-staff organization. A project is "a combination of human and nonhuman resources pulled together in a temporary organization to achieve a specified purpose."[16] The marketing of a new product and the construction of a new building are examples of projects. Because projects have a temporary life, a method of managing and organizing them was sought so that the existing organization structure would not be totally disrupted and would maintain some efficiency.

matrix structure
Hybrid organization structure in which individuals from different functional areas are assigned to work on a specific project or task.

Under the **matrix structure,** those working on a project are officially assigned to the project and to their original or base departments. A manager is given the authority and responsibility to meet the project objectives in terms of cost, quality, quantity, and time of completion. The project manager is then assigned the necessary personnel from the functional departments of the parent organization. Thus, a horizontal-line organization develops for the project within the parent vertical-line structure. Under such a system, the functional personnel are assigned to and evaluated by the project manager while they work on the project. When the project or their individual work on it is done, the functional personnel return to their departments or begin a new project, perhaps with a new project team. Figure 9.11 shows a matrix structure.

A major advantage of matrix structure is that the mix of people and resources can readily be changed as the project needs change. Other advantages include the emphasis placed on the project by use of a project team and the relative ease with which project members can move back into the functional organization once the project has ended. In addition, employees are challenged constantly, and interdepartmental cooperation develops along with expanded managerial talent due to the multitude of roles the project manager must undertake. Management Illustration 9.2 describes why Unilever has recently implemented a matrix structure.

FIGURE 9.11 **Illustrative Matrix Structure**

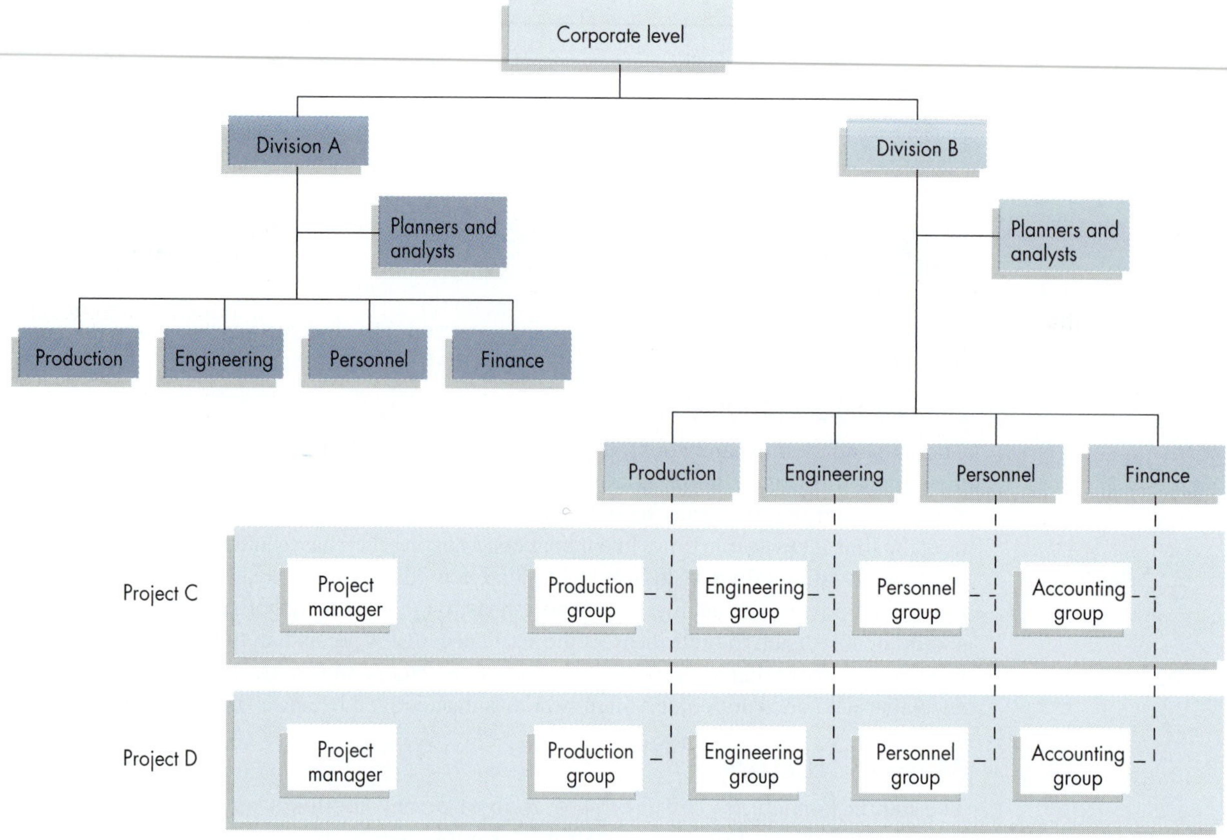

Source: From David Cleland and William King, *Systems Analysis and Project Management,* 3rd Edition, 1983. Reproduced with permission of The McGraw-Hill Companies.

One serious problem with the matrix structure is that it can violate the principle of unity of command. A role conflict can develop if the authority of the project manager is not clearly delineated from that of the functional managers. In such a case, the people assigned to the project may receive conflicting assignments from the project manager and their functional managers. A second problem occurs when the personnel assigned to a project are still evaluated by their functional manager, who usually has little opportunity to observe their work on the project. Third, they defy tradition, and put undue stress on communication networks.

Horizontal Structure

horizontal structure Consists of two groups. One group is composed of senior management who are responsible for strategic decisions and policies. The second group is composed of empowered employees working together in different process teams.

A relatively new type of structure is the **horizontal structure** (also called *team structure*). The pure form of a horizontal structure consists of two core groups. One group is composed of senior management who are responsible for strategic decisions and policies. The second group is composed of empowered employees working together in different process teams. Figure 9.12 illustrates a basic horizontal structure. Characteristics of a horizontal organization include the following:

1. The organization is built around three to five core processes, such as developing new products, with specific performance goals assigned. Each process has an owner or champion.
2. The hierarchy is flattened to reduce supervision.

Management Illustration 9.2

A NEW MATRIX STRUCTURE AT UNILEVER

Patrick Cescau became CEO of Unilever in September 2004. Unilever is one of Great Britain's largest consumer products companies with over 400 brands of products ranging from Dove soap to Ben and Jerry's ice cream. Profit before tax, which had been weak for some time, declined 36 percent for the full year of 2004.

Cescau believed that a dissonance between strategy and implementation is at the heart of Unilever's problems. In early 2005, Cescau stated, "Today we have an organization that is not sufficiently differentiating the roles of those who create the mix, prepare advertising and shape marketing, and those who execute in the market. As a result, we are too slow in rolling out big ideas; we spend too much time in discussion."

In an effort to overcome these problems, Cescau announced a new matrix structure for the company. The new matrix structure reduces the number of senior executives from 26 to 7 and hopefully will speed up Unilever's reaction to its markets. According to Cescau, 2005 will be "the year that we put the consumer back at the top of our agenda."

In November 2007, Unilever announced its third consecutive quarter of profit margin improvement, indicating that Cescau's restructuring efforts are producing results. Unilever stressed that all product categories, with the exception of ice cream, were showing sales and profit growth.

Sources: "Merely Splitting Hairs," *Marketing Week,* February 17, 2005; and Jenny Wiggins, "Unilever Gains as Recovery Continues," *Financial Times,* November 2, 2007, p. 19.

FIGURE 9.12
Horizontal Structure

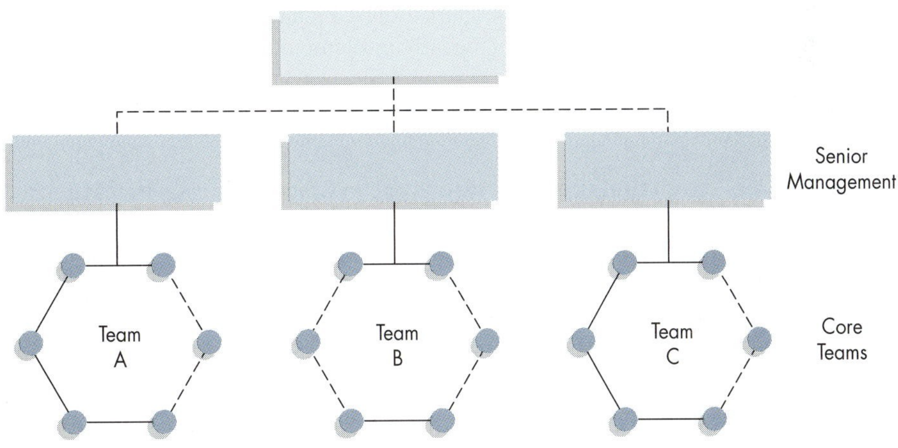

3. Teams manage everything, including themselves. They're held accountable for performance goals.
4. Customers, not stock appreciation or profitability, drive performance.
5. Team performance, not just the individual, is rewarded. Staffers are encouraged to develop multiple skills and are rewarded for it.
6. Customer contact is maximized with employees.
7. Emphasis is on informing and training all employees. "Don't just spoon-feed information on a 'need to know' basis."[17]

As suggested above, the horizontal organization emphasizes customer satisfaction, rather than focusing on financial or functional goals. Information is processed at the local level by process teams. Local problems can often be resolved quickly by the process team, thus permitting the organization to operate with flexibility and responsiveness.[18]

Additional advantages of the horizontal organization include increased efficiency, improved work culture and morale, and more satisfied customers. Kraft Foods, Ford Motor Company, General Electric, British Airways, AT&T, Motorola, Saab, Tesco, and American

Management Illustration 9.3

HORIZONTAL STRUCTURE IMPLEMENTED BY LONDON STOCK EXCHANGE

Some European stock exchanges operate "vertical silos" which incorporate a trading platform and post-trading services of clearing and settlement of trades. Silos such as these have been criticized as impeding competition because customers who choose lower-cost platforms find themselves faced with much higher costs for post-trading services. Europe's largest investment banks, who are the exchanges' prime customers, argue that a lack of competition created by these silos results in unnecessarily high exchange tariffs and post-trading costs.

In 2006, under pressure from investment banks, the European Commission issued a new code of conduct on interoperability among the different European stock exchanges. The code is aimed at forcing each exchange, clearing house, and settlement system to connect electronically with each other. Although all parties have agreed in principle to the code, there has been widespread skepticism about its actual implementation.

As a result of all the changes in the environment, the London Stock Exchange has vowed to pursue a "horizontal" structure in which it will own no post-trade services. Clearnet, Europe's largest clearing organization, is now the sole clearer for the London Stock Exchange.

Source: Norma Cohen, "LCH. Clearnet Launches Appeal for Bourses," *Financial Times,* August 10, 2007, p. 16.

Express Financial Advisors have all made efforts to implement a horizontal structure in at least a part of their organizations. Management Illustration 9.3 discusses why the London Stock Exchange has recently implemented a horizontal structure.

THE VIRTUAL ORGANIZATION

virtual organization
Temporary network of independent companies—suppliers, customers, and even rivals—linked by information technology to share skills, costs, and access to one another's markets.

A **virtual organization** is one in which business partners and teams work together across geographical or organizational boundaries by means of information technology.[19] In a virtual organization, co-workers often do not see each other on a regular basis. Three common types of virtual organizations have been identified.[20] One type exists when a group of skilled individuals form a company by communicating via computer, phone, fax, and videoconference. A second type occurs when a group of companies, each of which specializes in a certain function such as manufacturing or marketing, partner together. A third type occurs when one large company outsources many of its operations by using modern technology to transmit information to its partner companies so that it can focus on its specialty.

Virtual organizations create a network of collaborators that come together to pursue a specific opportunity. Once the opportunity has been realized, the collaborators usually disband and form new alliances to pursue new opportunities. Thus, virtual organizations are fluid, flexible, and constantly changing. Figure 9.13 illustrates a basic type of virtual organization.

FIGURE 9.13
Virtual Organization

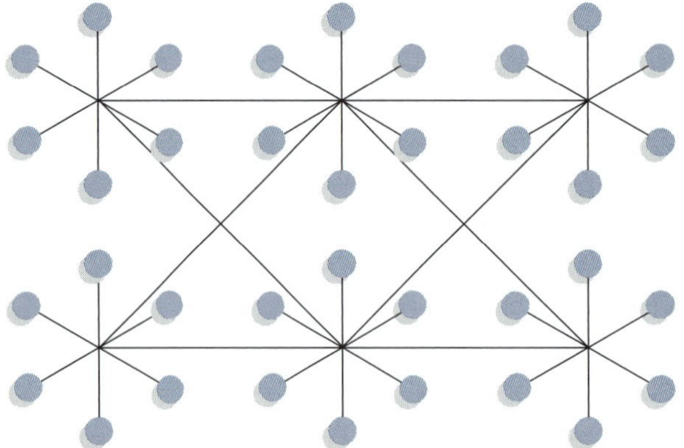

Suntech Data Systems is an intellectual processes outsourcing company and is also a virtual organization with headquarters in India, liasion offices in California and New Jersey, and clients around the globe. Suntech Data Systems, India Pvt., Ltd., is an intellectual processes outsourcing company based in Bangalore, India. It is also a virtual organization with affiliate offices in Boulder City, CO, and Phoenix, AZ. Suntech provides services to clients from around the world.

Technology plays a central role in allowing virtual organizations to form. Integrated computer and communication technology are the means by which the different collaborators are put together. To illustrate one example of how a virtual organization might work, suppose you head a large company.[21] It's Christmas season, and your company needs an additional 100 customer service representatives. Once the Christmas rush is over, these additional service representatives won't be needed, so it makes no sense to hire permanent employees. Instead, you hire 100 people who work at home and have their own computers. The physical locations of these *virtual employees* doesn't matter; they can be in Cleveland, Hong Kong, or Singapore. The virtual employees dial into the company's database and become an extension of the company. Whenever a customer calls in, all information about that customer appears on the computer screen of the virtual employee handling the call; hence, the widely scattered employees can operate as if they are all at the same location. Once the Christmas rush is over, the collaboration is dissolved.

As outlined in Figure 9.14, virtual organizations have many potential benefits and challenges. Many people believe that some form of virtual organization is the wave of the future. Management Illustration 9.4 describes one virtual organization and how it has created a virtual convention for its customers.

TRENDS IN ORGANIZATION STRUCTURE

flat structure
Organization with few levels and relatively large spans of management at each level.

tall structure
Organization with many levels and relatively small spans of management.

Several trends in organization structures have emerged over the last several decades. Beginning in the 1950s and 1960s, much attention was focused on the virtues of flat versus tall organization structures. A **flat structure** has relatively few levels and relatively large spans of management at each level; a **tall structure** has many levels and relatively small spans of management (see Figure 9.15). A classic study in this area was conducted by James Worthy.[22] Worthy studied the morale of over 100,000 employees at Sears, Roebuck during a 12-year period. His study noted that organizations with fewer levels and wider spans of management offered the potential for greater job satisfaction. A wide span of management also forced managers to delegate authority and develop more direct links of communication—another plus. On the other hand, Rocco Carzo and John Yanouzas found

FIGURE 9.14
Benefits and Challenges of Transitioning to a Virtual Organization

Sources: Maggie Biggs, "Tomorrow's Workforce," *Infoworld,* September 18, 2000, p. 59; and Sonny Ariss, Nick Nykodym, and Aimee A. Cole-Laramore, "Trust and Technology in the Virtual Organization," *S.A.M. Advanced Management Journal,* Autumn 2002, pp. 22–25.

Benefits	Challenges
Increases productivity.	Leaders must move from a control model to a trust method.
Decreases the cost of doing business.	New forms of communication and collaboration will be required.
Provides the ability to hire the best talent regardless of location.	Management must enable a learning culture and be willing to change.
Allows you to quickly solve problems by forming dynamic teams.	Staff reeducation may be required.
Allows you to more easily leverage both static and dynamic staff.	It can be difficult to monitor employee behavior.
Improves the work environment.	
Provides better balance for professional and personal lives.	
Provides competitive advantage.	

Management Illustration 9.4

VIRTUAL ORGANIZATION CREATES VIRTUAL CONVENTION

The Real Estate Cyberspace Society was founded in 1996 in Boston as a completely virtual organization. The for-profit society developed a system for delivering audiotapes and newsletters to help real estate professionals who were interested in using technology and the Internet to improve their businesses. After September 11, 2001, the Society's staff accurately predicted that member and exhibitor participation would decline at traditional in-person events. Leveraging its online experiences, the Society's leaders decided to produce an online convention in April 2002. The event was highly successful with some 22,000 real-estate professionals attending across five days. The attendees registered for the convention, listened to speakers, networked, and visited exhibitor booths—all online.

In April 2004, the convention was extended from five to seven days and 42,000 real estate professionals attended. During the seven days of the convention, participants could go to the exposition and view the exhibits at any time and have live chats with exhibitors. The conventions in 2005, 2006, and 2007 all drew over 40,000 attendees. The 2008 convention will be in an all new 3-D virtual convention center that is extremely immersive. The new center features a networking lounge that includes an array of discussion rooms at selected Expo Booths and a 24-hour "ticker tape" featuring special announcements regarding events and special drawings.

Sources: John M. Peckham III, "Virtual Society, Virtual Convention," *Association Management,* December 2004, p. 55; and "All New 3-D National Real Estate Cyber Convention & Exposition—February 11–17 in CyberSpace," Press Release, January 2008, accessed on January 21, 2008 @ http://www.recyber.com.

FIGURE 9.15
Flat versus Tall Structures

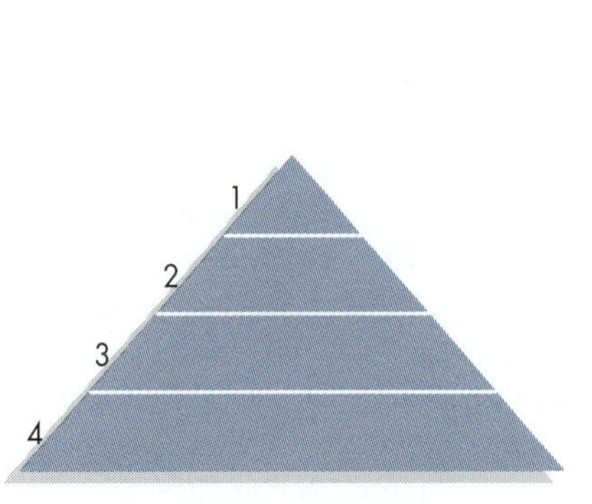

Span of management 8:1
Four levels
Flat structure

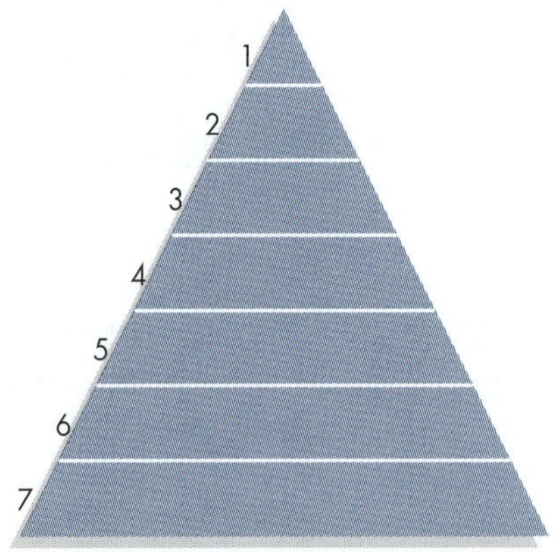

Span of management 5:1
Seven levels
Tall structure

that groups operating in a tall structure had significantly better performance than those operating in a flat structure.[23] Other studies have also shown conflicting results. Therefore, one cannot conclude that all flat structures are better than all tall structures, or vice versa.[24]

In general, Japanese organizations historically have had fewer middle managers and flatter structures than American organizations. For example, Toyota has historically had many fewer levels of management than has General Motors, Ford, or Chrysler. However, over the past 20 years many American organizations have experienced downsizing that has resulted in flatter structures with wider spans of control. Beginning in the early 1980s with the publication of the best-selling book *In Search of Excellence* by Thomas Peters and Robert Waterman, emphasis has shifted to the concept of a simple form and a lean staff. Historically, as organizations grow and experience success, they tend to evolve into increasingly complex structures. How this occurs varies; frequently, a major cause is an increase in staff positions, especially at high levels. Many managers seem to feel a need for more staff and a more complex structure as the organization grows. They seem inclined to equate staff size with success.

In their study, Peters and Waterman found that many of the best-performing companies had maintained simple structures with small staffs.[25] One reason is that a simple form with a lean staff allows an organization to adjust more rapidly to a fast-changing environment. It is also conducive to innovation. A simple form and a lean staff are naturally intertwined in that one breeds the other: A simple form requires fewer staff, and a lean staff results in a simple form.

More recently, many organizations have abandoned the more traditional line and staff structures in favor of horizontal structures and virtual organizations. All indications are that these trends will continue. As more and more employees become empowered, companies will put increased emphasis on managing through teams. Similarly, as communications technology continues to improve, many companies will evolve into virtual organizations.

COMMITTEES

committee
Organization structure in which a group of people are formally appointed, organized, and superimposed on the line, line and staff, or matrix structure to consider or decide certain matters.

Committees represent an important part of most traditional organization structures. A **committee** is a group of people formally appointed and organized to consider or decide certain matters. From a structural standpoint, committees are superimposed on the existing line, line and staff, or matrix structure. Committees can be permanent (standing) or temporary (ad hoc) and are usually in charge of, or supplementary to, the line and staff functions.

Teams are the counterpart to committees in nontraditional horizontal structures and virtual organizations. Because of their importance in today's organizations, the next chapter is devoted to understanding teams.

Using Committees Effectively

Managers can do many things to avoid the pitfalls and increase the efficiency of a committee. The first step is to define clearly its functions, scope, and authority. Obviously, the members must know the purpose of the committee to function effectively. If it is a temporary committee, the members should be informed of its expected duration. This will help avoid prolonging the life of the committee unnecessarily. Those responsible for establishing a committee should carefully communicate the limits of the committee's authority. This should be done very soon after the committee has been established.

In addition, careful thought should go into the selection of the committee members and chairperson. Size is always an important variable; generally, committees become more inefficient as they grow in size. A good rule of thumb is to use the smallest group necessary to get the job done. It is more important to select capable members than representative members when possible. It is also important to pick members from the same approximate organizational level. Members from higher levels may inhibit the actions and participation of the other members. Figure 9.16 lists several methods for selecting committee members and chairpeople and outlines advantages and disadvantages for each method.

board of directors
Carefully selected committee that reviews major policy and strategy decisions proposed by top management.

Boards of Directors

A **board of directors** is really a type of committee that is responsible for reviewing the major policy and strategy decisions proposed by top management. A board of directors can be characterized as either an inside or an outside board. On an *inside board,* a majority of the members hold management positions in the organization; on an *outside board,* a majority of the members do not hold or have not held a position with the organization. While

FIGURE 9.16
Methods of Selecting Committees

Method	Advantages/Disadvantages
Appointment of chairperson and members	Promotes sense of responsibility for all. May result in most capable members. Members may not work well together.
Appointment of chairperson who chooses members	Will probably get along well. Lack of sense of responsibility by members. May not be most capable or representative.
Appointment of members who elect chairperson	Lack of sense of responsibility by chairperson. May not choose best chairperson for the job. Election of chairperson may lead to split in the committee.
Volunteers	Will get those who have greatest interest in the outcome or those who are least busy. Lack of responsibility. Potential for splits among committee members is great.

insiders who are members of a board ordinarily have other duties related to the strategic management process by virtue of their corporate position, the role the board plays as an entity should be basically the same for both types. Board members do not necessarily need to own stock; they should be chosen primarily for what they can and will contribute to the organization.

Although most boards of directors restrict their inputs to the policy and strategy level and do not participate in the day-to-day operations of the organization, their degree of involvement varies widely from board to board. For many years, boards were used primarily as figureheads in many organizations, contributing little to the organization. However, this trend has been changing over the last several years. Lawsuits against boards of directors concerning their liabilities regarding the day-to-day operation of the organization have increased the risks of serving on boards.[26] Because of this, boards are becoming more active than they have been in the past. Moreover, some people now require liability insurance coverage before they will serve on a board of directors. An even more recent development is the tendency of shareholders to demand that the chairperson of the board be an outsider who is not employed in another capacity by the organization. Every diligent board of directors should address itself on behalf of the shareholders to this key issue: What is the standard of performance of the company's management—not what the company earned last year or this year, but what it *should* have earned?[27]

Summary

1. *Discuss the different stages an organization goes through as it grows and matures.* The first stage an organization goes through is the craft or family stage, which is characterized by the absence of formal policies, objectives, and structure. Operations at this stage generally center around one individual and one functional area. The second stage is the entrepreneurial stage, in which the organization grows first at an increasing and then at a decreasing rate. By the third stage, the entrepreneur has been replaced by a professional manager and profits are realized more from internal efficiency and less from a rapidly growing market.
2. *Explain what an organization chart is.* An organization chart uses a series of boxes connected with one or more lines to graphically represent the organization's structure.
3. *List several factors that can affect which structure is the most appropriate for a given organization.* Some of the most important variables that can affect an organization's structure are strategy, size, environment, and technology.

4. *Describe the general relationship between an organization's strategy and its structure.* Early research by Chandler reported that changes in strategy ultimately lead to changes in an organization's structure. Although subsequent research has supported the idea of some relationship between strategy and structure, it is clear that strategy is not the only variable that affects structure.
5. *Define outsourcing, and summarize its potential benefits as well as its potential drawbacks.* Outsourcing is the practice of subcontracting certain work functions to an outside entity. The potential benefits of outsourcing include allowing the organization to emphasize its core competencies; reducing operating costs; fewer personnel headaches; accessing top talent and state-of-the-art technology; and improving resource allocations. Potential drawbacks include loss of control; loss of in-house skills; and threats to the morale of employees.
6. *Describe a contingency approach to organizing.* The contingency approach to organization states that the most appropriate structure depends on many situational variables, including strategy, environment, size, technology, and employee characteristics. When taking a contingency approach, a manager should first analyze these variables and design a structure to fit the situation.
7. *Identify the different types of departmentalization.* Departmentalization refers to the grouping of activities into related work units. Departmentalization may be undertaken on the basis of work function, product, geography, customer, or time worked (shift). Hybrid departmentalization occurs when an organization simultaneously uses more than one type of departmentalization.
8. *Briefly describe each of the following types of organization structures: line structure, line and staff structure, matrix structure, horizontal structure, and virtual organization.* A line structure is the simplest organization structure; it has direct vertical links between the different organizational levels. The addition of staff specialists to a line organization creates a line and staff structure. A matrix structure is a structure in which individuals from different functional areas are assigned to work on a specific project or task. Under a matrix structure, those working on a project are officially assigned to the project and to their original or base departments. In its pure form, a horizontal structure consists of two core groups. One group is composed of senior management who are responsible for strategic decisions and policies. The second group is composed of empowered employees working together in different process teams. A virtual organization is one in which business partners and teams work together across geographical or organizational boundaries by means of information technology.
9. *Describe several trends that have taken place regarding the popularity of different types of organization structures.* Beginning in the 1950s and 1960s, much attention was focused on the virtues of flat versus tall organizations. In the early 1980s, emphasis shifted to the concept of a simple form and a lean staff. More recently, many organizations have abandoned the more traditional line and staff structures in favor of horizontal structures and virtual organizations.
10. *Describe how committees can be made more effective.* The first step is to define clearly the committee's functions, scope, and authority. The next step is to carefully review who will serve on the committee. Size and member capability are extremely important.
11. *Explain the difference between an inside and an outside board of directors.* With an inside board, a majority of the members hold management positions in the organization; with an outside board, a majority of the members do not hold or have not held a position with the organization.

Review Questions

1. Describe the different stages an organization goes through as it grows and matures.
2. What is an organization chart?
3. What several factors can affect an organization's structure?
4. Discuss the relationship between an organization's strategy and its structure.
5. Discuss the relationship between an organization's technology and its structure.
6. What is outsourcing?
7. What is the contingency approach to organizing?
8. Describe the following:
   a. Functional departmentalization
   b. Product departmentalization
   c. Geographic departmentalization
   d. Customer departmentalization
   e. Hybrid departmentalization
9. Explain the following:
   a. Line structure
   b. Line and staff structure
   c. Matrix structure
   d. Horizontal structure
   e. Virtual organization
10. What factors contribute to potential conflict between line and staff personnel in a line and staff organization?
11. What are the advantages of a flat structure? What are the advantages of a tall structure?
12. What types of organization structures have organizations moved toward in recent times?
13. How can committees be made more effective?

Skill-Building Questions

1. As a practicing manager, how could you justify the use of a matrix structure given that it potentially violates the unity of command principle?
2. Do you think the contingency approach to organizing is a useful concept that can be implemented, or is it really a cop-out?
3. Discuss this statement: When the appropriate organization structure is determined and implemented, a firm no longer has to worry about structure.
4. Recognizing that most organizations' staffs expand considerably as the organization grows, respond to the following statement: There is no way to grow and keep the corporate staff small.
5. If you were an employee and your company embarked on a large-scale outsourcing program, how do you think you would react?
6. Do you think that virtual organizations are going to become more and more prominent in the future? Why or why not?

SKILL-BUILDING EXERCISE 9.1
Applied Departmentalization

Suppose you have just been hired as the vice president in charge of sales at COMBO Enterprises, Inc. COMBO manufactures, sells, and distributes both land and water vehicles. The land vehicles are bicycles powered by a two-horsepower, two-cycle engine. Basically, you have developed a method to adapt an off-the-shelf chain saw motor to a popular French-produced bicycle. The water vehicles use the same chain saw motor adapted to a standard canoe, which is fitted with a special propeller and rudder.

The advantage over the existing competition is that, due to the light weight of the motor being used, the bicycles and canoes can also be used manually with very little loss of efficiency compared to nonmotorized bicycles and canoes. Your market surveys have shown that a large market exists for such a product.

COMBO serves both civilian and military markets for both the land and water vehicles. Presently COMBO has a plant in a medium-size eastern city and one in a medium-size western city. The eastern plant handles all business east of the Mississippi River, while the western plant handles business west of the Mississippi.

1. Design what you think would be the best way to organize the sales (marketing) division of the company.
2. Design an alternative structure for your division.
3. Why do you prefer one structure over the other?
4. Design a matrix structure for this situation (if you did not use one in question 1 or 2). What would be the pros and cons of such a structure in this situation?

SKILL-BUILDING EXERCISE 9.2

The Composition of Boards

Referring to the lists of most admired companies as identified by *Fortune* magazine (see Skill-Building Exercise 7.3, pages 151–153), go to the library or the Internet and research the board of directors for any five companies from the most admired list for 2007 and five from the most admired list for 2001. Determine how many outside directors and how many inside directors are serving each company. This information can be found in each company's annual report or in *Standard & Poor's Register of Corporations,* which is published annually.

1. Do most of these large, publicly held companies have a majority of inside or outside directors?
2. Are there any obvious differences in the composition of the boards of those companies from the 2007 list of the most admired companies as compared to those from the 2001 list?
3. Do you think the trend in large companies is toward more inside or more outside directors?

Case Incident 9.1

Who Dropped the Ball?

In October 2008, Industrial Water Treatment Company (IWT) introduced KELATE, a new product that was 10 times more effective than other treatments in controlling scale buildup in boilers. The instantaneous demand for KELATE required that IWT double its number of service engineers within the following year.

The sudden expansion caused IWT to reorganize its operations. Previously, each district office was headed by a district manager who was assisted by a chief engineer and two engineering supervisors. In 2009, this structure changed. The district manager now had a chief engineer and a manager of operations. Four engineering supervisors (now designated as group leaders) were established. They were to channel all work assignments through the manager of operations, while all engineering-related problems were to be handled by the chief engineer. Each group leader supervised 8 to 10 field service engineers (see Exhibit 1).

EXHIBIT 1 **Partial Organizational Chart for IWT**

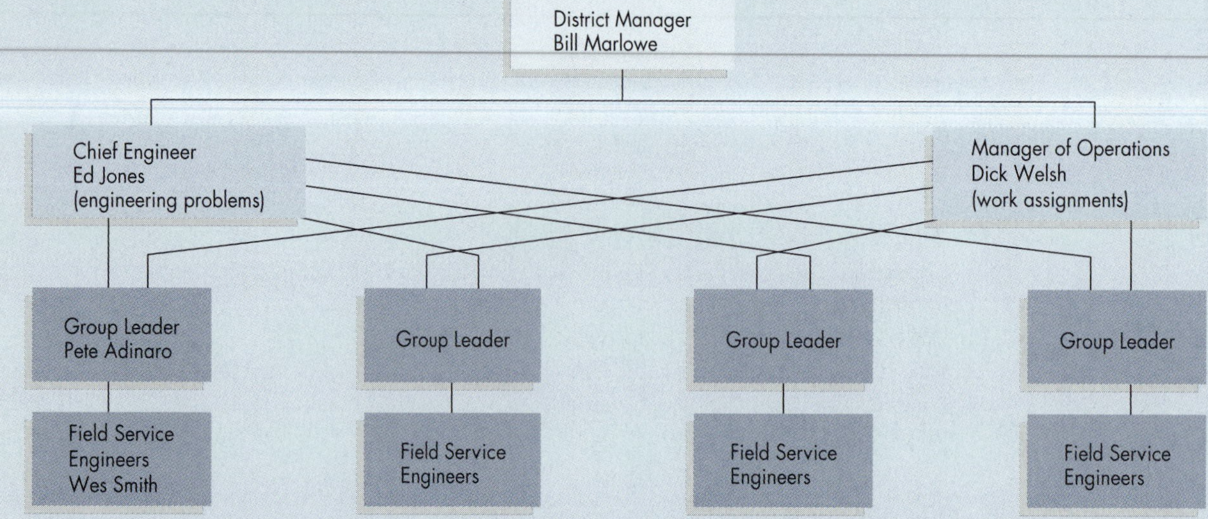

Bill Marlowe, district manager for the southeast district, has just received a letter from an old and very large customer, Sel Tex, Inc. The letter revealed that when Sel Tex inspected one of its boilers last week, it found the water treatment was not working properly. When Sel Tex officials contacted Wes Smith, IWT's service engineer for the area, they were told he was scheduled to be working in the Jacksonville area the rest of the week but would get someone else down there the next day. When no one showed up, Sel Tex officials were naturally upset; after all, they were only requesting the engineering service they had been promised.

Bill Marlowe, upset over the growing number of customer complaints that seemed to be crossing his desk in recent months, called Ed Jones, chief engineer, into his office and showed him the letter he had received from Sel Tex.

Ed: Why are you showing me this? This is a work assignment foul-up.

Bill: Do you know anything about this unsatisfactory condition?

Ed: Sure, Wes called me immediately after he found out. Their concentration of KELATE must have gone up, since they're getting corrosion and oxygen on their tubes. I told Peter Adinaro, Wes's group leader, about it, and I suggested he schedule someone to visit Sel Tex.

Bill: OK, Ed, thanks for your help. [Bill then calls Peter Adinaro into his office.] Peter, two weeks ago Ed asked you to assign someone to visit Sel Tex because of a tube corrosion problem they are having. Do you remember?

Peter: Oh, sure! As usual, Wes Smith called Ed instead of me. I left a message for Dick to assign someone there because my whole group was tied up and I couldn't spare anyone. I thought Dick would ask another group leader to assign someone to check it out.

Bill: Well, thanks for your help. Tell Dick to come on in here for a second.

Dick Welsh, manager of operations, came into Bill's office about 20 minutes later.

Bill: Dick, here's a letter from Sel Tex. Please read it and tell me what you know about the situation.

Dick: [After reading the letter] Bill, I didn't know anything about this.

Bill: I checked with Pete, Wes's group leader, and he tells me he left a message for you to assign someone since his group was all tied up. Didn't you get the message?

Dick: Have you taken a look at my desk lately? I'm flooded with messages.

Heck, I'm the greatest message handler of all times. If I could schedule my people without having all the engineering headaches unloaded on me, I wouldn't have all these messages. Sure, it's possible that he left a message, but I haven't seen it. I will look for it, though. Anyway, that letter sounds to me like they've got an engineering problem, and Ed should contact them to solve it.

Bill: I'll write Sel Tex myself and try to explain the situation to them. You and I will have to get together this afternoon and talk over some of these difficulties. See you later, Dick.

Questions

1. What problems does Bill Marlowe face?
2. Are the problems related to the way IWT is organized, or are they related to the employees?
3. How could these problems be resolved?

Case Incident 9.2

A New Organization Structure

Yesterday, Tom Andrews was officially promoted to his new job as hospital administrator for Cobb General Hospital. Cobb General is a 600-bed hospital located in a suburban area of Cincinnati. Tom is extremely excited about the promotion but at the same time has some serious doubts about it.

Tom has worked at Cobb General for three years and had previously served as the associate administrator of the hospital. Although associate administrator was his official job title, he was really more of an errand boy for the former administrator, Bill Collins. Because of Tom's educational background (which includes a master of hospital administration degree) and his enthusiasm for the hospital, Tom was offered the administrator's job last week after the hospital's board of directors had asked for Bill Collins's resignation.

Tom was now looking at the organization chart for the hospital, which had been pieced together over the years by Bill Collins (see Exhibit 2). In reality, each time a new unit had been added or a new function started, Bill merely had the person report directly to him. Tom is worried about his ability to handle all of the people currently reporting to him in his new position.

Questions

1. Do you agree with Tom's concern? Why?
2. How would you redraw the organizational chart?

EXHIBIT 2 Organization Structure—Cobb General Hospital

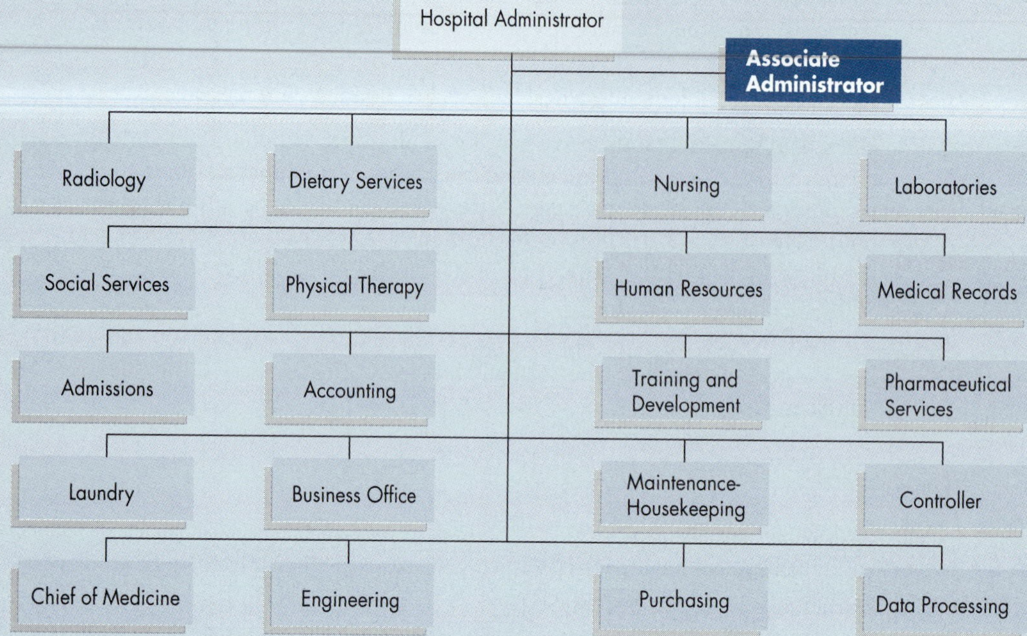

References and Additional Readings

1. Alan Filley and Robert House, *Managerial Process and Organizational Behavior* (Glenview, IL: Scott, Foresman, 1969), pp. 443–55.
2. A. D. Chandler, *Strategy and Structure* (Cambridge, MA: MIT Press, 1962).
3. Some relevant research includes J. Child, "Organization Structure, Environment, and Performance: The Role of Strategic Choice," *Sociology* 6 (1972), pp. 1–22; R. Rumelt, *Strategy, Structure, and Economic Performance* (Boston: Harvard Business School, Division of Research, 1974); and Stephen P. Robins, *Organization Theory: Structure, Design, and Application* (Englewood Cliffs, NJ: Prentice Hall, 1990).
4. Tom Burns and G. M. Stalker, *The Management of Innovation* (London: Tavistock Institute, 1962).
5. Paul Lawrence and Jay Lorsch, "Differentiation and Integration in Complex Organizations," *Administrative Science Quarterly,* June 1967, pp. 1–47; and Paul Lawrence and Jay Lorsch, *Organization and Environment* (Homewood, IL: Richard D. Irwin, 1969). Originally published in 1967 by Division of Research, Graduate School of Business Administration, Harvard University.
6. Robins, *Organization Theory.*
7. Joan Woodward, *Industrial Organization: Theory and Practice* (London: Oxford University Press, 1965).
8. Edward Harvey, "Technology and the Structure of Organizations," *American Sociological Review,* April 1968, pp. 247–59.
9. "International Association of Outsourcing Professionals Predicts Top Outsourcing Trends for 2008," *Business Wire,* December 28, 2007.
10. Jeremy Smerd, "The Philippines Vying to Become the Next India," *Workforce Management,* October 8, 2007, p. 6.
11. "Outsourcing Trends to Watch in '05," *Fortune,* March 21, 2005, pp. C1–C10.
12. Michael Corbett, "The Outsourcing Solution," *Fortune Small Business,* September 2005, p. 115.

13. Laure Edwards, "When Outsourcing Is Appropriate," *Wall Street and Technology,* July 1998, pp. 96–98; and "Outsourcing: What's In, What's Out," *Employee Benefits,* October 6, 2003, p. 39.
14. Ibid.
15. Kathleen Madigan and Michael J. Mandel, "Outsourcing Jobs: Is It Bad?" *BusinessWeek,* August 25, 2003, p. 36.
16. David Cleland and William King, *Systems Analysis and Project Management,* 3rd ed. (New York: McGraw-Hill, 1983), p. 187.
17. Cliff McGoon, "After Downsizing . . . Then What?" *Communication World,* May 1994, pp. 16–19.
18. Ronald K. Chung, "The Horizontal Organization: Breaking Down Functional Silos," *Business Credit,* May 1994, pp. 21–24; and Barbara Crawford-Cook, "Breaking Down Silos," *Canadian HR Reporter,* May 31, 2004, pp. 11–12.
19. Joyce Chutchian-Ferranti, "Virtual Corporation," *ComputerWorld,* September 1999, p. 33.
20. Ibid., p. 37.
21. This example is drawn from Sanuel E. Bleecker, "The Virtual Organization," *Futurist,* March–April 1994, p. 9.
22. James Worthy, "Organization Structure and Employee Morale," *American Sociological Review* 15 (1956), pp. 169–79.
23. Rocco Carzo, Jr., and John Yanouzas, "Effects of Flat and Tall Organization Structures," *Administrative Science Quarterly* 114 (1969), pp. 178–91.
24. Dan R. Dalton, William D. Todor, Michael J. Spendolini, Gordon J. Fielding, and Lyman W. Porter, "Organization Structure and Performance: A Critical Review," *Academy of Management Review,* January 1980, pp. 49–54.
25. Thomas J. Peters and Robert W. Waterman, Jr., *In Search of Excellence* (New York: Harper & Row, 1982), pp. 306–17.
26. Richard M. Miller, "The D&O Liability Dilemma," *Chief Executive,* November–December 1988, pp. 34–39; and Pamela W. Mason, "Portfolio D&O Insurance Can Leave Outside Directors in the Cold," *Venture Capital Journal,* October 1, 2005, p. 1.
27. Harold Geneen, *Managing* (Garden City, NY: Doubleday, 1984), p. 259.

Chapter Ten

Understanding Work Groups and Teams

Learning Objectives

After studying this chapter, you will be able to:

1. Describe formal and informal work groups.
2. Define group norms.
3. Explain group cohesiveness.
4. Define group conformity.
5. Outline the conditions under which individual members tend to conform to group norms.
6. Define groupthink.
7. Understand the concept of team building.
8. Explain idiosyncrasy credit.
9. Outline the phases in the life of teams.
10. Describe a quality circle.
11. Explain self-directed work teams.
12. Define virtual work teams.

Chapter Preview

Driving rain, pulled muscles, rescue helicopters and remote rocky slopes where very few people can hear you scream; if the Three Peaks Challenge doesn't bring colleagues closer together, nothing will. The event, where teams tried to climb Britain's three highest mountains in less than 24 hours, has become a well-established fundraiser for charities.

The aim for most of the 32 corporate teams was to raise money but, by the time they had all braved the harsh conditions, disparate groups of colleagues had become closely bonded units. They finished the first mountain in the dark, in torrential rain and everyone got soaked again on Scafell Pike in the Lake District.

Supporting slower walkers, and ensuring emergency equipment was working became essential to completing the challenge. People came to rely on each other in a way that could never occur in an office environment. One participant said, "It's changed our relationship from knowing one another to a feeling of much deeper understanding. "We've built links that will improve the way we work with each other."

From the planning stage onwards, the event encourages discussion and agreement, with people accepting responsibility for different tasks. Everyone feels accountable and sees how their individual objective fits in to the team objective.

Another participant said, "We thought we were a close-knit team before the event. Now we know."

Source: Adapted from Peter Crush, "Team Building or Time Wasting," *Human Resources,* December 2007, pp. 32–34.

Analyzing Management Skills

Why do you think climbing mountains builds teams? Is such an exercise applicable to all organizations?

Applying Management Skills

Go to the Internet and find other examples of organizations using a team-based organizational structure. What successes or failures did you find?

All organizations depend on groups to achieve success. In organizations, a group is two or more people who interact to meet a shared goal. Groups of students may organize fund-raising or social events. A shared sense of purpose sets a group apart from just a gathering of people. In general, organizations contain two kinds of groups: formal work groups and informal work groups. Work groups were introduced earlier in Chapter 8.

FORMAL WORK GROUPS

formal work group
Work group established and formally recognized by the organizing function of management.

Management establishes **formal work groups** to carry out specific tasks. Formal groups may exist for a short or long period of time. A task force is an example of a formal group. These groups have a single goal, such as resolving a problem or designing a new product.

A different type of formal work group is the *command,* or *functional,* group. This group consists of a manager and all the employees he or she supervises. Unlike a task group, the command group's work is ongoing and not confined to one issue or product.

INFORMAL WORK GROUPS

informal work group
Work group that results from personal contacts and interactions among people and is not formally recognized by the organization.

Informal work groups are formed voluntarily by members of an organization. They develop from personal contacts and interactions among people. Groups of employees who lunch together regularly and office cliques are examples of informal work groups.

A special type of informal group is the *interest group.* Its members share a purpose or concern. For example, women executives might form a group to share ideas about issues that women in management face.

Work is a social experience. Employees interact while performing job duties in offices, factories, stores, and other workplaces. Friendships emerge naturally from these contacts. Informal groups formed around mutual interests fill important social needs. In earlier centuries, groups like extended families, churches, and small towns met these needs. Today people socialize mostly with people they meet at work.

Informal work groups affect productivity, the morale of other employees, and the success of managers. They can be the result of—and can help create—a shared sense of loyalty. This is especially prevalent in high-risk occupations, such as fire fighting and police work.

Informal work groups often develop in areas where employees work close together (such as offices with cubicles) and among employees in the same field (such as accounting or graphic design). Employees may band together to share fears or complaints. In such cases, informal groups work against organization goals.

Studies have identified the power of informal work groups in organizations. The Hawthorne studies discovered that groups may set their own productivity levels and pressure workers to meet them. In one group, workers who produced more or less than the acceptable levels met with name-calling, sarcasm, ridicule, and in some cases, a blow on the arm. The Hawthorne studies concluded that informal organizations with their own social systems exist within formal organizations.

In general, management does not recognize informal groups that revolve around friendships, interests, or shared working space and tasks. Yet an understanding of these groups can improve managers' work with formal groups. Employees join informal groups to meet a social need. They often gain great satisfaction from these groups. Managers seek to duplicate this satisfaction in formal work groups.

GROUP NORMS

group norms
Informal rules a group adopts to regulate and regularize group members' behavior.

Group norms are the informal rules a group adopts to regulate the behavior of group members. They may be extremely simple—a group that lunches together may maintain a rigid seating order. They may include expectations that group members will remain loyal to each other under any circumstances. Whatever the norms, group members are expected to hold to them. Members who break the rules often are shut out.

Norms don't govern every action in a group, only those important for group survival. For instance, a working group's norms would affect its productivity levels, operating procedures, and other work-related activities. Norms may not be written down or even spoken. Rather, group members use their actions to show new members how to behave.[1]

GROUP BEHAVIOR

Think about the informal groups of friends and classmates you have belonged to at school or in your neighborhood. However they develop, informal work groups share similar types of behaviors. They include cohesiveness, conformity, and groupthink.

Group Cohesiveness

group cohesiveness
Degree of attraction each member has for the group, or the "stick-togetherness" of the group.

Group cohesiveness is the degree of attraction among group members, or how tightly knit a group is. The more cohesive a group, the more likely members are to follow group norms. A number of factors affect the cohesiveness of informal work groups—size, success, status, outside pressures, stability of membership, communication, and physical isolation.[2]

Size is a particularly important factor in group cohesiveness. The smaller the group, the more cohesive it is likely to be. A small group allows individual members to interact frequently. Members of large groups have fewer chances to interact; therefore, these groups tend to be less cohesive.

Think about how two close friends operate when they study together. Because they know each other well and talk easily, they have no trouble working together. Now imagine three new people in the study session. Everyone might not agree on the best way to cover material. It may be hard to work with different people. This might cause the study group to fall apart.

Success and status affect group cohesiveness. The more success a group experiences, the more cohesive it becomes. Several factors contribute to a group's status. For instance, highly skilled work groups tend to have more status than less-skilled groups. Like groups that meet their goals, high-status groups tend to be more cohesive than other informal work groups. These relationships are circular—success and status bring about cohesiveness, and cohesiveness brings about status and success.

Outside pressures, such as conflicts with management, can increase group cohesiveness. If a group sees management's requests as a demand or threat, it becomes more cohesive. In these situations, members may develop an "us against them" mentality.

A stable membership and easy lines of communication improve group cohesiveness. Long-standing members know each other well and are familiar with group norms. Employees who work in the same area socialize easily. In a production line, however, conversation is difficult and groups are less cohesive.

Finally, physical isolation from other employees may increase group cohesiveness. The isolation forces workers into close contact with each other and strengthens bonds.

Group Conformity

group conformity
Degree to which the members of the group accept and abide by the norms of the group.

Group conformity is the degree to which group members accept and follow group norms. A group generally seeks to control members' behavior for two reasons. First, independent behavior can cause disagreements that threaten a group's survival. Second, consistent behavior creates an atmosphere of trust that allows members to work together and socialize comfortably. Members are able to predict how others in the group will behave.

Individual members tend to conform to group norms under certain conditions:

- When group norms are similar to personal attitudes, beliefs, and behavior.
- When they do not agree with the group's norms but feel pressure to accept them.
- When the rewards for complying are valued or the sanctions imposed for noncompliance are devalued.

Group Pressure and Conformity

Researchers have studied the influence of group pressure on individual members. One study of group conformity took place at a textile firm in Virginia.[3] A textile employee began to produce more than the group norm of 50 units per day. After two weeks, the group started to pressure this worker to produce less, and she quickly dropped to the group's level. After three weeks, all the members of the group were moved to other jobs except for this worker. Once again, her production quickly climbed to double the group norm (see Figure 10.1).

FIGURE 10.1
Effect of Group Norms on a Member's Productivity

Source: Lester Coch and J. R. P. French, Jr., "Overcoming Resistance to Change," *Human Relations* (1948), pp. 519–20

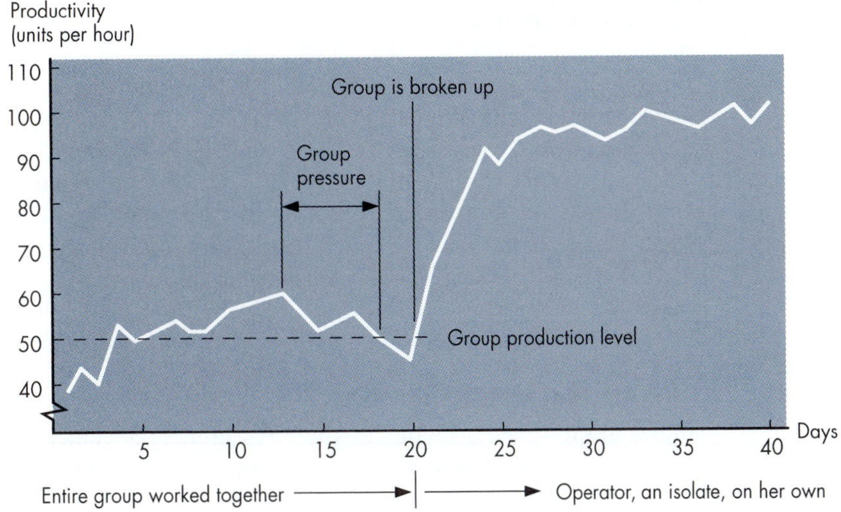

Management Illustration 10.1

MAKING WORK A MULTIPLAYER EXPERIENCE

In January 2006, Silvia Avella, communications project manager of Philips Electronics North America, and her fellow team members faced a complex challenge: According to internal company surveys, the North America region had the worst management communications ratings, and employees reported feeling neglected. The communications team needed a vehicle to solve both of these problems in one fell swoop, and it had to be innovative to the max. The solution they came up with was so outside the box that it, well, started with a box. They proposed to develop a video game to solve the issues at hand.

The basis of the game was simple: Simplicity Showdown, the name of the game, was a team-based competition that aimed to erase silos while building teamwork and camaraderie. It pitted departments across North America against each other in a collective journey to discover what "One Philips and Simplicity" was all about. Employees were tested on the company, the management agenda, and even a little bit of pop culture along the way, and managers had to take ownership of their teams' progress.

Managers were given the responsibility of going online, registering for the game and leading their team during the four-week competition. To get the managers on board in the first place, postcards were sent to their homes to get their attention when they weren't at work. The postcards highlighted the game and the prizes involved. The grand prize was a trip to the Bahamas. Then, to get the employees more engaged, they had to work in teams to play the game.

Source: Adapted from Anonymous, "Will the Real Mario Bros. Please Stand Up? Video Gaming Tech Backs PR's World," *PR News,* July 2, 2007, p. 1.

Groupthink

groupthink
Dysfunctional syndrome that cohesive groups experience that causes the group to lose its critical evaluative capabilities.

When group members lose their ability to think as individuals and conform at the expense of their good judgment, **groupthink** occurs. Members become unwilling to say anything against the group or any member, even if an action is wrong. William Golding explored the concept of groupthink in his novel *The Lord of the Flies.* This book illustrates what can happen when individuals are removed from society and are left to create their own rules.

Keeping a group together under any circumstance is a goal in itself. Groups with this goal believe that the group is indestructible and always right. Group members justify any action, stereotype outsiders as enemies of the group, and pressure unwilling members to conform. In business, groupthink is disruptive because it affects employees' ability to make logical decisions.

THE IMPORTANCE OF TEAMS

Teams play an important part in helping an organization meet its goals. Groups have more knowledge and information than individuals. They make communicating and solving problems easier. This creates a more efficient and effective company.

The importance of managing groups effectively is becoming recognized in the business world. Employees must work closely to improve production and maintain a competitive edge. Changes in the workforce are bringing men and women from different backgrounds together. Managers must work with groups to overcome cultural and gender differences. These, and other factors, make managing work groups one of management's most important tasks. Management Illustration 10.1 gives an interesting example of team building.

Influencing Work Groups

Studies at the Hawthorne plant, where researchers documented the existence of informal work groups, looked at the effects of various changes on workers' productivity.

FIGURE 10.2 Linchpin Concept

Source: From Renis Linkert, *New Patterns of Management*, 1961. Reproduced with permission of The McGraw-Hill Companies.

Researchers varied job factors, including the way workers were paid and supervised, lighting, the length of rest periods, and the number of hours worked. Productivity rose with each change.

Hawthorne effect
States that giving special attention to a group of employees (such as involving them in an experiment) changes their behavior.

This result led to the coining of the term **Hawthorne effect.** As you may remember from Chapter 2, the Hawthorne effect states that giving special attention to a group of employees changes the employees' behavior. The results of the studies show that when groups of employees are singled out for attention, they tend to work more efficiently.

Building Effective Teams

Members of informal work groups often develop a shared sense of values and group loyalty. Formal groups rarely share these qualities because they are assigned to rather than voluntary. Managers are responsible for developing shared values and group loyalty in formal work groups.

linchpin concept
Because managers are members of overlapping groups, they link formal work groups to the total organization.

The linchpin concept is one way of describing management's role in work groups. The **linchpin concept** holds that because managers are members of overlapping groups, they link formal work groups to the total organization. Managers improve communication and ensure that organizational and group goals are met. In other words, managers themselves are the linchpins (see Figure 10.2).

team building
Process by which the formal work group develops an awareness of those conditions that keep it from functioning effectively and then requires the group to eliminate those conditions.

Building effective formal work groups often is called team building. **Team building** is the process of establishing a cohesive group that works together to achieve its goals.[4] A team will be successful only if its members feel that working conditions are fair to all. A team can fail, even in a supportive organization, if a manager does not encourage fair play.

The success of a group or team can be measured in the same way as the success of organizations. Successful organizations and groups both meet their goals by using their resources well. Managers encourage teamwork by selecting group members carefully, creating a positive work environment, building trust, and increasing group cohesiveness. Figure 10.3 describes three steps to use in building productive teams. Management Illustration 10.2 shows how one company attempted to help its employees understand commitment.

Creating Groups

For a group to succeed, members must be able to perform the tasks assigned by management. Selecting the right individuals is key to the success of a group. The first step is to

Management Illustration 10.2

ROWING TOWARDS GREATER STAFF ENGAGEMENT

In 2006, engineering and electronics company Siemens announced a £3.2 million sponsorship deal with the British rowing squad to support the training and development of the Olympics team up to and including the 2012 games. From the start the deal was planned to have an employee engagement and team-building role. The most ambitious aspect of the sponsorship was the launch of the Siemens Indoor Rowing Regatta, open to all staff to enter individually, or as part of a team.

"We wanted to help teams with the notion of commitment and of being a winner," says Siemens head of talent management Teresa Frost. "We also wanted to get across the fact that, although we are 20 different businesses, we are all still part of the same organisation."

The event, using the usual type of gym rowing machines, has been an unexpected success. Regional heats in the build-up to the October final attracted more than 3,000 staff, representing more than one in seven of all, employees. This figure is comparable to the total number of UK-wide club-member rowers that enter the official annual British Indoor Rowing Championships.

"Employees really got involved, and it helped bring together staff who have never met before," said Frost. "Many of these have discovered they are working on similar projects and are sharing knowledge in a way we didn't originally expect." In rowing, performance is based on combined effort. It allows team members to provide the challenge required to improve everyone's performances. This is a great way of demonstrating some key concepts of team building.

Source: Adapted from Peter Crush, "Team Building or Time Wasting," *Human Resources*, December 2007, pp. 32–39.

FIGURE 10.3
Steps for Building Productive Teams

1. **Selecting Individuals**

   The first step in building an effective team is finding the right people. Group members need to have the right skills and the right personality fit.

2. **Building Trust**

   The second step is to build trust among group members and between the group and management.

3. **Encouraging Group Cohesiveness**

   The third step is to develop a cohesive group that conforms to group norms. Managers can improve group cohesiveness by keeping groups small, giving them clear goals, and rewarding them as a team.

identify qualified people. Then management must make the group attractive to these individuals.

For most employees, a formal work group is attractive because it increases pay and offers some satisfaction. If employees see that joining a formal group can provide them with the same satisfaction that an informal group can, they are more likely to participate willingly.

Environment also can be important to the success of a group. An important requirement for meeting group goals is a suitable place to work. How the office is laid out and other physical factors will affect the group's ability to work together successfully.

Building Trust

Trust is essential among group members and between groups and management. A successful group effort means sharing responsibilities and making decisions together. Group members must feel that the entire group is willing and able to work together successfully to achieve goals. Without trust, groups can't set or stick to production norms.

Management Illustration 10.3

THE BEST ADVICE I EVER GOT

Good advice often comes in the form of deeds, not words. The best advice I ever got came not by listening, but by observing one of my colleagues—by watching his behavior, coming to understand his philosophy, and then adapting it to my own style.

When I joined BCG as a consultant, Tom Lewis was a principal, and quickly became one of my role models, though he was only about five years my senior. On one of our earliest projects together, we worked for a high-technology client evaluating potential entry into new businesses. Tom was responsible for a remarkably mixed team: We had one person who was strong on organizational issues but incredibly weak with numbers, another who was a computer on legs—superb with analytics, much less so with anything else—and so on. Tom went about the task of turning that diverse set of individuals into a high-performing team—methodically, gradually, and quietly. Every week or so, he would engage us one-on-one to discuss how we perceived our performance, what we liked to do, what we thought would help the project go well, all in a nonthreatening way.

Source: Adapted from Daisy Wademan, "The Best Advice I Ever Got," *Harvard Business Review,* December 2007, p. 21.

Managers must have faith in their employees. They also must recognize the interests of the organization, the group, and the employees. Effective managers should become personally involved, take a real interest in group members, share information, and exhibit honesty.

Influencing Group Cohesiveness and Conformity

Think about teams you have belonged to at school or summer camp. These successful teams often are highly competitive and eager to succeed. Effective work groups share these characteristics. Both types of groups also draw their primary satisfaction from a sense of accomplishment, which comes from a job well done. Management Illustration 10.3 describes team building by one manager.

Managers can affect formal group performance levels by studying the degree of group conformity. Formal groups must be cohesive and dedicated to high performance norms in order to succeed. Managers can influence group cohesiveness by

- Keeping groups small.
- Selecting group members carefully.
- Finding a good personality fit between new and old employees.
- Developing an office layout that improves communication.
- Creating clear goals.
- Inspiring group competition.
- Rewarding groups rather than individuals.
- Isolating groups from each other.

idiosyncrasy credit
Phenomenon that occurs when certain members who have made or are making significant contributions to the group's goals are allowed to take some liberties within the group.

High individual performance with poor team performance is not what winning is about, either in sports or in business. Individuals must surrender their egos so that the end result is bigger than the sum of its parts. When this happens, the team works together like fingers on a hand.

Some members of groups will always be permitted to depart from group norms. This phenomenon is known as the idiosyncrasy credit. The **idiosyncrasy credit** occurs when individuals who have played a significant role in a group are allowed some freedom within the group. People in this position have often helped develop a group's norms. Because the

Management Illustration 10.4

QUALITY CIRCLE AT AUDI

Audi of America says its warranty claims have plunged 60 percent since 2002, a result of a companywide quality improvement program relying heavily on U.S. data. "The dollar amount reduction in warranty costs is similar to the drop in percentage of claims," says Marc Trahan, director of product quality and technical service for Audi of America.

Trahan attributes the drop in warranty costs and claims to the effectiveness of a group Audi calls its Quality Circle—about 60 people including board members and CEO Rupert Stadler who meet monthly at Audi AG headquarters in Ingolstadt, Germany. Trahan is a member representing the United States, the only market with its own seat, he says.

The United States has a seat because Audi has been paying careful attention to problems that surface here, "It was the realization we made a few years back that we could get more information from the United States than is available in other markets because of longer warranties and increased consumerism," says Trahan. "Also, the U.S. market has publications such as *Consumer Reports* and studies by J. D. Power and Associates that automakers watch closely. We have been able to apply the information worldwide," he says.

"Because of Quality Circle programs, Audi now can identify and fix problems within weeks—such as wheel alignment and power-seat defects that surfaced on the Q7 SUV when it was launched last year," says Trahan. "The problems were resolved within six weeks. I have to believe they were experiencing those problems in other markets, but we were the ones who caught it."

Source: Adapted from Diana T. Karyiko, "Audi: Quality Circle Cuts Warranty Claims 60%," *Automotive News,* May 14, 2007, p. 46.

group's norms often are the same as their own, those who could use the idiosyncrasy credit often do not.

Phases in the Life of Teams

Effective work teams go through four phases of development—forming, norming, storming, and performing. Phase one (forming) occurs when the team members first come together. Uncertainty and anxiety are common feelings that members of the team experience. Therefore, the focus of the forming phase is for members of the team to get to know each other and have their questions answered. Phase two (norming) involves developing the informal rules that the team adopts to regulate the behavior of the team members. In phase three (storming), members of the team begin to question the leadership and direction of the group. In phase four (performing), the team becomes an effective and high-performing team only if it has gone through the three previous phases.

Quality Circles

quality circle
Composed of a group of employees (usually from 5 to 15 people) who are members of a single work unit, section, or department; the basic purpose of a quality circle is to discuss quality problems and generate ideas that might help improve quality.

One type of formal work group is the quality circle. A **quality circle** is a group of employees, usually from 5 to 15 people, from a single work unit (such as a department) who share ideas on how to improve quality. The goal of a quality circle is to involve employees in decision making. Membership is almost always voluntary, and members share a common bond—they perform similar tasks. Management Illustration 10.4 describes a quality circle at Audi.

Japan has used quality circles since the early 1960s. The idea arrived in the United States after executives from Lockheed Corporation visited Japan in the 1970s and saw the circles in action. Lockheed used quality circles to improve quality and save several million dollars.

Quality circles have benefits other than increasing employee participation.[5] They encourage communication and trust among members and managers. They are an inexpensive way to provide employees with training while giving them a sense of control over their work lives. Most important, however, they may solve problems that have been around for years. Quality circles create strong lines of communication. "Me" becomes "us" in a good quality circle. A more current program on quality called a *six sigma* program is discussed in Chapter 20.

Self-Directed Work Teams

self-directed work teams (SDWT) Teams in which members are empowered to control the work they do without a formal supervisor.

Another type of formal work group is the **self-directed work team (SDWT).** SDWTs are empowered to control the work they do without a formal supervisor. Each SDWT has a leader who normally comes from the employees on the team. Most of these teams plan and schedule their work, make operational and personnel decisions, solve problems, set priorities, determine what employee does what work, and share leadership responsibilities. The positive and negative aspects of team decision making are discussed in more detail in Chapter 4.

Virtual Work Teams

virtual work teams Teams which mainly use technology-supported communication, with team members working and living in different locations.

Virtual work teams were largely nonexistent a decade ago. Today, globalization, technology, and fast responses to customer needs have led organizations to establish virtual work teams. Virtual work teams are responsible for making or implementing important decisions for the business, mainly using technology-supported communication, with the team members working and living in different locations. It is likely that this form of work team over time will be more widely used.

GROUPS AND LEADERS

When an informal group selects a leader, members choose the person most capable of satisfying the group's needs. The group gives the leader authority and can take this authority away at any time. This leader needs strong communication skills, especially in setting objectives for the group, giving directions, and summarizing information.

To see how informal groups choose leaders, imagine a group of people shipwrecked on an island. The group's first goal is to find food, water, and shelter. The individual best equipped to help the group survive would naturally become the leader. Later, the group's goal might change to getting off the island. The original leader may no longer be the best person to help meet this new goal, and a new leader could emerge. The process may continue through several leaders.

In an informal group, such as a group of people stranded on an island, leaders are chosen based on who could reach the newest goal. For instance, one person may be able to lead the group to find food and another may strategize how to build a shelter.

Gaining Acceptance

Managers assigned to formal work groups must work to gain acceptance as leaders. They generally do not have the same authority as leaders of informal groups. The formal authority granted by top management is no guarantee that a manager will effectively guide a group.

Think about how you respond to your teachers. You respect teachers who know their subject well, communicate information effectively, treat students with respect, and make fair judgments. Managers working with formal groups can use these same behaviors to gain the trust and respect of employees.

Managers must keep track of those changes within the organization that might affect the group. At times, they may have to modify group goals to meet new organizational goals. For example, an organization faced with strong competition may need to make decisions rapidly rather than rely on groups to come up with a solution. In these cases, managers must be ready to make immediate decisions for the group.

Encouraging Participation

Building an effective team requires a nontraditional managerial approach. In a traditional organizational structure, managers direct the employees who work for them. As part of a team, however, a manager encourages participation and shares responsibility, acting more like a coach than a manager.

One way of encouraging team spirit is to provide the group with a vision. People who organize groups to support social causes often use this approach. For example, one person may rally a community around a project such as reclaiming a vacant lot for a park. In the business world, managers can offer team members the possibility of designing a state-of-the-art product or service.

Managers lead by example. Their attitude and performance become the standard for group norms. A manager who believes that a group must listen to and support all members might create a group of top managers who share this feeling. Employees who see managers functioning within a cohesive group are more likely to work effectively in groups themselves.

Summary

1. *Describe formal and informal work groups.* Formal work groups are established by the organizing function. Their structure and membership are established and recognized by management. Informal work groups result from personal contacts and interactions of people within the organization and are not formally recognized by the organization.
2. *Define group norms.* Group norms are the informal rules a group adopts to regulate and regularize group members' behavior.
3. *Explain group cohesiveness.* Group cohesiveness refers to the degree of attraction each member has for the group, or the stick-togetherness of the group.
4. *Define group conformity.* Group conformity is the degree to which the members of a group accept and abide by the norms of the group.
5. *Outline conditions under which individual members tend to conform to group norms.* Members tend to conform to group norms when the norms are congruent with their personal attitudes, beliefs, and behavioral predispositions; when the norms are inconsistent with their personal attitudes, beliefs, or behavioral predispositions but the group exerts strong pressures to comply; and when the rewards for complying are valued or the sanctions imposed for noncompliance are devalued.
6. *Define groupthink.* Groupthink is a dysfunctional syndrome that cohesive groups experience that causes the group to lose its critical evaluative capabilities.
7. *Understand the concept of team building.* Team building is the process of establishing a cohesive group that works together to achieve its goals.
8. *Explain idiosyncrasy credit.* Idiosyncrasy credit refers to a phenomenon that occurs when certain members of a group who have made or are making significant contributions to the group's goals are allowed to take some liberties within the group.
9. *List the four phases in the life of teams.* Effective work teams go through four phases of development—forming, zooming, storming, and performing.
10. *Describe a quality circle.* A quality circle is composed of a group of employees (usually from 5 to 15 people) who are members of a single work unit, section, or

department and whose basic purpose is to discuss quality problems and generate ideas to help improve quality.

11. *Explain self-directed work teams.* SDWTs are empowered to control the work they do without a formal supervisor.
12. *Define virtual work teams.* Virtual work groups are responsible for making or implementing important decisions, using technology-supported communication, with the team members working and living in different locations.

Review Questions

1. Describe a formal work group.
2. Describe an informal work group.
3. What is the Hawthorne effect?
4. What is a group norm?
5. What is group cohesiveness?
6. What is group conformity?
7. What are some suggestions for building group cohesiveness?
8. Outline the conditions under which individual members of a group tend to conform to group norms.
9. What is idiosyncrasy credit?
10. List the four phases in the life of teams.
11. Explain the linking-pin concept.
12. What is team building?
13. What is a quality circle?
14. What is a self-directed work team?
15. Define virtual work teams.

Skill-Building Questions

1. Do you think it is possible to eliminate the need for informal work groups? Explain.
2. Discuss the following statement: The goals of informal work groups are never congruent with the goals of the formal organization.
3. Some employees are described as "marching to the beat of a different drummer." In light of the discussion in this chapter, what does this statement mean to you?
4. Cite one business example and one social example of what you perceive to be groupthink mentality.
5. Why do you think quality circles can be effective?

SKILL-BUILDING EXERCISE 10.1
PowerPoint Application on Self-Directed Work Teams

Work groups play an important role in helping an organization reach its goals. As you have learned, people working together can produce more than individuals working alone. Because groups have more knowledge and information, they can help a company become more efficient and effective.

The president of your firm has been impressed with the way you have implemented self-directed work teams in the department that you manage. He has asked that you make a brief presentation at the next quarterly meeting. This activity will involve your developing a PowerPoint presentation on self-directed work teams. You have been asked to present a description of these teams and summarize the benefits of using them.

First, develop a title slide. Then, develop at least three more slides to present your information. Use Clip Art on at least two of the slides. The examples below show various types of slides that you may want to use.

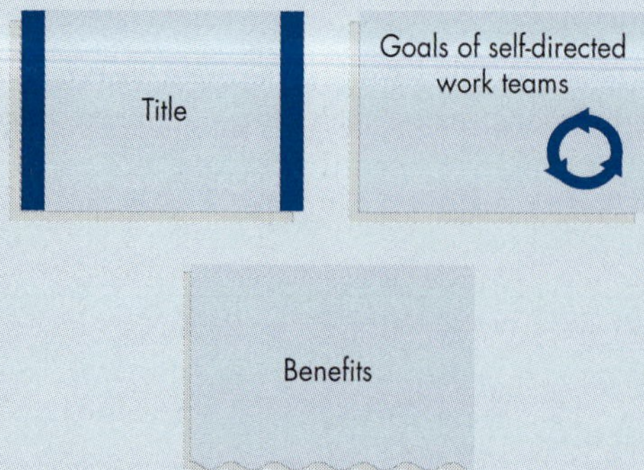

SKILL-BUILDING EXERCISE 10.2
Building a Team

The insurance company where you work is purchasing new software for the billing department. As head of the Information Technology Department, you are to lead the six-member team that will choose the new software. During the first two meetings, members of the group bickered constantly, and no one made any realistic suggestions. What can you do to make the team more effective?

In groups of five, discuss possible reasons for the group's behavior. Then discuss ways of building a more effective team that address those reasons. Prepare a presentation that describes your plan to create a more effective group.

SKILL-BUILDING EXERCISE 10.3
Characteristics of Effective Work Groups

You have been a member of many groups in your lifetime. Some of these groups include both formal and informal groups. Examples of such groups might include your Sunday school class, your neighborhood playmates when you were younger, your soccer or baseball team, and your co-workers at your summer job. Whether a formal or informal work group, all of us have been members of a group at some time. Some of the groups have been quite effective, and some have been quite ineffective.

Recall the most effective and the most ineffective groups of which you have been a member. Prepare a description of the characteristics of both groups. Be prepared to make a five-minute presentation of these characteristics in class.

SKILL-BUILDING EXERCISE 11.4
List of Questions

Darren Washington, an employee at AT&T, wants to start a volunteer tutoring program at a local school. His supervisor, Jackie, is pleased by this idea. AT&T encourages volunteerism and allows employees time to participate. Jackie wants to ensure that Darren will be an effective group leader.

Make a list of questions Jackie can ask that will help her determine whether Darren is a good candidate for team leader.

Case Incident 10.1

A Successful Baseball Manager

Bobby Cox, manager of the Atlanta Braves, has a better career winning percentage than Whitey Herzog, Sparky Anderson, Leo Durocher, and Casey Stengel. What has made Bobby Cox such a successful team manager?

Tom Glavine, pitcher for the Braves, says, "He has a knack for making people believe in the system and have pride in it, and of making people want to go out there and play hard for Bobby. . . . I've heard it from so many people who have come over from other organizations—it's just a joy to play for the guy. "

What does Bobby Cox actually do to make his players want to play hard and win for him? Players and co-workers give several reasons. First and foremost, he's a players' manager. Terry Mulholland, another Braves pitcher, says, "Bobby believes in his players. That's why you'll see, at a given moment, Keith Lockhart or Ozzie Guillen come in and get a big hit, or Eddie Perez be able to catch every game the rest of the way. Bobby has faith in everyone in this room. You can't help but want to play for Bobby Cox."

Otis Nixon, outfielder and veteran of nine other teams says, "Bobby let's you go out and play, and he'll let you use your particular abilities. He's laid back until you don't do the little things, which is when you'll see a different side of him."

Being a players' manager also means that he never criticizes a player to the press or other players or managers. "We have our confrontations," Cox says, "but they never become public because nobody knows about it."

Greg Myers, catcher and veteran of five other teams says, "Even if it's not in the paper, in other clubhouses you might get a sniff that a manager doesn't like a certain player. You don't hear that around here. Bobby pretty much treats everyone the same."

Bobby Cox also has very few rules for his players. They include: no music in the clubhouse (because everyone wants to listen to something different); sport coats are mandatory on team chartered flights; and batting practice has a uniform dress code (so we look like a unit). Pat Corrales, bench coach and former manager of three big league teams, says, "[By doing these things] it all blends. It all comes together. It's one of Bobby's things."

Finally, Bobby Cox puts his players' feelings first. "It's easy to support the players," Cox says. "They're human. I came up [with the Yankees] under Ralph Houk, and he could be as tough as they come, but he was also supportive. He was good at communicating with the guys who weren't playing; the superstars take care of themselves. I liked that style."

For example, Terry Mulholland remembers his first start with the Braves after being acquired from the Cubs. Bobby asked him if he could go another inning. "It'd been a long time since a manager left that decision up to me."

Another example of his player support is the praise he gives his players, even when they may not deserve it. "Sometimes I'll give up a bunch of hits," Tom Glavine says, "and read the next day where Bobby said I threw really well, and I'll think, 'What game was he watching?' "

Mark Bradley, sports columnist for the *Atlanta Journal-Constitution,* has this to say about Bobby Cox, which sums up his attributes as a great team manager, ". . . the managing that transpires during the games . . . is only a small part of the job. Bigger by far is the ability to choose a roster, to oversee a clubhouse, to keep a team functioning."

Questions

1. What attributes make Bobby Cox an effective team leader?
2. Do you feel that his rules are reasonable?
3. Why do players like to play for him?

Source: Glencoe: McGraw-Hill, used by permission.

Case Incident 10.2

Talkative Mike

Mike was an exceptionally friendly and talkative man—to the extent that he bothered his supervisor by frequently stopping the whole work crew to tell them a joke or a story. It didn't seem to bother Mike that it was during working hours or that somebody other than his crew might be watching. He just enjoyed telling stories and being the center of attention. The trouble was that the rest of the crew enjoyed him too.

The supervisor had just recently taken over the department, and he was determined to straighten out the crew. He thought he would have no problem motivating such a friendly person as Mike. Because the crew was on a group incentive, the supervisor believed he could get them to see how much they were losing by standing around and talking. But there was no question about it: Mike was the informal leader of the crew, and they followed him just as surely as if he were the plant manager.

Mike's crew produced extremely well. When they worked—and that was most of the time—their output could not be equaled. But the frequent nonscheduled storytelling breaks did bother the supervisor. Not only could that nonproductive time be converted to badly needed production, but they also were setting a poor example for the other crews and the rest of the department.

The supervisor called Mike in to discuss the situation. His primary emphasis was on the fact that Mike's crew could make more money by better using their idle time. Mike's contention was, "What good is money if you can't enjoy it? You sweat your whole life away to rake in money, and then all you've got to show for it is a lot of miserable years and no way of knowing how to enjoy what's left. Life's too short to spend every minute trying to make more money." The discussion ended with Mike promising the group would quiet down; if their production didn't keep up, the supervisor would let him know.

Things did improve for a while; but within a week or so, the old pattern was right back where it had been. The supervisor then arranged to talk with the other members of the crew individually. Their reactions were the same as Mike's. As before, some improvements were noted at first; then the crew gradually reverted to the old habits.

Questions

1. Do you agree with Mike and his group?
2. Does the supervisor really have a complaint in light of the fact that Mike's group produces well above average?
3. If you were the supervisor, what would you do next?

References and Additional Readings

1. David Greathatck and Timothy Clark, "Displaying Group Cohesiveness, Humour and Laughter in the Public Lectures of Management Gurus," *Human Relations,* December 2000, p. 15.
2. Lester Coch and John R. P. French, Jr., "Overcoming Resistance to Change," *Human Relations,* 1948, pp. 519–20.
3. Chris Bones, "Group-Think Doesn't Unite, It Divides," *Human Resources,* October 2005, p. 24.
4. See Paul E. Brauchle and David W. Wright, "Fourteen Team-Building Tips," *Training and Development Journal,* January 1992, pp. 32–36. Also see Mahmoud Salem, Harold Lazarus, and Joseph Cullen, "Developing Self-Managing Teams: Structure and Performance," *Journal of Management Development* 11 (1992), pp. 24–32.
5. Helene Fuhlfelder, "It's All about Improving Performance," *Quality Progress,* February 2000, pp. 49–53.

Staffing Skills

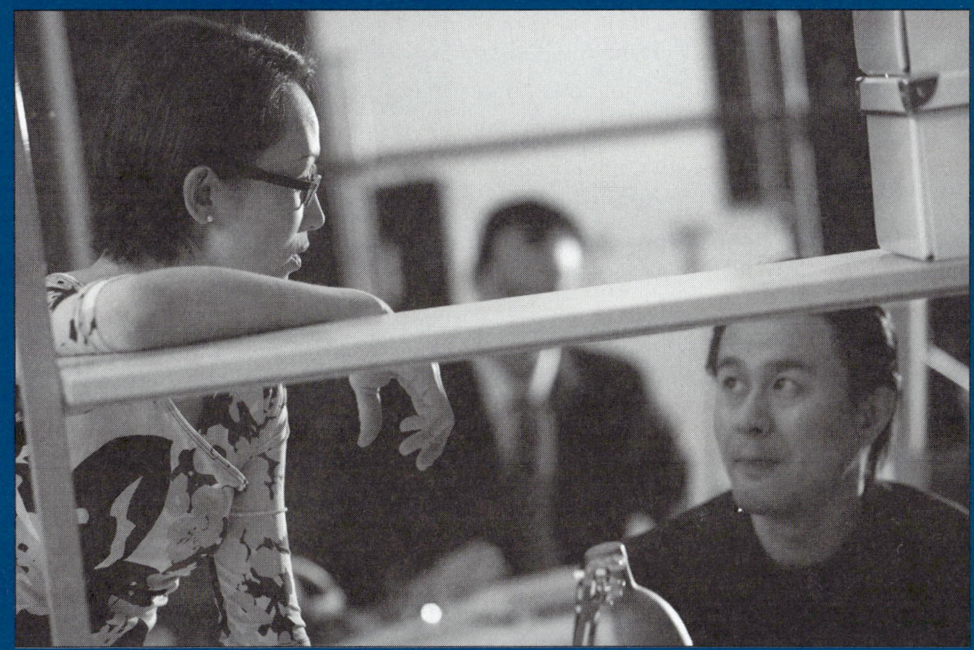

Chapter **Eleven**

Staffing

Learning Objectives

After studying this chapter, you will be able to:

1. Outline the human resource planning process.
2. Define job analysis, job description, job specification, and skills inventory.
3. Define equal employment opportunity.
4. Describe the recruitment process.
5. Define affirmative action plan.
6. Discuss reverse discrimination.
7. Define tests, test validity, and test reliability.
8. Discuss the different types of employment interviews.
9. Discuss potential problems in the interviewing process.

Chapter Preview

Offshoring information technology services is an emotive subject that incites mixed responses from most companies. Although Wall Street financial firms were among the early adopters of outsourcing, sending their back-office IT operations to offshore centers in India and other locations, the response from employees and U.S. lawmakers has been less than favorable.

Despite this, it does not appear to have stopped the major offshore IT outsourcing providers such as Infosys from reporting $1 billion-plus second-quarter revenues this year. Yet, while offshoring of IT may be here to stay, recent research commissioned by IT services company FDM and conducted by technology marketing agency Vanson Bourne indicates that companies are less than happy with the results. FDM's survey of 100 firms found that 44 percent of managers felt offshoring IT was damaging their business. Only 3 percent of managers reported encountering no problems with offshoring.

Julian Divert, chief operating officer of FDM, states as follows, "Firms that have outsourced IT resources offshore are beginning to realize that IT is not just a commodity and that you still need to have support and development." He adds that the cost benefits of offshoring have been overstated, as there are "hidden costs" associated with firms having to send managers to remote offshore locations.

Source: Adapted from Anita Hawser, "Offshoring Industry Faces New Opponents; Its Clients," *Global Finance,* November 2007, p. 6.

Analyzing Management Skills

What benefits do you think come from offshoring information technology?

Applying Management Skills

What are the hidden costs to offshoring information technology?

The staffing function of management involves securing and developing people to perform the jobs created by the organizing function. The goal of staffing is to obtain the best available people for the organization and to develop the skills and abilities of those people. Obtaining the best available people generally involves forecasting personnel requirements and recruiting and selecting new employees. Developing the skills and abilities of an organization's employees involves employee development as well as the proper use of promotions, transfers, and separations. The staffing function is complicated by numerous government regulations. Furthermore, many of these regulations are subject to frequent change.

Unfortunately, many staffing activities have traditionally been conducted by human resource departments and have been considered relatively unimportant by line managers. However, securing and developing qualified personnel should be a major concern of all managers because it involves the most valuable asset of an organization: human resources.

JOB ANALYSIS

job analysis
Process of determining, through observation and study, the pertinent information relating to the nature of a specific job.

job description
Written statement that identifies the tasks, duties, activities, and performance results required in a particular job.

job specification
Written statement that identifies the abilities, skills, traits, or attributes necessary for successful performance in a particular job.

skills inventory
Consolidates information about the organization's current human resources.

Job analysis is the process of determining, through observation and study, the pertinent information relating to the nature of a specific job. The end products of a job analysis are a job description and a job specification. A **job description** is a written statement that identifies the tasks, duties, activities, and performance results required in a particular job. The job description should be used to develop fair and comprehensive compensation and reward systems. In addition, the accuracy of the job description can help or hinder recruiters in their efforts to attract qualified applicants for positions within the company. A **job specification** is a written statement that identifies the abilities, skills, traits, or attributes necessary for successful performance in a particular job. In general, a job specification identifies the qualifications of an individual who could perform the job. Job analyses are frequently conducted by specialists from the human resource department. However, managers should have input into the final job descriptions for the jobs they are managing.

Skills Inventory

Through conducting job analysis, an organization defines its current human resource needs on the basis of existing or newly created jobs. A **skills inventory** consolidates information about the organization's current human resources. The skills inventory contains basic information about each employee of the organization, giving a comprehensive picture of the individual. Through analyzing the skills inventory, the organization can assess the current quantity and quality of its human resources.

Six broad categories of information that may be included in a skills inventory are:

1. Skills: education, job experience, training, etc.
2. Special qualifications: memberships in professional groups, special achievements, etc.
3. Salary and job history: present salary, past salary, dates of raises, various jobs held, etc.
4. Company data: benefit plan data, retirement information, seniority, etc.
5. Capacity of individual: scores on tests, health information, etc.
6. Special preferences of individual: location or job preferences, etc.

The primary advantage of a computerized skills inventory is that it offers a quick and accurate evaluation of the skills available within the organization. Combining the information provided by the job analysis and the skills inventory enables the organization to evaluate the present status of its human resources.

Specialized versions of the skills inventory can also be devised and maintained. One example would be the management inventory, which would separately evaluate the specific skills of managers such as strategy development, experiences (e.g., international experience or language skill), and successes or failures in administration or leadership.

In addition to appraising the current status of its human resources, the organization must consider anticipated changes in the current workforce due to retirements, deaths, discharges, promotions, transfers, and resignations. Certain changes in personnel can be estimated accurately and easily, whereas other changes are more difficult to forecast.

human resource planning (HRP)
Involves getting the right number of qualified people into the right jobs at the right time.

Human resource planning (HRP), also referred to as *personnel planning,* involves getting the right number of qualified people into the right jobs at the right time. Put another way, HRP involves matching the supply of people—internally (existing employees) and externally (those to be hired)—with the openings the organization expects to have for a given time frame.

HRP involves applying the basic planning process to the human resource needs of the organization. Once organizational plans are made and specific objectives set, the HRP process attempts to define the human resource needs to meet the organization's objectives.

The first basic question addressed by the planning process is: Where are we now? Human resource planning frequently answers this question by using job analysis and skills inventories.

Forecasting

human resource forecasting
Process that attempts to determine the future human resource needs of the organization in light of the organization's objectives.

The second basic question the organization addresses in the planning process is: Where do we want to go? **Human resource forecasting** attempts to answer this question with regard to the organization's human resource needs. It is a process that attempts to determine the future human resource needs of the organization in light of the organization's objectives. Some of the many variables considered in forecasting human resource needs include sales projections, skills required in potential business ventures, composition of the present workforce, technological changes, and general economic conditions. Given the critical role human resources play in attaining organizational objectives, all levels of management should be involved in the forecasting process.

Human resource forecasting is presently conducted largely on the basis of intuition; the experience and judgment of the manager are used to determine future human resource needs. This assumes all managers are aware of the future plans of the total organization. Unfortunately, this is not true in many cases.

Transition

In the final phase of human resource planning, the transition, the organization determines how it can obtain the quantity and quality of human resources it needs to meet its objectives as reflected by the human resource forecast. The human resource forecast results in a statement of what the organization's human resource needs are in light of its plans and objectives. The organization engages in several transitional activities to bring its current level of human resources in line with forecast requirements. These activities include recruiting and selecting new employees, developing current or new employees, promoting or transferring employees, laying off employees, and discharging employees. Given the current trend of downsizing in many organizations, some human resource departments now maintain a replacement chart for each employee. This confidential chart shows

FIGURE 11.1
Relationship between Job Analysis, Skills Inventory, Human Resource Planning, Recruitment, and Selection

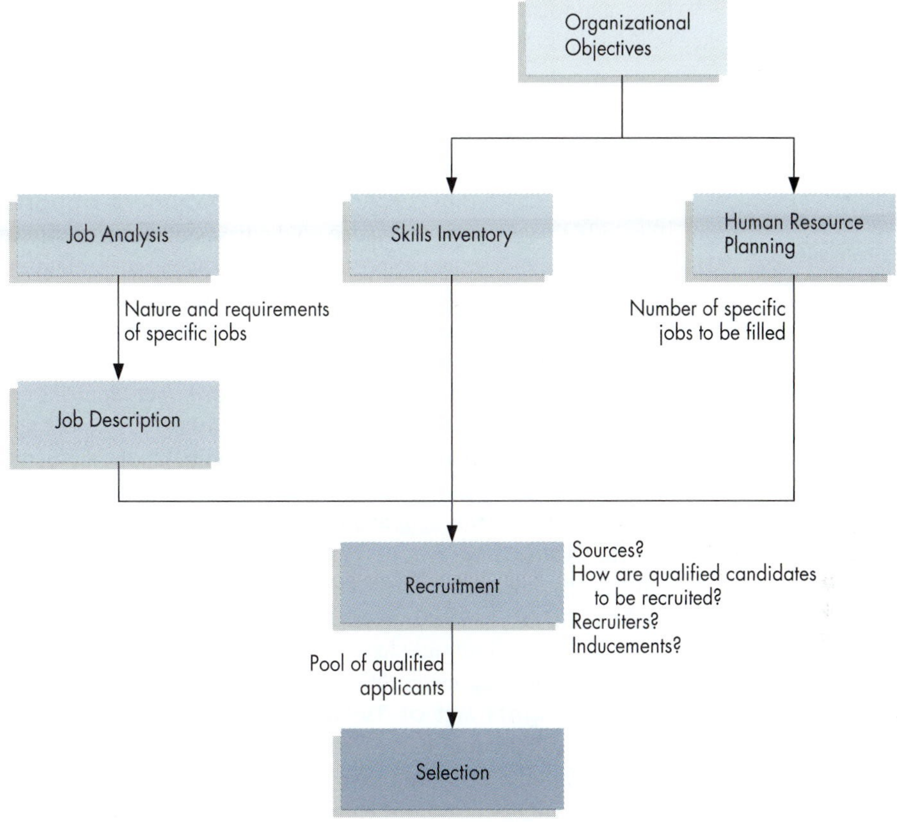

a diagram of each position in the management hierarchy and a list of candidates who would be qualified to replace a particular person should the need arise. Generally, the coordination of all the activities mentioned earlier is delegated to a human resource or personnel department within the organization. Figure 11.1 shows the relationship between job analysis, skills inventory, and human resource planning.

Equal Pay Act of 1963
Prohibits wage discrimination on the basis of sex.

Title VII of the Civil Rights Act of 1964
Designed to eliminate employment discrimination related to race, color, religion, sex, or national origin in organizations that conduct interstate commerce.

equal employment opportunity
The right of all people to work and to advance on the bases of merit, ability, and potential.

Legal Considerations

Due to discriminatory personnel practices by many organizations, government regulation now plays a vital role in human resource planning. The following paragraphs describe the significant government bills and laws that have affected human resource planning.

The **Equal Pay Act of 1963,** which became effective in June 1964, prohibits wage discrimination on the basis of sex. The law states,

> No employer . . . shall . . . discriminate . . . between employees on the basis of sex by paying wages . . . at a rate less than the rate at which he pays wages to employees of the opposite sex . . . for equal work on jobs the performance of which requires equal skill, effort, and responsibility and which are performed under similar working conditions.[1]

Title VII of the Civil Rights Act of 1964 is designed to eliminate employment discrimination related to race, color, religion, sex, or national origin in organizations that conduct interstate commerce. The act as amended covers the following types of organizations:

1. All private employers of 15 or more employees.
2. All educational institutions, public and private.

Age Discrimination in Employment Act
Passed in 1968, initially designed to protect individuals ages 40 to 65 from discrimination in hiring, retention, and other conditions of employment. Amended in 1978 to include individuals up to age 70. Specifically, forbids mandatory retirement at 65 except in certain circumstances.

Rehabilitation Act of 1973
Prohibits discrimination in hiring of persons with disabilities by federal agencies and federal contractors.

Americans with Disabilities Act (ADA) of 1990
Gives individuals with disabilities sharply increased access to services and jobs.

Civil Rights Act of 1991
Permits women, persons with disabilities, and persons who are religious minorities to have a jury trial and sue for punitive damages if they can prove intentional hiring and workplace discrimination. Also requires companies to provide evidence that the business practice that led to the discrimination was not discriminatory but was related to the performance of the job in question and consistent with business necessity.

Family and Medical Leave Act (FMLA)
Enables qualified employees to take prolonged unpaid leave for family- and health-related reasons without fear of losing their jobs.

3. State and local governments.
4. Public and private employment agencies.
5. Labor unions with 15 or more members.
6. Joint labor-management committees for apprenticeship and training.

Congress passed the Civil Rights Act to establish guidelines for ensuring equal employment opportunities for all people. **Equal employment opportunity** refers to the right of all people to work and to advance on the bases of merit, ability, and potential. One major focus of equal employment opportunity efforts has been to identify and eliminate discriminatory employment practices. Such practices are any artificial, arbitrary, and unnecessary barriers to employment when the barriers operate to discriminate on the basis of sex, race, or another impermissible classification.

The **Age Discrimination in Employment Act** went into effect on June 12, 1968. Initially it was designed to protect individuals 40 to 65 years of age from discrimination in hiring, retention, compensation, and other conditions of employment. In 1978, the act was amended and coverage was extended to individuals up to age 70. Specifically, the act now forbids mandatory retirement at age 65 except in certain circumstances.

The **Rehabilitation Act of 1973** prohibits discrimination in hiring of individuals with disabilities by federal agencies and federal contractors. The **Americans with Disabilities Act (ADA) of 1990** gives individuals with disabilities sharply increased access to services and jobs. Both acts have given citizens with disabilities protection in the workplace and increased opportunities to compete for jobs.

The **Civil Rights Act of 1991** permits women, minorities, persons with disabilities, and persons who are religious minorities to have a jury trial and sue for punitive damages of up to $300,000 if they can prove they are victims of intentional hiring or workplace discrimination. The law covers all employers with 15 or more employees. Prior to the passage of this law, jury trials and punitive damages were not permitted except in intentional discrimination lawsuits involving racial discrimination. The law places a cap on the amount of damages a victim of nonracial, intentional discrimination can collect. The cap is based on the size of the employer.

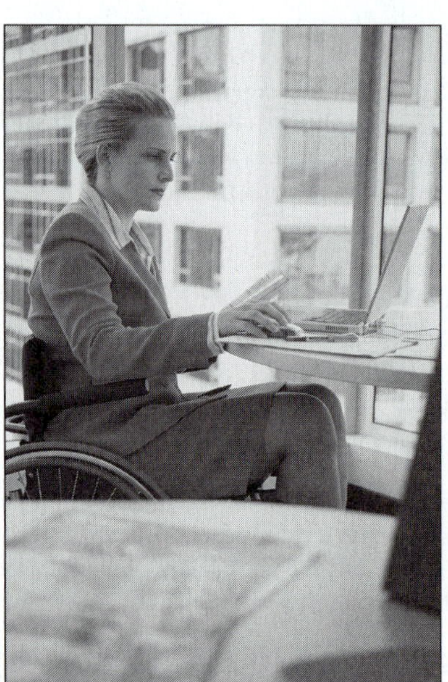

The Americans with Disabilities Act gives individuals with disabilities protection in the workplace and increased opportunities to compete for jobs.

A second aspect of this act concerned the burden of proof for companies with regard to intentional discrimination lawsuits. In a series of Supreme Court decisions beginning in 1989, the Court began to ease the burden-of-proof requirements on companies. This act, however, requires that companies provide evidence that the business practice that led to the discrimination was not discriminatory but was related to the performance of the job in question and consistent with business necessity.

The **Family and Medical Leave Act (FMLA)** was enacted in 1993 to enable qualified employees to take prolonged unpaid leave for family- and health-related reasons without fear of losing their jobs. Under the law, employees can use this leave if they are seriously ill, if an immediate family member is ill, or in the event of the birth, adoption, or placement for foster care of a child.

The results of discrimination are not always as obvious as hiring and firing practices. Communication, managerial and promotional career paths, and networking that are essential to employees' success in the workplace also can be affected by indirect discrimination.

Figure 11.2 summarizes the laws related to equal employment opportunity.

FIGURE 11.2 **Summary of Equal Opportunity Laws**

Law	Year	Intent	Coverage
Equal Pay Act	1963	Prohibits sexual-based discrimination in rates of pay for men and women working in the same or similar jobs.	Private employers engaged in commerce or in the production of goods for commerce and with two or more employees; labor organizations.
Title VII, Civil Rights Act (as amended in 1972)	1964	Prohibits discrimination based on race, sex, color, religion, or national origin.	Private employers with 15 or more employees for 20 or more weeks per year, educational institutions, state and local governments, employment agencies, labor unions, and joint labor–management committees.
Age Discrimination in Employment Act (ADEA)	1967	Prohibits discrimination against individuals who are 40 years of age and older.	Private employers with 20 or more employees for 20 or more weeks per year, labor organizations, employment agencies, state and local governments, and federal agencies with some exceptions.
Rehabilitation Act (as amended)	1973	Prohibits discrimination against persons with disabilities and requires affirmative action to provide employment opportunity for these individuals.	Federal contractors and subcontractors with contracts in excess of $2,500, organizations receiving federal financial assistance, federal agencies.
Vietnam-Era Veterans Readjustment Assistance Act	1974	Prohibits discrimination in hiring disabled veterans with 30 percent or more disability rating, veterans discharged or released for a service-connected disability, and veterans on active duty between August 5, 1964, and May 7, 1975. Also requires written affirmative action plans for certain employers.	Federal contractors and subcontractors with contracts in excess of $10,000. Employers with 50 or more employees and contracts in excess of $50,000 must have written affirmative action plans.
Pregnancy Discrimination Act (PDA)	1978	Requires employers to treat pregnancy just like any other medical condition with regard to fringe benefits and leave policies.	Same as Title VII, Civil Rights Act.
Immigration Reform and Control Act	1986	Prohibits hiring of illegal aliens.	Any individual or company.
Americans with Disabilities Act	1990	Increases access to services and jobs for persons with disabilities.	Private employers with 15 or more employees.
Civil Rights Act	1991	Permits women, minorities, persons with disabilities, and persons who are religious minorities to have a jury trial and to sue for punitive damages if they can prove intentional hiring and workplace discrimination. Also requires companies to provide evidence that the business practice that led to the discrimination was not discriminatory but was related to the position in question and consistent with business necessity.	Private employers with 15 or more employees.
Family and Medical Leave Act (FMLA)	1993	Enables qualified employees to take prolonged unpaid leave for family- and health-related reasons without fear of losing their jobs.	Private employers with 15 or more employees.

Management Illustration 11.1

RECRUITMENT AT THE UNIVERSITY OF MICHIGAN

The warmth and informal vibe at times felt closer to a house party than a business conference this weekend at the annual conference sponsored by black business students at the University of Michigan—though anyone looking for a job came sharply dressed. In its 32nd year, the event came against the backdrop of race being outlawed by voters in November 2006 as a consideration in school admission or hiring in the public sector. But the four-day conference and dozens of other events like it across the country show how committed corporations remain to diversity. The Black Business Students Association conference featured nearly two dozen sponsors who invested thousands of dollars, plus numerous senior faculty and administrators, and some 300 current and prospective students.

Companies as global—and disparate—as JPMorgan Chase financial services and Miller Brewing Co. sponsored receptions with food and open bars. Representatives spoke on the importance of drawing people in of all backgrounds at workshops and lectures meant not just to impress but arguably to empower.

While the federal government and some states including Michigan have scaled back race-specific measures aimed at leveling the playing field, corporations have plowed forward full force, partly because diversity is believed to make them more marketable and attractive to both customers and those in the workforce.

Source: Adapted from Alex P. Kellogg, "U-M. Students, Firms Come Together to Boost Diversity," *McClatchy-Tribune Business News*, January 28, 2008, Wire Feed.

Peter Principle
Tendency of individuals in a hierarchy to rise to their levels of incompetence.

With respect to internal promotions, one interesting proposition is the so-called Peter Principle. Proposed by Laurence J. Peter, the **Peter Principle** states that in a hierarchy such as a modern organization, individuals tend to rise to their levels of incompetence.[2] In other words, people routinely get promoted in organizations and ultimately reach a level at which they are unable to perform. Organizations that maintain tight control in the human resource area, adhere to skills inventories, and conduct careful job analyses can minimize this effect.

RECRUITMENT

recruitment
Seeking and attracting a supply of people from which qualified candidates for job vacancies can be selected.

Recruitment involves seeking and attracting a supply of people from which qualified candidates for job vacancies can be selected. The amount of recruitment an organization must do is determined by the difference between the forecasted human resource needs and the talent available within the organization. After the decision to recruit has been made, the sources of supply must be explored. Management Illustration 11.1 explains an approach used by companies in recruiting black business students at the University of Michigan.

An organization that has been doing an effective job of recruiting employees has one of the best sources of supply for filling job openings: its own employees. Promotion from within is very popular with growing and dynamic organizations. If internal sources prove to be inadequate, external sources are always available. Though usually more costly and time consuming to pursue, external sources such as employment agencies, consulting firms, employee referrals, and employment advertisements can be valuable resources for an organization. Figure 11.3 summarizes the advantages and disadvantages of using internal and external sources for human resource needs.

temporary help
People working for employment agencies who are subcontracted out to businesses at an hourly rate for a period of time specified by the businesses.

One of the fastest-growing areas of recruitment is **temporary help** hired through employment agencies. The agency pays the salary and benefits of the temporary help; the organization pays the employment agency an agreed-upon figure for the services of the temporary help. The use of temporary help is not dependent on economic conditions. When an organization is expanding, temporary employees are used to augment the current staff. When an organization is downsizing, temporary employees create a flexible staff that can be laid off easily and recalled when necessary. One obvious disadvantage of using temporary employees is their lack of commitment to the organization.

FIGURE 11.3
Advantages and Disadvantages of Internal and External Sources

Source	Advantages	Disadvantages
Internal	• Company has a better knowledge of strengths and weaknesses of job candidate. • Job candidate has a better knowledge of company. • Morale and motivation of employees are enhanced. • The return on investment that an organization has in its present workforce is increased.	• People might be promoted to the point where they cannot successfully perform the job. • Infighting for promotions can negatively affect morale. • Inbreeding can stifle new ideas and innovation.
External	• The pool of talent is much larger. • New insights and perspectives can be brought to the organization. • Frequently it is cheaper and easier to hire technical, skilled, or managerial employees from outside.	• Attracting, contacting, and evaluating potential employees is more difficult. • Adjustment or orientation time is longer. • Morale problems can develop among those employees within the organization who feel qualified to do the job.

employee leasing companies
Provide permanent staffs at customer companies.

Unlike temporary agencies, which normally place people in short-term jobs at various companies, **employee leasing companies** and PEOs (professional employer organizations) provide permanent staff at customer companies, issue the workers' paychecks, take care of personnel matters, ensure compliance with workplace regulations, and provide various employee benefits.[3] In addition, highly skilled technical workers such as engineers and information technology specialists are supplied for long-term projects under contract between a company and a technical services firm.

Legal Considerations in the Recruitment Process

The previously discussed legislation has also had a profound impact on the recruitment activities of organizations. For example, the courts have ruled reliance on word-of-mouth or walk-in methods of recruitment to be a discriminatory practice where females and minorities are not well represented at all levels within the organizations.[4]

The Equal Employment Opportunity Commission (EEOC) offers the following suggestions to help eliminate discrimination in recruitment practices:[5]

- Maintain a file of unhired female and minority applicants who are potential candidates for future openings. Contact these candidates first when an opening occurs.
- Utilize females and minorities in recruitment and in the entire human resource process.
- Place classified ads under "Help Wanted" or "Help Wanted, Male-Female" listings. Be sure the content of ads does not indicate any sex, race, or age preference for the job.
- Advertise in media directed toward women and minorities.
- All advertising should include the phrase "equal opportunity employer."

Research has shown that organizations that are aware of protective legislation and EEOC guidelines are more likely to promote diversity, conform to accepted hiring practices, be identity conscious in their recruitment efforts, and generally go beyond symbolic efforts to improve conditions for protected groups.[6] The diverse workplace is a reality, and growth-oriented companies use that fact as a positive rather than a negative influence on the staffing of their organizations.

SELECTION

The selection process involves choosing the individual most likely to succeed in the job from those persons available. The process is dependent on proper human resource planning and recruitment. Only when an adequate pool of qualified candidates is available can the selection process function effectively. The ultimate objective of the selection process is to match the requirements of the job with the qualifications of the individual.

Who Makes the Decision?

The responsibility for hiring is assigned to different levels of management in different organizations. Often the human resources/personnel department does the initial screening of recruits, but the final selection decision is left to the manager of the department with the job opening. Such a system relieves the manager of the time-consuming responsibility of screening out unqualified and uninterested applicants. Less frequently, the human resources/personnel department is responsible for both the initial screening and the final decision. Many organizations leave the final choice to the immediate manager, subject to the approval of higher levels of management. In small organizations, the owner or the top manager often makes the choice.

An alternative approach is to involve peers in the selection decision. Traditionally, peer involvement has been used primarily with professionals and those in upper levels of management, but it is becoming more popular at all levels of the organization. With this approach, co-workers have an input into the final selection decision.

Legal Considerations in the Selection Process

The selection process has been of primary interest to the government, as evidenced by the number of laws and regulations in effect that prohibit discrimination in the selection of employees. One action frequently required of organizations is the development of an affirmative action plan. An **affirmative action plan** is a written document outlining specific goals and timetables for remedying past discriminatory actions. All federal contractors and subcontractors with contracts over $50,000 and 50 or more employees are required to develop and implement written affirmative action plans, which are monitored by the Office of Federal Contract Compliance Programs (OFCCP). While Title VII and the EEOC require no specific type of affirmative action plan, court rulings have often required affirmative action when discrimination has been found.

affirmative action plan
Written document outlining specific goals and timetables for remedying past discriminatory actions.

A number of basic steps are involved in the development of an effective affirmative action plan. Figure 11.4 presents the EEOC's suggestions for developing such a plan.

Organizations without affirmative action plans will find it makes good business sense to identify and revise employment practices that have discriminatory effects before the federal government requires such action. Increased legal action and the record of court-required affirmative action has emphasized the advantages of writing and instituting an affirmative action plan.

However, the growing number of reverse discrimination suits may have a significant impact on affirmative action programs. **Reverse discrimination** is providing preferential treatment for one group (e.g., minority or female) over another group (e.g., white male) rather than merely providing equal opportunity. Management Illustration 11.2 illustrates a reverse discrimination charge.

reverse discrimination
Providing preferential treatment for one group (e.g., minority or female) over another group (e.g., white male) rather than merely providing equal opportunity.

The first real test case in this area was the *Bakke* case of 1978.[7] Allen Bakke, a white male, brought suit against the medical school of the University of California at Davis. He charged he was unconstitutionally discriminated against when he was denied admission to the medical school while some minority applicants with lower qualifications were accepted.

Management Illustration 11.2

REVERSE DISCRIMINATION

Opening arguments began in December 2007 in a federal civil trial in which two Drug Enforcement Administration agents are suing the Justice Department for reverse discrimination. The agents, George W. Marthers III and Jude T. McKenna, allege that their former superiors, Dempsey Jones and Johnny Fisher, subjected them to a hostile work environment and then retaliated against them after they filed a complaint with the Equal Employment Opportunity Commission. Marthers and McKenna are white; Jones and Fisher are black. An attorney for the Justice Department told jurors the case was simply an old-fashioned workplace dispute between employees and managers and had nothing to do with race.

Defense lawyer Colin M. Cherico said Jones and Fisher ruffled feathers after they arrived in Philadelphia in December 2001 and initiated new dress codes and attendance policies, and required agents to account for their whereabouts at all times. He said Marthers and McKenna were "problem agents" who were accustomed to "living the good life" and didn't like the new rules.

But plaintiffs' attorney Thomas G. Roth earlier told jurors that Jones and Fisher had a racial agenda, and, when the plaintiffs questioned it, they were repeatedly harassed. Roth said Marthers and McKenna eventually became so stressed out that they had to leave in March 2002, and Jones later "detailed" them out of their posts. The pair were off the job for 16 and 18 months.

The DEA required both men to be evaluated by doctors and they were found to be unfit for duty. A subsequent reevaluation in 2003 cleared both to return to work. Cherico said Marthers and McKenna received full pay and benefits while they were on leave and neither had been demoted or denied a promotion since returning to work. Roth said that shortly after Marthers and McKenna filed a complaint with the EEOC in March 2002, Fisher retaliated by telling EEOC investigators that the men were malcontents and created phony "disciplinary counseling memoranda" to mislead investigators. Marthers and McKenna are seeking $20 million in compensatory and punitive damages and restoration of their annual and sick leave.

Source: Adapted from Michael Hinkelman, "DEA Agents Sue for Race Bias," *McClatchy-Tribune Business News,* December 7, 2007, Wire Feed.

FIGURE 11.4
EEOC's Suggestions for Developing an Affirmative Action Plan

Source: *Affirmative Action and Equal Employment,* vol. 1 (Washington, DC: U.S. Equal Employment Opportunity Commission, 1974), pp. 16–64.

1. The chief executive officer of an organization should issue a written statement describing his or her personal commitment to the plan, legal obligations, and the importance of equal employment opportunity as an organizational goal.
2. A top official of the organization should be given the authority and responsibility to direct and implement the program. In addition, all managers and supervisors within the organization should clearly understand their own responsibilities for carrying out equal employment opportunity practices.
3. The organization's policy and commitment to the policy should be publicized both internally and externally.
4. Present employment should be surveyed to identify areas of concentration and underutilization and to determine the extent of underutilization.
5. Goals and timetables for achieving the goals should be developed to improve utilization of minorities, males, and females in each area where underutilization has been identified.
6. The entire employment system should be reviewed to identify and eliminate barriers to equal employment. Areas for review include recruitment, selection, promotion systems, training programs, wage and salary structure, benefits and conditions of employment, layoffs, discharges, disciplinary action, and union contract provisions affecting these areas.
7. An internal audit and reporting system should be established to monitor and evaluate progress in all aspects of the program.
8. Company and community programs that are supportive of equal opportunity should be developed. Programs might include training of supervisors regarding their legal responsibilities and the organization's commitment to equal employment and job and career counseling programs.

The Supreme Court ruled in Bakke's favor but at the same time upheld the constitutionality of affirmative action programs.

In another case in 1979, the Supreme Court heard a challenge brought by a white worker, Brian F. Weber, to an affirmative action plan collectively bargained by a union and an employer.[8] This case questioned whether Title VII of the Civil Rights Act of 1964 as amended prohibited private employers from granting racial preference in employment practices. The Court, in a 5-2 opinion, held that it did not and that the voluntary quota was permissible. The *Weber* decision also hinted at the Court's criteria for a permissible affirmative action plan: (1) The plan must be designed to break down old patterns of segregation; (2) it must not involve the discharge of innocent third parties; (3) it must not have any bars to the advancement of white employees; and (4) it must be a temporary measure to eliminate discrimination. However, in a 1989 case (*Martin v. Wilks*), the Supreme Court ruled that white employees could bring reverse discrimination claims against court-approved affirmative action plans.[9] In another case (*City of Richmond v. J. A. Crosan Company*), the Court ruled that government affirmative action programs that put whites at a disadvantage were illegal. Finally, in the case involving the University of Texas law school, the Court ruled that the school could not use race as a factor in admissions. As these examples indicate, managers must stay abreast of legislation and judicial rulings in this area, because constant changes and revised interpretations appear to be inevitable.

Selection Procedure

Figure 11.5 presents a suggested procedure for selecting employees. The preliminary screening and preliminary interview eliminate candidates who are obviously not qualified for the job. In the preliminary screening of applications, personnel data sheets, school records, work records, and similar sources are reviewed to determine characteristics, abilities, and the past performance of the individual. The preliminary interview is then used to screen out unsuitable or uninterested applicants who passed the preliminary screening phase.

tests
Provide a sample of behavior used to draw inferences about the future behavior or performance of an individual.

Testing

One of the most controversial areas of staffing is employment testing. **Tests** provide a sample of behavior that is used to draw inferences about the future behavior or performance of an individual. Many tests are available to organizations for use in the selection process.[10]

FIGURE 11.5
Steps in the Selection Process

Steps in Selection Process	Possible Criteria for Eliminating Potential Employee
• Preliminary screening from application form, résumé, employer records, etc.	Inadequate educational level or performance/experience record for the job and its requirements.
• Preliminary interview	Obvious disinterest and unsuitability for job and its requirements.
• Testing	Failure to meet minimum standards on job-related measures of intelligence, aptitude, personality, etc.
• Reference checks	Unfavorable reports from references regarding past performance.
• Employment interview	Inadequate demonstration of ability or other job-related characteristics.
• Physical examination	Lack of physical fitness required for job.
• Personal judgment	Intuition and judgment resulting in the selection of another employee. Inadequate demonstration of ability or other job-related characteristics.

Tests used by organizations can be grouped into the following general categories: aptitude, psychomotor, job knowledge and proficiency, interests, psychological, and polygraphs.

aptitude tests
Measure a person's capacity or potential ability to learn.

psychomotor tests
Measure a person's strength, dexterity, and coordination.

job knowledge tests
Measure the job-related knowledge possessed by a job applicant.

proficiency tests
Measure how well the applicant can do a sample of the work that is to be performed.

interest tests
Determine how a person's interests compare with the interests of successful people in a specific job.

psychological tests
Attempt to measure personality characteristics.

polygraph tests
Record physical changes in the body as the test subject answers a series of questions; popularly known as *lie detector tests.*

test validity
Extent to which a test predicts a specific criterion.

test reliability
Consistency or reproducibility of the results of a test.

Aptitude tests measure a person's capacity or potential ability to learn. **Psychomotor tests** measure a person's strength, dexterity, and coordination. **Job knowledge tests** measure the job-related knowledge possessed by a job applicant. **Proficiency tests** measure how well the applicant can do a sample of the work to be performed. **Interest tests** are designed to determine how a person's interests compare with the interests of successful people in a specific job. **Psychological tests** attempt to measure personality characteristics. **Polygraph tests,** popularly known as *lie detector tests,* record physical changes in the body as the test subject answers a series of questions. By studying recorded physiological measurements, the polygraph examiner then makes a judgment as to whether the subject's response was truthful or deceptive.

Employment testing is legally subject to the requirements of validity and reliability. **Test validity** refers to the extent to which a test predicts a specific criterion. For organizations, the criterion usually used is performance on the job. Thus, test validity generally refers to the extent to which a test predicts future job success or performance. The selection of criteria to define job success or performance is a difficult process, and its importance cannot be overstated. Obviously, test validity cannot be measured unless satisfactory criteria exist.

Test reliability refers to the consistency or reproducibility of the results of a test. Three methods are commonly used to determine the reliability of a test. The first method, called *test-retest,* involves testing a group of people and then retesting them later. The degree of similarity between the sets of scores determines the reliability of the test. The second method, called *parallel forms,* entails giving two separate but similar forms of the test. The degree to which the sets of scores coincide determines the reliability of the test. The third method, called *split halves,* divides the test into two halves to determine whether performance is similar on both halves. Again, the degree of similarity determines the reliability. All of these methods require statistical calculations to determine the degree of reliability of the test.

In the past, organizations have frequently used tests without establishing their validity or reliability. As a result of such practices, testing came under a great deal of attack. The previously discussed Civil Rights Act of 1964 includes a section specifically related to the use of tests:

> nor shall it be an unlawful employment practice for an employer to give and to act upon the results of any professionally developed ability test provided that such a test, its administration, or action upon the results is not designed, intended, or used to discriminate because of race, color, religion, sex, or national origin.[11]

Two Supreme Court decisions have had a profound impact on the use of testing by organizations. First, in the case of *Griggs v. Duke Power Company,* the Court ruled that any test that has an adverse impact on female or minority group applicants must be validated as job related, regardless of whether an employer intended to discriminate.[12] In *Albermarle Paper Company v. Moody,* the Supreme Court placed the burden on the employer to show that its tests are in compliance with EEOC guidelines for testing.

Finally, in 1978, the EEOC, the Civil Service Commission, the Department of Justice, and the Department of Labor adopted a document titled "Uniform Guidelines on Employee Selection Procedures." These guidelines established the federal government's position concerning discrimination in employment practices. The guidelines explain what private and public employers must do to prove their selection procedures, including testing, are nondiscriminatory. Management Illustration 11.3 discusses reliability and validity in more depth.

Management Illustration 11.3

RELIABLE AND VALID

No Child Left Behind, the education law passed under the Bush administration, requires that millions of students across the country be tested annually and that the tests produce "reliable and valid" data to measure how well they—and their schools—are doing. Testing experts say that one part of that equation is fairly easy to do, but the other . . . not so much.

Reliability essentially means that a test is, well, reliable; perfect reliability would mean that a student performs the same way on a test every time it is given. Things get in the way—including the health or frame of mind of the test-taker, the sampling of content on the test and scoring errors—but it is possible to quantify those mistakes and put error bands around a score that say how much it might vary. Many of the standardized tests being used can be considered reliable, experts say. But reliability alone doesn't mean much, said Bob Schaeffer, public education director of the National Center for Fair and Open Testing, a nonprofit group that advocates against standardized testing. "If you got on a scale, and every time you got on, it said it was 237 pounds, it would be reliable, even if you weighed 120," he said. "You could rely on it to say 237 pounds. But it's not accurate or meaningful."

And that's where the problem with validity comes into play, some educators say. Broadly, experts say, a valid test is one that measures what its authors say it will measure. Tests assess children in many different areas; validity is all about the specific purpose of the test. "A test itself is not valid or invalid," said Daniel Koretz, a professor of education at Harvard University. "The conclusion you base on the result is valid or invalid." "If indeed in the long run No Child Left Behind and the accountability movement is going to really have traction in improving education for kids in the United States, I think it's going to have to subject itself to a serious level of scrutiny," said Robert Pianta, director of the University of Virginia's Center for Advanced Study of Teaching and Learning.

What does validity actually mean in the context of student testing?

Source: Adapted from Valerie Straass, "Putting Assessments to the Test," *Washington Post,* March 26, 2007, p. B2.

Polygraph and Drug Testing

As noted earlier, polygraph tests can be used for screening job applicants. The *polygraph,* or lie detector, is a device that records physical changes in the body as the test subject answers a series of questions. The polygraph records fluctuations in blood pressure, respiration, and perspiration on a moving roll of graph paper. On the basis of the recorded fluctuations, the polygraph operator makes a judgment as to whether the subject's response was truthful or deceptive.

The use of a polygraph test rests on a series of cause-and-effect assumptions: Stress causes certain physiological changes in the body; fear and guilt cause stress; lying causes fear and guilt. The use of a polygraph test assumes that a direct relationship exists between the subject's responses to questions and the physiological responses recorded on the polygraph. However, the polygraph itself does not detect lies; it only detects physiological changes. The operator must interpret the data that the polygraph records. Thus, the real lie detector is the operator, not the device.

Serious questions exist regarding the validity of polygraph tests. Difficulties arise if a person lies without guilt (a pathological liar) or lies believing the response to be true. Furthermore, it is hard to prove that the physiological responses recorded by the polygraph occur only because a lie has been told. In addition, some critics argue that the use of the polygraph violates fundamental principles of the Constitution: the right of privacy, the privilege against self-incrimination, and the presumption of innocence. As a result of these questions and criticisms, Congress passed the Employee Polygraph Protection Act of 1988 that severely restricts the commercial use of polygraph tests. Those exempt from this restrictive law are (1) all local, state, and federal employees (however, state laws can be passed to restrict the use of polygraphs); (2) industries with national defense or security contracts; (3) businesses with nuclear power–related contracts with

Management Illustration 11.4

BACKGROUND CHECK LEADS TO JAIL

A 28-year-old man who went to the sheriff's office in Allendale, South Carolina, for a routine job interview background check landed in jail this week when deputies found he did have a criminal history—he was wanted for an armed robbery in North Augusta, according to officials. Sherman Desheell Harley, 28, of Allendale, is charged with two driving violations and armed robbery with a deadly weapon. Allendale officials ran the background check Tuesday when Harley requested one. He was transported back to Aiken County and jailed the same day, according to investigators in North Augusta.

The 28-year-old was linked to a Dec. 23, 2006, armed robbery at the Knox Avenue Tire Kingdom at which time two men, one armed with a handgun and the other with a shotgun, entered the store and ordered everyone to the ground, according to police documents. The incident reportedly occurred around 8 PM while there were several victims still in the store. The clerk told investigators at the time that one of the men ordered her to open the register and give him all the money. She said she complied with his demands, and the gunman then asked her where the rest of the money was kept. There wasn't any more money, she said, and the men left.

Source: Adapted from Karen Daily, "Routine Background Check for Job Puts Man in Jail; He's Wanted for Robbery," *McClatchy-Tribune Business News,* January 29, 2008, Wire Feed.

the Department of Energy; and (4) businesses and consultants with access to highly classified information.

Private businesses are also allowed to use polygraphs under certain conditions: when hiring private security personnel; when hiring persons with access to drugs; and during investigations of economic injury or loss by the employer.

In the past few years, there has also been a proliferation of drug-testing programs. Such programs have been instituted not only to screen job applicants but also to test current employees for drug use. It has been estimated that about 20 percent of the Fortune 500 companies have either instituted drug-testing programs or are contemplating their institution.

Numerous lawsuits have been filed to contest the legality of such programs. Generally, a drug-testing program is on stronger legal ground if it is limited to job applicants. Furthermore, current employees should not be subjected to drug testing on a random basis. A probable cause for drug testing, such as a dramatic change in behavior or a sudden increase in accident rates, should be established before testing. In addition, the results of drug testing should be protected to ensure confidentiality.

Background and Reference Checks

Background and reference checks usually fall into three categories: personal, academic, and past employment. Management Illustration 11.4 shows surprising information as discovered by a background check. Contacting personal and academic references is generally of limited value, because few people will list someone as a reference unless they feel that that person will give them a positive recommendation. Previous employers are in the best position to supply the most objective information. However, the amount and type of information that a previous employer is willing to divulge varies. Normally, most previous employers will provide only the following information—yes or no to the question if this applicant worked there, what the employee's dates of employment were, and what position he or she held.[13]

If a job applicant is rejected because of information in a credit report or another type of report from an outside reporting service, the applicant must be given the name and address of the organization that developed the report. The reporting service is *not* required by law to give the person a copy of his or her file, but it *must* inform the person of the nature and substance of the information.

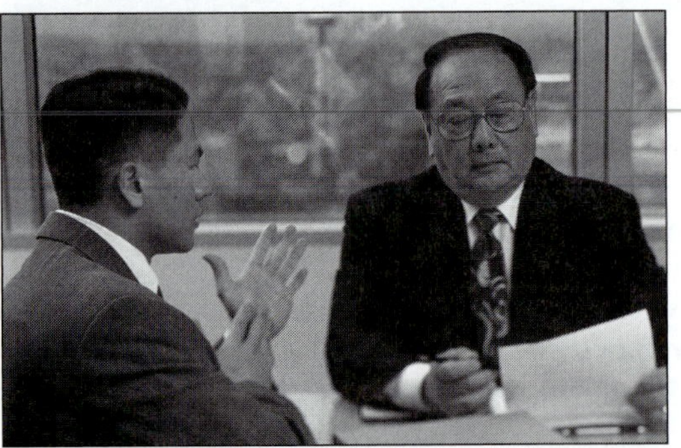

The purpose of an interview is to supplement information gained in other steps of the selection process to determine the suitability of a candidate for a specific opening in the organization.

Employment Interview

The employment interview is used by virtually all organizations as an important step in the selection process. Its purpose is to supplement information gained in other steps in the selection process to determine the suitability of an applicant for a specific opening in the organization. It is important to remember that all questions asked during an interview must be job related. Equal employment opportunity legislation has placed limitations on the types of questions that can be asked during an interview.

Types of Interviews

Organizations use several types of interviews. The *structured interview* is conducted using a predetermined outline. Through the use of this outline, the interviewer maintains control of the interview so that all pertinent information on the applicant is covered systematically. Structured interviews provide the same type of information on all interviewees and allow systematic coverage of all questions deemed necessary by the organization. The use of a structured interview tends to increase reliability and accuracy.

Two variations of the structured interview are the semistructured and the situational interview. In the *semistructured interview,* the interviewer prepares the major questions in advance but has the flexibility to use techniques such as probing to help assess the applicant's strengths and weaknesses. The *situational interview* uses projective techniques to put the prospective employee in action situations that might be encountered on the job. For example, the interviewer may wish to see how the applicant might handle a customer complaint or observe certain important decision-making characteristics. With either method, however, interviewer bias must be guarded against.

Unstructured interviews are conducted using no predetermined checklist of questions. This type of interview uses open-ended questions such as "Tell me about your previous job." Interviews of this type pose numerous problems, such as a lack of systematic coverage of information, and are also susceptible to the personal biases of the interviewer. This type of interview, however, does provide a more relaxed atmosphere.

Organizations have used three other types of interviewing techniques to a limited extent. The *stress interview* is designed to place the interviewee under pressure. In the stress interview, the interviewer assumes a hostile and antagonistic attitude toward the interviewee. The purpose of this type of interview is to detect whether the person is highly emotional. In the *board (or panel) interview,* two or more interviewers conduct the interview. The *group interview,* which questions several interviewees together in a group discussion, is also sometimes used. Board interviews and group interviews can involve either a structured or an unstructured format.

Problems in Conducting Interviews

Although interviews have widespread use in selection procedures, they can pose a host of problems. The first and one of the most significant problems is that interviews are subject to the same legal requirements of validity and reliability as other steps in the selection process. Furthermore, the validity and reliability of most interviews are questionable. One reason seems to be that it is easy for the interviewer to become either favorably or unfavorably impressed with the job applicant for the wrong reasons.

Several common pitfalls may be encountered in interviewing a job applicant. Interviewers, like all people, have personal biases, and these biases can play a role in the interviewing process. For example, a qualified male applicant should not be rejected merely because the interviewer dislikes long hair on males.

halo effect
Occurs when the interviewer allows a single prominent characteristic to dominate judgment of all other traits.

Closely related is the problem of the **halo effect,** which occurs when the interviewer allows a single prominent characteristic to dominate judgment of all other traits. For instance, it is often easy to overlook other characteristics when a person has a pleasant personality. However, merely having a pleasant personality does not ensure that the person will be a qualified employee.

Overgeneralizing is another common problem. An interviewee may not behave exactly the same way on the job that she or he did during the interview. The interviewer must remember that the interviewee is under pressure during the interview and that some people just naturally become nervous during an interview.

Conducting Effective Interviews

Problems associated with interviews can be partially overcome through careful planning. The following suggestions are offered to increase the effectiveness of the interviewing process.

First, careful attention must be given to the selection and training of interviewers. They should be outgoing and emotionally well-adjusted people. Interviewing skills can be learned, and the people responsible for conducting interviews should be thoroughly trained in these skills.

Second, the plan for the interview should include an outline specifying the information to be obtained and the questions to be asked. The plan should also include room arrangements. Privacy and some degree of comfort are important. If a private room is not available, the interview should be conducted in a place where other applicants are not within hearing distance.

Third, the interviewer should attempt to put the applicant at ease. The interviewer should not argue with the applicant or put the applicant on the spot. A brief conversation about a general topic of interest or offering the applicant a cup of coffee can help ease the tension. The applicant should be encouraged to talk. However, the interviewer must maintain control and remember that the primary goal of the interview is to gain information that will aid in the selection decision.

Fourth, the facts obtained in the interview should be recorded immediately. Generally, notes can and should be taken during the interview.

Finally, the effectiveness of the interviewing process should be evaluated. One way to evaluate effectiveness is to compare the performance ratings of individuals who are hired against assessments made during the interview. This cross-check can serve to evaluate the effectiveness of individual interviewers as well as that of the overall interviewing program.

Personal Judgment

The final step in the selection process is to make a personal judgment regarding which individual to select for the job. (Of course, it is assumed that at this point more than one applicant will be qualified for the job.) A value judgment using all of the data obtained in the previous steps of the selection process must be made in selecting the best person for the job. If previous steps have been performed correctly, the chances of making a successful personal judgment improve dramatically.

The individual making the personal judgment should also recognize that in some cases, none of the applicants is satisfactory. If this occurs, the job should be redesigned, more money should be offered to attract more qualified candidates, or other actions should be taken. Caution should be taken against accepting the "best" applicant if that person is not truly qualified to do the job.

TRANSFERS, PROMOTIONS, AND SEPARATIONS

The final step in the human resource planning process involves transfers, promotions, and separations. A transfer involves moving an employee to another job at approximately the same level in the organization with basically the same pay, performance requirements, and status. Planned transfers can serve as an excellent development technique. Transfers can also be helpful in balancing varying departmental workload requirements. The most common difficulty relating to transfers occurs when a "problem" employee is unloaded on an unsuspecting manager. Training, counseling, or corrective discipline of the employee may eliminate the need for such a transfer. If the employee cannot be rehabilitated, discharge is usually preferable to transfer.

A promotion moves an employee to a job involving higher pay, higher status, and thus higher performance requirements. The two basic criteria used by most organizations in promotions are merit and seniority. Union contracts often require that seniority be considered in promotions. Many organizations prefer to base promotions on merit as a way to reward and encourage performance. Obviously, this assumes the organization has a method for evaluating performance and determining merit. An organization must also consider the requirements of the job in question, not just the employee's performance in previous jobs. Success in one job does not automatically ensure success in another job. Both past performance and potential must be considered. This also lessens the probability that the Peter Principle effect will occur.

A separation involves either voluntary or involuntary termination of an employee. In voluntary separations, many organizations attempt to determine why the employee is leaving by using exit interviews. This type of interview provides insights into problem areas that need to be corrected in the organization. Involuntary separations involve terminations and layoffs. Layoffs occur when there is not enough work for all employees. Laid-off employees are called back if and when the workload increases. A termination usually occurs when an employee is not performing his or her job or has broken a company rule. Terminations should be made only as a last resort. When a company has hired an employee and invested resources in the employee, termination results in a low return on the organization's investment. Training and counseling often are tried before firing an individual. However, when rehabilitation fails, the best action is usually termination because of the negative impact a disgruntled or misfit employee can have on others in the organization.

Summary

1. *Outline the human resource planning process.* Human resource planning (HRP) is the process of getting the right number of qualified people into the right jobs at the right time. Once organizational plans are made and specific objectives are set, human resource planning attempts to define the human resource needs to meet the organization's objectives.
2. *Define job analysis, job description, job specification, and skills inventory.* Job analysis is the process of determining, through observation and study, the pertinent information relating to the nature of a specific job. A job description is a written statement that identifies the tasks, duties, activities, and performance results required in a particular job. A job specification is a written statement that identifies the abilities, skills, traits, or attributes necessary for successful performance in a particular job. A skills inventory contains basic information about all employees of the organization.
3. *Define equal employment opportunity.* Equal employment opportunity refers to the right of all people to work and to advance on the bases of merit, ability, and potential.

4. *Describe the recruitment process.* Recruitment involves the activities of seeking and attracting a supply of people from which to select qualified candidates for job vacancies.
5. *Define affirmative action plan.* An affirmative action plan is a written document outlining specific goals and timetables for remedying past discriminatory actions.
6. *Discuss reverse discrimination.* Reverse discrimination is the provision of alleged preferential treatment for one group (e.g., minority or female) over another group (e.g., white male) rather than merely providing equal opportunity.
7. *Define tests, test validity, and test reliability.* Tests provide a sample of behavior used to draw inferences about the future behavior or performance of an individual. Test validity refers to the extent to which a test predicts a specific criterion. Test reliability refers to the consistency or reproducibility of the results of a test.
8. *Discuss the different types of employment interviews.* A structured interview is conducted using a predetermined outline. Unstructured interviews are conducted using no predetermined checklist of questions. In the stress interview, the interviewer assumes a hostile and antagonistic attitude to place the interviewee under stress. In the board (or panel) interview, two or more interviewers conduct the interview. In a group interview, several interviewees are questioned together in a group discussion.
9. *Discuss potential problems in the interviewing process.* The biggest problem concerns validity and reliability; the interviewer may be legally required to show that the interviewing method used was valid, reliable, and not discriminatory. Second, the interviewer may be favorably or unfavorably impressed with the prospective employee for the wrong reasons and let personal biases enter into his or her judgment of the applicant. Third, the halo effect can cause the interviewer to make judgments based on a dominant favorable characteristic and therefore fail to see the total individual. Finally, overgeneralizing can be a problem. The interviewer must remember that the interview is different from the job itself and that the interviewee is likely to be nervous during the interview.

Review Questions

1. How does staffing relate to the organizing function?
2. What is human resource planning?
3. What is a job analysis? A job description? A job specification? A skills inventory?
4. What is human resource forecasting?
5. Describe the relationship between job analysis, skills inventory, and human resource planning.
6. Describe the purposes of the following government legislation:
   a. Equal Pay Act of 1963.
   b. Civil Rights Act of 1964.
   c. Age Discrimination in Employment Act of 1968, as amended in 1978.
   d. Rehabilitation Act of 1973.
   e. Americans with Disabilities Act of 1990.
   f. Civil Rights Act of 1991.
   g. Family and Medical Leave Act.

7. What is equal employment opportunity?
8. Define affirmative action plan.
9. What is recruitment? Describe some sources of recruitment.
10. What is selection? Describe the steps in the selection process.
11. What is test validity?
12. What is test reliability? What methods are commonly used to determine test reliability?
13. Describe two basic types of interviews.
14. Discuss some common pitfalls in interviewing.
15. What is a transfer? A promotion? A separation?

Skill-Building Questions

1. Discuss the following statement: An individual who owns a business should be able to hire anyone and shouldn't have to worry about government interference.
2. Discuss your feelings about reverse discrimination.
3. Many managers believe line managers should not have to worry about human resource needs and this function should be handled by the human resource department. What do you think?
4. One common method of handling problem employees is to transfer them to another department of the organization. What do you think about this practice?

SKILL-BUILDING EXERCISES 11.1
Interviewing Questions

Read the following job description.

Public Relations Manager

Responsibilities:

Responsible for managing the development, implementation, and coordination of internal and external public relations strategies with the goal of establishing and maintaining a favorable company image with investors, potential customers, employees, and the public.

Requirements:

Bachelor of Arts or Bachelor of Science degree. Strong communication skills, both writing and speaking. Two years public relations management in a technology company, preferable EDA. Ability to organize, multitask, and meet deadlines. Drives projects to completion and strives for continuous improvement. Works well with people without having direct supervisory control. Initiative to define and execute PR programs, projects, etc. Ability to understand corporate strategic objectives and support with a public relations plan.

Imagine that you are interviewing a person for the job of Public Relations Manager. Consider the job description above and write a list of questions you would ask to find out if the person you are interviewing is right for the job.

SKILL-BUILDING EXERCISE 11.2
Required Attributes of a Manager

The ads in Exhibit 1 were taken from the want ads section of a newspaper. All company names and locations have been disguised.

1. Choose the job that is most attractive to you.
2. Your instructor will form you into groups with other students that selected the same job as you did. Your group should then develop a list of required and desirable skills for the job.
3. Each group should be prepared to present and defend their list before the class.

EXHIBIT 1

CORPORATE MANAGER
CONSOLIDATIONS AND BUDGETS

Challenging career opportunity with moderate-size international machinery manufacturer with primary manufacturing locations overseas. Report to V.P.-Finance. Responsible for monthly consolidations, analysis, and financial reports. Prepare annual consolidated budgets and periodically monitor performance.

5 years' relevant experience in similar environment, familiarity with foreign exchange transactions preferred. Must be intelligent, self-disciplined, high-energy professional. We offer competitive compensation and benefits package. For prompt, totally confidential consideration please forward full resume including earnings history to: Vice President, Employee Relations.

A&B MODERN MACHINERY CO., INC.

An Equal Opportunity Employer M/F/HC

MANAGER SYSTEMS DEVELOPMENT

American Health Care Plans, which operates a number of HMOs across the country is seeking an experienced professional who can take a leadership role in the development of state-of-the-art claims processing systems. This position will report to the VP of MIS, and will involve extensive interaction with claims operational personnel as well as the programmer analysts who are implementing the new systems.

The ideal candidate will have a management, accounting, or computer science degree with a strong emphasis on information systems. The candidate's background should include at least five years in systems development and operational management in an insurance environment. Health insurance, experience and advanced degree are pluses.

We are looking for a very special person, who will bring intelligence, leadership, and creativity to the position. The selected candidate must also be able to take on expanding responsibilities as the company grows. We offer a competitive compensation package and a full range of benefits.

Qualified persons respond by sending resume and salary requirements to our Personnel Director.

American Health Care Plans

An Equal Opportunity Employer

Human Resource Manager

Jackson & Brown's Professional Products Division, the world leader in the development, manufacture, and sale of contact lenses, currently seeks a Human Resource Manager. Responsibilities will include managing personnel policies, practices, and procedures in the area of employee relations, training, organizational development, recruitment, and compensation.

The successful candidate will have a bachelor's degree, preferably in a business related field and 5 years' experience as a generalist in Human Resources. 1-2 years must be in a supervisory capacity. This highly visible position will report directly to the Vice President of Human Resources, Professional Products Division.

For immediate reply, send your resume to: Ms. Jane L. Doe, Professional Products Division.

Jackson & Brown

An Equal Opportunity Employer

VICE PRESIDENT OF MARKETING

... Office Automation Systems

Established Midwest manufacturer has an outstanding career opportunity available for an experienced, marketing professional.

You will be responsible for developing marketing plans and overseeing subsequent activities. Specific duties include:

- Market Analysis
- Product/Pricing Strategy
- Field Sales Support
- Advertising & Promotion
- Revenue Reporting and Projection

This is a prestigious opportunity to work in an industry-leading corporation, international in scope, to assure that our present and future products meet customers requirements and increase our market share. Career growth potential is exceptional. Benefits and salary are executive level. To apply, rush an outline of your qualification to the address below. All responses will be kept in inviolable secrecy. We are proud to be an equal opportunity employer.

SKILL-BUILDING EXERCISE 11.3
The Layoff

Two years ago, your organization experienced a sudden increase in its volume of work. At about the same time, it was threatened with an equal employment opportunity suit that resulted in an affirmative action plan. Under this plan, additional women and minority members have been recruited and hired.

Presently, the top level of management in your organization is anticipating a decrease in volume of work. You have been asked to rank the clerical employees of your section in the event a layoff is necessary.

Below you will find biographical data for the seven clerical people in your section. Rank the seven people according to the order in which they should be laid off, that is, the person ranked first is to be laid off first, and so on.

Burt Green: White male, age 45. Married, four children; five years with the organization. Reputed to be an alcoholic; poor work record.

Nan Nushka: White female, age 26. Married, no children, husband has a steady job; six months with the organization. Hired after the affirmative action plan went into effect; average work record to date. Saving to buy a house.

Johnny Jones: Black male, age 20. Unmarried; one year with organization. High performance ratings. Reputed to be shy—a "loner"; wants to start his own business some day.

Joe Jefferson: White male, age 24. Married, no children but wife is pregnant; three years with organization. Going to college at night; erratic performance attributed to work/study conflicts.

Livonia Long: Black female, age 49. Widow, three grown children; two years with the organization. Steady worker whose performance is average.

Ward Watt: White male, age 30. Recently divorced, one child; three years with the organization. Good worker.

Rosa Sanchez: Hispanic female, age 45. Six children, husband disabled one year ago; trying to help support her family; three months with the organization. No performance appraisal data available.

1. What criteria did you use for ranking the employees?
2. What implications does your ranking have in the area of affirmative action?

SKILL-BUILDING EXERCISE 11.4
Development Test

You will be given one minute to copy the letter *T* on a blank sheet of paper as many times as possible. The exercise is timed, and exactly one minute is permitted. A frequency distribution will then be developed by your instructor (or the class) to show how well the class performed.

1. What is the shape of the distribution?
2. Why is the distribution shaped in this manner?
3. Could this test be used as a selection device for certain jobs? If so, what types of jobs?
4. How would you demonstrate the validity of this test?

Case Incident 11.1
Accept Things As They Are?

Jane Harris came to work at the S&J department store two years ago. In Jane's initial assignment in the finance department, she proved to be a good and hard worker. It soon became obvious to both Jane and her department head, Rich Jackson, that she could handle a much more responsible job than the one she presently held. Jane discussed this matter with Rich. It was obvious to him that if a better position could not be found for Jane, S&J would lose a good employee. As there were no higher openings in the finance department, Rich recommended her for a job in the accounting department. She was hired.

Jane joined the accounting department as payroll administrator and quickly mastered her position. She became knowledgeable in all aspects of the job and maintained a good rapport with her two employees. A short time later, Jane was promoted to assistant manager of the accounting department. In this job, Jane continued her outstanding performance.

Two months ago, Bob Thomas suddenly appeared as a new employee in the accounting department. Ralph Simpson, vice president of administration for S&J, explained to Jane and Steve Smith, head of the accounting department, that Bob was a trainee. After Bob had learned all areas of the department, he would be used to take some of the load off both Jane and Steve and also to undertake special projects for the department. Several days after Bob's arrival, Jane learned that Bob was the son of a politician who was a close friend of the president of S&J. Bob had worked in his father's successful election campaign until shortly before he joined S&J.

Last week, Steve asked Jane to help him prepare the accounting department's budget for next year. While working on the budget, Jane got a big surprise. She found that Bob had been hired at a salary of $2,400 per month. At the time of Bob's hiring, Jane, as assistant manager of the accounting department, was making only $2,000 per month.

After considering her situation for several days, Jane went to see Ralph Simpson, the division head, about the problem. She told Ralph she had learned of the difference in salary while assisting Steve with the budget and stated it was not right to pay a trainee more than a manager. She reminded Ralph of what he had said several times: that Jane's position should pay $26,000 to $28,000 per year considering her responsibility, but S&J just could not afford to pay her that much. Jane told Ralph that things could not remain as they were at present, and she wanted to give S&J a chance to correct the situation. Ralph told Jane he would get back to her in several days.

About a week later, Ralph gave Jane a reply. He stated that while the situation was unfair, he did not think S&J could do anything about it. He told her that sometimes one has to accept things as they are, even if they are wrong. He further stated that he hoped this would not cause S&J to lose a good employee.

Questions

1. What options does Jane have?
2. What influence, if any, would the federal government have in this case?

Case Incident 11.2

The Employment Interview

Jerry Sullivan is the underwriting manager for a large insurance company located in the Southwest. Recently, one of his best employees had given him two weeks' notice of her intention to leave. She was expecting a baby soon, and she and her husband had decided she was going to quit work and stay home with her new baby and her other two young children.

Today, Jerry was scheduled to start interviewing applicants for this job. The first applicant was Barbara Riley. She arrived at the company's office promptly at 9 AM, the time scheduled for her interview. Unfortunately, just before she arrived, Jerry received a phone call from his boss, who had just returned from a three-week vacation. He wanted Jerry to bring him up to date on what had been going on. The telephone conversation lasted 30 minutes. During that time, Barbara Riley was seated in the company's reception room.

At 9:30, Jerry went to the reception room and invited her into his office. The following conversation occurred:

Jerry: Would you like a cup of coffee?

Barbara: No, I've already had one.

Jerry: You don't mind if I have a cup, do you?

Barbara: No, go right ahead. [*Jerry pauses, and rings his secretary Dorothy Cannon.*]

Jerry: Dorothy, would you fix me a cup of coffee?

Dorothy: I'll bring it in shortly. You have a call on line 1.

Jerry: Who is it?

Dorothy: It's Tom Powell, our IBM representative. He wants to talk to you about the delivery date on our new word processor.

Jerry: I'd better talk to him. [*Turning to Barbara.*] I'd better take this call. I'll only be a minute. [*He picks up his phone.*] Well, Tom, when are we going to get our machines?

This phone conversation goes on for almost 10 minutes. After hanging up, Jerry turns again to Barbara to resume the interview.

Jerry: I'm sorry, but I needed to know about those machines. We really do need them. We only have a short time, so why don't you just tell me about yourself.

At that point, Barbara tells Jerry about her education, which includes an undergraduate degree in psychology and an MBA, which she will be receiving shortly. She explains to Jerry that this will be her first full-time job. Just then the phone rings, and Jerry's secretary tells him that his next interviewee is waiting.

Jerry: [*Turns to Barbara.*] Thank you for coming in. I'll be in touch with you as soon as I interview two more applicants for this job. However, I need to ask you a couple of quick questions.

Barbara: OK.

Jerry: Are you married?

Barbara: I am divorced.

Jerry: Do you have children?

Barbara: Yes, two boys.

Jerry: Do they live with you?

Barbara: Yes.

Jerry: The reason I am asking is that this job requires some travel. Will this pose a problem?

Barbara: No.

Jerry: Thanks, and I'll be in touch with you.

Questions

1. Outline the inadequacies of this interview.
2. What information did Jerry learn?
3. What do you think of Jerry's last questions?

Case Incident 11.3

Problems in City Government

The city of Windsor, like most city governments, has a centralized human resource (HR) department. The HR department does the recruiting and testing and works with all operating departments in selecting new employees. Windsor employs a merit system for job selection and promotion.

Until recently, the Windsor HR department used the following process when a job was to be filled by hiring from outside the organization:

1. A job description was prepared and advertised. This description was very general and included all the tasks which the person might perform.

2. Minimum requirements were established. These requirements were based on what operating departments wanted and what the HR department thought was reasonable. It was not based on any demonstratable criteria.
3. Tests were given to those who met minimum requirements. Those who passed the tests were interviewed.
4. A register was established ranking the qualified applicants on a scale from 70 to 100.
5. Departments then chose one of the top three applicants on the register.

The operating departments want more control over who they can hire. The HR department wants to maintain the present system.

1. How could the present system be improved?
2. What do you think about the other departments making up their own systems for hiring?

References and Additional Readings

1. "Equal Pay for Equal Work under the Fair Labor Standards Act," *Interpractices Bulletin* (Washington, DC: U.S. Department of Labor, 1967), Title 29, pt. 800.
2. Laurence J. Peter and R. Hall, *The Peter Principle* (New York: Bantam Books, 1969). See also Laurence J. Peter, *Why Things Go Wrong* (New York: William Morrow and Company, 1985).
3. Jane Ester Bahls, "Employment for Rent," *Nation's Business,* June 1991, p. 36.
4. *Parham v. Southwestern Bell Telephone Company,* 433 F.2d 421 (8th Cir. 1970).
5. *Affirmative Action and Equal Employment,* vol. 1 (Washington, DC: U.S. Equal Employment Opportunity Commission, 1974), pp. 30–31.
6. Alison M. Konrad and Frank Linnehan, "Formalized HRM Structures: Coordinating Equal Employment Opportunity or Concealing Organizational Practices?" *Academy of Management Journal* 38, no. 3 (1995), p. 787.
7. *University of California Regents v. Bakke,* 483 U.S. 265 (1978).
8. *United Steelworkers v. Weber,* 99 S. Ct. 2721 (1979).
9. *Martin v. Wilks,* 104 L. Ed. 2d 835 (1989).
10. For a detailed description of a large number of tests, see *The Sixteenth Mental Measurements Yearbook,* edited by Robert A. Spics and Barbara S. Meke (Buros Institute/University of Nebraska Press, 2005) Lincoln, Nebraska.
11. Title VII, Section 703(h), Civil Rights Act of 1964.
12. *Griggs v. Duke Power Company,* 401 U.S. 424 (1971).
13. See Edward C. Andler, *The Complete Reference Checking Handbook: The Proven (and Legal) Way to Prevent Hiring Mistakes* (AMACOM, 2003). New York, NY.

Chapter Twelve

Employee Training and Development

Learning Objectives

After studying this chapter, you will be able to:

1. Define human asset accounting.
2. Describe the orientation process.
3. Define training.
4. Define needs assessment.
5. Discuss vestibule training, apprenticeship training, and computer-based instruction.
6. List and define the most popular methods of management development.
7. Describe an assessment center.
8. List the steps involved in the evaluation of training and management development.

Chapter Preview

The Cornell University ILR School (Industrial and Labor Relations) was founded in 1946, with the original mission "to improve industrial and labor conditions in the State through the provision of instruction, the conduct of research, and the dissemination of information in all aspects of industrial, labor, and public relations, affecting employers and employees." Today, more than 60 years later, the ILR School is a unique academic institution with national and international reach addressing the breadth of modern workplace issues. ILR focuses on advancing the world of work through cutting-edge research, excellence in teaching, and commitment to outreach to improve workplace practices and influence government policy—in New York state and throughout the world. ILR is the nation's only institution of higher education to offer a four-year undergraduate program focused on the workplace, several types of graduate degrees, and diverse continuing education programs and workshops. To learn more about the ILR School, visit www.ilr.cornell.edu.

eCornell, a wholly-owned subsidiary of Cornell University, provides many of the world's leading organizations with online, asynchronous professional and executive development in the areas of strategy, leadership and management development, human resources, financial management, and hospitality management. Its proven course development model and instructor-led course delivery provide for engaging, rigorous and interactive learning. For more information, visit www.ecornell.com/capability.

Source: Anonymous, "eCornel Offers First Online Strategic HR Management Certificate," *PR Newswire,* December 19, 2007.

Analyzing Management Skills

Do you feel that you would be more attracted to work for a company that has a good employee training program? Why or why not?

Applying Management Skills

Do you feel that management skills can be learned?

human asset accounting
Determining and recording the value of an organization's human resources in its statement of financial condition.

On an organization's balance sheet, such factors as cash, buildings, and equipment are listed as assets. One asset that is not listed is the value of the organization's human resources. However, businesses make huge investments in recruiting, hiring, training, and developing their human resources. **Human asset accounting** involves determining and recording the value of an organization's human resources in its statement of financial condition. Although human asset accounting is not an acceptable accounting practice for tax or financial reporting purposes, it does recognize that the quality of an organization's human resources is an important asset.

HUMAN RESOURCE DEVELOPMENT PROCESS

Enhancing the quality of an organization's human resources involves many activities. Newly hired employees must be introduced to the organization and to their jobs. They must be trained to perform their jobs. Employee assistance and union relations (if applicable) must be planned and managed. Also, current employees must regularly have their skills updated and must learn new skills. A business must also be concerned about developing the skills of its management team. Developing employee skills is a key managerial responsibility.

As Figure 12.1 shows, the human resource development process has many steps and functions. Most of these steps are not independent or mutually exclusive tasks. Instead, in the rapidly changing organization of the 2000s, the human resource department is a blend of all the needs that affect the company's workforce. The human resource department is at the heart of many important managerial decisions because of the increasing reliance on the department's skills in understanding, training, and providing tools with which to build and maintain a competitive workforce.

ORIENTATION

orientation
Introduction of new employees to the organization, their work units, and their jobs.

Orientation is the introduction of new employees to the organization, their work units, and their jobs. Orientation comes from co-workers and the organization. The orientation from co-workers is usually unplanned and unofficial, and it can provide the new employee with misleading and inaccurate information. This is one reason it is important that the organization provide an orientation. An effective orientation program has an immediate and lasting impact on the new employee and can make the difference between a new employee's success or failure.

FIGURE 12.1
Human Resource Wheel

Source: From P. A. McLagan, "Models for HRD Practice," *Training and Development Journal,* Volume 41, 1989, p. 53. Copyright © 1989 from Training & Development. With permission of American Society for Training & Development.

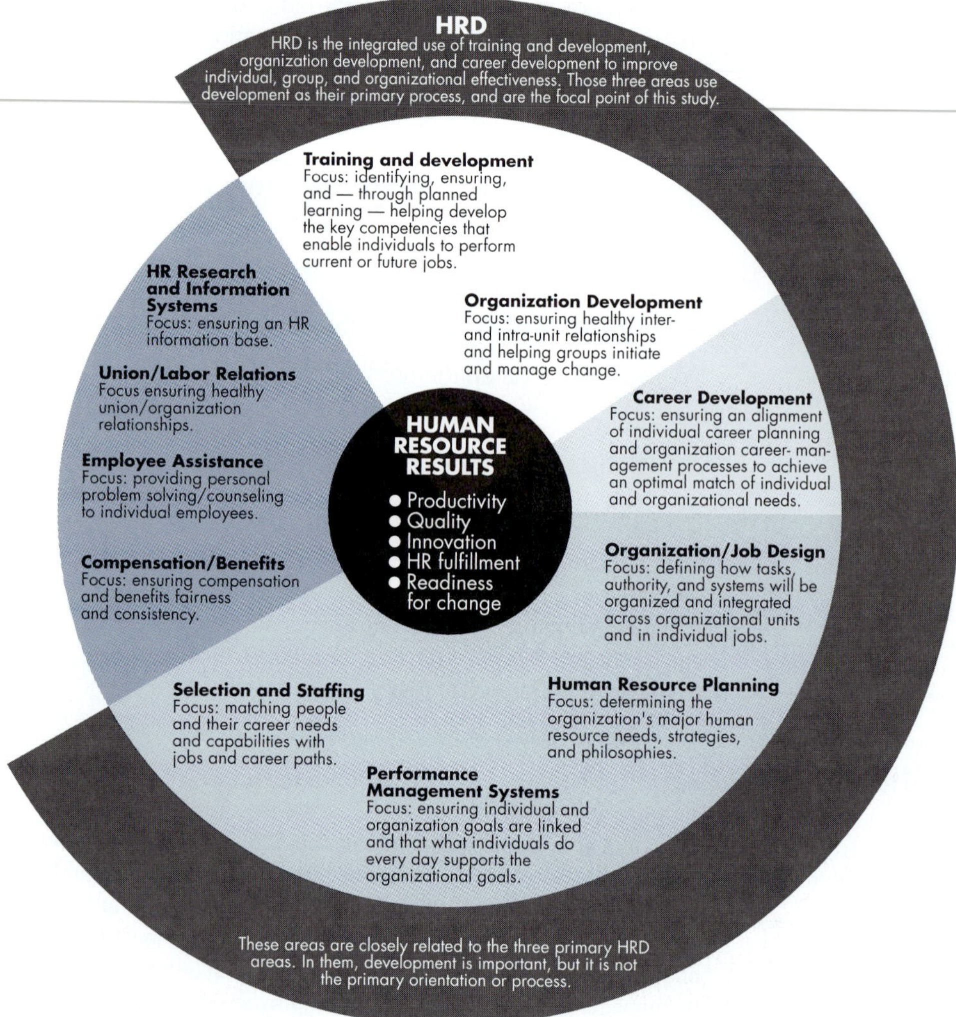

Job applicants get some orientation to the organization even before they are hired. Sometimes the orientation comes through the organization's reputation: how it treats employees and the types of products or services it provides. Also, during the selection process, applicants often learn about other general aspects of the organization and what their duties, working conditions, and pay will be. Commonly cited objectives of company orientation programs are (1) reduction of new employee stress, (2) lower start-up costs of integrating the new employee into the organization, (3) eventual reduction of turnover due to failure to understand the rules and culture of the organization, (4) reduced time required to integrate the employee into the job, and (5) helping the employee adjust to his or her work team or work environment more quickly.[1]

After the employee is hired, the organization's formal orientation program begins. For all types of organizations, orientation usually should be conducted at two distinct levels:

1. *General organizational orientation:* presents topics of relevance and interest to all employees.
2. *Departmental and job orientation:* covers topics unique to the new employee's specific department and job.

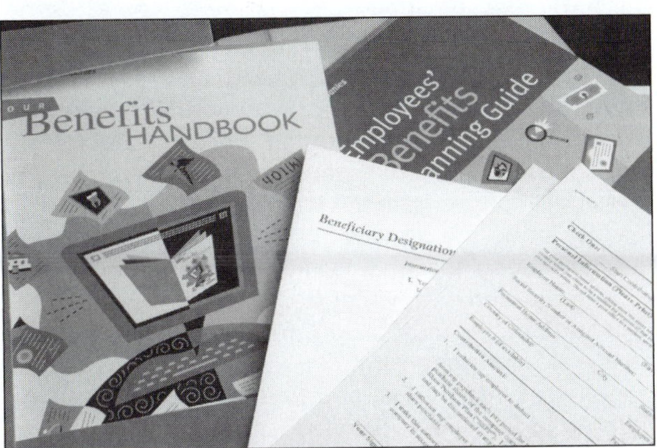

Many companies provide new employees with an orientation kit that contains materials such as a policy and procedure handbook, list of holidays and benefits, and telephone numbers of key personnel. This is useful to new employees to help them get acclimated to the company faster.

Normally, the general orientation is given by the human resource department. Departmental and job orientation are generally handled by the new employee's manager. Each new employee should receive a kit or packet of information to supplement the general organizational orientation program. This orientation kit is usually prepared by the human resource department and provides a wide variety of materials. It should be designed with care and provide only essential information. The orientation kit may include the following:

- Organizational chart.
- Map of the organization's facilities.
- Copy of policy and procedures handbook.
- List of holidays and fringe benefits.
- Copies of performance appraisal forms and procedures.
- Copies of other required forms (e.g., expense reimbursement form).
- Emergency and accident prevention procedures.
- Sample copy of company newsletter or magazine.
- Telephone numbers and locations of key company personnel (e.g., security).
- Copies of insurance plans.

Many organizations require employees to sign a form stating they have received and read the orientation kit. In unionized organizations, this protects the company if a grievance arises and the employee claims not to be aware of certain company policies and procedures. It is equally important that a form be signed in nonunionized businesses, particularly in light of an increase in wrongful discharge litigation. Whether signing a form actually encourages new employees to read the orientation kit is questionable, however.

Orientations do pose some difficulties. Commonly cited problems include information overload for the new employee, too much paperwork, unnecessary information, too much "selling" of the organization, lack of support of existing employees (e.g., seasoned co-workers telling new employees not to listen to the company line), lack of a long-term orientation (many orientations are done in only one day), lack of accurate follow-up, and failure to correct weaknesses in the orientation program. Reducing these difficulties is a real challenge for the human resource department.

Organizations should realize that the orientation, whether from co-workers or from the organization, will have a strong impact on the performance of new employees. Thus, it is in the company's best interest to have a well-planned, well-executed orientation program. Management Illustration 12.1 describes an orientation program for professors.

TRAINING EMPLOYEES

training
Acquiring skills or learning concepts to increase the performance of employees.

Training involves the employee acquiring skills or learning concepts to increase his or her performance. Generally, the new employee's manager has primary responsibility for training in how to perform the job. Sometimes this responsibility is delegated to a senior employee in the department. Regardless, the quality of this initial training can greatly influence the employee's job attitude and productivity.

Economic, social, technological, and governmental changes also influence the skills an organization needs. Changes in these areas can make current skills obsolete in a short time.

Management Illustration 12.1

ORIENTATION FOR PROFESSORS

At most colleges, orientation for new faculty members is one or two days of paperwork, awkward luncheons, and inspirational speeches, a barrage that typically leaves participants shell-shocked.

It used to be that way at Wheaton College in Massachusetts. In its one-day orientation program, new professors were "assaulted by newness," says the provost, Molly E. Smith. It seemed to her that they were bombarded with so much information that they barely had time to digest the basics, let alone get acquainted with the character of the small, liberal-arts college.

This year the college is taking a new approach. In addition to the usual rounds of meetings with department heads and human-resources personnel, the eight new tenure-track faculty members will participate all semester long in a seminar designed to immerse them in Wheaton's history, philosophy, and culture. Ms. Smith chose the seminar format in the hope that its emphasis on discussion and collaboration would encourage the newcomers to think of themselves as active participants in campus culture from the start.

Ms. Smith, the provost, hopes that the program will inspire among the new faculty members the sense of community and loyalty that freshmen experience in their orientations. For most faculty members in the seminar, it is a welcome opportunity to meet colleagues outside their own departments, and to share the experience of getting to know a new college, town, and campus culture. "They've already started making connections," says the provost. "We knew that would happen."

Source: Adapted from Paula Wasley, "Orientation for Professors," *The Chronicle of Higher Education,* September 28, 2007, p. A8.

Also, planned organizational changes and expansions can make it necessary for employees to update their skills or acquire new ones.

Needs Assessment

needs assessment Systematic analysis of the specific training activities a business requires to achieve its objectives.

Training must be directed toward the accomplishment of some organizational objective, such as more efficient production methods, improved quality of products or services, or reduced operating costs. This means an organization should commit its resources only to those training activities that can best help in achieving its objectives. **Needs assessment** is a systematic analysis of the specific training activities a business requires to achieve its objectives. In general, a needs assessment can be conducted in three ways: organizational analysis, functional unit or departmental analysis, and individual employee analysis.

At the organizational level, records on absenteeism, turnover, tardiness, and accident rates provide objective evidence of problems within the organization. When problems occur, these records should be examined carefully to determine if the problems could be partially resolved through training. Employee attitude surveys can also be used to uncover training needs at both the organizational and functional unit levels. Normally, most organizations bring in an independent party to conduct and analyze the survey.

Consumer or customer surveys can also indicate problem areas that may not be obvious to the employees of the organization. Responses to a customer survey may indicate needed areas of training for the organization as a whole or within functional units of the organization.

A popular approach to planning the assessment process includes the following steps:

1. Define the objectives of the assessment process (what is the purpose?).
2. Identify data necessary to conduct the assessment.
3. Select a method for gathering the data (questionnaires, interviews, surveys, etc.).
4. Gather the data.
5. Analyze and verify the data.
6. Prepare a final report.

These steps may be customized to fit the individual needs of the company, but a plan always helps to produce favorable results.

Management Illustration 12.2

TRAINING EMPLOYEES

Finley & Cook has six partners and has grown to 190 employees—a 50 percent increase in the past four years—throughout the company and has doubled its consulting staff from 10 to 20 in the past two years. This includes a 25 percent increase that occurred when the firm acquired Alaska-based Dudley Consulting in November 2006, and it expects to hire at least two more people this year. The increase has been so large that the firm had to expand to six offices.

Finley & Cook provides accounting software sales, implementation, and consulting services to roughly 300 nonprofit and government organizations in 27 states and outsources accounting services to Native American tribes and oil and gas companies.

Such selling success couldn't be accomplished without proper training, however. Linda O'Neal, manager at Finley & Cook, paid Sage Software to come to the firm's Shawnee office, where it trained 80 percent of the staff, and later sent others to the vendor in Austin, Texas.

Cough up the cash to give staff the proper training, and the numbers will come over time, even though it typically takes at least six months to see the return on investment, according to O'Neal.

Source: Alexandra DeFelice, "Training Employees," *Accounting Technology,* June 2007, p. S10.

Establishing Training Objectives

After training needs have been determined, objectives must be established for meeting these needs. Unfortunately, many organizational training programs have no objectives. "Training for training's sake" appears to be the maxim. This philosophy makes it virtually impossible to evaluate the strengths and weaknesses of a training program.

Effective training objectives should state what the organization, department, or individual is to be like when the training is completed. The outcomes should be in writing. Training objectives can be categorized as follows:

1. Instructional objectives:
   - What principles, facts, and concepts are to be learned in the training programs?
   - Who is to be taught?
   - When are they to be taught?
2. Organizational and departmental objectives:
   - What impact will the training have on organizational and departmental outcomes, such as absenteeism, turnover, reduced costs, and improved productivity?
3. Individual performance and growth objectives:
   - What impact will the training have on the behavioral and attitudinal outcomes of the individual trainee?
   - What impact will the training have on the personal growth of the individual trainee?

When clearly defined objectives are lacking, it is impossible to evaluate a program efficiently. However, sound training objectives can usually unlock the potential of an employee by identifying skill deficiencies and developmental opportunities, making good performance better, overcoming skill deficits, and helping the employee prepare for the future. Management Illustration 12.2 describes training employees in accounting software sales.

Methods of Training

Several methods can be used to satisfy the organization's training needs and accomplish its objectives. Some of the more commonly used methods include on-the-job training, job rotation, vestibule training, apprenticeship training, classroom training, and computer-assisted instruction.

On-the-Job Training and Job Rotation

on-the-job training (OJT)
Normally given by a senior employee or supervisor, training in which the trainee is shown how to perform the job and allowed to do it under the trainer's supervision.

On-the-job training (OJT) is normally given by a senior employee or supervisor. The trainee is shown how to perform the job and allowed to do it under the trainer's supervision.

One form of on-the-job training is *job rotation,* sometimes called *cross-training.* In job rotation, an employee learns several different jobs within a work unit or department and performs each job for a specified period. One main advantage of job rotation is that it allows flexibility in the department. For example, when one member of a work unit is absent, another can perform that job.

One advantage of OJT is that it requires no special facilities. Also, the new employee does productive work during the learning process. A major disadvantage is that the pressures of the workplace can cause training to be haphazard or neglected.

Vestibule Training

vestibule training
System in which procedures and equipment similar to those used in the actual job are set up in a special working area called a vestibule.

In **vestibule training,** procedures and equipment similar to those used in the actual job are set up in a special working area called a *vestibule.* The trainee is then taught how to perform the job by a skilled person and is able to learn the job at a comfortable pace without the pressures of production schedules.

The primary advantage of this method is that the trainer can stress theory and use of proper techniques rather than output, and the student can learn by actually doing the job. However, this method is expensive, and the employee still must adjust to the actual production environment. Vestibule training has been used to train word processor operators, bank tellers, clerks, and others in similar jobs.

Apprenticeship Training

apprenticeship training
System in which an employee is given instruction and experience, both on and off the job, in all of the practical and theoretical aspects of the work required in a skilled occupation, craft, or trade.

Apprenticeship training dates back to biblical times and is, in the simplest terms, training in those occupations requiring a wide and diverse range of skills and knowledge as well as independence of judgment. As practiced by organizations, **apprenticeship training** is a system in which an employee is given instruction and experience, both on and off the job, in all of the practical and theoretical aspects of the work required in a skilled occupation, craft, or trade. Most apprenticeship programs range from one to five years.

Classroom Training and Computer-Assisted Instruction

Classroom training is conducted off the job and is probably the most familiar method of training. Classroom training is an effective means of quickly getting information to large groups with limited or no knowledge of the subject being presented. It is useful for teaching actual material, concepts, principles, and theories. Portions of orientation programs, some aspects of apprenticeship training, and safety programs are usually presented with some form of classroom instruction. However, classroom training is used more frequently for technical, professional, and managerial employees. The most common classroom methods used for the general workforce are lecture, discussion, audiovisual methods, experiential methods, and computer-based training.

The lecture method is the simplest and least costly. A lecturer gives an oral presentation on a subject to an audience. The primary problems concern the skill of the lecturer and the ability of the audience to listen effectively. The lecture method is more effective when discussion is not only allowed but encouraged.

If expertise or lecture skills are lacking, audiovisual techniques can bring outside experts to the classroom via video or film. The method is most effective if a moderator allows periodic discussion or hands-on demonstration to complement the audiovisual presentation.

Occasionally, experiential methods, such as case studies or role playing, are effective for the general workforce. Though most commonly associated with management training, this method usually emphasizes creative thinking, problem solution, and human behavior skills.

Computer-based training is more effective than the old workbook method of answering questions, but it requires the use and understanding of certain computer skills.

computer-based training
Training that allows the trainee to absorb knowledge from a preset computer program and advance his or her knowledge in a self-paced format.

Computer-based training allows the employee to absorb information from a preset computer program and advance his or her knowledge in a self-paced format. This method is more effective than the old workbook method of answering questions, but it requires the use and understanding of computer equipment. Highly technical and computer-based manufacturing processes lend themselves to this method. The advantages of being able to use the full capabilities (especially the visually attractive CD-ROM feature) of the computer for learning usually outweigh the disadvantages associated with limited computer skills. One growing method of training is Internet-based training.

Making Training Meaningful

To make all types of training more meaningful, a manager should avoid several common pitfalls. Lack of reinforcement is one. An employee who is praised for doing a job well is likely to be motivated to do it well again. Praise and recognition can very effectively reinforce an employee's learning. Feedback regarding progress is critical to effective learning. Setting standards for trainees and measuring performance against the standards encourage learning.

The adage "practice makes perfect" definitely applies to the learning process. Too many managers try to explain the job quickly, then expect the person to do it perfectly the first time. Having trainees perform a job or explain how to perform it focuses their concentration and enhances learning. Repeating a job or task several times also helps. Learning is always aided by practice and repetition.

Managers sometimes also have preconceived and inaccurate ideas about what certain people or groups of people can or cannot do. A manager should realize that different people learn at different rates. Some learn rapidly; some learn more slowly. A manager should not expect everyone to catch on to the job right away. The pace of the training should be adjusted to the trainee. Also, a person who is not a fast learner will not necessarily always be a poor performer. The manager should take the attitude that all people can learn and want to learn.

MANAGEMENT DEVELOPMENT

management development
Process of developing the attitudes and skills necessary to become or remain an effective manager.

Management development is concerned with developing the attitudes and skills necessary to become or remain an effective manager. To succeed, it must have the full support of the organization's top executives. Management development should be designed, conducted, and evaluated on the basis of the objectives of the organization, the needs of the managers involved, and probable changes in the organization's management team.

Needs Assessment

Numerous methods have been proposed for use in assessing management development needs. The management development needs of any organization are composed of the aggregate, or overall, needs of the organization and the development needs of each manager within the organization.

Organizational Needs

The most common method for determining organizational management development needs is an analysis of problem areas within the organization. For example, increases in the number of grievances or accidents within an area of the organization often signal the need for management development. High turnover rates, absenteeism, or tardiness may also indicate management development needs. Projections based on the organization's objectives and on changes in its management team are also used to determine overall management development needs. Undertaking new business ventures, increased competitive threat (new competitors with new strategies), and a revised corporate vision or mission all usually call for a reevaluation of current management development. Top management must move forward through constant training, or it will begin to move backward and will lose its competitive edge that is so critical to successful business operation.

Needs of Individual Managers

The performance of the person is the primary indicator of individual development needs. Performance evaluations of each manager should be examined to determine areas that need strengthening. The existence of problem situations within a manager's work unit can also signal needs. Planned promotions or reassignments also often indicate the need for development. Outside motivators and consultants often can assist with the personal development and growth of the manager.

Establishing Management Development Objectives

After the management development needs of the organization have been determined, objectives for the overall management development program and for individual programs must be established to meet those needs. Both types of objectives should be expressed in writing and should be measurable. As mentioned earlier in this chapter, training objectives can be categorized within three broad areas: instructional, organizational and departmental, and individual performance and growth. This categorization scheme can also be used for management development objectives.

Instructional objectives might incorporate targets relating to the number of trainees to be taught, hours of training, cost per trainee, and time required for trainees to reach a standard level of knowledge. Furthermore, objectives are needed for the principles, facts, and concepts to be learned in the management development program(s). Organizational and departmental objectives are concerned with the impact the programs will have on organizational and departmental outcomes, such as absenteeism, turnover, safety, and number of grievances. Individual and personal growth objectives relate to the impact on the behavioral and attitudinal outcomes of the individual. They may also relate to the impact on the personal growth of the individuals involved in the programs.

After the overall management development objectives have been established, individual program objectives must be identified that specify the skills, concepts, or attitudes that should result. After these objectives are developed, course content and method of instruction can be specified. Figure 12.2 shows the relationship among needs assessment,

FIGURE 12.2
Relationship between Needs Assessment and Objectives in Management Development

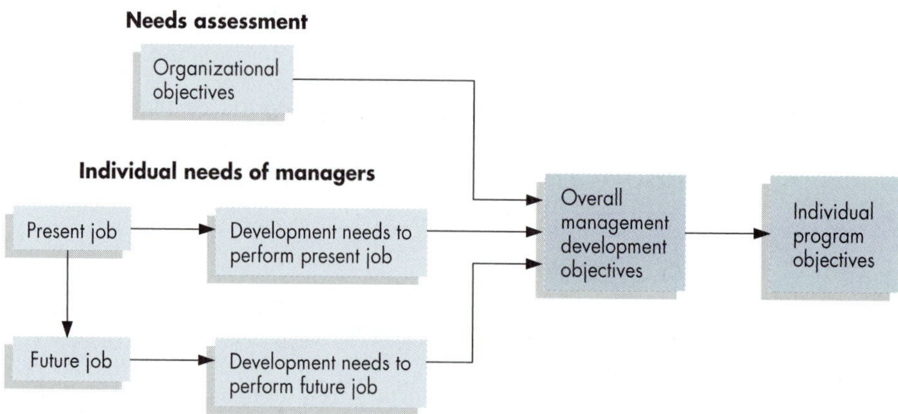

FIGURE 12.3
Methods Used in Management Development

On the Job	Off the Job
Understudy assignments	Classroom training
Coaching	Lectures
Job rotation	Case studies
Special projects and committee assignments	Role playing
	In-basket techniques
	Business games
	Assessment centers

objectives, identification of overall management development objectives, and identification of objectives for each individual management development program.

METHODS USED IN MANAGEMENT DEVELOPMENT

After the company's needs have been assessed and its objectives stated, management development programs can be implemented. This section examines some of the more frequently used methods of management development. As with employee training, management development can be achieved both on and off the job. Figure 12.3 summarizes some of the more commonly used methods of management development.

Understudy Assignments

Generally, *understudy assignments* are used to develop an individual's capabilities to fill a specific job. An individual who will eventually be given a particular job works for the incumbent. The title of the heir to the job is usually assistant manager, administrative assistant, or assistant to a particular manager.

The advantage of understudy assignments is that the heir realizes the purpose of the training and can learn in a practical and realistic situation without being directly responsible for operating results. On the negative side, the understudy learns the bad as well as the good practices of the incumbent. In addition, understudy assignments maintained over a long period can become expensive. If an understudy assignment system is used, it generally should be supplemented with one or more of the other management development methods.

Coaching

coaching
Carried out by experienced managers, emphasizes the responsibility of all managers for developing employees.

Coaching is carried out by experienced managers and emphasizes the responsibility of all managers for developing employees. Under this method of management development, experienced managers advise and guide trainees in solving managerial problems. The idea behind coaching should be to allow the trainees to develop their own approaches to management with the counsel of a more experienced person.

One advantage of coaching is that trainees get practical experience and see the results of their decisions. However, there is a danger that the coach will neglect the training responsibilities or pass on inappropriate management practices. The coach's expertise and experience are critical to the success of this method.

Job Rotation

job rotation
Process in which the trainee goes from one job to another within the organization, generally remaining in each job from six months to a year.

Job rotation is designed to give an individual broad experience through exposure to many different areas of the organization. With understudy assignments, coaching, and experience, the trainee generally receives training and development for one particular job. With **job rotation,** the trainee goes from one job to another within the organization, generally remaining in each job from six months to a year. This technique is used frequently by large organizations for training recent college graduates.

One advantage of job rotation is that the trainees can see how management principles can be applied in a cross section of environments. Also, the training is practical and allows the trainee to become familiar with the entire operation of the company. One serious disadvantage of this method is that the trainee is frequently given menial assignments in each job. Another disadvantage is the tendency to leave the trainee in each job longer than necessary. Both of these disadvantages can produce negative attitudes.

Special Projects and Committee Assignments

Special projects require the trainee to learn about a particular subject. For example, a trainee may be told to develop a training program on safety. This would require learning about the organization's present safety policies and problems and the safety training procedures used by other companies. The individual must also learn to work with and relate to other employees. However, it is critical that the special assignments provide a developmental and learning experience for the trainee and not just busywork.

Committee assignments, which are similar to special projects, can be used if the organization has regularly constituted or ad hoc committees. In this approach, an individual works with the committee on its regularly assigned duties and responsibilities. Thus, the person exercises skills in working with others and learns through the activities of the committee.

Classroom Training

With classroom training, the most familiar type of training, several methods can be used. Classroom training is used not only in management development programs but also in the orientation and training activities discussed earlier in this chapter. Therefore, some of the material in this section is also applicable to those activities.

Lectures

With lecturing, instructors have control over the situation and can present the material exactly as they desire. Although the lecture is useful for presenting facts, its value in changing attitudes and teaching skills is somewhat limited.

Case Studies

case study
Training technique that presents real and hypothetical situations for the trainee to analyze.

The **case study,** a technique popularized by the Harvard Business School, presents real and hypothetical situations for the trainee to analyze. Ideally, the case study should force the trainee to think through problems, propose solutions, choose among the alternatives, and analyze the consequences of the decision.

One primary advantage of the case method is that it brings a note of realism to the instruction. However, case studies often are simpler than the real situations managers face. Another drawback is that when cases are discussed, the participants often lack emotional involvement; thus, attitudinal and behavioral changes are less likely to occur. Also, the success of the case study method depends heavily on the skills of the instructor.

One variation of the case study is the *incident method.* The trainee is initially given only the general outline of a situation. The instructor then provides additional information as the trainee requests it. Theoretically, the incident method makes students probe the situations and seek additional information, much as they would be required to do in real life.

Role Playing

With role playing, trainees are assigned different roles and required to act out these roles in a realistic situation. The idea is for the participants to learn from playing out the assigned

Management Illustration 12.3

BUSINESS SIMULATION

On March 27, 2007, a new revolution in business simulation took place as the University of Maryland's Robert H Smith School of Business (College Park, MD, www.rhsmith.umd.edu), Delft University of Technology (Delft, the Netherlands, www.tudelft.nl) and Sun Microsystems Inc., (Santa Clara, CA, www.sun.com) launched a global supply chain game.

The Global Supply Chain Competition pitted 12 teams of business students from around the world in a real-time simulation of supply chain management. Each team of three students developed its own market and sourcing strategies and then went to market with a portfolio of four products. They responded to bids from virtual customers, set pricing, arranged deliveries, and fought for profit and market share against the other teams.

Students and professors tinkered with the game for 18 months prior to the competition in conjunction with classroom instruction on supply chain concepts. As students learned about inventory strategies, sourcing, transportation, marketing and procurement, they were able to see how these functions come into play when operating a real business. The March 27 competition was the first global event that put each team in direct competition.

With a portfolio of four high-tech products, each having a rapid depreciation rate, each team had to decide on a go-to-market strategy. Would they concentrate on the laptop product line, laptops and multimedia systems, or all of the products? Would they sell locally or globally? And, would they source locally or globally?

Source: Adapted from Perry A. Trunick, "What-If Game on a Global Scale," *Logistics Today,* April 2007, pp. 23–27.

roles. The success of this method depends on the ability of participants to assume the roles realistically. Videotaping allows for review and evaluation of the exercise to improve its effectiveness.

In-Basket Techniques

in-basket technique Simulates a realistic situation by requiring each trainee to answer one manager's mail and telephone calls.

The **in-basket technique** simulates a realistic situation by requiring each trainee to answer one manager's mail and telephone calls. Important duties are interspersed with routine matters. For instance, one call may come from an important customer who is angry, while a letter from a local civic club may request a donation. The trainees analyze the situations and suggest alternative actions. They are evaluated on the basis of the number and quality of decisions and on the priorities assigned to each situation. The in-basket technique has been used not only for management development but also in assessment centers, which are discussed later in this chapter.

Business Games

business game Generally provides a setting of a company and its environment and requires a team of players to make decisions involving company operations.

Business games generally provide a setting of a company and its environment and require a team of players to make decisions involving company operations. They also normally require the use of computer facilities. In a business game, several teams act as companies within a type of industry. This method forces individuals not only to work with other group members but also to function in an atmosphere of competition within the industry.

Advantages of business games are that they simulate reality, decisions are made in a competitive environment, feedback is provided concerning decisions, and decisions are made using less than complete data. The main disadvantage is that many participants simply attempt to determine the key to winning. When this occurs, the game is not used to its fullest potential as a learning device. Management Illustration 12.3 describes a business simulation.

Management Education

In addition to traditional on- and off-the-job training, manager development can occur within the confines of the academic or special (seminar) education environment. Expert

Management Illustration 12.4

ORGILL'S CORPORATE UNIVERSITY

Orgill started its university program on the sales side six years ago. The primary goal was to expand sales staffers' knowledge beyond merely information on vendors and products.

Now the program has grown to include two classes of employees, one remaining in the sales vein and another for corporate and administrative professionals. The program has grown to include multiple training modules and speakers from all sides of the industry.

Jerry Cardwell, vice president of Orgill, said, "For presenters for modules, we use both internal staff and external resources." For instance, I work very closely with the University of Memphis.

The corporate and administrative sector of the program starts with Orgill 101, an "overview" program that teaches administrative trainees about the 160-year history of the company. "We have a deep, rich heritage, and we're honored to be able to share that heritage with both existing and new employees," Cardwell said. Orgill 101 also teaches participants how Orgill fits into the home improvement and professional market as a whole.

A second portion of Orgill's corporate and administrative training program focuses on team building. Further programs include the "Advantage Development Program," known as ADP, a two-year long, seven-module training course that mixes online learning, help from local universities and sessions that "go beyond the scope of a typical corporate-executed program," Cardwell said.

Source: Kate Fazzini, "Orgill: Corporate University," *House Channel News,* August 13, 2007, pp. 25–28.

training can occur within additional undergraduate, MBA, executive MBA, or special seminar programs. These methods rely on sources outside the corporation to control and design the educational material for managers who wish to receive additional training. At their best, these programs can provide fresh ideas, strategies, and perspectives for the manager-student. At their worst, they may lack real-world application and be a waste of time. Among the chief complaints regarding the university-based programs are that they are too lengthy, drain the energy of employees, and may encourage career moves and employment changes. The last is a particularly distressing problem considering that many companies pay 80 percent of the tuition for advanced or additional degrees. Internet-based college courses are increasing rapidly. Management Illustration 12.4 describes a corporate university.

Assessment Centers

assessment center
Utilizes a formal procedure to simulate the problems a person might face in a real managerial situation to evaluate the person's potential as a manager and determine the person's development needs.

An **assessment center** utilizes a formal procedure to evaluate an employee's potential as a manager and determine that employee's developmental needs. Assessment centers are used for making decisions about promoting, evaluating, and training managerial personnel. Basically, these centers simulate the problems a person might face in a real managerial situation. In the typical center, 10 to 15 employees of about equal organizational rank are brought together for three to five days to work on individual and group exercises typical of a managerial job. Business games, in-basket techniques, and role playing are used to simulate managerial situations. These exercises involve the participants in decision making, leadership, written and oral communication, planning, organizing, and motivating. Assessors observe the participants, rate their performance, and provide feedback to them about their performance and developmental needs.

Assessors are often selected from management ranks several levels above those of the participants. Also, psychologists from outside the organization often serve as assessors. For a program to be successful, the assessors must be thoroughly trained in the assessment process, the mechanics of the exercises to be observed, and the techniques of observing and providing feedback.

Some operational problems can arise in using assessment centers. First, the organization must recognize that they are often more costly than other methods of management assessment. Problems can also occur when employees come from different levels in the organization. When their differences become apparent, lower-level participants often defer to those at higher levels during the group exercises; thus, the assessment results are biased. Finally, certain "canned" exercises may be only remotely related to the on-the-job activity at the organization in question. Care must be taken to ensure that exercises used in the assessment center bring out the specific skills and aptitudes needed in the position for which participants are being assessed.

EVALUATING EMPLOYEE TRAINING AND MANAGEMENT DEVELOPMENT ACTIVITIES

When the results of employee training and management development are evaluated, certain benefits accrue. Less effective programs can be withdrawn to save time and effort. Weaknesses within programs can be identified and remedied. Evaluation of training and management development activities can be broken down into four areas:

1. *Reaction.* How well did the trainees like the program?
2. *Learning.* What principles, facts, and concepts were learned in the program?
3. *Behavior.* Did the job behavior of the trainees change because of the program?
4. *Results.* What were the results of the program in terms of factors such as reduced costs or reduction in turnover?

Even when great care is taken in designing evaluation procedures, it is difficult to determine the exact effects of training on learning, behavior, and results.[2] Because of this, the evaluation of training is still limited and often superficial. However, if the management development programs are carefully tied to the focus of the corporate mission, related to the organization's strategic plan, and supported with sincere commitment on the part of senior management, they provide great benefits and move the organization in the direction of positive growth. Motivating employees usually is a function of opportunities for advancement and a corporate culture that encourages change and growth. In-house training, updated knowledge of computer technology, increased ability to create and implement strategy, and empowerment are no longer extras in which only some companies are interested. They are mandates for successful competition.

Summary

1. *Define human asset accounting.* Human asset accounting involves determining and recording the value of an organization's human resources in its statement of financial condition.
2. *Describe the orientation process.* Orientation is the introduction of new employees to the organization, their work units, and their jobs.
3. *Define training.* Training is a process that involves acquiring skills or learning concepts to increase the performance of employees.
4. *Define needs assessment.* Needs assessment is a systematic analysis of the specific training activities required to achieve the organization's objectives.
5. *Discuss vestibule training, apprenticeship training, and computer-based training.* In vestibule training, procedures and equipment similar to those used in the actual job are set up in a special working area called a *vestibule,* where the trainee learns the job at a comfortable pace without the pressures of production schedules. Apprenticeship

training generally lasts from two to five years and requires the trainee to work under the guidance of a skilled worker over this period. Computer-based training allows the trainee to absorb information from a preset computer program in a self-paced format.

6. *List and define the most popular methods of management development.* Understudy assignments require the person who will someday have a specific job to work for the incumbent to learn the job. With coaching, experienced managers advise and guide trainees in solving management problems. Job rotation exposes a manager to broad experiences in many different areas of the organization. Role playing requires trainees to act out assigned roles in a realistic situation. In-basket techniques require the trainee to answer one manager's mail and telephone calls. Business games generally provide settings of the company and its environment and require a team of players to make operating decisions.
7. *Describe an assessment center.* An assessment center utilizes a formal procedure to simulate the problems a person might face in a real managerial situation to evaluate the person's potential as a manager and determine the person's development needs.
8. *List the steps involved in the evaluation of training and management development.* The four steps in the evaluation of training and management development are (1) reaction (How well did the trainees like the program?), (2) learning (What principles, facts, and concepts were learned in the program?), (3) behavior (Did the job behavior of the trainees change because of the program?), and (4) results (What were the results of the program in terms of factors such as reduced costs or reduced turnover?).

Review Questions

1. What is human asset accounting?
2. What is orientation?
3. Describe the two distinct levels at which orientation is normally conducted within organizations.
4. What is training?
5. Describe the following methods of training:
   a. On-the-job.
   b. Job rotation.
   c. Vestibule.
   d. Apprenticeship.
   e. Computer-based training.
6. What is management development?
7. Describe the following methods used in management development:
   a. Understudy assignments.
   b. Coaching.
   c. Job rotation.
   d. Special projects and committee assignments.
   e. Classroom training.
8. What is an assessment center?
9. Describe four areas in the evaluation of training and management development.

Skill-Building Questions

1. Discuss the following statement: Why should we train our employees? It is a waste of money because they soon leave and another organization gets the benefits.
2. Outline a system for evaluating a development program for supervisors.
3. Discuss the following statement: Management games are fun, but you don't really learn anything from them.
4. Why are training programs generally one of the first areas to be eliminated when an organization must cut its budget?

SKILL-BUILDING EXERCISE 12.1 Training Methods

Summarized below are some methods that can be used in training both operative and managerial employees. Your professor will assign one of these methods for you to explain to your class. You are to prepare a five-minute presentation describing the method, how it works, and its strengths and weaknesses.

- Role playing
- Sensitivity training
- Simulation exercises
- Wilderness training
- In-basket technique
- Incident method
- Vestibule training
- Apprenticeship training

SKILL-BUILDING EXERCISE 12.2 OJT

Assume you are training director for a large, local retail company. The company has seven department stores in your city. One of your biggest problems is adequately training new salesclerks. Because salesclerks represent your company to the public, the manner in which they conduct themselves is highly important. Especially critical aspects of their job include knowledge of the computerized cash register system, interaction with the customers, and knowledge of the particular products being sold.

1. Design a three-day orientation/training program for these salesclerks. Be sure to outline the specific topics (subjects) to be covered and the techniques to be used.
2. Specify what methods could be used to evaluate the success of the program.
3. Be prepared to present your program to the class.

Case Incident 12.1

Starting a New Job

Jack Smythe, branch manager for a large computer manufacturer, has just been told by his marketing manager, Bob Sprague, that Otis Brown has given two weeks' notice. When Jack had interviewed Otis, he had been convinced of the applicant's tremendous potential in sales. Otis was bright and personable, an honor graduate in electrical engineering from Massachusetts Institute of Technology who had the qualifications the company looked for in computer sales. Now he was leaving after only two months with the company. Jack called Otis into his office for an exit interview.

Jack: Come in, Otis, I really want to talk to you. I hope I can change your mind about leaving.

Otis: I don't think so.

Jack: Well, tell me why you want to go. Has some other company offered you more money?

Otis: No. In fact, I don't have another job. I'm just starting to look.

Jack: You've given us notice without having another job?

Otis: Well, I just don't think this is the place for me!

Jack: What do you mean?

Otis: Let me see if I can explain. On my first day at work, I was told that my formal classroom training in computers would not begin for a month. I was given a sales manual and told to read and study it for the rest of the day.

The next day I was told that the technical library, where all the manuals on computers are kept, was in a mess and needed to be organized. That was to be my responsibility for the next three weeks.

The day before I was to begin computer school, my boss told me that the course had been delayed for another month. He said not to worry, however, because he was going to have James Chess, the branch's leading salesperson, give me some on-the-job training. I was told to accompany James on his calls. I'm supposed to start the computer school in two weeks, but I've just made up my mind that this place is not for me.

Jack: Hold on a minute, Otis. That's the way it is for everyone in the first couple months of employment in our industry. Any place you go will be the same. In fact, you had it better than I did. You should have seen what I did in my first couple of months.

Questions

1. What do you think about the philosophy of this company on a new employee's first few months on the job?
2. What suggestions do you have for Jack to help his company avoid similar problems of employee turnover in the future?

Case Incident 12.2

A New Computer System

John Brown, 52, has been at State Bank for 30 years. Over the past 20 years, he has worked in the bank's investment department. During his first 15 years, the department was managed by Lisa Adams. The department consisted of Lisa, John, and two other employees. Lisa made all decisions, while the others performed manual recordkeeping functions. When Lisa retired five years ago, John held the position of assistant cashier.

Tom Smith took over the investment department after Lisa Adams retired. Tom, 56, has worked for State Bank for the past 28 years. Shortly after taking control of the department, Tom recognized that it needed to be modernized and staffed with people capable of giving better service to the bank's customers. As a result, he increased the department workforce to 10 people and installed two different computer systems. Of the 10 employees, only John and Tom are older than 33.

When Tom took over the department, John was a big help because he knew all about how the department had been run in the past. Tom considered John to be a capable worker; after about a year, he promoted John to assistant vice president.

After he had headed the department for about a year and a half, Tom purchased a computer package to handle the bond portfolio and its accounting. When the new system was implemented, John said he did not like the computer system and would have nothing to do with it.

Over the next two years, further changes came about. As the other employees in the department became more experienced, they branched into new areas of investment work. The old ways of doing things were replaced by new, more sophisticated methods. John resisted these changes; he refused to accept or learn new methods and ideas. He slipped more and more into doing only simple but time-consuming activities.

Presently, a new computer system is being acquired for the investment section, and another department is being put under Tom's control. John has written Tom a letter stating he wants no part of the new computer systems but would like to be the manager of the new department. In his letter, John said he was tired of being given routine tasks while the "young people" got all the exciting jobs. John contended that since he has been with the bank longer than anyone else, he should be given first shot at the newly created job.

Questions

1. What suggestions do you have to motivate John to train on the new computer systems?
2. What methods of training would you recommend for John?

References and Additional Readings

1. See, for example, John P. Wanous and Arnon E. Aeichers, "New Employee Orientation Programs," *Human Resource Management Review,* Winter 2000, pp. 435–52.
2. For more information, see Jack McKillip, "Case Studies in Job Analysis and Training Evaluation," *International Journal of Training and Development,* December 2001, pp. 283–90.

After he had headed the department for about a year and a half, Tom purchased a computer package to handle the bond portfolio and its accounting. When the new system was implemented, John said he did not like the computer system and would have nothing to do with it.

Over the next two years, further changes came about. As the other employees in the department became more experienced, they branched into new areas of investment work. The old ways of doing things were replaced by new, more sophisticated methods. John resisted these changes; he refused to accept or learn new methods and ideas. He slipped more and more into doing only simple but time-consuming activities.

Presently, a new computer system is being acquired for the investment section, and another department is being put under Tom's control. John has written Tom a letter stating he wants no part of the new computer systems but would like to be the manager of the new department. In his letter, John said he was tired of being given routine tasks while the "young people" got all the exciting jobs. John contended that since he has been with the bank longer than anyone else, he should be given first shot at the newly created job.

Questions

1. What suggestions do you have to motivate John to train on the new computer systems?
2. What methods of training would you recommend for John?

References and Additional Readings

1. See, for example, John P. Wanous and Arnon E. Aeichers, "New Employee Orientation Programs," *Human Resource Management Review,* Winter 2000, pp. 435–52.
2. For more information, see Jack McKillip, "Case Studies in Job Analysis and Training Evaluation," *International Journal of Training and Development,* December 2001, pp. 283–90.

Directing Skills

13. Motivating Employees
14. Developing Leaderships Skills
15. Managing Conflict and Stress
16. Managing Change and Culture

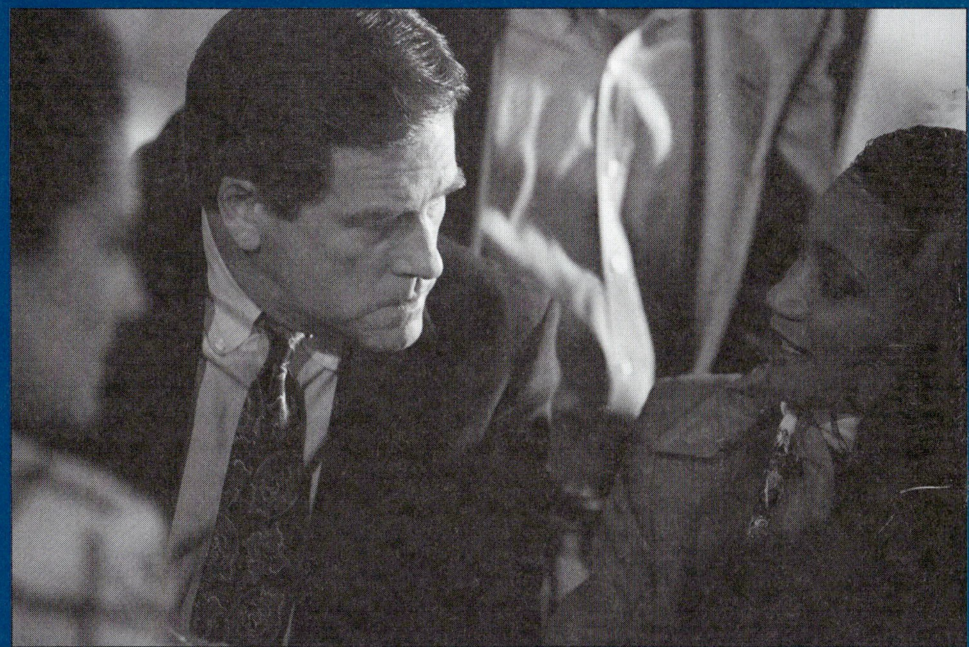

Chapter Thirteen

Motivating Employees

Learning Objectives

After studying this chapter, you will be able to:

1. Define motivation.
2. Explain the importance of trust in management in motivation.
3. Describe the scientific management approach to motivation.
4. Explain the equity approach to motivation.
5. Explain the hierarchy of needs.
6. Discuss the achievement-power-affiliation approach to motivation.
7. Discuss the motivation-maintenance approach to motivation.
8. Discuss the expectancy approach to motivation.
9. Explain the reinforcement approach to motivation.
10. Define job satisfaction and organizational morale.

Chapter Preview

Minimill steelmaker Nucor has nurtured one of the most dynamic and engaged workforces around. Nucor's flattened hierarchy and emphasis on pushing power to the front line lead its employees to adopt the mindset of owner-operators. It's a profitable formula: Nucor's 387 percent return to shareholders over the past five years handily beats almost all other companies in the Standard & Poor's 500 stock index. Legendary leader F. Kenneth Iverson's radical insight: that employees, even hourly clock-punchers, will make an extraordinary effort if you reward them richly, treat them with respect, and give them real power.

At Nucor, the art of motivation is about an unblinking focus on the people on the front line of the business. It's about talking to them, listening to them, taking a risk on their ideas, and accepting the occasional failure. At a time when many observers are busy hammering the final nail into the coffin of American heavy manufacturing, Nucor's business model is well worth considering. But Nucor's path is hard to follow. It requires managers to abandon the command-and-control model that has dominated American business for the better part of a century, trust their people, and do a much better job of sharing corporate wealth.

Source: Adapted from Nanette Byrnes and Michael Arndt, "The Art of Motivation," *BusinessWeek,* May 1, 2006, p. 56.

Analyzing Management Skills

What do you think of Nucor's art of motivation?

Applying Management Skills

Imagine that you own two coffee shops. Assume that the overall economy is declining. Shop 1 is losing money. Shop 2 is doing very well. What would you do to motivate employees at shop 1? Shop 2?

Statements and questions such as the following are often expressed by managers: Our employees are just not motivated. Half the problems we have are due to a lack of personal motivation. How do I motivate my employees?

The problem of motivation is not a recent development. Research conducted by William James in the late 1800s indicated the importance of motivation.[1] James found that hourly employees could keep their jobs by using approximately 20 to 30 percent of their ability. He also found that highly motivated employees will work at approximately 80 to 90 percent of their ability. Figure 13.1 illustrates the potential influence of motivation on performance. Highly motivated employees can bring about substantial increases in performance and substantial decreases in problems such as absenteeism, turnover, tardiness, strikes, and grievances.

motivation
Concerned with what activates human behavior, what directs this behavior toward a particular goal, and how this behavior is sustained.

The word **motivation** comes from the Latin word *movere,* which means to move. Numerous definitions are given for the term. Usually included are such words as *aim, desire, end, impulse, intention, objective,* and *purpose.* These definitions normally include three common characteristics of motivation. First, motivation is concerned with what activates human behavior. Second, motivation is concerned with what directs this behavior toward a particular goal. Third, motivation is concerned with how this behavior is sustained.

Motivation can be analyzed using the following causative sequence:

Needs → Drives or motives → Achievemennt of goals

In motivation, needs produce motives, which lead to the accomplishment of goals. Needs are caused by deficiencies, which can be either physical or psychological. For instance, a physical need exists when an individual goes without sleep for 48 hours. A psychological need exists when an individual has no friends or companions. Individual needs will be explored in much greater depth later in this chapter.

FIGURE 13.1
Potential Influence of Motivation on Performance

Source: P. Hersey and K. H. Blanchard, *Management of Organizational Behavior: Utilizing Human Resources,* 4th ed., Prentice Hall, 1982.

A motive is a stimulus that leads to an action that satisfies the need. In other words, motives produce actions. Lack of sleep (the need) activates the physical changes of fatigue (the motive), which produces sleep (the action or, in this example, inaction).

Achievement of the goal satisfies the need and reduces the motive. When the goal is reached, balance is restored. However, other needs arise, which are then satisfied by the same sequence of events. Understanding the motivation sequence in itself offers a manager little help in determining what motivates employees. The approaches to analyzing motivation described in this chapter help to provide a broader understanding of what motivates people. They include the following: scientific management, equity, hierarchy of needs, achievement-power-affiliation, motivation-maintenance, expectancy, and reinforcement.

IMPORTANCE OF TRUST IN MANAGEMENT

The importance of trust in management by employees cannot be stressed enough as being absolutely essential for the success (or failure) of all motivational efforts. Without trust in management, all organizational efforts to motivate employees for improved performance is suspect. The presence of trust gives management credibility when asking for more productivity from employees.

SCIENTIFIC MANAGEMENT APPROACH

The scientific management approach to motivation evolved from the work of Frederick W. Taylor and the scientific management movement that took place at the turn of the last century. Taylor's ideas were based on his belief that existing reward systems were not designed to reward individuals for high production. He believed that when highly productive employees discover they are being compensated basically the same as less productive employees, then the output of highly productive employees will decrease. Taylor's solution was quite simple. He designed a system whereby an employee was compensated according to individual production.

One of Taylor's problems was determining a reasonable standard of performance. Taylor solved the problem by breaking jobs down into components and measuring the time necessary to accomplish each component. In this way, Taylor was able to establish standards of performance "scientifically."

Taylor's plan was unique in that he had one rate of pay for units produced up to the standard. Once the standard was reached, a significantly higher rate was paid, not only for the units above the standard but also for all units produced during the day. Thus, under Taylor's system, employees could in many cases significantly increase their pay for production above the standard.

The scientific management approach to motivation is based on the assumption that money is the primary motivator of employees. Financial rewards are directly related to performance in the belief that if the reward is great enough, employees will produce more.

EQUITY APPROACH

Equity theory is based on the idea that people want to be treated fairly in relationship to others. The equity approach to job motivation is based on the work of J. Stacey Adams. **Inequity** exists when a person perceives his or her job inputs and rewards to be less than the job inputs and outcomes of another person. The important point to note in this definition

equity theory
Motivation theory based on the idea that people want to be treated fairly in relationship to others.

inequity
Exists when a person perceives his or her job inputs and outcomes to be less than the job inputs and outcomes of another person.

inputs
What an employee perceives are his or her contributions to the organization (i.e., education, intelligence, experience, training, skills, and the effort exerted on the job).

is that it is the person's *perception* of inputs and rewards, not necessarily the actual inputs and rewards. Furthermore, the other person in the comparison can be an employee in the person's work group or in another part of the organization, which forms the employee's internal equity perception. Likewise, an employee may compare his or her inputs and rewards to others outside the company in like jobs.

Inputs are what an employee perceives are his or her contributions to the organization (i.e., education, intelligence, experience, training, skills, and the effort exerted on the job). Outcomes are the rewards received by the employee (i.e., pay, rewards intrinsic to the job, seniority benefits, and status).

Equity theory also postulates that the presence of inequity in a person creates tension in that person that is proportional to the magnitude of the inequity. Furthermore, the tension will motivate someone to achieve equity or reduce inequity. The strength of the motivation varies directly with the amount of inequity. A person might take several actions to reduce inequity:

1. Increase inputs on the job if his or her inputs are low relative to the other person. For example, a person might work harder to increase his or her inputs on the job.
2. Reduce inputs if they are high relative to the other person's inputs and to his or her own outcomes.
3. Quit the job.
4. Request a pay increase.

HIERARCHY OF NEEDS

need hierarchy
Based on the assumption that individuals are motivated to satisfy a number of needs and that money can directly or indirectly satisfy only some of these needs.

The **hierarchy of needs** is based on the assumption that individuals are motivated to satisfy a number of needs and that money can directly or indirectly satisfy only some of these needs. The need hierarchy is based largely on the work of Abraham Maslow.[2] The hierarchy of needs consists of the five levels shown in Figure 13.2.

The physiological needs are basically the needs of the human body that must be satisfied in order to sustain life. These needs include food, sleep, water, exercise, clothing, shelter, and so forth.

Safety needs are concerned with protection against danger, threat, or deprivation. Since all employees have (to some degree) a dependent relationship with the organization, safety needs can be critically important. Favoritism, discrimination, and arbitrary administration of organizational policies are all actions that arouse uncertainty and therefore affect the safety needs.

The third level of needs is composed of the social needs. Generally categorized at this level are the needs for love, affection, belonging—all are concerned with establishing one's position relative to others. This need is satisfied by the development of meaningful personal relations and by acceptance into meaningful groups of individuals. Belonging to organizations and identifying with work groups are means of satisfying these needs in organizations.

The fourth level of needs is composed of the esteem needs. The esteem needs include both self-esteem and the esteem of others. These needs influence the development of various kinds of relationships based on adequacy, independence, and the giving and receiving of indications of esteem and acceptance.

The highest-order need is concerned with the need for self-actualization or self-fulfillment—that is, the need of people to reach their full potential in applying their abilities and interests to functioning in their environment. This need is concerned with the will to

FIGURE 13.2 Hierarchy of Needs

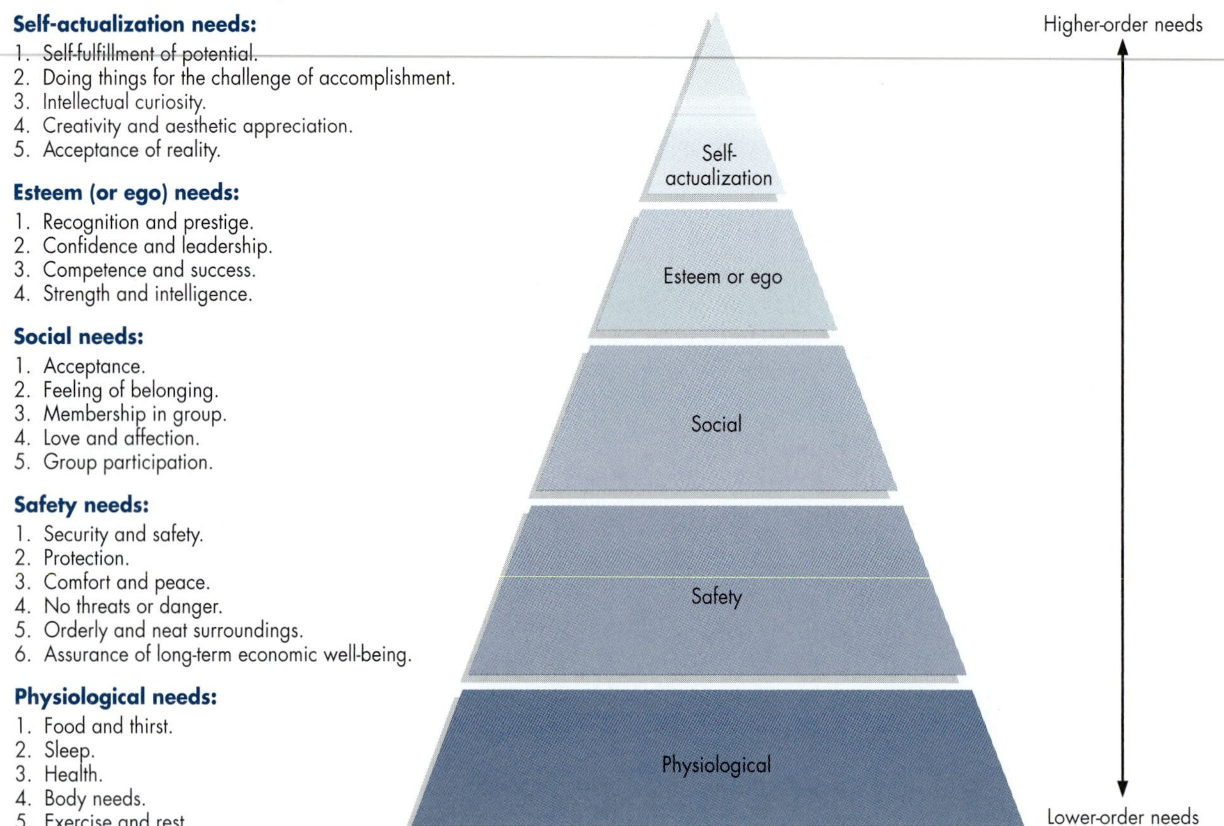

operate at the optimum. The need for self-actualization or self-fulfillment is never completely satisfied; one can always reach one step higher.

Self-actualization needs:
1. Self-fulfillment of potential.
2. Doing things for the challenge of accomplishment.
3. Intellectual curiosity.
4. Creativity and aesthetic appreciation.
5. Acceptance of reality.
Esteem (or ego) needs:
1. Recognition and prestige.
2. Confidence and leadership.
3. Competence and success.
4. Strength and intelligence.
Social needs:
1. Acceptance.
2. Feeling of belonging.
3. Membership in group.
4. Love and affection.
5. Group participation.
Safety needs:
1. Security and safety.
2. Protection.
3. Comfort and peace.
4. No threats or danger.
5. Orderly and neat surroundings.
6. Assurance of long-term economic well-being.
Physiological needs:
1. Food and thirst.
2. Sleep.
3. Health.
4. Body needs.
5. Exercise and rest.
Self-actualization
Esteem or ego
Social
Safety
Physiological
Higher-order needs
Lower-order needs

The hierarchy of needs adequately describes the general order or ranking of most people's needs. However, there are several other possibilities to be considered. First, although the needs of most people are arranged in the sequence shown in Figure 13.2, differences in the sequence can occur, depending on an individual's experience, culture, social upbringing, and numerous other personality aspects. Second, the strength or potency of a person's needs may shift back and forth under different situations. For instance, during bad economic times, physiological and safety needs might tend to dominate an individual's behavior; in good economic times, higher-order needs might dominate an individual's behavior.

The unconscious character of the various needs should be recognized. In addition, there is a certain degree of cultural specificity of needs. In other words, the ways by which the various needs can be met tend to be controlled by cultural and societal factors. For example, the particular culture may dictate one's eating habits, social life, and numerous other facets of life.

Finally, different methods can be used by different individuals to satisfy a particular need. Two individuals may be deficient in relation to the same physiological need; however, the way in which each chooses to satisfy that need may vary considerably.

As far as motivation is concerned, the thrust of the hierarchy of needs is that the lowest-level unsatisfied need causes behavior. The hierarchy represents what Maslow thought was the order in which unsatisfied needs would activate behavior.

Management Illustration 13.1

REWARDING EMPLOYEES

Gone are the days when a pat on the back for a job well done or a gold watch after 25 years of service are enough to keep employees happy, productive and profitable. Savvy CEOs and managers are spending time, money and resources on the "3Rs" of employee satisfaction—recognition, reward, and retainment. Increased spending on employee recognition and reward programs is now seen as an investment rather than an expense.

Manitoba Telecom Services has many ways to recognize employees says Marilyn Grayston of MTS Human Resources. There is a traditional service award program that marks milestones of 5 to 45 years, where employees select a gift from the different level categories, and at 25 or more years of service are honored with a formal dinner. The "tel-1-more" program rewards people for sales leads and allows them to accumulate points towards purchasing rewards.

Top MTS sales representatives who exceed specific revenue targets qualify to become part of the President's Sales Club and are often rewarded with all-expense paid trips to the Caribbean, Mexico, or the Dominican Republic. Other high achievers who exhibit superior performance at work or in the community may receive a President's Achievement Award and check for $5,000 for an individual or $12,500 for a team, with winners selected by a committee and announced at a special dinner.

The "You're A Star" peer recognition program at MTS allows employees or managers to acknowledge their colleagues who exhibit core company values and reward them with gift certificates of varied amounts.

Source: Adapted from Barbara Edie, "Rewarding Employees," *Manitoba Business,* June 2006, pp. 16–17.

Many of today's organizations are applying the logic of the needs hierarchy. For instance, compensation systems are generally designed to satisfy the lower-order needs—physiological and safety. On the other hand, interesting work and opportunities for advancement are designed to appeal to higher-order needs. So the job of a manager is to determine the need level an individual employee is attempting to satisfy and then provide the means by which the employee can satisfy that need. Obviously, determining the need level of a particular person can be difficult. All people do not operate at the same level on the needs hierarchy. All people do not react similarly to the same situation.

Little research has been conducted to test the validity of the hierarchy of needs theory. Its primary value is that it provides a structure for analyzing needs and, as will be seen later in this chapter, is used as a basis for other theories of motivation. Management Illustration 13.1 describes one firm's many approaches for motivating employees.

ACHIEVEMENT-POWER-AFFILIATION APPROACH

While recognizing that people have many different needs, David C. McClelland developed the achievement-power-affiliation approach to motivation, which focuses on three needs: (1) need to achieve, (2) need for power, and (3) need for affiliation.[3] The use of the term *need* in this approach is different from the hierarchy of needs approach in that, under this approach, the three needs are assumed to be learned, whereas the needs hierarchy assumes that needs are inherent.

The need for achievement is a desire to do something better or more efficiently than it has been done before—to achieve. The need for power is basically a concern for influencing people—to be strong and influential. The need for affiliation is a need to be liked—to establish or maintain friendly relations with others.

This approach assumes that most people have developed a degree of each of these needs, but the level of intensity varies among people. For example, an individual may be high in the need for achievement, moderate in the need for power, and low in the need for affiliation. This individual's motivation to work will vary greatly from that of another person who

FIGURE 13.3
Achievement-Power-Affiliation Needs

1. The Need for Power

Some people are strongly motivated by the need for power. They are likely to be happiest in jobs that give them control over budgets, people, and decision making.

2. The Need for Achievement

Other people are strongly motivated by the need for achievement. They are likely to be happiest working in an environment in which they can create something new.

3. The Need for Affiliation

Some people are strongly motivated by the need for affiliation. These people usually enjoy working with other people. They are motivated by the prospect of having people like them.

has a high need for power and low needs for achievement and affiliation. An employee with a high need for affiliation would probably respond positively to demonstrations of warmth and support by a manager; an employee with a high need for achievement would likely respond positively to increased responsibility. Finally, under this approach to motivation, when a need's strength has been developed, it motivates behaviors or attracts employees to situations where such behaviors can be acted out. However, this does not satisfy the need; it is more likely to strengthen it further. Figure 13.3 describes this approach to motivation.

MOTIVATION-MAINTENANCE APPROACH

motivation maintenance
An approach to work motivation that associates factors of high-low motivation with either the work environment or the work itself. Also called *motivation hygiene.*

Another approach to work motivation was developed by Frederick Herzberg and is referred to by several names: the **motivation-maintenance,** two-factor, or motivation-hygiene approach.[4] Initially, the development of the approach involved extensive interviews with approximately 200 engineers and accountants from 11 industries in the Pittsburgh area. In the interviews, researchers used what is called the critical incident method. This involved asking subjects to recall work situations in which they had experienced periods of high and low motivation. They were asked to recount specific details about the situation and the effect of the experience over time.

Analysis of the interviewees' statements showed that different factors were associated with good and bad feelings. The findings fell into two major categories. Those factors that were most frequently mentioned in association with a favorably viewed incident concerned the work itself. These factors were achievement, recognition, responsibility, advancement, and the characteristics of the job. But when subjects felt negatively oriented toward a work incident, they were more likely to mention factors associated with the work environment. These included status; interpersonal relations with supervisors, peers, and subordinates; technical aspects of supervision; company policy and administration; job security; working conditions; salary; and aspects of their personal lives that were affected by the work situation.

The latter set of factors was called *hygiene* or *maintenance* factors because the researchers thought that they are preventive in nature. In other words, they do not produce motivation but can prevent motivation from occurring. Thus, proper attention to maintenance factors is a necessary but not sufficient condition for motivation. The first set of factors were called *motivators.* The researchers contended that these factors, when present in addition to the maintenance factors, provide true motivation.

In summary, the motivation-hygiene approach contends that motivation comes from the individual, not from the manager. At best, proper attention to the maintenance factors keeps an individual from being highly dissatisfied but does not make that individual

Management Illustration 13.2

IT IS NOT THE MONEY

Money is not the prime key in attracting and motivating staff. Rewarding work and career progression are the biggest incentives, as the Computer Weekly/Computer People Salary and Benefits Survey makes clear.

Information Technology (IT) has long had a reputation as a profession that can offer high salaries for high flyers. But a major study by *Computer Weekly* and recruitment specialists Computer People shows that for most IT professionals, it is not how much they earn, but how challenging their job is that counts. The survey of nearly 3,000 *Computer Weekly* readers shows that engaging work, recognition for a job well done, job security, freedom to make decisions, and career prospects, all rank above salary in most important factors in any job.

The findings will have profound implications for employers who want to attract and retain the best people. Many are facing an uphill struggle to recruit qualified IT professionals, particularly those with business experience, as competition for staff heats up.

Source: Adapted from Bill Goodwin, "It's the Challenge That Pays," *Computer Weekly,* January 9, 2007, p. 26–27.

FIGURE 13.4
Motivation-Hygiene Factors

Hygiene Factors (Environmental)	Motivator Factors (Job Itself)
Policies and administration	Achievement
Supervision	Recognition
Working conditions	Challenging work
Interpersonal relations	Increased responsibility
Personal life	Opportunities for advancement
Money, status, security	Opportunities for personal growth

job enlargement
Giving an employee more of a similar type of operation to perform.

job rotation
Process in which the trainee goes from one job to another within the organization, generally remaining in each job from six months to a year.

job enrichment
Upgrading of the job by adding motivator factors.

expectancy approach
Based on the idea that employee beliefs about the relationship among effort, performance, and outcomes as a result of performance and the value employees place on the outcomes determine their level of motivation.

motivated. Both hygiene and motivator factors must be present in order for true motivation to occur. Figure 13.4 lists some examples of hygiene and motivator factors. Management Illustration 13.2 describes factors that rank higher than money.

Job enrichment programs have been developed in an attempt to solve motivational problems by using the motivation-maintenance theory. Unlike **job enlargement,** which merely involves giving an employee more of a similar type of operation to perform, or **job rotation,** which is the practice of periodically rotating job assignments, **job enrichment** involves an upgrading of the job by adding motivator factors. Designing jobs that provide for meaningful work, achievement, recognition, responsibility, advancement, and growth is the key to job enrichment.

As can be seen from Figure 13.5, the motivation-hygiene approach is very closely related to the hierarchy of needs approach to motivation and so is subject to many of the same criticisms.

What does a manager do in using the maintenance-hygiene theory when the manager has an employee that is not performing well? First, all hygiene factors should be checked to ensure that they are satisfactory. Then a motivation should be applied that meets the individual's needs and drives.

EXPECTANCY APPROACH

The **expectancy approach** to motivation was developed by Victor Vroom and is based on the idea that employee beliefs about the relationship among effort, performance, and outcomes as a result of performance and the value employees place on the outcomes determine their level of motivation.[5] Figure 13.6 outlines the expectancy approach to motivation.

FIGURE 13.5
Comparison of the Hierarchy of Needs with the Motivation-Hygiene Approach

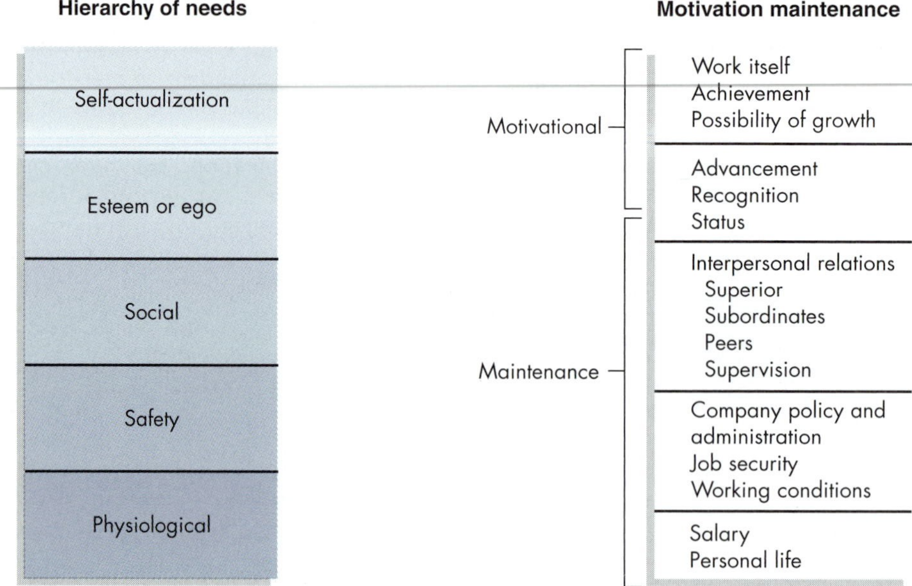

expectancy
Employee's belief that his or her effort will lead to the desired level of performance.

instrumentality
Employee's belief that attaining the desired level of performance will lead to desired rewards.

valence
Employee's belief about the value of the rewards.

The expectancy approach postulates that an employee's level of motivation depends on three basic beliefs: expectancy, instrumentality, and valence. **Expectancy** refers to the employee's belief that his or her effort will lead to the desired level of performance. **Instrumentality** refers to the employee's belief that attaining the desired level of performance will lead to certain rewards. **Valence** refers to the employee's belief about the value of the rewards. External factors are beyond the employee's control and often negatively influence expectancies and instrumentalities because they introduce uncertainty into the relationship. Company policies and efficiency of the equipment being used are examples of external factors.

The following example is intended to illustrate the expectancy approach. Assume John Stone is an insurance salesman for the ABC Life Insurance Company. John has learned over the years that he completes one sale for approximately every six calls he makes. John has a high expectancy about the relationship between his effort and performance. Since John is on a straight commission, he also sees a direct relationship between performance and rewards. Thus, his expectation that increased effort will lead to increased rewards is relatively high. Further, suppose that John's income is currently in a high tax bracket such that he gets to keep, after taxes, only 60 percent of his commissions. This being the case, he may not look on the additional money he gets to keep (the outcome) as being very

FIGURE 13.6
Expectancy Approach

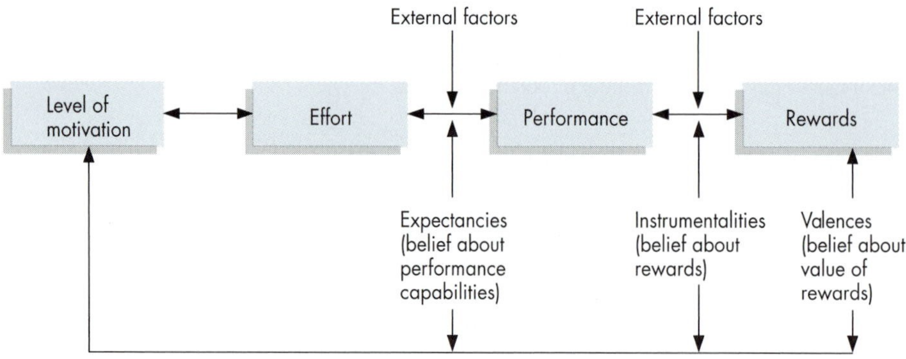

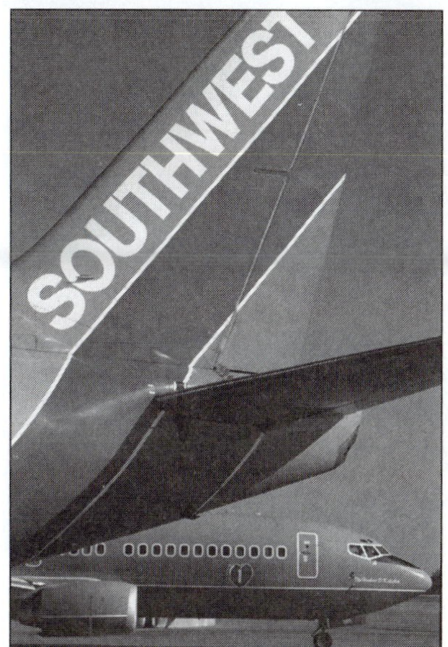

In order to maintain loyalty, high productivity, and innovation, Southwest has chosen to protect the jobs of its people even if it costs more than other options.

attractive. The end result is that John's belief about the value of the additional money (valence) may be relatively low. Thus, even when the expectation of receiving the additional money is high, his motivation to do additional work may be relatively low. Another way to illustrate this approach is as an equation: (expectancies) × (instrumentalities) × (valences), whereby if any of these variables are zero, the individual will not be motivated.

Each of the separate components of the expectancy approach can be affected by the organization's practices and management. The expectancy that increased effort will lead to increased performance can be positively influenced by providing proper selection, training, and clear direction to the workforce. The expectancy that increased performance will lead to desired rewards is almost totally under the control of the organization. Does the organization really attempt to link rewards to performance? Or are rewards based on some other variable, such as seniority? The final component—the preference for the rewards being offered—is usually taken for granted by the organization. Historically, organizations have assumed that whatever rewards are provided will be valued by employees. Even if this were true, some rewards are certainly more valued than others. Certain rewards, such as a promotion that involves a transfer to another city, may be viewed negatively. Organizations should solicit feedback from their employees concerning the types of rewards that are valued. Since an organization is going to spend a certain amount of money on rewards (salary, fringe benefits, and so on), it should try to get the maximum return from its investment.

REINFORCEMENT APPROACH

positive reinforcement
Providing a positive consequence as a result of desired behavior.

avoidance
Giving a person the opportunity to avoid a negative consequence by exhibiting a desired behavior. Also called *negative reinforcement.*

Developed by B. F. Skinner, the general idea behind the reinforcement approach to motivation is that the consequences of a person's present behavior influence his or her future behavior.[6] For example, behavior that leads to a positive consequence is likely to be repeated, while behavior that leads to a negative consequence is unlikely to be repeated.

The consequences of an individual's behavior are called *reinforcement.* Basically, four types of reinforcement exist—positive reinforcement, avoidance, extinction, and punishment. These are summarized in Figure 13.7. **Positive reinforcement** involves providing a positive consequence as a result of desired behavior. **Avoidance,** also called *negative reinforcement,* involves giving a person the opportunity to avoid a negative consequence by exhibiting a desired behavior. Both positive reinforcement and avoidance can be used to increase the frequency of desired behavior.

FIGURE 13.7
Types of Reinforcement

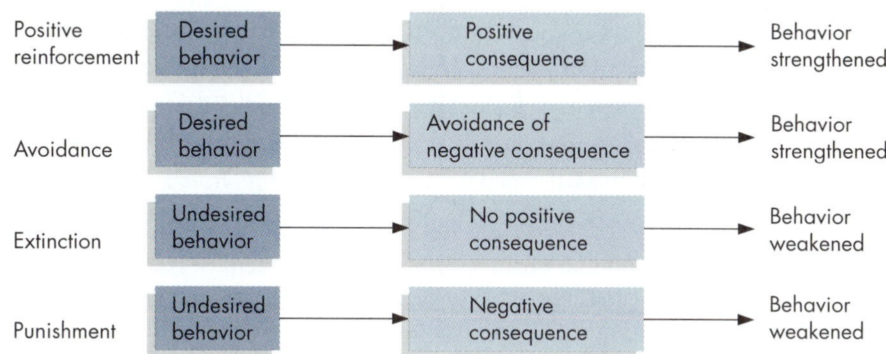

Management Illustration 13.3

FOUR STEPS TO BECOMING A PRAISER

1. Point out something that someone is doing right, every day. Make it a habit. This could be your spouse, your child, your pet, or a colleague. Let him or her know how appreciative you are. Remember—your praise has to be authentic, never phony or, heaven forbid, sarcastic. "Way to fix the fence, sport" won't do the trick when the fence is still falling apart!
2. Seek out good behavior in others that might not be repeated if it goes unnoticed. "Hey, I love the way you're standing up so straight and tall—you look beautiful" will work wonders for your teenage daughter who usually slumps, and it's much more effective than prodding her in the back all the time.
3. Make a list of your own "wins" over the past couple of months—big and small. Say a "good girl" to yourself for every one. Say it out loud if you like. Shout it from the window. Get used to how it feels.
4. Say "good girl" to yourself every chance you get from now on. Have fun with it. Sometimes just that verbal pat on the back will get you through times when things are so tough, everything feels like an effort. "Good girl to get out of bed!" "Good girl to put one foot in front of the other!" "Good girl to keep saying 'good girl!'"

Source: Adapted from Gail Blanke, "The Power of Praise," *Real Simple*, October 2007, p. 303.

extinction
Providing no positive consequences or removing previously provided positive consequences as a result of undesirable behavior.

punishment
Providing a negative consequence as a result of undesired behavior.

Extinction involves providing no positive consequences or removing previously provided positive consequences as a result of undesirable behavior. In other words, behavior that no longer pays is less likely to be repeated. **Punishment** involves providing a negative consequence as a result of undesired behavior. Both extinction and punishment can be used to decrease the frequency of undesired behavior.

The current emphasis on the use of reinforcement theory in management practices is concerned with positive reinforcement. Examples include increased pay for increased performance, and praise and recognition when an employee does a good job. Generally, several steps are to be followed in the use of positive reinforcement. These steps include:

1. Selecting reinforcers that are strong and durable enough to establish and strengthen the desired behavior.
2. Designing the work environment in such a way that the reinforcing events are contingent on the desired behavior.
3. Designing the work environment so that the employee has the opportunity to demonstrate the desired behavior.

The key to successful positive reinforcement is that rewards must result from performance. Several suggestions for the effective use of reinforcement have been proposed. These include the following:

1. All people should not be rewarded the same. In other words, the greater the level of performance by an employee, the greater should be the rewards.
2. Failure to respond to an employee's behavior has reinforcing consequences.
3. A person must be told what can be done to be reinforced.
4. A person must be told what he or she is doing wrong.
5. Reprimands should not be issued in front of others.
6. The consequences of a person's behavior should be equal to the behavior.

In addition, positive reinforcement generally is more effective than negative reinforcement and punishment in producing and maintaining desired behavior. Management Illustration 13.3 describes four steps to use in positive reinforcement.

FIGURE 13.8
The Relationship between Different Motivation Approaches

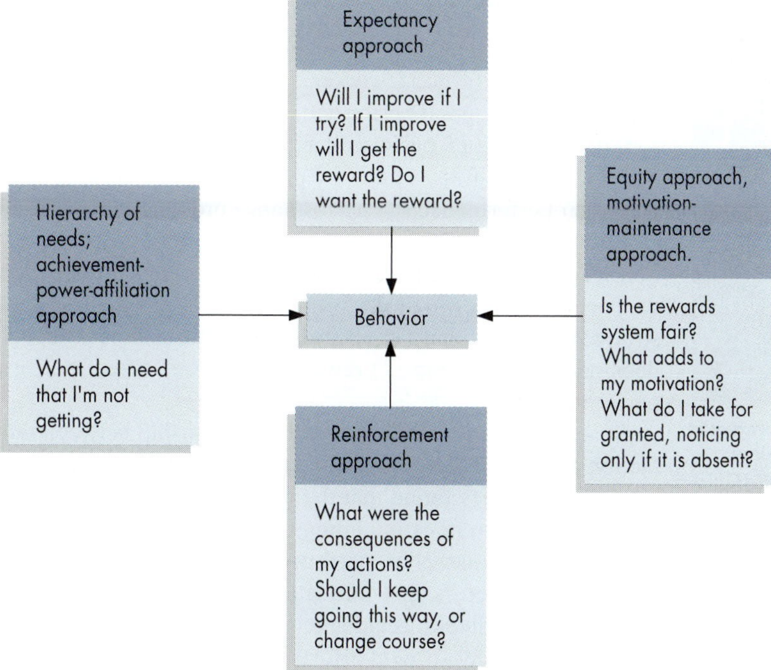

INTEGRATING THE APPROACHES TO MOTIVATION

There are many ways to look at motivation. Each approach emphasizes different contributors to motivation, or sees the same contributors from a different perspective (see Figure 13.8). No single approach provides all the answers, so it is sometimes necessary to utilize more than one approach.

JOB SATISFACTION

job satisfaction
An individual's general attitude about his or her job.

Job satisfaction is an individual's general attitude about his or her job. The five major components of job satisfaction are (1) attitude toward work group, (2) general working conditions, (3) attitude toward company, (4) monetary benefits, and (5) attitude toward supervision. Other major components that should be added to these five are the individual's attitudes toward the work itself and toward life in general. The individual's health, age, level of aspiration, social status, and political and social activities can all contribute to job satisfaction. Therefore, job satisfaction is an attitude that results from other specific attitudes and factors.

organizational morale
An individual's feeling of being accepted by, and belonging to, a group of employees through common goals, confidence in the desirability of these goals, and progress toward these goals.

Job satisfaction refers to the individual's mental set about the job. This mental set may be positive or negative, depending on the individual's mental set concerning the major components of job satisfaction. Job satisfaction is not synonymous with organizational morale. **Organizational morale** refers to an individual's feeling of being accepted by, and belonging to, a group of employees through common goals, confidence in the desirability of these goals, and progress toward these goals. Morale is related to group attitudes, whereas job satisfaction is more of an individual attitude. However, the two concepts are interrelated in that job satisfaction can contribute to morale and morale can contribute to job satisfaction.

Research generally rejects the more popular view that employee satisfaction leads to improved performance. The evidence does, however, provide moderate support for the view that performance causes satisfaction.

The Satisfaction-Performance Controversy

For many years, managers have believed for the most part that a satisfied worker will automatically be a good worker. In other words, if management could keep all the workers "happy," good performance would automatically follow. Many managers subscribe to this belief because it represents "the path of least resistance." Increasing employees' happiness is far more pleasant for the manager than confronting employees with their performance if a performance problem exists.

Research evidence generally rejects the more popular view that employee satisfaction leads to improved performance. The evidence does, however, provide moderate support for the view that performance causes satisfaction. The evidence also provides strong indications that (1) rewards constitute a more direct cause of satisfaction than does performance; and (2) rewards based on current performance cause subsequent performance.[7]

Research has also investigated the relationship between intrinsic and extrinsic satisfaction and performance for jobs categorized as being either stimulating or nonstimulating.[8] The studies found that the relationship did vary, depending on whether the job was stimulating or nonstimulating. These and other studies further emphasize the complexity of the satisfaction-performance relationship. One relationship that has been clearly established is that job satisfaction does have a positive impact on turnover, absenteeism, tardiness, accidents, grievances, and strikes.[9]

In addition, recruitment efforts by employees are generally more successful if the employees are satisfied. Satisfied employees are preferred simply because they make the work situation a more pleasant environment. So, even though a satisfied employee is not necessarily a high performer, there are numerous reasons for cultivating satisfied employees.

A wide range of both internal and external factors affect an individual's level of satisfaction. The top portion of Figure 13.9 summarizes the major factors that determine an individual's level of satisfaction (or dissatisfaction). The lower portion of the figure shows the organizational behaviors generally associated with satisfaction and dissatisfaction.

FIGURE 13.9
Determinants of Satisfaction and Dissatisfaction

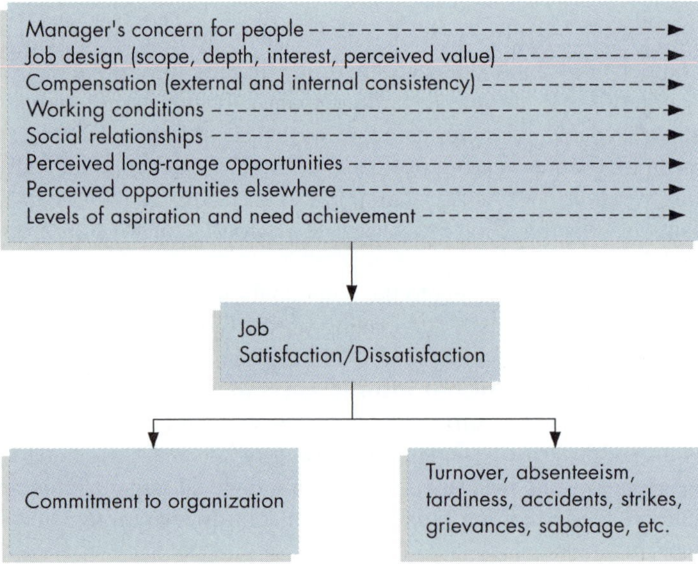

Management Illustration 13.4

EMPLOYEE STOCK OWNERSHIP PLANS (ESOPs) FOR THE HOSPITALITY INDUSTRY

Founded in Hawaii in 1941 by Robert Iwamoto, Sr., RHI has grown from a small, family-run business into a professionally managed, diversified transportation, tourism, and entertainment operation. RHI delivers first-class transportation, personalized sight-seeing tours and excursions around the state's four largest islands, and an exciting variety of attractions and activities. In addition, RHI offers dinner cruises, whale-watching cruises, the Magic of Polynesia show, and other leisure and entertainment alternatives.

The ESOP plan enables every RHI employee to move from simply collecting a paycheck to having an actual stake in the company's long-term success. "Our employees are a tremendous part of RHI's achievements," said Iwamoto. "Sharing ownership with them will not only reward their contribution, but also provide incentives for their continued dedication."

Introduced by Congress in 1972 and covered by ERISA, leveraged ESOPs—which transfer ownership interest in a company to employees—offer companies a unique tool to create alternative liquidity and access to associated tax benefits, while aligning employer and employee interests and creating valuable incentives for employees.

Source: Adapted from "Robert's Hawaii Entertains Its Employees: Part-Ownership of the Company; Company Implements Employee Stock Ownership Plan," *PR Newswire,* June 18, 2007.

Individual satisfaction leads to organizational commitment, while dissatisfaction results in behaviors detrimental to the organization (turnover, absenteeism, tardiness, accidents, etc.). For example, employees who like their jobs, supervisors, and other job-related factors will probably be very loyal and devoted employees. However, employees who strongly dislike their jobs or any of the job-related factors will probably be disgruntled and will often exhibit these feelings by being late, absent, or by taking more covert actions to disrupt the organization.

Satisfaction and motivation are not synonymous. Motivation is a drive to perform, whereas satisfaction reflects the individual's attitude or happiness with the situation. The factors that determine whether an individual is satisfied with the job differ from those that determine whether the individual is motivated. Satisfaction is largely determined by the comfort offered by the environment and the situation. Motivation, on the other hand, is largely determined by the value of rewards and their contingency on performance. The result of motivation is increased effort, which in turn increases performance if the individual has the ability and if the effort is properly directed. The result of satisfaction is increased commitment to the organization, which may or may not result in increased performance. This increased commitment will normally result in a decrease in problems, such as absenteeism, tardiness, turnover, and strikes. Management Illustration 13.4 describes one company's approach to having satisfied and motivated employees.

Summary

1. *Define motivation.* Motivation is concerned with what activates human behavior, what directs this behavior toward a particular goal, and how this behavior is sustained.
2. *Explain the importance of trust in management in motivation.* The presence of trust gives management credibility when asking for more productivity from employees.
3. *Describe the scientific management approach to motivation.* The scientific management approach to motivation is based on the assumption that money is the primary motivation of people: if the monetary reward is great enough, employees will work harder and produce more.

4. *Explain the equity approach to motivation.* The equity approach to motivation is based on the idea that people want to be treated fairly in relationship to others.
5. *Explain the hierarchy of needs.* The five levels of needs are physiological, safety, social, ego, and self-actualization. The physiological needs include food, sleep, water, exercise, clothing, and shelter. Safety needs are concerned with protection against danger, threat, or deprivation. Social needs are the needs for love, affection, and belonging. Ego needs include both self-esteem and the esteem of others. Self-actualization is the need of people to reach their full potential in applying their abilities and interests to functioning in their environment.
6. *Discuss the achievement-power-affiliation approach to motivation.* This approach focuses on three needs of people: achievement, power, and affiliation. The level of intensity of these needs varies among individuals, and people are motivated in situations that allow them to satisfy their most intense needs.
7. *Discuss the motivation-maintenance approach to motivation.* This approach postulates that all work-related factors can be grouped into two categories. The first category, maintenance factors, will not produce motivation but can prevent it. The second category, motivators, encourages motivation.
8. *Discuss the expectancy approach to motivation.* This approach holds that motivation is based on a combination of the individual's expectancy that increased effort will lead to increased performance, the expectancy that increased performance will lead to increased rewards, and the individual's preference for those rewards.
9. *Explain the reinforcement approach to motivation.* This approach is based on the idea that behavior that appears to lead to a positive consequence tends to be repeated, whereas behavior that appears to lead to a negative consequence tends not to be repeated.
10. *Define job satisfaction and organizational morale.* Job satisfaction is an individual's general attitude about his or her job. Organizational morale refers to an individual's feeling of being accepted by, and belonging to, a group of employees through common goals, confidence in the desirability of these goals, and progress toward these goals.

Review Questions

1. Explain the motivation sequence.
2. Describe the following approaches to motivation:
   a. Scientific management
   b. Equity
   c. Hierarchy of needs
   d. Achievement-power-affiliation
   e. Motivation maintenance
   f. Expectancy
   g. Reinforcement
3. What is job satisfaction? What are the major components of job satisfaction?
4. What is organizational morale?
5. Discuss the satisfaction-performance controversy.
6. From a managerial standpoint, what are the real benefits of having satisfied employees?

Skill-Building Questions

1. Discuss your views on this statement: Most people can be motivated with money.
2. Do you think a very loyal employee is necessarily a good employee?
3. As a manager, would you prefer a motivated or a satisfied group of employees? Why?
4. The XYZ Company has just decided to take all of its 200 employees to Las Vegas for a three-day, expense-paid weekend to show its appreciation for their high level of performance this past year. What is your reaction to this idea?
5. Discuss the following statement: A satisfied employee is one that is not being pushed hard enough.

SKILL-BUILDING EXERCISE 13.1
Motivation Maintenance

This exercise is designed to illustrate the motivation-maintenance theory in terms of your personal experiences.

1. Think of a time when you were extremely motivated or "turned on" by a job (the instance could have taken place yesterday or several years ago and it could have been on a full- or part-time job) and write a brief two- or three-sentence description of the situation. After you have completed the description, list the reasons this situation had a motivational effect on you. Don't sign your name, but do pass your paper forward.
2. After completing the above, repeat the same procedure for a situation that was highly demotivating. After all the papers have been passed forward, your instructor will help you analyze them.

SKILL-BUILDING EXERCISE 13.2
Does Money Motivate?

You will be divided into small groups. Your group will be assigned one of the two following statements:

1. Money is the primary motivator of people.
2. Money is not the primary motivator of people.

Your assignment is to prepare for a debate with another group on the validity of the statement that your group has been assigned. You will be debating a group that has the opposing viewpoint.

At the end of the debate, prepare a brief statement summarizing the key points made by your opposing group.

Case Incident 13.1
Our Engineers Are Just Not Motivated

You are a consultant to the manager of mechanical engineering for a large company (8,000 employees, $200 million annual sales) that manufactures industrial equipment. The manager has been in this position for six months, having moved from a similar position in a much smaller company.

Manager: I just can't seem to get these people to perform. They are all extremely competent, but they just don't seem to be willing to put forth the kind of effort that we expect and need if this company is going to remain successful.

Consultant: What type of work do they do?

Manager: Primarily designing minor modifications to existing equipment lines to keep up with our competition and to satisfy special customer requirements.

Consultant: How do you evaluate their performance?

Manager: Mainly on whether they meet project deadlines. It's hard to evaluate the quality of their work, since most of it is fairly routine and the designs are frequently altered later by the production engineers to facilitate production processes.

Consultant: Are they meeting their deadlines reasonably well?

Manager: No, that's the problem. What's worse is that they don't really seem too concerned about it.

Consultant: What financial rewards do you offer them?

Manager: They are all well-paid—some of the best salaries for mechanical engineers that I know of anywhere. Base pay is determined mainly on the basis of seniority, but there is also a companywide profit-sharing plan. At the end of each year, the company distributes 10 percent of its profits after taxes to the employees. The piece of the pie that you get is in proportion to your basic salary. This kind of plan was used in the company I used to work for, and it seemed to have a highly motivating effect for them. They also get good vacations, insurance plans, and all the other usual goodies. I know of no complaints about compensation.

Consultant: How about promotion possibilities?

Manager: Well, all I know is that I was brought in from the outside.

Consultant: If they are so lackadaisical, have you considered firing any of them?

Manager: Are you kidding? We need them too much, and it would be difficult and expensive to replace them. If I even threatened to fire any of them for anything short of blowing up the building, my boss would come down on me like a ton of bricks. We are so far behind on our work as it is. Besides, I'm not sure that it's really their fault entirely.

Questions

1. Why are the engineers not motivated?
2. What should management do to correct the situation?

Case Incident 13.2

The Long-Term Employee

Bill Harrison is 57 years old and has been with Ross Products for 37 years. He is on a top-paying machine-operator job and has been for the last 20 years. Bill is quite active in community affairs and takes a genuine interest in most employee activities. He is very friendly and well liked by all employees, especially the younger ones, who often come to him for advice. He is extremely helpful to these younger employees and never hesitates to help when asked. When talking with the younger employees, Bill never talks negatively about the company.

Bill's one shortcoming, as his supervisor Alice Jeffries sees it, is his tendency to spend too much time talking with other employees. This not only causes Bill's work to suffer but also, perhaps more importantly, hinders the output of others. Whenever Alice confronts Bill with the problem, Bill's performance improves for a day or two. It never takes long, however, for Bill to slip back into his old habit of storytelling and interrupting others.

Alice considered trying to have Bill transferred to another area where he would have less opportunity to interrupt others. However, Alice concluded she needs Bill's experience, especially since she has no available replacement for Bill's job.

Bill is secure in his personal life. He owns a nice house and lives well. His wife works as a librarian, and their two children are grown and married. Alice has sensed that Bill thinks he is as high as he'll ever go in the company. This doesn't seem to bother him since he feels comfortable and likes his present job.

Questions

1. What approach to motivation would you use to try to motivate Bill? Explain in detail what you would do?
2. Suppose Alice could transfer Bill. Would you recommend that she do it?

Case Incident 13.3

An Informative Coffee Break

On a Monday morning, April 28, George Smith was given the news that effective May 1, he would receive a raise of 13 percent. This raise came two months before his scheduled performance appraisal. He was informed by his manager, Tom Weeks, that the basis for the raise was his performance over the past several months and his potential worth to the company. He was told that this was a very considerable increase.

On the next day, Tuesday, a group of fellow workers in George's office were engaging in their normal coffee break. The course of conversation swung to salary increases. One of the group had received a performance review in April, but no indication of an impending salary adjustment had been given to him. George made a comment concerning the amount of any such increases, specifically questioning the range of increase percentages. A third individual immediately responded by saying how surprised he was in getting an "across the board" 12 percent increase last Friday. A fourth individual confirmed that he too had received a similar salary increase. Definitely astounded, George pressed for information, only to learn that several people had received increases of "around" 11 to 13 percent. George broke up the gathering by excusing himself.

That evening, George wrestled with his conscience concerning the forgoing discussion. His first impression of his raise was that it had been given based on performance. His second impression was decidedly sour. Several questions were bothering him:

1. Why did his boss tender the raise as a merit increase?
2. Is job performance really a basis for salary increases in his department?
3. Did his superior hide the truth regarding the raise?
4. Can he trust his boss in the future?
5. Upon what basis will further increases be issued?

Questions

1. What effect do you think that this new information will have on the effort put forth by George Smith?
2. What can Tom Weeks do to regain the confidence of George Smith?

References and Additional Readings

1. Cited in Paul Hersey and Kenneth H. Blanchard, *Management of Organizational Behavior: Utilizing Human Resources,* 4th ed. (Englewood Cliffs, NJ: Prentice Hall, 1982), p. 4.
2. Abraham H. Maslow, *Motivation and Personality,* 2nd ed. (New York: Harper & Row, 1970).
3. David C. McClelland, *The Achievement Motive* (New York: Halsted Press, 1976).

4. Frederick Herzberg, Bernard Mausner, and Barbara Snyderman, *The Motivation to Work* (New York: John Wiley & Sons, 1959).
5. Victor H. Vroom, *Work and Motivation* (New York: John Wiley & Sons, 1967).
6. B. F. Skinner, *Science and Human Behavior* (New York: Macmillan, 1953); and B. F. Skinner, *Beyond Freedom and Dignity* (New York: Knopf, 1972).
7. Charles N. Greene, "The Satisfaction–Performance Controversy," *Business Horizons,* October 1972, p. 31. Also see D. R. Norris and R. E. Niebuhr, "Attributional Influences on the Job Performance–Job Satisfaction Relationship," *Academy of Management Journal,* June 1984, pp. 424–31.
8. Greene, "The Satisfaction–Performance Controversy," p. 40.
9. John M. Ivancevich, "The Performance to Satisfaction Relationship: A Causal Analysis of Stimulating and Nonstimulating Jobs," *Organizational Behavior and Human Performance* 22 (1978), pp. 350–64.

Chapter Fourteen

Developing Leadership Skills

Learning Objectives

After studying this chapter, you will be able to:

1. Define power.
2. Describe the sources of power in organizations.
3. Define leadership.
4. Describe the self-fulfilling prophecy in management.
5. Define the trait theory of leadership.
6. List and define the basic leadership styles.
7. Understand the Managerial Grid.
8. Define the contingency approach to leadership.
9. Explain the path-goal approach to leadership.
10. Define the situational leadership theory.
11. Define transactional and transformational leadership.
12. Define servant leadership.
13. Discuss some of the lessons that can be learned from leadership research.

Chapter Preview

John Stewart, the 56-year-old chief executive of National Australia Bank Ltd., the country's biggest lender by assets, has overseen the bank's recovery after four rogue currency traders, aided by lax risk management and supervision at the bank, cost it the equivalent of roughly $270 million. At that time, the trading losses caused NAB's profit to tumble, led to the resignation of its chief executive and much of its board, including the chairman, and ultimately put the four traders in jail.

His early days at NAB were a tough time for the bank, with a wave of senior management being lost. Mr. Stewart had to address about 80 remedial actions mandated by the country's banking watchdog and mend a tattered regulatory relationship. He has been credited with changing the bank's culture and restoring its reputation, and he has returned it to profit growth. Today Mr. Stewart is considered one of Australia's most influential businesspeople.

Mr. Stewart was asked, "what are the three most important aspects of a good manager?" He responded, "the most important one is people skills. You need to be prepared to employ people who are better than you, and not be afraid of that, and make sure that you are managing through other people."

"Secondly, make sure you have the highest integrity. The third thing is to be a leader, not a manager. A lot of people can be managers but they aren't very effective. Leaders are people who can get great leaders around them."

Source: Adapted from Rebecca Tharlow, "An Avid Sailor Steers NAB Out of Choppy Waters," *The Wall Street Journal,* February 4, 2008, p. B5.

Analyzing Management Skills

Can a person be taught how to be a leader? Why or why not? What leadership skills do you feel can be taught?

Applying Management Skills

Think of the leader that you most admire. What unique leadership skills does he or she possess?

Leadership is probably researched and discussed more than any other topic in the field of management. New suggestions, methods, and tips for improving leadership skills are offered each year. Everyone seems to acknowledge the importance of leadership to managerial and organizational success. This chapter reviews the research on leadership and offers perspectives on leadership processes and styles.

POWER, AUTHORITY, AND LEADERSHIP

power
A measure of a person's potential to get others to do what he or she wants them to do, as well as to avoid being forced by others to do what he or she does not want to do.

Before undertaking a study of leadership, a clear understanding must be developed of the relationships among power, authority, and leadership. **Power** is a measure of a person's potential to get others to do what he or she wants them to do, as well as to avoid being forced by others to do what he or she does not want to do. Figure 14.1 summarizes several sources of power in organizations. The use of or desire for power is often viewed negatively in our society because power is often linked to the concepts of punishment, dominance, and control.

Power can have both a positive and negative form. Positive power results when the exchange is voluntary and both parties feel good about the exchange. Negative power results when the individual is forced to change. Power in organizations can be exercised upward, downward, or horizontally. It does not necessarily follow the organizational hierarchy from top to bottom.

FIGURE 14.1
Sources of Power

Organizational Sources	Basis
Reward power	Capacity to provide rewards.
Coercive power	Capacity to punish.
Legitimate power	Person's position in the organizational hierarchy.
Personal Sources	**Basis**
Expert power	The skill, expertise, and knowledge an individual possesses.
Referent power	The personal characteristics of an individual that make other people want to associate with the person.

Management Illustration 14.1

EXTRAVERT OR INTROVERT?

Extraverted leaders like to focus on the world outside their department or organization. They network, gather resources, and tend to know what is going on politically.

The strength of the extraverted leader is that their department or organization is unlikely to miss out through not knowing what is going on around it. If there is money going, the extravert will be there to pitch for it. If there are outside threats, the extravert will be the first to know. They prefer to be doing things rather than thinking about them, so ideas and plans are likely to leap into action fairly soon after their conception, if not before. Margaret Thatcher and Tony Blair are both examples of extraverted leaders.

Introverted leaders are more reflective and reserved, and their attention is more likely to center on the goings on within their domain. While they may well miss out on what is going on externally, they are likely to have their own department in order and be observant about the individuals within it. More inclined to listen than speak, they like to think things through before acting, and sometimes instead of acting. The result is that action may be slow in coming, but important decisions are likely to be sound.

If you saw the film *Fahrenheit 911* you will have seen the extraordinary moment when George Bush is told of the first, and then the second plane crash, into the twin towers. His response is complete stillness, while he inwardly digests the information, and there is not a trace of emotion on his face.

Source: Anonymous, "Leadership: Taking a Lead," *Chemist and Druggist,* December 1, 2007, p. 44.

authority
The right to issue directives and expend resources, related to power but narrower in scope.

leadership
Ability to influence people to willingly follow one's guidance or adhere to one's decisions.

leader
One who obtains followers and influences them in setting and achieving objectives.

Authority, which is the right to issue directives and expend resources, is related to power but is narrower in scope. Basically, the amount of authority a manager has depends on the amount of coercive, reward, and legitimate power the manager can exert. Authority is a function of position in the organizational hierarchy, flowing from the top to the bottom of the organization. An individual can have power—expert or referent—without having formal authority. Furthermore, a manager's authority can be diminished by reducing the coercive and reward power in the position.

Leadership is the ability to influence people to willingly follow one's guidance or adhere to one's decisions. Obtaining followers and influencing them in setting and achieving objectives makes a **leader.** Leaders use power in influencing group behavior. For instance, political leaders often use referent power. Informal leaders in organizations generally combine referent power and expert power. Some managers rely only on authority, while others use different combinations of power. Management Illustration 14.1 describes extraverted and introverted leaders.

LEADERSHIP AND MANAGEMENT

Leadership and management are not necessarily the same but are not incompatible. Effective leadership in organizations creates a vision of the future that considers the legitimate long-term interests of the parties involved in the organization, develops a strategy for moving toward that vision, enlists the support of employees to produce the movement, and motivates employees to implement the strategy. Management is a process of planning, organizing, staffing, motivating, and controlling through the use of formal authority. In practice, effective leadership and effective management must ultimately be the same.

It is important to note that some individuals may be more naturally charismatic than others and, thus, be natural leaders and/or managers. People do have the capacity to learn many of the elements of successful leadership. However, if one asks the question, can a

Management Illustration 14.2

SOURCES OF FUTURE LEADERS

Unless we challenge long-held assumptions about how business leaders are supposed to act and where they're supposed to come from, many people who could become effective global leaders will remain invisible, warns Harvard Business School professor Linda A. Hill.

Instead of assuming that leaders must exhibit take-charge behavior, broaden the definition of leadership to include creating a context in which other people are willing and able to guide the organization. And instead of looking for the next generation of global leaders in huge Western corporations and elite business schools, expand the search to developing countries.

Ms. Hill describes the changing nature of leadership and what we can learn from parts of the world where people have not, until recently, had opportunities to become globally savvy executives. In South Africa, for instance, the African National Congress has provided rigorous leadership preparation for many black executives.

Source: Anonymous, "Where Will We Find Tomorrow's Leaders? A Conversation with Linda A. Hill," *Harvard Business Review,* January 2008, p. 123.

person be taught how to be a leader? The answer is yes. Leadership strength can be evaluated. Leadership training in skills that are needed on the job can be implemented. And leadership training can be enhanced by other training through peer assessment and team building. Management Illustration 14.2 discusses sources of leaders.

LEADER ATTITUDES

Douglas McGregor developed two attitude profiles, or assumptions, about the basic nature of people. These attitudes were termed *Theory X* and *Theory Y;* they are summarized in Figure 14.2. McGregor maintained that many leaders in essence subscribe to either Theory X or Theory Y and behave accordingly. A Theory X leader would likely use a much more authoritarian style of leadership than a leader who believes in Theory Y assumptions. The real value of McGregor's work was the idea that a leader's attitude toward human nature has a large influence on how that person behaves as a leader.[1]

FIGURE 14.2
Assumptions about People

Source: From D. McGregor and W. Bennis, *The Human Side of Enterprise: 25th Aniversary Printing,* 1989. Reproduced with permission of The McGraw-Hill Companies.

Theory X

1. The average human being has an inherent dislike of work and will avoid it if possible.
2. Because of their dislike of work, most people must be coerced, controlled, directed, or threatened with punishment to get them to put forth adequate effort toward the achievement of organizational objectives.
3. The average human being prefers to be directed, wishes to avoid responsibility, has relatively little ambition, and wants security above all.

Theory Y

1. The expenditure of physical and mental effort in work is as natural as play or rest.
2. External control and the threat of punishment are not the only means for bringing about effort toward organizational objectives. Workers will exercise self-direction and self-control in the service of objectives to which they are committed.
3. Commitment to objectives is a function of the rewards associated with their achievement.
4. The average human being learns, under proper conditions, not only to accept but to seek responsibility.
5. The capacity to exercise a relatively high degree of imagination, ingenuity, and creativity in the solution of organizational problems is widely, not narrowly, distributed in the population.
6. Under the conditions of modern industrial life, the intellectual potentialities of the average human being are only partially utilized.

Management Illustration 14.3

THEORY X MANAGERS IN INDIA

While the West might benefit by sending out the so called "low-end" jobs to India, we will end up inheriting the problems of alienation. That is why I am convinced that it is time for a second QWL (quality of work life) movement and this time around, it has to be born in India! Make Theory Y assumptions. While every leader will swear that he makes Theory Y assumptions about his people, his actions are mostly Theory X.

Organizations love managers who run a tight ship, who micromanage, who are directive and quickly jump in when things are going wrong. Things like the Blackberry only make this easier. When you demonstrate Theory X assumptions, your people will live up to the prophecy of being irresponsible or at best do what is asked of them. Theory X managers can never create ownership. Given the pressures of performance and the lack of preparation for **leadership,** I am afraid that India faces the grave danger of breeding more and more Theory X managers.

Source: Adapted from Ganesh Chella, "Poor Ownership the Result of Poor Leadership," *Businessline,* February 4, 2008, p. 1.

self-fulfilling prophecy
The relationship between a leader's expectations and the resulting performance of subordinates.

The relationship between a leader's expectations and the resulting performance of subordinates has received much attention. Generally, it has been found that if a manager's expectations are high, productivity is likely to be high. On the other hand, if the manager's expectations are low, productivity is likely to be poor. McGregor called this phenomenon the **self-fulfilling prophecy.** It has also been called *Pygmalion in management.* Management Illustration 14.3 describes Theory X Management in India.

FRAMEWORK FOR CLASSIFYING LEADERSHIP STUDIES

Many studies have been conducted on leadership. One useful framework for classifying these studies is shown in Figure 14.3. *Focus* refers to whether leadership is to be studied as a set of traits or as a set of behaviors. *Traits* refer to what characteristics the leader possesses, whereas *behaviors* refer to what the leader does. The second dimension—*approach*—refers to whether leadership is studied from a universal or contingent approach. The universal approach assumes there is one best way to lead regardless of the circumstances. The contingent approach assumes the best approach to leadership is contingent on the situation. Each of the studies shown in Figure 14.3 is discussed in the following sections.

Trait Theory

trait theory
Stressed what the leader was like rather than what the leader did.

Early research efforts devoted to leadership stressed what the leader was *like* rather than what the leader did—a **trait theory** of leadership. Many personality traits (such as originality, initiative, persistence, knowledge, enthusiasm), social traits (tact, patience, sympathy, etc.), and physical characteristics (height, weight, attractiveness) have been examined to differentiate leaders.

FIGURE 14.3
Framework for Classifying Leadership Studies

Source: Arthur G. Yago, "Leadership Perspectives in Theory and Practice," *Management Science,* March 1982, p. 316.

	Approach	
Focus	**Universal**	**Contingent**
Traits	Trait theory	Fiedler's contingency theory
Behaviors	Leadership styles Ohio State studies Michigan studies Managerial Grid	Path–goal theory Situational theory

At first glance, a few traits do seem to distinguish leaders from followers. These include being slightly superior in such physical traits as weight and height and in a tendency to score higher on tests of dominance, intelligence, extroversion, and adjustment. But the differences seem to be small, with much overlap.

Thus, the research in this area has generally been fruitless—largely because the traits related to leadership in one case usually did not prove to be predictive in other cases. In general, it can be said that traits may to some extent influence the capacity to lead. But these traits must be analyzed in terms of the leadership situation (described in detail later in this chapter).

autocratic leader Makes most decisions for the group.

laissez-faire leader Allows people within the group to make all decisions.

democratic leader Guides and encourages the group to make decisions.

Basic Leadership Styles

Other studies dealt with the style of the leader. They found three basic leadership styles: autocratic, laissez-faire, and democratic. The main difference among these styles is where the decision-making function rests. Generally, the **autocratic leader** makes more decisions for the group; the **laissez-faire leader** allows people within the group to make all decisions; and the **democratic leader** guides and encourages the group to make decisions. More detail about each of the leadership styles is given in Figure 14.4. The figure implies

FIGURE 14.4
Relationship between Styles of Leadership and Group Members

Source: L. B. Bradford and R. Lippitt, "Building a Democratic Work Group," *Personnel* 22, no. 2, November 1945.

Autocratic Style

Leader

1. The individual is very conscious of his or her position.
2. He or she has little trust and faith in members of the group.
3. This leader believes pay is a just reward for working and the only reward that will motivate employees.
4. Orders are issued to be carried out, with no questions allowed and no explanations given.

Group members

1. No responsibility is assumed for performance, with people merely doing what they are told.
2. Production is good when the leader is present, but poor in the leader's absence.

Laissez-Faire Style

Leader

1. He or she has no confidence in his or her leadership ability.
2. This leader does not set goals for the group.

Group members

1. Decisions are made by whoever in the group is willing to do it.
2. Productivity generally is low, and work is sloppy.
3. Individuals have little interest in their work.
4. Morale and teamwork generally are low.

Democratic Style

Leader

1. Decision making is shared between the leader and the group.
2. When the leader is required or forced to make a decision, his or her reasoning is explained to the group.
3. Criticism and praise are given objectively.

Group members

1. New ideas and change are welcomed.
2. A feeling of responsibility is developed within the group.
3. Quality of work and productivity generally are high.
4. The group generally feels successful.

that the democratic style is the most desirable and productive. However, current research on leadership, discussed later in this chapter, does not necessarily support this conclusion. The primary contribution of this research was identifying the three basic styles of leadership.

Ohio State Studies

A series of studies on leadership was conducted at Ohio State University to find out the most important behaviors of successful leaders. The researchers wanted to find out what a successful leader does, regardless of the type of group being led: a mob, a religious group, a university, or a business organization. To do this, they developed a questionnaire called the **Leader Behavior Description Questionnaire (LBDQ).** Both the original form and variations of it are still used today.

Leader Behavior Description Questionnaire (LBDQ)
Questionnaire to determine what a successful leader does, regardless of the type of group being led.

consideration
Leader behavior of showing concern for individual group members and satisfying their needs.

initiating structure
Leader behavior of structuring the work of group members and directing the group toward the attainment of the group's goals.

In using the questionnaire, two leader behaviors emerged consistently as being the most important: consideration and initiating structure. The term **consideration** refers to the leader behavior of showing concern for individual group members and satisfying their needs. The term **initiating structure** refers to the leader behavior of structuring the work of group members and directing the group toward the attainment of the group's goals.

Since the Ohio State research, many other studies have been done on the relationship between the leader behaviors of consideration and initiating structure and their resulting effect on leader effectiveness. The major conclusions that can be drawn from these studies are[2]

1. Leaders scoring high on consideration tend to have more satisfied subordinates than do leaders scoring low on consideration.
2. The relationship between the score on consideration and leader effectiveness depends on the group being led. In other words, a high score on consideration was positively correlated with leader effectiveness for managers and office staff in a large industrial firm, whereas a high score on consideration was negatively correlated with leader effectiveness for production foremen.
3. There is also no consistent relationship between initiating structure and leader effectiveness; rather, the relationship varies depending on the group that is being led.

University of Michigan Studies

The Institute for Social Research of the University of Michigan conducted studies to discover principles contributing both to the productivity of a group and to the satisfaction derived by group members. The initial study was conducted at the home office of the Prudential Insurance Company in Newark, New Jersey.

Interviews were conducted with 24 managers and 419 nonmanagerial employees. Results of the interviews showed that managers of high-producing work groups were more likely

1. To receive general rather than close supervision from their superiors.
2. To like the amount of authority and responsibility they have in their job.
3. To spend more time in supervision.
4. To give general rather than close supervision to their employees.
5. To be employee oriented rather than production oriented.

Based on a study conducted at the home of the Prudential Insurance Company, supervisors of low-producing work groups generally gave close supervision and were more production oriented than were the supervisors of high-producing work groups.

Supervisors of low-producing work groups had basically opposite characteristics and techniques. They were production oriented and gave close supervision.

Rensis Likert, then director of the institute, published the results of his years of research in the book *New Patterns of Management,* which is a classic in its field.[3] Likert believes there are four patterns or styles of leadership or management employed by organizations. He has identified and labeled these styles as follows:

System 1: Exploitative authoritative. Authoritarian form of management that attempts to exploit subordinates.

System 2: Benevolent authoritative. Authoritarian form of management, but paternalistic in nature.

System 3: Consultative. Manager requests and receives inputs from subordinates but maintains the right to make the final decision.

System 4: Participative. Manager gives some direction, but decisions are made by consensus and majority, based on total participation.

Likert used a questionnaire to determine the style of leadership and the management pattern employed in the organization as a whole. The results of his studies indicated that system 4 was the most effective style of management and that organizations should strive to develop a management pattern analogous to this system.

Managerial Grid
A two-dimensional framework rating a leader on the basis of concern for people and concern for production.

The Managerial Grid

Robert Blake and Jane Mouton have also developed a method of classifying the leadership style of an individual.[4] The **Managerial Grid,** depicted in Figure 14.5, is a

FIGURE 14.5
The Managerial Grid

Source: Robert R. Blake and Jane Srygley Mouton, *The New Managerial Grid®* (Houston: Gulf Publishing, 1978), p. 11. Copyright © 1978 by Gulf Publishing Company. Reproduced by permission.

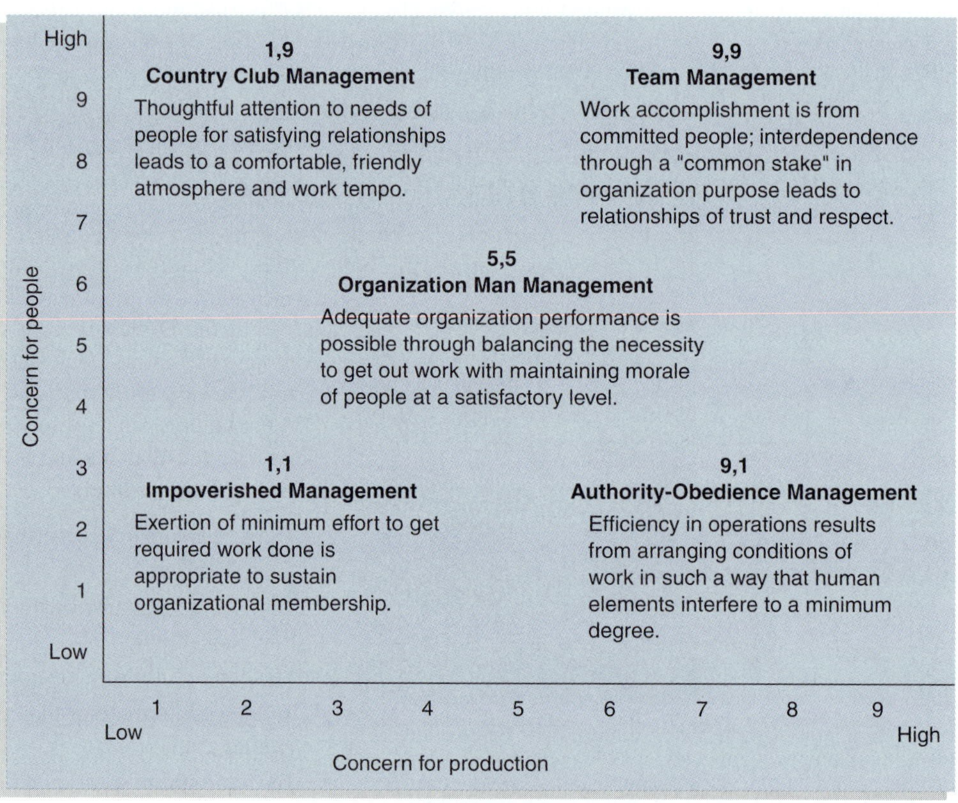

two-dimensional framework rating a leader on the basis of concern for people and concern for production. (Notice that these activities closely relate to the leader activities from the Ohio State studies—consideration and initiating structure.) A questionnaire is used to locate a particular style of leadership or management on the grid.

Blake and Mouton identified five basic styles of management using the Managerial Grid. *Authority-obedience*—located in the lower right-hand corner (9,1 position)—assumes that efficiency in operations results from properly arranging the conditions at work with minimum interference from other people. The opposite view, *country club management*—located in the upper left-hand corner (1,9)—assumes that proper attention to human needs leads to a comfortable organizational atmosphere and workplace. *Team management*—in the upper right-hand corner (9,9)—combines a high degree of concern for people with a high degree of concern for production. The other two styles on the grid are *impoverished management* (1,1) and *organization man management* (5,5). The Managerial Grid is intended to serve as a framework for managers to learn what their leadership style is and to develop a plan to move toward a 9,9 team management style of leadership.

Fiedler's Contingency Studies of Leadership

The leadership studies discussed so far are similar in that they did not specifically address the complex differences between groups (such as production workers versus accountants) and their influences on leader behavior. To imply that a manager should be employee-oriented rather than production-oriented (Michigan studies) or that the manager should exhibit concern for both production and people (Blake and Mouton) does not say much about what the manager should do in particular situations. Nor does it offer much guidance for daily leadership situations. As a result, research began to focus on the style of leadership that is most effective in particular situations. This is called the **contingency approach to leadership.**

contingency approach to leadership
Focuses on the style of leadership that is most effective in particular situations.

One of the first studies using the contingency approach was conducted by Fred Fiedler.[5] He studied the match between the leader's personality and the situation. Fiedler defined two basic leader personality traits—task and relationship motivation. Task-motivated leaders gain satisfaction from the performance of a task. Relationship-motivated leaders gain satisfaction from interpersonal relationships. Fiedler viewed task versus relationship as a leader trait that was relatively constant for any given person.

A scale, called the *least preferred co-worker scale* (LPC), was used to measure whether a person is a task- or relationship-oriented leader. Respondents were asked to think of all the people they had worked with and select the person with whom they could work least effectively. The respondents then described their least preferred co-worker on the LPC. Three sample items on the LPC are:

Pleasant	8	7	6	5	4	3	2	1	Unpleasant
Friendly	8	7	6	5	4	3	2	1	Unfriendly
Cooperative	8	7	6	5	4	3	2	1	Uncooperative

A person who described a least preferred co-worker in fairly favorable terms was presumed to be motivated to have close interpersonal relations with others; Fiedler classified these people as relationship-motivated leaders. On the other hand, people who rejected co-workers with whom they had difficulties were presumed to be motivated to accomplish or achieve the task; they were classified as task-oriented leaders.

FIGURE 14.6 **Fiedler's Classification of Situations**

Situation	1	2	3	4	5	6	7	8
Leader–member relations	Good	Good	Good	Good	Poor	Poor	Poor	Poor
Task structure	Structured	Structured	Unstructured	Unstructured	Structured	Structured	Unstructured	Unstructured
Position power	Strong	Weak	Strong	Weak	Strong	Weak	Strong	Weak
	Favorable for leader						*Unfavorable for leader*	

FIGURE 14.7 **Leadership Style and Leadership Situations**

Situation	1	2	3	4	5	6	7	8
Leader–member relations	Good	Good	Good	Good	Poor	Poor	Poor	Poor
Task structure	Structured	Structured	Unstructured	Unstructured	Structured	Structured	Unstructured	Unstructured
Leader position power	Strong	Weak	Strong	Weak	Strong	Weak	Strong	Weak
	Favorable for leader						*Unfavorable for leader*	
Most productive leadership style	Task	Task	Task	Relationship	Relationship	No data	Task or relationship	Task

leader-member relations
Degree that others trust and respect the leader and the leader's friendliness.

task structure
Degree to which job tasks are structured.

position power
Power and influence that go with a job.

Fiedler next turned to the situation in which the leader was operating. He placed leadership situations along a favorable–unfavorable continuum based on three major dimensions: leader–member relations, task structure, and position power. **Leader-member relations** refer to the degree others trust and respect the leader and to the leader's friendliness. This compares somewhat to referent power. **Task structure** is the degree to which job tasks are structured. For example, assembly-line jobs are more structured than managerial jobs. **Position power** refers to the power and influence that go with a job. A manager who is able to hire, fire, and discipline has more position power. Position power compares to coercive, reward, and legitimate power. Using these three dimensions, an eight-celled classification scheme was developed. Figure 14.6 shows this scheme along the continuum.

Figure 14.7 shows the most productive style of leadership for each situation. In both highly favorable and highly unfavorable situations, a task-motivated leader was found to be more effective. In highly favorable situations, the group is ready to be directed and is willing to be told what to do. In highly favorable situations, the group welcomes having the leader make decisions and direct the group. In moderately favorable situations, a relationship-motivated leader was found to be more effective. In situation 7 (moderately poor leader-member relations, unstructured task, and strong position power), the task and relationship styles of leadership were equally productive.

At Google, founders Sergey Brin and Larry Page have attempted to provide a supportive environment by creating a corporate headquarters where ability is revered and offices contain all the comforts of home and more.

Continuum of Leader Behaviors

Robert Tannenbaum and Warren Schmidt also contend that different combinations of situational elements

FIGURE 14.8 **Forces Affecting the Leadership Situation**

Forces in the Manager	Forces in the Subordinates	Forces in the Situation
Value system: How the manager personally feels about delegating, degree of confidence in subordinates. Personal leadership inclinations. Authoritarian versus participative. Feelings of security in uncertain situations.	Need for independence: Some people need and want direction, while others do not. Readiness to assume responsibility: Different people need different degrees of responsibility. Tolerance for ambiguity: Specific versus general directions. Interest and perceived importance of the problem: People generally have more interest in, and work harder on, important problems. Degree of understanding and identification with organizational goals: A manager is more likely to delegate authority to an individual who seems to have a positive attitude about the organization. Degree of expectation in sharing in decision making: People who have worked under subordinate-centered leadership tend to resent boss-centered leadership.	Type of organization: Centralized versus decentralized. Work group effectiveness: How effectively the group works together. The problem itself: The work group's knowledge and experience relevant to the problem. Time pressure: It is difficult to delegate to subordinates in crisis situations. Demands from upper levels of management. Demands from government, unions, and society in general.

require different styles of leadership. They suggest that there are three important factors, or forces, involved in finding the most effective leadership style: forces in the manager, the subordinate, and the situation. Furthermore, all of these forces are interdependent.[6]

Figure 14.8 describes in detail the forces that affect leadership situations. Since these forces differ in strength and interaction in differing situations, one style of leadership is not effective in all situations.

In fact, Tannenbaum and Schmidt argue that there is a continuum of behaviors that the leader may employ, depending on the situation (see Figure 14.9). These authors further conclude that successful leaders are keenly aware of the forces that are most relevant to their behavior at a given time. Successful leaders accurately understand not only

FIGURE 14.9 **Continuum of Leader Behavior**

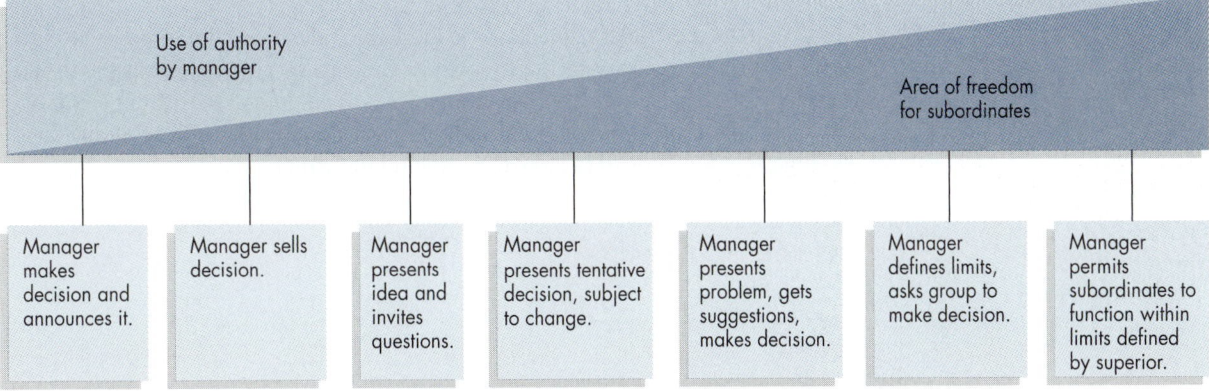
Use of authority
by manager
Area of freedom
for subordinates
Manager makes decision and announces it.
Manager sells decision.
Manager presents idea and invites questions.
Manager presents tentative decision, subject to change.
Manager presents problem, gets suggestions, makes decision.
Manager defines limits, asks group to make decision.
Manager permits subordinates to function within limits defined by superior.

Source: Reprinted by permission of *Harvard Business Review*. Exhibit from "How to Choose a Leadership Pattern," by Robert Tannenbaum and Warren H. Schmidt, May–June 1973.

themselves but also the other persons in the organizational and social environment, and they are able to behave correctly in light of these insights.

Path-Goal Theory of Leadership

path-goal theory of leadership
Attempts to define the relationships between a leader's behavior and the subordinates' performance and work activities.

The **path-goal theory of leadership** developed by Robert House attempts to define the relationships between a leader's behavior and the subordinates' performance and work activities. Leader behavior is acceptable to subordinates to the degree that they see it as a source of satisfaction now or as a step toward future satisfaction. Leader behavior influences the motivation of subordinates when it makes the satisfaction of their needs contingent on successful performance; and it provides the guidance, support, and rewards needed for effective performance. The path-goal theory of leadership and the expectancy theory of motivation, which was described in the previous chapter, are closely related in that leader behaviors can either increase or decrease employee expectancies.

In path-goal theory, leader behavior falls into one of the four basic types: role classification, supportive, participative, and autocratic. *Role classification leadership* lets subordinates know what is expected of them, gives guidance as to what should be done and how, schedules and coordinates work among the subordinates, and maintains definite standards of performance. *Supportive leadership* has a friendly, approachable leader who attempts to make the work environment more pleasant for subordinates. *Participative leadership* involves consulting with subordinates and asking for their suggestions in the decision-making process. *Autocratic leadership* comes from a leader who gives orders that are not to be questioned by subordinates.

Under this theory, each of these leadership behaviors results in different levels of performance and subordinate satisfaction, depending on the structure of the work tasks. Role clarification leads to high satisfaction and performance for subordinates engaged in unstructured tasks. Supportive leadership brings the most satisfaction to those who work on highly structured tasks. Participative leader behavior enhances performance and satisfaction for subordinates engaged in ambiguous tasks. Autocratic leadership behavior has a negative effect on both satisfaction and performance in both structured and unstructured task situations.

Situational Leadership Theory

situational leadership theory
As the level of maturity of followers increases, structure should be reduced while socioemotional support should first be increased and then gradually decreased.

Paul Hersey and Kenneth Blanchard include maturity of the followers as an important factor in leader behavior.[7] According to the **situational leadership theory,** as the level of maturity of followers increases, structure (task) should be reduced while socioemotional support (relationship) should first be increased and then gradually decreased. The maturity level of the followers is determined by their relative independence, their ability to take responsibility, and their achievement-motivation level.

Figure 14.10 shows the cycle of the basic leadership styles that should be used by the leader, depending on the maturity of the followers. The situational leadership theory proposes that as the followers progress from immaturity to maturity, the leader's behavior should move from: (1) high task–low relationships to (2) high task–high relationships to (3) low task–high relationships to (4) low task–low relationships.

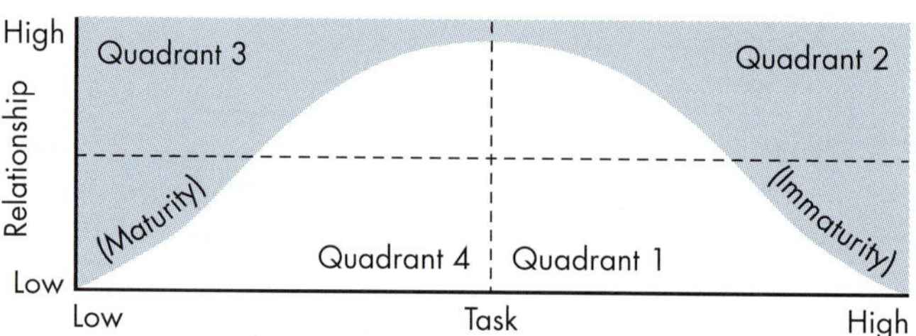

FIGURE 14.10
Situational Leadership Theory

Transformational and Transactional Leaders

Another approach to the analysis of leadership has been based on how leaders and followers influence one another. Under this approach, leadership is viewed as either a transactional or transformational process. **Transactional leadership** takes the approach that leaders engage in a bargaining relationship with their followers. Under this approach, the leader (manager)

transactional leadership
Takes the approach that leaders engage in a bargaining relationship with their followers.

1. Tells employees what they need to do to obtain rewards.
2. Takes corrective action only when employees fail to meet performance objectives.

transformational leadership
Involves cultivating employee acceptance of the group mission.

Transformational leadership involves cultivating employee acceptance of the group mission. The manager-employee relationship is one of mutual stimulation and is characterized by charisma on the part of the leader, inspiration by the leader, consideration by the leader of individual needs, and intellectual stimulation between the leader and followers. Transformational leaders go beyond transacting with their followers and transform not only the situation but also the followers.

Servant Leadership

Servant leadership is based on the belief that the leader exists to meet the needs of the people who he or she nominally leads. The servant leader takes the fulfillment of followers' needs as his or her primary aim. The servant leader believes that the business exists as much to provide meaningful work to employees as it does to provide a quality product or service to the customer.

LESSONS FROM LEADERSHIP STUDIES

How can all of these leadership theories be made relevant to the organization's need for effective managers? First, given the situational factors discussed in this chapter, it appears unlikely that a selection process will be developed to accurately predict successful leaders. The dynamic, changing nature of managerial roles further complicates the situation. Even if the initial process could select effective leaders, the dynamics of the managerial situation might make the selection invalid. Further, contrary to the conclusions of many studies, most leadership training today seems to assume there is one best way to lead.

However, leadership training designed to help leaders or potential leaders identify the nature of the leadership situation appears to have potential in developing more effective leaders. Such training is not so much a process of changing individual traits as it is one of ensuring that the person is operating in an appropriate situation or of teaching the individual how to act in a given situation. The following points on effective leadership can tentatively be made:

1. High consideration and initiating structure often provide a successful leadership style.
2. Under emergency or high-pressure situations, emphasis on initiating structure is desirable and often preferred by subordinates.
3. When the manager is the only information source for subordinates regarding their tasks, they often expect the manager to structure their behavior.
4. Subordinates have differing preferences regarding the degree of consideration and initiating structure exhibited by their managers.
5. Higher management often has set preferences regarding the leadership styles employed by lower-level managers.
6. Some managers can adjust their behavior to fit the situation; while others, in attempting to make this adjustment, appear to be fake and manipulative.

Management Illustration 14.4

BUILDING TRUST

Last winter, the author took one of several groups of leaders to the top of a 12,400 foot mountain. They were visiting with him in his Colorado home to learn how to make breakthroughs in their skiing and leadership skills. The qualities of a great leader are courage, authenticity, service, truthfulness, love, and effectiveness. Learning how to ski double-black diamonds in one day is the mountain equivalent of transforming leadership style and corporate culture and passion in a short period of time—both are within the reach of those who are passionate and yearning to grow as leaders.

Skiing is a metaphor. I teach intermediate skiers how to ski double-black diamond runs in one day. Most skiers say it can't be done, but we do it as routine. First, we ask skiers to open themselves to new ideas and thinking and to let go of their existing, outmoded beliefs and techniques. This requires courage. Then we teach them how to be authentic on the mountain. We ask them to model service and to tell the truth (I am cold, I'm afraid, I'm hungry). We model a loving teaching style and ask them to be loving in interactions with each other and to be effective.

Source: Adapted from Lance Secretan, "Building Trust," *Leadership Excellence,* January 2008, p. 16.

The book *The Leadership Challenge* by James M. Kouzes and Barry Z. Posner was published in 2006. In their book, Kouzes and Posner discuss the four qualities that people believe are essential to exemplary leadership, and on which all great leadership is built. The majority of people believe a leader must be 1) honest, 2) forward-looking, 3) competent, and 4) inspiring. But above all else they want leaders who are credible. People must be able to believe that their leaders' words can be trusted, they'll do what they say, that they're personally excited and enthusiastic about the future, and that they have the knowledge and skill to lead. Because this finding in their research has been so pervasive and so consistent, in the book the authors refer to "Credibility" and "Integrity" as the First Laws of Leadership. Management Illustrations 14.4 describes one approach to building trust.

Summary

1. *Define power.* Power is a measure of a person's potential to get others to do what he or she wants them to do, as well as to avoid being forced by others to do what he or she does not want to do.
2. *Describe the sources of power in organizations.* The sources of power in organizations are reward, coercive, legitimate, expert, and referent.
3. *Define leadership.* Leadership is the ability to influence people to willingly follow one's guidance or adhere to one's decisions.
4. *Describe the self-fulfilling prophecy in management.* The self-fulfilling prophecy basically postulates that what a manager expects of subordinates and the way he or she treats subordinates influence their performance and career progress.
5. *Define the trait theory of leadership.* The trait theory of leadership emphasizes what the leader is like rather than what the leader does. Personality traits and physical characteristics are examined to differentiate leaders. Few studies have been able to support this theory.
6. *List and define the basic leadership styles.* The autocratic leader makes most decisions for the group. The laissez-faire leader allows people within the group to make all decisions. The democratic leader guides and encourages the group to make decisions.
7. *Understand the Managerial Grid.* The Managerial Grid is a two-dimensional framework rating a leader on the basis of concern for people and concern for production.

8. *Define the contingency approach to leadership.* The contingency approach to leadership defines two basic styles of leadership: task-motivated and relationship-motivated. In both highly favorable and highly unfavorable situations, a task-motivated leader was found to be more effective. In moderately favorable situations, a relationship-motivated leader was found to be more effective.
9. *Explain the path-goal approach to leadership.* The path-goal theory of leadership attempts to define the relationships between a leader's behavior and the subordinates' performance and work activities. Leader behavior influences the motivation of subordinates when it makes the satisfaction of their needs contingent on successful performance; and it provides the guidance, support, and rewards needed for effective performance.
10. *Define the situational leadership theory.* According to the situational leadership theory, as the maturity of followers increases, structure (task) should be reduced while socioemotional support (relationship) should first be increased and then gradually decreased.
11. *Define transactional and transformational leadership.* Transactional leadership takes the approach that leaders engage in a bargaining relationship with their followers. Transformational leadership involves cultivating employee acceptance of the group mission.
12. *Define servant leadership.* Servant leadership is based on the belief that the leader exists to meet the needs of the people whom he or she nominally leads.
13. *Discuss some of the lessons that can be learned from leadership research.* The following lessons can be learned from leadership research:

    High consideration and initiating structure often provide a successful leadership style.

    Under emergency or high-pressure situations, emphasis on initiating structure is desirable and often preferred by subordinates.

    When the manager is the only information source for subordinates regarding their tasks, they often expect the manager to structure their behavior.

    Subordinates have differing preferences regarding the degree of consideration and initiating structure exhibited by their managers.

    Higher management often has set preferences regarding the leadership styles employed by lower-level managers.

    Some managers can adjust their behavior to fit the situation; while others, in attempting to make this adjustment, appear to be fake and manipulative.

Review Questions

1. Define power.
2. Describe sources of power in organizations.
3. Define leadership.
4. Describe in detail the following three leadership styles:
    a. Autocratic
    b. Laissez-faire
    c. Democratic
5. What was the purpose of the Ohio State leadership studies? What were the results of the Ohio State studies?

6. What was the purpose of the University of Michigan leadership studies? Explain the results of the Michigan studies.
7. Describe the Managerial Grid.
8. What is Fiedler's contingency approach to leadership?
9. Describe three important forces, or factors, that Tannenbaum and Schmidt think should be considered in determining which leadership style is most effective.
10. What is the path-goal theory of leader effectiveness?
11. What is the situational leadership theory?
12. Define transactional and transformational leadership.
13. Describe some of the implications of the studies on leadership for organizations and managers.

Skill-Building Questions

1. Discuss the following statement: Leaders are born and cannot be developed.
2. Do you agree or disagree with this statement: Leaders must have courage. Why?
3. Do you think the variance in leadership styles of such people as Adolf Hitler, Franklin D. Roosevelt, and Martin Luther King, Jr., can be explained by any of the theories discussed in this chapter? Elaborate on your answer.
4. Explain what people mean when they use this statement: Leaders lead by example. Do you believe it? Explain your answer.

SKILL-BUILDING EXERCISE 14.1
Insubordination?

The company installed a new performance management system this year. You distributed the information and forms several weeks ago, and they were due to be completed in two weeks. One manager reporting to you has not yet returned his. This morning, you ran into him in the parking lot and asked him about it. He reacted angrily with: "I haven't had time to do it—I don't have enough time to get my job done as it is, much less to take the time necessary to have my people write a bunch of meaningless information."

You asked him to stop by your office later to discuss it. As you think about how to handle this situation in the meeting, you consider several alternatives.

1. In view of his attitude and behavior, it clearly is appropriate to exercise your authority. Tell him, in no uncertain terms, that this must be done if he expects to continue as a supervisor.
2. Tell him why this program is important and use your best persuasion technique to sell him on doing it willingly.
3. Remind him that no salary increases, including his own, will be processed until the forms are completed. Establish another deadline and let him know you expect it to be done then.
4. Explain to him that appraising employee performance is a part of every supervisor's job and that he himself is being evaluated on his performance in implementing this program.
5. Tell him you understand the difficulties of his job and the shortage of time available to do it, but remind him that this is a mandatory program that has top management's backing.

Other alternatives may be open to you, but assume these are the only ones you have considered. *Without discussion* with anyone, choose one of them and be prepared to defend your choice.

SKILL-BUILDING EXERCISE 14.2
Leadership Situations

Under the situational approach to leadership, different situations call for different leadership styles. Assuming this approach is correct, outline specific situations in which you would employ an autocratic style of leadership. In addition, outline situations in which you would employ a participative style of leadership. Be specific in describing the situation. Be prepared to present your list of situations for both leadership styles to the class.

SKILL-BUILDING EXERCISE 14.3
Test Your Leadership Style

Read both statements in each entry in the following list and circle either *a* or *b* to indicate whichever best describes you—or is the least incorrect about you. You must answer every question to arrive at a proper score.

1. *a.* You are the person people most often turn to for help.
   b. You are aggressive and look after your best interests first.
2. *a.* You are more competent and better able to motivate others than most people.
   b. You strive to reach a position where you can exercise authority over large numbers of people and sums of money.
3. *a.* You try hard to influence the outcome of events.
   b. You quickly eliminate all obstacles that stand in the way of your goals.
4. *a.* There are few people you have as much confidence in as yourself.
   b. You have no qualms about taking what you want in this world.
5. *a.* You have the ability to inspire others to follow your lead.
   b. You enjoy having people act on your commands and are not opposed to making threats if you must.
6. *a.* You do your best to influence the outcome of events.
   b. You make all the important decisions, expecting others to carry them out.
7. *a.* You have a special magnetism that attracts people to you.
   b. You enjoy dealing with situations requiring confrontation.
8. *a.* You would enjoy consulting on the complex issues and problems that face managers of companies.
   b. You would enjoy planning, directing, and controlling the staff of a department to ensure the highest profit margins.
9. *a.* You want to consult with business groups and companies to improve effectiveness.
   b. You want to make decisions about other people's lives and money.
10. *a.* You could deal with level upon level of bureaucratic red tape and pressure to improve performance.
    b. You could work where money and profits are more important than other people's emotional well-being.
11. *a.* You typically must start your day before sunrise and continue into the night six to seven days a week.
    b. You must fire unproductive employees regularly and expediently to achieve set targets.
12. *a.* You must be responsible for how well others do their work (and you will be judged on their achievements, not yours).
    b. You have a workaholic temperament that thrives on pressure to succeed.
13. *a.* You are a real self-starter and full of enthusiasm about everything you do.
    b. Whatever you do, you have to do it better than anyone else.
14. *a.* You are always striving to be the best, the tops, the first at whatever you do.
    b. You have a driving, aggressive personality and fight hard and tough to gain anything worth having.
15. *a.* You have always been involved in competitive activities, including sports, and have won several awards for outstanding performance.
    b. Winning and succeeding are more important to you than playing just for enjoyment.
16. *a.* You will stick to a problem when you are getting nowhere.
    b. You quickly become bored with most things you undertake.
17. *a.* You are naturally carried along by some inner drive or mission to accomplish something that has never been done.
    b. Self-demanding and a perfectionist, you are always pressing yourself to perform to the limit.

18. *a.* You maintain a sense of purpose or direction that is larger than yourself.
    b. Being successful at work is the most important thing to you.
19. *a.* You would enjoy a job requiring hard and fast decisions.
    b. You are loyal to the concepts of profit, growth, and expansion.
20. *a.* You prefer independence and freedom at work to a high salary or job security.
    b. You are comfortable in a position of control, authority, and strong influence.
21. *a.* You firmly believe that those who take the most risks with their own savings should receive the greatest financial rewards.
    b. There are few people's judgment you would have as much confidence in as your own.
22. *a.* You are seen as courageous, energetic, and optimistic.
    b. Being ambitious, you are quick to take advantage of new opportunities.
23. *a.* You are good at praising others and you give credit readily when it's due.
    b. You like people but have little confidence in their ability to do things the right way.
24. *a.* You usually give people the benefit of the doubt, rather than argue openly with them.
    b. Your style with people is direct, "tell it like it is" confrontation.
25. *a.* Although honest, you are capable of being ruthless if others are playing by devious rules.
    b. You grew up in an environment that stressed survival and required you to create your own rules.

Find Your Score

Count all the *a* responses you circled and multiply by 4 to get your percentage for leadership traits. Do the same with *b* answers to arrive at manager traits.

Leader (number of *a*'s) ______ × 4 = ______%

Manager (number of *b*'s) ______ × 4 = ______%

Interpret Your Score

Consider yourself a leader if you score more than 65 percent in the leader tally above; consider yourself a manager if you score more than 65 percent in the manager tally. If your scores cluster closer to a 50-50 split, you're a leader/manager.

The Leader

Your idea of fulfilling work is to motivate and guide co-workers to achieve their best and to reach common goals in their work by functioning in harmony. You are the sort of person who simply enjoys watching people grow and develop. You are commonly described as patient and encouraging in your dealings with people and a determined self-starter in your own motivation. Since you have a natural ability for inspiring top performances, there's usually little turnover among your employees, and staff relations are harmonious. At times, however, you may be too soft on people or overly patient when their performance lags. Where people are concerned, you may be too quick to let emotions get in the way of business judgments. Overall, you're the visionary type, not the day-to-day grinder.

The Manager

You are capable of getting good work out of people, but your style can be abrasive and provocative. You are especially competent at quickly taking charge, bulldozing through corporate red tape, or forcing others to meet tough work demands. Driven partly by a low threshold for boredom, you strive for more complexity in your work. But you love the "game" of power and the sense of having control over others. Also, your confidence in your own ideas is so strong that you may be frustrated by working as part of a team. Your tendency to see your progress as the battle of a great mind against mediocre ones is not the best premise for bringing out the best in others. Therefore, the further up the corporate ladder you go, the more heavily human-relations problems will weigh against you.

The Leader/Manager Mix

As a 50-50 type, you probably do not believe in the need to motivate others. Instead, you maintain that the staff should have a natural desire to work as hard as you do, without needing somebody to egg them on. You do your job well, and you expect the same from your subordinates. This means that while your own level of productivity is high, you are not always sure about how to motivate others to reach their full potential. Generally, however, you do have the ability to get others to do as you wish, without being abrasive or ruffling feathers. You may pride yourself on being surrounded by a very competent, professional staff that is self-motivated, requiring little of your own attention. But don't be too sure: almost everyone performs better under the right sort of encouraging leadership.

Source: Adapted from Michael Clugston, "Manager," *Canadian Business,* June 1988, pp. 268, 270.

Case Incident 14.1

Changes in the Plastics Division

Ed Sullivan was general manager of the Plastics Division of Warner Manufacturing Company. Eleven years ago, Ed hired Russell (Rusty) Means as a general manager of the Plastics Division's two factories. Ed trained Rusty as a manager and thinks Rusty is a good manager, an opinion based largely on the fact that products are produced on schedule and are of such quality that few customers complain. In fact, for the past eight years, Ed has pretty much let Rusty run the factories independently.

Rusty believes strongly that his job is to see that production runs smoothly. He feels that work is work. Sometimes it is agreeable, sometimes disagreeable. If an employee doesn't like the work, he or she can either adjust or quit. Rusty, say the factory personnel, "runs things. He's firm and doesn't stand for any nonsense. Things are done by the book, or they are not done at all." The turnover in the factories is low; nearly every employee likes Rusty and believes that he knows his trade and that he stands up for them.

Two months ago, Ed Sullivan retired and his replacement, Wallace Thomas, took over as general manager of the Plastics Division. One of the first things Thomas did was call his key management people together and announce some major changes he wanted to implement. These included (1) bring the operative employees into the decision-making process; (2) establish a planning committee made up of three management members and three operative employees; (3) start a suggestion system; and (4) as quickly as possible, install a performance appraisal program agreeable to both management and the operative employees. Wallace also stated he would be active in seeing that these projects would be implemented without delay.

After the meeting, Rusty was upset and decided to talk to Robert Mitchell, general manager of sales for the Plastics Division.

Rusty: Wallace is really going to change things, isn't he?

Robert: Yeah, maybe it's for the best. Things were a little lax under Ed.

Rusty: I liked them that way. Ed let you run your own shop. I'm afraid Wallace is going to be looking over my shoulder every minute.

Robert: Well, let's give him a chance. After all, some of the changes he's proposing sound good.

Rusty: Well, I can tell you our employees won't like them. Having them participate in making decisions and those other things are just fancy management stuff that won't work with our employees.

Questions

1. What different styles of leadership are shown in this case?
2. What style of leadership do you think Wallace will have to use with Rusty?
3. Do you agree with Rusty? Discuss.

Case Incident 14.2

Does the Congregation Care?

You are talking with a young pastor of an independent church with 300 adult members. The pastor came directly to the church after graduating from a nondenominational theological school and has been in the job for eight months.

Pastor: I don't know what to do. I feel as if I've been treading water ever since the day I got here; and frankly, I'm not sure that I will be here much longer. If they don't fire me, I may leave on my own. Maybe I'm just not cut out for the ministry.

You: What has happened since you came to this church?

Pastor: When I arrived, I was really full of energy and wanted to see how much this church could accomplish. The very first thing I did was to conduct a questionnaire survey of the entire adult membership to see what types of goals they wanted to pursue. Unfortunately, I found that the members had such mixed (and perhaps apathetic) feelings about the goals that it was hard to draw any conclusions. There were also a few who strongly favored more emphasis on internal things, such as remodeling the sanctuary, developing our music program, and setting up a day care center for the use of the members. Most of the members, however, didn't voice any strong preferences. A lot of people didn't return the questionnaire, and a few even seemed to resent my conducting the survey.

You: What have you done since you took the survey?

Pastor: To be honest about it, I've kept a pretty low profile, concentrating mainly on routine duties. I haven't tried to implement or even push any major new programs. One problem is that I've gotten the impression, through various insinuations, that my being hired was by no means an overwhelmingly popular decision. Evidently, a fairly substantial segment of the congregation was skeptical of my lack of experience and felt that the decision to hire me was railroaded through by a few members of the Pastoral Search Committee. I guess I am just reluctant to assume a strong leadership role until some consensus has developed concerning the goals of the church and I've had more time to gain the confidence of the congregation. I don't know how long that will take, though; and I'm not sure I can tolerate the situation much longer.

Questions

1. Analyze and explain the situation using any of the theories of leadership discussed in this chapter.
2. What would you recommend the young pastor do?

References and Additional Readings

1. For another view on Theory X and Theory Y, see T. C. Carbone, "Theory X and Theory Y Revisited," *Managerial Planning,* May–June 1981, pp. 24–27. See also Michael P. Bobie and William Eric Davis, "Why So Many Newfangled Management Techniques Quickly Fail," *Journal of Public Administration Research and Theory,* July 2003, p. 239.
2. Victor H. Vroom, "Leadership," in *Handbook of Industrial and Organizational Psychology,* ed. Marvin D. Dunnette (Skokie, IL: Rand McNally, 1976), p. 1531.
3. Rensis Likert, *New Patterns of Management* (New York: McGraw-Hill, 1961).
4. Robert R. Blake and Jane Srygley Mouton, *The New Managerial Grid* (Houston: Gulf Publishing, 1978); and Robert R. Blake and Jane S. Mouton, "How to Choose a Leadership Style," *Training and Development Journal,* February 1982, pp. 38–45.
5. Fred E. Fiedler, *A Theory of Leadership Effectiveness* (New York: McGraw-Hill, 1967).
6. Robert Tannenbaum and Warren Schmidt, "HBR Highlights: Excerpts from How to Choose a Leadership Pattern," *Harvard Business Review,* July–August 1986, p. 131.
7. Paul Hersey and Kenneth Blanchard, "Life-Cycle Theory of Leadership," *Training and Development Journal,* June 1979, pp. 94–100. See also George William Yeatrey, *Hersey and Blanchard's Situational Leadership Theory, Applications in the Military* (Nova Southeastern University, 2002). Ft. Lauderdale, FL.

Chapter Fifteen

Managing Conflict and Stress

Learning Objectives

After studying this chapter, you will be able to:

1. Define conflict.
2. Discuss the useful effects of conflict.
3. Outline the stages of conflict development.
4. Name the five major types of conflict based on the entities involved.
5. Name five approaches for resolving interpersonal conflict.
6. Name and briefly discuss one method of positively managing conflicts created by diversity in the workforce.
7. Define stress and technostress.
8. Define burnout.
9. Describe what is a sabbatical.
10. Outline the basic elements of a violence-prevention program.
11. Explain the three basic types of employee assistance programs.
12. Explain wellness programs.

Chapter Preview

In 1997, operations at United Parcel Service (UPS) were severely hampered when unionized drivers and truck loaders went on strike. Before the strike, UPS did not appear to be a likely candidate for a strike. The company had worked collaboratively with the Teamsters Union for 82 years—ever since UPS founder Jim Casey extended the invitation to the teamsters, saying that employees could be both good Teamsters and good "UPSers." After a stormy two-week strike, a settlement was reached and a new contract was signed. Recognizing the importance of individual contact between customers and drivers, the company was careful not to create negative images of its striking drivers during and after the strike. The company concentrated not only on rebuilding its customer base but also on rebuilding the relationship with its employees. First up was a video presentation to employees by chairman and CEO James Kelly. The theme of the video was to move forward and concentrate on what the company does best—deliver packages. At this same time, the management team held meetings in all of the 60 UPS districts around the country. They met with employees and held question-and-answer sessions.

Despite all the efforts by top management to diffuse hard feelings, relations between first-level supervisors and employees have continued to be strained in some areas. Many supervisors who crossed the picket lines to keep the company going were subjected to harsh language and even threats. Some of these supervisors have found it hard to forget.

The 1997 strike was still having repercussions five years later in the spring and summer of 2002. During this time, UPS's volume of business fell significantly because of a threatened strike by the Teamsters. Mindful of the 1997 strike and as a precautionary act, many customers took their business elsewhere. A strike was averted and many of the customers came back—but not all.

In early 2005, UPS pilots threatened a strike if certain concessions were not made by the company. Negotiations continued throughout the year and were resolved in mid 2006. With the trauma and costs of the 1997 strike still in their minds, UPS and the Teamsters opened negotiations on their labor contract in September 2006, a full two years before the contract expired. "This is our most important contract, one we want to work on without the pressure of a strike," said James Hoffa, the Teamsters' general president. "You don't want to be doing this under the gun." UPS and the Teamsters reached an agreement in October 2007.

Sources: Robert J. Grossman, "Trying to Heal the Wounds," *HR Magazine,* September 1998, pp. 85–92; Richard Thompson, "Some United Parcel Customers Fear Strike, Turn to Other Carriers," *Knight Ridder Tribune Business News,* July 24, 2002, p. 1; "UPS, Pilots Plan New Talks," *Journal of Commerce,* November 8, 2005, p. 1; Corey Dade, "UPS, Teamsters Begin Negotiations; Both Sides Hope to Avoid Type of Contentious Battle That Led to 1997 Walkout," *The Wall Street Journal,* September 20, 2006, p. A13; and Larry Kahaner, "Strike Averted at UPS," *Fleet Owner,* December 2007, p. 8.

Analyzing Management Skills

Why do you think conflict arises between parties that have had a good relationship for years? What might have happened if UPS had used press coverage and other means to portray its drivers negatively during and after the strike?

Applying Management Skills

Have you ever witnessed a dispute between friends or co-workers that turned out badly? Outline a set of guidelines that might be followed to help resolve such a dispute.

conflict
Overt behavior that results when an individual or a group of individuals thinks a perceived need of the individual or group has been blocked or is about to be blocked.

Conflict is an overt behavior that results when an individual or group of individuals thinks a perceived need of the individual or group has been blocked or is about to be blocked. Conflict occurs because individuals have different perceptions, beliefs, and goals. From an organizational perspective, conflict can be viewed as anything that disrupts the "normal" routine.[1]

Conflict in organizations is often assumed to be unnatural and undesirable, something to be avoided at all costs. Conflict can lead to rigidity in the system in which it operates, distort reality, and debilitate the participants in the conflict situation. Therefore, many organizations approach the management of conflict with the following assumptions:

1. Conflict is avoidable.
2. Conflict is the result of personality problems within the organization.
3. Conflict produces inappropriate reactions by the persons involved.
4. Conflict creates a polarization within the organization.

FIGURE 15.1
Myths and Truths about Conflict

Source: Jerry Wisinski, *Resolving Conflicts on the Job* (New York: American Management Association, 1993).

Myth	Truth
Conflict in the workplace is always dysfunctional.	Conflict is a normal part of life within an organization.
All conflicts can be resolved.	Most conflicts can be managed.
Conflict tends to go away if it is ignored.	Conflict can motivate change.
Conflicts always result in winners and losers.	Conflict can help build relationships between people.

However, conflict is perfectly natural and should be expected to occur. Management must know when to eliminate conflict and when to build on it. Today's managers must accept the existence of conflict and realize that to attempt to stop all conflict is a mistake. The general consensus is that conflict itself is not undesirable; rather, it is a phenomenon that can have constructive or destructive effects.[2]

For example, in a struggle between two people for a promotion, the winner will probably think the conflict was most worthwhile, while the loser will likely reach the opposite conclusion. However, the impact of the conflict on the organization must also be considered. If the conflict ends in the selection and promotion of the better-qualified person, the effect is good from the organization's viewpoint. If, by competing, the parties have produced more or made improvements within their areas of responsibility, the effect is also positive. At the same time, there may be destructive effects. The overall work of the organization may have suffered during the conflict. The loser may resign or withdraw as a result of the failure. The conflict may become chronic and inhibit the work of the organization. In extreme cases, the health of one or both participants may be impaired.

The destructive effects of conflict are often obvious, whereas the constructive effects may be more subtle. The manager must be able to see these constructive effects and weigh them against the costs. Some potentially useful effects of conflict include the following:

1. Conflict energizes people. Even if not all of the resulting activity is constructive, it at least wakes people up and gets them moving.
2. Conflict is a form of communication; the resolution of conflict may open new and lasting channels.
3. Conflict often provides an outlet for pent-up tensions, resulting in catharsis. With the air cleansed, the participants can again concentrate on their primary responsibilities.
4. Conflict may actually be an educational experience. The participants may become more aware and more understanding of their opponents' functions and the problems with which they must cope.

Figure 15.1 summarizes some general myths and truths about conflict.

PROGRESSIVE STAGES OF CONFLICT

A manager must be aware of conflict's dynamic nature. Conflict usually does not appear suddenly. It passes through a series of progressive stages as tensions build. These stages of development are as follows:

1. *Latent conflict:* At this stage, the basic conditions for conflict exist but have not yet been recognized. For example, racial differences may preclude basic communication channels between two employees.

2. *Perceived conflict:* One or both participants recognize the cause of the conflict. For example, an employee begins to complain that his or her manager doesn't like him or her.
3. *Felt conflict:* Tension is beginning to build between the participants, although no real struggle has begun. When employees become short-tempered with one another, this form of conflict begins to emerge.
4. *Manifest conflict:* The struggle is under way, and the behavior of the participants makes the existence of the conflict apparent to others not directly involved. Arguments or damaged feelings are no longer privately held. Disruptions begin to arise in public.
5. *Conflict aftermath:* The conflict has been ended through resolution or suppression. This establishes new conditions that will lead either to more effective cooperation or to a new conflict that may be more severe than the first. This form of conflict can result in firings, punishments, or future difficulties. In some instances, resolution can be positive and serve to end the issue.

Conflict does not always pass through all of these stages. Furthermore, the parties in conflict may not be at the same stage simultaneously. For example, one participant may be at the manifest stage of conflict while the other is at the perceived stage.

ANALYZING CONFLICT

Conflict can be analyzed from many different perspectives. One approach is based on the entities involved: intrapersonal, interpersonal, intergroup, organizational, or political. Each of these types of conflict is discussed in the following sections.

Intrapersonal Conflict

intrapersonal conflict
Conflict internal to the individual.

Intrapersonal conflict is internal to the individual. It is probably the most difficult form of conflict to analyze. Intrapersonal conflict can result when barriers exist between the drive and the goal. When a drive or a motive is blocked before the goal is reached, frustration and anxiety can occur. Barriers can be either overt (rules and procedures) or covert (mental hang-ups). When a barrier exists, people tend to react with defense mechanisms, which are behaviors used to cope with frustration and anxiety. Figure 15.2 lists some typical defense mechanisms.

Responses to frustration and anxiety vary and can be expressed through withdrawal behavior (higher absenteeism and turnover rates), aggression (sabotage and other destructive work acts), excessive drinking, drug abuse, and more subtle responses such as ulcers or heart trouble.

Intrapersonal conflict can also result from goal conflict. Goal conflict occurs when an individual's goal has both positive and negative aspects or when goals exist. There are three basic forms of goal conflict:

1. *Conflicting positive goals.* This situation occurs when a person must choose between two or more positive goals. For example, say that a person is offered two equally attractive jobs. Suppose that a manager in Company A is approached by the human resources manager of Company B and offered a managerial job in Company B. If the manager likes the present job but also thinks that the new job would be very good, he or she is faced with conflicting positive goals. This situation produces intrapersonal conflict.
2. *Goals with both positive and negative aspects.* This situation occurs when a person is confronted by a goal that has both positive and negative aspects. For example, an

FIGURE 15.2 Reactions to Frustration and Anxiety

Adjustive Reactions	Psychological Process	Illustration
Compensation	Individual devotes himself or herself to a pursuit with increased vigor to make up for some feeling of real or imagined inadequacy.	Zealous, hardworking president of the 25-Year Club who has never advanced very far in the company hierarchy.
Conversion	Emotional conflicts are expressed in muscular, sensory, or bodily symptoms of disability, malfunctioning, or pain.	A disabling headache keeping a staff member off the job the day after a cherished project has been rejected.
Displacement	Redirects pent-up emotions toward persons, ideas, or objects other than the primary source of the emotion.	Roughly rejecting a simple request from a subordinate after receiving a rebuff from the boss.
Fantasy	Daydreaming or other forms of imaginative activity provide an escape from reality and imagined satisfactions.	An employee's daydream of the day in the staff meeting when he corrects the boss's mistakes and is publicly acknowledged as the real leader of the group.
Negativism	Active or passive resistance, operating unconsciously.	The manager who, having been unsuccessful in getting out of a committee assignment, picks apart every suggestion anyone makes in the meetings.
Rationalization	Justifies inconsistent or undesirable behavior, beliefs, statements, and motivations by providing acceptable explanations for them.	Padding the expense account because "everybody does it."
Regression	Individual returns to an earlier and less mature level of adjustment in the face of frustration.	A manager, having been blocked in some administrative pursuit, busies himself with clerical duties or technical details more appropriate for his subordinates.
Repression	Completely excludes from consciousness impulses, experiences, and feelings that are psychologically disturbing because they arouse a sense of guilt or anxiety.	An employee "forgetting" to tell his boss the circumstances of an embarrassing situation.
Resignation, apathy, and boredom	Breaks psychological contact with the environment, withholding any sense of emotional or personal involvement.	Employee who, receiving no reward, praise, or encouragement, no longer cares whether or not he does a good job.
Flight or withdrawal	Leaves the field in which frustration, anxiety, or conflict is experienced, either physically or psychologically.	The salesman's big order falls through, and he takes the rest of the day off; constant rebuff or rejection by superiors and colleagues pushes an older employee toward being a loner and ignoring whatever friendly gestures are made.

Source: From *Psychology in Administration: A Research Orientation,* by T. W. Costello and S. S. Zalkind. Copyright © 1963 by Pearson Education, Inc. Reprinted by permission of Pearson Education, Inc., Upper Saddle River, NJ.

employee may be offered a job promotion that requires the employee to relocate. The employee may really want the promotion but may also not want to move. Thus, a conflict internal to the employee emerges.

3. *Goals that have only negative aspects.* This situation occurs when a person is confronted with two or more negative goals. For example, a person may be working at a job he or she dislikes but may consider quitting and looking for another job just as undesirable.

dissonance
Feeling of conflict felt by individual trying to make a decision.

Since goal conflict forces the person to make a decision, decision making often creates a feeling of conflict within the individual. This **dissonance** or disharmony is a danger sign that managers must watch for, since it can lead to a loss of mental concentration and productivity in the workplace.

An extension of goal conflict is *cognitive conflict,* in which ideas or thoughts are perceived as incompatible in a given situation, and *affective conflict,* in which feelings or emotions are incompatible and the result is usually anger at the other person.

Managers can help deal with intrapersonal conflict only if they can identify when and why it is occurring. Therefore, managers must learn to identify intrapersonal conflict not only within employees but also within themselves.

Interpersonal Conflict

interpersonal conflict
Conflict between two or more individuals.

Interpersonal conflict, or conflict between two or more individuals, may result from many factors. Opposing personalities often result in interpersonal conflict. Some people simply rub each other the wrong way. The extrovert and the introvert, the boisterous individual and the reserved one, the optimist and the pessimist, the impulsive person and the deliberate person, are but a few possible combinations that may spark conflict.

Prejudices based on personal background or ethnic origin can also cause interpersonal conflict. Obvious examples are racial and religious conflicts, but other, more subtle, prejudices exist. Examples include the college graduate versus the person with only a high school education, the married person versus the divorced person, and the longtime employee versus the new hire.

Another cause of interpersonal conflict arises when individuals become dissatisfied with their roles relative to the roles of others. For example, an employee may be perfectly satisfied with the relationship with both his or her managers and co-workers. However, if a peer is promoted to a management job, the employee may have difficulty accepting his or her role in relation to the former peer.

In a classic discussion of role conflict, Robert L. Kahn revealed that each individual organizational member has numerous roles to play. In many instances, role conflict occurs because of job overload (especially at the managerial level). In attempting to deal with role conflict, employees may cut themselves off from peers and support groups, suffer high anxiety, reduce their productivity, and eventually become demotivated.[3]

Intergroup (Structural) Conflict

intergroup (structural) conflict
Conflict that results from the organizational structure; may be relatively independent of the individuals occupying the roles within the structure.

The organizational structure may be the cause of **intergroup** or **structural conflict.** Such conflict may be relatively independent of the individuals occupying the roles within the structure. For example, structural conflict between marketing and production departments is fairly common. The marketing department, being customer oriented, may believe some exceptions can and should be made in production for the sake of current and future sales. The production department may view such exceptions as unreasonable and not in the best interests of the organization. Hence, a structural conflict occurs. The conflict situation can be even more intense if the managers of each department are also experiencing interpersonal conflict. The following sections discuss various types of structural conflict.

Goal Segmentation and Rewards

Each functional unit of an organization has different functional goals. These can cause conflict that, when it emerges, may seem to be personality clashes. The classic problem of inventory levels illustrates this dilemma. The marketing department would like to keep finished-goods inventories high to supply all of the customers' needs on short notice. The finance department would like to keep inventories low because of the cost of maintaining these inventories. The end result is often a conflict between departments.

The reward system is a key source for reducing this type of conflict. A reward system that stresses the separate performances of the departments feeds the conflict. However, rewarding the combined efforts of the conflicting departments reduces the conflict.

Nevertheless, inadequate reward systems that lead to conflict are still very common. Four factors generally inhibit implementing effective reward systems:

- Insistence on an objective criterion (i.e., rewards are linked to one objective when in fact many objectives come into play).
- Overemphasis on highly visible behaviors (for example, difficult-to-observe concepts such as team building are rarely rewarded).
- Hypocrisy (having a reward system that actually encourages one type of behavior while claiming to encourage another).
- Emphasis on morality or equity rather than efficiency (many situations are not just either-or situations).[4]

Mutual Departmental Dependence

Sometimes two departments or units of an organization are dependent on each other to accomplish their respective goals, creating a potential for structural conflict. For instance, the marketing department's sales depend on the volume of production from the production department; at the same time, the production department's quotas are based on the sales of the marketing department. This type of mutual dependence exists in many organizations.

Unequal Departmental Dependence

Often departmental dependence is unequal and fosters conflict. In most organizations, for instance, staff groups are more dependent on line groups. The staff generally must understand the problems of the line, cooperate with the line, and sell ideas to the line. However, the line does not have to reciprocate. One tactic in this form of conflict is an attempt by the more dependent unit to interfere with the work performance of the independent group. In doing so, the more dependent group hopes the other group will cooperate once it realizes how the dependent group can hinder progress.

Functional Unit and the Environment

Functional units obviously perform different tasks and cope with different parts of the environment. Research has shown that the more the environments served by functional units differ, the greater the potential for conflict. Paul Lawrence and Jay Lorsch have developed four basic dimensions to describe these differences: (1) structure—the basic type of managerial style employed; (2) environment orientation—the orientation of the unit to the outside world; (3) time span orientation—the unit's planning-time perspectives; and (4) interpersonal orientation—the openness and permissiveness of interpersonal relationships.[5]

Role Dissatisfaction

Role dissatisfaction may also produce structural conflict. Professionals in an organizational unit who receive little recognition and have limited opportunities for advancement may initiate conflict with other units. Purchasing agents often demonstrate this form of conflict.

Role dissatisfaction and conflict often result when a group that has low perceived status sets standards for another group. For example, within academic institutions, administrators—whom the faculty may view as having less status—often set standards of performance and make administrative decisions that affect the faculty.

Role Ambiguity

Ambiguities in the description of a particular job can lead to structural conflict. When the credit or blame for the success or failure of a particular assignment cannot be determined between two departments, conflict is likely to result. For instance, improvements

FIGURE 15.3
Summary of Types of Intergroup (or Structural) Conflict

Type	Example
Goal segmentation and reward	Different inventory levels are desired by different functional departments.
Mutual departmental dependence	Marketing department's sales are dependent on the volume of production from the production department.
Unequal departmental dependence	Staff departments are generally more dependent on line departments.
Functional unit and environment	The environment faced by an applied research department and a sales department are different and can lead to conflict between these departments.
Role dissatisfaction	Professionals in an organizational unit who receive little attention.
Role ambiguities	When the credit or blame for the success or failure of a particular assignment cannot be determined between two departments.
Common resource dependence	Two departments competing for computer time.
Communication barriers	Purchasing agents and engineers may use different language to describe similar materials, and conflict can result from those semantic differences.

in production techniques require the efforts of the engineering and production departments. After the improvements are made, credit is difficult to assign; thus, conflict often results between these two departments.

Common Resource Dependence

When two organizational units are dependent on common but scarce resources, potential for conflict exists. This often occurs when two departments are competing for budget money. Each naturally believes its projects are more important and should be funded.

Communication Barriers

Semantic differences can cause conflict. For instance, purchasing agents and engineers generally use different language to describe similar materials, which leads to conflict. Communication-related conflict also occurs when a physical or organizational barrier to effective communication exists. Company headquarters and branch offices frequently suffer from this problem.

Figure 15.3 summarizes types of intergroup or structural conflict.[6]

Organizational Conflict

organizational conflict
Conflict between employees and the organization itself.

Organizational conflict is conflict between employees and the organization itself. Organizational conflict pits employees or groups of employees against the organization. Changes in policies that negatively affect employees, such as a cutback in benefits offered, are one source of organizational conflict. Reorganizations, corporate downsizing, layoff of employees, and tightening of expenses are other examples of sources of organizational conflict. Management Illustration 15.1 describes layoffs recently experienced by one company.

Political Conflict

Intrapersonal, interpersonal, intergroup, and organizational conflict generally are not planned; they simply develop as a result of existing circumstances. But political (sometimes called *strategic*) conflict is started purposely and is often undertaken with an elaborate battle plan. Such conflict usually results from the promotion of self-interests on the part of an individual or a group. The instigator(s) has a clear goal, and those who stand in

Management Illustration 15.1

LAYOFFS AT ENTENMANN'S BAKERY

On January 23, 2008, Entenmann's Bakery of Bay Shore, New York, announced that approximately 250 employees would be laid off over the next two months. In January 2007, Entenmann's parent company, George Weston Bakeries, announced that cookie and cake baking operations would move out of Bay Shore to Albany, New York, and to Pennsylvania, respectively. The result of these moves was a reduction of 350 employees at the Bay Shore plant. Doughnut production was previously moved to Pennsylvania in 2003.

Lou Minella, a spokesperson for George Weston Bakeries, estimated that the total number of jobs cut since January of 2007 was about 550. Of the 550 job cuts, about 200 were eliminated through attrition. The rising cost of ingredients coupled with a decline in sales volume made the cutbacks a necessity. The Bay Shore plant was built in 1961 and is in need of modernization and also has higher energy costs. It is easy to imagine the conflicts created by layoff situations such as described above—how many to lay off, whom to lay off, when to lay them off, and so on.

Source: Michael Amon and Keiko Morris, "Entenmann's Eliminating 250 More Jobs," *McClatchy-Tribune Business News,* January 23, 2008.

the way are the adversary. In organizations, the goal is usually to gain an advantage over the opponent within the reward system. The potential reward may be a bonus or commission, a choice assignment, a promotion, or an expansion of power. Whatever it is, usually one of the participants will receive it (or the greatest portion of it). As an example, the vice presidents of an organization may find themselves in a political conflict situation as the retirement of the president nears. An ambitious vice president, in an attempt to better his or her personal chances for the presidency, may create a political conflict with one or more of the other vice presidents.

Political conflict does not always imply that the participants are dishonest or unethical. Indeed, rewards are there to be pursued with vigor. But such conflicts can degenerate into unfair play because the participants cannot resist the temptation to win at all costs.

MANAGING CONFLICT

As described earlier, conflict is an inherent part of any organization. Even though some conflict may be beneficial to an organization, unresolved conflict or conflict that is resolved poorly usually results in negative consequences such as job withdrawal behaviors, unionization activity, low morale, and lower levels of goal attainment.[7] Successful resolution of conflict among employees often depends on the employees' immediate manager or managers. The objective of the manager is not to force a resolution to the conflict but act as a referee and counselor in helping the participant(s) reach an acceptable solution. Understanding the type of conflict—intrapersonal, interpersonal, intergroup, organizational, or political—and the stage of the conflict cycle will aid the manager.

Resolving Conflict Situations

Managers most frequently are faced with intrapersonal, interpersonal, and intergroup conflict. Therefore, these forms of conflict are discussed in more depth in this section.

As was stated earlier, intrapersonal conflict is often difficult to analyze. Managers should not go around looking for intrapersonal conflict in every situation. However, when an employee asks to discuss a personal problem, the manager should look for signs of *intrapersonal conflict.* When a manager detects what he or she believes to be an intrapersonal conflict situation with an employee, the employee should normally be referred to a person specifically trained in handling such matters.

Five general approaches can be used to deal with interpersonal conflict situations: (1) compromising, (2) smoothing over the conflicts, (3) withdrawal of one or more of the participants, (4) forcing the conflict to a conclusion, and (5) confrontation. Each of these methods is discussed below.

Compromising

Compromising occurs when both sides give some of what they want. Compromising is effective in dealing with interpersonal conflict when it benefits both parties. It can be used when the issue in question is not very important. It can also be used to expedite solutions under time pressures or to obtain temporary solutions to complex problems. Unfortunately, compromising often leaves the real cause of the conflict unsolved and provides the groundwork for future conflict.

Smoothing over the Conflict

Smoothing over the conflict happens when the manager acts like the conflict does not exist. Managers using this approach often pretend "we are all one big happy family." This approach rarely leads to long-term solutions and generally results in more conflict.

Withdrawal

Withdrawal of one or more of the participants involves actions such as firing, transferring, or having an employee quit. Another form of withdrawal is having one or more of the participants refuse to discuss the conflict. Withdrawal rarely addresses the underlying cause of the conflict and usually provides the basis for future conflict.

Forcing a Solution

Forcing a solution occurs when the manager or another third party steps in and forces a solution on the conflicting parties. For example, a manager, observing a conflict between two employees, might step in and say, "this is the way it is going to be, and that ends it." Like the previous methods, this one may only sow the seeds for future conflict.

Confrontation

Confrontation occurs when both parties confront each other with what is really bothering them. With this method, each party discusses their true feelings and also listens to what the other parties have to say.

Although each of the above methods can work in certain situations, confrontation is generally considered to be the most effective method of resolving conflict; third-party intervention has been found to be the least effective method.[8] One reason for this is that resolutions reached through confrontation tend to be more long lasting.

If two parties are in conflict with one another and have a confrontation to discuss their true feelings and also listen to what the other party has to say, the resolution tends to be longer lasting. Why is this?

In some instances, however, the profiles of the parties involved in conflict fall into the category of "difficult people." Figure 15.4 suggests some rather interesting tactics for dealing with these personalities. The general rule for the manager is to ensure that each situation involving interpersonal conflict is dealt with based on the individuals' and the situation's basic characteristics.[9]

Much intergroup conflict results from interdependencies among organizational units that are inherent in the organizational structure. Some of this conflict potential may be removed by decoupling the conflicting units by reducing their common resource dependencies; giving each control over its own resources; introducing buffer inventories; or invoking impersonal, straightforward rules for resource allocation. Decoupling may also occur by

FIGURE 15.4
Tactics for Managing Interpersonal Conflict with Difficult People

Source: From *Coping with Difficult People* by Robert M. Bramson. Copyright © 1981 by Robert Bramson. Used by permission of Doubleday, a division of Random House, Inc.

Hostile-Aggressives

Stand up for yourself.
Give them time to run down.
Use self-assertive language.
Avoid a direct confrontation.

Complainers

Listen attentively.
Acknowledge their feelings.
Avoid complaining with them.
State the facts without apology.
Use a problem-solving mode.

Clams

Ask open-ended questions.
Be patient in waiting for a response.
Ask more open-ended questions.
If no response occurs, tell clams what you plan to do, because no discussion has taken place.

Superagreeables

In a nonthreatening manner, work hard to find out why they will not take action.
Let them know you value them as people.
Be ready to compromise and negotiate, and do not allow them to make unrealistic commitments.
Try to discern the hidden meaning in their humor.

Negativists

Do not be dragged into their despair.
Do not try to cajole them out of their negativism.
Discuss the problem thoroughly, without offering solutions.
When alternatives are discussed, bring up the negative side yourself.
Be ready to take action alone, without their agreement.

Know-It-Alls

Bulldozers:
Prepare yourself.
Listen and paraphrase their main points.
Use the questioning form to raise problems.

Balloons:
State facts or opinions as your own perceptions of reality.
Find a way for balloons to save face.
Confront balloons alone, not in public.

Indecisive Stallers

Raise the issue of why they are hesitant.
If you are the problem, ask for help.
Keep the action steps in your own hands.
Possibly remove the staller from the situation.

duplicating facilities for dependent departments. However, this approach may be too expensive for the organization. A more affordable approach to reducing interdependencies is the use of a "linking" position between dependent departments. The purpose is to ease communication and coordination among interdependent and potentially conflicting departments. Another approach is to design the work flow so that the system reflects more logical and complete work units in which responsibility and authority are more consistent. Finally, the matrix organization can offer a means for constructive confrontation, which, as stated earlier, is the most effective method of conflict resolution.[10]

The Conflict Interface

Besides acting as referees in enforcing these rules, managers can give valuable assistance to the participants without interfering with their responsibility to resolve the conflict. Managers can help the participants understand why the conflict exists and what underlying issues must be resolved. They can also help obtain information needed to reach a solution. To maximize the constructive aspects of the conflict and speed its resolution while minimizing the destructive consequences, the manager should make sure the participants are aware of the following ground rules for constructive confrontations:

1. Before the confrontation begins, review the past actions of the participants, and clarify the issues causing the conflict.
2. Encourage the participants to communicate freely. They should get their personal feelings out in the open and should not hold back grievances.

3. Don't try to place blame. This only polarizes the participants.
4. Don't surprise either party with confrontations for which either party is not prepared.
5. Don't attack sensitive areas of either party that have nothing to do with the specific conflict.
6. Keep to specific issues; do not argue aimlessly.
7. Identify areas of mutual agreement.
8. Emphasize mutual benefits to both parties.
9. Don't jump into specific solutions too quickly.
10. Encourage all of the participants to examine their own biases and feelings.
11. Maintain the intensity of the confrontation and ensure that all participants say all they want to say. If the basic issues have been resolved at this point, agree on what steps are to be taken toward resolving the conflict.

In interpersonal conflict, managers can regulate somewhat the frequency of contacts between the participants and perhaps establish a problem-solving climate when they meet. A manager's most important contribution, however, is to keep the individuals working toward a true resolution of the conflict. Confrontation of the conflict situation within the ground rules just described should encourage constructive conflict within the organization.[11]

Conflict and Diversity

Conflict can and does arise in the workplace when differences in thinking styles, speech patterns, lifestyles, national origins, ethnicity, religion, age, functional expertise, company experience, and a host of other variables are present.[12] The key to using these differences to the organization's advantage is to properly manage the potential conflict. One method of positively managing the conflicts created by diversity is to use organizational diplomacy. **Organizational diplomacy** is broadly defined as strategies used to minimize conflict in a diverse workplace, in both domestic and international settings. Organizational diplomacy is based on a proactive, unifying approach to diversity, as opposed to a reactive and superficial approach. The model shown in Figure 15.5 outlines the causes and resulting solutions that accompany both a reactive and a proactive approach. Under the reactive or pacification approach, organizations do only the minimum required by law; diversity is viewed as a necessary evil to procure government contracts or to avoid litigation. The results produced by this approach are usually negative in the form of lawsuits, reduced competitiveness, turnover, and so on. With the proactive approach, employees work together toward mutually acceptable solutions, and differences among the organization's members are used to the organization's advantage. One of the primary tenets of the proactive approach using organizational diplomacy is to encourage employee suggestions for improving organizational climate and policies.

organizational diplomacy
Strategies used to minimize conflict in a diverse workplace.

WORKPLACE STRESS

Just as conflict is an integral part of organizational life, so is stress. Stress is part of living and can contribute to personal growth, development, and mental health. However, excessive and prolonged stress generally becomes quite negative. For example, the American Institute of Stress reports that stress costs U.S. businesses about $300 billion a year in lost productivity, increased employee compensation claims, increased turnover, and increased health care costs.[13] Additionally, the institute reports that stress is a factor in up to 80 percent of all work-related injuries, a major factor in 40 percent of all turnovers, and a major contributor in 75 to 90 percent of primary care physician visits. This same group reports that 60 to 80 percent of accidents on the job are stress related.[14]

FIGURE 15.5 A Model of Organizational Diplomacy

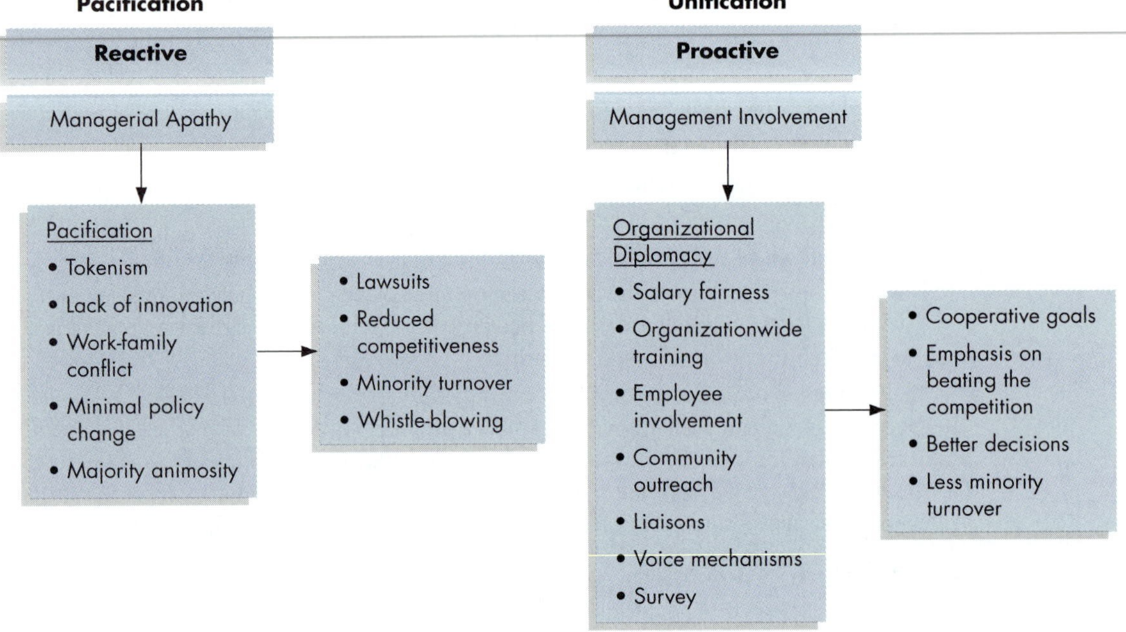

Source: Jacqueline A. Gilbert and John M. Ivancevich, "Organizational Diplomacy: The Bridge for Managing Diversity," *Human Resource Planning,* Vol. 22, No. 3, 1999, p. 30. Reprinted with permission.

stress
Mental or physical condition that results from a perceived threat of danger (physical or emotional) and the pressure to remove it.

Stress is the mental or physical condition that results from a perceived threat of danger (physical or emotional) and the pressure to remove it. The potential for stress exists when an environmental situation presents a demand that threatens to exceed the person's capabilities and resources for meeting it, under conditions in which the person expects a substantial difference in rewards and costs resulting from meeting the demand versus not meeting it. Numerous surveys conducted over the last 15 years have all reported that a significant percentage of employees feel stress related to their jobs.[15] These same studies have also reported that many employees view their job as the number-one stressor in their lives. While workplace violence (workplace violence is discussed later in this chapter) culminating in bloodshed gets the most publicity, shouting matches and lost tempers occur much more frequently. One survey by the Marlin Group found that 42 percent of employees have jobs where yelling and verbal abuse occur frequently.[16]

In its earliest stages, stress manifests itself in exaggerated behavior such as cynical attitudes and increased use of alcohol, tobacco, and medications.[17] If allowed to continue, stress affects employees on the job in several ways, including increased absenteeism, job turnover, lower productivity, and mistakes on the job. In addition, prolonged excessive stress can result in both physical and emotional problems. Some common stress-related disorders include tension and migraine headaches; coronary heart disease; high blood pressure; and muscle tightness in the chest, neck, and lower back. From a psychological perspective, inordinate or prolonged stress can impair concentration, memory, sleep, appetite, motivation, mood, and the ability to relate to others. In addition, several studies have shown that stress at work is carried to the home environment. Soon the employee becomes surrounded by stress and becomes dysfunctional.[18]

Stress strikes all levels of employees. While there is no single course of workplace stress, much of today's stress-related illnesses worldwide is the result of added demands

FIGURE 15.6
Common Sources and Suggested Causes of Organizational Stress

Source: Charles R. Stoner and Fred L. Fry, "Developing a Corporate Policy for Managing Stress," *Personnel*, May–June 1983, p. 70.

Common Sources	Suggested Causes
Job mismatch	Job demands skills or abilities the employee does not possess (job incompetence). Job does not provide opportunity for the employee to fully utilize skills or abilities (underutilization).
Conflicting expectations	The formal organization's concept of expected behavior contradicts the employee's concept of expected behavior. The informal group's concept of expected behavior contradicts the employee's concept. The individual employee is affected by two (or more) strong influences.
Role ambiguity	Employee is uncertain or unclear about how to perform on the job. Employee is uncertain or unclear about what is expected in the job. Employee is unclear or uncertain about the relationship between job performance and expected consequences (rewards, penalties, and so forth).
Role overload	Employee is incompetent at job. Employee is asked to do more than time permits (time pressure).
Fear/responsibility	Employee is afraid of performing poorly or failing. Employee feels pressure for high achievement. Employee has responsibility for other people.
Working conditions	The job environment is unpleasant; there is inadequate lighting or improper regulation of temperature and noise, for example. The requirements of the job may unnecessarily produce pacing problems, social isolation, and so forth. The machine design and maintenance procedures create pressure. The job involves long or erratic work hours.
Working relationships	Individual employees have problems relating to, or working with, superiors, peers, or subordinates. Employees have problems working in groups.
Alienation	There is limited social interaction. Employees do not participate in decision making.

placed on employees because of downsizing and the difficulties that women in particular face in juggling the demands of work and family.[19] In the face of reductions in workforces due to downsizing and reengineering, many employees have had to increase their job scopes and responsibilities. Those who experience "good job fit" do not seem to experience as much stress as those who are mismatched or overmatched in their expanded positions.[20] Figure 15.6 lists some of the more common sources and suggested causes of job-related stress.

The Workplace Stress Audit

The first step in managing workplace stress is to determine what the specific sources of stress are since they can and usually do vary from situation to situation. One method of doing this is to undertake a stress audit. A stress audit attempts to identify any work-related causes of stress. A stress audit can be undertaken by outside consultants, by internal personnel, and even online. Stress audits can be in the form of questionnaires filled out by employees or personal interviews conducted by qualified persons. Information can also be gathered on such factors as absenteeism, sick leave, and tardiness. When a company undertakes a stress audit, management is acknowledging that the workplace can be a source of stress and that it is not just the individual employee's personal problems. Management Illustration 15.2 describes a newly available online tool for conducting a stress audit.

Management Illustration 15.2

NEW ONLINE TOOL FOR STRESS AUDITS

CIGNA Behavioral Health (CBH), the benefit management arm of CIGNA Group Insurance, has recently launched a new tool, called Personal Stress Navigator, to help organizations combat stress-related costs. Personal Stress Navigator is an online questionnaire that determines the causes of employee stress and also offers solutions on both an individual and aggregate level. Recommendations that might be suggested vary from flextime for better work/life balance to brown bag seminars on various topics such as financial planning or weight loss.

The Personal Stress Navigator provides data that helps companies measure the impact stress has on its bottom line. The program also provides return-on-investment calculations to quantify a suggested solution's value to the company.

Some companies are offering employees incentives, such as gift cards or a reduction in an employee's monthly insurance contribution, to participate in this program.

Source: Donna M. Airoldi, "Decompressing the Bottom Line," *Incentive,* June 2005, p. 18.

Organizational Guidelines for Managing Stress

Once the sources of stress have been identified, solutions for reducing the stress should be explored. There are many actions that organizations can take to reduce the amount of job-related stress experienced by their employees. Among these actions are

- Shortening hours of direct contact with customers.
- Granting special leaves (sabbatical programs).
- Introducing early retirement programs.
- Installing on-site exercise facilities.
- Actively involving employees in the decision-making processes.
- Fulfilling the realistic expectations of employees.
- Introducing flextime or telecommuting where possible.
- Insisting that employees take vacation time.
- Clearly defining employee jobs.
- Providing well-thought-out training programs.
- Introducing changes gradually.
- Integrating wholesome humor into the workplace.

Naturally, some of these actions are more appropriate in some situations than in others. For any of these actions to work, the organization must first have an awareness of its potential for dealing with stress-related problems. For example, in the case of North Sea oil rig workers, audits discovered that major sources of stress included long amounts of time away from the family, the foul weather and its effect on transporting and working conditions, living conditions, and a lack of opportunity for relaxing and exercising during free time.[21] Although all of these sources of stress seemed inherent to the job, remedies were discovered. The shift system could be rearranged, and exercise facilities, no-smoking areas, quiet rooms, and more private sleeping areas could be provided. Even the stress of having to fly back and forth to the rigs could be lessened by providing more information about the safety of helicopters. Management Illustration 15.3 discusses how and why some companies are encouraging wholesome humor in the workplace.

Managing Personal Stress

In addition to reducing stress inherent in the industry and job, managers should learn to personally manage stress on a daily basis. The old strategy of waiting for an annual one- or

Management Illustration 15.3

WHOLESOME HUMOR IN THE WORKPLACE

Wholesome and appropriate humor in the workplace can help reduce employee stress and improve productivity. The type of humor referred to here does not include jokes featuring religion, sexuality, politics, or ethnic backgrounds but rather well-timed and light anecdotes such as the befuddled customer who forgot his address. Such anecdotes can be the perfect icebreaker to dispel tension in many situations. While timing is always important, experts agree that laughter in the workplace can be a real asset to profitability and productivity.

Many companies of all sizes, services, and products are hiring professional humor consultants to encourage employees to lighten up and get serious about laughing. Many modern medical experts agree that laughter in the workplace is good. A hearty belly laugh can lower blood pressure, exercise the lungs, pump more oxygen into the bloodstream, and activate endorphins that make people feel good. General Electric, IBM, and AT&T are some companies that actively encourage laughter in the workplace.

Source: Elaine Ambrose, "How to Get Serious about Humor in the Workplace," *Boulder County Business Report,* November 9–November 22, 2007, p. 43A.

two-week vacation to wind down is no longer a solution.[22] One or two weeks off rarely counterbalance 50 weeks of stress. Furthermore, many people don't take vacation time, even when it is available. One study by the Families and Work Institute reported that 36 percent of employees did not plan to take their full vacations and that 37 percent took less than a week of vacation in a year.[23]

The first step in reducing personal stress is to determine if your life is reasonably balanced. The following behaviors are indications that your life may be out of balance:

- Hurrying everywhere; walking, talking, driving faster.
- Feeling depressed, apathetic, or bored most of the time.
- Changes in sleeping or eating patterns.
- Difficulty enjoying social activities.
- Emphasis on how much you get done, rather than how well you do it.
- Inability to accept praise or affection, even when you want it.
- More frequent accidents than usual.[24]

Recognizing the above signs in your life will let you know that you should search for ways of restoring balance. The following five-step approach can help you regain your balance:

1. Counter every yes with a no. If you add a new unscheduled activity to your day, cancel another. If you decide to make an unscheduled stop at the grocery store, reschedule your plan to stop at the post office.
2. Schedule only 80 percent of your time. Leave some breathing space for unpredictable events; remember most things take longer than you think.
3. Practice giving in. Constantly making decisions places demands on your time and energy. Occasionally giving in and letting someone else make the decisions can take the pressure off.
4. Be realistic. Set realistic deadlines and workloads. Usually, no one expects as much of you as yourself.
5. Focus on the five Fs. To find balance, focus on faith, family, finances, friends, and fitness. Examine each of these areas and balance your schedule each week by including activities in all five areas.[25]

FIGURE 15.7 The Path to Professional Burnout

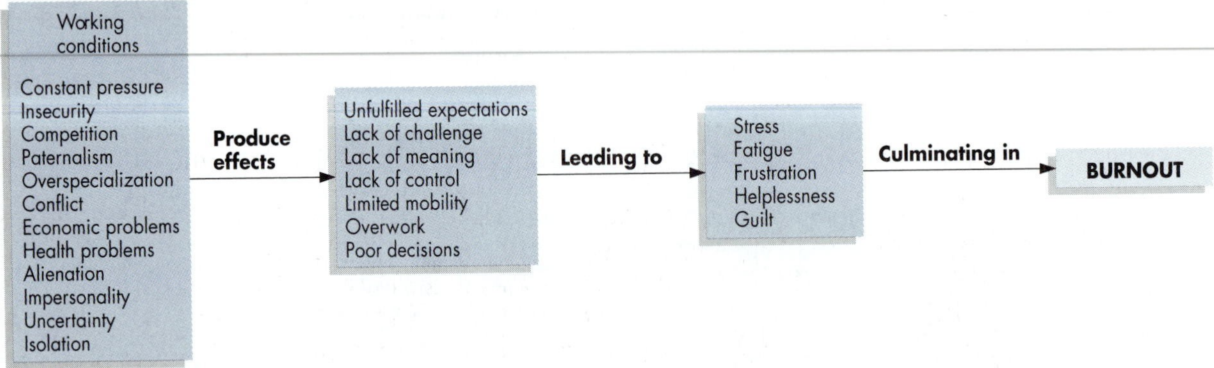

Source: Reprinted by permission from *State of Business Magazine,* "Helping Employees Cope with Burnout," by Donald P. Rogers, October–December 1984. Copyright © 1984 by the Robinson College of Business, Georgia State University, Atlanta.

technostress
Personal stress generated by reliance on technological devices, a panicky feeling when they fail, a state of near-constant stimulation, or being constantly "plugged-in."

burnout
Condition that occurs when work is no longer meaningful to a person.

Technostress

Computers and advanced communications in the form of laptops, handheld computers, cellphones, blackberries, and similar devices have added a new dimension of stress for today's employees. While these devices certainly are useful, they also allow employees to work from anywhere, be called upon at any time, and essentially have no downtime. With these devices, it can be very difficult to ever get "totally away." **Technostress** can be defined as personal stress generated by reliance on technological devices, a panicky feeling when they fail, a state of near-constant stimulation, or being constantly "plugged-in."[26] In summary, technostress is stress resulting from interacting with high-technology devices. The effects of technostress are essentially the same as those resulting from any other type of job-related stress.

Burnout

Burnout occurs when work is no longer meaningful to a person. Research has shown that chronic stress, rather than acute crises, and prolonged personal contact tend to bring about the highest degrees of burnout.[27] Figure 15.7 illustrates the sequence of events that often leads to professional burnout. As burnout has become more recognized, certain related myths have surfaced.[28]

Myth 1: Burnout is just a newfangled notion that gives lazy people an excuse not to work. Although *burnout* is a relatively new term, the behavior has been around for centuries. History abounds with examples of workers, such as writers, artists, and scientists, who gradually or suddenly stopped producing.

Myth 2: As long as people really enjoy their work, they can work as long and hard as they want and never experience burnout. Any work that inherently includes significant and continuing frustration, conflict, and pressure can lead to burnout.

Myth 3: Individuals know when they are burning out, and when they do, all they need to do is take off for a few days or weeks and then they will be as good as new. Unfortunately, most people do not realize that burnout is occurring until it reaches its later stages.

Myth 4: Individuals who are physically and psychologically strong are unlikely to experience burnout. Physically and psychologically strong individuals may indeed be able to work harder than less strong people.

Some possibilities to reduce burnout on the job include redesigning the job, clarifying expectations, improving physical working conditions, and training the jobholders.

FIGURE 15.8
Methods for Increasing Career Motivation

Sources: M. London and E. M. Moore, *Career Management and Survival in the Workplace* (San Francisco: Jossey-Bass, 1987), p. 5; and K. N. Wexley and J. Hinricks, eds., *Developing Human Resources* (Washington, DC: BNA Books, 1991), pp. 51–59.

1. Review your accomplishments and give yourself credit for them.
2. Take a moderate risk—one from which there will be some benefit.
3. Show others you can cooperate but that you also have your own ideas.
4. Inquire about how well you are doing.
5. Ask for information about career opportunities.
6. Set specific career goals for next year and general goals for the next five years.
7. Create your own job challenge by redesigning your job and generating new assignments.
8. If you want to be a leader, try it. Initiate and delegate work.
9. Take actions toward your goals.

However, without proper stress skills, the inordinate amount of work can cause serious damage.

Myth 5: Job burnout is always job related. Burnout usually results from a combination of work, family, social, and personal factors.

Since chronic stress is one of the major causes of burnout, following the guidelines previously discussed for reducing workplace and personal stress should reduce burnout. A second step in reducing burnout is to identify those jobs with the highest potential for burnout. Certain jobs are more likely to lead to burnout than others. Once those jobs have been identified, several actions are possible. Some of the possibilities include redesigning the jobs, clarifying expectations, improving physical working conditions, and training the jobholders.

For top- and mid-level managers, a chief source of burnout is the "career plateau" (the point at which further promotion or advancement no longer seems possible). Studying career resilience, examining how one gains insight or learns about a career, and carefully matching individuals with their careers through career identity can dramatically reduce burnout. Figure 15.8 identifies several methods for increasing career motivation.

Sabbaticals

One way that some companies are trying to reduce burnout is to use sabbaticals. **Sabbatical** is a word derived from *Sabbath* and literally means a recurring period of rest and renewal. Most sabbaticals granted by today's organizations allow the recipient to take time off, often with some pay cut, while retaining benefits. The length and terms of sabbaticals vary considerably among those organizations that offer them. Figure 15.9 presents the sabbaticals currently offered by several different organizations.

sabbatical
Derived from Sabbath and literally means a recurring period of rest and renewal.

FIGURE 15.9
Sabbatical Plans Offered by Different Companies

Source: From *The Wall Street Journal* by Erin White and Jeffrey A. Trachtenberg, "Sabbaticals: The Pause That Refreshes," August 2, 2005. Copyright © 2005 by Dow Jones & Co., Inc. Reproduced with permission of Dow Jones & Co., Inc. via Copyright Clearance Center.

Procter & Gamble	Eligible for an unpaid sabbatical of up to 12 weeks after only one year, and every 7 years thereafter. Employees continue to receive benefits.
Newsweek	Reporters and editors are eligible for 6 months of sabbatical at half-salary after 15 years.
Random House	Available to North American employees who have over 10 years service. After 10 years they get 4 weeks off; after 20 years, they get 5 weeks off and so on.
Nike	Eligible for 5 weeks off after 10 years; after first sabbatical employees are eligible for future sabbaticals every 5 years from the start of the last one.
Intel	Employees get 8 weeks for every 7 years of service.

Management Illustration 15.4

REDUCING BURNOUT AT MOTEK

Motek is a Beverly Hills, California–based software firm that has taken some unusual actions to help reduce employee burnout. Employees at Motek are eligible for $100 bonuses to supplement their five weeks of paid vacation per year. In addition, for employees that take three consecutive weeks of vacation, the company provides a set of luggage and a $5,000 stipend for hotels and airfare.

Motek's CEO, Ann Price, believes the more vacation, the better. Recently, Price was quoted as saying, "Take one week off, you may as well not go anywhere. If you never reach the third week, you never reach vacation." Price leads by example and has taken a two-month vacation every year. Price also prohibits working on weekends. Motek's office door has a tracker that lets Price know if someone is working after hours.

In 2007 Motek was named to Food Logistics magazine's esteemed Food Logistics 100, a listing of technology providers that best solve critical logistical issues in the food, beverage, and consumer packaged goods industry.

Sources: Kelly M. Butler, "Faced With Worker Burnout, Employers Pay Employees to Get Away," *Employee Benefit News,* June 1, 2005, p. 1; and "Motek Awarded 2007 Food Logistics Top 100; Motek Cited as Top Technology Provider for Critical Logistical Challenges in Food, Beverage and Consumer Packaged Goods," *PR Newswire,* December 19, 2007.

A 2007 survey conducted by the Society of Human Resources Management (SHRM) reported that about 16 percent of employers offered unpaid sabbatical leaves and 4 percent offered sabbaticals with pay.[29] Employees returning from a sabbatical generally report that they return with a deeper commitment to their job and a feeling of more purpose than before. Management Illustration 15.4 describes the actions taken by one software company to help reduce burnout.

Workaholism

workaholism
Working to the exclusion of everything else in one's life.

Workaholism is related to stress in that it can be a cause of stress. **Workaholism** is working to the exclusion of everything else in one's life.[30] It is an addiction that causes a person to become so obsessed with work that he or she is crippled emotionally and physically. Workaholics constantly think about work, work long hours, and often sacrifice sleep, food, exercise, family, and friends in favor of work.

One might think that having an organization full of workaholics would be desirable from the organization's viewpoint. However, a workaholic environment creates stress, burnout, and low morale. Also, workaholics are often not the most efficient employees because they frequently engage in doing unnecessary things.

Workplace Violence

The U.S. Bureau of Labor Statistics defines workplace violence as "an act of physical assault, threat of assault, harassment, intimidation, or bullying toward a person at work or on duty."[31] Violence in the workplace has become a real concern. Consider the following statistics for the United States: An average of 5,500 incidents of workplace violence occur every day; an average of at least three people are murdered at work each day; and 13,000 women are assaulted, stalked, or murdered at work by a significant other each year.[32] Also, since the events of September 11, 2001, the threat of terrorism in the workplace has become a reality.

For many organizations, the danger from workplace violence comes not only from extreme violence, like shootings, but from nonfatal assaults, verbal threats, harassment and intimidation, sexual harassment, and other erratic behaviors suggesting emotional instability. Figure 15.10 shows the incidence of workplace violence found in a survey conducted by the Society for Human Resources Management (SHRM).

FIGURE 15.10
Violence Incidents in the Workplace

Source: "Safe, Not Sorry, Is the Best Approach," *HR Focus*, April 2000, pp. 51, 54.

Incidents	Percentage
Verbal threats	41
Pushing/shoving	19
Burglary/robbery	9
Fistfight	9
Stalking	9
Bomb threat	7
Shooting	1
Stabbing	1

A 2004 survey by the American Society of Safety Engineers (ASSE) reported that 80 percent of respondents had some type of written policies addressing workplace violence, but that 39 percent had no procedures at all for preventing workplace violence.[33]

While there is no way to guarantee that an organization will not be victimized, the establishment of a workplace violence-prevention program can greatly reduce the probability of a problem. A comprehensive workplace violence-prevention program should include the following elements:[34]

- A written policy statement that communicates a clear commitment to promoting a workplace safe from violence, that prohibits threats and violence of every sort, and that requires employees to immediately report to management all circumstances that create a concern for safety from violence.
- A management response team that represents diverse segments of the organization, trained and charged with the responsibility of investigating and managing all reports of circumstances that raise a concern for an employee.
- A meaningful reporting and response mechanism that establishes clear lines of communication and responsibility for issues involving violence and ensures that the organization is both promptly notified of potential security risks and can take immediate steps to resolve underlying concerns.
- Clear standards of behavior that prohibit threats and violence of every sort and that require prompt, appropriate discipline of employees who breach safety rules.
- A wide array of other security, employment, legal, and administrative practices can help an organization prevent and manage on-site threats and violence. Such practices include a security inventory to assess the particular risks faced by the organization from violence; the development of security protocols to manage threats and violence in depth, preemployment background checks; and the pursuit of legal remedies such as restraining orders (when needed) to guard against third-party threats.
- A system of periodic employee training addressing such issues as workplace policies; warning signs of violence; the requirement that employees report threats to management; methods for properly investigating complaints made under the workplace violence policy; defusing hostile situations; and strategies for addressing domestic violence.

A survey by the U.S. Bureau of Labor Statistics found that more than 80 percent of employers that experienced an incident of workplace violence between September 2004 and September 2006 did not change their workplace violence program or policy afterwards.[35]

Employee Assistance Programs (EAPs)

Many large organizations and a growing number of smaller ones are attempting to help employees with stress, burnout, and other personal problems that include not only alcohol and drug abuse but also depression, anxiety, domestic trauma, financial problems, and other psychiatric/medical problems. This help is not purely altruistic; it is based largely on cost savings. The help is generally offered in the form of an **employee assistance program (EAP).**

employee assistance program (EAP)
Program sponsored by the organization that attempts to help employees with stress, burnout, and other personal problems that include alcohol and drug abuse, depression, anxiety, domestic trauma, financial problems, and other psychiatric/medical problems.

A primary result of personal problems brought to the workplace is reduced productivity. According to the National Mental Health Association, untreated mental illness alone costs the United States $105 billion in lost productivity annually, with U.S. employers funding up to $44 billion of the bill.[36] Absenteeism and tardiness also tend to increase with personal problems. Increased costs of insurance programs, including sickness and accident benefits, are a direct result of personal problems brought to the workplace. Lower morale, more friction among employees, more friction between supervisors and employees, and more grievances also result from troubled employees. Permanent loss of trained employees due to disability, retirement, and death is also associated with troubled employees. Frequently cited work-related stress problems that affect the employee's feeling of self-worth are lack of supervisor trust and respect, conflict between job performance and reward, job communication, supervisor action or inaction, and job nonperformance (lack of control over job).[37] An intangible but very real cost associated with troubled employees is the loss of business and damaged public image.

Until recently, organizations attempted to avoid employees' problems that were not job related. Although aware of the existence of these problems, organizations did not believe they should interfere with employees' personal lives. In the past, organizations tended to get rid of troubled employees. In recent years, however, cost considerations, unions, and government legislation have altered this approach. The accepted viewpoint today is that employees' personal problems are private until they begin affecting their job performance. When and if that happens, personal problems become a matter of concern for the organization.

Studies have shown that absenteeism can be significantly reduced by employee assistance programs. EAPs have also been found to help reduce on-the-job accidents and grievances. Workers' compensation premiums, sickness and accident benefits, and trips to the infirmary also tend to decrease with an EAP.

Several types of employee assistance programs exist. In one type, which is rarely used, diagnosis and treatment of the problem are provided directly by the organization. This type of in-house EAP is used only in very large organizations. In a second type of program, the organization hires a qualified person to diagnose the employee's problem; then the employee is referred to the proper agency or clinic for treatment. The third and most common type of program employs a coordinator who evaluates the employee's problem only sufficiently to make a referral to the proper agency or clinic for diagnosis. Oftentimes the coordinator serves only as a consultant to the organization and is not a full-time employee. This type of program is especially popular with smaller employers and branch operations of large employers.

Variations of these basic types of EAPs include the use of the telephone or the Internet as a referral tool. Both the telephone and the Internet can provide a fast and convenient way to link employees with an EAP. In addition to being convenient, some people feel more at ease confiding over the phone or with their computer than talking face-to-face with an EAP specialist. Management Illustration 15.5 describes how Bridgestone Americas has integrated teletherapy into its EAP with great success.

To be successful, an EAP must first be accepted by the employees; they must not be afraid to use it. Experience has shown that certain elements are critical to the success of an EAP. Figure 15.11 summarizes several of the most important characteristics of an EAP.

Management Illustration 15.5

TELETHERAPY AT BRIDGESTONE AMERICAS

For several years, companies have used telephone hotlines to link employees with appropriate EAP professionals who would subsequently provide face-to-face help. More recently, some companies have taken this process one step further by integrating telephone therapy into their EAP offerings. Ron Tepner is vice president of human resources at BPS Retail and Commercial Operations, a subsidiary of Bridgestone Americas. Tepner provides EAP to 22,000 employees in 2,000 Bridgestone tire stores throughout the United States. Originally Tepner was skeptical of anything other than a traditional face-to-face counseling. However, face-to-face counseling is relatively expensive and employees weren't inclined to use it because they didn't want people in human resources knowing they had a problem, didn't want to wait days for an appointment, or, in smaller towns, didn't want their cars seen in the parking lot of the town psychologist.

Tepner heard about teletherapy being used by Wal-Mart and Kroger and decided to try it. The change has paid off. Once teletherapy was introduced, EAP use jumped 70 percent with about 9.6 percent of employees calling in during a given year. Before teletherapy Bridgestone Americas EAP effectiveness—described as the percentage of people who get better—was 30–50 percent; now it's about 92 percent!

Source: Michelle V. Rafter, "EAPs Tout the Benefits of Dial-Up Counseling in Place of Face-to-Face." *Workforce Management*, November 2004, pp. 75–77.

Wellness Programs

wellness program
Company-implemented program designed to prevent illness and enhance employee well-being.

In addition to the EAPs discussed in the previous section, many companies have installed programs designed to prevent illness and enhance employee well-being. These programs are referred to as **wellness programs** and include such things as periodic medical exams, stop-smoking clinics, education on improved dietary practices, hypertension detection and control, weight control, exercise and fitness, stress management, accident-risk reduction, immunizations, and cardiopulmonary resuscitation (CPR) training. Some of the documented results of wellness programs include fewer sick days, reduced coronary heart disease, and lower major medical costs. Many also believe that employee productivity increases for employees who participate in exercise and fitness programs. Numerous studies have reported a very attractive return on investment for most types of wellness programs.[38]

FIGURE 15.11
Ten Critical Elements of an EAP

Source: Adapted from F. Dickman and W. G. Emener, "Employee Assistance Programs: Basic Concepts, Attributes, and an Evaluation," *Personnel Administrator*, August 1982, p. 56.

Element	Significance
Management backing	Without this at the highest level, key ingredients and overall effect are seriously limited.
Labor support	The EAP cannot be meaningful if it is not backed by the employees' labor unit.
Confidentiality	Anonymity and trust are crucial if employees are to use an EAP.
Easy access	For maximum use and benefit.
Supervisor training	Crucial to employees needing understanding and support during receipt of assistance.
Union steward training	A critical variable is employees' contact with the union—the steward.
Insurance involvement	Occasionally assistance alternatives are costly, and insurance support is a must.
Breadth of service components	Availability of assistance for a wide variety of problems (e.g., drugs, alcoholism, family, personal, financial, grief, medical).
Professional leadership	A skilled professional with expertise in helping who must have credibility in the eyes of the employee.
Follow-up and evaluation	To measure program effectiveness and overall improvement.

FIGURE 15.12
Specific Company Benefits of Wellness Programs

Source: Nancy Hatch Woodward, "Exercise Options, *HR Magazine*, June 2005, pp. 78–83.

- DuPont Corporation reported absences from illness unrelated to the job declined 14 percent at 41 individual sites where the company offered a wellness program. This compared to a 5.8 percent decline at the 19 sites where a wellness program was not offered.
- Pacific Bell found that absentee days decreased by 0.8 percent after its FitWorks program was put in place. This resulted in a $2 million savings in one year. Employees who participated in the program spent 3.3 fewer days on short-term disability, saving the company an additional $4.7 million.
- The Coca-Cola Company reported a $500 reduction in annual health care claims for each employee who participated in its Health Works fitness program.

Figure 15.12 summarizes some benefits obtained from wellness programs by specific companies. Experts in the wellness field report that even small companies can offer wellness programs and that such programs do not have to be expensive.

In addition to the companies mentioned in Figure 15.12, the Adolph Coors Company has a very successful wellness program. Coors claims that its 25,000-square-foot wellness facility, designed for employees and their spouses, has helped the company save more than $2 million annually in medical claims and other health-related factors. The Coors program is designed around a six-step behavioral change model: awareness, education, incentives, programs, self-education, and follow-up and support. Chief among the elements that are critical for successful wellness programs are CEO support and direction, accessibility, inclusion of family, needs assessment, staffing with specialists, and establishment of a separate budget for wellness activities.[39]

Summary

1. *Define conflict.* Conflict is overt behavior that results when an individual or a group of individuals think a perceived need or needs of the individual or group has been blocked or is about to be blocked.
2. *Discuss the useful effects of conflict.* Some potentially useful effects of conflict are that it energizes people; is a form of communication; often provides an outlet for pent-up tensions, resulting in catharsis; and may actually be an educational experience.
3. *Outline the stages of conflict development.* The stages of conflict development are latent conflict, perceived conflict, felt conflict, manifest conflict, and conflict aftermath.
4. *Name the five major types of conflict based on the entities involved.* The five major types of conflict based on the entities involved are intrapersonal, interpersonal, intergroup, organizational, and political.
5. *Name five approaches for resolving interpersonal conflict.* There are five general approaches for resolving interpersonal conflict: (1) compromising for the sake of ending the conflict; (2) smoothing over the conflict and pretending it does not exist; (3) withdrawal of one or more of the participants; (4) forcing the conflict to a conclusion through third-party intervention; and (5) forcing a confrontation between the participants in an effort to solve the underlying source of conflict.
6. *Name and briefly discuss one method of positively managing conflicts created by diversity in the workplace.* One method for positively managing conflicts created by diversity in the workplace is organizational diplomacy. Organizational diplomacy is based on a proactive, unifying approach to diversity, as opposed to a reactive and superficial approach.
7. *Define stress and technostress.* Stress is the mental or physical condition that results from a perceived threat of danger (physical or emotional) and the pressure to remove

it. Technostress is personal stress generated by reliance on technological devices, a panicky feeling when they fail, a state of near-constant stimulation, or being constantly "plugged-in." In summary, technostress is stress resulting from interacting with high-technology devices.

8. *Define burnout.* Burnout is a condition that occurs when work is no longer meaningful to a person.
9. *Describe what is a sabbatical.* Sabbatical is a word derived from "Sabbath" and literally means a recurring period of rest and renewal. Most sabbaticals granted by today's organizations allow the recipient to take time off with some pay cut while retaining benefits.
10. *Outline the basic elements of a violence-prevention program.* The basic elements of a comprehensive violence-prevention program are a written policy statement communicating a clear commitment to promoting a workplace safe from violence; a management response team; a meaningful reporting and response mechanism; clear standards of behavior; a wide array of other security, employment, legal, and administrative practices; and a system of periodic employee training covering violence-prevention issues.
11. *Explain the three basic types of employee assistance programs.* In one type of EAP, diagnosis and treatment of the problem are provided directly by the organization. In a second type, the organization hires a qualified person to diagnose the employee's problem and then refers the employee to a proper agency or clinic for treatment. The third and most common type employs a coordinator who evaluates the employee's problem only sufficiently to make a referral to the proper agency or clinic for diagnosis.
12. *Explain wellness programs.* Wellness programs are company-implemented programs designed to prevent illness and enhance employee well-being.

Review Questions

1. What is conflict?
2. Describe some potentially useful effects of conflict.
3. Identify the five stages of conflict.
4. What causes intrapersonal conflict?
5. What are some typical defense mechanisms used when an individual is frustrated?
6. What are some causes of interpersonal conflict?
7. Name at least four types of intergroup conflict.
8. What is organizational conflict?
9. What is political conflict?
10. What are some methods that can be used to resolve interpersonal conflict?
11. Outline some key questions that need to be answered in conflict resolution.
12. What is organizational diplomacy?
13. Name several ways that stress can manifest itself in the workplace.
14. What is a workplace stress audit?
15. List several actions an organization can take to reduce job-related stress of its employees.
16. What is technostress?
17. What is burnout?

18. What are sabbaticals?
19. What is workaholism?
20. What is a workplace violence-prevention program?
21. What are three basic types of employee assistance programs?
22. What is a wellness program?

Skill-Building Questions

1. Should managers attempt to avoid conflict at all times? Explain.
2. "Conflict is inevitable." Do you agree or disagree with this statement? Discuss.
3. How can managers reduce destructive stress in organizations?
4. How would you handle a situation in which you have two people working for you who "just rub each other the wrong way"?
5. Examine your personal situation and identify some ways that you might reduce stress in your day-to-day activities.

SKILL-BUILDING EXERCISE 15.1 The Workplace Stress Scale

Thinking about your current job, how often does each of the following statements describe how you feel?

	Never	Rarely	Sometimes	Often	Very Often
A. Conditions at work are unpleasant or sometimes even unsafe.	1	2	3	4	5
B. I feel that my job is negatively affecting my physical or emotional well being.	1	2	3	4	5
C. I have too much work to do and/or too many unreasonable deadlines.	1	2	3	4	5
D. I find it difficult to express my opinions or feelings about my job conditions to my superiors.	1	2	3	4	5
E. I feel that job pressures interfere with my family or personal life.	1	2	3	4	5
F. I have adequate control or input over my work duties.	5	4	3	2	1
G. I receive appropriate recognition or rewards for good performance.	5	4	3	2	1
H. I am able to utilize my skills and talents to the fullest extent at work.	5	4	3	2	1

To get your score, add the numbers you answered to all of the eight questions and see how you compare.

Interpreting Workplace Stress Scale Scores

Total score of 15 or lower (33 percent of us are in this category): Chilled out and relatively calm. Stress isn't much of an issue.

Total score 16 to 20 (35 percent): Fairly low. Coping should be a breeze, but you probably have a tough day now and then. Still, count your blessings.

Total score 21–25 (21 percent): Moderate stress. Some things about your job are likely to be pretty stressful, but probably not much more than most people experience and are able to cope with. Concentrate on seeing what can be done to reduce items with the worst scores.

Total score 26–30 (9 percent): Severe. You may still be able to cope, but life at work can sometimes be miserable. Several of your scores are probably extreme. You could be in the wrong job, or even in the right job but at the wrong time, and might benefit from counseling.

Total score 31–40 (2 percent): Stress level is potentially dangerous—the more so the higher your score. You should seek professional assistance, especially if you feel your health is affected, or you might need to consider a job change.

Workplace Stress Scale Scores by Demographic

Overall: 18.4
Men: 18.6
Women: 18.1
Ages 18–34: 17.6
Ages 35–49: 19.2
Ages 50+: 18.4

Source: Reprinted with permission of The American Institute of Stress.

SKILL-BUILDING EXERCISE 15.2
Self-Evaluation: The Glazer Stress Control Lifestyle Questionnaire

As you can see, each scale below is composed of a pair of adjectives or phrases separated by a series of horizontal lines. Each pair has been chosen to represent two contrasting behaviors. Each of us belongs somewhere along the line between the two extremes. Since most of us are neither the most competitive nor the least competitive person we know, put a check mark where you think you belong between the two extremes.

	1	2	3	4	5	6	7	
1. Doesn't mind leaving things temporarily unfinished	___	___	___	___	___	___	___	Must get things finished once started
2. Calm and unhurried about appointments	___	___	___	___	___	___	___	Never late for appointments
3. Not competitive	___	___	___	___	___	___	___	Highly competitive
4. Listens well, lets others finish speaking	___	___	___	___	___	___	___	Anticipates others in conversation (nods, interrupts, finishes sentences for the other)
5. Never in a hurry, even when pressured	___	___	___	___	___	___	___	Always in a hurry
6. Able to wait calmly	___	___	___	___	___	___	___	Uneasy when waiting
7. Easygoing	___	___	___	___	___	___	___	Always going full speed ahead
8. Takes one thing at a time	___	___	___	___	___	___	___	Tries to do more than one thing at a time; thinks about what to do next
9. Slow and deliberate in speech	___	___	___	___	___	___	___	Vigorous and forceful in speech (uses a lot of gestures)
10. Concerned with satisfying himself or herself, not others	___	___	___	___	___	___	___	Wants recognition by others for a job well done
11. Slow doing things	___	___	___	___	___	___	___	Fast doing things (eating, walking, etc.)
12. Easygoing	___	___	___	___	___	___	___	Hard driving
13. Expresses feelings openly	___	___	___	___	___	___	___	Holds feelings in
14. Has a large number of interests	___	___	___	___	___	___	___	Few interests outside work

		1	2	3	4	5	6	7	
15.	Satisfied with job	___	___	___	___	___	___	___	Ambitious; wants quick advancement on job
16.	Never sets own deadlines	___	___	___	___	___	___	___	Often sets own deadlines
17.	Feels limited responsibility	___	___	___	___	___	___	___	Always feels responsible
18.	Never judges things in terms of numbers	___	___	___	___	___	___	___	Often judges performance in terms of numbers (how much, how many)
19.	Casual about work	___	___	___	___	___	___	___	Takes work very seriously (works weekends, brings work home)
20.	Not very precise	___	___	___	___	___	___	___	Very precise (careful about detail)

Source: Unknown to the authors.

Scoring

Assign a value from 1 to 7 for each score. Total them. The categories are as follows:

Total Score	Type	Explanation
110–140:	A_1	If you are in this category, and especially if you are over 40 and smoke, you are likely to have a high risk of developing cardiac illness.
80–109:	A_2	You are in the direction of being cardiac prone, but your risk is not as high as the A_1. You should, nevertheless, pay careful attention to the advice given to all type A's.
60–79:	AB	You are an admixture of A and B patterns. This is a healthier pattern than either A_1 or A_2, but you have the potential for slipping into A behavior and you should recognize this.
30–59:	B_2	Your behavior is on the less-cardiac-prone end of the spectrum. You are generally relaxed and cope adequately with stress.
0–29:	B_1	You tend to the extreme of noncardiac traits. Your behavior expresses few of the reactions associated with cardiac disease.

SKILL-BUILDING EXERCISE 15.3 Social Readjustment Rating Scale

Everybody is confronted by both major and minor changes in the workplace and in their private lives. Some of these changes are predictable and some are not; some can be controlled and others cannot. The following list contains 43 life events. Please record the frequency with which you have confronted each of these within the past 12 months.

Life Events	Life Change Units		Number of Events in Past 12 Months		Total
Death of spouse	100	×	_____	=	_____
Divorce	73	×	_____	=	_____
Marital separation	65	×	_____	=	_____
Jail term	63	×	_____	=	_____
Death of close family member	63	×	_____	=	_____
Personal injury or illness	53	×	_____	=	_____
Marriage	50	×	_____	=	_____
Fired at work	47	×	_____	=	_____
Marital reconciliation	45	×	_____	=	_____
Retirement	45	×	_____	=	_____
Change in health of family member	44	×	_____	=	_____
Pregnancy	40	×	_____	=	_____
Sex difficulties	39	×	_____	=	_____
Gain of new family member	39	×	_____	=	_____

Business readjustment	39	×	_____	=	_____
Change in financial state	38	×	_____	=	_____
Death of a close friend	37	×	_____	=	_____
Change to different line of work	36	×	_____	=	_____
Change in number of arguments with spouse	35	×	_____	=	_____
Mortgage over $100,000*	31	×	_____	=	_____
Foreclosure of mortgage or loan	30	×	_____	=	_____
Change in responsibility at work	29	×	_____	=	_____
Son or daughter leaving home	29	×	_____	=	_____
Trouble with in-laws	29	×	_____	=	_____
Outstanding personal achievement	28	×	_____	=	_____
Spouse begins or stops work	26	×	_____	=	_____
Begin or end school	26	×	_____	=	_____
Change in living conditions	25	×	_____	=	_____
Revision of personal habits	24	×	_____	=	_____
Trouble with boss	23	×	_____	=	_____
Change in work hours or conditions	20	×	_____	=	_____
Change in residence	20	×	_____	=	_____
Change in schools	20	×	_____	=	_____
Change in recreation	19	×	_____	=	_____
Change in church activities	19	×	_____	=	_____
Change in social activities	18	×	_____	=	_____
Mortgage or loan less than $100,000*	17	×	_____	=	_____
Change in sleeping habits	16	×	_____	=	_____
Change in number of family get-togethers	15	×	_____	=	_____
Change in eating habits	15	×	_____	=	_____
Vacation	13	×	_____	=	_____
Christmas or High Holy Days	12	×	_____	=	_____
Minor violations of the law	11	×	_____	=	_____
Life change units total				=	_____

*Figures adjusted by authors to reflect inflation.

Source: Reprinted from *Journal of Psychosomatic Research,* Vol. 11, by Holmes, "The Social Readjustment Rating Scale."

After you have gone through the list, compute your score by multiplying the assigned points times the number of times a specific event has occurred and summing the totals. Use the following information to interpret your score:

Score	**More Susceptible to Illness Than Following Percentage of General Population**
350–400	90%
300–349	80%
200–299	50%
150–199	37%
Up to 150	Low stress level

If your total score is under 150, your level of stress, based on life change, is low. If your score is between 150 and 300, your stress levels are borderline—you should minimize other changes in your life at this time. If your score is over 300, your life change level of stress is high—you should not only minimize any other changes in your life and work but should strive to practice some stress intervention techniques.

Case Incident 15.1

The Young College Graduate and the Old Superintendent

You are a consultant to the manager of a garment manufacturing plant in a small southern town. The manager has been having trouble with two employees: Ralph, the plant superintendent, and Kevin, the production scheduler. Ralph is 53 years old and has been with the company since he was released from a two-year stint in the army. He started in the warehouse with a tenth-grade education and worked his way up through the ranks. Until recently, Ralph handled—along with his many other duties—the production scheduling function. He was proud of the fact that he could handle it all "in my head." As the volume of production and the number of different products grew, however, the plant manager thought significant savings could be attained through a more sophisticated approach to scheduling. He believed he could save on raw materials by purchasing in larger quantities and on production setup time by making longer runs. He also wanted to cut down on the frequency of finished-goods stock-outs; when backlogs did occur, he wanted to be able to give customers more definite information as to when goods would be available. He wanted to have a planned schedule for at least two months into the future, with daily updates.

Kevin is 24 years old and grew up in the Chicago area. This is his first full-time job. He earned a master of science degree in industrial engineering from an eastern engineering school. He jumped right into the job and set up a computer-assisted scheduling system, using a time-sharing service with a teletype terminal in his office. The system is based on the latest production scheduling and inventory control technology. It is very flexible and has proven to be quite effective in all areas that were of interest to the plant manager.

Plant manager: Sometimes I just want to shoot both Ralph and Kevin. If those two could just get along with each other, this plant would run like a well-oiled machine.

Consultant: What do they fight about?

Manager: Anything and everything that has to do with the production schedule. Really trivial things in a lot of cases. It all seems so completely senseless!

Consultant: Have you tried to do anything about it?

Manager: At first, I tried to minimize the impact of their feuds on the rest of the plant by stepping in and making decisions that would eliminate the point of controversy. I also tried to smooth things over as if the arguments were just friendly disagreements. I thought that after they had a chance to get accustomed to each other, the problem would go away. But it didn't. It got to the point that I was spending a good 20 percent of my time stopping their fights. Furthermore, I began to notice that other employees were starting to take sides. The younger people seemed to support Kevin; everybody else sided with Ralph. It began to look as if we might have our own little war.

Consultant: What's the current situation?

Manager: I finally told them both that if I caught them fighting again, I would take very drastic action with both of them. I think that move was a mistake though, because now they won't even talk to each other. Kevin just drops the schedule printouts on Ralph's desk every afternoon and walks away.

Ralph needs some help in working with those printouts, and Kevin needs some feedback on what's actually going on in the plant. Frankly, things aren't going as well production-wise now as when they were at each other's throats. And the tension in the plant as a whole is even worse. They are both good people and outstanding in their respective jobs. I would really hate to lose either of them, but if they can't work together, I may have to let one or both of them go.

Questions

1. Why is this conflict occurring?
2. What method did the manager use in dealing with this conflict situation? Was it effective?
3. Recommend an approach for resolving the conflict.

Case Incident 15.2

Problems at the Hospital

Smith County is a suburban area near a major midwestern city. The county has experienced such a tremendous rate of growth during the past decade that local governments have had difficulty providing adequate service to the citizens.

Smith County Hospital has a reputation for being a first-class facility, but it is inadequate to meet local needs. During certain periods of the year, the occupancy rates exceed the licensed capacity. There is no doubt in anyone's mind that the hospital must be expanded immediately.

At a recent meeting of the Hospital Authority, the hospital administrator, Kaye Austin, presented the group with a proposal to accept the architectural plans of the firm of Watkins and Gibson. This plan calls for a 100-bed addition adjacent to the existing structure. Kaye announced that after reviewing several alternative plans, she believed the Watkins and Gibson plan would provide the most benefit for the expenditure.

At this point, Randolph (Randy) Lewis, the board chairperson, began questioning the plan. Randy made it clear he would not go along with the Watkins and Gibson plan. He stated that the board should look for other firms to serve as the architects for the project.

The ensuing argument became somewhat heated, and a 10-minute recess was called to allow those attending to get coffee as well as allow tempers to calm down. Kaye was talking to John Rhodes, another member of the Hospital Authority board, in the hall and said, "Randy seems to fight me on every project."

Randy, who was talking to other members of the board, was saying, "I know that the Watkins and Gibson plan is good, but I just can't stand for Kaye to act like it's her plan. I wish she would leave so we could get a good administrator from the community whom we can identify with."

Questions

1. Is Randy's reaction uncommon? Explain.
2. What type of conflict exists between Kaye and Randy?
3. What methods would you use to reduce or resolve the conflict?
4. Could Kaye have done anything in advance of the meeting to maximize her chances of success? Explain.

References and Additional Readings

1. William Cottringer, "Conflict Management," *Executive Excellence,* August 1997, p. 6.
2. See Kenneth Thomas, "Conflict and Conflict Management," in *Handbook of Industrial and Organizational Psychology,* ed. Marvin D. Dunnette (New York: John Wiley & Sons, 1983); and Jim Dawson, "Making Conflict Work for You," *Cost Engineering,* October 2005, pp. 7–8.
3. Robert L. Kahn, "Role Conflict and Ambiguity in Organizations," *Personnel Administrator,* March–April 1964, pp. 8–13.
4. Steven Kerr, "On the Folly of Rewarding A, While Hoping for B," *Academy of Management Journal* 18 (1975), pp. 769–83.
5. P. R. Lawrence and J. W. Lorsch, *Organization and Environment* (Boston: Harvard Business School, Division of Research, 1967).
6. For more information, see Dean Tjosvold, Valerie Dann, and Choy Wong, "Managing Conflict between Departments to Serve Customers," *Human Relations,* October 1992, pp. 1035–54.
7. Julie Olson-Buchanan, Fritz Drasgow, Philip J. Moberg, Alan D. Mead, et al., "Interactive Video Assessment of Conflict Resolution Skills," *Personnel Psychology,* Spring 1998, pp. 1–24.
8. See also Philip B. DuBose and Charles D. Pringle, "Choosing a Conflict Management Technique," *Supervision,* June 1989, pp. 10–12.
9. R. M. Bramson, *Coping with Difficult People* (New York: Dell, 1981).
10. See also Evert Van de Vliert and Boris Kabanoff, "Toward Theory-Based Measures of Conflict Management," *Academy of Management Journal,* March 1990, pp. 199–209.
11. See also, Kenneth Thomas, "Conflict and Conflict Management: Reflections and Update," *Journal of Organizational Behavior,* May 1992, pp. 263–74; and "Taking a Positive Approach to Resolving Conflicts," *Association Management,* September 2005, p. 23.
12. Much of this section is drawn from Jacqueline A. Gilbert and John M. Ivancevich, "Organizational Diplomacy: The Bridge for Managing Diversity," *Human Resource Planning* 22, no. 3 (1999), pp. 29–39.
13. Allison Bruce, "Stress on the Job Proves to Be Costly," *Knight Ridder Tribune Business News,* March 22, 2005, p. 1.
14. http://www.stress.org/job.html. Accessed on January 26, 2008.
15. Several of these are summarized by the American Institute of Stress at http://www.stressorg/job.html. Accessed on January 26, 2008.
16. Terry Schraeder, "Battling Workplace Stress," *PIM's Papermaker,* June 2001, p. 30.
17. "How to Reduce Workplace Stress," *Worklife Report* 10, no. 3 (1997), pp. 4–5.
18. Victoria J. Doby and Robert D. Caplan, "Organizational Stress as Threat to Reputation: Effects on Anxiety at Work and Home," *Academy of Management Journal* 38, no. 4 (1995), pp. 1105–23.
19. "Workplace Stress Equals Health Distress," *Worklife Report* 11, no. 1 (1997), p. 10.
20. Jia Lin Xie and Gary Johns, "Job Scope and Stress: Can Job Scope Be Too High?" *Academy of Management Journal* 38, no. 5 (1995), pp. 1288–1309.
21. "How to Reduce Workplace Stress."
22. Much of this section is drawn from Cecilia MacDonald, "Frayed to the Breaking Point," *Credit Union Management,* June 1996, pp. 30–31.
23. Allison Bruce, op. cit.
24. Cecilia MacDonald, op. cit.
25. Ibid.
26. Peter E. Brillhart, "Technostress in the Workplace: Managing Stress in the Electronic Workplace," *Journal of the American Academy of Business, Cambridge,* September 2004, pp. 302–07.
27. C. Maslach, *Burnout—The Cost of Caring* (Englewood Cliffs, NJ: Prentice Hall, 1982).
28. Michael E. Cavanagh, "What You Don't Know about Stress," *Personnel Journal,* July 1988, pp. 56–57.

29. Joann S. Lublin, "How One Executive Used a Sabbatical to Fix His Career," *The Wall Street Journal,* January 8, 2008, p. B1.
30. Much of this section is drawn from Kathryn Tyler, "Spinning Wheels," *HR Magazine,* September 1999, pp. 34–40.
31. "The Real Situation with Workplace Violence Events v. Media Coverage," *HR Focus,* March 2007, p. 3.
32. Paul Viollis, "Most Workplace Violence Avoidable," *Business Insurance,* April 11, 2005, p. 10.
33. Ibid.
34. Rebecca A. Speer, "Can Workplace Violence Be Prevented?" *Occupational Hazards,* August 1998, pp. 26–30.
35. "Most Employers Don't Change Policies After Workplace Violence Occurs," *HR Focus,* January 2007, p. 9.
36. Mari Edlin, "Depression Can Be a Detriment to Workplace Productivity," *Managed Healthcare Executive,* October 2006, p. 48.
37. H. Richard Priesmeyer, *Organization and Chaos* (Westport, CT: Quorum Books, 1992), pp. 164–65.
38. For example, "Wellness Programs Yield Sizeable Savings on Health-Care Expenses," *Contractor's Business Management Report,* November 2005, p. 9.
39. Shari Caudron and Michael Rozek, "The Wellness Payoff," *Personnel Journal,* July 1990, pp. 54–62, as described in John M. Ivancevich, *Human Resource Management* (Burr Ridge, IL: Richard D. Irwin, 1995), pp. 636–37.

Chapter Sixteen

Managing Change and Culture

Learning Objectives

After studying this chapter, you will be able to:

1. Identify the three major categories of organizational change.
2. List the three steps in Lewin's model for change.
3. Discuss several reasons employees resist change.
4. Identify several prescriptions for reducing resistance to change.
5. Describe an approach that managers can use to lead change.
6. Summarize the four phases of an organizational development (OD) program.
7. Briefly describe the four essential principles that organizations must follow to manage innovation.
8. Explain what a learning organization is.
9. Define corporate culture.
10. Describe the generic types of organizational culture.
11. Identify two common sources of organizational subcultures.

Chapter Preview

Everybody knows FedEx, the $23 billion company that initiated the overnight package delivery business. Since its beginning in 1971, FedEx has expanded internationally and into low-cost ground shipping and freight. More recently, FedEx acquired Kinko's copy stores and is partnering with Kinko's to offer a combined copy and ship service.

Fred Smith, FedEx's founder, was recently interviewed about FedEx's approach to managing change, and specifically how to get employees to embrace change. Fred's response is shown below:

> To be able to change effectively, you have to have a high degree of trust and outstanding communications capability. When we got into the ground business, we didn't want our employees at FedEx to feel threatened. So we put a tremendous effort into communicating with them. I got onto our corporate television network. I gave speeches. I went on road trips. We talked to them in e-mails and publications. Anything to make them feel they were part of the change and explain why we were changing. We're doing the same thing with Kinko's. We didn't walk in there and say, Okay, guess what: A lot of people are

> laid off. We managed it cautiously. You have to spend that time and effort to communicate why change is necessary. If you can put that into a culture that knows change is inevitable and an opportunity, not a threat, then I think you have the potential to have a company that can grow to a very large size.

As of late 2007 FedEx was introducing another major change in its ground businesses—the introduction of hybrid vehicles in some of its ground delivery trucks. These hybrid vehicles have already been introduced to some extent in the United States, Asia, and Europe. The aim is to cut fuel use in half while significantly lowering engine emissions.

Sources: Ellen Florian, "I Have a Cast-Iron Stomach," *Fortune,* March 8, 2004, pp. 91–97; and "FedEx Ground, Parker Hannifin to Test Hydraulic Hybrid," *Logistics Today,* January 2008, p. 10.

Analyzing Management Skills

Do you believe that most organizations do a good job of preparing their employees for change? What are some specific things that managers can do to better prepare their employees for change?

Applying Management Skills

Pick a specific industry of interest to you. How was this industry affected by the tragic events of September 11, 2001? How has the industry responded to the changes brought about by these events?

In his book *Thriving on Chaos,* Tom Peters stresses the importance of change to the modern corporation: "To up the odds of survival, leaders at all levels must become obsessive about change." He adds, "Change must become the norm, not cause for alarm."[1] Similarly, Jack Welch, the well-known former CEO of GE, has been quoted as saying, "When the rate of change on the outside exceeds the rate of change on the inside, the end is in sight."[2] What does *change* mean from these perspectives? Simply put, it means that unless managers have changed something, they have not earned their paychecks. This bold view is somewhat foreign to many organizations today.

Today, managing change and dealing with its impact on the corporate culture are essential skills that the manager must master if the organization is to compete globally. Furthermore, the manager must learn these skills rapidly, since change is occurring at an ever-increasing rate. The new bottom line for the twenty-first century will be to assess each and every action in light of its contribution to an increased corporate capacity for change.

An organization's affinity for change and its corporate culture are intrinsically intertwined; each affects the other. It is because of this interdependency that both of these topics are discussed in this chapter.

MANAGING CHANGE

Organizations today are beset by change. Many managers find themselves unable to cope with an environment or an organization that has become substantially different from the one in which they received their training and gained their early experience. Other managers have trouble transferring their skills to a new assignment in a different industry. A growing organization, a new assignment, changing customer needs, changing employee expectations, and changing competition may all be encountered by today's managers. To be successful, managers must be able to adapt to these changes.

Change as a Global Issue

One of the driving pressures for change is the desire to compete globally. Since America's global trading partners (notably Japan, China, and Europe) have adopted change as an essential ingredient of their long-term strategies, corporate America must follow suit. When asked about change in the international environment, Eric A. Cronson, vice president and managing director of Thomas Group Europe, commented, "Change has to be radical—if you stay in your comfort zone, you will not be internationally competitive."[3] Similarly, Joseph V. Marulli, president of information services at Eunetcom, commented at an international conference on change, "Transformation has to be in the leader's heart, in your heart, and in the hearts of all the senior people."[4] From comments such as these, the manager must understand that the challenge to compete is really the challenge to change.

Types of Change

technological changes Changes in such things as new equipment and new processes.

environmental changes All nontechnological changes that occur outside the organization.

internal changes Budget adjustments, policy changes, personnel changes, and the like.

Change as it applies to organizations can be classified into three major categories: (1) technological, (2) environmental, and (3) internal to the organization. **Technological changes** include such things as new equipment and new processes. The technological advances since World War II have been dramatic, with computers and increased speed of communication being the most notable. **Environmental changes** are all the nontechnological changes that occur outside the organization. New government regulations, new social trends, and economic changes are all examples of environmental change. An organization's **internal changes** include such things as budget adjustments, policy changes, diversity adjustments, and personnel changes. Figure 16.1 lists several examples of each major type of change affecting today's organizations.

Any of the three types of changes can greatly affect a manager's job. Both technological and environmental changes occur outside an organization and can create the need for internal change. Internal change can also occur because of performance issues (such as conflict, quality, lack of productivity, and so forth) or as a result of regular self-assessment as part of the strategic management process.

Any of the three types of change can create the need for unplanned change or planned change. Since managers can control planned change, they should be periodically analyzing what changes are necessary. Thus, by being proactive rather than reactive, managers can have much more control over the change process.

FIGURE 16.1
Types of Changes Affecting Organizations

Technological	Environmental	Internal
Machines	Laws	Policies
Equipment	Taxes	Procedures
Processes	Social trends	New methods
Automation	Fashion trends	Rules
Computers	Political trends	Reorganization
New raw materials	Economic trends	Budget adjustment
Robots	Interest rates	Restructuring of jobs
Cell phones	Consumer trends	Personnel
Blackberries	Competition	Management
	Suppliers	Ownership
	Population trends	Products/services sold

Management Illustration 16.1

CHANGING EATING HABITS

One of Kurt Lewin's most significant examples of his theory at work occurred as a result of a commission from the U.S. government to develop a program to change the eating habits of American families during World War II. To help the war effort, the government was encouraging families, and especially housewives, to buy more of the visceral organs and less of the more normal muscle cuts of beef. The government attempted to explain the facts and logically tell the housewives why it was necessary to support this program—patriotism, economy, and nutrition. However, the government underestimated the restraining forces; people were simply not used to preparing or eating tongue, heart, and lungs. As a result, the housewives resisted the change until Lewin came in and developed a program to counteract the restraining forces. The cornerstone of the program was a grassroots campaign that organized discussion groups throughout the country where housewives could meet and discuss the issue. Once housewives actually got involved with the nature of the problem, they gradually broadened their thinking and came to understand how their change of diet could help the war effort. The result was that they did change their buying habits.

Source: Stephen Covey, "Work It Out Together," *Incentive*, April 1997, p. 26.

THE CHANGE PROCESS

As first discussed in the late 1940s by social psychologist Kurt Lewin, change is a function of the forces that support or promote the change and those forces that oppose or resist the change (Lewin referred to this approach as *force field analysis*). Change forces introduce something different about the organization over time. Resistance forces support the status quo, or keeping things as they are. The sum total of these forces determines the extent to which a change will be successfully implemented.

Lewin's Three-Step Model for Change

Lewin developed a three-step model for successfully implementing change:

1. Lewin's first step, *unfreezing,* deals with breaking down the forces supporting or maintaining the old behavior. These forces can include such variables as the formal reward system, reinforcement from the work group, and the individual's perception of what is proper role behavior.
2. The second step, *presenting a new alternative,* involves offering a clear and attractive option representing new patterns of behavior.
3. The third step, *refreezing,* requires that the change behavior be reinforced by the formal and informal reward systems and by the work group. It is in this step that the manager can play a pivotal role by positively reinforcing employee efforts to change.

Implicit in Lewin's three-step model is the recognition that the mere introduction of change does not ensure the elimination of the prechange conditions or that the change will be permanent. Unsuccessful attempts to implement lasting change can usually be traced to a failure in one of Lewin's three steps. Management Illustration 16.1 describes one of Lewin's early applications of his theory.

Resistance to Change

Most people profess to be modern and up to date. However, their first reaction is usually to resist change. This is almost always true when the change affects their jobs. Resistance to change is a natural, normal reaction; it is not a reaction observed only in troublemakers. For example, most employees are apprehensive when there is a change in their immediate manager. It is usually not that the employees dislike the new manager but rather that they don't know what he or she will be like. All change requires adjustment; in fact, the adjustment may concern employees more than the actual change.

Resistance to change may be very open, or it may be very subtle. The employee who quits a job because of a change in company policy is showing resistance to change in an open and explicit manner. For example, when Holiday Inn entered the gambling industry in the 1970s, several managers left because they did not condone gambling. Other employees who stay but become sullen are resisting in a more passive manner.

Because organizations are composed of individuals, often there is organizational resistance to change. Organizational resistance to change occurs when the organization, as an entity, appears to resist change. For example, obsolete products or services and inappropriate organization structure are often the result of organizational resistance to change.

Reasons for Resisting Change

Employees resist change for many reasons. Some of the most frequent reasons are as follows.

1. *Fear of the unknown.* It is natural human behavior to fear the unknown. With many changes, the outcome is not foreseeable. When it is, the results are often not made known to all of the affected employees. For example, employees may worry about and resist a new computer if they are not sure what its impact will be on their jobs. Similarly, employees may resist a new manager simply because they don't know what to expect. A related fear is the uncertainty employees may feel about working in a changed environment. They may fully understand the change yet really doubt whether they will be able to handle it. For example, an employee may resist a change in procedure because of a fear of being unable to master it.
2. *Economics.* Employees fear any change they think threatens their jobs or incomes. The threat may be real or only imagined. In either case, the result is resistance. For example, a salesperson who believes a territory change will result in less income will resist the change. Similarly, production workers will oppose new standards they believe will be harder to achieve.
3. *Fear that skills and expertise will lose value.* Everyone likes to feel valued by others, and anything that has the potential to reduce that value will be resisted. For example, an operations manager may resist implementation of a new, more modern piece of equipment for fear the change will make him or her less needed by the organization.
4. *Threats to power.* Many employees, and especially managers, believe a change may diminish their power. For example, a manager may perceive a change to the organization's structure as weakening his or her power within the organization.
5. *Additional work and inconvenience.* Almost all changes involve work, and many result in personal inconveniences to the affected employees. If nothing else, they often have to learn new ways. This may mean more training, school, or practice. A common reaction by employees is that "it isn't worth the extra effort required."
6. *Threats to interpersonal relations.* The social and interpersonal relationships among employees can be

One of the many reasons employees resist change is that they may have to learn new ways of doing things. What are some other reasons why employees resist change?

quite strong. These relationships may appear unimportant to everyone but those involved. For example, eating lunch with a particular group may be very important to the involved employees. When a change, such as a transfer, threatens these relationships, the affected employees often resist. Employees naturally feel more at ease when working with people they know well. Also, the group may have devised methods for doing the work based on the strengths and weaknesses of group members. Any changes in the group would naturally disrupt the routine.

Reducing Resistance to Change

As discussed previously, most employees' first reaction to change is resistance. However, how employees perceive the change's impact greatly affects their reaction to the change. While many variations are possible, four basic situations usually occur:

1. If employees cannot foresee how the change will affect them, they will resist the change or be neutral at best. Most people shy away from the unknown, believing that change may make things worse.
2. If employees perceive that the change does not fit their needs and hopes, they will resist the change. In this instance, employees are convinced the change will make things worse.
3. If employees see that the change is inevitable, they may first resist and then resign themselves to the change. The first reaction is to resist. Once the change appears imminent, employees often see no other choice but to go along with it.
4. If employees view the change as being in their best interests, they will be motivated to make the change work. The key here is for the employees to feel sure the change will make things better. Three out of four of these situations result in some form of resistance to change. Also, the way in which employees resist change can vary greatly. For example, an employee may not actively resist a change but may never actively support it. Similarly, an employee may mildly resist by acting uninterested in the change. At the other extreme, an employee may resist by trying to sabotage the change.

Figure 16.2 summarizes how employees might respond to change.

Before a manager can reduce resistance to a change, she or he must try to determine how the employees will react to the change. The following steps are recommended before issuing a change directive.

1. Determine the response needed from the employee to accomplish the task effectively.
2. Estimate the expected response if the directive is simply published or orally passed to the employee (as many are).
3. If a discrepancy exists between the needed response and the estimated response, determine how the two responses can be reconciled (opposition is never an acceptable response).[5]

The following paragraphs present several suggestions for reducing resistance to change and helping employees to accept and even commit themselves to change.

Build Trust If employees trust and have confidence in management, they are much more likely to accept change. If an air of distrust prevails, change is likely to be strongly resisted. Management's day-to-day and long-term actions determine the degree of trust among employees. Managers can go a long way toward building trust if they discuss upcoming changes with employees and actively involve employees in the change process.

Discuss Upcoming Changes Fear of the unknown is one of the major barriers to change. This fear can be greatly reduced by discussing any upcoming changes with the affected

FIGURE 16.2
Employee Response Model

Source: Waldron Berry, "Overcoming Resistance to Change," *Supervisory Management,* February 1983.

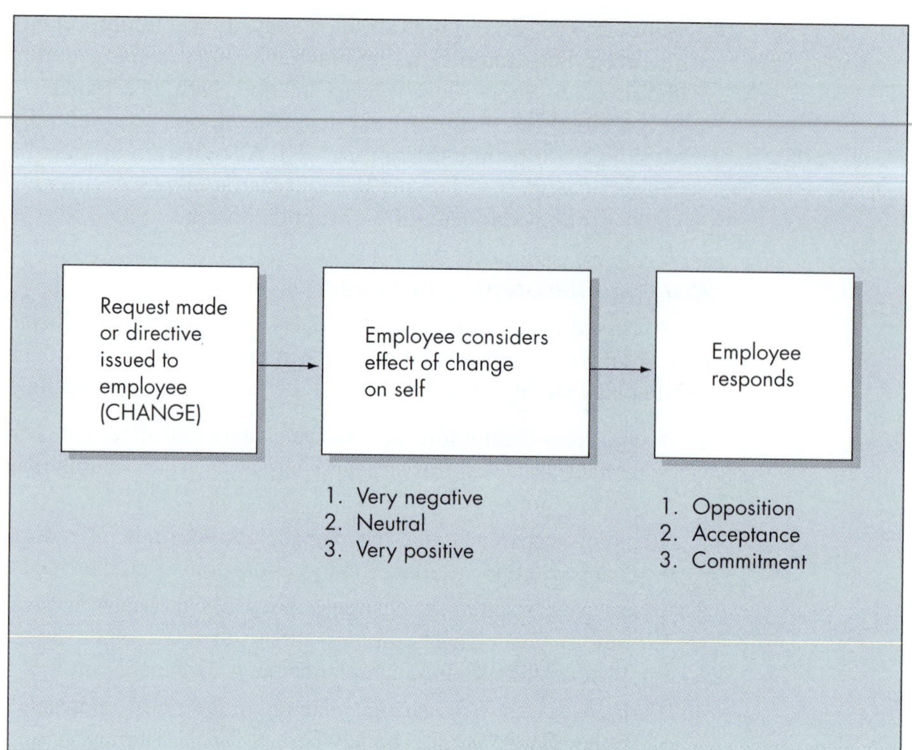

employees. During this discussion, the manager should be as open and honest as possible. The manager should explain not only what the change will be but also why the change is being made. The manager should also outline the impact of the change on each affected employee. Figure 16.3 presents a classical approach to change resistance that can help a manager who is attempting to explain and discuss an upcoming change.

Involve the Employees Involving employees means more than merely discussing the upcoming changes with them. The key is to involve employees personally in the entire change process. It is natural for employees to want to go along with a change they have helped devise and implement. A good approach is to ask for employees' ideas and input as early as possible in the change process.

Make Sure the Changes Are Reasonable The manager should always do everything possible to ensure that any proposed changes are reasonable. Often proposals for changes come from other parts of the organization. These proposals are sometimes not reasonable because the originator is unaware of all the pertinent circumstances.

Avoid Threats The manager who attempts to force change through the use of threats is taking a negative approach. This is likely to decrease rather than increase employee trust. Most people resist threats or coercion. Such tactics also usually have a negative impact on employee morale.

Follow a Sensible Time Schedule A manager can often influence the timing of changes. Some times are doubtless better than others for making certain changes. If nothing else, the manager should always use common sense when proposing a time schedule for implementing a change.

FIGURE 16.3 **Methods of Overcoming Resistance to Change**

Approach	Commonly Used in Situations	Advantages	Drawbacks
Education + communication	Where there is a lack of information or inaccurate information and analysis.	Once persuaded, people will often help with the implementation of the change.	Can be time-consuming if lots of people are involved.
Participation + involvement	Where the initiators do not have all the information they need to design the change, and where others have considerable power to resist.	People who participate will be committed to implementing change, and any relevant information they have will be integrated into the change plan.	Can be time-consuming if participators design an inappropriate change.
Facilitation + support	Where people are resisting because of adjustment problems.	No other approach works as well with adjustment problems.	Can be time-consuming and expensive and still fail.
Negotiation + agreement	Where someone or some group will clearly lose out in a change, and where that group has considerable power to resist.	Sometimes it is a relatively easy way to avoid major resistance.	Can be too expensive in many cases if it alerts others to negotiate for compliance.
Manipulation + co-optation	Where other tactics will not work or are too expensive.	It can be a relatively quick and inexpensive solution to resistance problems.	Can lead to future problems if people feel manipulated.
Explicit + implicit coercion	Where speed is essential and the change initiators possess considerable power.	It is speedy and can overcome any kind of resistance.	Can be risky if it leaves people mad at the initiators.

Source: Reprinted by permission of *Harvard Business Review,* Exhibit from "Choosing Strategies for Change," by John P. Kotter and Leonard A. Schlesinger, March–April 1979.

Most of the above suggestions for reducing resistance to change relate to the manner in which management communicates a change. It is often not the change itself that determines its acceptability but rather the manner in which the change is implemented. The importance of the manager's role in this process was reinforced by the finding of a late 1990s study conducted by Watson Wyatt Worldwide. The study of more than 9,000 working Americans concluded that the three biggest barriers to managing change are (1) lack of management visibility and support, (2) inadequate management skills, and (3) employee resistance to change.[6] It is interesting to note that two relate directly to management and only one relates directly to employees. Management Illustration 16.2 describes how one company reduced its employees' resistance to the implementation of a new computer system.

Leading Change

Today's competitive world requires that managers at all levels be constantly looking for improvements via change. This fact, coupled with the realization that most people's natural reaction is to resist change, means that successful change implementation requires that managers make a conscious effort to lead change efforts. John Kotter has developed the eight-step method for leading change shown in Figure 16.4.[7] Each of these steps is discussed in the following paragraphs.

Establish a Sense of Urgency Because so many large and small companies have a tendency to become complacent, managers must constantly be on the lookout for needed change. Success and the comfort of doing everything the same way are two frequently encountered reasons that organizations become complacent. Successful managers are constantly looking for the need to change, and once a need is identified, they establish an urgency for making it happen.

Management Illustration 16.2

REDUCING RESISTANCE TO CHANGE AT AMERICAN LEATHER

Two critical departments within today's manufacturing organizations, the plant floor and the information technology (IT) department, are often worlds apart. The major mitigating factors are language barriers, misaligned goals and resistance to change. Companies that have successfully overcome these problems have done so through cross-training, team building, definition of common goals, and improved communication.

A few years ago, American Leather Company experienced a major change when it implemented a new Oracle computer system to operate its financial affairs. Approximately one year later, the company expanded the project to include a new Oracle system for the plant floor, replacing an old automation system. Team building helped to smooth the transition during the implementation of the new system on the plant floor. American Leather made sure that meetings included not only IT personnel but also the vice president of operations, consultants, and plant employees. The attitude taken by American Leather was that the IT personnel were not there to tell the plant employees what they needed or how to do their job but rather IT was presented as an enabler. "IT isn't here to tell you how you need to run your business. IT is here to enable what your requirements are," stated Bruce Weinberg, CFO and COO of American Leather.

Source: Jonathan Katz, "Bridging the Great Divide," *Industry Week,* August 2007, p. 32.

Create a Guiding Coalition Most successful change efforts require the participation and support of several managers and employees from many different levels in the organization. A group or coalition of managers and employees must be formed to lead the change. Most major changes are initiated by top management, but to be successful they must eventually involve middle managers, supervisors, and employees.

FIGURE 16.4
Model for Leading Change

Source: Reprinted by permission of Harvard Business School Press. From *Leading Change,* by J. Kotter. Boston, MA 1996. Copyright © 1996 by the Harvard Business School Publishing Corporation; all rights reserved.

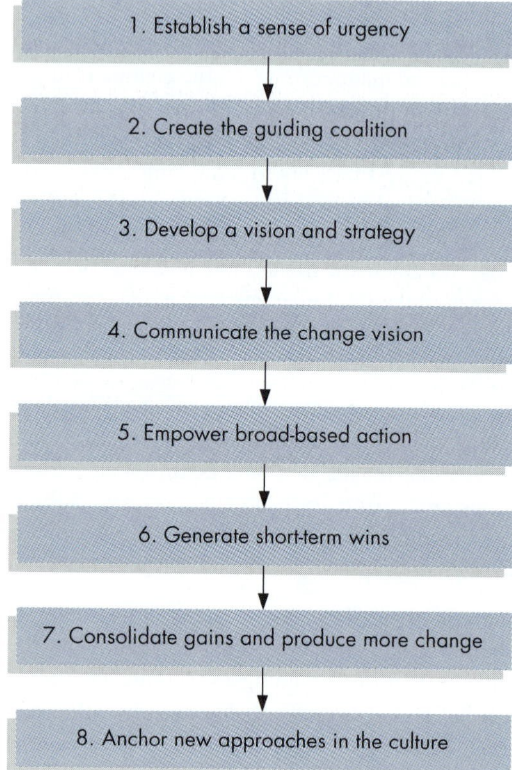
1. Establish a sense of urgency
2. Create the guiding coalition
3. Develop a vision and strategy
4. Communicate the change vision
5. Empower broad-based action
6. Generate short-term wins
7. Consolidate gains and produce more change
8. Anchor new approaches in the culture

Develop a Vision and Strategy As discussed earlier in this chapter, most people are much more accepting of change when they can visualize its ultimate impact. Therefore, it is important that change leaders develop a clear image of what the results of the change will be and what the transition process will involve.

Communicate the Change Vision Change leaders should use every available means to communicate the change vision to organizational members and affected parties. All too often managers assume that employees have the same vision about a change that they do. The best approach is to use multiple channels and opportunities to communicate the change vision.

Empower Broad-Based Action The idea here is to actively involve managers and employees at all levels in the change process. Eliminate obstacles to the change process and empower employees to take the actions necessary to implement the change.

Generate Short-Term Wins Once the successes associated with a change are seen, even those who initially resisted will usually get on board. The key here is to not wait for the ultimate realization of the vision but rather to recognize and celebrate numerous small successes along the way. Take the opportunity to publicly recognize successes and the people responsible. Everyone likes to be a member of a winning team.

Consolidate Gains and Produce More Change Don't rest on your laurels along the way. Maintain the ultimate vision, and don't get sidetracked or satisfied with the small successes. As you approach the original ultimate vision, look for new projects and changes.

Anchor New Approaches in the Culture Take actions to ensure that the organization and its members don't slowly revert back to the old ways. Emphasize the positive results of the changes, and continually give credit to those who participated in the change process.

ORGANIZATIONAL DEVELOPMENT

The previous sections emphasized the change process from the viewpoint of individual managers. This section looks at the change process from the viewpoint of the entire organization.

organizational development (OD)
Organizationwide, planned effort, managed from the top, to increase organizational performance through planned interventions.

Organizational development (OD) is an organizationwide, planned effort managed from the top, with a goal of increasing organizational performance through planned interventions in the organization. In particular, OD looks at the human side of organizations. It seeks to change attitudes, values, and management practices in an effort to improve organizational performance. The ultimate goal of OD is to structure the organizational environment so that managers and employees can use their skills and abilities to the fullest.

An OD effort starts with a recognition by management that organizational performance can and should be improved. Following this, most OD efforts include the following phases:

1. Diagnosis
2. Change planning
3. Intervention/education
4. Evaluation

Diagnosis

The first decision to be made in the OD process is whether the organization has the talent and available time necessary to conduct the diagnosis. If not, an alternative is to hire an outside consultant. Once the decision has been made regarding who will do the diagnosis, the next step is to gather and analyze information. Some of the most frequently used methods for doing this are the following.

1. *Review available records.* The first step is to review any available records or documents that may be pertinent. Personnel records and financial reports are two types of generally available records that can be useful.
2. *Survey questionnaires.* The most popular method of gathering data is through questionnaires filled out by employees. Usually the questionnaires are intended to measure employee attitudes and perceptions about certain work-related factors.
3. *Personal interviews.* In this approach, employees are individually interviewed regarding their opinions and perceptions and certain work-related factors. This method takes more time than the survey questionnaire method but can result in better information.
4. *Direct observation.* In this method, the person conducting the diagnosis observes firsthand the behavior of organizational members at work. One advantage of this method is that it allows observation of what people actually do as opposed to what they say they do.

In the diagnosis stage, one should collect data for a reason. A plan for analyzing the data should be developed even before the data are collected. Too often data are collected simply because they are available and with no plan for analysis.

Change Planning

The data collected in the diagnosis stage must be carefully interpreted to determine the best plan for organizational improvement. If a similar diagnosis has been done in the past, it can be revealing to compare the data and look for any obvious differences. Because much of the collected data are based on personal opinions and perceptions, there will always be areas of disagreement. The key to interpreting the data is to look for trends and areas of general agreement. The end result of the change-planning process is to identify specific problem areas and outline steps for resolving the problems.

Intervention/Education

The purpose of the intervention/education phase is to share the information obtained in the diagnostic phase with the affected employees and help them realize the need for change. A thorough analysis in the change-planning phase often results in the identification of the most appropriate intervention/education method to use. Some of the most frequently used intervention/education methods are discussed next.

direct feedback
Process in which the change agent communicates the information gathered through diagnosis directly to the affected people.

team building
Process by which a work group develops awareness of conditions that keep it from functioning effectively and takes action to eliminate these conditions.

sensitivity training
Method used in OD to make one more aware of oneself and one's impact on others.

Direct Feedback With the **direct feedback** method, the change agent communicates the information gathered in the diagnostic and change-planning phases to the involved parties. The change agent describes what was found and what changes are recommended. Then workshops are often conducted to initiate the desired changes.

Team Building The objective of **team building** is to increase the group's cohesiveness and general group spirit. Team building stresses the importance of working together. Some of the specific activities used include (1) clarifying employee roles, (2) reducing conflict, (3) improving interpersonal relations, and (4) improving problem-solving skills.[8] Team building was discussed in depth in Chapter 12.

Sensitivity Training **Sensitivity training** is designed to make one more aware of oneself and one's impact on others. Sensitivity training involves a group, usually called a *training group* or *T-group,* that meets and has no agenda or particular focus. Normally the group has between 10 and 15 people who may or may not know one another. With no planned structure or no prior common experiences, the behavior of individuals in trying to deal with the lack of structure becomes the agenda. While engaging in group dialogue, members are encouraged to learn about themselves and others in the nonstructured environment.

Sensitivity training has been both passionately criticized and vigorously defended as to its relative value for organizations. In general, the research shows that people who have undergone sensitivity training tend to show increased sensitivity, more open communication, and increased flexibility.[9] However, these same studies indicate that while the outcomes of sensitivity training are beneficial in general, it is difficult to predict the outcomes for any one person.

Evaluation

Probably the most difficult phase in the OD process is the evaluation phase.[10] The basic question to be answered is: Did the OD process produce the desired results? Unfortunately, many OD efforts begin with admirable but overly vague objectives such as improving the overall health, culture, or climate of the organization. Before any OD effort can be evaluated, explicit objectives must be determined. Objectives of an OD effort should be outcome oriented and should lend themselves to the development of measurable criteria.

A second requirement for evaluating OD efforts is that the evaluation effort be methodologically sound. Ideally, an OD effort should be evaluated using hard, objective data. One approach is to compare data collected before the OD intervention against data collected after the OD intervention. An even better approach is to compare "before" and "after" data with similar data from a control group. When using this approach, two similar groups are identified, an experimental group and a control group. The OD effort is then implemented with the experimental group but not with the control group. After the OD intervention has been completed, the before and after data from the experimental group are compared with the before and after data from the control group. This approach helps to rule out changes that may have resulted from factors other than the OD intervention. Figure 16.5 summarizes the OD process.

FIGURE 16.5 Model for the Management of Organizational Development

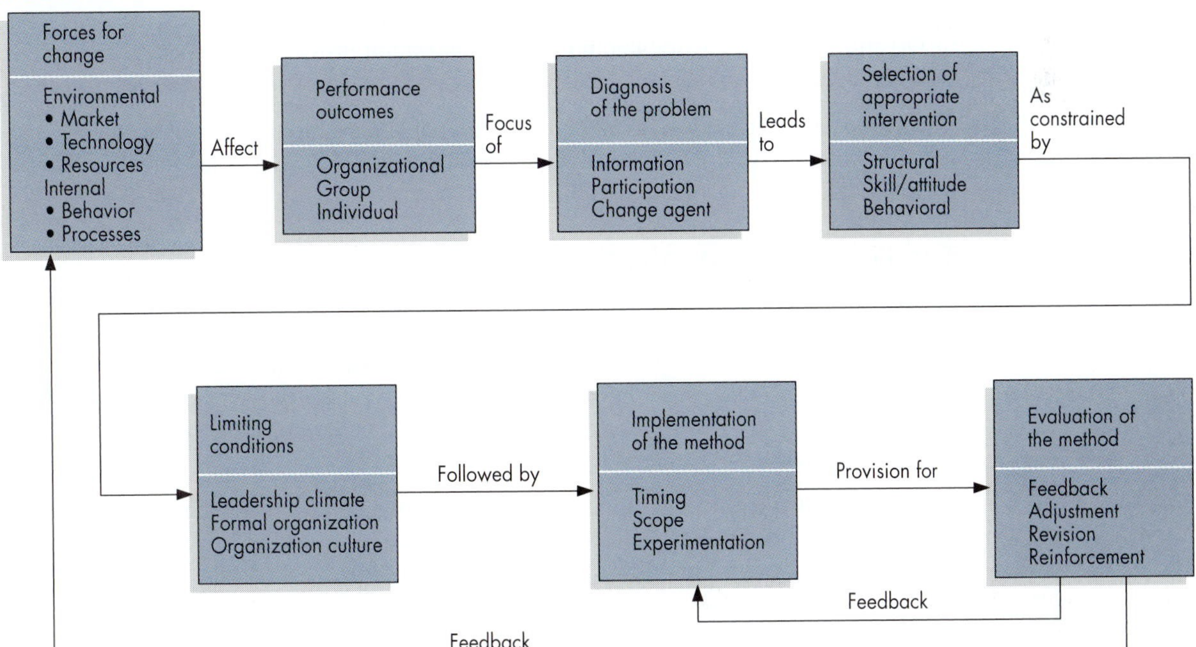

Source: James L. Gibson, John M. Ivancevich, and James H. Donnelly, Jr., *Organizations* (Burr Ridge, IL: Richard D. Irwin, 1994), p. 668.

Managing Innovation

The concept of innovation was briefly introduced in Chapter 4 as part of the discussion on creativity. As defined in Chapter 4, innovation refers to doing new things that inherently involve change. Many management experts today believe that innovation is an organization's best sustainable source of growth, competitive advantage, and new wealth.[11]

Because what worked in the past may not work today, many organizations are having to create new ways to foster innovation. Robert Tucker, author of the international best-seller *Managing the Future,* believes that organizations that successfully innovate in the future must embrace four essential principles. These four principles are discussed below.

1. An organization's approach to innovation must be comprehensive. Innovation cannot be confined to a few departments or to a small group of "innovations." Innovation must permeate the entire organization, and it must encompass all aspects of organization.
2. Innovation must include systematic, organized, and continual search for new opportunities. Traditionally, top management was the only organizational entity concerned with questions such as, What do these developments mean to our company? How could we take advantage of these developments? What threats are on the horizon that we must respond to now if we are going to capitalize on this development? The rapid pace of change today dictates much broader participation than just top management in these decisions.
3. Organizations must involve everyone in the innovation process. Up until very recent times, many employees were not asked or expected to innovate in their jobs. In some instances, employees were encouraged *not* to innovate. The dormant creativity of employees across the organization must be tapped.
4. An organization must work constantly on improving its climate for innovation. As used here, climate refers to the "feeling in the air" you get when you work for or visit an organization. Does the feeling in the air foster innovation and encourage employees to take risks? What happens when someone fails? Innovative climates expect a certain degree of failure, learn from failures, and share the learning throughout the organization. As the old saying goes, If you haven't failed, you haven't taken sufficient risks. Organization with favorable climates for innovation provide the context for people to collaborate in groups, teams, divisions, and departments without boundaries of fear.

As the rate of change increases for today's organizations, the ability to innovate becomes more and more critical. By subscribing to the above principles, managers at all levels can positively affect an organization's ability to innovate and remain competitive.

The Learning Organization

If organizations are to encourage change and innovation, they must establish environments that support these actions. Learning organizations establish such an environment. A learning organization has been defined as an organization skilled at creating, acquiring, and transferring knowledge, and in modifying behavior to reflect the new knowledge.[12] Peter Senge, whose book *The Fifth Discipline* popularized the learning organization, has identified five principles for creating a learning organization:[13]

1. *Systems thinking.* Managers must learn to see the big picture and not concentrate only on their part; they must learn to recognize the effects of one level of learning on another.
2. *Personal mastery.* Individual managers and employees must be empowered to experiment, innovate, and explore.
3. *Mental models.* Managers and employees should be encouraged to develop mental models as ways of stretching their minds to find new and better ways of doing things.

Management Illustration 16.3

TOP-RATED LEARNING ORGANIZATIONS—WORLDWIDE

The list below encompasses the top 20 companies that the American Society of Training and Development (ASTD) identified as the most outstanding learning organizations for 2007. According to ASTD, these organizations create, support, and champion learning opportunities for results and a deep learning culture within their respective organizations. It is interesting to note the different countries represented in the list.

Rank	Organization	Corporate Headquarters	Number of Employees	Industry
1.	Satyam Computer Services	Hyderabad, India	42,000	Information technology
2.	Sanofi-Aventis U.S.	Bridgewater, New Jersey	16,000	Pharmaceuticals
3.	TELUS Communications	Vancouver, British Columbia, Canada	28,900	Telecommunications
4.	BD (Becton, Dickinson & Co)	Franklin Lakes, New Jersey	27,000	Health care
5.	Deloitte & Touche USA LLP	New York, New York	40,000	Professional services
6.	U.S. Army Armament Research Development and Engineering Center	Picatinny Arsenal, New Jersey	2,940	Research and engineering services
7.	Equity Residential	Chicago, Illinois	5,200	Real estate property management
8.	Wachovia	Charlotte, North Carolina	108,000	Financial services
9.	The Home Depot	Atlanta, Georgia	364,000	Retail
10.	Air Products and Chemicals	Allentown, Pennsylvania	18,112	Manufacturing
11.	Wipro Technologies	Bangalore, India	48,891	Information technology
12.	EMC Corporation	Hopkinton, Massachusetts	30,500	Information management & storage
13.	Checkfree Services Inc.	Norcross, Georgia	3,600	Financial e-commerce services
14.	Telkom SA Limited	Pretoria, South Africa	27,273	Telecommunications
15.	BB&T	Winston-Salem, North Carolina	28,900	Financial services
16.	UT-Battelle, LLC–Oak Ridge National Laboratory	Oak Ridge, Tennessee	4,100	Research & development
17.	Ruby Tuesday Inc.	Maryville, Tennessee	53,080	Food services
18.	Tata Consultancy Services Limited	Mumbai, India	93,000	Information technology
19.	BJC Healthcare	St. Louis, Missouri	26,622	Health care
20.	Caterpillar	Peoria, Illinois	94,593	Manufacturing

Source: "Better Than the Rest," *T & D,* October 2007, pp. 27–29.

4. *Shared vision.* Managers should develop and communicate a shared vision that can be used as a framework for addressing problems and opportunities.
5. *Team learning.* Team learning is the process of aligning a team so as to avoid wasted energy and to get the desired results.

Honda, Corning, and General Electric are examples of companies that have become good learning organizations.[14] In these organizations, learning, in whatever form, becomes an inescapable way of life for both managers and employees alike. These and other learning organizations are gaining the commitment of their employees at all levels by continually expanding their capacity to learn and change. Management Illustration 16.3 lists the

20 top learning organizations for 2007 as identified by the American Society of Training and Development.

MANAGING CORPORATE CULTURE

culture
Set of important understandings (often unstated) that members of a community share.

corporate culture
Communicates how people in an organization should behave by establishing a value system conveyed through rites, rituals, myths, legends, and actions.

The word *culture* is derived in a roundabout way from the Latin verb *colere,* which means "to cultivate."[15] In later times, *culture* came to indicate a process of refinement and breeding in domesticating a particular crop. The modern-day meaning draws on this agricultural derivation: It relates to society's control, refinement, and domestication of itself. A contemporary definition of **culture** is "the set of important understandings (often unstated) that members of a community share in common."[16]

Culture in an organization compares to personality in a person. Humans have fairly enduring and stable traits that help them protect their attitudes and behaviors. So do organizations. In addition, certain groups of traits or personality types are known to consist of common elements. Organizations can be described in similar terms. They can be warm, aggressive, friendly, open, innovative, conservative, and so forth. An organization's culture is transmitted in many ways, including long-standing and often unwritten rules; shared standards regarding what is important; prejudices; standards for social etiquette and demeanor; established customs for relating to peers, subordinates, and superiors; and other traditions that clarify to employees what is and is not appropriate behavior. Thus, corporate culture communicates how people in the organization should behave by establishing a value system conveyed through rites, rituals, myths, legends, and actions. Simply stated, **corporate culture** means "the way we do things around here."[17]

Cultural Forms of Expression

Culture has two basic components: (1) substance, the meanings contained in its values, norms, and beliefs; and (2) forms, the practices whereby these meanings are expressed, affirmed, and communicated to members.[18]

Executives at Walt Disney Company reportedly pick up litter on the grounds without thinking because of the Disney vision of an immaculate Disneyland.

How Does Culture Originate?

There is no question that different organizations develop different cultures. What causes an organization to develop a particular type of culture? Many organizations trace their culture to one person who provided a living example of the major values of the organization. Robert Wood Johnson of Johnson & Johnson, Harley Procter of Procter & Gamble, Walt Disney of Walt Disney Company, Thomas J. Watson, Sr., of IBM, and Phil Knight of Nike all left their imprints on the organizations they headed. Research indicates, however, that fewer than half of a new company's values reflect the values of the founder or chief executive. The rest appear to develop in response both to the environment in which the business operates and to the needs of the employees.[19] Four distinct factors contribute to an organization's culture: its history, its environment, its selection process, and its socialization processes.[20]

History

Employees are aware of the organization's past, and this awareness builds culture. Much of the "way things are done" is a continuation of how things have always been done. The existing values that a strong leader may have established originally are constantly and subtly reinforced by experiences. The status quo is also protected by the human tendency to fervently embrace beliefs and values and to resist changes. Executives at Walt Disney Company reportedly pick up litter on the grounds without thinking because of the Disney vision of an immaculate Disneyland.

Environment

Because all organizations must interact with their environments, the environment plays a role in shaping their cultures. Deregulation of the telecommunications industry in the 1980s dramatically altered its environment. Before deregulation, the environment was relatively risk averse and noncompetitive. Increases in costs were automatically passed on to customers. As a result of deregulation, the environment changed overnight to become highly competitive and much more dynamic. No longer sheltered by a regulated environment, the cultures of the telecommunications companies were forced to change. Recently there has been significant reconsolidation in the telecommunications industry. It will be interesting to see if these changes also result in culture changes.

Staffing

Organizations tend to hire, retain, and promote people who are similar to current employees in important ways. A person's ability to fit in can be important in these processes. This "fit" criterion ensures that current values are accepted and that potential challengers of "how we do things" are screened out. Adjustment has to be carefully managed. For example, when Bill George took over Medtronic, a leading producer of pacemakers in 1991, he quickly found out that to survive in the rapidly growing high-tech health care business, he needed a change—but not at the expense of what had historically worked for the company. He opted for a merger with another company. The merger brought in "new blood" that was free-spirited and experimental in nature and teamed them with a highly disciplined, methodical existing culture. Though it was hard work, empowerment of people and a merger of cultures helped the company halve its development time and remain competitive in the industry.[21]

Entry Socialization

While an organization's values, norms, and beliefs may be widely and uniformly held, they are seldom written down. The new employee, who is least familiar with the culture, is most likely to challenge it. It is therefore important to help the newcomer adopt the organization's culture. Companies with strong cultures attach great importance to the process of introducing and indoctrinating new employees. This process is called **entry socialization.** Entry socialization not only reduces threats to the organization from newcomers but also lets new employees know what is expected of them. It may be handled in a formal or informal manner, as well as on an individual or group basis.

entry socialization
Adaptation process by which new employees are introduced and indoctrinated into the organization.

Strong and Weak Corporate Cultures

A strong corporate culture is clearly defined, reinforces a common understanding about what is important, and has the support of management and employees. Such a culture contributes greatly to an organization's success by creating an understanding about how employees should behave. Figure 16.6 identifies the characteristics of a strong corporate culture.

Weak cultures have the opposite characteristics. In a weak corporate culture, individuals often act in ways that are inconsistent with the company's way of doing things. Figure 16.7

FIGURE 16.6
Characteristics of a Strong Corporate Culture

Source: Terrence E. Deal and Allan A. Kennedy, *Corporate Cultures: The Rites and Rituals of Corporate Life* (Reading, MA: Addison-Wesley, 1982).

- Organizational members share clear values and beliefs about how to succeed in their business.
- Organizational members agree on which beliefs about how to succeed are most important.
- Different parts of the organization have similar beliefs about how to succeed.
- The rituals of day-to-day organizational life are well organized and consistent with company goals.

summarizes some characteristics of a weak culture. Management Illustration 16.4 describes the strong culture developed by Southwest Airlines.

Identifying Culture

Researchers have identified seven characteristics that, taken together, capture the essence of an organization's culture:[22]

1. *Individual autonomy.* The degree of responsibility, independence, and opportunities for exercising initiative that individuals in the organization have.
2. *Structure.* The number of rules and regulations and the amount of direct supervision that is used to oversee and control employee behavior.
3. *Support.* The degree of assistance and warmth provided by managers to their subordinates.
4. *Identification.* The degree to which members identify with the organization as a whole rather than with their particular work group or field of professional expertise.
5. *Performance-reward.* The degree to which reward allocations (i.e., salary increases, promotions) in the organization are based on performance criteria.
6. *Conflict tolerance.* The degree of conflict present in relationships between peers and work groups, as well as the willingness to be honest and open about differences.
7. *Risk tolerance.* The degree to which employees are encouraged to be aggressive, innovative, and risk seeking.

Each of these traits should be viewed as existing on a continuum ranging from low to high. A picture of the overall culture can be formed by evaluating the organization on each of these characteristics. The learning organization, discussed earlier in this chapter, is in essence a type of organization culture.

There are as many distinct cultures as there are organizations. Most can be grouped into one of four basic types, determined by two factors: (1) the degree of risk associated with the organization's activities and (2) the speed with which the organization and its employees get feedback indicating the success of decisions. Figure 16.8 shows in matrix form the four generic types of culture.[23]

FIGURE 16.7
Characteristics of a Weak Corporate Culture

Source: Terrence E. Deal and Allan A. Kennedy, *Corporate Cultures: The Rites and Rituals of Corporate Life* (Reading, MA: Addison-Wesley, 1982).

- Organizational members have no clear values or beliefs about how to succeed in their business.
- Organizational members have many beliefs as to how to succeed but cannot agree on which are most important.
- Different parts of the organization have fundamentally different beliefs about how to succeed.
- Those who personify the culture are destructive or disruptive and don't build on any common understanding about what is important.
- The rituals of day-to-day organizational life are disorganized or working at cross-purposes.

Management Illustration 16.4

UNUSUAL CULTURE AT SOUTHWEST AIRLINES

When Dallas-based Southwest Airlines started in 1971 it was obvious from the start that the organizational culture would be different. Originally flight attendants wore hot pants and were selected for their good looks and sense of humor. Today, the hot pants are gone but employees often dress casually in shorts, polo shirts, and sneakers and they are still encouraged to tell jokes and have fun on the job. Herb Kelleher, chairman and cofounder, has been called the "High Priest of Ha Ha" by *Fortune* magazine for making fun as much a part of the company's successful business strategy as its low fares.

The company even has a committee on company culture and sends cards to all of its 32,847 employees on their birthdays, the anniversary of their employment, and Thanksgiving and Christmas. The company also periodically sponsors Halloween costume contests, poem contests, and chili cookoffs. As summarized by Alan Bender, an airline economist, "The philosophy of the company has always been that it is the job of the employee to serve the customer and the principal job of management to serve their employees."

"Hire for attitude and train for skill" is Southwest's philosophy according to Colleen Barrett, president of Southwest.

Sources: Jim Mckay, "Southwest's Culture Includes Cards, Contests," *Knight Ridder Tribune Business News,* January 6, 2005, p. 1; and Elizabeth Bryant, "Leadership Southwest Style," T&D, December 2007, pp. 36–39.

FIGURE 16.8
Generic Types of Organization Culture

		Degree of Risk	
		High	Low
Speed of Feedback	Rapid	Tough-person, macho culture	Work-hard/play-hard culture
	Slow	Bet-your-company culture	Process culture

Tough-Person, Macho Culture

tough-person, macho culture
Characterized by individuals who take high risks and get quick feedback on whether their decisions are right or wrong.

The **tough-person, macho culture** is characterized by individualists who regularly take high risks and get quick feedback on whether their decisions are right or wrong. Teamwork is not important, and every colleague is a potential rival. In this culture, the value of cooperation is ignored; there is no chance to learn from mistakes. People who do best in this culture are those who need to gamble and who can tolerate all-or-nothing risks because they need instant feedback. Companies that develop large-scale advertising programs for major clients would be characterized by the tough-person, macho culture; these advertising programs are usually high-budget with rapid acceptance or failure.

Work-Hard/Play-Hard Culture

work-hard/play-hard culture
Encourages employees to take few risks and to expect rapid feedback.

The **work-hard/play-hard culture** encourages employees to take few risks and to expect rapid feedback. In this culture, activity is the key to success. Rewards accrue to persistence and the ability to find a need and fill it. Because of the need for volume, team players who are friendly and outgoing thrive. Companies that are sales based such as real estate companies often have a work-hard/play-hard culture.

Bet-Your-Company Culture

bet-your-company culture
Requires big-stakes decisions; considerable time passes before the results are known.

The **bet-your-company culture** requires big-stakes decisions, with considerable time passing before the results are known. Pressures to make the right decisions are always present in this environment. Companies involved in durable goods manufacturing are often characterized by a bet-your-company culture.

Process Culture

process culture
Involves low risk with little feedback; employees focus on how things are done rather than on the outcomes.

The **process culture** involves low risk coupled with little feedback; employees must focus on how things are done rather than on the outcomes. Employees in this atmosphere become cautious and protective. Those who thrive are orderly, punctual, and detail oriented. Companies in regulated or protected industries often operate in this type of culture.

Organizational Subcultures

In addition to its overall culture, organizations often have multiple subcultures. It is not uncommon for the values, beliefs, and practices to vary from one part of the organization to another. For example, newly acquired components of a company often have cultural differences that must be worked out over time. Global companies also tend to be faced with multiple cultures. Such factors as language, social norms, values, attitudes, customs, and religion naturally vary throughout the world.

The presence of different subcultures within an organization does not preclude the development of areas of commonality and compatibility.[24] For example, a company's emphasis on quality can be embedded in the local culture at sites throughout the world. At the same time, however, successful companies have learned to look at the compatibility of cultures when considering acquisitions and mergers and new locations. Extreme cultural differences can make it very difficult for an acquisition or an expansion to be successful.

Changing Culture

Executives who have successfully changed organization cultures estimate that the process usually takes from 6 to 15 years.[25] Because organization culture is difficult and time consuming to change, any attempts should be well thought-out.

Allan Kennedy, an expert on organization culture, believes only five reasons justify a large-scale cultural change:[26]

1. The organization has strong values that do not fit into a changing environment.
2. The industry is very competitive and moves with lightning speed.
3. The organization is mediocre or worse.
4. The organization is about to join the ranks of the very large companies.
5. The organization is small but growing rapidly.

Some organizations attempt to change their cultures only when they are forced to do so by changes in their environments or economic situations; others anticipate a necessary change. While massive cultural reorientation may be reasonable in most situations, it is usually possible to strengthen or fine-tune the current situation. A statement of corporate mission consistently reinforced by systems, structures, and policies is a useful tool for strengthening the culture.

Because of the cost, time, and difficulty involved in changing culture, many people believe it is easier to change, or physically replace, the people. This view assumes most organizations promote people who fit the prevailing norms of the organization. Therefore, the easiest if not the only way to change an organization's culture is to change its people.

Summary

1. *Identify the three major categories of organizational change.* The three major categories of organizational change are technological changes, environmental changes, and changes internal to the organization.
2. *List the three steps in Lewin's model for change.* Lewin's model for change involves three steps: unfreezing, presenting a new alternative, and refreezing.

3. *Discuss several reasons employees resist change.* Employees resist change for many reasons. Six of the most frequently encountered reasons are (1) fear of the unknown, (2) economics, (3) fear that expertise and skills will lose value, (4) threats to power, (5) inconvenience, and (6) threats to interpersonal relations.
4. *Identify several prescriptions for reducing resistance to change.* Just as there are many reasons employees resist change, there are many approaches for reducing resistance to change. Several suggestions for reducing resistance to change include (1) building trust between management and employees; (2) discussing upcoming changes with affected employees; (3) involving employees in the change process as early as possible; (4) ensuring that the proposed changes are reasonable; (5) avoiding threats; and (6) following a sensible time schedule for implementing the change.
5. *Describe an approach that managers can use to lead change.* John Knotter has developed an eight-step method for leading change in organizations: (1) establish a sense of urgency, (2) create a guiding coalition, (3) develop a vision and strategy, (4) communicate the change vision, (5) empower broad-based action, (6) generate short-term wins, (7) consolidate gains and produce more change, and (8) anchor new approaches in the culture.
6. *Summarize the four phases of an organizational development (OD) program.* Most OD efforts include a diagnosis phase, a change-planning phase, an intervention/education phase, and an evaluation phase. Diagnosis involves gathering and analyzing information to determine the areas of the organization in need of improvement. Change planning involves developing a plan for organization improvement. Intervention/education involves the sharing of diagnostic information with the people affected by it and helping them to realize the need for change. The evaluation phase attempts to determine the effects the OD effort has had on the organization.
7. *Briefly describe four essential principles that organizations must follow to manage innovation.* Essential principles for successfully innovating are (1) have a comprehensive approach; (2) include a systematic, organized, and continued search for new opportunities; (3) involve everyone in the innovation process, and (4) work constantly on improving the organization's climate for innovation.
8. *Explain what a learning organization is.* A learning organization is skilled at creating, acquiring, and transferring knowledge, and in modifying behavior to reflect the new knowledge. Learning organizations gain the commitment of their employees at all levels by continually expanding their capacity to learn and change.
9. *Define corporate culture.* Corporate culture communicates how people in the organization should behave by establishing a value system conveyed through rites, rituals, myths, legends, and actions. Simply stated, corporate culture means "the way we do things around here."
10. *Describe the generic types of organizational culture.* The tough-person, macho culture is characterized by individualists who regularly take high risks and get quick feedback on whether they are right or wrong. The work-hard/play-hard culture encourages employees to take few risks and to expect rapid feedback. The bet-your-company culture requires big-stakes decisions with considerable time lags before the results are known. The process culture involves low risk coupled with little feedback; employees must focus on how things are done rather than on the outcomes.
11. *Identify two common sources of organizational subcultures.* Two common sources of organizational subcultures are (1) acquisitions/mergers and (2) global or international operations.

Review Questions

1. Name the three major categories of change that apply to organizations.
2. Describe Lewin's model for change.
3. Name six common barriers (reasons for resistance) to change.
4. Describe the four basic reactions of employees to change.
5. Discuss six approaches to reducing resistance to change.
6. List Kotter's eight steps for leading change.
7. What is organizational development?
8. What principles can organizations follow to successfully innovate?
9. What is a learning organization?
10. What organizational characteristics determine corporate culture?
11. How is corporate culture originated and maintained?
12. Name and briefly define the four generic types of corporate culture.
13. What is an organizational subculture?

Skill-Building Questions

1. Take a position on the following statement and be prepared to defend it: Most people resist change, not because the change is harmful but because they are lazy.
2. Check recent literature (*BusinessWeek, The Wall Street Journal,* and other library sources), and identify two or three industries that are currently experiencing major changes. How is each industry responding to the changes? Are these industries likely to be stronger or weaker as a result of these changes?
3. Pick an organization or industry you think will need to change its culture if it is to thrive in the future (as the telecommunication companies had to do in the 1980s and the airlines have had to do since September 11, 2001). Be prepared to explain why you think this change must occur.
4. Pick a company that you think has been particularly innovative. Why do you think they have been successful at promoting innovation?

SKILL-BUILDING EXERCISE 16.1
Change in the Airline Industry

Many organizations have had to change the way they do business since the tragic events of September 11, 2001. The airline industry has certainly been one of the most affected industries. Your instructor will divide the class into groups of four to six students per group. Once the groups have been formed, each group should respond to the following:

1. Identify what major changes have been implemented by or in the airline industry since September 11, 2001.
2. Does your group feel that these changes are positive or negative for the flying public? For airline employees?
3. Why does the group feel that these changes were not implemented before the tragic events took place?

After each group has answered the above questions, your instructor will ask each group to share their answers with the class.

SKILL-BUILDING EXERCISE 16.2
Real Changes

1. Plastic is a post–World War II invention. Suppose everything made of plastic or a derivative of plastic was removed from your life. Make a list of what things in your life would go away.
2. The first personal computer came on the market in 1976. Suppose all computers were instantly removed from your life today. Make a list of things that would be affected in your day-to-day life by this removal.

SKILL-BUILDING EXERCISE 16.3
Resisting Change

One of the problems you face in your firm involves mistakes being made by employees who perform a particular operation. The same mistakes seem to occur in more than one department. You believe a training program for the people concerned will help reduce errors.

You are aware, however, that your supervisors may defend existing procedures simply because the introduction of training may imply criticism of the way they have been operating. You realize, too, that the supervisors may fear resistance by employees afraid of not doing well in the training program. All in all, you plan to approach the subject carefully.

1. Add a recommendation to the agenda of your weekly staff meeting that training be undertaken to help reduce errors.
2. Talk to all your supervisors individually and get their attitudes and ideas about what to do before bringing the subject up in the weekly staff meeting.
3. Ask the corporate training staff to come in, determine the training needs, and develop a program to meet those needs.
4. Since this training is in the best interests of the company, tell your supervisors they will be expected to implement and support it.
5. Appoint a team to study the matter thoroughly, develop recommendations, then bring it before the full staff meeting.

Other alternatives may be open to you, but assume these are the only ones you have considered. *Without discussion* with anyone, choose one of them and be prepared to defend your choice.

SKILL-BUILDING EXERCISE 16.4
The Performance of Learning Organizations

Pick one of the 20 companies listed in Management Illustration 16.3. Once you have made your choice, research the company and find out how it has performed over the last several years. Has it outperformed the averages for its industry? Do you think the company's performance has been influenced by any of the characteristics of learning organizations listed on pages 348–349. Why or why not?

Case Incident 16.1
The Way We Do Things

Fitzgerald Company manufactures a variety of consumer products for sale through retail department stores. For over 30 years, the company has held a strong belief that customer relations and a strong selling orientation are the keys to business success. As a result, all top executives have sales backgrounds and spend much of their time outside the company with customers. Because of the strong focus on the customer, management at Fitzgerald emphasizes new-product development projects and growth in volume. The company rarely implements cost reduction or process improvement projects.

Between 1975 and 1985, Fitzgerald's 10 percent share of the market was the largest in the industry. Profitability was consistently better than the industry average. However, in the last 10 years, the markets for many of Fitzgerald's products have matured, and Fitzgerald has dropped from market share leader to the number three company in the industry. Profitability has steadily declined since 1991, although Fitzgerald offers a more extensive line of products than any of its competitors. Customers are complaining that Fitzgerald's prices are higher than those of other companies.

In June 1996, Jeff Steele, president of Fitzgerald Company, hired Valerie Stevens of Management Consultants, Inc., to help him improve the company's financial performance. After an extensive study of Fitzgerald Company and its industry group, Valerie met with Jeff and said, "Jeff, I believe the Fitzgerald Company may have to substantially change its culture."

Questions

1. Describe, in general terms, the corporate culture at Fitzgerald Company.
2. What does Valerie mean when she says Fitzgerald Company may have to change its culture? What are some of the necessary changes?
3. Discuss the problems the company may encounter in attempting to implement changes.

Case Incident 16.2

Upgrading Quality

Judy Franklin, the plant manager of Smart Manufacturing Company, was reviewing the Quality Control Department figures with despair. Once again, the department's figures indicated quality improvements were not being made. Judy was annoyed. "I don't understand it," she thought. "I've been stressing to my staff for over a year that I want to see some quality improvements, but it just doesn't seem to be happening. Quality may actually be worse now than it was a year ago!"

Judy called in David Berg, the quality control manager, and production manager Stuart Lewicki. "Look," Judy said, "I told both of you over a year ago I wanted to see some improvements in quality around here, and we've talked about it at every staff meeting since then. But nothing has happened. What's going on?"

David spoke up. "My department just inspects the products. The quality problems occur in production. All I can do is what I've been doing all along—tell Stuart about the problems we are seeing. I've already told him that 50 percent of the quality problems are caused by worker carelessness."

"I know," said Stuart. "I don't understand it. I've been stressing to my shift supervisors that we need to see quality improvements. They have all told me they are coming down really hard on quality problems and are telling their people they need to work harder on getting out a quality product. Just the other day, Frances Stanfield threatened to fire Joe Duncan if she got any more complaints from quality control about Joe's work."

Questions

1. Why have efforts to improve quality failed?
2. Design a quality improvement program that would have a better chance of being successful if used by Judy.

References and Additional Readings

1. Tom Peters, *Thriving on Chaos* (New York: Alfred A. Knopf, 1987), p. 464.
2. Lon Matejczyk, "Commentary: Everyone Responsible for Ensuring Change," *The Colorado Springs Business Journal,* October 21, 2005, p. 1.
3. "The 1995 *BusinessWeek* Europe Forum of Financial Directors," *BusinessWeek,* January 15, 1996.
4. Ibid.
5. Waldron Berry, "Overcoming Resistance to Change," *Supervisory Management,* February 1983, pp. 25–30.
6. Margaret Boles and Brenda Paik Sunoo, "Three Barriers to Managing Change," *Workforce,* January 1998, p. 25.
7. John Kotter, *Leading Change* (Boston: Harvard Business School Press, 1996).
8. Arthur G. Bedeian, *Management* (Hinsdale, IL: Dryden Press, 1986).

9. Michael Beer, "The Technology of Organizational Development," in *Handbook of Industrial and Organizational Psychology,* ed. Marvin D. Dunnette (New York: John Wiley & Sons, 1983), p. 941; and Michael Beer, *Organizational Change and Development: A Systems View* (Santa Monica, CA: Goodyear Publishing, 1980), pp. 194–95.
10. Much of this section is drawn from David E. Terpstra, "The Organization Development Evaluation Process: Some Problems and Proposals," *Human Resource Management,* Spring 1981, p. 24.
11. Much of this section is drawn from Robert B. Tucker, "Innovation Discipline," *Executive Excellence,* September 2001, pp. 3–4; Robert B. Tucker, "Innovation: The New Core Competency," *Strategy and Leadership,* January–February 2001, pp. 11–14; and Robert B. Tucker, "Generating Ideas," *Executive Excellence,* December 2003, p. 19.
12. David Garvin, "Building a Learning Organization," *Harvard Business Review,* July 1993, p. 78.
13. Peter M. Senge, *The Fifth Discipline: The Art and Practice of the Learning Organization* (New York: Doubleday, 1990); and Peter M. Senge, "Learning Organizations," *Executive Excellence,* September 1991, pp. 7–8.
14. Garvin, "Building a Learning Organization."
15. Roy Wagner, *The Invention of Culture,* rev. ed. (Chicago: University of Chicago Press, 1981), p. 21.
16. Vijay Sathe, "Implications of Corporate Culture: A Manager's Guide to Action," *Organizational Dynamics,* Autumn 1983, p. 6.
17. Terrence E. Deal and Allan A. Kennedy, *Corporate Cultures: The Rites and Rituals of Corporate Life* (Reading, MA: Addison-Wesley, 1982), p. 4.
18. Harrison M. Trice and Janice M. Beyer, "Studying Organizational Cultures through Rites and Ceremonials," *Academy of Management Review* 9, no. 4 (1984), p. 645.
19. "The Corporate Culture Vultures," *Fortune,* October 17, 1983, p. 72.
20. Stephen P. Robbins, *Essentials of Organizational Behavior* (Englewood Cliffs, NJ: Prentice Hall, 1984), pp. 174–76.
21. Ron Stodghill, "One Company, Two Cultures," *BusinessWeek,* January 22, 1996, p. 88.
22. Robbins, *Essentials of Organizational Behavior,* p. 171. © 1984; reprinted by permission of Prentice Hall, Inc.
23. This section is drawn from Deal and Kennedy, *Corporate Cultures,* pp. 107, 129–35.
24. Arthur A. Thompson, Jr., A. J. Strickland III, and John E. Gamble, *Crafting and Executing Strategy* (New York: McGraw-Hill/Irwin, 2007), p. 420.
25. "The Corporate Culture Vultures," p. 70.
26. Ibid.

Controlling Skills

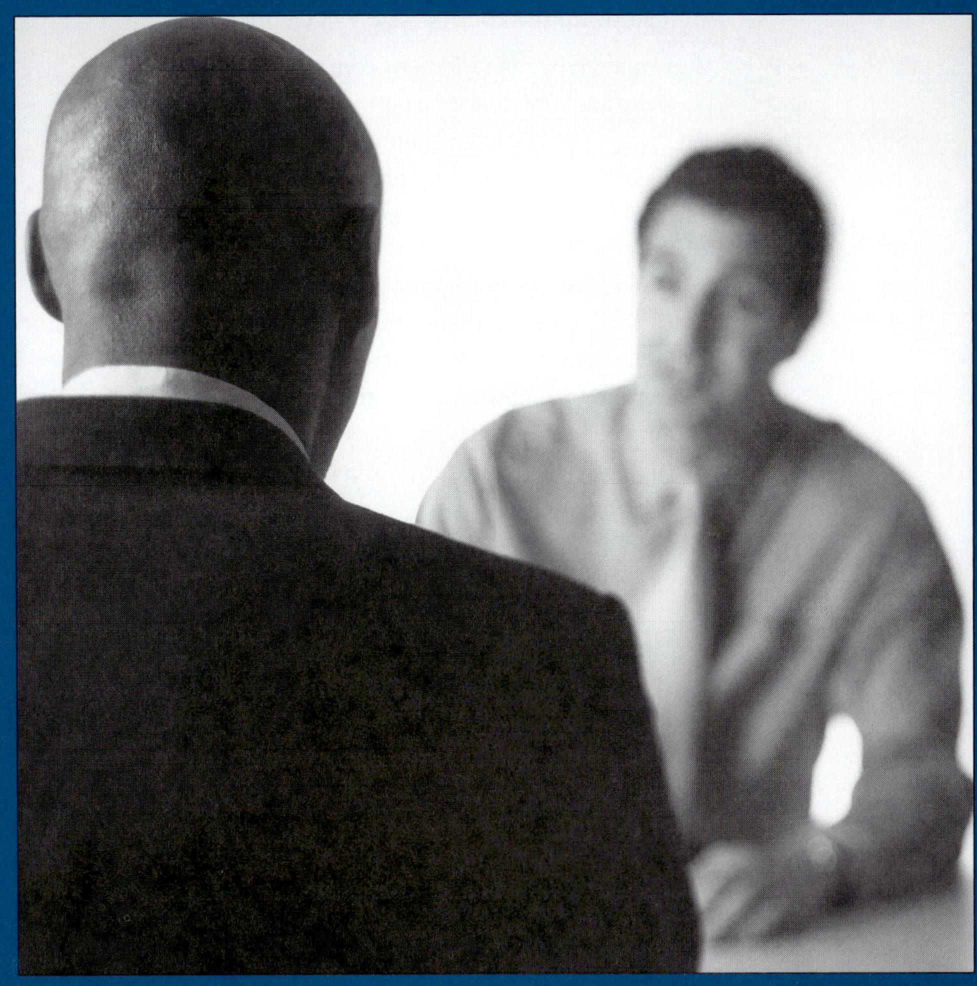

Chapter Seventeen

Management Control

Learning Objectives

After studying this chapter, you will be able to:

1. Explain why management controls are necessary.
2. Describe a feedback system.
3. Discuss the basic requirements of the control process.
4. Describe the control pyramid.
5. Identify the factors that affect how much control should be exercised in an organization.
6. Discuss the two categories of control methods.
7. Differentiate between preliminary, concurrent, and postaction controls.
8. List several methods or systems of control commonly used by managers.
9. List the four basic types of financial ratios.
10. Summarize the Sarbanes-Oxley Act of 2002.
11. Discuss the basic purpose of a break-even chart.

Chapter Preview

Well into 2001 Enron was flying high. The company was listed as number seven on the Fortune 500 list, had a total capitalization of $63 billion, was building a new $339 million office tower, and had obtained the naming rights of the Houston Astros' field, calling it "Enron Field." Founded in 1985, Enron had become the nation's largest and most innovative energy trader. Enron had brought high-tech and complex finance to energy trading and had been ultrasuccessful.

In a matter of weeks, if not days, Enron's stock fell from $90 a share to 61 cents a share, over 4,000 employees were laid off, and the company filed for bankruptcy. How could this possibly happen?

As it turned out, Enron businesses depended on the borrowing of lots of money. Institutions were anxious to lend Enron money as long as the company seemed healthy. However, when suspicions arose after some partnership problems were made public, the lenders began to become hesitant to lend money. What began as a trickle very soon became a flood. All of this was exacerbated by the failure of Enron's outside auditors, Arthur Andersen, to expose the problems.

Since Enron filed for bankruptcy in December 2001, Arthur Andersen has ceased to exist and several banks have agreed to significant settlements for their roles in the

Enron debacle. In mid-January 2008, Enron shareholders learned that they would receive an average of $6.79 per share for common stock.

Sources: Allen Sloan, "Lights Out for Enron," *Newsweek,* December 10, 2001, pp. 50–51; and "Payouts Set for Former Enron Shareholders," *The Wall Street Journal,* January 17, 2008, p. Al3.

Analyzing Management Skills

How might Enron have prevented its problems? Why do you think a company as large as Enron might not have adequate controls?

Applying Management Skills

Suppose you have been elected treasurer of your sorority, fraternity, or some other social group of interest to you. What type of controls could you install to guard against any type of fraud by other officers or members of the organization? How do you think the other officers or members might react to your controls?

control
Process of ensuring that organizational activities are going according to plan; accomplished by comparing actual performance to predetermined standards or objectives, then taking action to correct any deviations.

The basic premise of organizations is that all activities will function smoothly; however, the possibility that this will not be the case gives rise to the need for control. **Control** simply means knowing what is actually happening in comparison to preset standards or objectives and then making any necessary corrections. The overriding purpose of all management controls is to alert the manager to an existing or a potential problem before it becomes critical. Control is accomplished by comparing actual performance to predetermined standards or objectives and then taking action to correct any deviations from the standard. However, control is a sensitive and complex part of the management process.

Controlling is similar to planning. It addresses these basic questions: Where are we now? Where do we want to be? How can we get there from here? But controlling takes place after the planning is completed and the organizational activities have begun. Whereas most planning occurs before action is taken, most controlling takes place after the initial action has been taken. This does not mean control is practiced only after problems occur. Control decisions can be preventive, and they can also affect future planning decisions.

WHY PRACTICE MANAGEMENT CONTROL?

As we just noted, management controls alert the manager to potentially critical problems. At top management levels, a problem occurs when the organization's goals are not being met. At middle and lower levels, a problem occurs when the objectives for which the manager is responsible are not being met. These may be departmental objectives, production standards, or other performance indicators. All forms of management controls are designed to give the manager information regarding progress. The manager can use this information to do the following:

1. *Prevent crises.* If a manager does not know what is going on, it is easy for small, readily solvable problems to turn into crises.
2. *Standardize outputs.* Problems and services can be standardized in terms of quantity and quality through the use of good controls.
3. *Appraise employee performance.* Proper controls can provide the manager with objective information about employee performance.

Management Illustration 17.1

LAX CONTROLS HELP CONCEAL HUGE LOSSES
www.mandtbank.com

Allied Irish Banks PLC (AIB) has portrayed itself as the victim of a clever fraud that resulted in huge currency-trading losses at its Baltimore unit, Allfirst Financial Inc. However, there are signs that a lack of controls at Allfirst may have led to the problems. Initial evidence suggested that Allfirst's risk controls were not very sophisticated.

Allfirst's currency trader, John Rusnak, fraudulently concealed losses of over $690 million over a five-year period. Larry Smith, Allfirst's back-office employee responsible for verifying the trades made by Rusnak, told investigators that his bosses instructed him not to bother confirming any trades involving banks in Asia. Furthermore, because Smith didn't always have access to a computer screen displaying currency rates, he sometimes had to ask Rusnak for verification. This situation obviously prevented independent verification. Another factor that helped disguise the extent of Rusnak's poor trading was that he used more than one prime broker to clear and settle his trades. This system may have helped conceal the extent of his trading from his colleagues.

Rusnak pleaded guilty to one count of bank fraud and is serving a 7½-year sentence in federal prison. In April 2005, a shareholder lawsuit against former executives and officers of Allfirst was resurrected after the Maryland Court of Appeals agreed to hear the case later in the year. The case alleges that directors and senior managers at Allfirst were negligent in their supervision of Rusnak and oversight of the trading department.

It is interesting to note that the former chairman of the U.S. Federal Reserve, Alan Greenspan, suggested in 2000 that banks enforce a simple internal risk control for their trading desks—that all traders be forced to take a two-week vacation. The theory is that "perpetration of an embezzlement of any substantial size usually requires the constant presence of the embezzler in order to manipulate records, respond to inquiries from customers or other employees, and otherwise prevent detection." Those who investigated Rusnak's fraud agreed that the "two-week vacation rule" would probably have detected Rusnak's fraud.

Sources: Alessandra Galloni, Michael R. Sesit, and Benjamin Pedley, "Lax Controls May Explain Trading Loss at Allied Irish," *The Wall Street Journal,* March 8, 2002, p. 8; and Andrew Hill, "Fraud-Free Fortnight," *Financial Times,* January 29, 2008, p. 18.

4. *Update plans.* Even the best plans must be updated as environmental and internal changes occur. Controls allow the manager to compare what is happening with what was planned.
5. *Protect the organization's assets.* Controls can protect assets from inefficiency, waste, and pilferage.

Management Illustration 17.1 illustrates what can happen to an organization when controls are inadequate.

TWO CONCERNS OF CONTROL

When practicing control, the manager must balance two major concerns: stability and objective realization. To maintain stability, the manager must ensure that the organization is operating within its established boundaries of constraint. The boundaries of constraint are determined by policies, budgets, ethics, laws, and so on. The second concern, objective realization, requires constant monitoring to ensure that enough progress is being made toward established objectives.

A manager may become overly worried about one concern at the expense of another. Most common is a manager who becomes preoccupied with the stability of the operation and neglects the goal. This manager is overly concerned with day-to-day rules and policies and forgets about his or her goals. A manager who is obsessed with the manner or style in which a job is done is an example. On the other hand, a manager may lose sight of stability and have glamorous but short-lived success. A manager who sets production records by omitting safety checks is an example of this behavior.

THE MANAGEMENT CONTROL PROCESS

Figure 17.1 is a simple model of the management control process. Outputs from the activity are monitored by some type of sensor and compared to preset standards (normally set during the planning process). The manager acts as the regulator; he or she takes corrective action when the outputs do not meet the standards. The manager's actions may be directed at the inputs to the activity or at the activity itself.

feedback system
System in which outputs from the system affect future inputs or future activities of the system.

Such a system, in which outputs from the system affect future inputs into or future activities of the system, is called a **feedback system.** In other words, a feedback system is influenced by its own past behaviors. The heating system of a house is a common example of a mechanical feedback system. The thermostat sensor compares the temperature resulting from heat previously generated by the system to some predetermined standard (the desired temperature setting) and responds accordingly. Feedback is a vital part of the control process. Although preventive, before-the-fact steps can often aid the control process, total control cannot be practiced without feedback. Managers may receive and act on facts about the inputs or the activity itself. But in the end, they must know what is happening in the organization; feedback gives them this information.

Three Requirements for Control

The process of control has three basic requirements: (1) establishing standards, (2) monitoring results and comparing them to standards, and (3) correcting deviations. The first step, setting standards, comes from the planning process, whereas the latter two, monitoring and correcting, are unique to the control process. All three are essential to effective control.

Setting Standards

standard
Value used as a point of reference for comparing other values.

A **standard** is a value used as a point of reference for comparing other values. As such, a standard outlines what is expected of the job or the individual. When used in management control, standards often come directly from objectives. In some instances, objectives may be used directly as standards. In other instances, performance indicators may be derived from the objectives. In certain situations, a standard may be determined by methods analysts, industrial engineers, or recognized experts. In any case, standards should be easy to measure and define. The more specific and measurable an objective is, the more likely it

FIGURE 17.1
The Control Process

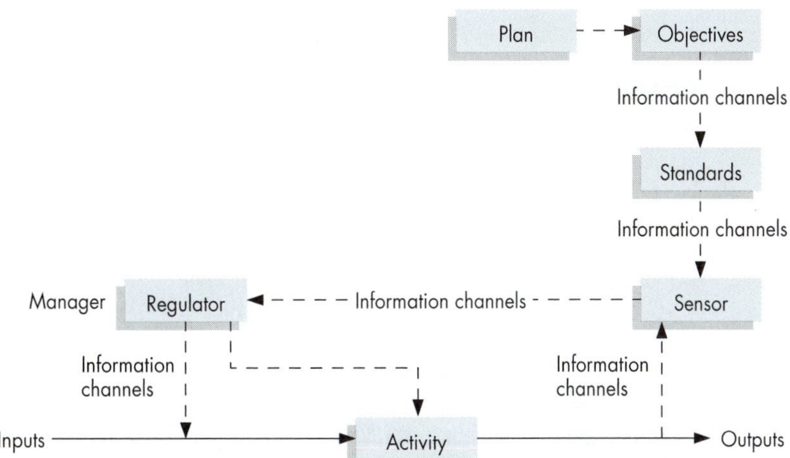

can be directly used as a standard. Standards may deal with output per hour, quality level, inventory level, or other indicators of individual or organizational performance.

Monitoring Performance

Obviously, the overall control system is no better than the information on which it operates, and much of this information is gathered from the monitoring process. Monitoring is often considered to be synonymous with control. In fact, it is only one part of the total control process. The main purpose of monitoring performance is to gather data and detect problem areas. The type of standards used often dictates the type of checks to be made.

The major problem in monitoring performance is deciding when, where, and how often to inspect or check. Checks must be made often enough to provide needed information. However, some managers become obsessed with the checking process. Monitoring can be expensive if overdone, and it can result in adverse reactions from employees. Timing is equally important. The manager must recognize a problem in time to correct it.

Correcting for Deviations

Too often, managers set standards and monitor results but do not follow up with actions. The first two steps are of little value if corrective action is not taken. The action needed may be simply to maintain the status quo. Action of this type would depend on standards being met in a satisfactory manner. If standards are not being met, the manager must find the cause of the deviation and correct it. It is not enough to treat only the symptoms. This action is comparable to replacing a car battery when the real problem is a faulty alternator. In a short time, the battery will go dead again. The manager must determine why the deviation occurred. The deviation may be because a false assumption was made in the planning function or because of poor execution. It is also possible that a careful analysis of the deviation will require a change in the standard. The standard may have been improperly set, or changing conditions may dictate a change. Figure 17.2 lists some potential causes of deviations between desired and actual performance.

Tools used to correct for deviations should have the following characteristics:

1. The tools should be used to eliminate the root causes of a problem (as in the battery example above).
2. Tools should be capable of correcting defects (which are bound to occur).
3. Tools should be relatively simple and straightforward so that all employees can use them (e.g., monitoring a gauge, turning a dial, reading a simple report).
4. Tools should be easy for employees to tie to goals or standards for improvement.
5. Tools should be applied totally, not piecemeal.[1]

Control Tolerances

Actual performance rarely conforms exactly to standards or plans. A certain amount of variation will normally occur. Therefore, the manager must set limits on the acceptable degree of deviation from the standard. In other words, how much variation from standard

FIGURE 17.2
Potential Causes of Performance Deviations

- Faulty planning.
- Lack of communication within the organization.
- Need for training.
- Lack of motivation.
- Unforeseen forces outside the organization, such as government regulation or competition.

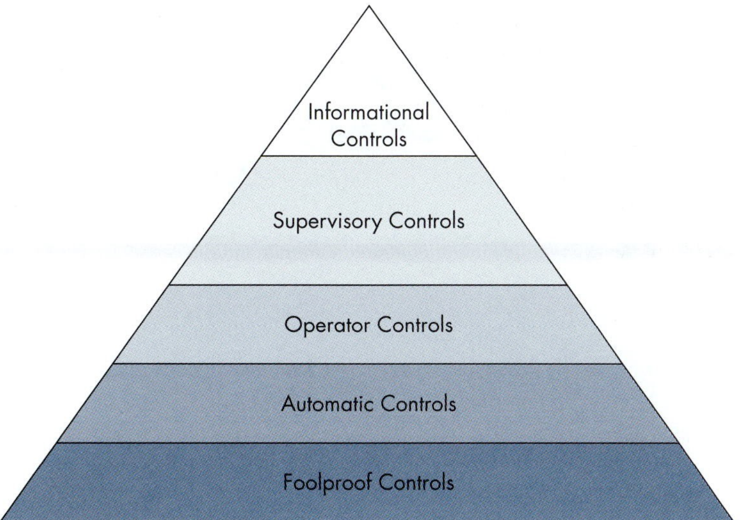

FIGURE 17.3
The Control Pyramid

Source: From J. Juran, *Managerial Breakthrough,* 2nd Edition, 1995. Reproduced with permission of The McGraw-Hill Companies.

control tolerances
Variation from the standard that is acceptable to the manager.

is tolerable? For example, by how much can expenses be allowed to exceed expectations before the manager becomes alarmed? The manner in which the manager sets **control tolerances** depends on the standard and methods being used. If sampling is being used to monitor the activity, statistical control techniques can be used. The tolerance levels may be formalized, or they may merely exist in the mind of the manager. The important point is that the manager must develop some guidelines as to what deviation is acceptable (in control) and what is not acceptable (out of control).

The Control Pyramid

The control pyramid provides a method for implementing controls in the organization.[2] The idea is to implement simple controls first and then move to more complex controls at a later time. The first area to be considered using this method would be *foolproof controls,* wherein the control deals with repetitive acts and requires little thought (e.g., turning off lights). Surprisingly, many of these acts and controls already exist in an organization's normal course of business. The second area to consider is *automatic controls,* wherein a feedback loop can exist without much human interaction (e.g., regulation of plant temperature). These systems require monitoring, but the control can be machine or computer based. The third area is *operator controls,* which require a human response (e.g., a salesperson checking records). The key to this form of control is to make it meaningful for the controller. The fourth area is *supervisory control,* the layer that controls the person or persons implementing the controls (e.g., a department head checking an employee's reports). The organization must make sure that this form of control gets results and is not redundant. The final area is *informational controls* (e.g., report summaries). This is the ultimate feedback loop, wherein the manager must pull together all the information provided by the other controls.[3] Seeing the process as a whole helps the manager get a feel for how interrelated the control process is and how it must be synchronized. Figure 17.3 shows how these different types of controls relate to each other.

Informational controls are the final feedback loop wherein the manager must pull together all the information provided by other controls.

How Much Control?

The effectiveness of any control system is a function of the number and types of controls that are used. When deciding just how much control should be

FIGURE 17.4
General Relationship between Control Cost and Benefits

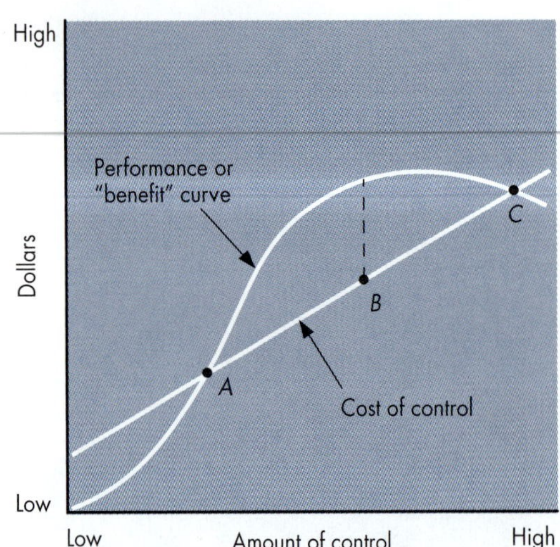

exercised in an organization, three major factors must be appraised: (1) economic considerations, (2) behavioral considerations, and (3) flexibility and innovation considerations.

Economic Considerations

Installing and operating control systems cost money. A good quality control system, for instance, requires additional labor, if nothing else. The equipment costs of sophisticated electronic and mechanical control systems can be significant. Ideally, control systems should be installed as long as they save more than they cost. Figure 17.4 shows the general relationship between control costs and the benefits gained. The straight, upward-sloping line represents the costs associated with implementing and maintaining the controls (up-front installation expenses, labor costs, and so on). The S-shaped curve represents the performance or benefits received as a result of having the controls. Analyzing Figure 17.4, several points can be seen:

- There is some minimum amount of control necessary before the benefits of more control outweigh the costs (point A).
- There is some optimal amount of control (point B).
- There is some maximum amount of control that, if exceeded, can cost more than its worth (point C).

The costs of implementing a control system can usually be estimated or calculated much more accurately than the benefits. For example, it is difficult to quantify and measure the true benefits of a quality control system. A good quality control system supposedly increases goodwill; but how does one measure this attribute? The decision is obviously much easier when the costs of not maintaining control are either very high or very low. For example, because the cost of low quality control is so high, airlines go to great expense to ensure high control of quality. Despite the measurement problems, management should regularly attempt to evaluate the economic costs versus the benefits of controls.

Behavioral Considerations

Managers need to be aware of the potential impact of the control system on employees. Most people do not like to work where they think their every move is being watched or questioned. For example, most salespeople do not like to have to account for every penny spent on meals and entertainment. At the same time, however, very few people like to work where no control exists; an absence of control creates an environment in which people do not know what is expected of them.

Flexibility and Innovation Considerations

Too much control may restrict the flexibility and innovation required to be competitive. Overly restrictive controls can stifle the entrepreneurial spirit of employees and discourage them from trying new and creative options. The key is to maintain control without squelching innovation.

Many managers tend to increase controls whenever things are not going according to plan. Figure 17.5 shows a simplified version of a model developed by Alvin Gouldner that explains this behavior. Gouldner's model begins with top management's demand for control over operations. This is attempted through the use and enforcement of general and impersonal rules regarding work procedures. These rigid rules are meant to be guides for the behavior of the organization members; they also have the unintended effect of showing minimum acceptable behavior. In organizations where there is little congruence between individual and organizational objectives or acceptance of organizational objectives is not high, the effect is a reduction of performance to the lowest acceptable level: People who are not highly committed to organizational objectives will perform at the lowest acceptable level. Managers view such behavior as resulting from inadequate control; they therefore respond with closer supervision and tighter controls. This increases the visibility of power, which in turn raises the level of interpersonal tension in the organization. Raising the tension level brings even stricter enforcement of the general and impersonal formal rules. Hence, the cycle repeats itself. The overall effect is increased control, increased interpersonal tension, and a lowering of performance.

One problem in deciding on the proper amount of control is that different people react differently to similar controls. Research suggests that reactions differ according to personality and prior experiences.[4] Problems can occur from unforeseen reactions to control due to both compliance and resistance.[5] Problems from compliance arise when people adhere

FIGURE 17.5
Simplified Gouldner Model of Organization Control

Source: From James G. March and Herbert A. Simon, *Organizations,* 2nd ed. Reprinted with permission of Blackwell Publishing Ltd.

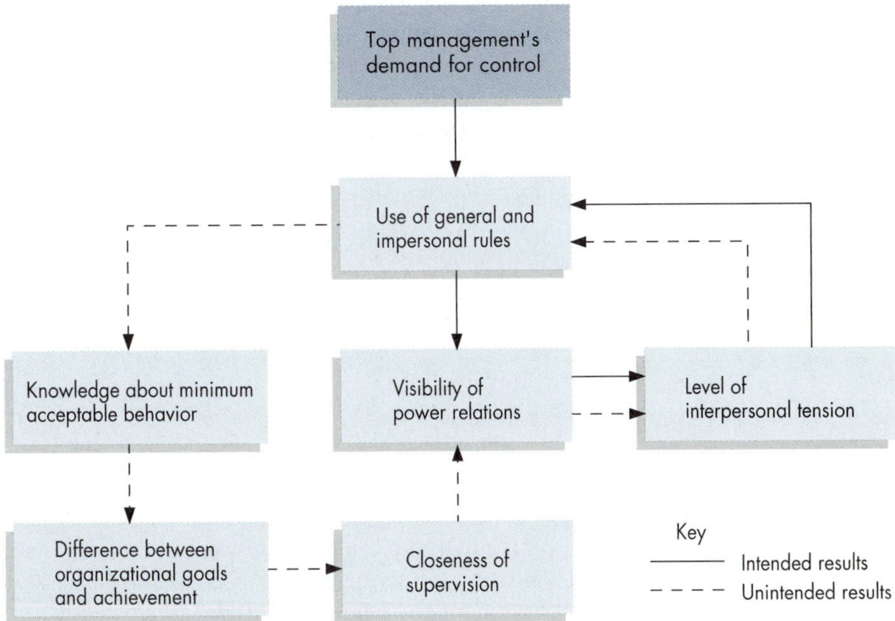

to the prescribed behavior even when it is inappropriate. The salesperson who will not vary from prescribed procedures to satisfy a customer complaint is an example of this. Problems resulting from resistance to controls arise when individuals attempt to preempt, work around, or sabotage the controls. Distorting a report and padding the budget are forms of control resistance.

Several things can be done to lessen negative reactions to controls. Most approaches are based on good common sense. However, they require a concerted effort by the manager. The tendency is to take these suggestions for granted. Some guidelines are as follows:

1. Make sure the standards and associated controls are realistic. Standards set too high or too low turn people off. Make sure the standards are attainable yet challenging.
2. Involve employees in the control-setting process. Many of the behavioral problems associated with controls result from a lack of understanding of the nature and purpose of the controls. People naturally resist anything new, especially if they do not understand why it is being used. Solicit and listen to suggestions from employees.
3. Use controls only where needed. As the Gouldner model suggests, there is a strong tendency to overcontrol. Periodically evaluate the need for different controls. A good rule of thumb is to evaluate every control at least annually. Changing conditions can make certain controls obsolete. Remember, overcontrol can produce negative results.

Where Should Control Reside?

For years, it was believed that control in organizations is a fixed commodity that should rest only in the hands of top management. This viewpoint naturally favored a highly centralized approach to decision making and controlling. However, as decentralized organizations have become more common, controls have been pushed farther and farther down the hierarchy. It is now recognized that where the controls reside is an important factor in how much control is desirable.

James Champy, author of *Reengineering Management,* believes the modern approach to control should involve more "enabling" or learning to control at lower levels.[6] Supporting this idea, Leon Royer, director of Learning Services at 3M, found that learning and enabling go hand in hand. Lower-level employees are valuable controllers if they are allowed to learn how to control.[7] The difficulty with enabling, however, is that it means senior management must be willing to relinquish control. One reason for pushing controls down in the organization is that the controllers then are close to the actual situations that require control.

Building on this material, evidence favors relatively tight controls as long as they are placed as far down in the organization as possible.[8] This approach has several advantages. First, it keeps higher-level managers from getting too involved in details. Second, it shows why the control is necessary. Third, it elicits commitment from lower-level managers. When controls are spread through many levels of an organization, caution must be taken to ensure that there are no disagreements about how the controls are distributed. In other words, managers at every level should clearly understand their authority and responsibility.

behavior (personal) control
Based on direct, personal surveillance.

TYPES OF CONTROL

output (impersonal) control
Based on the measurement of outputs.

There are two categories of control methods: behavior control and output control. **Behavior** or **personal control** is based on direct, personal surveillance. The first-line supervisor who maintains a close personal watch over employees is using behavior control. **Output** or **impersonal control** is based on the measurement of outputs. Tracking production records and monitoring sales figures are examples of output controls.

Research shows that these two categories of control are not substitutes for each other in the sense that a manager uses one or the other.[9] The evidence suggests that output control occurs in response to a manager's need to provide an accurate measure of performance. On the other hand, behavior control is exerted when performance requirements are well known and personal surveillance is needed to promote efficiency and motivation. In most situations, organizations need to use a mix of output and behavior controls because each serves different organizational needs.

preliminary (steering) control
Method of exercising control to prevent a problem from occurring.

concurrent (screening) control
Focuses on process as it occurs; designed to detect a problem when it occurs.

postaction control
Designed to detect an existing or a potential problem before it gets out of hand.

Preliminary, Concurrent, or Postaction Control?

In general, methods for exercising control can be described as either preliminary, concurrent, or postaction. **Preliminary control** methods, sometimes called **steering controls,** attempt to prevent a problem from occurring. Requiring prior approval for purchases of all items over a certain dollar value is an example. **Concurrent controls,** also called **screening controls,** focus on things that happen as inputs are being transformed into outputs. They are designed to detect a problem as it occurs. Personal observation of customers being serviced is an example of a concurrent control. **Postaction control** methods are designed to detect existing problems after they occur but before they reach crisis proportions. Written or periodic reports represent postaction control methods. Most controls are based on postaction methods.

Budgetary Control

budget
Statement of expected results or requirements expressed in financial or numerical terms.

Budgets are probably the most widely used control devices. A **budget** is a statement of expected results or requirements expressed in financial or numerical terms. Budgets express plans, objectives, and programs of the organization in numerical terms. Preparation of the budget is primarily a planning function; however, its administration is a controlling function.

Many different types of budgets are in use. Figure 17.6 outlines some of the most common types. Some may be expressed in terms other than dollars. For example, an equipment budget may be expressed in numbers of machines; material budgets may be expressed in pounds, pieces, gallons, and so on. Budgets not expressed in dollars can usually be translated into dollars for inclusion in an overall budget.

While budgets are useful for planning and control, they are not without their dangers. Perhaps the greatest danger is inflexibility. This is a special threat to organizations operating in an industry with rapid change and high competition. Rigidity in the budget can also lead to ignoring organizational goals for budgetary goals. The financial manager who won't go $5 over budget to make $500 is a classic example. Budgets can hide inefficiencies. The fact that a certain expenditure has been made in the past often becomes justification for continuing the practice even when the situation has greatly changed. Managers may also

FIGURE 17.6
Types and Purposes of Budgets

Type of Budget	Purpose
Revenue and expense budget	Provides details for revenue and expense plans.
Cash budget	Forecasts cash receipts and disbursements.
Capital expenditure budget	Outlines specific expenditures for plant, equipment, machinery, inventories, and other capital items.
Production, material, or time budget	Expresses physical requirements of production, or material, or the time requirements for the budget period.
Balance sheet budgets	Forecasts the status of assets, liabilities, and net worth at the end of the budget period.

pad budgets because they anticipate that their budgets will be cut by superiors. Since the manager is never sure how severe the cut will be, the result is often an inaccurate, if not unrealistic, budget.

The answer to effective budget control may be to make the manager and any concerned employees accountable for their budgets. Performance incentives can be tied to budget control, accuracy, and fulfillment. In other words, if it is worth budgeting, it is worth budgeting right! Others believe budgets should also be tied not only to financial data but also to customer satisfaction. Budgeting for what it takes to satisfy the customer would be the rule of thumb for this logic. Managers can get so hung up on measuring themselves by sticking to their own sets of rules, focusing internally, and watching their budgets that they forget their customers.[10] Yet the customer is what business is all about. Generally managers meet on a periodic basis (usually monthly or quarterly) with accounting officials to discuss planned finances versus actual expenses.

Zero-Base Budgeting

Zero-base budgeting was designed to stop basing this year's budget on last year's budget. **Zero-base budgeting** requires each manager to justify an entire budget request in detail. The burden of proof is on each manager to justify why any money should be spent. Under zero-base budgeting, each activity under a manager's discretion is identified, evaluated, and ranked by importance. Then each year every activity in the budget is on trial for its life and is matched against all the other claimants for an organization's resources.

zero-base budgeting
Form of budgeting in which the manager must build and justify each area of a budget. Each activity is identified, evaluated, and ranked by importance.

Financial Controls

In addition to budgets, many managers use other types of financial information for control purposes. These include balance sheets, income statements, and financial ratios. Regardless of the type of financial information used, it is meaningful only when compared with either the historical performance of the organization or the performances of similar organizations. For example, knowing that a company has a net income of $100,000 this year doesn't reveal much by itself. However, when compared to last year's net income of $500,000 or to an industry average of $500,000, much more can be determined about the company's performance.

Financial Ratio Analysis

Financial ratios can be divided into four basic types: profitability, liquidity, debt, and activity ratios. *Profitability ratios* indicate the organization's operational efficiency, or how well the organization is being managed. Gross profit margin, net profit margin, and return on investment (ROI) are all examples of profitability ratios. *Liquidity ratios* are used to judge how well an organization will be able to meet its short-term financial obligations. The current ratio (current assets divided by current liabilities) and the quick ratio (current assets minus inventories divided by current liabilities) are examples of liquidity ratios. *Debt* (sometimes called *leverage*) *ratios* measure the magnitude of owners' and creditors' claims on the organization and indicate the organization's ability to meet long-term obligations. The debt to equity ratio and total debt to total assets ratio are two common debt ratios. *Activity ratios* evaluate how effectively an organization is managing some of its basic operations. Asset turnover, inventory turnover, average collection period, and accounts receivable turnover represent some commonly used activity ratios.

As mentioned earlier, financial ratios are meaningful only when compared to past ratios and to ratios of similar organizations. Also, financial ratios reflect only certain specific information, and therefore they should be used in conjunction with other management controls. Figure 17.7 presents a summary of several financial ratio calculations.

FIGURE 17.7 Summary of Financial Ratio Calculations

Ratio	Calculation	Purpose
Profitability Ratios		
Gross profit margin	$\frac{\text{Sales} - \text{Cost of goods sold}}{\text{Sales}} \times 100$	Indicates efficiency of operations and product pricing
Net profit margin	$\frac{\text{Net profit after tax}}{\text{Sales}} \times 100$	Indicates efficiency after all expenses are considered
Return on investment (ROI)	$\frac{\text{Net profit after tax}}{\text{Total investment}} \times 100$	Shows productivity of investment
Return on assets (ROA)	$\frac{\text{Net profit after tax}}{\text{Total assets}} \times 100$	Shows productivity of assets
Return on equity (ROE)	$\frac{\text{Net profit after tax}}{\text{Stockerholders' equity}} \times 100$	Shows earnings power of equity
Liquidity Ratios		
Current ratio	$\frac{\text{Current assets}}{\text{Current liabilities}}$	Shows short-run debt-paying ability
Quick ratio	$\frac{\text{Current assets} - \text{Inventories}}{\text{Current liabilities}}$	Shows short-term Liquidity
Debt Ratios		
Debt to equity	$\frac{\text{Total liabilities}}{\text{Stockholders' Equity}}$	Indicates long-term liquidity
Total debt to total assets (debt ratio)	$\frac{\text{Total liabilities}}{\text{Total assets}}$	Shows percentage of assets financed through borrowing
Activity Ratios		
Asset turnover	$\frac{\text{Sales}}{\text{Total assets}}$	Shows efficiency of asset utilization
Inventory turnover	$\frac{\text{Cost of goods sold}}{\text{Average inventory}}$	Shows management's ability to control investment in inventory
Average collection period	$\frac{\text{Receivables} \times 365 \text{ days}}{\text{Annual credit sales}}$	Shows effectiveness of collection and credit policies
Accounts receivable turnover	$\frac{\text{Annual credit sales}}{\text{Receivables}}$	Shows effectiveness of collection and credit policies

Sarbanes-Oxley Act of 2002

As introduced in Chapter 5, the Sarbanes-Oxley Act (SOX) was passed in 2002. SOX, which has been called the most dramatic change to federal securities laws since the 1930s, radically redesigned federal regulation of public company corporate governance and reporting obligations. The law also significantly tightens accountability standards for corporate directors and officers, auditors, securities, analysts, and legal counsel. The purpose of the act is to prevent the kind of accounting and financial maneuvering that caused the meltdowns experienced at Enron (see the chapter preview) and WorldCom.

One major concern related to SOX is its hefty compliance costs. A 2004 survey by Financial Executives International (FEI) reported that large public companies spent thousands of hours and an average of $4.4 million each to comply with SOX.[11] More recent data show that SOX compliance costs, after dropping slightly in 2005, increased in 2006 for both large and small public companies.[12] In response to concerns about the costs of complying for smaller businesses, the Securities and Exchange Commission delayed

Management Illustration 17.2

UNEXPECTED BENEFITS OF SARBANES-OXLEY ACT

Despite the fact that most CEO's are complaining about the costs of complying with the Sarbanes-Oxley Act, a few companies have discovered some unexpected benefits:

For years Pitney Bowes Inc. had been trying to create central offices for accounts receivable, billing, payroll, and seven other functions that its business units were doing on their own. Being forced by Sarbanes-Oxley to review its internal controls turbocharged that move. The early results are promising with Pitney Bowes expecting to save more than $500,000 in 2005 by combining four accounts receivable offices into one.

At Genentech, Inc., the generation of detailed reports on financial controls "sped up by several months" the installation of a new computer system that consolidates its financial data, according to Elaine Yang, director of general audit. The new computer system allows managers to spend more time analyzing, rather than gathering, data.

While Cisco Systems Inc. spent $50 million and 240,000 hours on its first-year audit of internal controls, the effort did reveal opportunities to streamline steps for ordering products and service, thus making it easier for customers to do business with Cisco. According to Amy Kwan, senior director of finance, compliance "forced us to make sure that when a customer calls, sales and support are integrated."

Source: Amy Borrus, "Learning to Love Sarbanes-Oxley," *BusinessWeek,* November 21, 2005, p. 126.

implementation of key sections of the act until 2007 for companies with less than $75 million in market capitalization.[13]

A silver lining to the act is that some companies have realized unexpected benefits. Management Illustration 17.2 describes some of the unexpected benefits that some companies have realized as a result of complying with the Sarbanes-Oxley Act.

Direct Observation

A store manager's daily tour of the facility, a company president's annual visit to all branches, and a methods study by a staff industrial engineer are all examples of control by direct observation. Although time-consuming, personal observation is sometimes the only way to get an accurate picture of what is really happening. One hazard is that employees may misinterpret a superior's visit and consider such action meddling or eavesdropping. A second hazard is that behaviors change when people are being watched or monitored. Another potential inaccuracy lies in the interpretation of the observation. The observer must be careful not to read into the picture events that did not actually occur. Visits and direct observation can have positive effects when viewed by employees as a display of the manager's interest.

Visits and direct observations by managers can have positive effects when viewed by employees as a display of the managers' interest. Why might an employee take one of these visits negatively?

Written Reports

Written reports can be prepared on a periodic or an as-necessary basis. There are two basic types of written reports: analytical and informational. Analytical reports interpret the facts they present; informational reports present only the facts. Preparing a report is a four- or five-step process, depending on whether it is informational or analytical. The steps are (1) planning what is to be done, (2) collecting the facts, (3) organizing the facts, (4) interpreting the facts (this step is omitted with informational reports), and (5) writing the report.[14] Most reports should be prepared for the benefit of the reader and not the writer. In most cases, the reader wants useful information not previously available.

Management Illustration 17.3

THE BALANCED SCORECARD AT FOSTERS BREWING GROUP

The Fosters Brewing Group grew from a local Canadian brewery in the mid-1960s into an international company by the mid-1980s. By the 1990s, however, the company was in serious decline with both short-term and long-term problems threatening its survival. In March 1992, Ted Kunkel was made president and CEO of Fosters.

As part of Fosters's recovery effort, Kunkel introduced the Balanced Scorecard (BSC) approach for measuring and controlling performance. The four perspectives of performance used by Fosters's BSC were (1) financial perspective, (2) customer perspective, (3) internal business process perspective, and (4) learning and growth perspective. By implementing the BSC system, Kunkel was able to align individual organization and cross-departmental objectives and to establish a flexible structure that allowed the company to quickly adapt to its changing environment.

As a result of the BSC and other initiatives, Fosters, under Kunkel's leadership, has emerged as one of the world's leading brewers and leading premium wine companies. The company employs more than 13,000 people and enjoys annual revenues of approximately $5 billion. The stock price also reflects that the company has been able to reverse its decline.

Source: Sanjoy Bose and Keith Thomas, "Applying the Balanced Scorecard for Better Performance of Intellectual Capital," *Journal of Intellectual Capital* 8, Issue 4, 2007, p. 653.

Electronic Monitors

Today, a number of different types of electronic devices can be used to monitor what is going on. Examples include electronic cash registers that keep a record of what items are sold and when; video cameras that record employee and customer movements; phones that record how long each customer was engaged; and Internet programs that track where and how long an employee or customer is at certain Internet sites.

Management by Objectives

Management by objectives (MBO) was discussed in Chapter 7 as an effective means for setting objectives. The development of an MBO system is part of the planning function. However, once such a system has been developed, it can be used for control purposes.

Balanced Scorecard

The Balanced Scorecard (BSC) system is a measurement and control system that is similar to management by objectives and based on the idea that financial measures alone do not adequately indicate how an organization or organizational unit is performing. BSC attempts to balance traditional financial measures with measures relating to customer service, internal processes, and potential for learning and innovation. The idea is to balance these four categories of measures on both the short and long term.

A significant advantage of the BSC is that it is based on participation and commitment at all levels within the organization. Under BSC, operational managers develop scorecards at every level in the organization so that each manager can see how his or her job duties relate to and contribute to the higher-level objectives and strategies. The key is that the scorecards at one level are derived from the scorecards at the next level up. Once the scorecards have been developed, managers and employees use them to periodically assess how they are doing and what, if any, corrective actions should be taken.

While balanced scorecarding is relatively new, its use has grown significantly in the last several years and is expected to increase at a rapid rate.[15] Management Illustration 17.3 describes how the Fosters Brewing Group used the BSC approach to help turn around the company.

Management Illustration 17.4

EXTERNAL AUDIT REVEALS PROBLEMS

An audit conducted by the U.S. Office of Inspector General found that the city of Fort Lauderdale had possibly mismanaged $5.1 million in federal grants intended for poor and impoverished families. The audit criticizes the city for using federal money to purchase land that remains unused years after its purchase. The audit also revealed sloppy recordkeeping for federally funded community services, including street improvements, parks, and programs for seniors. The audit reported that "the city lacked effective management controls" over its Community Development Block grants.

The audit orders the city to prove that the grant money was used according to the federal rules and that the land purchased will help low-income people. If the city can't meet these requirements, the money must be paid back with nonfederal funds.

Had the audit not been conducted, it is unlikely that the identified problems would ever have been uncovered. City officials maintain that there was no staff negligence but rather a lack of staff that caused the problems.

Source: Brittany Wallman, "Federal Audit Demands Fort Lauderdale Account for Grants—Or Pay Them Back," *McClatchy-Tribune Business News,* February 5, 2008.

Management Information Systems

As discussed in Chapter 4, management information systems (MISs) are computerized systems designed to produce information needed for successful management of a process, department, or business. Usually, the information provided by an MIS is in the form of periodic reports, special reports, and outputs of mathematical simulations.[16]

Audits

audit
Method of control normally involved with financial matters; also can include other areas of the organization.

Audits can be conducted by either internal or external personnel. External audits are normally done by outside accountants and are usually limited to financial statements. Normally, external audits are performed by certified public accountants (CPAs). Most are conducted to certify that the organization's accounting methods are fair, are consistent, and conform to existing practices. Internal audits are performed by the organization's own personnel. Management Illustration 17.4 describes how an external audit uncovered some problems in the city of Fort Lauderable.

management audit
Attempts to evaluate the overall management practices and policies of the organization.

An audit that looks at areas other than finance and accounting is known as a **management audit.** Management audits attempt to evaluate the overall management practices and policies of the organization. They can be conducted by outside consultants or inside staff; however, a management audit conducted by inside staff can easily result in a biased report.

Break-Even Charts

break-even chart
Depicts graphically the relationship of volume of operations to profits.

Break-even charts depict graphically the relationship of volume of operations to profits. The break-even point (BEP) is the point at which sales revenues exactly equal expenses. Total sales below the BEP result in a loss; total sales above the BEP result in a profit.

Figure 17.8 shows a typical break-even chart. The horizontal axis represents output; the vertical axis represents expenses and revenues. Though not required, most break-even charts assume there are linear relationships and all costs are either fixed or variable. Fixed costs do not vary with output, at least in the short run. They include rent, insurance, and administrative salaries. Variable costs vary with output. Typical variable costs include direct labor and materials. The purpose of the chart is to show the break-even point and the effects of changes in output. A break-even chart is useful for showing whether revenue and costs are running as planned.

FIGURE 17.8
Break-Even Chart

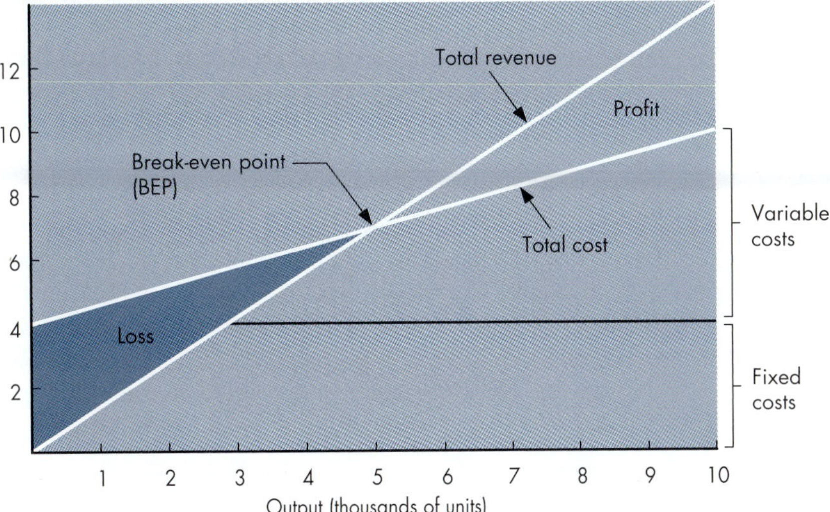

Summary

1. *Explain why management controls are necessary.* The overriding purpose of all management controls is to alert the manager to an existing or a potential problem before it becomes critical. Specifically, management controls can be used to (1) prevent crises, (2) standardize outputs, (3) appraise employee performance, (4) update plans, and (5) protect an organization's assets.
2. *Describe a feedback system.* Any system in which the outputs from the system affect future inputs or future activities of the system is called a feedback system; in other words, a feedback system is influenced by its own past behavior.
3. *Discuss the basic requirements of the control process.* The control process has three basic requirements: (1) establishing standards, (2) monitoring results and comparing them to standards, and (3) correcting for any deviations between the standard and actual results.
4. *Describe the control pyramid.* The control pyramid is a method for implementing control in the organization. It consists of control through foolproofing, automatic controls, operator controls, control by personal supervision, and informational controls.
5. *Identify the factors that affect how much control should be exercised in an organization.* When deciding how much control should be exercised in an organization, three major factors must be appraised: (1) economic considerations, (2) behavioral considerations, and (3) flexibility and innovation considerations.
6. *Discuss the two categories of control methods.* Control methods can be either of two kinds: (1) behavior control or (2) output control. Behavior (or personal) control is based on direct, personal surveillance. Output (or impersonal) control is based on the measurement of outputs.
7. *Differentiate between preliminary, concurrent, and postaction controls.* Preliminary (steering) controls are designed to prevent a problem from occurring. Concurrent (screening) controls focus on things that happen as inputs are being transformed into outputs. They are designed to detect a problem as it occurs. Postaction controls are designed to detect existing or potential problems after they occur but before they reach crisis proportions.

8. *List several methods or systems of control commonly used by managers.* Many control methods or systems are in use today. Some of the most popular control methods/systems include all types of budgets, financial controls (balance sheets, income statements, and financial ratios), direct observations, written reports, electronic monitors, management by objectives, balanced scorecards, management information systems, audits, break-even charts, and time-related charts and techniques.
9. *List the four basic types of financial ratios.* The four basic types of financial ratios are profitability, liquidity, debt, and activity ratios.
10. *Summarize the Sarbanes-Oxley Act of 2002.* The Sarbanes-Oxley Act of 2002 radically redesigned federal regulation of public company corporate governance and reporting obligations. The law also significantly tightens accountability standards for corporate directors and officers, auditors, securities analysts, and legal counsel.
11. *Discuss the basic purpose of a break-even chart.* A break-even chart graphically depicts the relationship of volume of operations to profits.

Review Questions

1. What is management control? What are the two major concerns in management control?
2. Describe a model of the management control process.
3. Outline the three basic requirements of control.
4. How much control should be exercised in an organization?
5. Describe the two categories of control methods.
6. Define preliminary, concurrent, and postaction controls.
7. Describe the following control methods and systems:
   a. Budgets
   b. Financial ratios
   c. Direct observation
   d. Written reports
   e. Electronic monitors
   f. Management by objectives
   g. Balanced scorecards
   h. Management information
   i. Audits
   j. Break-even charts
8. Outline the major points of the Sarbanes-Oxley Act of 2002.

Skill-Building Questions

1. If you were implementing a new control system designed to track more closely the expenses of your salespeople, what actions might you take to minimize negative reactions?
2. Why are many managers reluctant to take the actions necessary to correct for deviations?
3. How should you deal with managers who are so "married" to their departmental budgets that they will not let you spend $1 to make $10?
4. Give an example of how you might enable a subordinate to control something at the production line level. What might be the benefits of enabling?

SKILL-BUILDING EXERCISE 17.1

Breaking Even

As of January 1, 2009, UND Family Health Service Center had 8 employees with a total annual salary budget of $400,000. The annual maintenance cost was estimated at $80,000. Based on 2008 data, the monthly patient service in 2009 was forecast to be 180 patients per month. For each patient serviced, the average variable cost incurred (e.g., paperwork, treatment materials, equipment depreciation, utility consumption) was estimated at $10, and average revenue per patient was projected to be $230.

1. Based on the above information, do you think the center manager can balance annual costs and annual revenues? Explain. What would you suggest to the manager?
2. If, by implementing more efficient operations management, the center's operating (variable) cost can be reduced to $8 per patient, do you think the center could balance its annual budget?
3. If dismissing employees becomes necessary to balance the budget, how many employees would you recommend be let go? Why?
4. At the end of June 2009, the manager showed you the following report:

	Jan.	Feb.	March	April	May	June
Number of patients	150	140	152	145	130	145

What comments would you make to the manager?

Source: This exercise was written by Jiaqin Yang, assistant professor, the University of North Dakota.

SKILL-BUILDING EXERCISE 17.2

Staying on Budget

As manager of the Ace Division of the Triple-A Company, you agreed to the following budget at the beginning of the current fiscal year: This budget was based on forecast sales of 30,000 units during the year.

Fixed costs	$80,000
Subcontracting costs (variable, per unit)	$4
Other variable costs (per unit)	$2
Sales price	$10

You are six months into the fiscal year and have collected the following sales data:

Month	*Actual Sales (units)*
1	2,000
2	2,200
3	1,700
4	1,800
5	2,300
6	2,200

By shopping around, you have held your subcontracting costs to an average of $3.60 per unit. The fixed and other variable costs are conforming to budgets.

1. What was the break-even point based on the original forecast in sales for the Ace Division?
2. What is the revised break-even point?
3. What trends in the above information, if any, concern you?
4. Based on the preceding information, prepare a brief report for your boss, summarizing the current status of the Ace Division.

Case Incident 17.1

"Bird-Dogging" the Employee

Ace Electronics, Inc., is a small company located in Centerville. It is owned and operated by Al Abrams, a highly experienced electronics person who founded the company.

Ace's basic product is a walkie-talkie that is sold primarily to the U.S. military. The walkie-talkie units are relatively simple to produce; Ace merely purchases the parts—cables, wires, transistors, and so on—and assembles them with hand tools. Due to this moderate level of complexity, Ace employs semiskilled workers at low wage rates.

Although Ace has made a profit each year since it started production, Al Abrams was becoming increasingly concerned. Over the past six years, he had noticed a general decline in employee morale; furthermore, he had observed a decline in his employees' productivity and his company's profit margin.

As a result of his concern, Al asked his supervisors to keep a closer watch on the workers' hour-to-hour activities. In the first week, they discovered two workers in the restroom reading magazines. This "bird-dogging" technique, as management called it, or "slave driving," as the workers called it, failed to increase either production or productivity.

Al recognized that the lack of performance on the part of some employees was affecting the production of everyone. This phenomenon was caused by the balanced assembly line under which the walkie-talkies were assembled. If an employee next to a normally productive employee did not work fast enough, walkie-talkies would back up on the line. Instead of having a backup, however, the assembly line was usually readjusted to the production rate of the slower employees.

In addition, another situation developed to lower productivity and increase unit costs. Ace was required by the government to meet monthly production and delivery schedules. If it failed, a very substantial financial penalty could result. In recent years, the production and delivery schedule had become more difficult to meet. For the last eight months, Al had scheduled overtime to meet the production and delivery schedule and thus avoid the financial penalty. This overtime increased unit production costs and caused another problem: Many employees began to realize that if they worked more slowly at the beginning of the month, they could receive more overtime at the end of the month. Even the senior employees were slowing down to increase their overtime wages.

Al was very reluctant to fire employees, especially senior employees. Even if he was inclined to do so, it was difficult to catch employees slowing down or provide any reasonable evidence for such a rash action. Al was frustrated and perplexed.

Questions

1. Describe in detail the control dilemma at Ace Electronics.
2. Are Al Abrams and the employees getting the same feedback? Why or why not?
3. What should Al do?

Case Incident 17.2

Mickey Mouse Controls

Jean: Hey, John, I could sure use some help. We regional supervisors are caught in the middle. What do you do about all this red tape we're having to put up with? The accounting department is all bothered about the way people are padding their expenses and about the cost of luncheons and long-distance calls. You know—their answer is nothing but more red tape.

John: Well, Jean, I don't know. I'm feeling the heat too. Upper management wants us to maintain our contacts with our brokers and try to get the money out in loans. So we push the district supervisors to see our best contacts or at least call them frequently. Yet lately, I've been having a heck of a time getting my people reimbursed for their expenses. Now the accounting department is kicking because we spend a few bucks taking someone to lunch or making a few long-distance calls.

Jean: I really don't know what to do, John. I'll admit that some of my people tend to charge the company for expenses that are for their personal entertainment. But how can I tell whether they're buttering up a broker or just living it up on the company? The accounting department must have some receipts and records to support expenses. Yet I think that getting a receipt from a parking lot attendant is carrying this control stuff too far. As a matter of fact, the other day, I caught a taxi at the airport and failed to get a receipt—I'll bet I have a hard time getting that money from the company even if I sign a notarized affidavit.

John: Well, the way I handle those things is to charge the company more for tips than I actually give—and you know they don't require receipts for tips. I just don't know how to decide whether those reimbursement receipts that I sign for my people are legitimate. If I call people up and ask about some items on a reimbursement request, they act as though I'm making a charge of grand larceny. So far, I've decided to sign whatever requests they turn in and leave the accounting department to scream if it wants to. The trouble is that I don't have any guidelines as to what is reasonable.

Jean: Yeah, but I don't want to ask questions about that because it would just result in more controls! It isn't up to me to be a policeman for the company. The accounting department sits back looking at all those figures—it should watch expenses. I ran into someone from the department the other day on what she called an internal audit trip, and she told me that they aren't in a position to say whether a $40 lunch at a restaurant is necessary to sell a loan. She said that the charge was made by one of my people and that I should check it out! Am I a regional production person or am I an accountant? I've got enough to do meeting my regional quota with my five district salespeople. I can't go snooping around to find out whether they're taking advantage of the company. They may get the idea that I don't trust them, and I've always heard that good business depends on trust. Besides, our department makes the company more money than any other one. Why shouldn't we be allowed to spend a little of it?

John: Well, I say that the brass is getting hot about a relatively small problem. A little fudging on an expense account isn't going to break the company. I learned the other day that the accounting department doesn't require any receipts from the securities department people. They just give them a per diem for travel and let them spend it however they want to, just so long as they don't go over the allotted amount for the days that they're on trips.

Jean: Now that sounds like a good idea. Why can't we do that? It sure would make my life easier. I don't want to get a guilt complex about signing reimbursement requests that may look a little out of line. Why should I call an employee on the carpet for some small expense that may be the reason we got the deal? Performance is our job, so why can't the company leave us alone? They should let us decide what it takes to make a deal. If we don't produce the loans, we should catch flak about something that's important—not about these trifling details.

John: Jean, I've got to run now. But honestly, if I were you, I wouldn't worry about these Mickey Mouse controls. I'm just going to do my job and fill in the form in order to stay out of trouble on the details. It's not worth getting upset about.

Questions

1. Has the company imposed overly restrictive controls? Explain why or why not.
2. Do you think the company has a good conception of control tolerances? Why or why not?
3. What should Jean do?

References and Additional Readings

1. Jeremy Main, *Quality Wars* (New York: Free Press, 1994), pp. 132–33.
2. J. M. Juran, *Managerial Breakthrough,* rev. ed. (New York: McGraw-Hill, 1995), pp. 203–205.
3. Ibid.
4. For a discussion of some relevant studies, see Arnold S. Tannenbaum, "Control in Organizations: Individual Adjustment in Organization Performance," *Administrative Science Quarterly,* September 1962, pp. 241–46; Klaus Bartolke, Walter Eschweiler, Dieter Flechsenberger, and Arnold S. Tannenbaum, "Worker Participation and the Distribution of Control as Perceived by Members of Ten German Companies," *Administrative Science Quarterly* 27 (1982), pp. 380–97; and Almerinda Forte, "Locus of Control and the Moral Reasoning of Managers," *Journal of Business Ethics,* May 2005, p. 65.
5. Gene W. Ealton and Paul R. Lawrence, *Motivation and Control in Organizations* (Homewood, IL: Richard D. Irwin, 1971), p. 8.
6. James Champy, *Reengineering Management* (New York: Harper Business, 1995), p. 130; and James Champy, "Ambition: Root of Achievement," *Executive Excellence,* March 2000, pp. 5–6.
7. Champy, *Reengineering Management,* p. 130.
8. Timothy J. McMahon and G. W. Perritt, "Toward a Contingency Theory of Organizational Control," *Academy of Management Journal,* December 1973, pp. 624–35.
9. William G. Ouchi and Mary Ann Maguire, "Organizational Control: Two Functions," *Administrative Science Quarterly,* December 1975, pp. 559–71; and William G. Ouchi, "The Transmission of Control through Organizational Hierarchy," *Academy of Management Journal,* June 1978, pp. 174–76.
10. Champy, *Reengineering Management,* p. 140.
11. "Sarbanes-Oxley Act Improves Investor Confidence, but at a Cost," *The CPA Journal,* October 2005, p. 19.
12. Tom Henderson, "Study: Sarbanes-Oxley Compliance Cost Grew in '06," *Crain's Detroit Business,* August 13, 2007, p. 25.
13. Deborah Solomon, "Corporate Governance: At What Price? Critics Say the Cost of Complying with Sarbanes-Oxley Is a Lot Higher Than It Should Be," *The Wall Street Journal,* October 17, 2005, p. R3.
14. C. W. Wilkinson, Dorothy Wilkinson, and Gretchen Vik, *Communicating through Letters and Reports,* 9th ed. (Homewood, IL: Richard D. Irwin, 1986).
15. William Stratton, Raef Lawson, and Toby Hatch, "Scorecarding as a Management Coordination and Control System," *Cost Management,* May–June 2004, pp. 36–42.
16. James A. Senn, *Information Technology in Business,* 2nd ed. (Englewood Cliffs, NJ: Prentice Hall, 1998), p. 615; and Raymond McLeod, Jr., *Management Information Systems,* 4th ed. (New York: Macmillan, 1990), p. 30.

Chapter Eighteen

Appraising and Rewarding Performance

Learning Objectives

After studying this chapter, you will be able to:

1. Define performance.
2. Explain the determinants of performance.
3. Define performance appraisal.
4. Describe the major performance appraisal methods.
5. Explain the contents of a job description.
6. Discuss common errors made in performance appraisals.
7. Suggest ways to make performance appraisal systems more legally acceptable.
8. Define compensation.
9. Outline desirable preconditions for implementing a merit pay program.

Chapter Preview

Candy making is a fun business, and so it's no surprise that it's fun to work at the Jelly Belly Candy Company of Fairfield, California. But at this family-owned company, there's no fooling around when it comes to promoting employee performance and job satisfaction. So when Jelly Belly decided to overhaul and automate its antiquated employee performance management (EPM) process, it was looking for a serious solution to help give its employees across the United States fair, accurate appraisals.

The Jelly Belly Candy Company makes Jelly Belly brand jelly beans in 50 flavors, as well as candy corn and other treats. Introduced in 1976 and named by former U.S. president Ronald Reagan as his favorite candy, the company's jelly beans are exported worldwide. Herman Goelitz Candy was founded in 1869 by Albert and Gustav Goelitz, whose great-grandsons own and run Jelly Belly today.

A committee set up by the company selected Halogen eAppraisal™, a Web-based employee performance and talent management application from Halogen Software. "We liked the way it looked, and we really liked the user-friendliness of it. It's easy for the managers to use and it's customizable without overwhelming them," Poulos said. After two days of training by Halogen staff, four members of Jelly Belly's HR team set out to train the company's supervisors on the new system. About 50 managers received a crash course in using Halogen eAppraisal, and then used it to complete annual evaluations in May. Jelly Belly's HR team is now customizing the software to include more relevant competencies and to respond to comments from managers and staff on the new system.

The new automated employee performance appraisal system has completely formalized and organized Jelly Belly's employee evaluation process. "It allows us to standardize competencies across job classifications, add signature and comment sections to make our process more interactive, and increase accessibility for remote managers," Brown said.

Under Jelly Belly's old system, employees conducting reviews started from scratch once a year with new performance journals. Halogen eAppraisal will let them log notes throughout the year and regularly update their on-line appraisals. Employees use one consistent form to add comments and to sign their appraisals.

Source: Adapted from Web site of Halogen Software, "A Sweet Employee Performance Appraisal System for Jelly Belly," www.halogensoftware.com.

Analyzing Management Skills

Do you feel that a person's pay should be based on his or her performance? Why or why not?

Applying Management Skills

Recall a time when you were rewarded for an activity based on how well you completed the task. Did the reward motivate you to do a better job?

UNDERSTANDING PERFORMANCE

performance
Degree of accomplishment of the tasks that make up an employee's job.

Performance refers to the degree of accomplishment of the tasks that make up an employee's job. It reflects how well an employee is fulfilling the requirements of the job. Often confused with effort, which refers to energy expended, performance is measured in terms of results. Because many organizations have become very results oriented in the last decade, more and more emphasis is being placed on measuring performance.

Determinants of Performance

effort
Results from being motivated; refers to the amount of energy an employee uses in performing a job.

abilities
Personal characteristics used in performing a job.

role perception
Direction in which employees believe they should channel their efforts on their jobs.

Job performance is the net effect of an employee's effort as modified by abilities, role perceptions, and results produced. This implies that performance in a given situation can be viewed as resulting from the interrelationships among effort, abilities, role perceptions, and results produced.

Effort, which results from being motivated, refers to the amount of energy an employee uses in performing a job. **Abilities** are personal characteristics used in performing a job. Abilities usually do not fluctuate widely over short periods of time. **Role perception** refers to the direction in which employees believe they should channel their efforts on their jobs. The activities and behavior employees believe are necessary in the performance of their jobs define their role perceptions. The results produced are usually measured by standards created by the degree of attainment of management-directed objectives.

To attain an acceptable level of performance, a minimum level of proficiency must exist in each of the performance components. Similarly, the level of proficiency in any one of the performance components can place an upper boundary on performance. Studies indicate

Management Illustration 18.1

MEASURING PERFORMANCE OF THE CEO AT BANK OF AMERICA

As a result of new government regulations, stockholders now have more information available to them than ever about how a firm measures CEO performance and how those measures are used to determine compensation. Instead of just reporting the compensation of their top five executives, companies now must include a "discussion" section that explains how compensation is determined. The new disclosure requirements took effect with annual proxy statements filed with the Securities and Exchange Commission after December 2006. Those statements began showing up in the mailboxes of shareholders in the spring 2007 reporting season.

For example, in its most recent proxy statement, Bank of America's compensation committee sets forth—in an easy-to-read table—five "performance measures" and the "reasons" that the committee uses those measures. The measures are: revenue, net income, operating earnings per share, shareholder value added, and total stockholder return. "Our financial success begins with our ability to grow revenue," the proxy explains, but it also emphasizes that revenue growth is not sufficient "unless it leads to growth in our net income."

In explaining operating earnings per share, the proxy states that the compensation committee looks "to this measure to make sure that our net income growth is being achieved over time in a manner that is accretive for our stockholders." It goes on to say that the inclusion of shareholder added value as a metric "places specific focus on whether the investments we make in our businesses generate returns in excess of the costs of capital associated with those investments." The proxy also states that Bank of America uses the metric of total stockholder return which takes into account both stock price performance and dividends "as the ultimate means to compare our performance for our stockholders relative to our competitors."

Source: Adapted from Anonymous, "The Art and Science of Measuring CEO Performance," *Better Investing,* December 2007, pp. 45–47.

that the level of performance can be improved and boundaries raised if management empowers employees to become more active in determining and evaluating their performance measures and standards. To accomplish this, however, management has to erase the natural fear of and resistance to empowerment and become advocates of employee involvement. Management Illustration 18.1 describes how the performance of the CEO of Bank of America is measured.

Performance Appraisal Process

Performance appraisal systems that are directly tied to an organization's reward system provide a powerful incentive for employees to work diligently and creatively toward achieving organizational objectives. When properly conducted, performance appraisals not only let employees know how well they are presently performing but also clarify what needs to be done to improve performance.[1]

performance appraisal
Process that involves determining and communicating to employees how they are performing their jobs and establishing a plan for improvement.

Performance appraisal is a process that involves determining and communicating to employees how they are performing their jobs and establishing a plan for improvement. Some of the more common uses of performance appraisals are to make decisions related to merit pay increases, promotions, layoffs, and firings. For example, the present job performance of an employee is often the most significant consideration for determining whether to promote the person. While successful performance in the present job does not necessarily mean an employee will be an effective performer in a higher-level job, performance appraisals do provide some predictive information.

Performance appraisal information can also provide needed input for determining both individual and organizational training and development needs. For example, it can be used to identify individual strengths and weaknesses. These data can then be used to help determine the organization's overall training and development needs. For an individual employee, a completed performance appraisal should include a plan outlining a specific training and development program.

Another important use of performance appraisals is to encourage performance improvement. In this regard, performance appraisals are used as a means of communicating to employees how they are doing and suggesting needed changes in behavior, attitude, skill, or knowledge. This type of feedback clarifies for employees the job expectations the manager holds. Often, this feedback must be followed by coaching and training by the manager to guide an employee's work efforts.

To work effectively, performance appraisals must be supported by documentation and a commitment by management to make them fair and effective. Typical standards for the performance appraisal process are that it be fair, accurate (facts, not opinions, should be used), include as much direct observation as possible, be consistent, and contain as much objective documentation as possible. The amount and types of documentation necessary to support decisions made by management vary, but the general rule of thumb is to provide enough varied documentation to allow anyone evaluating the performance of an employee to generally come to the same conclusion as the manager.

An additional concern in organizations is how often to conduct performance appraisals. No real consensus exists on this question, but the usual answer is as often as necessary to let employees know what kind of job they are doing and, if performance is not satisfactory, the measures they must take to improve. For many employees, this cannot be accomplished through one annual performance appraisal. Therefore, it is recommended that for most employees, informal performance appraisals should be conducted two or three times a year in addition to the annual performance appraisal.

PERFORMANCE APPRAISAL METHODS

An early method of performance appraisal used in the United States was described as follows:

> On the morning following each day's work, each workman was given a slip of paper informing him in detail just how much work he had done the day before, and the amount he had earned. This enabled him to measure his performance against his earnings while the details were fresh in his mind.[2]

This method of performance appraisal was effective in that it gave immediate feedback and tied pay to performance. Since then, the number and variety of performance appraisal methods have dramatically increased. The following sections describe the performance appraisal methods used in businesses today.

Goal Setting, or Management by Objectives (MBO)

In addition to being a useful method for directing the organization's objective-setting process, management by objectives (MBO) can also be used in the performance appraisal process. The value of linking the MBO program to the appraisal process is that employees tend to support goals if they agree the goals are acceptable and if they expect to be personally successful in their efforts. Employee acceptance (by giving the employee a stake in the MBO process) is certainly a powerful motivator for considering the MBO process. The typical MBO process consists of:

1. Establishing clear and precisely defined statements of objectives for the work an employee is to do.
2. Developing an action plan indicating how these objectives are to be achieved.
3. Allowing the employee to implement this action plan.

FIGURE 18.1
Sample Objectives

To answer all customer complaints in writing within three days of receipt of complaint.
To reduce order-processing time by two days within the next six months.
To implement the new computerized accounts receivable system by August 1.

4. Appraising performance based on objective achievement.
5. Taking corrective action when necessary.
6. Establishing new objectives for the future.

If an employee is to be evaluated on the objectives set in the MBO process, several requirements must be met. First, objectives should be quantifiable and measurable; objectives whose attainment cannot be measured or at least verified should be avoided where possible. Objectives should also be challenging, yet achievable, and they should be expressed in writing and in clear, concise, unambiguous language. Figure 18.1 lists some sample objectives that meet these requirements.

Production Standards

production standards approach
Performance appraisal method most frequently used for employees who are involved in physically producing a product; is basically a form of objective setting for these employees.

The **production standards approach** to performance appraisal is most frequently used for employees who are involved in physically producing a product and is basically a form of objective setting for these employees. It involves setting a standard or an expected level of output and then comparing each employee's performance to the standard. Generally, production standards should reflect the normal output of an average person. Production standards attempt to answer the question of what is a fair day's output. Several methods can be used to set production standards. Figure 18.2 summarizes some of the more common methods.

An advantage of the production standards approach is that the performance review is based on highly objective factors. Of course, to be effective, the standards must be viewed by the affected employees as being fair. The most serious criticism of production standards is a lack of comparability of standards for different job categories.

Essay Appraisal

essay appraisal method
Requires the manager to describe an employee's performance in written narrative form.

The **essay appraisal method** requires the manager to describe an employee's performance in written narrative form. Instructions are often provided to the manager as to the topics to be covered. A typical essay appraisal question might be, "Describe, in your own words, this employee's performance, including quantity and quality of work, job knowledge, and ability to get along with other employees. What are the employee's strengths and weaknesses?"

FIGURE 18.2
Frequently Used Methods for Setting Production Standards

Method	Areas of Applicability
Average production or work	When tasks performed by all employees are the same or approximately the same.
Performance of specially selected employees	When tasks performed by all employees are basically the same, and it would be cumbersome and time-consuming to use the group average.
Time study	Jobs involving repetitive tasks.
Work sampling	Noncyclical types of work in which many different tasks are performed and there is no set pattern or cycle.
Expert opinion	When none of the more direct methods (described above) applies.

The primary problem with essay appraisals is that their length and content can vary considerably (depending on the manager) and the method can be very subjective (whereas objective measures are more defensible). For instance, one manager may write a lengthy statement describing an employee's potential and saying little about past performance; another manager may concentrate on the employee's past performance. Thus, essay appraisals are difficult to compare. The writing skill of a manager can also affect the appraisal. An effective writer can make an average employee look better than the actual performance warrants.

Critical-Incident Appraisal

critical-incident appraisal
Requires the manager to keep a written record of incidents, as they occur, involving job behaviors that illustrate both satisfactory and unsatisfactory performance of the employee being rated.

The **critical-incident appraisal** method requires the manager to keep a written record of incidents, as they occur, involving job behaviors that illustrate both satisfactory and unsatisfactory performance of the employee being rated. As they are recorded over time, the incidents provide a basis for evaluating performance and providing feedback to the employee.

The main drawback to this approach is that the manager is required to jot down incidents regularly, which can be a burdensome and time-consuming task. Also, the definition of a critical incident is unclear and may be interpreted differently by different managers. Some believe this method can lead to friction between the manager and employees when the employees think the manager is keeping a "book" on them.

Graphic Rating Scale

graphic rating scale
Requires the manager to assess an employee on factors such as quantity of work, dependability, job knowledge, attendance, accuracy of work, and cooperativeness.

With the **graphic rating scale** method, the manager assesses an employee on factors such as quantity of work, dependability, job knowledge, attendance, accuracy of work, and cooperativeness. Graphic rating scales include both numerical ranges and written descriptions. Figure 18.3 gives an example of some of the items that might be included on a graphic rating scale that uses written descriptions.

The graphic rating scale method is subject to some serious weaknesses. One potential weakness is that managers are unlikely to interpret written descriptions in the same manner because of differences in background, experience, and personality. Another potential problem relates to the choice of rating categories. It is possible to choose categories that have little relationship to job performance or omit categories that have a significant influence on job performance.

Checklist

checklist
Requires the manager to answer yes or no to a series of questions concerning the employee's behavior.

With the **checklist** method, the manager answers yes or no to a series of questions concerning the employee's behavior. Figure 18.4 lists some typical questions. The checklist can also have varying weights assigned to each question.

Normally, the scoring key for the checklist method is kept by the human resource department; the manager is generally not aware of the weights associated with each question. But because the manager can see the positive or negative connotation of each question, bias can be introduced. Additional drawbacks to the checklist method are that it is time-consuming to assemble the questions for each job category; a separate listing of questions must be developed for each job category; and the checklist questions can have different meanings for different managers.

Behaviorally Anchored Rating Scales (BARS)

behaviorally anchored rating scale (BARS)
Assesses behaviors required to successfully perform a job.

The **behaviorally anchored rating scale (BARS)** method of performance appraisal is designed to assess behaviors required to successfully perform a job. The focus of BARS (and, to some extent, the graphic rating scale and checklist methods) is not on performance

FIGURE 18.3 Sample Items on a Graphic Rating Scale Evaluation Form

Quantity of work (the amount of work an employee does in a workday)

( )	( )	( )	( )	( )
Does not meet requirements.	Does just enough to get by.	Volume of work is satisfactory.	Very industrious, does more than is required.	Superior production record.

Dependability (the ability to do required jobs with a minimum of supervision)

( )	( )	( )	( )	( )
Requires close supervision; is unreliable.	Sometimes requires prompting.	Usually completes necessary tasks with reasonable promptness.	Requires little supervision; is reliable.	Requires absolute minimum of supervision.

Job knowledge (information that an employee should have on work duties for satisfactory job performance)

( )	( )	( )	( )	( )
Poorly informed about work duties.	Lacks knowledge of some phases of job.	Moderately informed; can answer most questions about the job.	Understands all phases of job.	Has complete mastery of all phases of job.

Attendance (faithfulness in coming to work daily and conforming to work hours)

( )	( )	( )	( )	( )
Often absent without good excuse, or frequently reports for work late, or both.	Lax in attendance or reporting for work on time, or both.	Usually present and on time.	Very prompt; regular in attendance.	Always regular and prompt; volunteers for overtime when needed.

Accuracy (the correctness of work duties performed)

( )	( )	( )	( )	( )
Makes frequent errors.	Careless; often makes errors.	Usually accurate; makes only average number of mistakes.	Requires little supervision; is exact and precise most of the time.	Requires absolute minimum of supervision; is almost always accurate.

outcomes but on behaviors demonstrated on the job. The assumption is that these behaviors result in effective performance on the job.

To understand the use and development of a BARS, several key terms must be understood. First, most behaviorally anchored rating scales use the term *job dimension* to mean those broad categories of duties and responsibilities that make up a job. Each job is likely to have several job dimensions, and separate scales must be developed for each one.

Figure 18.5 illustrates a BARS written for rating hotel managers' communication skills. Scale values appear on the left side of the table and define specific categories of performance. Anchors, which appear on the right side of the table, are specific written statements

FIGURE 18.4 Sample Checklist Questions

	Yes	No
1. Does the employee lose his or her temper in public?	____	____
2. Does the employee play favorites?	____	____
3. Does the employee praise people in public when they have done a good job?	____	____
4. Does the employee volunteer to do special jobs?	____	____

FIGURE 18.5 **BARS for Rating Hotel Managers' Communication Skills**

Relevant behavior: Attending departmental staff meetings and involving subordinates in discussions; visiting with executive committee regularly on personal basis; using memos to communicate special instructions and policies to departments; disseminating financial and other operating information to subordinates; conducting periodic meetings with employees.

Scale Values		Anchors
Communicates effectively with staff members and attends meetings frequently	7.00	This manager calls a "town hall" meeting to explain why the hotel will be cutting back staff. Employees are permitted to ask questions and discuss why certain positions in the hotel are being eliminated.
	6.00	During a busy expansion program, this manager increases the frequency of policy committee meetings to improve communications and coordination of the project.
	5.00	
Communicates satisfactorily with staff members and attends some meetings	4.00	Once a week, this manager invites several line employees into his or her office for an informal talk about hotel activities.
	3.00	This manager neglects to discuss with his or her front-office manager the problem of overstaffed bellmen during certain periods of the day, yet expresses concern to the resident manager.
	2.00	
Experiences difficulty in communicating with staff members and attends meetings infrequently	1.00	This manager misses departmental meetings and fails to visit with subordinates individually, but leaves memos around the hotel with instructions on what should be done.
		During weekly executive committee meetings, this manager dismisses most subordinate comments as stupid.

Source: From Terry W. Umbreit, Robert W. Eder, and Jon P. McConnell, "Performance Appraisals: Making Them Fair and Making Them Work," *The Cornell Hotel and Restaurant Administration Quarterly,* February 1986, Vol. 64, No. 4, p. 65. Copyright © 1986 by Sage Publications, Inc. Reprinted by permission of Sage Publications, Inc.

of actual behaviors that, when exhibited on the job, indicate the level of performance on the scale opposite that particular anchor. As the anchor statements appear beside each scale value, they are said to "anchor" the respective scale values along the scale.

Rating performance using a BARS requires the manager to read the list of anchors on each scale to find the group of anchors that best describes the employee's job behavior during the period being reviewed. The scale value opposite that group of anchors is then checked. This process is followed for all of the identified dimensions on the job. A total evaluation is obtained by combining the scale values checked for all of the job dimensions.

A BARS is normally developed through a series of meetings attended by both the manager and employees who are actually performing the job. Three steps are usually followed:

1. Manager and job incumbents identify the relevant job dimensions for the job.
2. Manager and job incumbents write behavioral anchors for each job dimension. As many anchors as possible should be written for each dimension.
3. Manager and job incumbents reach a consensus concerning the scale values to be used and the grouping of anchor statements for each scale value.

The use of a BARS can result in several advantages. First, such scales are developed through the active participation of both the manager and the job incumbents. This increases the likelihood that the method will be accepted. Second, the anchors are developed from the observations and experiences of employees who actually perform the job. Finally, a BARS can be used to provide specific feedback concerning an employee's job performance. One major drawback to the use of such scales is that they take considerable time and commitment to develop. Furthermore, separate rating scales must be developed for different jobs.

FIGURE 18.6
Sample Forced-Choice Set of Statements

Instructions: Rank the following statements according to how they describe the manner in which this employee carries out duties and responsibilities. Rank 1 should be given to the most descriptive and rank 4 to the least descriptive. No ties are allowed.

Rank	Description
_____	Easy to get acquainted with
_____	Places great emphasis on people
_____	Refuses to accept criticism
_____	Thinks generally in terms of money
_____	Makes decisions quickly

Forced-Choice Rating

forced-choice rating
Requires the manager to rank a set of statements describing how an employee carries out the duties and responsibilities of the job.

Many variations of the **forced-choice rating** method exist. The most common practice requires the manager to rank a set of statements describing how an employee carries out the duties and responsibilities of the job. Figure 18.6 illustrates a group of forced-choice statements. The statements are normally weighted, and the weights are generally not known to the manager. After the manager ranks all of the forced-choice statements, the human resource department applies the weights and computes a score. This method attempts to eliminate bias by forcing the manager to rank statements that are seemingly indistinguishable or unrelated. However, the forced-choice method can irritate managers who think they are not being trusted. Furthermore, the results of the forced-choice appraisal can be difficult to communicate to employees.

Ranking Methods

When it becomes necessary to compare the performance of two or more employees, ranking methods can be used. Three of the more commonly used ranking methods are alternation, paired comparison, and forced distribution.

Alternation Ranking

In this ranking method, the names of the employees to be evaluated are listed down the left side of a sheet of paper. The manager is then asked to choose the most valuable employee on the list, cross that name off the left-hand list, and put it at the top of the column on the right side of the paper. The manager is then asked to select and cross off the name of the "least valuable" employee from the left-hand column and move it to the bottom of the right-hand column. The manager then repeats this process for all of the names on the left-hand side of the paper. The resulting list of names in the right-hand column gives a ranking of the employees from most to least valuable.

Paired Comparison Ranking

This method is best illustrated with an example. Suppose a manager is to evaluate six employees. The names of these employees are listed on the left side of a sheet of paper. The manager then compares the first employee with the second employee on a chosen performance criterion, such as quantity of work. If the manager thinks the first employee has produced more work than the second employee, she or he places a check mark by the first employee's name. The first employee is then compared to the third, fourth, fifth, and sixth employees on the same performance criterion. A check mark is placed by the name of the employee who produced the most work in each of these paired comparisons. The process is repeated until each employee has been compared to every other employee on all of the chosen performance criteria. The employee with the most check marks is considered to be the

Management Illustration 18.2

MICROSOFT'S PERFORMANCE APPRAISAL SYSTEM

Microsoft's 78,565 employees generated revenue of $51.12 billion for fiscal year 2007, which ended June 30, continuing a long pattern of enviable growth and profitability. But the company's performance management system fueled widespread dissatisfaction among employees and managers.

Employees receive two ratings in performance reviews—one based on current performance and used to determine merit increases, and one for potential or future performance that's used to set stock awards.

Under the old system, managers assigned current performance ratings of 0 to 5 in half-point increments based on a forced distribution. Because current performance ratings not only determine annual salary increases but also come into play when employees apply for another position within the company, the forced distribution approach was a sore spot. "We also discovered that the old system was not fully effective in creating teamwork because of the forced distribution," Ritchie notes.

Consequently, Microsoft trashed its 0–5 rating scale and adopted a three-point "commitment" scale of "exceeded," "achieved," and "underperformed," with no forced distribution. "Distribution under the new system is about what we expected," Ritchie reports. In the last full cycle, 37 percent of employees received a rating of "exceeded," 58 percent received an "achieved" rating, and 5 percent were rated "underperformed." The general rule is that the top group receives a merit increase 50 percent higher than average performers.

Source: Adapted from Fay Hansen, "Lackluster Performance," *Workforce Management,* November 5, 2007, p. 40.

FIGURE 18.7
Forced Distribution Curve

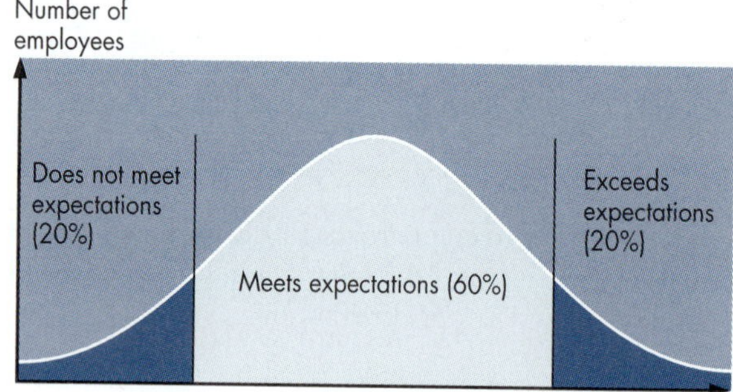

best performer. Likewise, the employee with the fewest check marks is the lowest performer. One major problem with the paired comparison method is that it becomes unwieldy when comparing large numbers of employees.

Forced Distribution

This method requires the manager to compare the performances of employees and place a certain percentage of employees at various performance levels. It assumes the performance level in a group of employees is distributed according to a bell-shaped, or "normal," curve. Figure 18.7 illustrates how the forced distribution method works. The manager is required to rate 60 percent of the employees as meeting expectations, 20 percent as exceeding expectations, and 20 percent as not meeting expectations.

One problem with the forced distribution method is that for small groups of employees, a bell-shaped distribution of performance may not be applicable. Even where the distribution approximates a normal curve, it is probably not a perfect curve. This means some employees will probably not be rated accurately. Also, ranking methods differ dramatically from the other methods in that one employee's performance evaluation is a function of the performance of other employees in the job. Management Illustration 18.2 describes a forced distribution system used by Microsoft.

360-Degree Feedback Assessment

360-degree feedback
Method of performance appraisal that uses input from an employee's managers, peers, customers, suppliers, or colleagues.

In the **360-degree feedback** process, individuals receive ratings from three or four different sources: They assess themselves, and receive assessments from supervisors, peers, and from subordinates. It provides for performance feedback from the full circle of daily contacts that an employee might have, ranging from mailroom personnel to customers to bosses to peers.

Organizations primarily use 360-degree feedback for developmental purposes, to provide information to individuals being rated about how raters perceive their leadership and work behaviors. They suggest that the advantages of using multiple raters include the ability to observe and rate various job facets of each person being rated, greater reliability, enhanced fairness, and increased acceptance. 360-degree feedback furthers management or leadership development. Providing feedback to managers about how they are viewed by direct subordinates, peers, and customers should prompt behavior change. By increasing managerial self-awareness through formalized 360-degree feedback, an organization's culture will become more participatory and will be able to react more quickly to the needs of internal and external customers.

SELECTING A PERFORMANCE APPRAISAL METHOD

Whatever performance appraisal method an organization uses, it must be job related. Therefore, before selecting a performance appraisal method, job analyses must be conducted and job descriptions written. Normally, job analyses are performed by trained specialists with the organization's human resource department or by outside consultants. Figure 18.8 summarizes the information a job analysis provides.

Job analysis involves not only determining job content but also reporting the results of the analysis. One product of a job analysis is a job description, a formal written document, usually one to three pages long, that should include the following:

- Date written.
- Job status (full-time or part-time).
- Job title.
- Supervision received (to whom the jobholder reports).
- Supervision exercised (who reports to this employee).
- Job summary (a synopsis of the job responsibilities).
- Detailed list of job responsibilities.

FIGURE 18.8
Information Provided by Job Analysis

Area of Information	Contents
Job title and location within company	
Organizational relationship	A brief explanation of the number of persons supervised (if applicable) and the job title(s) of the position(s) supervised; a statement concerning supervision received.
Relation to other jobs	Describes and outlines the coordination required by the job.
Job summary	Condensed explanation of the content of the job.
Information concerning job requirements	Varies greatly from job to job and from organization to organization; typically includes information on such topics as machines, tools, and materials; mental complexity and attention required; physical demands; and working conditions.

- Principal contacts (in and outside the organization).
- Competency or position requirements.
- Required education or experience.
- Career mobility (position or positions employee may qualify for next).

leniency
Grouping of ratings at the positive end of the scale instead of spreading them throughout the scale.

After a job description is written, the most appropriate performance appraisal method can be determined.[3]

POTENTIAL ERRORS IN PERFORMANCE APPRAISALS

central tendency
Tendency of raters to rate most employees as doing average or above-average work.

recency
Occurs when performance evaluations are based on work performed most recently, generally work performed one to two months before evaluation.

Several common errors have been identified in performance appraisals. **Leniency** is the grouping of ratings at the positive end of the performance scale instead of spreading them throughout the scale. **Central tendency** occurs when performance appraisal statistics indicate that most employees are evaluated similarly as doing average or above-average work. **Recency** occurs when performance evaluations are based on work performed most recently, generally work performed one to two months before evaluation. Leniency, central tendency, and recency errors make it difficult, if not impossible, to separate the good performers from the poor performers. In addition, these errors make it difficult to compare ratings from different managers. For example, it is possible for a good performer who is evaluated by a manager committing central tendency errors to receive a lower rating than a poor performer who is rated by a manager committing leniency errors.

Another common error in performance appraisals is the **halo effect.**[4] This occurs when managers allow a single prominent characteristic of an employee to influence their judgment on each separate item in the performance appraisal. This often results in the employee receiving approximately the same rating on every item.

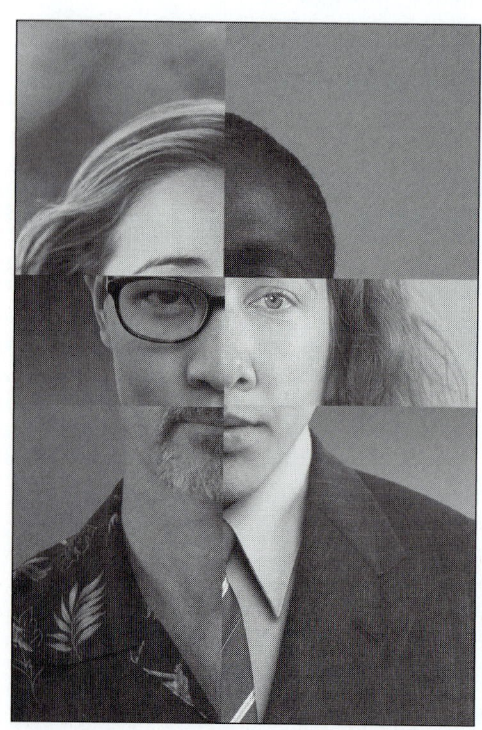

Appearance, social status, dress, race, and sex have influenced many performance appraisals. What better way is there to evaluate employees?

Personal preferences, prejudices, and biases can also cause errors in performance appraisals. Managers with biases or prejudices tend to look for employee behaviors that conform to their biases. Appearance, social status, dress, race, and sex have influenced many performance appraisals. Managers have also allowed first impressions to influence later judgments of an employee. First impressions are only a sample of behavior; however, people tend to retain these impressions even when faced with contradictory evidence.

Because of all the potential problems just cited, some critics of the traditional process suggest that there may be a better way to evaluate employees. Tom Peters suggests that job descriptions and traditional evaluations are relevant only in stable, predictable, and very vertically oriented (functional) organizations.[5] Peters believes organizations that are better able to respond to dynamic competition are adopting "fluidity" concepts and are seriously reviewing the traditional forms of control (performance standards, MBO, and job descriptions).[6] Why? The reasoning is as follows. First, the focus should be on what is important (e.g., flexibility rather than rigidity). Second, the processes should be "living" ones that will encourage change on the part of both the organization and the employee. Third, a simple written contract will encourage creativity and reduce unnecessary and costly layers of bureaucracy.[7] Time will determine whether these ideas have merit.

CONDUCTING EFFECTIVE PERFORMANCE APPRAISALS

halo effect
Occurs when the interviewer allows a single prominent characteristic to dominate judgment of all other traits.

A promising approach to conducting effective performance appraisals is to improve the skills of managers. Suggestions on the specific training managers should receive are often vague, but they usually emphasize that managers should be given training to observe behavior more accurately and judge it fairly.

More research is needed before a definitive set of topics for manager training can be established. However, at a minimum, managers should receive training in (1) the performance appraisal method(s) of the company, (2) the importance of the manager's role in the total appraisal process, (3) the use of performance appraisal information, and (4) the communication skills necessary to provide feedback to the employee.

General dos and don'ts of the performance appraisal process can help managers to not only prevent but reduce the errors that always seem to plague the process. The dos include the following:

1. Base performance appraisal on job performance only and not other factors unrelated to the job.
2. Use only those rating scales that are relevant to the job itself and are indicators of objective performance and attainment.
3. Sincerely work at the appraisal interview process.
4. Be problem solving oriented.

The don'ts include the following:

1. Don't criticize. Be proactive.
2. Carefully avoid the halo effect and leniency errors.
3. Dominate conversations about performance. Encourage employees to speak and to address issues in the evaluation process themselves.
4. Avoid general prescriptions to fix performance. Always present concrete and realizable objectives. Performance goals are the foundation of productivity.

PROVIDING FEEDBACK THROUGH THE APPRAISAL INTERVIEW

After one of the previously discussed methods for developing an employee's performance appraisal has been used, the results must be communicated to the employee. Unless this interview is properly conducted, it can and frequently does result in an unpleasant experience for both manager and employee. Following are some of the more important factors influencing success or failure of appraisal interviews:

- The more employees participate in the appraisal process, the more satisfied they are with the appraisal interview and with the manager and the more likely they are to accept and strive to meet performance improvement objectives.
- The more a manager uses positive motivational techniques (e.g., recognizing and praising good performance), the more satisfied the employee is likely to be with the appraisal interview and with the manager.
- The mutual setting by the manager and the employee of specific performance improvement objectives results in more improvement in performance than does a general discussion or criticism.
- Discussing and solving problems that may be hampering the employee's current job performance improve the employee's performance.

Management Illustration 18.3

BAXTER STOREY'S PERFORMANCE APPRAISAL SYSTEM

Baxter Storey is the UK's largest independent food service operator, providing restaurant and catering services to blue-chip companies including Barclays, ITV, and Oracle. The vast majority of Baxter Storey's employees work remotely on client sites, rather than at the company's Reading headquarters. For the company's HR team, led by HR director Linda Halliday, that raises obvious challenges in terms of coordinating the appraisal process and identifying talent in individual units that may be located several hundred miles away. It was then that they came across Talent Toolbox from Learnpurple, and it seemed to fit the bill by making appraisals faster and simpler. Talent Toolbox is a Web-based communications platform that provides a review and appraisal system that can be customized to fit the needs of an individual company and its employees. The toolbox has been such a success for Baxter Storey that the company is now planning to extend its use of the system.

When appraisals are ready for online completion, the system prompts line managers and their employees via an e-mail that provides a link to the Talent Toolbox system. The employees grade themselves against a predefined list of competencies, and their line manager also grades them. Comments can be added, along with examples to support the grades given. Talent Toolbox then generates a single form showing both sets of grades and comments. This is used at a formal appraisal meeting between the employee and manager, at which the employee's performance is analyzed and their training needs discussed.

Finally, the manager inputs the details of this discussion and the results are fed back to Halliday and her team. Throughout the process, they can track who has completed the necessary forms, how many meetings have been held, and which appraisals have been completed.

Source: Adapted from Jessica Twentyman, "The Golden Ingredient," *Personnel Today,* November 20, 2007, pp. 32–33.

- Areas of job performance needing improvement that are most heavily criticized are less likely to be improved than similar areas of job performance that are less heavily criticized.
- The more employees are allowed to voice their opinions during the interview, the more satisfied they will be with the interview.
- The amount of thought and preparation employees independently devote before the interview increases the benefits of the interview.
- The more the employee perceives that performance appraisal results are tied to organizational rewards, the more beneficial the interview will be.

The interviewer must also be aware that many employees are skeptical about the appraisal process because of its potential association with punishment. Research has shown that this most often happens because the employee does not trust the manager's motivation; the feedback is unclear; the employee does not respect the manager's judgment; the feedback is inconsistent with the opinions of others; and the employee has had negative past experiences with the evaluation, appraisal, or feedback process. Most of these problems can be overcome by simply accentuating the positive as the basis for the interview, feedback, and correction processes.[8] Management Illustration 18.3 describes the feeedback system at Baxter Storey.

DEVELOPING PERFORMANCE IMPROVEMENT PLANS

Earlier in this chapter, we stated that a completed performance appraisal should include a performance improvement plan. This important step is often ignored. However, managers must recognize that an employee's development is a continuous cycle of setting performance goals, providing training necessary to achieve the goals, assessing performance as to the accomplishment of the goals, and then setting new, higher goals. A performance improvement plan consists of the following components:

1. *Where are we now?* This question is answered in the performance appraisal process.
2. *Where do we want to be?* This requires the evaluator and the person being evaluated to mutually agree on the areas that can and should be improved.
3. *How does the employee get from where he or she is now to where he or she wants to be?* This component is critical to the performance improvement plan. Specific steps to be taken must be agreed on. The steps may include training the employee will need to improve his or her performance and should also include how the evaluator will help the employee achieve the performance goals.

PERFORMANCE APPRAISAL AND THE LAW

Title VII of the Civil Rights Act permits the use of a bona fide performance appraisal system. Performance appraisal systems generally are not considered to be bona fide when their application results in adverse effects on minorities, women, or older employees.

A number of court cases have ruled that performance appraisal systems used by organizations were discriminatory and not job-related. In one case involving layoffs, *Brito et al. v. Zia Company,* Spanish-surnamed workers were reinstated with back pay because the company had used a performance appraisal system of unknown validity in an uncontrolled and unstandardized manner. In *Mistretta v. Sandia Corporation,* performance appraisals were used as the main basis of layoff decisions affecting a disproportionate number of older employees. The judge awarded the plaintiffs double damages plus all court costs.

In *Chamberlain v. Bissel, Inc.,* an evaluator expressed dissatisfaction with an employee's performance but did not inform the employee that his job was in jeopardy. On being terminated, the emloyee sued the company claiming he had never been warned that he might be dismissed. The Michigan state court ruled the company had been negligent in not informing the employee that he might be fired and awarded the employee $61,354 in damages.

In *Price Waterhouse v. Hopkins,* the plaintiff, Ann Hopkins, charged she was denied a partnership at Price Waterhouse because of sexual stereotyping. Although Hopkins had generated more new business and logged more billable hours than any other candidate for partner, she was denied partnership consideration because the partners concluded she lacked the proper interpersonal skills. The court ruled that the interpersonal skills category was a legitimate performance evaluation measure, but it found that some of the evaluations of Hopkins were sexual stereotyping. For example, one member of the firm advised Hopkins to walk, talk, and dress in a more feminine fashion. In its decision, the Supreme Court found that Price Waterhouse had violated Title VII of the Civil Rights Act and stated that evaluating employees by assuming or insisting that they match a stereotype was illegal.

The recent wave of layoffs has produced lawsuits in which former employees have alleged discrimination as a cause of termination.

Many suggestions have been offered for making performance appraisal systems more legally acceptable. Some of these include (1) deriving the content of the appraisal system from job analyses; (2) emphasizing work behaviors rather than personal traits; (3) ensuring that the results of appraisals are communicated to employees; (4) ensuring that employees are allowed to give feedback during the appraisal interview; (5) training managers in how to conduct proper evaluations; (6) ensuring that appraisals are written, documented, and retained; and (7) ensuring that personnel decisions are consistent with the performance appraisals.

REWARDING PERFORMANCE

The previously described systems and methods of appraising employee performance are useful only if they are closely tied to the organization's reward system. Appraising performance without a system that ties the results of the appraisal to the organization's reward system creates an environment where employees are poorly motivated.

Organizational Reward System

The organizational reward system consists of the types of rewards the organization offers. **Organizational rewards** include all types of rewards, both intrinsic and extrinsic, that are received as a result of employment by the organization. **Intrinsic rewards** are internal to the individual and are normally derived from involvement in work activities. Job satisfaction and feelings of accomplishment are examples of intrinsic rewards. Most **extrinsic rewards** are directly controlled and distributed by the organization and are more tangible than intrinsic rewards. Figure 18.9 provides examples of both intrinsic and extrinsic rewards.

organizational rewards
All types of rewards, both intrinsic and extrinsic, received as a result of employment by the organization.

intrinsic rewards
Rewards internal to the individual and normally derived from involvement in work activities.

extrinsic rewards
Rewards that are directly controlled and distributed by the organization.

compensation
Composed of the extrinsic rewards offered by the organization and consists of the base wage or salary, any incentives or bonuses, and any benefits employees receive in exchange for their work.

Though intrinsic and extrinsic rewards are different, they are also closely related. Often an extrinsic reward provides the recipient with intrinsic rewards. For example, an employee who receives an extrinsic reward in the form of a pay raise may also experience feelings of accomplishment (an intrinsic reward) by interpreting the pay raise as a sign of a job well done.

Compensation consists of the extrinsic rewards offered by the organization and includes the base wage or salary, any incentives or bonuses, and any benefits employees receive in exchange for their work. The base wage or salary is the hourly, weekly, or monthly pay employees receive. Incentives are rewards offered in addition to the base wage or salary and are usually directly related to performance. Benefits are rewards employees receive because of their employment with the organization. Paid vacations, health insurance, and retirement plans are examples of benefits.

Relating Rewards to Performance

The free enterprise system is based on the premise that rewards should depend on performance. This performance-reward relationship is desirable not only at the corporate level but also at the individual employee level. The underlying idea is that employees will be motivated when they believe good performance will lead to rewards. Unfortunately, many extrinsic rewards provided by organizations do not lend themselves to being related to performance. For example, paid vacations, insurance plans, and paid holidays are usually determined by organizational membership and seniority rather than by performance.

Other rewards, such as promotion, can and should be related to performance. However, opportunities for promotion may occur only rarely. When available, the higher positions may be filled on the basis of seniority or by someone outside the organization.

FIGURE 18.9
Intrinsic versus Extrinsic Rewards

Intrinsic Rewards	Extrinsic Rewards
Sense of achievement	Formal recognition
Feelings of accomplishment	Fringe benefits
Informal recognition	Incentive payments
Job satisfaction	Base wages
Personal growth	Promotion
Status	Social relationships

Management Illustration 18.4

QUARTERLY PERFORMANCE APPRAISALS

Trufast, a $40 million manufacturer of fasteners in Bryan, Ohio, had a problem. Staff turnover had hit 30 percent, and unmotivated employees were keeping profit margins stuck in the single digits. CEO Brian Roth needed to retain his best workers and boost everyone's productivity, but traditional annual reviews weren't helping. "The only thing the review did was cover the previous two weeks of performance," says Roth. "Then it motivated the employee for another two weeks with a 3 percent raise. Basically, it was worthless."

Roth decided to assess and reward more frequently. Working with Gary Harpst, CEO of the consulting firm Six Disciplines, he launched a quarterly review system for his 80 factory employees. At the end of each quarter workers meet with their managers, who award them up to 25 points in each of four categories: initiative, aptitude, flexibility, and attitude. Those with a score of 70 or higher receive incentive pay from a pool funded with 10 percent of pretax profits. The higher the score, the higher the bonus. The average recipient collects about 75 additional cents for every hour worked during the previous quarter, but some top-tier performers land an extra $1.50 per hour. More than 90 percent of Trufast's line workers now receive some bonus, but there's a stick with that carrot: Those who score below 70 two quarters in a row are terminated. The bonus program costs Trufast $250,000 a year, and Roth calculates a return on investment of 15 to 18 percent.

The new system has been well received, says Chris Whalen, a material handler at Trufast for three years. "Truthfully, a review once a year didn't mean anything," Whalen says. "Quarterly reviews are more targeted with reality. We get a clear view of what's expected, we know where we stand, and we get more money if we do a good job."

Roth would like to use them elsewhere in the business but says it's tricky for jobs in quality engineering or management, where the duties aren't easily defined. "My employees keep asking when the next review is and what they need to do to score well on it," he says. "That tells me all I need to know."

Source: Adapted from Scott Westcott, "Putting an End to End-of-Year Reviews," *Inc.*, December 2007, p. 58.

A key organizational variable that can be used to reward individuals and reinforce performance is basing an employee's pay raise on his or her performance (often referred to as *merit pay*). Management Illustration 18.4 describes how one company relates pay to performance.

If relating rewards to performance is desirable, why is it not more widespread? One answer is that it is not easy to do; it is much easier to give everybody the same thing, as evidenced by the ever-popular across-the-board pay increase. Relating rewards to performance requires that performance be accurately measured, and this is not easy. It also requires discipline to actually match rewards to performance. Another reason is that many union contracts require that certain rewards be based on totally objective variables, such as seniority. While no successful formula for implementing a merit pay program has been developed, a number of desirable preconditions have been identified and generally accepted:[9]

1. *Trust in management.* If employees are skeptical of management, it is difficult to make a merit pay program work.
2. *Absence of performance constraints.* Because pay-for-performance programs are usually based on individual ability and effort, the job must be structured so that an employee's performance is not hampered by factors beyond his or her control.
3. *Trained managers.* Managers must be trained in setting and measuring performance standards.
4. *Good measurement systems.* Performance should be based on criteria that are job specific and focus on results achieved.
5. *Ability to pay.* The merit portion of the salary-increase budget must be large enough to get employees' attention.

6. *Clear distinction between cost of living, seniority, and merit pay.* In the absence of strong evidence to the contrary, employees will naturally assume a pay increase is an economic or a longevity increase.
7. *Well-communicated total pay policy.* Employees must have a clear understanding of how merit pay fits into the total pay picture.
8. *Flexible reward schedule.* It is easier to establish a credible pay-for-performance plan if all employees do not receive pay adjustments on the same date.

Summary

1. *Define performance.* Performance refers to the degree of accomplishment of the tasks that make up an employee's job.
2. *Explain the determinants of performance.* Job performance is the net effect of an employee's effort in terms of abilities, role perceptions, and results produced. This implies that performance in a given situation can be viewed as resulting from the interrelationships among effort, abilities, role perceptions, and results produced. Effort refers to the amount of energy an employee expends in performing a job. Abilities are personal characteristics used in performing a job. Role perception refers to the direction in which employees believe they should channel their efforts on their jobs.
3. *Define performance appraisal.* Performance appraisal involves determining and communicating to an employee how he or she is performing the job and establishing a plan for improvement.
4. *Describe the major performance appraisal methods.*
   a. Evaluation by objectives involves using the objectives set in the management-by-objectives process as a basis for performance appraisal.
   b. The production standards approach involves setting a standard or expected level of output and then comparing each employee's performance to the standard.
   c. The essay appraisal method requires the manager to describe an employee's performance in written narrative form.
   d. The critical-incident appraisal method requires the manager to keep a written record of incidents, as they occur, involving job behaviors that illustrate both satisfactory and unsatisfactory performance by the employee being rated.
   e. The graphic rating scale method requires the manager to assess an individual on factors such as quantity of work, dependability, job knowledge, attendance, accuracy of work, and cooperativeness.
   f. The checklist method requires the manager to answer yes or no to a series of questions concerning the employee's behavior.
   g. The behaviorally anchored rating scale (BARS) method is designed to assess behaviors required to successfully perform a job.
   h. The forced-choice rating method requires the manager to rank a set of statements describing how an employee carries out the duties and responsibilities of the job.
   i. Ranking methods (alternation, paired comparison, and forced distribution) require the manager to compare the performance of an employee to the performance of other employees.
   j. 360-degree feedback involves managers, peers, customers, suppliers, or colleagues completing questionnaires on the employee being assessed.
5. *Explain the contents of a job description.* A job description should include the following: date written, job status, job title, supervision received, supervision exercised, job

summary, detailed list of job responsibilities, principal contacts, competency or position requirements, required education or experience, and career mobility.

6. *Discuss common errors made in performance appraisals.* Leniency is the grouping of ratings at the positive end of the performance scale instead of spreading them throughout the scale. Central tendency occurs when performance appraisal statistics indicate that most employees are evaluated similarly as doing average or above-average work. Recency occurs when performance evaluations are based on work performed most recently. The halo effect occurs when managers allow a single prominent characteristic of an employee to influence their judgment on each separate item in the performance appraisal.
7. *Suggest ways to make performance appraisal systems more legally acceptable.* Some suggestions include deriving the content of the appraisal system from job analyses; emphasizing work behaviors rather than personal traits; ensuring that the results of the appraisals are communicated to employees; ensuring that employees are allowed to give feedback during the appraisal interview; training managers in conducting proper evaluations; ensuring that appraisals are written, documented, and retained; and ensuring that personnel decisions are consistent with performance appraisals.
8. *Define compensation.* Compensation consists of the extrinsic rewards offered by the organization and includes the base wage or salary, any incentives or bonuses, and any benefits employees receive in exchange for their work.
9. *Outline desirable preconditions for implementing a merit pay program.* Desirable preconditions are trust in management; absence of performance constraints; trained managers; good measurement systems; ability to pay; a clear distinction among cost-of-living, seniority, and merit pay; a well-communicated total pay policy; and a flexible reward schedule.

Review Questions

1. Define performance appraisal.
2. What is performance? What factors influence an employee's level of performance?
3. Identify at least three uses of performance appraisal information.
4. Describe the following methods used in performance appraisal:
   a. Evaluation by objectives
   b. Production standards
   c. Essay
   d. Critical incident
   e. Graphic rating scale
   f. Checklist
   g. Behaviorally anchored rating scale
   h. Forced-choice rating
   i. Ranking methods
   j. 360-degree feedback
5. Define the following types of performance appraisal errors:
   a. Leniency
   b. Central tendency
   c. Recency
   d. Halo effect

6. Outline some factors that influence the success or failure of performance appraisal interviews.
7. Describe some suggestions for making performance appraisal systems more legally acceptable.
8. Identify three basic components of compensation and give examples of each.
9. Outline some preconditions for implementing a merit pay program.

Skill-Building Questions

1. What are your thoughts on discussing salary raises and promotions during the performance appraisal interview?
2. Which method of performance appraisal do you think is the fairest? Why? (You may have to cite an example to explain your reason.) Under which method would you like to work? Why?
3. It has been said that incentive plans work for only a relatively short time. Do you agree or disagree? Why?
4. Why do you think management frequently uses across-the-board pay increases?

SKILL-BUILDING EXERCISE 18.1

Developing a Performance Appraisal System

A large public utility has been having difficulty with its performance evaluation program. The organization has an evaluation program in which all operating employees and clerical employees are evaluated semiannually by their supervisors. The form they have been using is given in Exhibit 1. It has been in use for 10 years. The form is scored as follows: excellent = 5; above average = 4; average = 3; below average = 2; and poor = 1. The scores for each facet are entered in the right-hand column and are totaled for an overall evaluation score.

In the procedure used, each supervisor rates each employee on July 30 and January 30. The supervisor discusses the rating with the employee and then sends the rating to the personnel department. Each rating is placed in the employee's personnel file. If promotions come up, the cumulative ratings are considered at that time. The ratings are also supposed to be used as a check when raises are given.

The system was designed by Joanna Kyle, the personnel manager, who retired two years ago. Her replacement was Eugene Meyer. Meyer graduated 15 years ago with a degree in commerce from the University of Texas. Since then he's had a variety of experiences, mostly in utilities. For about five of these years, he did personnel work.

Eugene has been reviewing the evaluation system. Employees have a mixture of indifferent and negative feelings about it. An informal survey has shown that about 60 percent of the supervisors fill out the forms, give about three minutes to each form, and send them to personnel without discussing them with the employees. Another 30 percent do a little better. They spend more time completing the forms but communicate about them only briefly and superficially with their employees. Only about 10 percent of the supervisors seriously try to do what was intended.

Eugene also found that the forms were rarely used for promotion or pay-raise decisions. Because of this, most supervisors may have thought the evaluation program was a useless ritual. In his previous employment, Eugene had seen performance evaluation as a much more useful experience. It included giving positive feedback to employees, improving future employee performance, developing employee capabilities, and providing data for promotion and compensation.

Eugene has had little experience with design of performance evaluation systems. He believes he should seek advice on the topic.

Write a report summarizing your evaluation of the strengths and weaknesses of the present appraisal system. Recommend some specific improvements or data-gathering exercises to develop a better system for Eugene Meyer.

EXHIBIT 1 Performance Evaluation Form

Performance Evaluation

Supervisors: When you are asked to do so by the personnel department, please complete this form on each of your employees. The supervisor who is responsible for 75 percent or more of an employee's work should complete this form on him or her. Please evaluate each facet of the employee separately. Circle the rating for each facet.

Facet	Rating				
Quality of work	Excellent	Above average	Average	Below average	Poor
Quantity of work	Poor	Below average	Average	Above average	Excellent
Dependability at work	Excellent	Above average	Average	Below average	Poor
Initiative at work	Poor	Below average	Average	Above average	Excellent
Cooperativeness	Excellent	Above average	Average	Below average	Poor
Getting along with co-workers	Poor	Below average	Average	Above average	Excellent

Supervisor's signature ______________________

Employee name ______________________

Employee number ______________________

SKILL-BUILDING EXERCISE 18.2

Who Are "Normal" Employees?

Assume your company has just adopted the form shown in Skill-Building Exercise 18.1 for its performance evaluation system. Assume further that your company has also instituted a policy that every manager's performance appraisals must conform to the accompanying bell-shaped curve. Using this curve, a manager that has 10 employees would have one that would be ranked as excellent, one that would be ranked above average, six that would be ranked average, one that would be ranked as below average, and one that would be ranked unsatisfactory.

Prepare a 10-minute presentation summarizing the problems, advantages, and disadvantages of using such a system.

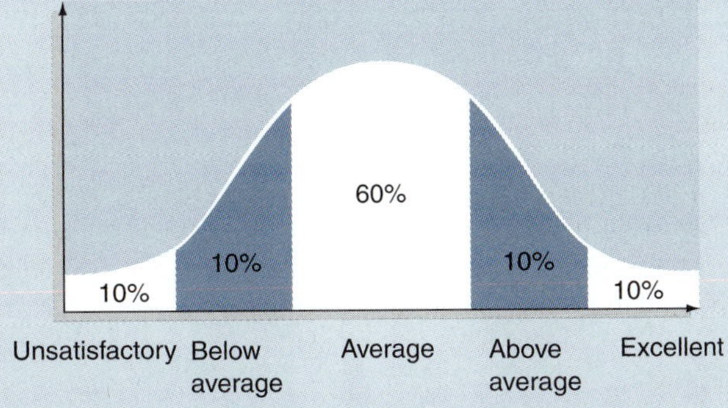

SKILL-BUILDING EXERCISE 18.3

Generally, at your college or university at the end of the semester or quarter you will be asked to complete a form to give your evaluation of the professor. Exhibit 2 gives an example of such a form.

1. Prepare a list of the pluses and minuses of such a system.
2. Suppose there are 60 students in the class and only 34 complete the form. Does this invalidate the evaluation?

EXHIBIT 2

Item	(5) Strongly agree	(4) Agree	(3) Partly agree & partly disagree	(2) Disagree	(1) Strongly disagree	N/A	No of resp.	Inter-polated median
1. Course seemed well planned and organized								
2. Good job covering course objectives/content								
3. Explained complex material clearly								
4. Was approachable and willing to assist								
5. Encouraged students to consult with him/her								
6. Class attendance important in promoting learning of material								
7. Number of assignments was reasonable								
8. Exams covered course content/objectives								
9. Exams were of appropriate difficulty								
10. Instructor was an effective teacher								

Student comments about the class or instructor ______________________________

____

3. What does performance mean in evaluating a professor?

   Be prepared to discuss your answers in class.

Case Incident 18.1

Determining Pay Raises

About four months ago, Judy Holcomb was promoted to supervisor of the claims department for a large, eastern insurance company. It is now time for all supervisors to make their annual salary increase recommendations. Judy doesn't feel comfortable in making these recommendations because she has been in her job only a short time. To further complicate the situation, the former supervisor has left the company and is unavailable for consultation.

There are no formal company restrictions on the kind of raises that can be given, but Judy's boss has said the total amount of money available to Judy for raises would be 8 percent of Judy's payroll for the past year. In other words, if the sum total of the salaries for all of Judy's employees was $200,000, then Judy would have $16,000 to allocate for raises. Judy is free to distribute the raises any way she wants, within reason.

Summarized below is the best information on her employees that Judy can find from the files of the former supervisor of the claims department. This information is supplemented by feelings Judy has developed during her short time as supervisor.

John Thompson: John has been with Judy's department for only five months. In fact, he was hired just before Judy was promoted into the supervisor's job. John is single and seems to be a carefree bachelor. His job performance, so far, has been above average, but Judy has received some negative comments about John from his co-workers. Present salary, $28,000.

Carole Wilson: Carole has been on the job for three years. Her previous performance appraisals have indicated superior performance. However, Judy does not believe the previous evaluations are accurate. She thinks Carole's performance is, at best, average. Carole appears to be well liked by all of her co-workers. Just last year, she became widowed and is presently the sole support for her five-year-old child. Present salary: $29,000.

Evelyn Roth: Evelyn has been on the job for four years. Her previous performance appraisals were all average. In addition, she had received below-average increases for the past two years. However, Evelyn recently approached Judy and told her she believes she was discriminated against in the past due to both her age and sex. Judy thinks Evelyn's work so far has been satisfactory but not superior. Most employees don't seem to sympathize with Evelyn's accusations of sex and age discrimination. Present salary: $27,000.

Jane Simmons: As far as Judy can tell, Jane is one of her best employees. Her previous performance appraisals also indicate she is a superior performer. Judy knows Jane badly needs a substantial salary increase because of some personal problems. She appears to be well respected by her co-workers. Present salary: $28,500.

Bob Tyson: Bob has been performing his present job for eight years. The job is very technical, and he would be difficult to replace. However, as far as Judy can discern, Bob is not a good worker. He is irritable and hard to work with. Despite this, Bob has received above-average pay increases for the past two years. Present salary: $23,000.

Questions

1. Indicate the size of the raise you would give each of these employees.
2. What criteria did you use in determining the size of the raise?
3. What do you think would be the feelings of the other people in the group if they should find out what raises you recommend?
4. Do you think the employees would eventually find out what raises others received? Would it matter?

Case Incident 18.2

Conducting a Performance Appraisal

Plant manager Paul Dorn wondered why his boss, Leonard Hech, had sent for him. Paul thought Leonard had been tough on him lately; he was slightly uneasy at being asked to come to Leonard's office at a time when such meetings were unusual. "Close the door and sit down, Paul," invited Leonard. "I've been wanting to talk to you." After preliminary conversation, Leonard said that because Paul's latest project had been finished, he would receive the raise he had been promised on its completion.

Leonard went on to say that since it was time for Paul's performance appraisal, they might as well do that now. Leonard explained that the performance appraisal was based on four criteria: (1) the amount of high-quality merchandise manufactured and shipped on time, (2) the quality of relationships with plant employees and peers, (3) progress in maintaining employee safety and health, and (4) reaction to demands of top management. The first criterion had a relative importance of 40 percent; the rest had a weight of 20 percent each.

On the first item, Paul received an excellent rating. Shipments were at an all-time high, quality was good, and few shipments had arrived late. On the second item, Paul also was rated excellent. Leonard said plant employees and peers related well to Paul, labor relations were excellent, and there had been no major grievances since Paul had become plant manager.

However, on attention to matters of employee safety and health, the evaluation was below average. His boss stated that no matter how much he bugged Paul about improving housekeeping in the plant, he never seemed to produce results. Leonard also rated Paul below average on meeting demands from top management. He explained that Paul always answered yes to any request and then disregarded it, going about his business as if nothing had happened.

Seemingly surprised at the comments, Paul agreed that perhaps Leonard was right and that he should do a better job on these matters. Smiling as he left, he thanked Leonard for the raise and the frank appraisal.

As weeks went by, Leonard noticed little change in Paul. He reviewed the situation with an associate:

> It's frustrating. In this time of rapid growth, we must make constant changes in work methods. Paul agrees but can't seem to make people break their habits and adopt more efficient ones. I find myself riding him very hard these days, but he just calmly takes it. He's well liked by everyone. But somehow, he's got to care about safety and housekeeping in the plant. And when higher management makes demands he can't meet, he's got to say, "I can't do that and do all the other things you want, too." Now he has dozens of unfinished jobs because he refuses to say no.
>
> As he talked, Leonard remembered something Paul had told him in confidence once. "I take Valium for a physical condition I have. When I don't take it, I get symptoms similar to a heart attack. But I only take half as much as the doctor prescribed." Now, Leonard thought, I'm really in a spot. If the Valium is what is making him so lackadaisical, I can't endanger his health by asking him to quit taking it. And I certainly can't fire him. Yet, as things stand, he really can't implement all the changes we need to fulfill our goals for the next two years.

Questions

1. Do you think a raise was justified in Paul's situation? Explain.
2. What could have been done differently in the performance appraisal session?
3. What can be done now to change the situation?

Case Incident 18.3

The College Admissions Office

Bob Luck was hired to replace Alice Carter as administrative assistant in the admissions office of Claymore Community College. Before leaving, Alice had given a month's notice to the director of admissions, hoping this would allow ample time to locate and train her replacement. Alice's responsibilities included preparing and mailing transcripts at the request of students, mailing information requested by people interested in attending the college, answering the telephone, assisting students or potential enrollees who came to the office, and general supervision of clerical personnel and student assistants.

After interviewing and testing many people for the position, the director hired Bob, mainly because his credentials were good and he made a favorable impression. Alice spent many hours during the next 10 days training Bob. He appeared to be quite bright and seemed to quickly pick up the procedures involved in operating a college admissions office. When Alice left, everyone thought Bob would do an outstanding job.

However, little time had elapsed before people realized that Bob had not caught on to his job responsibilities. Bob seemed to have personal problems that were severe enough to stand in the way of his work. He asked questions about subjects that Alice had covered explicitly; he should have been able to answer these himself if he had comprehended her instructions.

Bob appeared to constantly have other things on his mind. He seemed to be preoccupied with such problems as his recent divorce, which he blamed entirely on his ex-wife, and the distress of his eight-year-old daughter, who missed her father terribly. His thoughts also dwelled on his search for peace of mind and some reasons for all that had happened to him. The director of admissions was aware of Bob's preoccupation with his personal life and his failure to learn the office procedures rapidly.

Questions

1. What would you do at this point if you were the director of admissions?
2. Describe how you might effectively use a performance appraisal in this situation.

References and Additional Readings

1. Patricia M. Buhler, "The Performance Appraisal Process," *Supervision,* November 2005, pp. 14–17.
2. Frederick W. Taylor, *Scientific Management* (New York: Harper & Row, 1911), p. 52.
3. Noel Amerpohl, "Who Writes Your Job Description?" *Pro,* October–November 2005, pp. 8–11.
4. See John W. Rogers, "Halo Effect," *Forbes,* September 26, 2005, p. 246.
5. Tom Peters, *Thriving on Chaos,* (New York: Alfred A. Knopf, 1987), p. 500.
6. Ibid., p. 501.
7. Ibid., 494.
8. Linda Henman, "Putting the Praise in Appraisals," *Security Management,* August 2005, pp. 28–32.
9. Frederick S. Hills, Robert M. Madigan, K. Dow Scott, and Steven E. Markham, "Tracking the Merit of Merit Pay," *Personnel Administrator,* March 1987, pp. 56–57. See also Mary Jo Ducharme, Prabudyal Singh, and Marc Podolsky, "Exploring the Links between Performance Appraisals and Pay Satisfaction," *Compensation and Benefits Review,* September–October 2005, pp. 46–53.

Part **Seven**

Operations Management

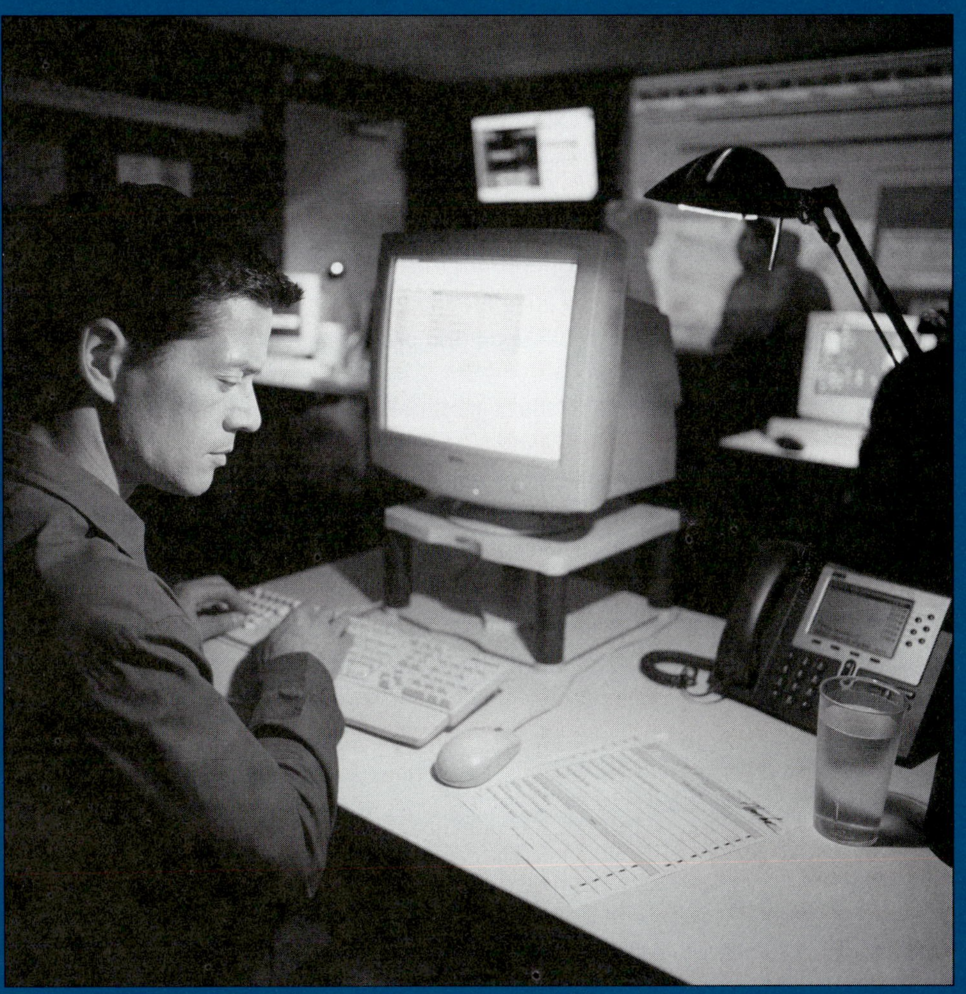

Chapter Nineteen

Operations Management and Planning

Learning Objectives

After studying this chapter, you will be able to:

1. Define operations management.
2. Describe an operating system, and identify the two basic types of operating systems.
3. Differentiate among product/service design, process selection, and site selection decisions.
4. Explain what a materials-handling system is.
5. Describe and give an example of the three basic classifications of facilities layouts.
6. Explain the sociotechnical approach to job design.
7. Describe several computer-related technologies that are currently playing major roles in production/operations management.
8. Outline the three major steps in developing an aggregate operations plan.
9. Summarize the differences between resource allocation and activity scheduling.
10. Distinguish between Gantt charts, the critical path method (CPM), and the program evaluation and review technique (PERT).

Chapter Preview

Igus Inc., whose flagship factory is located in Cologne, Germany, makes more than 28,000 different products that are used in everything from assembly lines to the movable stage for Broadway's *Beauty and the Beast*. Because of the unpredictability of its customers' needs, Igus has to be able to react quickly and is in a state of almost constant innovation. What's different about Igus is the plant's design that enables it to operate exceptionally flexibly. Employees buzz around the plant's enormous space—about the size of three football fields—on shiny scooters. Very little equipment is bolted down, so machines and modular furniture can be rearranged in a moment's notice. Easily accessible, exposed overhead electrical wiring and few obstructive support columns allow Igus to expand, shrink, or relocate departments with minimal disruption. Glass walls separate the factory floor from the office area, which eliminates any real or perceived barriers between departments. The plant has only one cafeteria, one set of restrooms, and one entrance. Additionally, the parking lot has no designated spaces for managers. According to Frank Blasé, Igus's president, "We're trying to be a different kind of company, and our building helps us tremendously in doing that. It creates a holistic system for how to behave."

Blasé also believes the physical environment affects employee creativity: "How can you be creative if you aren't inspired to think differently about a problem? At Igus, all employees have to do is look around: Their factory looks different for a reason." Igus's factory in the United Kingdom has also recently moved into a more modern facility that the company hopes will benefit customers and employees alike.

Sources: Chuck Salter, "This Is One Fast Factory," *Fast Company,* August 2001, pp. 32–33; Michelle Porter, "Fast and Fluid Factory," *Plants, Sites and Parks,* October–November 2001, p. 8; and "Production World: Igus Open Day," *Metalworking Production,* May 22, 2006, p. 9.

Analyzing Management Skills

To what extent do you think the layout and physical facilities of the workplace are important?

Applying Management Skills

Suppose you were designing a small store for selling office supplies to college students. What are some of the major factors you would want to consider in your design?

operations management
Application of the basic concepts and principles of management to those segments of the organization that produce its goods or services.

operations planning
Designing the systems of the organization that produce goods or services; planning the day-to-day operations within those systems.

Operations management, which evolved from the field of production or manufacturing management, deals with the application of the basic concepts and principles of management to those segments of the organization that produce the organization's goods or services. Traditionally, the term *production* brings to mind such things as smokestacks, machine shops, and the manufacture of real goods. Operations management is the management of the production function in any organization—private or public, profit or nonprofit, manufacturing or service.

Operations planning is concerned with designing the systems of the organization that produce the goods or services and with the planning of the day-to-day operations within those systems. The design of the systems that produce the goods or services is a long-range and strategic planning issue, whereas the planning of the day-to-day operations is a short-range and tactical planning issue. This chapter introduces some basic concepts related to operations management, discusses the basic design-related aspects of operations, and covers the day-to-day planning of operations.

THE IMPORTANCE OF OPERATIONS MANAGEMENT

The operations function is only one part of the total organization; however, it is a very important part. The production of goods or services often involves the bulk of an organization's financial assets, personnel, and expenses. The operations process also usually takes up an appreciable amount of time. Thus, because of the resources and time consumed by operations, the management of this function plays a critical role in achieving the organization's goals.

Most operations managers no longer manage in a stable environment with standard products. Changing technology and a strong emphasis on low costs have altered the technical and administrative problems they confront. The modern operations manager must deal not only with low costs but also with product diversity, a demand for high quality, short lead times, and a rapidly changing technology. As a result, an operations manager's problems are now greater and require much more managerial talent than ever before.

OPERATING SYSTEMS AND ACTIVITIES

operating systems
Consist of the processes and activities necessary to turn inputs into goods or services.

Operating systems consist of the processes and activities necessary to turn inputs into goods or services. Operating systems exist in all organizations; they are made up of people, materials, facilities, and information. The end result of an operating system is to add value by improving, enhancing, or rearranging the inputs. Many operating systems take a collection of parts and form them into a more valuable whole. For example, an automobile is a group of separate parts formed into a more valuable whole.

In some situations, the operating system breaks something down from a larger quantity to smaller quantities with more value. A metal shop cuts smaller parts from larger sheets of metal; a butcher produces steaks, hamburger, and other cuts from a side of beef. Both break down a larger quantity into smaller quantities with more value.

A third type of operating system produces services by turning inputs into more useful outputs. Here more emphasis is usually placed on labor and less on materials. For example, an electronics repair shop uses some materials, but the primary value results from the repairer's labor.

Figure 19.1 presents a simplified model of an operating system. The operating system is broader and more inclusive than just the conversion or transformation process. It includes not only the design and operation of the process but also many of the activities needed to get the various inputs (such as product design and scheduling) into the transformation process. Inputs can take on numerous forms (such as managers, workers, equipment, facilities, materials, or information). Many of the activities necessary to get the outputs out of the transformation process (such as inventory control and materials distribution) are also

FIGURE 19.1
Simplified Model of an Operating System

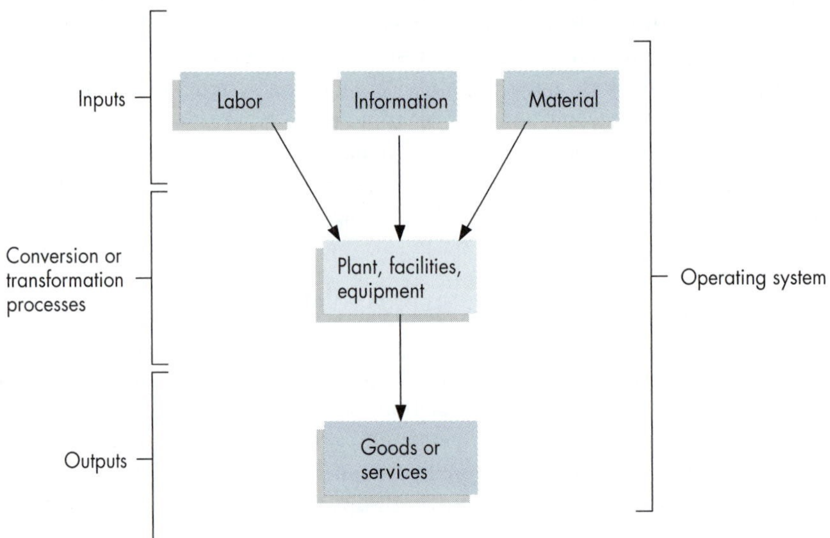

Management Illustration 19.1

THE TOYOTA PRODUCTION SYSTEM
www.toyotaproductionsystem.net

The most famous operating system in the automotive industry is the Toyota production system (TPS). Initially established in the late 1940s, the Toyota operating system is based on the concept of "lean manufacturing." Lean manufacturing is an approach to manufacturing that attempts to minimize everything, from work in process, to part counts, to labor hours. This approach not only reduces costs, it also increases pressure to get things done more quickly as well as correctly. (Lean manufacturing is discussed further in Chapter 20.)

One of the fundamental elements that make TPS successful is the commitment to the customer-first philosophy. However, Toyota views the customer as not only the entity that purchases the final product at the end of the process but each succeeding process or workstation or department in the production process. Under the TPS there are no artificial barriers that wall off one area from another or one department from another. Rather, the entire organization shares problems and must work together to ensure that a solution is found.

The TPS system is still working well for Toyota. According to a 2005 study by Harbour Consulting, Toyota's manufacturing efficiency reached an even higher level by reinvigorating its TPS. The study reported that Toyota's labor productivity lead equated to a $350- to $500-per-vehicle cost advantage relative to other domestic U.S. manufacturers.

In 2007, Toyota passed Ford and became, behind General Motors, the second biggest seller of automobiles in the United States. Ford had held the second position for 75 years.

Sources: "Toyota Still Tops in Operations," *Industrial Engineer,* August 2005, p. 10; Gary Convis, "Learning to Think Lean: Role of Management in a Lean Manufacturing Environment," *Automotive Manufacturing and Production,* July 2001, pp. 64–65; Gary S. Vasilash, "Going Places and Getting Things Done: Think Operating Systems," *Automotive Manufacturing and Production,* April 1998, pp. 62–65; and "Toyota Breaks Ford's 75-Year Lock as 2nd Biggest Auto Seller in the U.S.," *Financial Wire,* January 3, 2008.

included. Management Illustration 19.1 discusses the most famous operating system in the automotive industry.

Basic Types of Operating Systems

continuous flow system
Operating system used by companies that produce large amounts of similar products/services flowing through similar stages of the operating system.

intermittent flow system
Operating system used when customized products and services are produced.

There are two basic types of operating systems. One is based on continuous flows and the other on intermittent flows. Organizations with a **continuous flow system** generally have a standardized product or service. This product or service is often advertised and is immediately available to the customer. The post office, paper mills, petroleum refineries, assembly plants, and fast-food outlets with standardized products (such as McDonald's) are examples. The continuous type of operation has relatively large volumes of identical or similar products or services flowing through similar stages of the operating system.

The second type of operating system, the **intermittent flow** (or *job shop*) **system,** produces customized products and services. Because of its customized nature, organizations using an intermittent operating system usually do not keep an inventory of finished products or offer standardized services. Intermittent flow systems include special-order fabrication shops, hospitals, advertising agencies, and dental offices. Technological advances in the last several years have lowered the per-unit costs associated with many intermittent flow systems.

The continuous flow system usually results in lower unit costs than the intermittent flow system because of economies of scale, specialized labor, and high equipment use. However, continuous flow systems usually require special-purpose equipment that is less flexible and usually more expensive than general-purpose equipment. An example is the customized equipment and machinery used in an automobile assembly plant. Inputs can take on numerous forms (such as managers, workers, equipment, facilities, materials, or information).

To understand the difference between the two types of operating systems, consider the difference between McDonald's and Taco Bell. McDonald's uses a continuous flow operating system. It makes a certain number of products, based on sales history, and hopes people will buy them. Taco Bell uses an intermittent flow operating system. It does not produce anything until a customer places an order.

PRODUCT/SERVICE DESIGN

An organization's product or service determines the design of its operating systems. The design of a new product/service or the redesign of an existing product/service may lead to extensive systems redesign, equipment changes, new personnel, and other modifications. Consider the redesign necessary just to change from one year's automobile models to the next year's models. The design can be functionally sound, yet not economical to produce. Of course, specific functional design objectives must be achieved; however, several alternative designs are often available. When such choices exist, production costs should certainly be one criterion used in the decision.

Historically, design engineers have encountered conflict with operations managers. Design engineers are technically oriented and sometimes lack concern for production methods and costs. On the other hand, operations managers may care more about the production costs and requirements than about the functional requirements of the product. A good example of these differences occurred at Boeing Aircraft in the mid-1990s. During this period, Boeing won a $1.2 billion order from SAS; a chief component of the deal was Boeing's promise to slash the cost of its planes by one-third. However, cutting prices without knowing where the matching savings would come from was not only a gamble but an operations manager's nightmare. When asked to comment, CEO Frank Shrontz said, "We have been technically excellent but [production] process-poor, and we have to change. Now common goals and close communication between design and operations is not only a necessity at Boeing but a mandate."[1] Close communication that fosters an appreciation by both engineers and managers for the common objective of producing a functional product or service at minimum cost is certainly in the best interest of Boeing.

PROCESS SELECTION

process selection
Specifies in detail the processes and sequences required to transform inputs into products or services.

Process selection includes a wide range of decisions about the specific process to be used, the basic sequences of the process, and the equipment to be employed. As suggested earlier, the product/service design decisions and the process selection decisions should be closely coordinated.

The processes and equipment used can play a large role in whether the product or service is competitive. The importance of the process selection decision has become magnified in some industries with the advent of robotics. This is clearly evident in the steel and automotive industries; the Japanese steel and automotive industries have much more modern production processes than their American counterparts. At the most basic level, the types of processes that are normally considered in managerial planning can be categorized as follows: (1) conversion processes (e.g., changing iron ore into steel sheets), (2) fabrication processes (e.g., changing raw materials into some specific form, such as in making sheet metal into a car bumper), (3) assembly processes (e.g., assembling a fender to a car), and (4) testing processes (not usually functional processes but incorporated to ensure quality control).[2] Understanding which process is needed or is in operation is thought to be a key to efficiently organizing production.

Once the overall type of operations process has been selected, specific decisions are needed regarding such factors as whether to use general- or special-purpose equipment, whether to make or buy the components, and how much to automate. In equipment decisions, several factors beyond normal cost should be considered:

1. Availability of operators.
2. Training required for operators.
3. Maintenance record and potential.
4. Availability of parts and services.
5. Supplier assistance in installation and debugging.
6. Compatibility with existing equipment.
7. Flexibility of equipment in handling product variation.
8. Safety of equipment.
9. Expected delivery date.
10. Warranty coverage.

In process selection, the overriding objective is to specify in detail the most economical processes and sequences required to transform the inputs into the desired product or service.

FACILITIES LAYOUT

facilities layout
Process of planning the optimal physical arrangement of facilities, including personnel, operating equipment, storage space, office space, materials-handling equipment, and room for customer or product movement.

After the product/service design has been established, the facilities layout should be planned. **Facilities layout** is essentially the process of planning the optimal physical arrangement of facilities, which includes personnel, operating equipment, storage space, office space, materials-handling equipment, and room for customer service and movement. Facilities layout integrates all of the previous planning of the design process into one physical system. Facilities layout decisions are needed for a number of reasons, including

1. Construction of a new or an additional facility.
2. Obsolescence of current facilities.
3. Changes in demand.
4. Development of a new or redesigned product or process.
5. Personnel considerations: frequent accidents, poor working environment, or prohibitive supervisory costs.

Demand forecasts for the product or service must be considered in establishing the productive capacity of the organization. The costs of running short on space and equipment must be balanced against the costs of having idle space and equipment. A good approach is to match space needs with estimates of future demand but purchase equipment only as it is needed. This allows quick capacity expansion and avoids the costs of idle equipment.

Materials Handling

The materials used and how they are moved around in manufacturing a product or producing a service can have a significant influence on the facility layout. The size, shape, weight, density, and even the flexibility of the materials used can affect the layout. Some materials require special handling and storage with regard to factors such as temperature, humidity, light, dust, and vibration. A materials-handling system is the entire network that receives materials, stores materials, moves materials between processing points and between buildings, and positions the final product or service for delivery to the ultimate customer.

Process selection and the production scheduling and control systems should incorporate materials-handling system needs and limitations (such as wide aisles in the plant to accommodate forklifts).

The design and layout of the facilities must be closely coordinated with the design of the materials-handling system. Process selection and the production scheduling and control systems should incorporate materials-handling system needs and limitations (such as wide aisles in the plant to accommodate forklifts) as part of their design. This view of the materials-handling function includes attention to the (1) handling unit and container design, (2) micromovement (within a production workplace), (3) macromovement (between operations), (4) staging and storage of materials, and (5) control system for directing and tracking activity.[3] While the design of any materials-handling system depends on the specifics of the situation, the principles outlined in Figure 19.2 generally apply.

Basic Layout Classifications

Most layouts are one of three types: product layout, process layout, or fixed-position layout. Which type of layout is used usually depends on the type of product or service produced.

Product layouts usually occur in continuous flow operating systems. In a **product layout,** equipment or services are arranged according to the progressive steps by which the product is made or the customer is serviced. A product layout is generally used when a standardized product is made in large quantities. The assembly line is the ultimate product layout. Automobile assembly plants, cafeterias, and standardized testing centers are normally product layout oriented. In a product layout, all the equipment or services necessary to produce a product or completely serve a customer are located in one area.

product layout
Facilities layout that arranges equipment or services according to the progressive steps by which the product is made or the customer is served.

A product layout is efficient because it simplifies production planning. It also allows workers to specialize in a small number of simple tasks. This kind of layout can cause problems. First, workers who perform a limited number of repetitive tasks often grow bored. Second, an assembly line can move only as fast as the slowest link in the chain.

Process layouts are generally used in intermittent flow operating systems. In a **process layout,** equipment or services of a similar functional type are arranged or grouped together. All X-ray machines are grouped together; all reproduction equipment is grouped together; all drilling machines are grouped together; and so forth. Custom fabrication shops, hospitals, and restaurants are usually arranged in this fashion. With a process layout, a product/customer moves from area to area in the desired sequence of functional

process layout
Facilities layout that groups together equipment or services of a similar functional type.

FIGURE 19.2
Materials-Handling Principles

Source: From *Production & Operations Management,* 5th edition—HSIE 5th ed., by Norman Gaither. Copyright © 1992. Reprinted with permission of SouthWestern College Publishing, a division of Thomson Learning.

1. Materials should move through the facility in direct flow patterns, minimizing zigzagging or backtracking.
2. Related production processes should be arranged to provide for direct material flows.
3. Mechanical materials-handling devices should be designed and located, and material storage locations should be selected so that human effort expended through bending, reaching, lifting, and walking is minimized.
4. Heavy or bulky materials should be moved the shortest distance through locating the processes that use them near receiving and shipping areas.
5. The number of times each material is moved should be minimized.
6. Systems flexibility should allow for unexpected situations such as materials-handling equipment breakdowns, changes in production system technology, and future expansion of production capacities.
7. Mobile equipment should carry full loads at all times; empty and partial loads should be avoided.

operations. When the product or service is not standardized or when the volume of similar products or customers in service at any one time is low, a process layout is preferred because of its flexibility.

The main advantage of the process layout is that employees perform a wider variety of tasks than do people working on assembly lines. As a result, they are less likely to become bored at their jobs and more likely to perform well. A disadvantage of the process layout is that it requires high-skilled workers.

fixed-position layout
A type of facilities layout where the product is too large to move and remains in one place.

The third type of layout is the **fixed-position layout.** In this, the product is too large to move and remains in one place. Manufacturing of very large products, such as ships or airplanes, and construction of most houses and buildings use a fixed-position layout. A disadvantage of the fixed-position layout is that it is not always as efficient as a product layout or process layout.

Computer-based simulations and related models are available to help managers visualize and generate different facility layouts.[4] Most of these simulations and models seek to minimize overall materials-handling costs and floor space requirements.

SITE SELECTION

Management should carefully consider site location. It is easy to become overly engrossed in the operating details and techniques and ignore the importance of site location. Location is an ongoing question; it does not arise only when a facility is outgrown or obsolete. Location decisions relate to offices, warehouses, service centers, and branches, as well as the parent facility. The site selection decision is usually critical for most retail establishments, restaurants, and other organizations that come into direct contact with customers. Each site selection decision involves the total production/distribution system of the organization. Therefore, not only the location of new facilities should be examined; the location of present facilities should also be regularly reviewed for the most effective production/distribution system.

Several options exist for expanding capacity when the present facility is overcrowded:

1. Subcontract work.
2. Add another shift.
3. Work overtime.
4. Move operation to a larger facility.
5. Expand the current facility.
6. Keep the current facility and add another facility elsewhere.

A decision to expand on site, move the entire operation to a larger facility, or add another facility elsewhere means management faces a location decision. A survey of Fortune 500 firms showed that 45 percent of expansions were on site, 43 percent were in new plants at new locations, and only 12 percent were relocations. The popularity of on-site expansions was thought to be due to the advantages of keeping management together, reducing construction time and costs, and avoiding splitting up operations. However, there are arguments for building new plants or relocating. According to Lee Krajewski and Larry Ritzman, reasons for taking these actions might be poor materials handling, employee "job bumping," increasingly complex production control, and a simple lack of space.[5]

Two primary concerns still tend to dominate the location decision, however. The first is financial in nature. Figure 19.3 indicates the principal considerations affecting the financial decision. The second, and no less important, concern is the quality-of-life factor. Most firms are finding out, as Saturn Corporation did when it located in Spring Hill, Tennessee,

Management Illustration 19.2

HOW MANY RESTAURANT CHAINS ARE SELECTING NEW SITE LOCATIONS

By better understanding their best customers and plugging that information into their criteria for selecting new sites, some restaurant chains are enjoying great success in completely new geographical areas. These companies are using a process called "customer segmentation analysis" which infuses their statistical sales forecasts or new-site modeling software with information about the dining, shopping, and commuting habits of their most frequent customers. Traditionally, many chains have used statistical modeling and sales forecasting techniques that relied heavily on Census Bureau data to decipher the demographic characteristics of a given ZIP code area. In contrast, customer segmentation analysis uses what the operators already know about their best customers from focus groups, credit card data, Web site questionnaires, and feedback from blogs to determine the attractiveness of certain areas. Dunkin' Brands, Logan's Roadhouse, Buffalo Wild Wings, McAlister's Deli, Papa Murphy's, IHOP, and Cereality are some of the brands successfully using customer segmentation analysis to identify new sites.

Source: Milford Prewitt, "Customer Data Mining Aids in Quests for Lucrative New Sites," *Nation's Restaurant News,* April 30, 2007, p. 1.

FIGURE 19.3
Factors to Be Considered in Site Location

1. Revenue
   a. Location of customers and accessibility
   b. Location of competitors
2. Operating costs
   a. Price of materials
   b. Transportation costs: materials, products, people
   c. Wage rates
   d. Taxes: income, property, sales
   e. Utility rates
   f. Rental rates
   g. Communication costs
3. Investment
   a. Cost of land
   b. Cost of construction
4. Other limiting factors
   a. Availability of labor with appropriate skills
   b. Availability of materials, utilities, supplies
   c. Union activity
   d. Community attitudes and culture
   e. Political situation
   f. Pollution restrictions
   g. Climate
   h. General living conditions

that attractiveness of location (beauty, terrain, climate, etc.), business climate and community interest, proximity to sources of quality education, availability of well-established employee training facilities and resources, and a climate conducive to innovative entrepreneurship are factors that cannot be ignored in a location decision.[6] The final choice of the site should be a compromise on all the above factors. Management Illustration 19.2 describes a method being used by many restaurant chains to select new site locations.

JOB DESIGN

job design
Designates the specific work activities of an individual or a group of individuals.

Job design specifies the work activities of an individual or a group of individuals. Job design answers the question of how the job is to be performed, who is to perform it, and where it is to be performed.

The job design process generally proceeds in three phases:

1. The specification of individual tasks.
2. The specification of the method of performing each task.
3. The combination of individual tasks into specific jobs to be assigned to individuals.[7]

Phases 1 and 3 determine the content of the job; phase 2 identifies the specific methods to be used to perform the job.

FIGURE 19.4
Advantages and Disadvantages of Specialization of Labor

Source: Richard B. Chase, F. Robert Jacobs, and Nicholas J. Aquilano, *Operations Management for Competitive Advantage,* 11th ed., 2006. Reproduced with permission of The McGraw-Hill Companies.

Advantages of Specialization

To Management	To Labor
1. Rapid training of the workforce. 2. Ease in recruiting new workers. 3. High output due to simple and repetitive work. 4. Low wages due to ease of substitutability of labor. 5. Close control over work flow and workloads.	1. Little or no education required to obtain work. 2. Ease in learning job.

Disadvantages of Specialization

To Management	To Labor
1. Difficulty in controlling quality since no one person has responsibility for entire product. 2. Worker dissatisfaction leading to hidden costs arising from turnover, absenteeism, tardiness, grievances, and intentional disruption of production process. 3. Reduced likelihood of improving the process because of workers' limited perspective. 4. Limited flexibility to change the production process to produce new or improved products.	1. Boredom stemming from repetitive nature of work. 2. Little gratification from work itself because of small contribution to each item. 3. Little or no control over the workplace, leading to frustration and fatigue (in assembly-line situations). 4. Little opportunity to progress to a better job since significant learning is rarely possible on fractionated work.

job content
Aggregate of all the work tasks the jobholder may be asked to perform.

job method
Manner in which the human body is used, the arrangement of the workplace, and the design of the tools and equipment used.

Job Content

Job content is the sum of all the work tasks the jobholder may be asked to perform. Starting with the scientific management movement, job design focused on the most efficient way to do a job. This usually meant minimizing short-run costs by minimizing unit operation time. Thus, the number of tasks a jobholder was assigned was small. The obvious problem with this approach is that the job can become overly routine and repetitive, which leads to motivational problems in the form of boredom, absenteeism, turnover, and perhaps low performance. One fact greatly complicates the job design process: Different people react differently to similar jobs. In other words, what is boring and routine to one person is not necessarily boring and routine to another. Figure 19.4 illustrates the most commonly recognized advantages and disadvantages of job specialization.

This keyboard has been designed to be ergonomically correct in order to make jobs as physically easy as possible.

Job Methods

The next step in the job design process is to determine the precise methods to be used to perform the job. The optimal **job method** is a function of the manner in which the human body is used, the arrangement of the workplace, and the design of the tools and equipment used.[8] The main purpose of job method design is to find the one best way to do a job. Normally, job methods are determined after the basic process and physical layout have been established.

Motion study is used in designing jobs. It involves determining the necessary motions and movements to perform a job or task and then designing the most efficient method for putting these motions and movements together.

ergonomics
Study of the interface between people and machines.

Ergonomics is the study of the interface between people and machines. Ergonomics, also called human engineering, is concerned with improving productivity and safety by designing workplaces, tools, instruments, and furniture that take into account the physical abilities of people. A primary concern of ergonomics is that the equipment and the workplace be designed to make jobs as physically easy as possible.

Job methods designers have traditionally concentrated on manual tasks. However, the basic concept of finding the one best way applies to all types of jobs.

Job Characteristics

Job design can also be described in terms of five key characteristics:

- Skill variety
- Task identity
- Task significance
- Autonomy
- Feedback

Skill variety refers to the number of different skills an employee needs to perform a job. Security officers who only check people's bags as they enter a building have little skill variety in their jobs. People whose jobs demand little skill variety often become bored at work.

Task identity refers to the degree to which a job allows an employee to complete an entire task rather than just part of the task. Mechanics who work at small garages have a high degree of task identity because they are responsible for every aspect of the job of repairing cars. In contrast, mechanics on assembly lines that do nothing but check transmissions have a lower degree of task identity.

Task significance refers to the level of impact a job has on the whole organization. Employees who feel that their work affects the organization generally have high job satisfaction. Employees who feel that their jobs do not affect others rarely share this feeling.

Autonomy refers to the independence employees have to make decisions about how to perform their jobs. Checkout clerks in supermarkets have almost no job autonomy. In contrast, supermarket store managers are able to decide how they spend their time. They evaluate the tasks they need to accomplish during the day and perform them in the order they choose. Most people prefer to have some autonomy in their jobs.

Feedback involves the extent to which managers let employees know how they are performing. Feedback was discussed in depth in Chapter 18. In general, employees like to receive feedback about their job performance.

Jobs that rank high in these five characteristics tend to be more desirable than those that don't.

The Physical Work Environment

The physical work environment—temperature, humidity, ventilation, noise, light, color, and so on—can affect employee performance and safety. Studies clearly show that adverse physical conditions do have a negative impact on performance, but the degree of influence varies from person to person.

Occupational Safety and Health Act (OSHA) of 1970
Federal legislation designed to reduce job injuries; established specific federal safety guidelines for almost all U.S. organizations.

The importance of safety in the design process was reinforced by the **Occupational Safety and Health Act (OSHA) of 1970.** Designed to reduce job injuries, the act gives very specific federal safety guidelines for almost all U.S. organizations.

In general, the work area should allow for normal lighting, temperature, ventilation, and humidity. Baffles, acoustical wall materials, and sound absorbers should be used to reduce unpleasant noises. Exposure to less than ideal conditions should be limited to short periods. All of these measures will minimize potential physical or psychological damage to employees.

Sociotechnical Approach

sociotechnical approach
Approach to job design that considers both the technical system and the accompanying social system.

The sociotechnical concept was introduced in the 1950s by Eric Trist and his colleagues at the Tavistock Institute of Human Relations in London.[9] The **sociotechnical approach** rests on two premises. First, in any organization that requires people to perform certain tasks, a joint system is operating; this joint system combines the social and technological systems. Second, the environment of every sociotechnical system is influenced by a culture, its values, and a set of generally accepted practices.[10] The concept stresses that the technical system, the related social system, and the general environment should all be considered when designing jobs.

The sociotechnical approach is very situational; few jobs have identical technical requirements, social surroundings, and environments. This approach requires that the job designer carefully consider the role of the worker within the system, the task boundaries, and the autonomy of the work group. Using the sociotechnical approach, Louis Davis has developed the following guidelines for job design:

1. The need for the content of a job to be reasonably demanding for the employee in terms other than sheer endurance and yet provide some variety (but not necessarily novelty).
2. The need to be able to learn on the job and go on learning.
3. The need for some minimum area of decision making that the individual can call his or her own.
4. The need for some minimum degree of social support and recognition at the workplace.
5. The need to be able to relate what the individual does and what he or she produces to the person's social life.
6. The need to feel that the job leads to some sort of desirable future.[11]

COMPUTER TECHNOLOGY AND THE DESIGN PROCESS

computer-aided design (CAD)
Generates various views of different components and assemblies.

computer-aided engineering (CAE)
Uses a product's characteristics to analyze its performance under different parameters.

computer-aided manufacturing (CAM)
Uses stored data regarding various products to provide instructions for automated production equipment.

In recent years, computers have come to play a major role in production/operations technology. The term *factories of the future* has become popular and generally refers to the use of computers in various parts of the operating system. **Computer-aided design (CAD)** may be defined as carrying out all structural or mechanical design processes of a product or component at a specially equipped computer terminal.[12] CAD can be used to generate various views of different components and assemblies. With CAD, designs can be developed, analyzed, and changed much faster than by using conventional drawing methods. Management Illustration 19.3 discusses how one company is realizing substantial cost savings by using a new online CAD system.

Engineering analysis, when performed at a computer terminal with a CAD system, is called **computer-aided engineering (CAE).** CAE uses a product's characteristics from a CAD database and analyzes its performance under different parameters.[13] For example, several designs could be subjected to different tests and comparisons made by computer instead of actually making and testing different prototypes.

Computer-aided manufacturing (CAM) basically refers to control of the manufacturing process by computers.[14] CAM uses stored data regarding various products to provide instructions for automated production equipment. When CAD provides the design formation used by CAM, the result is called *computer-aided design and manufacturing (CAD/CAM).*

Management Illustration 19.3

ONLINE CAD SYSTEM SHORTENS DESIGN TIME
www.nookindustries.com

While the manufacture of many standard products has moved out of the United States to places where the labor is cheaper, many U.S. manufacturers have identified a competitive opportunity in the important and growing area of customization. Nook Industries Inc. of Cleveland produces linear motion components and linear actuators used in medical machinery, military equipment, and packaging equipment. "Everything we sell is customized," said vice president Chris Nook. "We have a standard catalog of items we sell, but every customer orders a modified version of an item. The challenge is to get it in the customer's hand as fast as you can."

In the past, Nook's salespeople held meetings with customers to determine the customers' needs. Then, engineers created each specialized part using in-house computer-aided design software. The overall process took about two weeks. Starting in about 2002, Nook brought in online CAD software that allows customers to design their own actuators at the Nook Industries Web site. With this new system customized parts can be designed in minutes as opposed to weeks. Nook's system works because their engineers have put in considerable time behind the scenes creating the CAD drawings to be modified by the online customers. By 2005 Chris Nook estimated that the online CAD system had cut sales costs by about $426,000 per year, while increasing sales by about 35 percent.

In 2005 and 2006, Nook Iindustries received several awards and widespread recognition for its Web site and configurable 2D and 3D CAD model downloads at its Web site: http://www.nookindustries.com.

Sources: Jean Thilmany, "Made Your Way," *Mechanical Engineering,* October 2005, pp. 40–42; "Nook Industries Receives Network World's 2005 Enterprise All-Star Award," *PR Newswire,* November 30, 2005, p. 1; and "Nook Industries Website Reviewed in MarketingSherpa Case Study," *PR Newswire,* March, 7, 2006, p. 1.

computer-integrated manufacturing (CIM)
Uses computer technology to incorporate all of the organization's production-related functions into an integrated computer system to assist, augment, or automate most functions.

Finally, **computer-integrated manufacturing (CIM)** uses computer technology to incorporate all of the organization's production-related functions into an integrated computer system to assist, augment, or automate most operations.[15] With CIM, the output of one activity or operation serves as the input to the next activity, and this system pervades the entire organization. In essence, CIM involves the integration of product design, engineering, process planning, and manufacturing through the use of computer systems. The overall goal of using CIM is to link various parts of an organization to achieve rapid response to customer orders or product changes, to allow fast production, and to reduce indirect labor costs.[16]

There is little doubt that operations design and planning are moving more and more toward the use of computer technology. For example, sales of mechanical CAD/CAM/CAE software have increased significantly over the past several years. Many believe that in the near future, CIM will become a reality for most manufacturers.

DAY-TO-DAY OPERATIONS PLANNING

production planning
Concerned primarily with aggregate operations planning, resource allocation, and activity scheduling.

Designing an effective operating system does not ensure that the system will operate efficiently. The day-to-day operations must also be planned and then carried out. This process is called **production planning** and includes aggregate operations planning, resource allocation, and scheduling. Its overriding purpose is to maintain a smooth, constant flow of work from start to finish so that the product or service will be completed in the desired time at the lowest possible cost.

Aggregate Operations Planning

Aggregate operations planning (also known as *aggregate production planning*) deals with overall operations and with balancing the major parts of the operating system. The

aggregate operations planning Concerned with overall operations and balancing major sections of the operating system; matches the organization's resources with demands for its goods and services.

objective of the aggregate operations plan is to minimize the cost of resources required to meet demand over the period covered.[17] This is achieved by matching the organization's resources with the demands for its goods or services. Specifically, the plan should find the production rates that satisfy demand requirements while minimizing the costs of workforce and inventory fluctuations. Aggregate operations plans generally look 6 to 18 months into the future.

The first step in developing an aggregate operations plan is to obtain a demand forecast for the organization's goods or services. The second step involves evaluating the impact of the demand forecasts on the organization's resources—plant capacity, workforce, raw materials, and the like. The final step is to develop the best plan for using the organization's current and expected resources to meet the forecast demand. The aggregate operations plan determines production rates, workforce needs, and inventory levels for the entire operating system over a specified period.

Gantt chart Planning and controlling device that graphically depicts work planned and work accomplished in their relation to each other and to time.

One of the oldest and simplest methods of graphically showing both expected and completed production is the Gantt chart. Developed by Henry L. Gantt in the early 1900s, the main feature of the **Gantt chart** is that it shows work planned and work accomplished in relation to time. Figure 19.5 presents a typical Gantt chart.

From a planning perspective, Gantt charts require operations managers to clearly think through the sequence of events necessary to complete the tasks being charted. From a control perspective, Gantt charts emphasize the element of time by readily pointing out

FIGURE 19.5
Sample Gantt Chart

Source: Adapted from Elwood S. Buffa, *Modern Production Management,* 4th ed. (New York: John Wiley & Sons, Inc., 1973), p. 576.

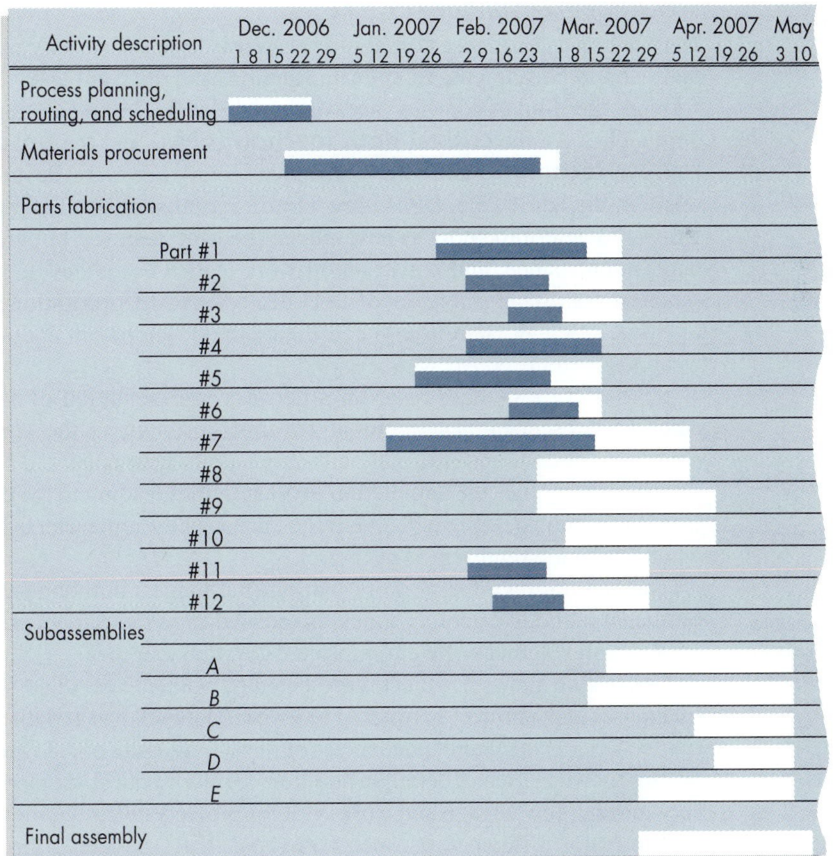

Key: White bars represent work planned.
Shaded bars represent work accomplished.

any actual or potential slippages. One criticism of the Gantt chart is that it can require considerable time to incorporate scheduling changes such as rush orders. To accommodate such scheduling changes rapidly, mechanical boards using movable pegs or cards have been developed.

Resource Allocation

resource allocation
Efficient allocation of people, materials, and equipment to meet the demand requirements of the operating system.

Resource allocation is the efficient allocation of people, materials, and equipment to meet the demand requirements of the operating system. It is the natural outgrowth of the aggregate production plan. The materials needed must be determined and ordered; the work must be distributed to the different departments and workstations; personnel must be allocated; and time allotments must be set for each stage of the process.

Due to resource scarcities, resource allocation has become critical in recent times. Increased competition, both domestic and foreign, has also heightened its importance. Proper resource allocation can mean great cost savings, which can give the needed competitive edge.

Numerous mathematical and computer-assisted tools and techniques can assist in resource allocation. Linear programming, the critical path method (CPM), and the program evaluation and review technique (PERT) are some of the most often used approaches. The last two are discussed in the following section.

Critical Path Method (CPM) and Program Evaluation and Review Technique (PERT)

critical path method (CPM)
Planning and control technique that graphically depicts the relationships among the various activities of a project; used when time durations of project activities are accurately known and have little variance.

program evaluation and review technique (PERT)
Planning and control technique that graphically depicts the relationships among the various activities of a project; used when the durations of the project activities are not accurately known.

Network analysis focuses on finding the most time-consuming path through a network of tasks and identifying the relationships among the different tasks. The Gantt chart concept formed the foundation for network analysis.[18] The most popular network analysis approaches are the **critical path method (CPM)** and the **program evaluation and review technique (PERT).** These two techniques were developed almost simultaneously in the late 1950s. CPM grew out of a joint study by DuPont and Remington Rand Univac to determine how to best reduce the time required to perform routine plant overhaul, maintenance, and construction work.[19] PERT was developed by the Navy in conjunction with representatives of Lockheed Aircraft Corporation and the consulting firm of Booz, Allen, & Hamilton to coordinate the development and production of the Polaris weapons system.

CPM and PERT both result in a network representation of a project. The network is composed of sequential activities and events. An activity is the work necessary to complete a particular event, and it usually consumes time. Events denote a point in time, and their occurrence signifies the completion of all activities leading to the event. All activities originate and terminate at events. Activities are usually represented by arrows in a network, while events are represented by a circle.

The path through the network that has the longest duration (based on a summation of estimated individual activity times) is referred to as the *critical path.* If any activity on the critical path lengthens, the entire project duration lengthens.

Figure 19.6 shows a project represented by both a Gantt chart (which was introduced in Chapter 2) and a project network. The project network has two distinct advantages over the Gantt chart: (1) the interdependencies of the activities are noted explicitly, and (2) the activities are shown in greater detail. In addition, from a practical standpoint, Gantt charts become very difficult to visualize and work with for projects involving more than 25 activities.

The major difference between CPM and PERT concerns the activity time estimates. CPM is used for projects whose activity durations are accurately known and whose variance in performance time is negligible. PERT is used when the activity durations are more

Management Illustration 19.4

CERTIFIED PROJECT MANAGERS

In 2003, the Standish Group reported that the lost dollar value for U.S. projects in 2002 was estimated at $38 billion, with another $17 billion in cost overruns, making a total project waste of $55 billion compared with $255 billion in total project spending. Thus, the potential savings from good project management is substantial.

Today more than 16 million people in the world call themselves project managers. According to *Certification* magazine, the project management professional (PMP) is now one of the top 10 certifications in the world. Yet, only 200,000, or just over 1 percent, are certified. Not only is the PMP certification valued in the private sector but, today, many government contracts require project managers to have the PMP credential. Statistics also show that the salaries of PMP certified project managers are 17.2 percent higher than their noncredentialed counterparts.

Source: Michelle LaBrosse, "The Evolution of Project Management," *Employment Relations Today,* Spring 2007, p. 97.

FIGURE 19.6 **Project Represented by Gantt Chart and a Project Network**

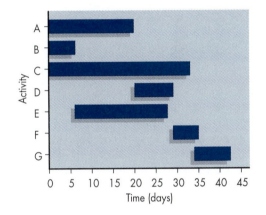

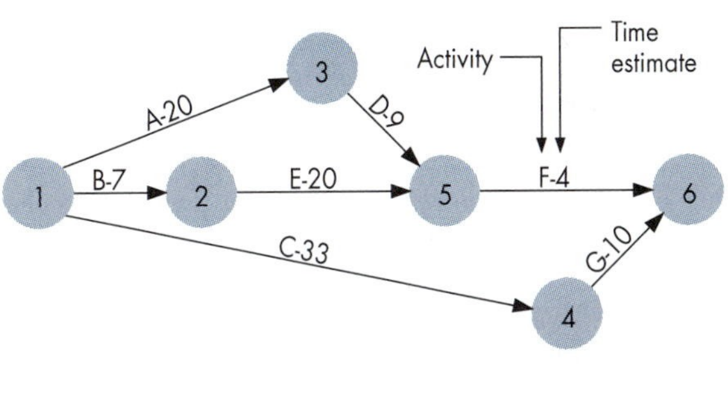

uncertain and variable. CPM is based on a single estimate for an activity duration, whereas PERT is based on three time estimates for each activity: an optimistic (minimum) time, a most likely (modal) time, and a pessimistic (maximum) time.

CPM and PERT can also be used for controlling once the plans have been put into action. By tracking actual progress compared to planned progress, activities that fall behind schedule can quickly be spotted.

Project network analysis can provide information beyond simple project planning and control. By knowing the critical activities, the project manager can best allocate limited resources and can make more accurate time-cost trade-offs. Management Illustration 19.4 provides some interesting information related to project management.

Routing

routing
Finds the best path and sequence of operations for attaining a desired level of output with a given mix of equipment and personnel.

Routing finds the best path and sequence of operations for attaining a desired level of output with a given mix of equipment and personnel. Routing looks for the best use of existing equipment and personnel through careful assignment of these resources. An organization may or may not have to analyze its routing system frequently; it depends on the variety of products or services it offers.

Flowcharts and diagrams are used to locate and end inefficiencies in a process by analyzing the process in a step-by-step fashion. Most charting procedures divide the actions in

FIGURE 19.7
Flowcharting Activities

Source: From H. B. Maynard, *Industrial Engineering Handbook,* 3rd ed., 1963. Reproduced with permission of The McGraw-Hill Companies.

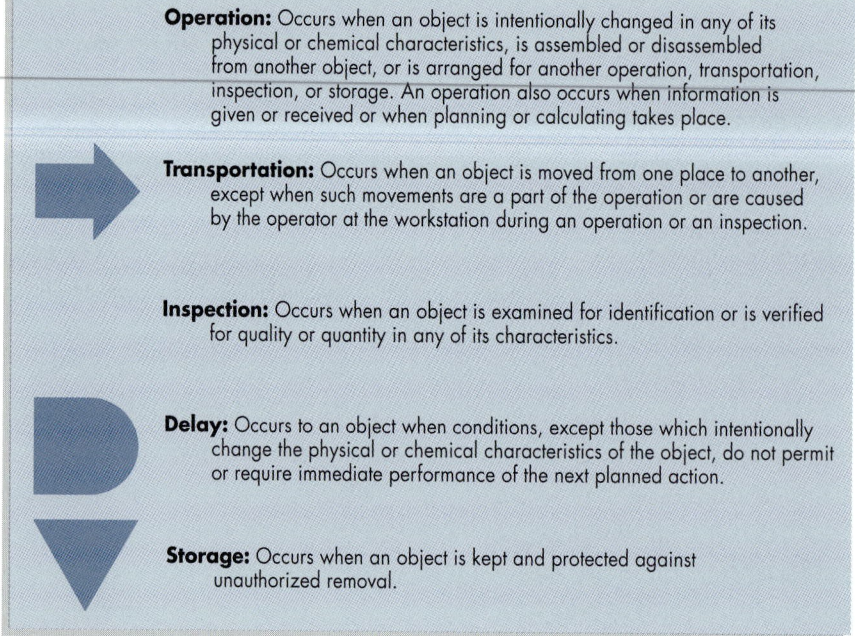

a given process into five types: operation, transportation, inspection, delay, and storage. Figure 19.7 defines each of these types of actions.

Operation: Occurs when an object is intentionally changed in any of its physical or chemical characteristics, is assembled or disassembled from another object, or is arranged for another operation, transportation, inspection, or storage. An operation also occurs when information is given or received or when planning or calculating takes place.
Transportation: Occurs when an object is moved from one place to another, except when such movements are a part of the operation or are caused by the operator at the workstation during an operation or an inspection.
Inspection: Occurs when an object is examined for identification or is verified for quality or quantity in any of its characteristics.
Delay: Occurs to an object when conditions, except those which intentionally change the physical or chemical characteristics of the object, do not permit or require immediate performance of the next planned action.
Storage: Occurs when an object is kept and protected against unauthorized removal.

Two types of charts frequently used are the assembly chart and the flow process chart. An **assembly chart** depicts the sequence and manner in which the various parts of a product or service are assembled. A **flow process chart** outlines what happens to the product as it moves through the operating facility. Flow process charts can also map the flow of customers through a service facility. Figure 19.8 shows a flow process chart for the processing of a form for an insurance company.

assembly chart
Depicts the sequence and manner in which the various components of a product or service are assembled.

flow process chart
Outlines what happens to a product or service as it progresses through the facility.

activity scheduling
Develops the precise timetable to be followed in producing a product or service.

Activity Scheduling

Activity scheduling develops the precise timetable to be followed in producing the product or service. It also includes dispatching work orders and expediting critical and late orders. Scheduling does not involve deciding how long a job will take (which is part of job design); rather, it determines when the work is to be done. Scheduling is the link between system design and operations planning and control. Once the initial schedule has been set, the system is ready for operation. Of course, scheduling is an ongoing activity in an operating system.

A scheduling system design must be based on knowledge of the operating system for which it is being designed. Scheduling for intermittent systems is very complex because of the larger number of individual orders or customers that must flow through the system. Many types of scheduling tools, such as the Gantt chart, the critical path method, and the program evaluation and review technique, have been developed to help overcome scheduling problems.

Scheduling for high-volume continuous flow systems is often a process of matching the available resources to the production needs as outlined by the aggregate plan. Computer simulation is used to assist in the scheduling of continuous flow systems by estimating the impact of different scheduling decisions on the system.

FIGURE 19.8
Flow Process Chart: Present Method for Completing Authorization-to-Investigate Form

Source: From *Production and Operations Management*, 6th edition—HSIE 6th ed., by Norman Gaither. Copyright © 1994. Reprinted with permission of SouthWestern College Publishing, a division of Thomson Learning.

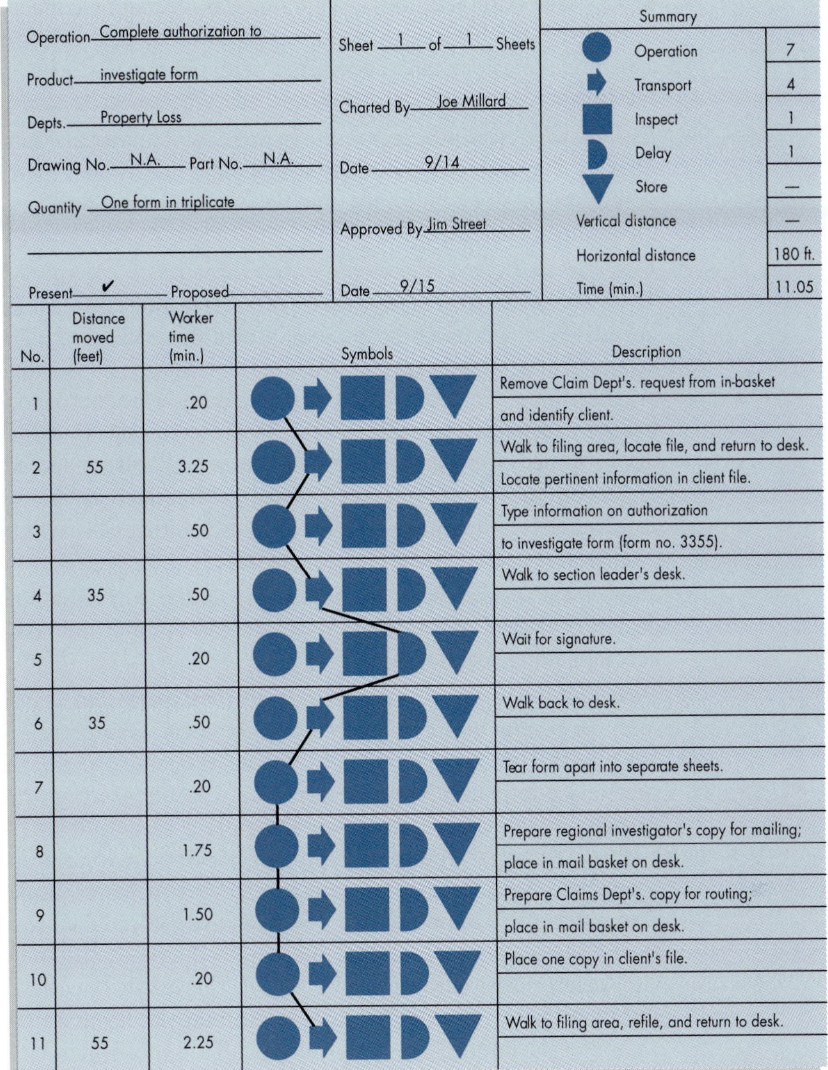

Operation Complete authorization to
Product investigate form
Depts. Property Loss
Drawing No. N.A. Part No. N.A.
Quantity One form in triplicate
Present ✔ Proposed

Sheet 1 of 1 Sheets
Charted By Joe Millard
Date 9/14
Approved By Jim Street
Date 9/15

Summary	
Operation	7
Transport	4
Inspect	1
Delay	1
Store	—
Vertical distance	—
Horizontal distance	180 ft.
Time (min.)	11.05

No.	Distance moved (feet)	Worker time (min.)	Symbols	Description
1		.20		Remove Claim Dept's. request from in-basket and identify client.
2	55	3.25		Walk to filing area, locate file, and return to desk. Locate pertinent information in client file.
3		.50		Type information on authorization to investigate form (form no. 3355).
4	35	.50		Walk to section leader's desk.
5		.20		Wait for signature.
6	35	.50		Walk back to desk.
7		.20		Tear form apart into separate sheets.
8		1.75		Prepare regional investigator's copy for mailing; place in mail basket on desk.
9		1.50		Prepare Claims Dept's. copy for routing; place in mail basket on desk.
10		.20		Place one copy in client's file.
11	55	2.25		Walk to filing area, refile, and return to desk.

Summary

1. *Define operations management.* Operations management is the application of the basic concepts and principles of management to those segments of the organization that produce its goods or services.
2. *Describe an operating system, and identify the two basic types of operating systems.* An operating system consists of the processes and activities necessary to transform various inputs into goods or services. The two basic types of operating systems are those based on continuous flows and those based on intermittent flows. Continuous flow systems generally have a standardized product or service. Intermittent flow systems usually produce customized products and services.
3. *Differentiate among product/service design, process selection, and site selection decisions.* Product/service design decisions deal with how the product or service will be designed. The design must be such that it can be economically produced.

Process selection includes a wide range of decisions concerning the specific process to be used, the basic sequences of the process, and the equipment to be used. Site selection decisions are concerned with where to locate a new or an additional facility.

4. *Explain what a materials-handling system is.* A materials-handling system is the entire network that receives materials, stores materials, moves materials between processing points and between buildings, and positions the final product or service for delivery to the ultimate customer.
5. *Describe and give an example of the three basic classifications of facilities layouts.* The three basic types of layouts are process layouts, product layouts, and fixed-position layouts. With a process layout, equipment or services of a similar functional type are arranged or grouped together. Custom fabrication shops and hospitals are examples of organizations that use process layouts. With a product layout, the equipment or services are arranged according to the progressive steps by which the product is made or the customer is serviced. Automobile assembly plants and cafeterias are examples of organizations that use product layouts. With a fixed-position layout the product is too large to move and remains in place. Manufacturing of very large products such as ships or airplanes use the fixed-position layout.
6. *Explain the sociotechnical approach to job design.* The sociotechnical approach to job design considers not only the technical system and the task to be done but also the accompanying social system.
7. *Describe several computer-related technologies that are currently playing major roles in production/operations management.* Computer-aided design is carrying out all structural or mechanical design processes of a product or component at a specially equipped computer terminal. CAD is used in product design to generate various views of different components and assemblies. CAE is when engineering analysis is performed at a computer terminal with a CAD system. CAE uses a product's characteristics to analyze its performance under different parameters. Computer-aided manufacturing (CAM) uses stored data regarding various products to provide instructions for automated production equipment. When CAD provides the design information used by CAM, the result is called computer-aided design and manufacturing (CAD/CAM). Computer-integrated manufacturing (CIM) uses computer technology to incorporate all of the organization's production-related functions into an integrated computer system to assist, augment, or automate most operations.
8. *Outline the three major steps in developing an aggregate operations plan.* The first step in developing an aggregate operations plan is to obtain a demand forecast for the organization's goods or services. The second step involves evaluating the impact of the demand forecasts on the organization's resources. The third step is to develop the best plan for using the organization's current and expected resources to meet the forecast demand.
9. *Summarize the differences between resource allocation and activity scheduling.* Resource allocation is concerned with the efficient allocation of people, materials, and equipment to meet the demand requirements of the operating system. This includes distributing the workload and determining how much time should be allotted for each stage in the production process. Activity scheduling develops the precise timetable to be followed when producing the product or service. Activity scheduling does not involve determining how long a job will take; rather, it determines when the work is to be done.

10. *Distinguish between Gantt charts, the critical path method (CPM), and the program evaluation and review technique (PERT).* Gantt charts graphically depict work planned and work accomplished in relation to time. CPM and PERT both result in a network representation of a project or a group of activities. CPM and PERT have two distinct advantages over Gantt charts: (1) The interdependencies of the activities are noted explicitly, and (2) the activities are shown in greater detail. The major difference between CPM and PERT centers on activity time estimates. CPM is used for projects whose activity durations are accurately known. PERT is used when the activity durations are more uncertain and variable.

Review Questions

1. What is operations management?
2. Describe an operating system.
3. Describe the two basic types of operating systems.
4. What is the overriding objective of the process selection decision?
5. At the most basic level of process selection, what are the four primary types?
6. Discuss several factors that should be considered in site location.
7. What is a process-oriented layout? A product-oriented layout? A fixed-position layout?
8. What is a materials-handling system?
9. Identify the three phases of the job design process.
10. Define ergonomics.
11. What is the sociotechnical approach to job design? Using the sociotechnical approach, give some guidelines for job design.
12. Define CAD, CAE, CAM, and CIM.
13. What is production planning?
14. Define aggregate operations planning.
15. What is the difference between resource allocation and activity scheduling?

Skill-Building Questions

1. Explain how you might take a production line approach (transferring the concepts and methodologies of operations management) to a service organization such as a branch bank.
2. Does process selection in service industries such as restaurants and hotels differ from process selection in manufacturing? If so, how?
3. Why should all of the phases in designing an operating system be integrated?
4. Discuss the following statement: Most production planning is a waste of time because it all depends on demand forecasts, which are usually inaccurate.
5. What can the computer do to help with modern assembly-line planning? How might simulations be used?

SKILL-BUILDING EXERCISE 19.1
Analyzing the Layout

Visit a local fast-food restaurant (McDonald's, Burger King, Hardee's, Wendy's, etc.) and sketch the basic layout of the facility on a single sheet of 8½-by-11-inch paper. Observe the flow of customers and employees through the store. Identify what specific aspects of the layout you think are particularly good. Try to identify one or more aspects of the layout that you think could be improved. Why do you think this improvement has not been made previously? Write down your findings and be prepared to discuss them in class.

SKILL-BUILDING EXERCISE 19.2
Disseminating Confidential Information

Every month, you are responsible for collating and stapling 500 copies of a four-page document. The documents must then be placed in manila envelopes, sealed, and have the word *CONFIDENTIAL* written on each. The four pages are printed on one side only and are numbered sequentially.

1. Assume you have a manual stapler and a felt marker at your disposal. Draw a sketch of how you would arrange your workplace for doing this task and describe the procedure you would use.
2. Assume you have the authority (within reason) to make changes in the equipment, materials, and processes used, as long as the basic task of organizing the information and labeling it as confidential is accomplished. What suggestions would you make?

SKILL-BUILDING EXERCISE 19.3
Drawing a CPM Logic Network

Based upon the following narrative description of a project, draw a CPM logic network that accurately shows the natural dependencies among the activities involved. Be prepared to share your network with the class.

The Sheffield Manufacturing Company is considering the introduction of a new product. The first step in this project will be to design the new product. Once the product is designed, a prototype can be built and engineers can design the process by which the product will be produced on a continuous basis. When the prototype is completed, it will be tested. Upon completing the process design, an analysis will be made of the production cost per unit for the new product. When the prototype testing and the production cost analysis are both finished, the results will be submitted to an executive committee, which will make the final go-ahead decision on the product introduction and establish the price to be charged.

Assuming that the committee's decision is positive, several steps can be taken immediately. The marketing department will begin designing sales literature. The production department will obtain the equipment to be used in the manufacture of the new product, hire the additional personnel needed to staff the process, and obtain an initial stock of raw materials. After sales literature has been designed, it will be printed. The new equipment obtained for the production process will have to be modified slightly. The production personnel will be trained as soon as the equipment modifications are complete, all necessary personnel have been hired, and the initial stock of materials has been obtained. When the printing of the sales literature is completed and the production personnel have been trained, the sales literature will be distributed to the salespersons and the product introduction will be considered complete.

Questions

1. What specific benefits do you think that a CPM network would provide on this project?
2. What information does the CPM network that you created provide that would not be provided by a Gantt chart of the same project?

Case Incident 19.1
The Lines at Sam's

Sam Baker owns and manages a cafeteria on Main Street in Dawsonville. During his two years of operation, Sam has identified several problems he has been unable to solve. One is the line that always seems to develop at the checkout register during the rush hour. Another is customers' constant complaints that the size of the helpings and the size of the pie slices vary tremendously from customer to customer. A third problem is the frequency with which the cafeteria runs out of "choice" dishes. The final problem is that every Sunday at noon, when a large crowd arrives after church, Sam invariably runs short of seating space.

Sam had worked at other food establishments for the previous 15 years, and most of them experienced similar problems. In fact, these and other related problems have come to be expected and are therefore accepted practice for the industry. After all, Sam's former boss used to say, "You can't please everybody all the time." Sam is wondering if he should take the industry's position and just accept these problems as an inherent part of the business.

Questions

1. What are Sam's options?
2. How might Sam improve his present situation?
3. Do you have any further suggestions for Sam? If so, what are they?
4. What other service-oriented industries can you think of that seem to take the same view toward their problems that Sam's industry does?

Case Incident 19.2

A New Building for Tot-Two

The Tot-Two Company manufactures clothes for children up to age five. Tot-Two has been growing rapidly for the past several years and is planning to build a new plant in a recently developed industrial park on the north side of town. Shirley Shaver, the plant's operations manager, has been assigned the task of drawing up a new physical layout subject to the constraints that the new building cannot exceed 7,000 square feet, including office space, and that it must be a perfect rectangle to minimize construction costs. Shirley developed the following list of departments with their respective approximate space requirements:

Shipping (400 square feet)—area for shipping all finished goods.

Receiving (400 square feet)—area for receiving all materials and supplies.

Materials supply room (300 square feet)—storage area for all incoming materials.

Spreading and cutting area (1,600 square feet)—area containing three 40-foot tables for spreading and then cutting the cloth. Many layers of cloth are spread on top of each other and cut at the same time with large portable cutters.

Pattern-making area (200 square feet)—area in which patterns are made.

Assembly area (1,200 square feet)—area for sewing the various clothing parts.

Packing area (400 square feet)—area for packing the finished goods into boxes for shipping.

Finished goods storage (500 square feet)—area for storing finished goods before shipping.

Design area (200 square feet)—area occupied by designers.

Office space (800 square feet)—space for secretaries and company officers.

Wash facilities (300 square feet)—area containing men's and women's bathrooms.

Lunch/break area (400 square feet)—area with vending machines and lunch tables.

Shirley then drew up an initial layout as illustrated below.

Designers (200 sq. ft.)
Lunch/break (400 sq. ft.)
Wash facilities (300 sq. ft.)
Shipping (400 sq. ft.)
Pattern making (200 sq. ft.)
Office (800 sq. ft.)
Packing (400 sq. ft.)
Finished goods storage (500 sq. ft.)
Material supply (300 sq. ft.)
Receiving (400 sq. ft.)
Assembly (1,200 sq. ft.)
Spreading and cutting (1,600 sq. ft.)

Questions

1. What are the strong points of Shirley's layout? What are the weak points?
2. Redesign the layout, based on your answers to question 1.

References and Additional Readings

1. Howard Banks, "Moment of Truth," *Forbes,* May 22, 1995, pp. 51–62.
2. Richard B. Chase, F. Robert Jacobs, and Nicholas J. Aquilano, *Operations Management for Competitive Advantage,* 11th ed. (Burr Ridge, IL: Richard D. Irwin, 2006), p. 210.
3. James M. Apple and Leon F. McGinnis, "Innovation in Facilities and Materials Handling Systems: An Introduction," *Industrial Engineering,* March 1987, pp. 33–38.
4. B. Gopalakrishnan, R. Turuvekere, and D.P. Gupta, "Computer Integrated Facilities Planning and Design," *Facilities* 22, issue 7–8, 2004, p. 199.
5. Lee J. Krajewski and Larry P. Ritzman, *Operations Management,* 3rd ed. (Reading, MA: Addison-Wesley, 1993), p. 348.
6. James L. Lewardowski and William P. MacKinnon, "What We Learned at Saturn," *Personnel Journal,* December 1992, pp. 30–32.
7. Louis E. Davis, "Job Design and Productivity: A New Approach," *Personnel,* March 1957, p. 420.
8. Richard A. Johnson, William T. Newell, and Roger C. Vergin, *Production and Operations Management: A Systems Concept* (Boston: Houghton Mifflin, 1974), p. 204.
9. Peter B. Vaill, "Industrial Engineering and Socio-Technical Systems," *Journal of Industrial Engineering,* September 1967, p. 535.
10. Louis E. Davis and James C. Taylor, *Design of Jobs,* 2nd ed. (Santa Monica, CA: Goodyear Publishing, 1979), pp. 98–99.
11. Louis E. Davis, *Job Satisfaction—a Socio-Technical View,* report no. 515-1-69 (Los Angeles: University of California, 1969), p. 14.
12. Mark M. Davis, Nicholas J. Aquilano, and Richard B. Chase, *Fundamentals of Operations Management,* 4th ed. (New York: McGraw-Hill/Irwin, 2003), p. 125.
13. Roberta S. Russell and Bernard W. Taylor III, *Operations Management,* 4th ed. (Upper Saddle River, NJ: Prentice Hall, 2003), p. 101.
14. Ibid.

15. Mikell P. Groover, *Automation, Production Systems and Computer Integrated Manufacturing* (Englewood Cliffs, NJ: Prentice Hall, 1980), pp. 721–22; and James B. Dilworth, *Production and Operations Management,* 5th ed. (New York: McGraw-Hill, 1993), pp. 609–13.
16. William J. Stevenson, *Operations Management,* 7th ed. (New York: McGraw-Hill/Irwin, 2002), p. 228.
17. Richard B. Chase, F. Robert Jacobs, and Nicholas J. Aquilano, *Operations Management for Competitive Advantage,* 11th ed. (New York: McGraw-Hill/Irwin, 2006), p. 560.
18. Evidence indicates there were other forerunners to CPM and PERT. See Edward R. Marsh, "The Harmonogram of Karol Adamiecki," *Academy of Management Journal,* June 1975, pp. 358–64.
19. Joseph J. Moder and Cecil R. Phillips, *Project Management with CPM and PERT* (New York: Van Nostrand Reinhold, 1970), p. 6.

Chapter Twenty

Operations Control

Learning Objectives

After studying this chapter, you will be able to:

1. Understand the basic requirements for controlling operating costs.
2. Define quality from the perspective of an operations manager.
3. List the eight common dimensions of design quality.
4. Explain the concept of quality assurance.
5. Explain the concept of total quality management (TQM).
6. Define the following terms: *continuous improvement*, *kaizen*, *quality at the source*, *lean manufacturing*, *six sigma*, and *lean six sigma*.
7. Describe ISO 9000, ISO 14000, and the zero-defects approaches to quality.
8. Identify and define the two major types of quality control.
9. Recount the major reasons for carrying inventories.
10. Explain the concept of just-in-time (JIT) inventory.
11. Describe the ABC classification system for managing inventories.
12. Summarize the economic order quantity (EOQ) concept.
13. Describe the basic purposes of material requirements planning (MRP).

Chapter Preview

Leiner Health Products, a California-based company, is the nation's second-largest supplier of over-the-counter Pharmaceuticals in the food, drug, mass merchant, and warehouse club retail markets. Wal-Mart, Sam's Club, and Costco are three of Leiner's biggest customers.

Early in 2007, an employee of the Fort Mill, South Carolina, plant of Leiner complained to the Food and Drug Administration about certain lab practices at the plant. A subsequent unplanned government inspection visit found problems with the plant's manufacturing practices. The exact nature of the problems has not been stated publicly but in April 2007 the company did shut down drug production at its plants nationwide. A company official has said that the problems were mostly related to shelf-life issues. In June 2007, Leiner announced it was laying off about 540 employees at the Fort Mill plant, closing down manufacturing and packaging operations and keeping about 35 people for distribution.

On September 5, 2007, Leiner learned that the U.S. Department of Justice was investigating if the company had committed any wrongdoing in the way it produced and distributed over-the-counter drugs at its Fort Mill Facility.

In November 2007, Leiner reported a net loss of $26.3 million for its second quarter compared with a net income of $6.1 million for the same period in the previous year. Sales for the same period were down 36.6 percent from the previous year.

Sources: Rebecca Sulock, Adam O'Daniel, and Zettler Clay, "Leiner to Lay Off 500 Workers: Fort Mill Plant to Cease Manufacturing and Packaging Operations; 75 Workers to Stay On," *Knight Ridder Tribune Business News,* June 8, 2007, p. 1; Matt Garfield, "Justice Department Investigating Leiner Plant in Fort Mill," *Knight Ridder Tribune Business News,* September 12, 2007; and "Leiner Health Products Reports Second Quarter 2008 Results," *Business Wire,* November 8, 2007.

Analyzing Management Skills

Why do you think that cost, quality, or inventory problems are often allowed to get "relatively out of control"? What can managers do to help prevent this from happening?

Applying Management Skills

Think of a retail store that you have visited in the last month that provided poor service to you. If you were manager of this store (or department), what would you do to improve the service to customers?

There are two aspects to an effective operating system: design and control. These aspects are related in that after a system has been designed and implemented, day-to-day operations must be controlled. With respect to efficient operation, the system processes must be monitored; quality must be assured; inventories must be managed; and all of these tasks must be accomplished within cost constraints. In addition to ensuring that things do not get out of control, good operations control can be a substitute for resources. For example, good quality control can reduce scrap and wasted materials, thus cutting costs. Similarly, effective inventory control can reduce the investment costs in inventories.

Effective operations control is attained by applying the basic control concepts to the operations function of the organization. Operations controls generally relate to one of three areas: costs, quality, or inventories.

CONTROLLING OPERATIONS COSTS

Ensuring that operating costs do not get out of hand is one of the primary jobs of the operations manager. The first requirement for controlling costs is to understand the organization's accounting and budgeting systems. Operations managers are primarily concerned with costs relating to labor, materials, and overhead. Figure 20.1 describes the major components of each of these costs. **Variable overhead expenses** change with the level of production or service. **Fixed overhead expenses** do not change appreciably with the level of production or service.

variable overhead expenses
Expenses that change in proportion to the level of production or service.

fixed overhead expenses
Expenses that do not change appreciably with fluctuations in the level of production or service.

Normally, operations managers prepare monthly budgets for each of the major cost areas. Once these budgets have been approved by higher levels of management, they are put into effect. By carefully monitoring the ensuing labor, material, and overhead costs, the operations manager can compare actual costs to budgeted costs. The methods used to monitor costs naturally vary, but typically they include direct observation, written reports, break-even charts, and so on.

Usually a cost control system indicates only when a particular cost is out of control; it does not address the question of *why* it is out of control. For example, suppose an

FIGURE 20.1
Budget Costs: The Basis for Cost Control

Source: N. Gaither, *Production and Operations Management* (Fort Worth: Dryden Press, 1980).

Type of Cost	Components
Direct labor—variable	Wages and salaries of employees engaged in the direct generation of goods and services. This typically does not include wages and salaries of support personnel.
Materials—variable	Cost of materials that become a tangible part of finished goods and services.
Production overhead—variable	Training new employees, safety training, supervision and clerical, overtime premium, shift premium, payroll taxes, vacation and holiday, retirement funds, group insurance, supplies, travel, repairs and maintenance.
Production overhead—fixed	Travel, research and development, fuel (coal, gas, or oil), electricity, water, repairs and maintenance, rent, depreciation, real estate taxes, insurance.

operations manager determines from the monthly cost report that the labor costs on product X are exceeding budget by 20 percent. The manager must then attempt to determine what is causing the cost overrun. The causes could be many, including unmotivated employees, several new and untrained employees, low-quality raw materials, or equipment breakdowns. The wise manager not only investigates the cause but also plans for prevention. The logical conclusion of a monitoring process is the implementation of prevention measures.[1]

Determining the cause may require only a simple inspection of the facts, or it may call for an in-depth analysis. Whatever the effort required, the operations manager must ultimately identify the source of the problem and then take the necessary corrective action. If the same cost problems continue to occur, chances are the manager has not correctly identified the true cause of the problem or the necessary corrective action has not been taken.

QUALITY MANAGEMENT

quality
For the operations manager, quality is determined in relation to the specifications or standards set in the design stages—the degree or grade of excellence specified.

Quality is a relative term that means different things to different people. The consumer who demands quality may have a different concept than the operations manager who demands quality. The consumer is concerned with service, reliability, performance, appearance, and so forth. The operations manager's primary concern is that the product or service specifications be achieved, whatever they may be. For the operations manager, **quality** is determined in relation to the specifications or standards set in the design stages. Thus, design quality refers to the inherent value of the product or service in the marketplace.[2] Figure 20.2 lists the six common dimensions of design quality. From the overall organizational perspective, quality can be defined as "meeting or exceeding customer expectations."

FIGURE 20.2
The Dimensions of Design Quality

Source: From Richard B. Chase, F. Robert Jacobs, and Nicholas J. Aquilano, *Operations Management for Competitive Advantage,* 11th ed., 2006. Reproduced with permission of the McGraw-Hill Companies.

Dimension	Meaning
Performance	Primary product or service characteristics
Features	Added touches; bells and whistles; secondary characteristics
Reliability/durability	Consistency of performance over time; probability of failing; useful life
Serviceability	Ease of repair
Aesthetics	Sensory characteristics (sound, feel, look, and so on)
Reputation	Past performance and other intangibles (perceived quality)

The quality of an organization's goods and services can affect the organization in many ways. Some of the most important of these areas are (1) loss of business, (2) liability, (3) costs, and (4) productivity.[3] The reputation of an organization is often a direct reflection of the perceived quality of its goods or services. In today's legalistic environment, an organization's liability exposure can be significant and the associated costs can be high. Higher-quality goods and services generally have less liability exposure than lower-quality goods and services. In addition to liability costs, quality can affect other costs, including scrap, rework, warranty, repair, replacement, and other similar costs. Productivity and quality are often closely related.[4] Poor-quality equipment, tools, parts, or subassemblies can cause defects that hurt productivity. Similarly, high-quality equipment, tools, parts, and subassemblies can boost productivity.

Because of the many different ways quality can affect an organization, it is often difficult to determine precisely the costs associated with different quality levels. Also, it must be realized that consumers and customers are willing to pay for quality only up to a point. In response, many firms have instituted a total customer response program in which quality in the workplace is transferred to dealings with customers. To implement the program, firms must (1) develop a new attitude toward customers, (2) reduce management layers so that managers are in contact with customers, (3) link quality and information systems to customer needs and problems, (4) train employees in customer responsiveness, (5) integrate customer responsiveness throughout the entire distribution channel, and (6) use customer responsiveness as a marketing tool.[5]

Quality Assurance

For years, the responsibility for quality in almost all organizations rested with a quality control department.[6] The idea under this approach was to identify and remove defects or correct mistakes before they got to the customer. Some systems emphasized finding and correcting defects at the end of the line; others focused on detecting defects during the production process. Both approaches focused on only the production part of the process; they gave little or no consideration to the design of the products/services or to working with suppliers. Suppliers were usually treated as adversaries.

Today's quality management emphasizes the prevention of defects and mistakes rather than finding and correcting them. The idea of "building in" quality as opposed to "inspecting it in" is also known as *quality assurance.* This approach views quality as the responsibility of all employees rather than the exclusive domain of a quality control department. Furthermore, suppliers are treated as partners.

While there have been many individuals who have championed the prevention approach to quality, W. Edwards Deming is perhaps most responsible. Deming was a statistics professor at New York University in the 1940s who went to Japan after World War II to assist in improving quality and productivity. While he became very much revered in Japan, Deming remained almost unknown to U.S. business leaders until the 1980s when Japan's quality and productivity attracted the attention of the world. Figure 20.3 presents a list compiled by Deming of 14 points he believed are needed to achieve quality in any organization. The underlying philosophy of Deming's work in this area is that the cause of poor quality and low productivity is the system and not the employees. He also stressed that it is management's responsibility to correct the system so that the desired results can be achieved.

Total Quality Management

Total quality management (TQM) is a management philosophy that emphasizes "managing the entire organization so that it excels in all dimensions of products and services that are important to the customer."[7] TQM, in essence, is an organizationwide emphasis on quality

FIGURE 20.3
Deming's 14 Points

Source: From W. Edwards Deming, *Out of the Crisis*, 1986. Copyright © 1986 by The MIT Press. Reprinted with permission.

1. Create and publish to all employees a statement of the aims and purposes of the company or other organization. The management must demonstrate constantly their commitment to this statement.
2. Learn the new philosophy, top management and everybody.
3. Understand the purpose of inspection, for improvement of processes and reduction of cost.
4. End the practice of awarding business on the basis of price tag alone.
5. Improve constantly and forever the system of production and service.
6. Institute training.
7. Teach and institute leadership.
8. Drive out fear. Create trust. Create a climate for innovation.
9. Optimize toward the aims and purposes of the company the efforts of teams, groups, and staff.
10. Eliminate exhortations for the workforce.

11a. Eliminate numerical quotas for production. Instead learn and institute methods for improvement.

11b. Eliminate management by objective. Instead learn the capabilities of processes and how to improve them.

12. Remove barriers that rob people of pride of workmanship.
13. Encourage education and self-improvement for everyone.
14. Take action to accomplish the transformation.

A major part of any total quality management program is to keep customers satisfied. This often involves integrating the customers' voice in the decision-making process through the use of surveys, focus groups, or interviews.

as defined by the customer. Under TQM, everyone from the CEO on down to the lowest-level employee must be involved. TQM can be summarized by the following actions:[8]

1. Find out what customers want. This might involve the use of surveys, focus groups, interviews, or some other technique that integrates the customer's voice in the decision-making process.
2. Design a product or service that will meet (or exceed) what customers want. Make it easy to use and easy to produce.
3. Design a production process that facilitates doing the job right the first time. Determine where mistakes are likely to occur, and try to prevent them. When mistakes do occur, find out why so that they are less likely to occur again. Strive to mistake-proof the process.
4. Keep track of results, and use those results to guide improvement in the system. Never stop trying to improve.
5. Extend these concepts to suppliers and to distribution.

As stated previously, TQM is an organizationwide emphasis on quality as defined by the customer. It is not a collection of techniques but a philosophy or way of thinking about how people view their jobs and quality throughout the organization.

Implementing TQM

Today's managers are bombarded with advice and literature telling them how to implement TQM. Three of the most popular approaches for implementing TQM are the Deming method, the Juran method, and the Crosby method, each named after the person who championed the respective approach. These three men, W. Edwards Deming, Joseph M. Juran, and Philip Crosby, are known as the "quality gurus." The Deming method emphasizes statistical quality control through employee empowerment. The Juran method emphasizes the reformulation of attitudes, comprehensive controls, and annual objective reviews. The Crosby method emphasizes conformance to requirements and zero defects. All of these approaches are sound; however, the best approach for implementing TQM is to custom-tailor the process for each application. In a study conducted by Frank Mahoney, the following initiatives were those most often cited by senior executives who had successfully implemented TQM.[9]

1. Demonstrate top-down commitment and involvement-push.
2. Set *tough* improvement goals, not just stretch goals.
3. Provide appropriate training, resources, and human resource backup.
4. Determine critical measurement factors; benchmark and track progress.
5. Spread success stories, especially those about favorable benchmarking; always share financial progress reports.
6. Identify the costs of quality and routes to improvement; prove the case that quality costs decline with quality progress.
7. Rely on teamwork, involvement, and all-level leadership.
8. Respect the "gurus," but tailor every initiative for a good local fit.
9. Allow time to see progress, analyze the system's operation, reward contributions, and make needed adjustments.
10. Finally, recognize that the key internal task is a culture change and the key external task is a new set of relationships with customers and suppliers.

Although it would seem to make good sense to transform an organization in the direction of total quality management, there is still resistance from the traditionalists. Figure 20.4 compares traditional organizations with those using TQM. The most often cited barriers to adopting TQM are (1) a lack of consistency of purpose on the part of management, (2) an emphasis on short-term profits, (3) an inability to modify personnel review systems, (4) mobility of management (job hopping), (5) lack of commitment to training and failure to instill leadership that is change oriented, and (6) excessive costs.[10]

FIGURE 20.4
Comparison of Traditional Organizations with Those Using TQM

Source: From William J. Stevenson, *Production and Operations Management,* 4th ed., 1992. Reproduced with permission of The McGraw-Hill Companies.

Aspect	Traditional	TQM
Overall mission	Maximize return on investment	Meet or exceed customer satisfaction
Objectives	Emphasis on short term	Balance of long term and short term
Management	Not always open; sometimes inconsistent objectives	Open; encourages employees' input; consistent objectives
Role of manager	Issue orders; enforce	Coach, remove barriers, build trust
Customer requirements	Not highest priority; may be unclear	Highest priority; important to identify and understand
Problems	Assign blame; punish	Identify and resolve
Problem solving	Not systematic; by individuals	Systematic; by teams
Improvement	Erratic	Continual
Suppliers	Adversarial	Partners
Jobs	Narrow, specialized; much individual effort	Broad, more general; much team effort
Focus	Product oriented	Process oriented

Specific Approaches for Improving Quality

Continuous improvement, kaizen, quality at the source, six sigma, and *lean manufacturing* are all terms that have particular relevance to TQM. Each of these approaches is discussed in the following sections.

continuous improvement
Refers to an ongoing effort to make improvements in every part of the organization relative to all of its products and services.

Continuous improvement in general refers to an ongoing effort to make improvements in every part of the organization relative to all of its products and services.[11] With regard to TQM, it means focusing on continuous improvement in the quality of the processes by which work is accomplished. The idea here is that the quest for better quality and better service is never ending.

kaizen
"Good change"; a process of continuous and relentless improvement.

Kaizen is a philosophy for improvement that originated in Japan and that has recently enjoyed widespread adoption throughout the world. Many people consider *kaizen* and *continuous improvement* to be synonymous terms; others consider kaizen to be a subset of or a particular type of continuous improvement. The word *kaizen* comes from two Japanese words: *kai,* meaning "change," and *zen,* meaning "good."[12] Hence, *kaizen* literally means "good change," and in today's context it describes a process of continuous and relentless improvement. Kaizen is not based on large technical leaps but on the incremental refining of existing processes. Kaizen is basically a system of taking small steps to improve the workplace. It is based on the belief that the system should be customer driven and involve all employees through systematic and open communication. Under kaizen, employees are viewed as the organization's most valued asset. This philosophy is put into practice through teamwork and extensive employee participation. In summary, kaizen applies the principles of participatory management toward incremental improvement of the current methods and processes. Kaizen does not focus on obtaining new and faster machines but rather on improving the methods and procedures used in the existing situation.

quality at the source
The philosophy of making each employee responsible for the quality of his or her own work.

Quality at the source refers to the philosophy of making each employee responsible for the quality of his or her work.[13] In effect, this approach views every employee as a quality inspector for his or her own work. A major advantage of this approach is that it removes the adversarial relationship that often exists between quality control inspectors and production employees. It also encourages employees to take pride in their work.

lean manufacturing
A systematic approach to identifying and eliminating waste and non-value-added activities.

Lean methods or lean manufacturing was introduced in Management Illustration 19.1 in the previous chapter. **Lean manufacturing** is a systematic approach to identifying and eliminating waste and non-value-added activities.[14] The essence of lean manufacturing is to look at the entire production or service process to eliminate waste or unnecessary activities wherever possible. Lean approaches focus on reducing cost through optimizing the processes being used. Management Illustration 20.1 describes some of the successes that Boeing has experienced with lean manufacturing at its Mesa, Arizona, helicopter plant.

six sigma
Both a precise set of statistical tools and a rallying cry for continuous improvement.

Six sigma is both a precise set of statistical tools and a rallying cry for continuous improvement.[15] Six sigma was pioneered by Motorola during the 1980s and literally means, in statistical terms, six standard deviations from the mean. The philosophy of six sigma is that in order to realize the very high level of quality demanded by six sigma (most processes traditionally have used three sigma), the entire production or service system must be examined and improved. Customer focus and data-driven rigor are at the heart of six sigma. Six sigma addresses the question of "what does the customer want in the way of quality." The answer to this question is then translated into statistical terms and rigorously analyzed.

Although it's most often thought of as applying to manufacturing processes, six sigma can be applied to any business process where the quality of the result may be quantified and the results of each process tracked.[16] Processes such as shipping, pickup and delivery of goods, order taking, and credit management readily lead themselves to six sigma.

lean six sigma
A combination of lean methods and six sigma; draws on the philosophies, principles, and tools of both approaches. Goal is growth and not just cost-cutting.

Lean six sigma is a combination of lean methods and six sigma.[17] Lean six sigma draws on the philosophies, principles, and tools of both approaches. Lean six sigma's goal

Management Illustration 20.1

LEAN MANUFACTURING AT BOEING

When Boeing Company's Mesa, Arizona, manufacturing facility began assembling a new generation of Apache Longbow helicopters in 1998, the plant's overall performance declined and cycle times increased. Unlike what one would expect, every aircraft literally took longer to build than the previous one. To attack the problem, the plant initially installed a single lean production line to manufacture the Longbow helicopter in 1999. This lean framework used a system that identified the key processes associated with the Longbow production. The system allowed the necessary flexibility to meet customer demand by providing necessary resources to mechanics at point of use, and working to standard repeatable processes that enable a single-piece flow.

Since implementing lean manufacturing, the Mesa plant has enjoyed dramatic improvement in its manufacturing measurements: On-time delivery has been 100 percent; overall production hours per aircraft have decreased by more than 48 percent; the number of internal defects has gone down more than 58 percent since the year 2000; the cost of internal defects (rework, repair, and scrap) has declined more than 61 percent; and the lost workday case rate has declined more than 58 percent since the year 2000.

Boeing has recently implemented lean manufacturing at its Boeing Satellite Development Center in El Segundo, California and in the assembly of the 787 plane at its Everett, Washington, plant.

Sources: Patrick Waurzyniak, "Lean Machine," *Manufacturing Engineering,* November 2005, pp. L1–L4; Michael Mecham, "Commercial Payoff," *Aviation Week & Space Technology,* April 9, 2007, pp. 55–57; and Guy Norris, "Lean, Mean Dream Machine," *Flight International,* June 12–June 18, 2007, pp. 56–58.

is growth and not just cost-cutting. Furthermore, its aim is effectiveness and not just efficiency. Figure 20.5 shows how lean six sigma relates to both lean methods and six sigma. Some companies retain the term six sigma even though they have incorporated lean features in their program. Caterpillar, discussed in Management Illustration 20.2, is one such company.

All of the above terms (*continuous improvement, kaizen, quality at the source, lean manufacturing, six sigma,* and *lean six sigma*) are approaches for improving quality of the product or service offered. These approaches are not mutually exclusive but rather are complementary; the differences are that each offers a different emphasis. It should also be pointed out that each of these approaches can be applied in nonmanufacturing environments such as service, education, and government.

FIGURE 20.5
Lean Six Sigma Incorporates the Key Methods, Tools, and Techniques of Its Predecessors.

Source: George Byrne, Dave Lubowe, and Amy Blitz, "Using a Lean Six Sigma Approach to Drive Innovation," *Strategy & Leadership* 35, November 2, 2007, p. 8.

Lean focuses on waste elimination in existing processes.

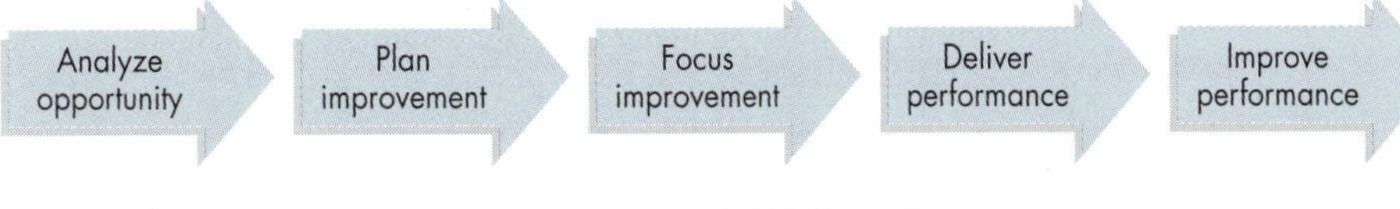

Six sigma focuses on continuous process improvement (DMAIC) to reduce variation in existing processes.

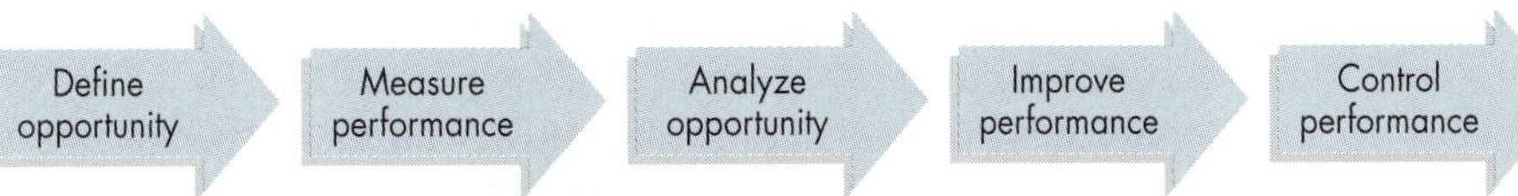

Six sigma also focuses on new process design/complete redesign (DMEDI) for wholesale redesign of processes as well as new products and services.

Define opportunity → Measure requirements → Explore solutions → Develop solutions → Implement solutions

Management Illustration 20.2

SIX SIGMA AT CATERPILLAR

On a technical level, six sigma represents six standard deviations from the mean or 3.4 defects per million opportunities. At Caterpillar, Inc., six sigma is a broad cultural philosophy to drive continuous improvement throughout the company. Caterpillar's managers view its six sigma program as a fact-based, data-driven methodology used to improve processes, enhance quality, cut costs, expand business, and deliver greater value to its customers.

Caterpillar made the decision to use six sigma at an August 2000 strategic management conference of top managers. The company began aggressively implementing six sigma corporatewide in January 2001. The payback was almost immediate with first-year gains exceeding first-year deployment costs. As of mid-2005, over 30,000 Caterpillar employees were involved in its six sigma program.

Caterpillar's success with six sigma has been summarized by Vice President and CFO Dave Burritt:

> Caterpillar's competitiveness has improved . . . Six Sigma has been applied to increase our percent of industry in all of our principal lines of business. The machine, the engine, and financial products businesses have all benefited from the rigor of Six Sigma. Without question, we are in the best of times at Caterpillar and the improvements would have been much less without Six Sigma.

Sources: James W. Owens, "Featured Company: Caterpillar Inc.," *ASQ Six Sigma Forum Magazine*, August 2005, p. 56; and George Byrne, Dave Lubowe, and Amy Blitz, "Using a Lean Six Sigma Approach to Drive Innovation," *Strategy and Leadership*, 35, no. 2, 2007, pp. 5–10.

As stated earlier, TQM is an organizationwide emphasis emphasis on quality as defined by the customer. It is not a collection of techniques but a philosophy or way of thinking about how people view their jobs and quality through the organization.

Reengineering

reengineering Searching for and implementing radical change in business processes to achieve breakthroughs in costs, speed, productivity, and service.

Some people confuse the concept of reengineering with TQM. **Reengineering,** also called *business process engineering,* is "the search for and implementation of radical change in business processes to achieve breakthrough results in costs, speed, productivity, and service."[18] Unlike TQM, reengineering is not a program for making marginal improvements in existing procedures. Reengineering is rather a onetime concerted effort, initiated from the top of the organization, to make major improvements in processes used to produce products or services. The essence of reengineering is to start with a clean slate and redesign the organization's processes to better serve its customers.

Other Quality Standards

While TQM is a highly effective, organizationwide philosophy about quality, there are other techniques and approaches that organizations may adopt to encourage quality. Most of these can be used alone or in conjunction with TQM. Quality circles were discussed in Chapter 10. Three additional approaches are discussed below.

ISO 9000

ISO 9000 A set of quality standards for international business.

ISO 9000 is a set of quality standards created in 1987 by the International Organization for Standardization (ISO), in Geneva, Switzerland. ISO is currently composed of the national standards bodies of over 152 countries with the major objective of promoting the development of standardization and facilitating the international exchange of goods and services. The American National Standards Institute (ANSI) is the member body representing the United States in the ISO.

Originally the ISO published five international standards designed to guide internal quality management programs and to facilitate external quality assurance endeavors. The original 1987 standards were slightly revised in 1994. In essence, ISO 9000:1994 outlined the quality system requirements necessary to meet quality requirements in varying situations. ISO 9000:1994 focused on the design and operation processes, not on the end product or service. ISO 9000:1994 required extensive documentation in order to demonstrate the consistency and reliability of the processes being used. In summary, ISO 9000:1994 certification did not relate to the quality of the actual end product or service, but it guaranteed that the company had fully documented its quality control procedures. While ISO issues the standards, it does not regulate the program internally; regulation is left to national accreditation organizations such as the U.S. Register Accreditation Board (RAB). RAB and other such boards then authorize registrars to issue ISO 9000 certificates.

New ISO 9000 standards were implemented beginning in fall 2000. The new standards emphasize international organization and in-house performance, rather than engineering, as the best way to deliver a product or service. In essence the new ISO 9000:2000 focuses more on continuous improvement and customer satisfaction. ISO 9000:2000, like its predecessor, is really a series of interrelated standards. In ISO 9000:2000 there are three interrelated standards. ISO 9000:2000 deals with fundamentals and vocabulary; ISO 9001:2000 states the requirements for the new system; and ISO 9004:2000 provides guidance for implementation. Because ISO 9001:2000 represents the heart of the new standards, this entire set of standards is sometimes referred to as ISO 9001:2000 as opposed to ISO 9000:2000.

Organizations previously certified under ISO 9000:1994 are required to update their quality systems in order to meet the new standard's requirement. As of the end of 2006 at least 897,866 organizations in 170 countries had been certified in ISO 9001:2000.[19] This represented an increase of 16 percent over the previous year.

ISO 14000

ISO 14000
Addition to the ISO 9000 to control the impact of an organization's activities and outputs on the environment.

Sparked by the success of ISO 9000, ISO developed a similar series of international standards for environmental management. **ISO 14000** is a series of voluntary international standards covering environmental management tools and systems. While many countries have developed environmental management system standards, these standards are often not compatible. The goal of ISO 14000 is to provide international environmental standards that are compatible. Similar to ISO 9000, which does not prescribe methods to integrate quality processes into an organization, ISO 14000 does not prescribe environmental policies. ISO 14000 does provide an international standard for environmental management systems so that organizations will have a systematic framework for their environmental activities. ISO 14000 focuses heavily on strategic issues such as setting goals and developing policies. ISO 14000 certification requires compliance in four organizational areas: (1) implementation of an environmental management system, (2) assurance that procedures are in place to maintain compliance with laws and regulations, (3) commitment to continual improvement, and (4) commitment to waste minimization and prevention of pollution.

Although the ISO 14000 series will ultimately include 20 separate standards covering everything from environmental auditing to environmental labeling to assessing life cycles of products, ISO 14001 is the first standard released. ISO 14001, Environmental Management Systems–Specification with Guidance for Use, is the standard companies will use to establish their own environmental management systems. As of December 31, 2006, 129,199 companies in 140 countries had been certified for ISO 14001.[20] This represents an increase of 16 percent over the previous year.

Zero-Defects

zero-defects program
Increasing quality by increasing everyone's impact on quality.

The name *zero-defects* is somewhat misleading in that this approach doesn't literally try to cut defects or defective service to zero. Such an approach would obviously be very cost ineffective in many situations. A **zero-defects program** attempts to create a positive attitude toward the prevention of low quality. The objective of a zero-defects program is to

Management Illustration 20.3

BALDRIGE RECIPIENTS FOR 2007

On November 20, 2007, President George W. Bush and Commerce Secretary Carlos Gutierrez announced five organizations as recipients of the 2007 Malcolm Baldrige National Quality Award. For the first time in the history of the Baldrige award, nonprofit organizations were selected.

The 2007 Baldrige award recipients—listed with their category—were:

- PRO-TEC Coating Company, Leipsic, Ohio (small business)
- Mercy Health System, Janesville, Wisconsin (health care)
- Sharp Healthcare, San Diego, California (health care)
- City of Coral Springs, Coral Springs, Florida (nonprofit)
- U.S. Army Armament Research, Development & Engineering Center (ARDEC), Picatinny Arsenal, New Jersey (nonprofit)

"I am pleased to join President Bush in congratulating the five outstanding organizations that have been named to receive this year's Baldrige award," said Secretary Gutierrez. "The organizations we recognize today have given us superb examples of innovation, excellence and world-class performance. They serve as role models for organizations of all kinds striving to improve effectiveness and increase value to their customers."

The 2007 Baldrige award recipients were selected from a field of 84 applicants. All of the applicants were evaluated rigorously by an independent board of examiners in seven areas: leadership; strategic planning; customer and market focus; measurement, analysis and knowledge management; workforce focus; process management; and results.

Source: http://www.nist.gov/public_affairs/releases/2007baldrigerecipients.html.

heighten awareness of quality by making everyone aware of his or her potential impact on quality. Naturally, this should lead to more attention to detail and concern for accuracy.

Most successful zero-defects programs have the following characteristics:

1. Extensive communication regarding the importance of quality—signs, posters, contests, and so on.
2. Organizationwide recognition—publicly granting rewards, certificates, and plaques for high-quality work.
3. Problem identification by employees—employees point out areas where they think quality can be improved.
4. Employee goal setting—employees participate in setting quality goals.[21]

The Malcolm Baldrige National Quality Award

Malcolm Baldrige Award
Recognition of U.S. companies' achievements in quality.

In 1987, the U.S. Congress passed the Malcolm Baldrige National Quality Improvement Act. The purpose of this legislation was to inspire increased efforts by U.S. businesses to improve the quality of their products and services. The **Malcolm Baldrige Award** is named after the late Malcolm Baldrige, who was a successful businessman and a former U.S. secretary of commerce. The award is administered by the National Institute of Standards and Technology and can only be awarded to businesses located in the United States. The purpose of the award is to encourage efforts to improve quality and to recognize the quality achievements of U.S. companies. A maximum of two awards may be given annually in each of five categories: manufacturing, service, small business (500 or less employees), education, and health care. Education and health care were added as categories in 1999. In October 2004, President Bush signed legislation that expands the Baldrige Award to include nonprofit and government organizations. Management Illustration 20.3 describes the Baldrige Award winners for 2007.

Types of Quality Control

product quality control
Relates to inputs or outputs of the system; used when quality is evaluated with respect to a batch of existing products or services.

Quality control relating to the inputs or outputs of the system is referred to as **product quality control** (sometimes called *acceptance control*). Product quality control is used when the quality is being evaluated with respect to a batch of products or services that already exists, such as incoming raw materials or finished goods. Product quality control lends itself to acceptance sampling procedures, in which some portion of a batch of outgoing items (or incoming materials) is inspected to ensure that the batch meets specifications with regard to the percentage of defective units that will be tolerated in the batch. With acceptance sampling procedures, the decision to accept or reject an entire batch is based on a sample or group of samples.

process control
Relates to equipment and processes used during the production process; used to monitor quality while the product or service is being produced.

Process control concerns monitoring quality while the product or service is being produced. Process control relates to the control of the equipment and processes used during the production process. Under process control, periodic samples are taken from a process and compared to a predetermined standard. If the sample results are acceptable, the process is allowed to continue. If the sample results are not acceptable, the process is halted and adjustments are made to bring the machines or processes back under control.

acceptance sampling
Statistical method of predicting the quality of a batch or a large group of products by inspecting a sample or group of samples.

Acceptance sampling is a method of predicting the quality of a batch or a large group of products from an inspection of a sample or group of samples taken from the batch. Acceptance sampling is used for one of three basic reasons:

1. The potential losses or costs of passing defective items are not great relative to the cost of inspection; for example, it would not be appropriate to inspect every match produced by a match factory.
2. Inspection of some items requires destruction of the product being tested, as is the case when testing flash bulbs.
3. Sampling usually produces results more rapidly than does a census.

Acceptance sampling draws a random sample of a given size from the batch or lot being examined. The sample is then tested and analyzed. If more than a certain number (determined statistically) are found to be defective, the entire batch is rejected, as it is deemed to have an unacceptably large percentage of defective items. Because of the possibility of making an incorrect inference concerning the batch, acceptance sampling always involves risks. The risk the producer is willing to take of rejecting a good batch is referred to as the *producer's risk.* The risk of accepting a bad batch is referred to as the *consumer's risk.* Obviously, one would desire to minimize both the producer's risk and the consumer's risk. However, the only method of simultaneously lowering both of these risks is to increase the sample size, which also increases the inspection costs. Therefore, the usual approach is to decide on the maximum acceptable risk for both the producer and the consumer and design the acceptance sampling plan around these risks.

process control chart
Time-based graphic display that shows whether a machine or a process is producing items that meet preestablished specifications.

A **process control chart** is a time-based graphic display that shows whether a machine or a process is producing output at the expected quality level. If a significant change in the variable being checked is detected, the machine is said to be out of control. Control charts do not attempt to show why a machine is out of control, only whether it is out of control.

The most frequently used process control charts are called *mean* and *range charts.* Mean charts (also called *X-charts*) monitor the mean or average value of some characteristic (dimension, weight, etc.) of the items produced by a machine or process. Range charts (also called *R-charts*) monitor the range of variability of some characteristic (dimension, weight, etc.) of the items produced by a machine or process.

The quality control inspector, using control charts, first calculates the desired level of the characteristic being measured. The next step is to calculate statistically the upper and lower

FIGURE 20.6
Mean Chart

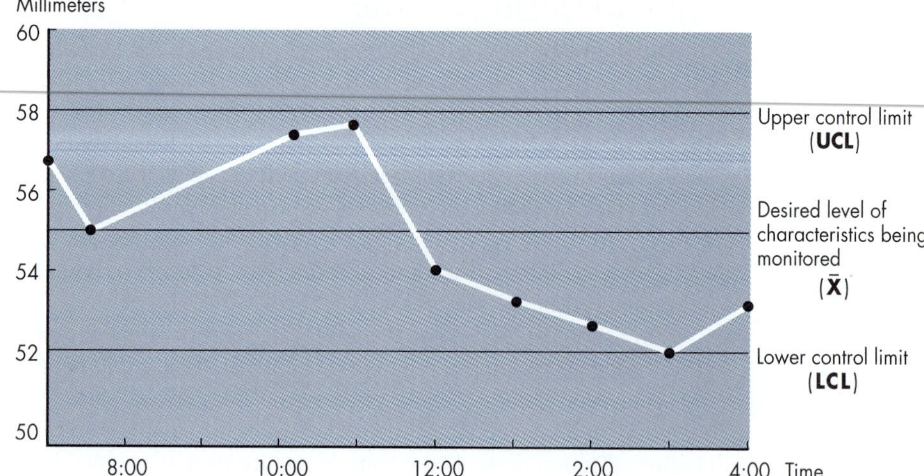

control limits, which determine how much the characteristic can vary from the desired level before the machine or process is considered to be out of control. Once the control chart has been set up, the quality control inspector periodically takes a small sample from the machine or process outputs. Depending on the type of chart being used, the mean or range of the sample is plotted on the control chart. By plotting the results of each sample on the control chart, it is easy to identify quickly any abnormal trends in quality. Figure 20.6 shows a sample mean chart. A range chart looks like a mean chart; the only difference is that the range, as opposed to the mean, of the characteristic being monitored is plotted.

A mean or range chart used by itself can easily lead to false conclusions. For example, the upper and lower control limits for a machined part might be 0.1000 millimeter and 0.0800 millimeter, respectively. A sample of four parts of 0.1200, 0.1100, 0.0700, and 0.0600 would yield an acceptable mean of 0.0900; yet every element of the sample is out of tolerance. For this reason, when monitoring variables, it is usually desirable to use mean and range charts simultaneously to ensure that a machine or a process is under control.

INVENTORY CONTROL

inventory
Quantity of raw materials, in-process goods, or finished goods on hand; serves as a buffer between different rates of flow associated with the operating system.

Inventories serve as a buffer between different rates of flow associated with the operating system. **Inventories** are generally classified into one of three categories, depending on their location within the operating system: (1) raw material, (2) in process, or (3) finished goods. Raw material inventories serve as a buffer between purchasing and production. In-process inventories are used to buffer differences in the rates of flow through the various production processes. Finished-goods inventories act as a buffer between the final stage of production and shipping.

Inventories add flexibility to the operating system and allow the organization to do the following:

1. Purchase, produce, and ship in economic lot sizes rather than in small jobs.
2. Produce on a smooth, continuous basis even if the demand for the finished product or raw material fluctuates.
3. Prevent major problems when forecasts of demand are in error or when unforeseen slowdowns or stoppages in supply or production occur.

FIGURE 20.7
Benefits of JIT System

Source: N. Gaither, *Production and Operations Management* (Fort Worth: Dryden Press, 1992).

1. Inventory levels are drastically lowered.
2. The time it takes products to go through the production facility is greatly reduced. This enables the organization to be more flexible and more responsive to changing customer demands.
3. Product/service quality is improved and the cost of scrap is reduced because defective parts and services are discovered earlier.
4. With smaller product batches, less space is occupied by inventory and materials-handling equipment. This also allows employees to work closer together, which improves communication and teamwork.

If it were not so costly, every organization would attempt to maintain very large inventories to facilitate purchasing, production scheduling, and distribution. However, many costs are associated with carrying inventory. Potential inventory costs include such factors as insurance, property taxes, storage costs, obsolescence costs, spoilage, and the opportunity cost of the money invested in the inventory. The relative importance of these costs depends on the specific inventory being held. For example, with women's fashions, the obsolescence costs are potentially high. Similarly, the storage costs for dangerous chemicals may be high. Thus, management must continually balance the costs of holding the inventory against the costs of running short of raw materials, in-process goods, or finished goods.

Just-in-Time Inventory Control

just-in-time inventory control (JIT)
Inventory control system that schedules materials to arrive and leave as they are needed.

Just-in-time inventory control (JIT) was pioneered in Japan but has become popular in the United States. JIT systems are sometimes referred to as *zero inventory systems, stockless systems,* or *kanban systems.* JIT is actually a philosophy for production to ensure that the right items arrive and leave as they are needed. Traditionally, incoming raw materials are ordered in relatively few, large shipments and stored in warehouses until needed for production or for providing a service.

Under JIT, organizations make smaller and more frequent orders of raw materials. JIT depends on the elimination of set-up time between the production of different batches of different products. JIT can be viewed as an operating philosophy whose basic objective is to eliminate waste. In this light, waste is "anything other than the minimum amount of equipment, materials, parts, space, and workers' time which are absolutely essential to add value to the product or service."[22]

Traditionally raw materials were ordered in relatively few, large shipments and stored in warehouses until needed. Under JIT (just-in-time inventory control), organizations make smaller and more frequent orders of raw materials.

The JIT philosophy applies not only to inventories of incoming raw materials but also to the production of subassemblies or final products. The idea is not to produce an item or a subassembly until it is needed for shipment. JIT is called a *demand pull system* because items are produced or ordered only when they are needed (or pulled) by the next stage in the production process. Figure 20.7 summarizes the benefits of JIT. One potential hazard is that the entire production line can be shut down if the needed parts or subassemblies are not available when needed. JIT has been successfully implemented by many American companies, including Hewlett-Packard, Motorola, Black & Decker, General Motors, Ford, Chrysler, General Electric, Goodyear, and IBM.[23]

Despite the popularity of JIT in American business, it is not a quick fix for all the quality and operations problems a company may face. In fact, JIT may take many years to really catch hold in a company. Beginning in the early 1960s, it took Toyota over 20 years to fully implement the concept.[24] Although JIT was a key to Toyota's lean production system, it also exposed

Management Illustration 20.4

TOYOTA REAFFIRMS BELIEF IN ITS JIT SYSTEM

The Toyota production system (TPS) was introduced in Management Illustration 19.1 in the previous chapter. Toyota learned early on that increasing productivity by itself was not enough. Just-in-time (JIT) manufacturing was introduced to complement increases in productivity. JIT resulted in less overproduction, inventory, and other wastes. JIT manufacturing helped Toyota transform itself from a traditional *push* company based on forecasts and multiple scheduling into a customer demand based *pull* system.

In July 2007 Toyota announced it was temporarily shutting down all 12 of its domestic plants after Riken Corporation, a supplier of $1.50 piston rings, was damaged by a 6.8 magnitude earthquake that hit Japan on July 16. Riken's closure forced nearly 70 percent of Japan's auto production to temporarily shut down. Despite the production setbacks, Katsuaki Watanabe, president of Toyota, reiterated his belief in the JIT system stating, "We've been implementing this strategy (JIT) for decades . . . and we'll keep on with it." Mr. Watanabe did say that the company will look for ways to become less dependent on single suppliers.

Source: Amy Chozick, "Toyota Sticks by 'Just In Time' Strategy after Quake," *The Wall Street Journal,* July 24, 2007, p. A2.

many defects in the inventory system, because JIT enables easier detection of defective inventory. Fixing these forms of defects (finding where and how the defects occurred) is sometimes time-consuming and difficult to accomplish. Management Illustration 20.4 discusses how Toyota recently reaffirmed its belief in its JIT system.

Tom Peters offers a new twist on JIT. He believes that instead of using JIT just to assist suppliers in improving their products (i.e., resulting in fewer defective parts), a company can push JIT forward in the distribution channel to proactively seek out opportunities to assist customers (using some variant of JIT as a marketing strategy) and link them to the company's processes. In other words, by examining and solving customers' problems by supplying them with exactly what they need, the company not only improves its quality control but also builds ties to its customer base.[25]

Tracking Inventory

Before computers, tracking inventory was a tedious and time-consuming task. It was difficult to keep accurate inventory records. Employees recorded every sale and purchase, and a bookkeeper would subtract all sales and add all purchases at the end of the week. This determined how much inventory remained in stock. However, employees often forgot to record transactions. Bookkeepers frequently made mistakes computing figures. Both kinds of errors made it difficult for businesses to know how much inventory they actually had in stock.

Bar Code Technology

Technology has improved inventory tracking. Most items are marked with *bar codes,* patterns of bars and spaces that an electronic scanner recognizes. Bar coding has reduced errors in tracking inventory. When a company purchases or sells an item, an employee scans the item's bar code. A computer program recognizes the information contained in the bar code and automatically adds or subtracts the item from inventory.

Physical Inventory

physical inventory Counting the number of units of inventory a company holds in stock.

Even if computers track inventory, managers need to take physical inventory. A **physical inventory** involves actually counting the number of units of inventory a company holds in stock. Most businesses perform a physical inventory once or twice a year.

Managers need to conduct physical inventories because actual inventory is often different from the level of inventory tracked. The discrepancy may reflect errors or unauthorized

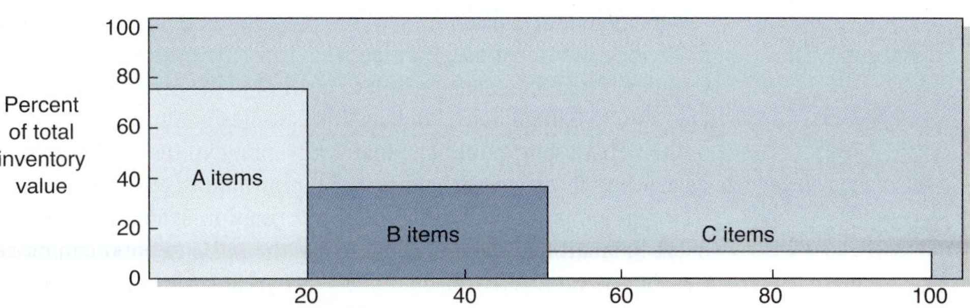

FIGURE 20.8
ABC Inventory Classification
Shows the inventory value for each group versus the group's portion of the total list.

Source: From Richard B. Chase, F. Robert Jacobs, and Nicholas J. Aquilano, *Operation Management for Competitive Advantage,* 11th ed., 2006. Copyright © 2004. Reproduced with permission of The McGraw-Hill Companies.

withdrawals, including theft. Managers who do not adjust their inventory occasionally may experience shortages.

Independent versus Dependent Demand Items

independent demand items
Finished goods ready to be shipped out or sold.

dependent demand items
Subassembly or component parts used to make a finished product; their demand is based on the number of finished products being produced.

Independent demand items are finished goods or other end items. For the most part, independent demand items are sold or shipped out as opposed to being used in making another product. Examples of independent demand environments include most retail shops, book publishing, and hospital supplies.[26] **Dependent demand items** are typically subassemblies or component parts that will be used in making some finished product. In these cases, the demand for the items depends on the number of finished products being produced. An example is the demand for wheels for new cars. If the car company plans to make 1,000 cars next month, it knows it must have 5,000 wheels on hand (allowing for spares).[27] With independent demand items, forecasting plays an important role in inventory stocking decisions. With dependent demand items, inventory stocking requirements are determined directly from the production plan.

ABC Classification System

ABC classification system
Method of managing inventories based on their total value.

One of the simplest and most widely used systems for managing inventories is the ABC approach. The **ABC classification system** manages inventories based on the total value of their usage per unit of time. In many organizations, a small number of products or materials, group A, account for the greatest dollar value of the inventory; the next group of items, group B, accounts for a moderate amount of the inventory value; and group C accounts for a small amount of the inventory value. Figure 20.8 illustrates this concept. The dollar value reflects both the cost of the item and the item's usage rate. For example, an item might be put into group A through a combination of either low cost and high usage or high cost and low usage.

Grouping items in this way establishes appropriate control over each item. Generally, the items in group A are monitored very closely; the items in group B are monitored with some care; and the items in group C are checked only occasionally. Items in group C are usually not subject to the detailed paperwork of items in groups A and B. In an automobile service station, gasoline would be considered a group A item and monitored daily. Tires, batteries, and transmission fluid would be group B items and might be checked weekly or biweekly. Valve stems, windshield wiper blades, radiator caps, hoses, fan belts, oil and gas additives, car wax, and so forth would be group C items and might be checked and ordered only every two or three months.[28]

One potential shortcoming of the ABC method is that although the items in group C may have very little cost/usage value, they may be critical to the operation. It is possible, for instance, for an inexpensive bolt to be vital to the production of a costly piece of machinery. One way to handle items such as this is to designate them as group A or B items regardless of their cost/usage value. The major advantage of the ABC method is that it concentrates on controlling those items that are most important to the operation.

With computer technology and information systems becoming increasingly commonplace in small and medium-size firms, the ABC method can be computerized and categories can be monitored or changed with greater skill and accuracy. An additional value of computerizing the operation and control of the classification system is the power it brings to ordering cycles and stock control.

Safety Stocks

safety stocks Inventory maintained to accommodate unexpected changes in demand and supply and allow for variations in delivery time.

Most organizations maintain **safety stocks** to accommodate unexpected changes in demand and supply and allow for variations in delivery time. The optimal size of the safety stock is determined by the relative costs of a stock-out of the item versus the costs of carrying the additional inventory. The cost of a stock-out of the item is often difficult to estimate. For example, the customer may choose to go elsewhere rather than wait for the product. If the product is available at another branch location, the stock-out cost may be simply the cost of shipping the item from one location to another.

The Order Quantity

Most materials and finished products are consumed one by one or a few units at a time; however, because of the costs associated with ordering, shipping, and handling inventory, it is usually desirable to purchase materials and products in large lots or batches.

When determining the optimal number of units to order, the ordering costs must be balanced against the cost of carrying the inventory. *Ordering costs* include such things as the cost of preparing the order, shipping costs, and setup costs. The capacity to order online has reduced the ordering costs for many organizations. *Carrying costs* include storage costs, insurance, taxes, obsolescence, and the opportunity costs of the money invested in the inventory. The smaller the number of units ordered, the lower the carrying costs (because the average inventory held is smaller) but the higher the ordering costs (because more orders must be placed). The optimal number of units to order, referred to as the **economic order quantity (EOQ),** is determined by the point at which ordering costs equal carrying costs, or where total cost (ordering costs plus carrying costs) is at a minimum.

economic order quantity (EOQ) Optimal number of units to order at one time.

The greatest weakness of the EOQ approach is the difficulty in accurately determining the actual carrying and ordering costs. However, research has shown that the total costs associated with order sizes that are reasonably close to the economic order quantity do not differ appreciably from the minimum total costs associated with the EOQ.[29] Thus, as long as the estimated carrying and ordering costs are in the ballpark, this approach can yield meaningful results. Variations of this basic model have been developed to take into account such things as purchase quantity and other special discounts.

material requirements planning (MRP) Dependent inventory planning and control system that schedules the right amount of materials needed to produce the final product on schedule.

Material Requirements Planning

Material requirements planning (MRP) is a special type of inventory system in which the needed amount of each component of a product is figured on the basis of the amount of the final product to be produced. When each component is needed depends on when the

FIGURE 20.9
Potential Advantages of Material Requirements Planning (MRP)

Source: From James B. Dilworth, *Production and Operations Management*, 4th ed., McGraw-Hill, 1989. Reprinted with permission of the author.

1. Reduces the average amount of inventory for dependent demand items (raw material, parts, and work-in-progress inventory).
2. Improves work flow, resulting in reduced elapsed time between the start and finish of jobs.
3. Enables delivery promises to be more reliable.
4. Minimizes parts shortages.
5. Keeps priorities of work items up to date so that shop work is more effective and appropriate.
6. Helps plan the timing of design changes and aids in their implementation.
7. Can simulate and evaluate changes in the master schedule.
8. Tells management ahead of time if desired delivery dates appear achievable.
9. Changes (expedites or deexpedites) due dates for orders.
10. Facilitates capacity requirements planning.

final assembly is needed and the lead time required to incorporate the component into the assembly.

The purpose of MRP is to get the right materials to the right places at the right times. It does little good to have some of the parts needed to produce a product if the organization does not have all of them. Because carrying parts that are not being used is costly, the idea behind MRP is to provide either all or none of the necessary components. Figure 20.9 outlines some of the advantages of MRP.

Japanese organizations have used MRP to support their highly productive manufacturing and assembly process. Their planning systems include strategic industrial outsourcing. Under this concept, help with the MRP process is gained by relying on strategic partners to supply critical components. From their traditional vertically integrated system, entry and exit of resources and products are extremely efficient. Most suppliers' modernization attempts have been aided by the parent manufacturer so that the outsourcer and the manufacturer's systems match. Once the MRP systems are in alignment, significant gains can be made in cost savings and production efficiency.[30]

Almost all MRP systems, regardless of the competitive system in which they operate, utilize a computer because of its ability to store inventory records, production sequences, and production lead times and then rapidly convert these data into period-by-period production schedules and inventory levels.

MRP utilizes three basic documents: (1) the master production schedule, (2) the bill of materials, and (3) the inventory status file. The *master production schedule* is derived from the aggregate production plan and forecasts the number of end products to be produced for a given period. The *bill of materials* is a listing of all parts and subassemblies that make up each end product. The *inventory status file* is a record of parts currently in inventory.

The MRP system uses these three files to create schedules that identify the specific parts and materials required to produce end items, the precise numbers needed, and the dates when orders for these materials should be placed and be received or completed. For example, if the master production schedule determines that a manufacturer needs to have 100 end items assembled and ready for shipment by June, the company may need to order some subcomponents in April and make additional subcomponent orders in May. Use of an MRP system allows a production planner to take the requirements for end items and "back schedule" the production and ordering of subcomponents. The MRP printout would indicate how much of each subcomponent and when to order so as to meet the end item production

FIGURE 20.10
Overall View of the Inputs to a Standard Material Requirements Planning Program and the Reports Generated by the Program

Source: From Richard B. Chase, F. Robert Jacobs, and Nicholas J. Aquilano, *Operations Management for Competitive Advantage,* 11th ed., 2006. Reproduced with permission of The McGraw-Hill Companies.

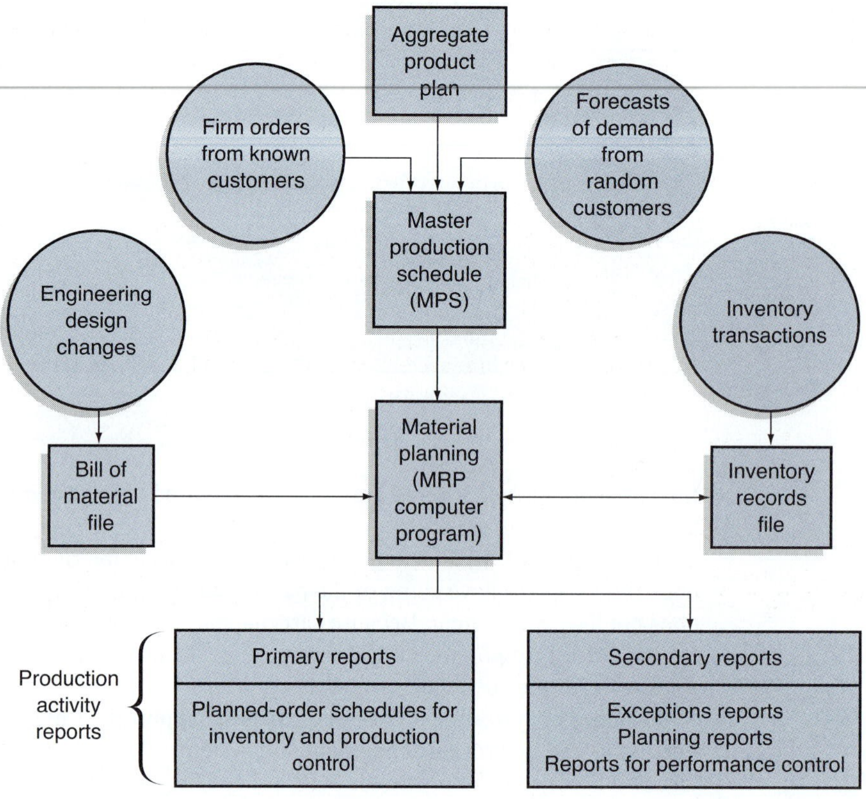

requirements. Figure 20.10 presents an overall view of the inputs to and the reports generated by a basic MRP system.

MRP differs from JIT in that MRP generally produces to forecasts (a push system) rather than to actual demands (a pull system). MRP allows for large batch production of parts, whereas JIT strives for small batches. Many companies combine elements of both MRP and JIT.[31] In these instances, companies use basic MRP for ordering purposes and materials management and then execute using JIT procedures. Figure 20.11 provides a general comparison between JIT and MRP.

FIGURE 20.11
Differences between JIT and MRP

Source: From Nicholas J. Aquilano and Richard B. Chase, *Fundamentals of Operations Management,* 1991, p. 582. Reproduced with permission of The McGraw-Hill Companies.

Operating System Characteristics	JIT	MRP
Focus	Physical operations	Information system
Rates of output	Level schedule	Variable production plan
Work authorization	Kanban pull	Master schedule push
Data philosophy	Minimize data captured	Capture all data
Problem response	Resolve and fix	Regenerate
Clerical personnel	Decreased	Increased
Forms of control	Shop floor, visual, line workers	Middle management reports, staff
Capacity adjustment	Visual, immediate	Capacity requirements planning, deferred

Summary

1. *Understand the basic requirements for controlling operating costs.* The first requirement for controlling costs is to understand the organization's accounting and budgeting system. Once the budgets have been put into effect, they must be carefully monitored for any unexpected cost variances. Any cost variances detected must then be analyzed to determine the cause.
2. *Define quality from the perspective of an operations manager.* The operations manager's primary concern is that the product or service specifications be achieved. For the operations manager, quality is determined in relation to the specifications or standards set in the design stages.
3. *List the eight common dimensions of design quality.* The eight common dimensions of design quality are performance, features, reliability, durability, serviceability, response, aesthetics, and reputation.
4. *Explain the concept of quality assurance.* Quality assurance refers to the idea of "building in" quality as opposed to "inspecting it in."
5. *Explain the concept of total quality management (TQM).* Total quality management is a management philosophy that emphasizes managing the entire organization so that it excels in all dimensions of products and services that are important to the customer. In essence, TQM is an organizationwide emphasis on quality as defined by the customer.
6. *Define the following terms: continuous improvement, kaizen, quality at the source, lean manufacturing, six sigma*, and *lean six sigma*. Continuous improvement refers to an ongoing effort to make improvements in every part of the organization relative to all of its products and services. Kaizen is a philosophy for improvement that originated in Japan and that literally means "good change." Kaizen is basically a system of taking small steps to improve the workplace. Quality at the source refers to the philosophy of making each employee responsible for the quality of his or her work. Lean manufacturing is a systematic approach to identifying and eliminating waste and non-value-added activities. Six sigma is a precise set of statistical tools and a rallying cry for continuous improvement. The philosophy of six sigma is that in order to realize the very high level of quality demanded by six sigma (most processes traditionally have used three sigma), the entire production or service system must be examined and improved. Lean six sigma is a combination of lean methods and six sigma and draws on the philosophies, principles, and tools of both approaches. Lean six sigma's goal is growth and not just cost-cutting.
7. *Describe ISO 9000, ISO 14000, and the zero-defects approach to quality.* ISO 9000 is a series of quality standards originally established in 1987 by the International Organization for Standardization (ISO). ISO 9000 focuses on the design and operations processes and not on the end product or service. ISO 9000 requires extensive documentation in order to demonstrate the consistency and reliability of the processes being used. The ISO 14000 series was developed to control the impact of an organization's activities and outputs on the environment. A zero-defects program attempts to create a positive attitude toward the prevention of low quality.
8. *Identify and define the two major types of quality control.* The two major types of quality control are product quality control and process control. Product quality control is used when the quality is being evaluated with respect to a batch of products or services that already exist, such as incoming raw materials or finished goods. Under process control, machines or processes are periodically checked to detect significant changes in the quality produced by the process.

9. *Recount the major reasons for carrying inventories.* Inventories add flexibility to the operating system and allow the organization to do the following:
   - Purchase, produce, and ship in economic lot sizes rather than in small jobs.
   - Produce on a smooth, continuous basis even if the demand for the finished product or raw material fluctuates.
   - Prevent major problems when forecasts of demand are in error or when unforeseen slowdowns or stoppages in supply or production occur.
10. *Explain the concept of just-in-time (JIT) inventory.* JIT is a philosophy for scheduling so that the right items arrive and leave at the right time. The basic idea under JIT is to have materials arrive just as they are needed.
11. *Describe the ABC classification system for managing inventories.* The ABC classification system is a method of managing inventories based on the total value of their usage per unit of time. In many organizations, a small number of products, group A, account for the greater dollar value of the inventory; the next group of items, group B, accounts for a moderate amount of the inventory value; and group C accounts for a small amount of the inventory value. The purpose of grouping items in this way is to establish appropriate control over each item. Generally, the items in group A are monitored closely; the items in group B are monitored with some care; and the items in group C are checked only occasionally.
12. *Summarize the economic order quantity (EOQ) concept.* When determining the optimal number of units to order, the ordering costs must be balanced against the cost of carrying the inventory. Ordering costs include such things as the cost of preparing the order, shipping costs, and setup costs. Carrying costs include storage costs, insurance, taxes, obsolescence, and the opportunity costs of the money invested in the inventory. The smaller the number of units ordered, the lower the carrying costs (because the average inventory held is smaller) but the higher the ordering costs (because more orders must be placed). The optimal number of units to order, referred to as the economic order quantity (EOQ), is determined by the point where ordering costs equal carrying costs, or where total cost (ordering costs plus carrying costs) is at a minimum.
13. *Describe the basic purposes of material requirements planning (MRP).* Material requirements planning is a special type of inventory system in which the needed amount of each component of a product is figured on the basis of the amount of the final product to be produced. When each component is needed depends on when the final assembly is needed and the lead time required to incorporate the component into the assembly. The purpose of MRP is to get the right materials to the right places at the right times.

Review Questions

1. Name the three major categories of costs that usually concern operations managers from a control standpoint. Give several examples of each category.
2. What is the difference between fixed and variable overhead expenses?
3. What are the eight common dimensions of design quality?
4. Define quality assurance.
5. Explain the concept of total quality management.
6. Define continuous improvement and kaizen. How are they related?
7. Define lean manufacturing, six sigma, and lean six sigma.

8. What is the meaning of "quality at the source"?
9. What is reengineering?
10. Explain the thrust of ISO 9000 and of ISO 14000.
11. What is the objective of a zero-defects program?
12. What is the Malcolm Baldrige Award?
13. Differentiate between product quality control and process quality control.
14. What are the purposes of inventories?
15. What is just-in-time inventory control?
16. Explain the difference between independent and dependent demand items.
17. How does the ABC classification system work?

Skill-Building Questions

1. Given that quality is a relative concept, how does a manager ever know if the quality level is optimal?
2. Total quality management has gotten a lot of attention over the last several years. How do you account for this phenomenon? Do you think it is justified or just a lot of hype about nothing new?
3. What do you think are the most significant barriers to the implementation of TQM programs? What would you recommend to fix the problems?
4. Suppose you are manager of a drive-in restaurant and your business fluctuates dramatically from season to season as well as from day to day within a season. Discuss the production control problems such a situation presents.
5. It has been said that good inventory management can make the difference between success and failure in certain industries. Name several industries in which this statement is particularly applicable, and discuss the reasons for your answer.

SKILL-BUILDING EXERCISE 20.1
Out of Control?

Situation 1

The manager of a fast-food hamburger chain must ensure that the hamburger advertised as a quarter-pounder is actually 4 ounces, more or less. The company policy states that the quarter-pounder must come within 3/10 of an ounce of being 4 ounces in order to be used. The following chart reflects the expected weight of the patty (4 ounces), the upper control limit (4.3 ounces), and the lower control limit (3.7 ounces). A sample of patties has been taken each day for the last eight days, and the average weight recorded for each day is recorded on the chart.

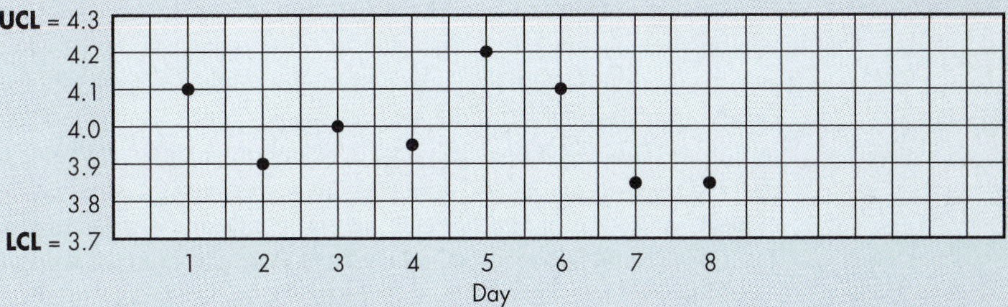

1. Should the patty preparation process be investigated?
2. Why do you think so?

Situation 2

You are the owner of a car repair shop that specializes in tune-ups. On each work order, the mechanic records the time at which he began the tune-up and the time when finished. From these data, you can determine how long each mechanic spends on each job. You expect each job to take about 40 minutes; however, you know that if someone were in a hurry, the job could be done in as few as 20 minutes. Also, you believe that under no circumstances should a tune-up take over one hour. A recently hired mechanic has recorded the times shown on the following chart for his last 11 tune-up jobs:

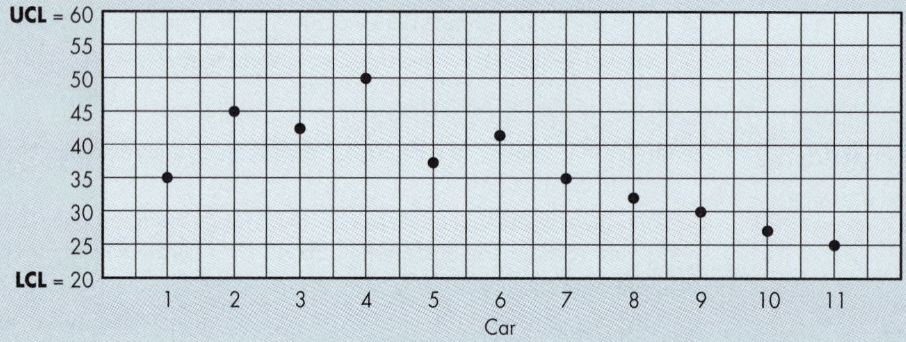

1. Should you have a talk with this mechanic? Is there a problem?
2. Why do you think so?

Source: This exercise is adapted from Henry L. Tosi and Jerald W. Young, *Management Experiences and Demonstrations* (Homewood, IL: Richard D. Irwin, 1982), pp. 45–47.

SKILL-BUILDING EXERCISE 20.2

How Important Is Quality?

Think of the last product or service that you purchased that cost at least $500. What role did quality play in making your decision to purchase the item or service? Now that you have used the product or service, are you satisfied with its quality? If you could go through the selection process again, would you make the same choice? What, if anything, would you do differently?

Case Incident 20.1

Production Problems

Braddock Company of Sea Shore City fabricates stamped metal parts used in the production of wheelbarrows. Braddock fabricates two basic styles of wheelbarrow trays: One is for a deep, four-cubic-foot construction model, and the other is for a shallow, two-cubic-foot homeowner's model. Braddock's process is simple. Raw metal sheets are picked up from inventory (Braddock presently maintains about 7 days' worth of the large metal sheets for the construction model and about 10 days' worth of the smaller sheets for the homeowner's model) and fed into a large machine that bends and shapes the metal into the desired tray. The trays are then inspected and packaged, 10 to a box, for shipping.

In the past few days, Braddock has been experiencing quality problems with both tray styles. Undesirable creases have been forming in the corners following the stamping operation. However, the problem with the construction model tray is more pronounced and appeared almost three full days before it did on the homeowner's model.

Several incidents have occurred at Braddock during the past week that Hal McCarthy, the operations manager, thinks may have a bearing on the problem. Shorty McCune, a machine operator and labor activist, was accused of drinking on the job and released a few days before the problem began. Since his release, Shorty has been seen in and around the plant talking to several other employees. About two weeks ago, Braddock also began receiving raw metal from a new supplier because of an attractive price break.

The only inspection the company performs is the postfabrication inspection.

Questions

1. What do you think is causing Braddock's problem?
2. Why is the problem more pronounced on the construction model than on the homeowner's model?
3. How can Braddock eliminate its problem?

Case Incident 20.2

The Purchasing Department

The buyers for a large airline company were having a general discussion with the manager of purchasing in her office Friday afternoon. The inspection of received parts was a topic of considerable discussion. Apparently, several parts had recently been rejected six months or more after being received. Such a rejection delay was costing the company a considerable amount of money, since most of the items were beyond the standard 90-day warranty period. The current purchasing procedures state that the department using the parts is responsible for the inspection of all parts, including stock and nonstock items. The company employs an inspector who is supposedly responsible for inspecting all aircraft parts, in accordance with FAA regulations. However, the inspector has not been able to check those items purchased as nonaircraft parts because he is constantly overloaded. Furthermore, many of the aircraft parts are not being properly inspected because of insufficient facilities and equipment.

One recent example of the type of problem being encountered was the acceptance of a batch of plastic forks that broke easily when in use. The vendor had shipped over 100 cases of the forks of the wrong type. Unfortunately, all the purchase order specified was "forks." Another example was the acceptance of several cases of plastic cups with the wrong logo. The cups were put into use for in-flight service and had to be used because no other cups were available. A final example was the discovery that several expensive radar tubes in stock were found to be defective and with expired warranties. These tubes had to be reordered at almost $900 per unit.

It was apparent that the inspection function was inadequate and unable to cope with the volume of material being received. Purchasing would have to establish some guidelines as to what material should or should not be inspected after being processed by the material checker. Some of the buyers thought the material checker (who is not the inspector) should have more responsibility than simply checking quantity and comparing the packing sheet against purchase orders. Some believed the checker could and should have caught the obvious errors in the logo on the plastic cups. Furthermore, if the inspector had sampled the forks, they would have been rejected immediately. As for the radar tubes, they should have been forwarded by the inspector to the avionics shop for bench check after being received. Such a rejection delay was costing the company a considerable amount of money, since most of the items were beyond the standard 90-day warranty period. The current purchasing procedures state that the department using the parts is responsible for the inspection before the part is placed in stock. Some buyers thought the inspector should be responsible for inspection of all materials received, regardless of its function or usage. It was pointed out, however, that several landing gears had been received from the overhaul/repair vendor and tagged by the inspector as being acceptable. These gears later turned out to be defective and unstable and had to be returned for repair. This generated considerable discussion concerning the inspector's qualifications, testing capacity, workload, and responsibility for determining if the unit should be shop-checked.

Much of the remaining discussion centered around what purchasing should recommend for the inspection of material. One proposal was that everything received be funneled through the Inspection Department. Another proposal was that all material be run through inspection except as otherwise noted on the purchase order. Other questions were also raised. If purchasing required all material to be inspected, would this demand additional inspection personnel? Who would be responsible for inspection specifications? Furthermore, who should determine what items should be shop-checked?

The meeting was finally adjourned until the following Friday.

Questions

1. What do you think of the current system of inspection?
2. Do you think the inspector is at fault? Explain.
3. What would you suggest happen at the meeting next Friday?

References and Additional Readings

1. Y. S. Chang, George Labovitz, and Victor Rosansky, *Making Quality Work* (New York: Harper Business, 1993), p. 65.
2. Richard B. Chase, F. Robert Jacobs, and Nicholas J. Aquilano, *Operations Management for Competitive Advantage,* 11th ed. (New York: McGraw-Hill/Irwin, 2006), p. 322.
3. William J. Stevenson, *Production/Operations Management,* 4th ed. (Burr Ridge, IL: Richard D. Irwin, 1993), p. 99.
4. Ibid., p. 100.
5. Tom Peters, *Thriving on Chaos* (New York: Alfred A. Knopf, 1987), pp. 118–19.
6. Parts of this section were drawn from Stevenson, *Production/Operations Management,* p. 101.
7. Chase, Jacobs, and Aquilano, *Operations Management for Competitive Advantage,* p. 320.
8. Stevenson, *Production/Operations Management,* pp. 104–105.
9. Adapted from Francis X. Mahoney and Carl G. Thor, *The TQM Trilogy* (New York: AMACOM, 1994), pp. 132–37. Excerpted by permission of the publisher. All rights reserved.
10. Ibid., p. 134.
11. Richard B. Chase and Nicholas J. Aquilano, *Production and Operations Management: A Life Cycle Approach,* 6th ed. (Homewood, IL: Richard D. Irwin, 1992), p. 196; other parts of this section are drawn from this source.
12. Vivienne Walker, "Kaizen—The Art of Continual Improvement," *Personnel Management,* August 1993, pp. 36–38.
13. Stevenson, *Production/Operations Management,* p. 105.
14. Esther Durkalski, "Lean Times Call for Lean Concepts," *Official Board Markets,* October 26, 2002, p. 38.
15. Erik Einset and Julie Marzano, "Six Sigma Demystified," *Tooling and Production,* April 2002, p. 43.
16. Ken Cowman, "Six Sigma: What, Where, When, Why and How," *Materials Management and Distribution,* October 2005, p. 69.

17. Much of this section is drawn from George Byrne, Dave Lubowe, and Amy Blitz, "Using a Lean Six Sigma Approach to Drive Innovation," *Strategy & Leadership* 35, No. 2, 2007, pp. 5–10.
18. Thomas B. Clark, "Business Process Reengineering," Working Paper, Georgia State University, November 1997, p. 1.
19. http://www.iso.org/iso/pressrelease.html?refid=Ref1089. Accessed on February 10, 2008.
20. Ibid.
21. Chase and Aquilano, *Production and Operations Management,* pp. 654–55.
22. Nicholas J. Aquilano and Richard B. Chase, *Fundamentals of Operations Management* (Homewood, IL: Richard D. Irwin, 1991), p. 586.
23. Norman Gaither, *Production and Operations Management,* 5th ed. (Forth Worth: Dryden Press, 1992), p. 377.
24. Jeremy Main, *Quality Wars* (New York: Free Press, 1994), p. 115.
25. Peters, *Thriving on Chaos,* p. 117.
26. Chase and Aquilano, *Production and Operations Management,* p. 481.
27. Stevenson, *Production/Operations Management,* p. 585.
28. Chase, Jacobs, and Aquilano, *Operations Management for Competitive Advantage,* p. 611.
29. John F. Magee, "Guides to Inventory Policy: I. Functions and Lot Size," *Harvard Business Review,* January–February 1956, pp. 49–60.
30. Adapted from a book review by Paul Shrivastava found in the *Academy of Management Review* 21, no. 1 (1996), p. 286, of Toshibiro Nishiguchi, *Strategic Industrial Sourcing: The Japanese Advantage* (New York: Oxford University Press, 1994).
31. Aquilano and Chase, *Fundamentals of Operations Management,* p. 581.

Glossary of Key Terms

A

ABC classification system Method of managing inventories based on their total value.

abilities Personal characteristics used in performing a job.

absolute advantage The ability to produce more of a good than another producer.

acceptance sampling Statistical method of predicting the quality of a batch or a large group of products by inspecting a sample or group of samples.

active listening Absorbing what another person is saying and responding to the person's concerns.

activity scheduling Develops the precise timetable to be followed in producing a product or service.

affirmative action plan Written document outlining specific goals and timetables for remedying past discriminatory actions.

Age Discrimination in Employment Act of 1968 Passed in 1968, initially designed to protect individuals ages 40 to 65 from discrimination in hiring, retention, and other conditions of employment. Amended in 1978 to include individuals up to age 70. Specifically, forbids mandatory retirement at 65 except in certain circumstances.

aggregate operations planning Concerned with overall operations and balancing major sections of the operating system; matches the organization's resources with demands for its goods and services.

Americans with Disabilities Act of 1990 (ADA) Gives individuals with disabilities sharply increased access to services and jobs.

apprenticeship training System in which an employee is given instruction and experience, both on and off the job, in all of the practical and theoretical aspects of the work required in a skilled occupation, craft, or trade.

aptitude tests Measure a person's capacity or potential ability to learn.

assembly chart Depicts the sequence and manner in which the various components of a product or service are assembled.

assessment center Utilizes a formal procedure to simulate the problems a person might face in a real managerial situation to evaluate the person's potential as a manager and determine the person's development needs.

audit Method of control normally involved with financial matters; also can include other areas of the organization.

authority Legitimate exercise of power; the right to issue directives and expend resources; related to power but narrower in scope.

autocratic leader Makes most decisions for the group.

avoidance Giving a person the opportunity to avoid a negative consequence by exhibiting a desirable behavior. Also called *negative reinforcement.*

B

balance of trade Difference between the value of the goods a country exports and the value of the goods it imports.

behavior (personal) control Based on direct, personal surveillance.

behaviorally anchored rating scale (BARS) Assesses behaviors required to successfully perform a job.

bet-your-company culture Requires big-stakes decisions; considerable time passes before the results are known.

board of directors Carefully selected committee that reviews major policy and strategy decisions proposed by top management.

bottom-up management Philosophy popularized by William B. Given that encouraged widespread delegation of authority to solicit the participation of all employees from the bottom to the top of the organization.

brainstorming Presenting a problem to a group and allowing group members to produce a large quantity of ideas for its solution; no criticisms are allowed initially.

brainwriting Technique in which a group is presented with a problem situation and members anonymously write down ideas, then exchange papers with others who build on ideas and pass them on until all members have participated.

break-even chart Depicts graphically the relationship of volume of operations to profits.

budget Statement of expected results or requirements expressed in financial or numerical terms.

burnout Condition that occurs when work is no longer meaningful to a person.

business game Generally provides a setting of a company and its environment and requires a team of players to make decisions involving company operations.

business strategies Focus on how to compete in a given business.

C

case study Training technique that presents real and hypothetical situations for the trainee to analyze.

central tendency Tendency of raters to rate most employees as doing average or above-average work.

centralization Little authority is delegated to lower levels of management.

checklist Requires the manager to answer yes or no to a series of questions concerning the employee's behavior.

Civil Rights Act of 1991 Permits women, persons with disabilities, and persons who are in religious minorities to have a jury trial and sue for punitive damages if they can prove intentional hiring and workplace discrimination. Also requires companies to provide evidence that the business practice that led to the discrimination was not discriminatory but was related to the performance of the job in question and consistent with business necessity.

coaching Carried out by experienced managers, emphasizes the responsibility of all managers for developing employees.

code of ethics A document that outlines the principles of conduct to be used in making decisions within an organization.

combination strategy Used when an organization simultaneously employs different strategies for different parts of the company.

committee Organization structure in which a group of people are formally appointed, organized, and superimposed on the line, line and staff, or matrix structure to consider or decide certain matters.

communication The act of exchanging information.

comparative advantage Exists when a country can produce goods more efficiently or cheaply than other countries because of its specific circumstance.

compensation Composed of the extrinsic rewards offered by the organization and consists of the base wage or salary, any incentives or bonuses, and any benefits employees receive in exchange for their work.

competitive advantage Sometimes called *business-specific advantage;* refers to some proprietary characteristic of the business, such as a brand name, that competitors cannot imitate without substantial cost and risk.

computer-aided design (CAD) Generates various views of different components and assemblies.

computer-aided engineering (CAE) Uses a product's characteristics to analyze its performance under different parameters.

computer-aided manufacturing (CAM) Uses stored data regarding various products to provide instructions for automated production equipment.

computer-based training Training that allows the trainee to absorb knowledge from a preset computer program and advance his or her knowledge in a self-paced format.

computer-integrated manufacturing (CIM) Uses computer technology to incorporate all of the organization's production-related functions into an integrated computer system to assist, augment, or automate most functions.

conceptual skills Involve understanding the relationship of the parts of a business to one another and to the business as a whole. Decision making, planning, and organizing are specific managerial activities that require conceptual skills.

concurrent (screening) control Focuses on process as it occurs; designed to detect a problem when it occurs.

conflict Overt behavior that results when an individual or a group of individuals thinks a perceived need or needs of the individual or group have been blocked or are about to be blocked.

consideration Leader behavior of showing concern for individual group members and satisfying their needs.

contingency approach to leadership Focuses on the style of leadership that is most effective in particular situations.

contingency approach to management Theorizes that different situations and conditions require different management approaches.

contingency (situational) approach to organization structure States that the most appropriate structure depends on the technology used, the rate of environmental change, and other dynamic forces.

contingency plans Address the what-ifs of the manager's job; get the manager in the habit of being prepared and knowing what to do if something does go wrong.

continuous flow system Operating system used by companies that produce large amounts of similar products/services flowing through similar stages of the operating system.

continuous improvement Refers to an ongoing effort to make improvements in every part of the organization relative to all of its products and services.

contract An agreement between two parties to carry out a transaction.

control Process of ensuring that organizational activities are going according to plan; accomplished by comparing actual performance to predetermined standards or objectives, then taking action to correct any deviations.

control tolerances Variation from the standard that is acceptable to the manager.

controlling Measuring performance against objectives, determining the causes of deviations, and taking corrective action where necessary.

copyright The protection provided to a creative work.

corporate culture Communicates how people in an organization should behave by establishing a value system conveyed through rites, rituals, myths, legends, and actions.

corporate strategies See *grand strategies.*

corporation A business formed under state or federal statutes that is authorized to act as a legal person.

creativity Coming up with an idea that is new, original, useful, or satisfying to its creator or to someone else.

critical-incident appraisal Requires the manager to keep a written record of incidents, as they occur, involving job behaviors that illustrate both satisfactory and unsatisfactory performance of the employee being rated.

critical path method (CPM) Planning and control technique that graphically depicts the relationships among the various activities of a project; used when time durations of project activities are accurately known and have little variance.

culture Set of important understandings (often unstated) that members of a community share.

customer departmentalization Defining organizational units in terms of customers served.

D

data processing Capture, processing, and storage of data.

decentralization A great deal of authority is delegated to lower levels of management.

decision making In its narrowest sense, the process of choosing from among various alternatives.

decision process Process that involves three stages: intelligence, design, and choice. Intelligence is searching the environment for conditions requiring a decision. Design is inventing, developing, and analyzing possible courses of action. Choice is the actual selection of a course of action.

defensive (retrenchment) strategy Used when a company wants or needs to reduce its operations.

democratic leader Guides and encourages the group to make decisions.

departmentalization Grouping jobs into related work units.

dependent demand items Subassembly or component parts used to make a finished product; their demand is based on the number of finished products being produced.

direct feedback Process in which the change agent communicates the information gathered through diagnosis directly to the affected people.

dissonance Feeling of conflict felt by individual trying to make a decision.

diversity Including people of different genders, races, religions, nationalities, ethnic groups, age groups, and physical abilities.

E

economic order quantity (EOQ) Optimal number of units to order at one time.

effort Results from being motivated; refers to the amount of energy an employee uses in performing a job.

embargo Involves stopping the flow of exports to or imports from a foreign country.

employee assistance program (EAP) Program sponsored by the organization that attempts to help employees with stress, burnout, and other personal problems that include alcohol and drug abuse, depression, anxiety, domestic trauma, financial problems, and other psychiatric/medical problems.

employee leasing companies Provide permanent staffs at customer companies.

empowerment Form of decentralization in which subordinates have authority to make decisions.

entrepreneur An individual who conceives the idea of what product or service to produce, starts the organization, and builds it to the point where additional people are needed.

entry socialization Adaptation process by which new employees are introduced and indoctrinated into the organization.

environmental changes All nontechnological changes that occur outside the organization.

equal employment opportunity The right of all people to work and to advance on the bases of merit, ability, and potential.

Equal Pay Act of 1963 Prohibits wage discrimination on the basis of sex.

equity theory Motivation theory based on the idea that people want to be treated fairly in relationship to others.

ergonomics Study of the interface between humans and machines.

essay appraisal method Requires the manager to describe an employee's performance in written narrative form.

ethics A set of moral principles or values that govern behavior.

evaluation phase Third phase in strategic management, in which the implemented strategic plan is monitored, evaluated, and updated.

exception principle States that managers should concentrate on matters that deviate significantly from normal and let subordinates handle routine matters; also called *management by exception.*

expectancy Employee's belief that his or her effort will lead to the desired level of performance.

expectancy approach Based on the idea that employees' beliefs about the relationship among effort, performance, and outcomes as a result of performance and the value employees place on the outcomes determine their level of motivation.

exports Goods and services that are sold abroad.

external environment Consists of everything outside the organization.

extinction Providing no positive consequences or removing previously provided positive consequences as a result of undesirable behavior.

extrinsic rewards Rewards that are directly controlled and distributed by the organization.

F

facilities layout Process of planning the optimal physical arrangement of facilities, including personnel, operating equipment, storage space, office space, materials-handling equipment, and room for customer or product movement.

Family and Medical Leave Act (FMLA) Enables qualified employees to take prolonged unpaid leave for family- and health-related reasons without fear of losing their jobs.

feedback The flow of information from the receiver to the sender.

feedback system System in which outputs from the system affect future inputs or future activities of the system.

fixed overhead expenses Expenses that do not change appreciably with fluctuations in the level of production or service.

fixed-position layout A type of facilities layout where the product is too large to move and remains in one place.

flat structure Organization with few levels and relatively large spans of management at each level.

flow process chart Outlines what happens to a product or service as it progresses through the facility.

forced-choice rating Requires the manager to rank a set of statements describing how an employee carries out the duties and responsibilities of the job.

formal plan Written, documented plan developed through an identifiable process.

formal work group Work group established and formally recognized by the organizing function of management.

formulation phase First phase in strategic management, in which the initial strategic plan is developed.

free trade area A region within which trade restrictions are reduced or eliminated.

functional departmentalization Defining organizational units in terms of the nature of the work.

functional plans Originate from the functional areas of an organization such as production, marketing, finance, and personnel.

functional strategies Concerned with the activities of the different functional areas of the business.

G

Gantt chart Planning and controlling device that graphically depicts work planned and work accomplished in their relation to each other and to time.

geographic departmentalization Defining organizational units by territories.

glass ceiling Refers to a level within the managerial hierarchy beyond which very few women and minorities advance.

global economy Economy in which companies compete actively with businesses from around the world.

Gordon technique Differs from brainstorming in that no one but the group leader knows the exact nature of the real problem under consideration. A key word is used to describe a problem area.

grand or corporate strategies Address which businesses an organization will be in and how resources will be allocated among those businesses.

grapevine Informal channels of communication within an organization.

graphic rating scale Requires the manager to assess an employee on factors such as quantity of work, dependability, job knowledge, attendance, accuracy of work, and cooperativeness.

group cohesiveness Degree of attraction each member has for the group, or the "stick-togetherness" of the group.

group conformity Degree to which the members of the group accept and abide by the norms of the group.

group norms Informal rules a group adopts to regulate and regularize group members' behavior.

groupthink Dysfunctional syndrome that cohesive groups experience that causes the group to lose its critical evaluative capabilities.

growth strategy Used when the organization tries to expand, as measured by sales, product line, number of employees, or similar measures.

H

halo effect Occurs when the interviewer allows a single prominent characteristic to dominate judgment of all other traits.

Hawthorne effect States that giving special attention to a group of employees (such as involving them in an experiment) changes their behavior.

Hawthorne studies Series of experiments conducted in 1924 at the Hawthorne plant of Western Electric in Cicero, Illinois; production increased in relationship to psychological and social conditions rather than to the environment.

horizontal or lateral communication Communication across the lines of the formal chain of command.

horizontal structure Consists of two groups. One group is composed of members of senior management who are responsible for strategic decisions and policies. The second group is composed of empowered employees working together in different process teams.

human asset accounting Determining and recording the value of an organization's human resources in its statement of financial condition.

human relations skills Involve understanding people and being able to work well with them.

human resource forecasting Process that attempts to determine the future human resource needs of the organization in light of the organization's objectives.

human resource planning (HRP) Process of getting the right number of qualified people into the right jobs at the right time. Also called *personnel planning.*

hybrid departmentalization Occurs when an organization simultaneously uses more than one type of departmentalization.

I

idiosyncrasy credit Phenomenon that occurs when certain members who have made or are making significant contributions to the group's goals are allowed to take some liberties within the group.

implementation phase Second phase in strategic management, in which the strategic plan is put into effect.

importing The purchasing of goods from a foreign company.

imports Goods and services purchased abroad.

In Search of Excellence Book by Thomas J. Peters and Robert H. Waterman, Jr., that identifies 36 companies with an excellent 20-year performance record. The authors identified eight characteristics of excellence after interviewing managers in each company.

in-basket technique Simulates a realistic situation by requiring each trainee to answer one manager's mail and telephone calls.

income tax A tax levied against a business's profits.

independent demand items Finished goods ready to be shipped out or sold.

inequity Exists when a person perceives his or her job inputs and outcomes to be less than the job inputs and outcomes of another person.

informal organization Aggregate of the personal contacts and interactions and the associated groupings of people working within the formal organization.

informal work group Work group that results from personal contacts and interactions among people and is not formally recognized by the organization.

initiating structure Leader behavior of structuring the work of group members and directing the group toward the attainment of the group's goals.

innovation Process of applying a new and creative idea to a product, service, or method of operation.

inputs What an employee perceives are his or her contributions to the organization (e.g., education, intelligence, experience, training, skills, and the effort exerted on the job).

instrumentality Employee's belief that attaining the desired level of performance will lead to desired rewards.

intellectual property Ownership of ideas; gives creators of the intellectual property the exclusive right to market and sell their work.

interest tests Determine how a person's interests compare with the interests of successful people in a specific job.

intergroup (structural) conflict Conflict that results from the organizational structure; may be relatively independent of the individuals occupying the roles within the structure.

intermittent flow system Operating system used when customized products and services are produced.

internal changes Budget adjustments, policy changes, personnel changes, and the like.

international trade The exchange of goods and services by different countries.

Internet A global collection of independently operating, but interconnected, computers.

interpersonal communication An interactive process between individuals that involves sending and receiving verbal and nonverbal messages.

interpersonal conflict Conflict between two or more individuals.

intranet A private, corporate, computer network that uses Internet products and technologies to provide multimedia applications within organizations.

intrapersonal conflict Conflict internal to the individual.

intrapreneurship Entrepreneurship within a large or medium-size company.

intrinsic rewards Rewards internal to the individual and normally derived from involvement in work activities.

intuitive approach Approach used when managers make decisions based largely on hunches and intuition.

inventory Quantity of raw materials, in-process goods, or finished goods on hand; serves as a buffer between different rates of flow associated with the operating system.

ISO 9000 A set of quality standards for international business.

ISO 14000 Addition to the ISO 9000 to control the impact of an organization's activities and outputs on the environment.

J

job analysis Process of determining, through observation and study, the pertinent information relating to the nature of a specific job.

job content Aggregate of all the work tasks the jobholder may be asked to perform.

job depth Refers to the freedom of employees to plan and organize their own work, work at their own pace, and move around and communicate as desired.

job description Written statement that identifies the tasks, duties, activities, and performance results required in a particular job.

job design Designates the specific work activities of an individual or a group of individuals.

job enlargement Giving an employee more of a similar type of operation to perform.

job enrichment Upgrading the job by adding motivator factors.

job knowledge tests Measure the job-related knowledge possessed by a job applicant.

job method Manner in which the human body is used, the arrangement of the workplace, and the design of the tools and equipment used.

job rotation Process in which the trainee goes from one job to another within the organization, generally remaining in each job from six months to a year.

job satisfaction An individual's general attitude about his or her job.

job scope Refers to the number of different types of operations performed on the job.

job specification Written statement that identifies the abilities, skills, traits, or attributes necessary for successful performance in a particular job.

just-in-time inventory control (JIT) Inventory control system that schedules materials to arrive and leave as they are needed.

K

kaizen "Good change"; a process of continuous and relentless improvement.

L

laissez-faire leader Allows people within the group to make all decisions.

law of comparative advantage Producers should produce the goods they are most efficient at producing and purchase from others the goods they are less efficient at producing.

layoff Occurs when there is not enough work for all employees; employees will be called back if and when the workload increases.

leader One who obtains followers and influences them in setting and achieving objectives.

Leader Behavior Description Questionnaire (LBDQ) Questionnaire designed to determine what a successful leader does, regardless of the type of group being led.

leader-member relations Degree to which others trust and respect the leader and the leader's friendliness.

leadership Ability to influence people to willingly follow one's guidance or adhere to one's decisions.

leading Directing and channeling human behavior toward the accomplishment of objectives.

lean manufacturing A systematic approach to identifying and eliminating waste and non-value-added activities.

lean six sigma A combination of lean methods and six sigma; draws on the philosophies, principles, and tools of both approaches. Goal is growth and not just cost-cutting.

leniency Grouping of ratings at the positive end of the scale instead of spreading them throughout the scale.

level of aspiration Level of performance that a person expects to attain; determined by the person's prior successes and failures.

limited liability company (LLC) Similar to a corporation, owners have limited personal liability for the debts and actions of the LLC.

limited liability partnership (LLP) A partnership where liability is limited to the amount of money invested in the business or any guarantees given.

linchpin concept Because managers are members of overlapping groups, they link formal work groups to the total organization.

line and staff structure Organization structure that results when staff specialists are added to a line organization.

line functions Functions and activities directly involved in producing and marketing the organization's goods or services.

line structure Organization structure with direct vertical lines between the different levels of the organization.

long-range objectives Go beyond the current fiscal year; must support and not conflict with the organizational mission.

long-range plans Typically span at least three to five years; some extend as far as 20 years into the future.

M

Malcolm Baldrige Award Recognition of U.S. companies' achievements in quality.

management A process of deciding the best way to use an organization's resources to produce goods or provide services.

management audit Attempts to evaluate the overall management practices and policies of the organization.

management by objectives (MBO) MBO is a philosophy based on converting organizational objectives into personal objectives. It assumes that establishing personal objectives elicits employee commitment, which leads to improved performance.

management development Process of developing the attitudes and skills necessary to become or remain an effective manager.

management information system (MIS) Integrated approach for providing interpreted and relevant data that can help managers make decisions.

management theory jungle Term developed by Harold Koontz referring to the division of thought that resulted from the multiple approaches to studying the management process.

Managerial Grid A two-dimensional framework rating a leader on the basis of concern for people and concern for production.

material requirements planning (MRP) Dependent inventory planning and control system that schedules the right amount of materials needed to produce the final product on schedule.

matrix structure Hybrid organization structure in which individuals from different functional areas are assigned to work on a specific project or task.

maximax approach Selecting the alternative whose best possible outcome is the best of all possible outcomes for all alternatives; sometimes called the *optimistic* or *gambling approach* to decision making.

maximin approach Comparing the worst possible outcomes for each alternative and selecting the one that is least undesirable; sometimes called the *pessimistic approach* to decision making.

McCormick multiple-management plan Developed by Charles McCormick, a plan that uses participation as a training and motivational tool by selecting promising young employees from various company departments to form a junior board of directors.

mechanistic systems Organizational systems characterized by a rigid delineation of functional duties, precise job descriptions, fixed authority and responsibility, and a well-developed organizational hierarchy through which information filters up and instructions flow down.

middle management Responsible for implementing and achieving organizational objectives; also responsible for developing departmental objectives and actions.

mission Defines the basic purpose(s) of an organization: why the organization exists.

motivation Concerned with what activates human behavior, what directs this behavior toward a particular goal, and how this behavior is sustained.

motivation maintenance An approach to work motivation that associates factors of high-low motivation with either the work environment or the work itself. Also called *motivation hygiene.*

multinational corporation (MNC) Business that maintains a presence in two or more countries, has a considerable portion of its assets invested in and derives a substantial portion of its sales and profits from international activities, considers opportunities throughout the world, and has a worldwide perspective and orientation.

N

need hierarchy Based on the assumption that individuals are motivated to satisfy a number of needs and that money can directly or indirectly satisfy only some of these needs.

needs assessment Systematic analysis of the specific training activities a business requires to achieve its objectives.

nominal group technique (NGT) Highly structured technique for solving group tasks; minimizes personal interactions to encourage activity and reduce pressures toward conformity.

nonprogrammed decisions Decisions that have little or no precedent; they are relatively unstructured and generally require a creative approach by the decision maker.

North American Free Trade Agreement (NAFTA) NAFTA allows businesses in the United States, Mexico, and Canada to sell their products anywhere in North America without facing major trade restrictions.

O

objectives Statements outlining what the organization is trying to achieve; give an organization and its members direction.

Occupational Safety and Health Act (OSHA) of 1970 Federal legislation designed to reduce job injuries; established specific federal safety guidelines for almost all U.S. organizations.

on-the-job training (OJT) Normally given by a senior employee or supervisor, training in which the trainee is shown how to perform the job and allowed to do it under the trainer's supervision.

operating systems Consist of the processes and activities necessary to turn inputs into goods or services.

operations management Application of the basic concepts and principles of management to those segments of the organization that produce its goods or services.

operations or tactical planning Short-range planning; done primarily by middle- to lower-level managers, it concentrates on the formulation of functional plans.

operations planning Designing the systems of the organization that produce goods or services; planning the day-to-day operations within those systems.

optimizing Selecting the best possible alternative.

optimizing approach Includes the following steps: recognize the need for a decision; establish, rank, and weigh criteria; gather available information and data; identify possible alternatives; evaluate each alternative with respect to all criteria; and select the best alternative.

organic systems Organizational systems characterized by less formal job descriptions, greater emphasis on adaptability, more participation, and less fixed authority.

organization Group of people working together in some concerted or coordinated effort to attain objectives.

organization structure Framework that defines the boundaries of the formal organization and within which the organization operates.

organizational conflict Conflict between employees and the organization itself.

organizational development (OD) Organizationwide, planned effort, managed from the top, to increase organizational performance through planned interventions.

organizational diplomacy Strategies used to minimize conflict in a diverse workplace.

organizational morale An individual's feeling of being accepted by, and belonging to, a group of employees through common goals, confidence in the desirability of these goals, and progress toward these goals.

organizational rewards All types of rewards, both intrinsic and extrinsic, received as a result of employment by the organization.

organizing Grouping activities, assigning activities, and providing the authority necessary to carry out the activities.

orientation Introduction of new employees to the organization, their work units, and their jobs.

orientation kit Normally prepared by the human resource department, provides a wide variety of materials to supplement the general organizational orientation.

output (impersonal) control Based on the measurement of outputs.

outsourcing Practice of subcontracting certain work functions to an independent outside source.

P

paralanguage A form of nonverbal communication that includes the pitch, tempo, loudness, and hesitations in verbal communication.

parity principle States that authority and responsibility must coincide.

partnership An association of two or more persons who jointly own a for-profit business.

patent The document the federal government issues to inventors and companies that gives them the exclusive right to their inventions for 17 years.

path-goal theory of leadership Attempts to define the relationships between a leader's behavior and the subordinates' performance and work activities.

perception The mental and sensory processes an individual uses in interpreting information received.

performance Degree of accomplishment of the tasks that make up an employee's job.

performance appraisal Process that involves determining and communicating to employees how they are performing their jobs and establishing a plan for improvement.

period of solidification A period in the 1920s and 1930s in which management became recognized as a discipline.

Peter Principle Tendency of individuals in a hierarchy to rise to their levels of incompetence.

physical inventory Counting the number of units of inventory a company holds in stock.

planning Process of deciding what objectives to pursue during a future time period and what to do to achieve those objectives.

policies Broad, general guides to action that constrain or direct the attainment of objectives.

polygraph A device that records physical changes in the body as the test subject answers a series of questions.

polygraph tests Record physical changes in the body as the test subject answers a series of questions; popularly known as *lie detector tests.*

position power Power and influence that go with a job.

positive reinforcement Providing a positive consequence as a result of desirable behavior.

postaction control Designed to detect an existing or a potential problem before it gets out of hand.

power Ability to influence, command, or apply force; a measure of a person's potential to get others to do what he or she wants them to do, as well as to avoid being forced by others to do what he or she does not want them to do.

preliminary (steering) control Method of exercising control to prevent a problem from occurring.

principle A basic truth or law.

principle of bounded rationality Assumes people have the time and cognitive ability to process only a limited amount of information on which to base decisions.

principle of individual rights Involves making decisions based on protecting human dignity.

problem solving Process of determining the appropriate responses or actions necessary to alleviate a problem.

procedure Series of related steps or tasks expressed in chronological order for a specific purpose.

process approach to management Focuses on the management functions of planning, controlling, organizing, staffing, and leading.

process control Relates to equipment and processes used during the production process; used to monitor quality while the product or service is being produced.

process control chart Time-based graphic display that shows whether a machine or a process is producing items that meet preestablished specifications.

process culture Involves low risk with little feedback; employees focus on how things are done rather than on the outcomes.

process layout Facilities layout that groups together equipment or services of a similar functional type.

process selection Specifies in detail the processes and sequences required to transform inputs into products or services.

product departmentalization Grouping all activities necessary to produce and market a product or service under one manager.

product layout Facilities layout that arranges equipment or services according to the progressive steps by which the product is made or the customer is served.

product quality control Relates to inputs or outputs of the system; used when quality is evaluated with respect to a batch of existing products or services.

production planning Concerned primarily with aggregate operations planning, resource allocation, and activity scheduling.

production standards approach Performance appraisal method most frequently used for employees who are involved in physically producing a product; is basically a form of objective setting for these employees.

professional manager Career manager who does not necessarily have a controlling interest in the organization and bears a responsibility to employees, stockholders, and the public.

proficiency tests Measure how well the applicant can do a sample of the work that is to be performed.

program evaluation and review technique (PERT) Planning and control technique that graphically depicts the relationships among the various activities of a project; used when the durations of the project activities are not accurately known.

programmed decisions Decisions that are reached by following an established or systematic procedure.

property tax Tax levied against the property, buildings, and land owned by a business.

psychological tests Attempt to measure personality characteristics.

psychomotor tests Measure a person's strength, dexterity, and coordination.

punishment Providing a negative consequence as a result of undesirable behavior.

Q

quality For the operations manager, quality is determined in relation to the specifications or standards set in the design stages—the degree or grade of excellence specified.

quality at the source The philosophy of making each employee responsible for the quality of his or her own work.

quality circle Composed of a group of employees (usually from 5 to 15 people) who are members of a single work unit, section, or department; the basic purpose of a quality circle is to discuss quality problems and generate ideas that might help improve quality.

quota Establishes the maximum quantity of a product that can be imported or exported during a given period.

R

recency Occurs when performance evaluations are based on work performed most recently, generally work performed one to two months before evaluation.

recruitment Seeking and attracting a supply of people from which qualified candidates for job vacancies can be selected.

reengineering Searching for and implementing radical change in business processes to achieve breakthroughs in costs, speed, productivity, and service.

regulations Rules that government agencies issue to implement laws.

Rehabilitation Act of 1973 Prohibits discrimination in hiring of persons with disabilities by federal agencies and federal contractors.

reinforcement theory States that the consequences of a person's present behavior influence future behavior.

resource allocation Efficient allocation of people, materials, and equipment to meet the demand requirements of the operating system.

responsibility Accountability for the attainment of objectives, the use of resources, and the adherence to organizational policy.

reverse discrimination Providing preferential treatment for one group (e.g., minority or female) over another group (e.g., white male) rather than merely providing equal opportunity.

risk-averting approach Choosing the alternative with the least variation among its possible outcomes.

role Set of behaviors associated with a particular job.

role perception Direction in which employees believe they should channel their efforts on their jobs.

routing Finds the best path and sequence of operations for attaining a desired level of output with a given mix of equipment and personnel.

rules Require specific and definite actions to be taken or not to be taken in a given situation.

S

sabbatical Derived from Sabbath and literally means a recurring period of rest and renewal.

safety stocks Inventory maintained to accommodate unexpected changes in demand and supply and allow for variations in delivery time.

satisficing Selecting the first alternative that meets the decision maker's minimum standard of satisfaction.

scalar principle States that authority in the organization flows through the chain of managers one link at a time, ranging from the highest to the lowest ranks; also called *chain of command.*

Scanlon plan Incentive plan developed in 1938 by Joseph Scanlon to give workers a bonus for tangible savings in labor costs.

scientific management Philosophy of Frederick W. Taylor that sought to increase productivity and make the work easier by scientifically studying work methods and establishing standards.

self-directed work teams (SDWT) Teams in which members are empowered to control the work they do without a formal supervisor.

self-fulfilling prophecy The relationship between a leader's expectations and the resulting performance of subordinates.

semantics The science or study of the meanings of words and symbols.

sensitivity training Method used in OD to make one more aware of oneself and one's impact on others.

short-range objectives Generally tied to a specific time period of a year or less and are derived from an in-depth evaluation of long-range objectives.

short-range plans Generally cover up to one year.

situation of certainty Situation that occurs when a decision maker knows exactly what will happen and can often calculate the precise outcome for each alternative.

situation of risk Situation that occurs when a decision maker is aware of the relative probabilities of occurrence associated with each alternative.

situation of uncertainty Situation that occurs when a decision maker has very little or no reliable information on which to evaluate the different possible outcomes.

situational leadership theory As the level of maturity of followers increases, structure should be reduced while socioemotional support should first be increased and then gradually decreased.

six sigma Both a precise set of statistical tools and a rallying cry for continuous improvement.

skills inventory Consolidates information about the organization's current human resources.

small business A company that is independently owned and operated and is not dominant in its field; generally has fewer than 100 employees.

social audit A method used by management to evaluate the success or lack of success of programs designed to improve the social performance of the organization.

social responsibility The obligation that individuals or businesses have to help solve social problems.

sociotechnical approach Approach to job design that considers both the technical system and the accompanying social system.

soldiering Describes the actions of employees who intentionally restrict output.

sole proprietorship A business owned by a single individual, or proprietor.

span of management Number of subordinates a manager can effectively manage; also called *span of control.*

stability strategy Used when the organization is satisfied with its present course (status quo strategy).

staff functions Functions that are advisory and supportive in nature; designed to contribute to the efficiency and maintenance of the organization.

staffing Determining human resource needs and recruiting, selecting, training, and developing human resources.

stakeholders The people—employees, customers, suppliers, and the community—who are affected by the actions of a business.

standard Value used as a point of reference for comparing other values.

strategic business unit (SBU) Distinct business that has its own set of competitors and can be managed reasonably independently of other businesses within the organization.

strategic management Formulation, proper implementation, and continuous evaluation of strategic plans; determines the long-run directions and performance of an organization. The essence of strategic management is developing strategic plans and keeping them current.

strategic planning Analogous to top-level long-range planning; covers a relatively long period; affects many parts of the organization.

strategy Outlines the basic steps management plans to take to reach an objective or a set of objectives; outlines how management intends to achieve its objectives.

stress Mental or physical condition that results from a perceived threat of danger (physical or emotional) and the pressure to remove it.

subsidies or subsidized protection Widely used practice of government support of domestic industries to make their prices cheaper than the prices of imports.

supervisory management Manages operative employees; generally considered the first level of management.

synectics Creative problem-solving technique that uses metaphorical thinking to "make the familiar strange and the strange familiar."

systems approach to management A way of thinking about the job of managing that provides a framework for visualizing internal and external environmental factors as an integrated whole.

T

tall structure Organization with many levels and relatively small spans of management.

tariffs Government-imposed taxes charged on goods imported into a country.

task structure Degree to which job tasks are structured.

team building Process by which the formal work group develops an awareness of those conditions that keep it from functioning effectively and then requires the group to eliminate those conditions.

technical skills Involve being able to perform the mechanics of a particular job.

technological changes Changes in such things as new equipment and new processes.

technostress Personal stress generated by reliance on technological devices—a panicky feeling when they fail, a state of near-constant stimulation, or being constantly "plugged in."

temporary help People working for employment agencies who are subcontracted out to businesses at an hourly rate for a period of time specified by the businesses.

test reliability Consistency or reproducibility of the results of a test.

test validity Extent to which a test predicts a specific criterion.

tests Provide a sample of behavior used to draw inferences about the future behavior or performance of an individual.

Theory Z A theory developed by William Ouchi that attempts to integrate American and Japanese management practices by combining the American emphasis on individual responsibility with the Japanese emphasis on collective decision making, slow evaluation and promotion, and holistic concern for employees.

360-degree feedback Method of performance appraisal that uses input from an employee's managers, peers, customers, suppliers, or colleagues.

Title VII of the Civil Rights Act of 1964 Designed to eliminate employment discrimination related to race, color, religion, sex, or national origin in organizations that conduct interstate commerce.

top or senior management Establishes the objectives of the organization, formulates the actions necessary to achieve them, and allocates the resources of the organization to achieve the objectives.

tough-person, macho culture Characterized by individuals who take high risks and get quick feedback on whether their decisions are right or wrong.

trademark A word, name, symbol, or slogan a business uses to identify its own goods.

training Acquiring skills or learning concepts to increase the performance of employees.

trait theory Stressed what the leader was like rather than what the leader did.

transactional leadership Takes the approach that leaders engage in a bargaining relationship with their followers.

transaction-processing system Substitutes computer processing for manual recordkeeping procedures.

transformational leadership Involves cultivating employee acceptance of the group mission.

U

unity of command principle States that an employee should have one, and only one, immediate manager.

V

valence Employee's belief about the value of the rewards.

value A conception, explicit or implicit, that defines what an individual or a group regards as desirable. People are not born with values; rather, they acquire and develop them early in life.

value-added chain Process by which a business combines the raw material, labor, and technology into a finished product, markets the product, and distributes the product.

variable overhead expenses Expenses that change in proportion to the level of production or service.

vestibule training System in which procedures and equipment similar to those used in the actual job are set up in a special working area called a vestibule.

virtual organization Temporary network of independent companies—suppliers, customers, and even rivals—linked by information technology to share skills, costs, and access to one another's markets.

virtual work teams Teams which mainly use technology-supported communication, with team members working and living in different locations.

W

wellness program Company-implemented program designed to prevent illness and enhance employee well-being.

workaholism Working to the exclusion of everything else in one's life.

work-hard/play-hard culture Encourages employees to take few risks and to expect rapid feedback.

Z

zero-base budgeting Form of budgeting in which the manager must build and justify each area of a budget. Each activity is identified, evaluated, and ranked by importance.

zero-defects program Increasing quality by increasing everyone's impact on quality.

Photo Credits

Page 1 Comstock/PictureQuest
Page 9 © Comstock/PictureQuest
Page 12 © Joel Anderson
Page 27 © Underwood & Underwood/Corbis
Page 31 Courtesy of The Lincoln Electric Company
Page 51 © John A. Rizzo/Getty Images
Page 56 © Getty Images
Page 72 © Photodisc/Getty Images
Page 76 © Keith Brofsky/Getty Images
Page 91 arabianEye/PunchStock
Page 117 © Erica Simone Leeds
Page 120 Photograph and the HOLIDAY INN® name appear courtesy of Intercontinental Hotels Group
Page 129 Beathan/Corbis
Page 133 © PunchStock
Page 136 © Steve Cole/Getty Images
Page 165 © Images.com/Corbis
Page 181 © The McGraw-Hill Companies/Lars A. Niki, photographer
Page 213 ABC/Photofest
Page 219 Comstock/PictureQuest
Page 224 © Digital Vision
Page 234 © Getty Images
Page 247 © The McGraw-Hill Companies/Jill Braaten, photographer
Page 251 © Geoff Manasse/Getty Images
Page 263 Royalty-Free/Corbis
Page 273 © Louie Psihoyos
Page 276 © PhotoLink/Getty Images
Page 289 © Roy McMahon/zefa/Corbis
Page 292 © Catherine Karnow/Corbis
Page 313 © Eric Audras/Photoalto/PictureQuest
Page 320 © Teo Lannie/Getty Images
Page 340 © Roz Woodward/Getty Images
Page 350 © Richard Klune/Corbis
Page 361 BananaStock/PictureQuest
Page 367 © C Squared Studios/Getty Images
Page 374 © Digital Vision/Getty Images
Page 394 © Royalty Free/Corbis
Page 409 Ryan McVay/Getty Images
Page 416 © Alistair Berg/Photodisc/Getty Images
Page 419 Courtesy of Microsoft Corporation
Page 438 © Digital Vision/Getty Images
Page 447 © John A. Rizzo/Getty Images

Name Index

A page number with an f indicates a figure; an n, notes.

N

O

P

Subject Index

A page number with an f indicates a figure; an n, notes.

D

N

O